Concept Clips

Expanded to now include audio, Concept Cl...
videos that walk students through the mor...
the American government course (such as t... ...college,
Supreme Court procedures, or how to evaluate a public opinion poll).

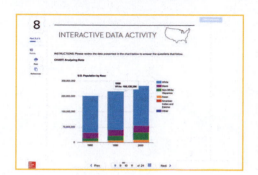

Interactive Data Analysis

Help your students consume political data in a meaningful way. Students in the American Government course now have the ability to interact with political data visualizations to gain insight into important factors that shape our political process. Students can review electoral turnout over time or contemplate how demographic shifts in the American population will impact future elections. These interactive charts and maps are paired with auto-grade and critical thinking questions to enhance student understanding.

87%

of college students report that access to learning analytics can positively impact their learning experience.

75%

of students using adaptive technology report that it is "very helpful" or "extremely helpful" in aiding their ability to retain new concepts.

"I can honestly say that he first time I used SmartBook after reading a chapter I understood what I had just read better than I ever had in the past."

– Nathan Herrmann, Oklahoma State University

"I really enjoy how it has gotten me engaged in the course and it is a great study tool without having to carry around a heavy textbook."

– Madeline Uretsky, Simmons College

Professors spend:

Less time on administrative tasks

75%

90%

More time on active learning

"Connect keeps my students engaged and motivated. Requiring Connect assignments has improved student exam grades."

– Sophia Garcia, Tarrant County College

Because learning changes everything.™

To learn more about American Government visit the McGraw-Hill Education American Government page: bit.ly/MHEAmGov

AM G★V

SIXTH EDITION

JOSEPH LOSCO
Ball State University and Loyola University Chicago

RALPH BAKER
State College of Florida

AM GOV, SIXTH EDITION

Published by McGraw-Hill Education, 2 Penn Plaza, New York, NY 10121. Copyright © 2019 by McGraw-Hill Education. All rights reserved. Printed in the United States of America. Previous editions © 2017, 2015, 2013, and 2011. No part of this publication may be reproduced or distributed in any form or by any means, or stored in a database or retrieval system, without the prior written consent of McGraw-Hill Education, including, but not limited to, in any network or other electronic storage or transmission, or broadcast for distance learning.

Some ancillaries, including electronic and print components, may not be available to customers outside the United States.

This book is printed on acid-free paper.

2 3 4 5 6 QVS 22 21 20 19

ISBN 978-1-259-91244-3 (bound edition)
MHID 1-259-91244-2 (bound edition)
ISBN 978-1-260-16597-5 (loose-leaf edition)
MHID 1-260-16597-3 (loose-leaf edition)

Portfolio Manager: *Jason Seitz*
Product Development Manager: *Dawn Groundwater*
Marketing Manager: *Will Walter*
Content Project Managers: *Rick Hecker/George Theofanopoulos*
Buyer: *Sandy Ludovissy*
Design: *Matt Diamond*
Content Licensing Specialist: *Ann Marie Jannette*
Cover Image: © *Pixtal/AGE Fotostock.*

Compositor: *Aptara®, Inc.*

All credits not appearing on page or at the end of the book are considered to be an extension of the copyright page.

Library of Congress Cataloging-in-Publication Data

Names: Losco, Joseph, author. | Baker, Ralph, 1942- author.
Title: Am gov 2019-2020 / Joseph Losco, Ball State University and Ralph
   Baker, State College of Florida.
Other titles: American government 2019-2020
Description: Sixth edition. | New York : McGraw-Hill Education, [2019]
Identifiers: LCCN 2018036948| ISBN 9781259912443 (alk. paper) | ISBN
   1259912442 (alk. paper)
Subjects: LCSH: United States—Politics and government—Textbooks.
Classification: LCC JK276 .L67 2019 | DDC 320.473—dc23 LC record available at
https://lccn.loc.gov/2018036948

The Internet addresses listed in the text were accurate at the time of publication. The inclusion of a website does not indicate an endorsement by the authors or McGraw-Hill Education, and McGraw-Hill Education does not guarantee the accuracy of the information presented at these sites.

AM G★V

Brief Contents

©Zach Gibson/Getty Images

©Robert W. Kelley/The LIFE Images Collection/Getty Images

©Corbis/PunchStock

Contents

©Sandy Macys/Alamy Stock Photo

4 Civil Liberties: Citizens' Rights
Versus Security 67

Civil Liberties Versus Civil Rights: A Sweet Dispute 67

©Amos Aikman/Getty Images

©Bettmann/Getty Images

©Chris Pizzello/AP Images

©Bettmann/Getty Images

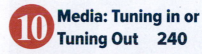

©Spencer Platt/Getty Images

©Robert Emerson/Alamy Stock Photo

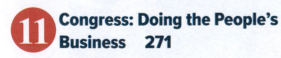

©Stephen Chernin/Getty Images

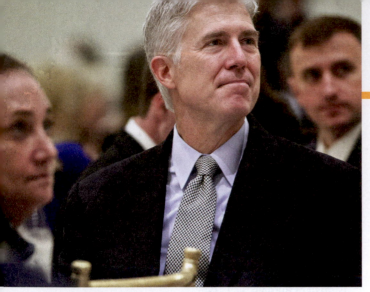

©Andrew Harrer/Bloomberg via Getty Images

©Tony Comiti/Corbis via Getty Images

What's in *AM GOV*

Ralph Baker, State College of Florida, and Joseph Losco, Ball State University and Loyola University Chicago.
Courtesy of Ball State University

AM GOV was created with one simple premise in mind: Students will learn only if the content is engaging and current, if the design is visually attractive, and if the price is affordable.

With this premise in mind, we, the authors, set out to discover from you—students and faculty—how best to create a program that students would read and faculty would eagerly assign. We interviewed dozens of faculty and hundreds of students at colleges throughout the country. Students told us they wanted resources with innovative visual appeal, interactive digital technology, an integrated approach, and relevant content designed according to the way they learn. Instructors told us they wanted a way to engage their students without compromising on high-quality content.

We listened. The result is *AM GOV,* an American government program that started a revolution. Our goal in *AM GOV* is to engage students in the story of people's relationship to government and how an active and informed citizenry is essential in making democracy meaningful. We want students to recognize how their choices about government affect their lives.

AM GOV marries our commitment to scholarly content with the value that currency, presentation, adaptive technology, and reasonable price have for students. Frequent updates of both political events and scholarship keep the program vital and relevant. We gave *AM GOV* this visually rich design because our research taught us that, in our visual culture, it makes student learning excel and American government memorable. Students even gave *AM GOV* its name.

And we continue to listen. Using the latest technology to track student usage and comprehension, *AM GOV* pinpoints those content areas students find most challenging with heat maps. This technology is used to help us rework presentations to make the material more comprehensible and meaningful to students. Available adaptive technologies, like LearnSmart® and SmartBook®, put students in control of the learning experience, allowing them to learn from peer responses and create a personal reading experience that's all their own.

You started *AM GOV.* You convinced us that there had to be a better way to get across the fundamental concepts of American democracy and what it means to be an American citizen.

We listened. And we continue to learn from you.

About the Authors

Joseph Losco is professor emeritus of political science at Ball State University, director emeritus of the Bowen Center for Public Affairs, and currently adjunct professor of political science at Loyola University of Chicago. He teaches courses in political theory and American government. Losco has published in the areas of public policy and political theory. His publications include *Political Theory: Classic and Contemporary Readings* (Oxford University Press) and *Human. Nature and Politics,* co-edited with Albert Somit (JAI Press). At the Bowen Center, Losco founded and directed the annual Hoosier Survey of public opinion and shared responsibility for the Voting System Technical Oversight Program (VSTOP), which conducts voting system studies for the Indiana secretary of state. His research has been funded by grants from the Pew Charitable Trusts and the U.S. Election Assistance Commission. He serves as consultant to VSTOP and as an expert in voting system technology. Losco received his B.A. and M.A. from Pennsylvania State University and his Ph.D. from Temple University. He has been married to his wife Marcia for over 40 years and has a son, Michael, who practices international arbitration law in New York City.

Ralph Baker is an adjunct professor of political science at the State College of Florida, where he teaches Introduction to American Government courses. Before moving to Florida, he was a political science professor at Ball State University, specializing in American government, constitutional law, constitutional liberties, judicial politics, criminal justice policy, and media and politics. Raised in central Illinois, he attended Bradley University for his undergraduate degree and the University of Illinois for his M.A. and Ph.D.

He is the author of numerous books and articles, including *The Criminal Justice Game, Evaluating Alternative Law Enforcement Policies, Determinants of Law Enforcement Policies, State Policy Problems,* and *Women Government Officials in Indiana* and articles concerning the Supreme Court, gender policy, the chilly climate in academia, media and politics, and police professionalism. With Joe Losco, Baker produced over twenty political science videos that resulted in *Telly Awards* for "The 1996 Campaign," "The 2000 Campaign," and an *Axiem Award* for "Case Studies in American Government." At Ball State University, Baker won the Outstanding Teacher Award and served several terms as the president of the Indiana Political Science Association.

Foundational Content and

AM GOV is a **relatable, informative,** and **visual** introduction to American politics. Designed with **today's students** in mind, AM GOV is a **concise, magazine style** program that teaches students *how to* **think critically,** and **politically.** With an emphasis on current events, AM GOV engages its readers through **approachable content** and **digital tools** that are proven to help students better understand and connect with the concepts and language used in the American government course.

Better Data, Smarter Revision, Improved Results

Students helped inform the revision strategy:

STEP 1. Over the course of three years, data points showing concepts that caused students the most difficulty were anonymously collected from McGraw-Hill Education's Connect® American Government's SmartBook for AM GOV.

STEP 2. The data from SmartBook was provided to the authors in the form of a ***heat map,*** which graphically illustrated "hot spots" in the text that impacted student learning (see image to left).

STEP 3. The authors used the ***heat map*** data to refine the content and reinforce student comprehension in the new edition. Additional quiz questions and assignable activities were created for use in Connect American Government to further support student success.

RESULT: Because the ***heat map*** gave the authors empirically based feedback at the paragraph and even sentence level, they were able to develop the new edition using precise student data that pinpointed concepts that caused students the most difficulty.

Heat map data also inform the activities and assessments in Connect American Government, McGraw-Hill Education's assignable and assessable learning platform. Where the heat map data show students struggle with specific learning objectives or concepts, we created new Connect assets—Concept Clips, Applied Critical Thinking (ACT), and NewsFlash current event activities—to provide another avenue for students to learn and master the content.

Fueled by LearnSmart, SmartBook is the first and only adaptive reading experience currently available.

Make It Effective. SmartBook creates a personalized reading experience by highlighting the most impactful concepts a student needs to learn at that moment in time. This ensures that every minute spent with SmartBook is returned to the student as the most value added minute possible.

Make It Informed. The reading experience continuously adapts by highlighting content based on what the student knows and doesn't know. Real-time reports quickly identify the concepts that require more attention from individual students—or the entire class. SmartBook detects the content a student is most likely to forget and brings it back to improve long-term knowledge retention.

New to this edition, SmartBook is now optimized for mobile and tablet and is accessible for students with disabilities. And as part of any American government

SMARTBOOK®

course, SmartBook now focuses on the broader context for and building blocks of the political system. Specifically, it has been enhanced with improved learning objectives to ensure that students gain foundational knowledge while also learning to make connections for broader understanding of government institutions, events, and behavior. SmartBook personalizes learning to individual student needs, continually adapting to pinpoint knowledge gaps and focus learning on topics that need the most attention. Study time is more productive and, as a result, students are better prepared for class and coursework. For instructors, SmartBook tracks student progress and provides insights that can help guide teaching strategies.

Informing and Engaging Students on American Government Concepts

Using Connect American Government, students can learn the course material more deeply and study more effectively than ever before.

At the *remember* and *understand* levels of Bloom's taxonomy, **Concept Clips** help students break down key concepts in American government. Using easy-to-understand audio narration, visual cues, and colorful animations, Concept Clips provide a step-by-step presentation that aids in student retention. New Concept Clips for this edition include the following:

- What are the Types of Government?
- Federalists and Antifederalists
- What is Devolution?
- Regulation of the Media
- Who Participates?
- Presidency: Going Public
- U.S. Foreign Policy

In addition to the concept-based clips, the new edition also offers several skills-based clips that equip students for work within and outside the classroom. These skills-based clips include the following:

- Evaluating the News
- Critical Thinking
- How to Read a Court Case
- How to Understand Charts and Graphs
- Political Cartoons
- How to Avoid Plagiarism

Also at the *remember* and *understand* levels of Bloom's, **NewsFlash** exercises tie current news stories to key American government concepts and learning objectives. After interacting with a contemporary news story, students are assessed on their ability to make the connections between real-life events and

course content. Examples include the 2018 midterm election results, 2017 tax reform legislation, and trade tariffs.

Deepen understanding of how politics happens in the real world by leveraging the most popular podcasts available with our new **Podcast Assignments**. These assignments, allow you to bring greater context and nuance to your courses while engaging students through the storytelling power of podcasts.

At the ap*ply, analyze,* and *evaluate* levels of Bloom's taxonomy, **critical thinking activities** allow students to engage with the political process and learn by doing. Examples include the following:

- Quiz: What is your political ideology?
- Poll: Americans' Confidence in the Police
- Research: Find Your Senator
- Infographic: Compare the Courts

Practice Government, McGraw-Hill's educational game focused on the American political system, is fully integrated inside of Connect American Government! A set of focused introductory missions are paired with auto-graded and critical thinking assessments.

Relevant Content

AM GOV presents content in an approachable, meaningful way, designed to engage students.

- **Thinking It Through Activities:** Our discussions at the American Government symposia conducted across the country, as well as survey feedback, made it clear that critical thinking is an essential skill for which instructors need additional support. Now with additional scaffolding, every chapter concludes with a "Thinking It Through" activity tied to a learning objective for the chapter that challenges students to go beyond the basics to think through a problem and formulate possible solutions. Examples include "Media and Political Campaigns" (Chapter 10) and "The Path to the Presidency" (Chapter 12).
- **Citizenship Quizzes:** In these quizzes, students are invited to take the U.S. Citizenship Test to check their understanding of institutions such as the courts, behavior such as voting rights, and the number of amendments to the Constitution.
- **Current Controversy:** These features examine controversial issues, ranging from "Attacks on Journalists and Journalism" (Chapter 10) to "Lower Federal Courts and the Travel Bans" (Chapter 14).
- **Challenges Ahead:** These features examine the political challenges following the 2016 elections and beyond. Topics range from "The Changing American Identity" (Chapter 1) to "Cell Phones and Civil Liberties" (Chapter 4).

- **Global Perspectives:** These features compare the United States to other nations by interpreting charts and graphs. Topics include "Changing Patterns of Political Participation" (Chapter 7) and "Defense Spending" (Chapter 16).

As mentioned earlier, the authors revised the text in response to student heat map data that pinpointed the topics and concepts with which students struggle the most. This heat-map-directed revision is reflected primarily in Chapters 9, 11, 13, and 14.

Chapter 1—Citizenship in Our Changing Democracy

- Revised opening vignette, "Millennials: You're in Charge Now: Where Will You Take Us?"
- New content on government surveillance and social media
- New poll results on power and influence in Washington
- Updated data on trust in national governments worldwide
- Expanded discussion of the nature and role of political ideologies
- Expanded coverage of the relationship between economic stratification and political engagement
- New Challenges Ahead feature, "The Changing American Identity"
- Expanded discussion of service learning programs
- New figure, "Freshman Class Survey: Essential or Very Important Personal Objectives"

Chapter 2—The Constitution: The Foundation of Citizens' Rights

- New opening vignette, "Our Constitution: Time for a Change?"
- Expanded discussion of the Bill of Rights' applicability to the states
- New "Current Controversy" feature, "An Arcane Provision Comes to Life," addressing the emoluments clause and the Trump presidency

Chapter 3—Federalism: Citizenship and the Dispersal of Power

- New opening vignette on sanctuary cities, "At Odds over Immigration"
- Revised discussion of the evolution of federalism
- New "Portrait of an Activist" feature, "Climate Change Activists"
- New "Challenges Ahead" feature, "A Clash of Wills: Cities Push Back on Preemption"

Chapter 4—Civil Liberties: Citizens' Rights Versus Security

- New opening vignette on the Masterpiece Cakeshop case, "Civil Liberties Versus Civil Rights: A Sweet Dispute"
- Refined explanation of selective incorporation
- New coverage of the NFL football player protests and the right to free speech
- Updated coverage of the role of religion in American life, the relationship between religious and political affiliation, and the separation of church and state
- Updated coverage of campaign contributions as free speech
- Updated data on incarceration rates
- Updated search and seizure cases

- New Challenges Ahead feature, "Cell Phones and Civil Liberties: Can You Hear Me Now?"
- New "Current Controversy" feature, "More Than a Few Scraped Knees"

Chapter 5—Civil Rights: Toward a More Equal Citizenry
- New opening vignette, "Sexual Assaults on College Campuses"
- Updated information on economic disparities between racial groups in America
- Updated information on perceptions of police and of racial privilege
- Revised explanation of judicial tests regarding discrimination
- Revised discussion of affirmative action, including recent court cases
- Revised coverage of Hispanic Americans, including population growth, college enrollment rates, and immigration
- Update coverage on same-sex marriage
- New "Challenges Ahead" feature, "Voter Suppression and the 2016 Election"
- Updated coverage of pay equity for women
- Updated coverage of sexual harassment

Chapter 6—Public Opinion
- New opening vignette, "Changing Tides of Public Opinion," on the Obama voters who voted for Trump
- Updated discussion of partisan polarization and partisan clustering
- Updated coverage of the political divide between urban and rural residents
- Revised coverage of the accuracy of polling, including a new Challenges Ahead feature, "Is Polling in Crisis?"
- Updated discussion of trust in government in America
- Updated coverage of support for democratic values
- Revised discussion of ideological divisions, including ideological leanings by generation
- Revised discussion of deliberative polling
- New "Current Controversy" feature on opinion persistence

Chapter 7—Political Participation: Equal Opportunities and Unequal Voices
- New opening vignette, "Millennials Rising," on young mayors across the nation
- Updated coverage of factors related to political participation
- Updated information on factors affecting voter turnout
- Updated discussion of unconventional political participation, including a new "Global Perspectives" feature
- New "Portrait of an Activist" feature, "Allie Armstrong and the H-CAN Community Moms"

Chapter 8—Interest Groups in America
- New opening vignette, "The National Rifle Association and the Status Quo"
- New figure, "Lobbying Expenditures by the Pharmaceuticals and Health Products Industry"
- Coverage of lobbying and the Trump administration

- New figure, "Total Lobbying Spending and Number of Lobbyists"
- New content on the role of outside money and dark money in the 2016 election

Chapter 9—Parties and Political Campaigns: Putting Democracy into Action

- New opening vignette, "Separate Tables, Please," on avoiding our partisan adversaries
- Revised explanation of the functions of political parties
- Updated discussion of partisan realignment and the partisan divide
- Updated coverage of campaign spending and campaign advertising
- New Challenges Ahead feature, "Tamping Down the Cost of Elections"

Chapter 10—Media: Tuning In or Tuning Out

- New opening vignette, "How to Restore Confidence," addressing a recent study on trust in the media
- Updated coverage of differing news media habits across generations
- Updated discussion of the political divide in favored news sources, including a new figure
- Updated polls on the public perception of media bias, including data on the partisan divide on the issue
- New coverage of Facebook and the 2016 election
- Discussion of press coverage of the Trump administration
- New Current Controversy feature, "Attacks on Journalists and Journalism"

Chapter 11—Congress: Doing the People's Business

- New opening vignette, "Last Man Standing," on challenges to male dominance in Congress
- Complete coverage of 2018 midterm elections
- New Portrait of an Activist feature, "Meet Jonathan Castañeda" (former congressional staffer)
- Extensive revisions and updates to the section on congressional procedures
- Updated suggestions for improving the efficacy and public image of Congress

Chapter 12—The Presidency: Power and Paradox

- New opening vignette, "The Unprecedented President"
- Coverage of historical continuities and discontinuities of the Trump presidency throughout the chapter
- Analysis of electoral factors contributing to the Trump victory
- Coverage of how Trump exercises presidential powers including appointments, executive orders, diplomacy and foreign policy, and Trump's legislative success record
- New Challenges Ahead feature, "It's Two Minutes 'til Midnight."
- Analysis of Trump's presidential style
- Coverage of Russian interference in the 2016 election and the role Facebook played

Chapter 13—Bureaucracy: Citizens as Owners and Consumers

- Updates throughout opening vignette, "Student Loans, Debt, and Bureaucracy"

- New Current Controversy feature, "The Special Counsel: Outside Regular Bureaucratic Boundaries"
- New Challenges Ahead feature, "The FCC and Net Neutrality"
- Updated examples of whistle-blowing and of judicial controls on bureaucratic power

Chapter 14—The Courts: Judicial Power in a Democratic Setting

- New opening vignette, "The Tortuous Selection of a Supreme Court Justice," on the appointment of Judge Gorsuch
- Refinements and clarifications throughout the section on Supreme Court decision making
- New Current Controversy feature, "Lower Federal Courts and the Travel Bans"
- Updated Challenges Ahead feature, "Confidence in the Supreme Court"

Chapter 15—Public Policy: Responding to Citizens

- Updated opening vignette, "The Widening Gap," on income inequality
- Updates on greenhouse gas pollution
- Material on the Trump administration's policies on the environment, poverty, health care, economics, and trade
- Updated statistics on poverty levels in America

Chapter 16—Foreign and Defense Policy: Protecting American Interests in the World

- New opening vignette, "Flight and Fight," on the world refugee crisis
- Material on the Trump administration's national security and foreign relations policies and procedures
- Updates on current world conflicts

American Government Symposia

Since 2006, McGraw-Hill Education has conducted several American Government symposia for instructors from across the country. These events offered a forum for instructors to exchange ideas and experiences with colleagues they might not have met otherwise. They also provided an opportunity for editors from McGraw-Hill Education to gather information about what instructors of American Government need and the challenges they face. The feedback we have received has been invaluable and has contributed—directly and indirectly—to the development of *AM GOV*. We would like to thank the participants for their insights:

Melvin Aaron, *Los Angeles City College*
Yan Bai, *Grand Rapids Community College*
Robert Ballinger, *South Texas College*
Nancy Bednar, *Antelope Valley College*
Jeffrey Birdsong, *Northeastern Oklahoma A&M College*
Amy Brandon, *San Jacinto College-North*
Jane Bryant, *John A. Logan College*
Dan R. Brown, *Southwestern Oklahoma State University*
Monique Bruner, *Rose State College*

Anita Chadha, *University of Houston–Downtown*
John Clark, *Western Michigan University–Kalamazoo*
Kathleen Collihan, *American River College*
Steven Collins, *Oklahoma State University–Oklahoma City*
John Davis, *Howard University*
Kevin Davis, *North Central Texas College*
Paul Davis, *Truckee Meadows Community College*
Vida Davoudi, *Lone Star College–Kingwood*
Robert De Luna, *Saint Philips College*

Jeff DeWitt, *Kennesaw State University*

Kevin Dockerty, *Kalamazoo Valley Community College*

Cecil Dorsey, *San Jacinto College–South*

Hien Do, *San Jose State University*

Jay Dow, *University of Missouri–Columbia*

Manar Elkhaldi, *University of Central Florida*

Karry Evans, *Austin Community College*

Pearl Ford, *University of Arkansas–Fayetteville*

John Forshee, *San Jacinto College–Central*

Ben Riesner Fraser, *San Jacinto College*

Daniel Fuerstman, *Dutchess Community College*

Marilyn Gaar, *Johnson County Community College*

Jarvis T. Gamble, *Owens Community College*

Michael Gattis, *Gulf Coast Community College*

William Gillespie, *Kennesaw State University*

Dana K. Glencross, *Oklahoma City Community College*

Larry Gonzalez, *Houston Community College–Southwest*

Nirmal Goswami, *Texas A&M University–Kingsville*

Daniel Gutierrez, *El Paso Community College*

Richard Gutierrez, *University of Texas, El Paso*

Michelle Kukoleca Hammes, *St. Cloud State University*

Cathy Hanks, *University of Nevada, Las Vegas*

Wanda Hill, *Tarrant County Community College*

Joseph Hinchliffe, *University of Illinois at Urbana–Champaign*

John Hitt, *North Lake College*

Mark Jendrysik, *University of North Dakota*

Brenda Jones, *Houston Community College–Central*

Franklin Jones, *Texas Southern University*

Lynn Jones, *Collin County Community College*

James Joseph, *Fresno City College*

Jason Kassel, *Valdosta State University*

Manoucher Khosrowshahi, *Tyler Junior College*

Rich Kiefer, *Waubonsee Community College*

Robert J. King, *Georgia Perimeter College*

Melinda Kovacs, *Sam Houston State University*

Chien-Pin Li, *Kennesaw State University*

Fred Lokken, *Truckee Meadows Community College*

John Mercurio, *San Diego State University*

Janna Merrick, *University of South Florida*

Joe Meyer, *Los Angeles City College*

Eric Miller, *Blinn College*

Kent Miller, *Weatherford College*

Charles Moore, *Georgia State University*

Eduardo Munoz, *El Camino College*

Kay Murnan, *Ozarks Technical Community College*

Carolyn Myers, *Southwestern Illinois College*

Blaine Nelson, *El Paso Community College*

Theresa Nevarez, *El Paso Community College*

James A. Norris, *Texas A&M International University*

Kent Park, *U.S. Military Academy at West Point*

Eric Rader, *Henry Ford Community College*

Elizabeth Rexford, *Wharton County Junior College*

Tara Ross, *Keiser University*

Carlos Rovelo, *Tarrant Community College–South*

Ryan Rynbrandt, *Collin County Community College*

Ray Sandoval, *Richland College*

Craig Scarpelli, *California State University–Chico*

Louis Schubert, *City College of San Francisco*

Edward Senu-Oke, *Joliet Junior College*

Mark Shomaker, *Blinn College*

Thomas Simpson, *Missouri Southern University*

Henry Sirgo, *McNeese State University*

Amy Smith, *North Lake College*

Daniel Smith, *Northwest Missouri State University*

John Speer, *Houston Community College–Southwest*

Jim Startin, *University of Texas at San Antonio*

Sharon Sykora, *Slippery Rock University*

Tressa Tabares, *American River College*

Beatrice Talpos, *Wayne County Community College*

Alec Thomson, *Schoolcraft College*

Judy Tobler, *Northwest Arkansas Community College*

Steve Tran, *Houston Community College*

Beth Traxler, *Greenville Technical College*

William Turk, *University of Texas–Pan American*

Ron Vardy, *University of Houston*

Sarah Velasquez, *Fresno City College*

Ron VonBehren, *Valencia Community College–Osceola*

Albert C. Waite, *Central Texas College*

Van Allen Wigginton, *San Jacinto College–Central*

Charlotte Williams, *Pasadena City College*

Ike Wilson, *U.S. Military Academy*

Paul Wilson, *San Antonio College*

John Wood, *University of Central Oklahoma*

Robert Wood, *University of North Dakota*

Larry Wright, *Florida A&M University*

Ann Wyman, *Missouri Southern State University*

Kathryn Yates, *Richland College*

Citizenship
In Our Changing Democracy

MILLENNIALS: YOU'RE IN CHARGE NOW. WHERE WILL YOU TAKE US?

Millennials, young adults between 18 and 34 years of age, are now the largest living generation in the United States. They have surpassed in numbers the generation of baby boomers (those born between 1946 and 1964) who long dominated American politics and culture. The millennial population, already at 83.1 million and representing more than a quarter of the U.S. population, is projected to peak in 2036, surpassing the baby boom generation, which reached 78.8 million in 1999.[1]

Tens of thousands of students across the nation walked out of class in protest of school violence in Parkland, Florida following the shooting death of 17 students at Marjory Stoneman Douglas High School. The students made clear by their actions that they will "never again" tolerate government inaction on gun control and school safety

©Zach Gibson/Getty Images

The millennial generation is the most diverse generation in U.S. history, with 44.2 percent being members of a minority race or ethnic group.[2] Millennials are better educated than previous generations as well. Four in ten millennial workers ages 25 to 29 had at least a bachelor's degree in 2016, compared with smaller percentages of earlier generational cohorts. Women, in particular, have made substantial education gains; almost half (46 percent) of employed millennial women ages 25 to 29 hold at least a bachelor's degree, up substantially from previous generations.[3]

This group is having a substantial effect on the way the country works and lives. Young people in large numbers are substituting bikes for cars, multiple job holding in the gig economy for full time employment, Amazon for Macy's, streaming for network TV, and Facebook posts for newspaper subscriptions. As we learn more about this emerging majority, some of the stereotypes associated with them are falling way. For example, although the Great Recession forced millennials to postpone some life choices, recent data show the older members of this cohort are now forming families, buying homes, and settling into communities just as their elders did.[4] Although voter turnout among millennials had been sluggish, this age group was the only one to see turnout increases since 2012, especially among older members. This is what political scientists would expect, and it fits the pattern that turnout increases with age.[5]

As You READ

- **What kinds of citizen involvement fuel democracies?**
- **What ideals fuel American democracy?**
- **What are some of the changes and challenges facing America today?**

Millennials who are attending college or who are college age, remain more civic minded than their immediate predecessors in Generation X. Compared to their elders, they volunteer in their communities at higher rates, are more tolerant of lifestyle differences, are more supportive of equal opportunities for all, and are less likely to support military solutions to international problems.[6] They are also more likely to express support for nontraditional forms of participation. For example, hundreds of thousands of millennial women have joined women's marches across the country in recent years demanding that their voices be heard on policy issues from health care to sexual harassment. And even younger adults have shown their political prowess by organizing demonstrations across the country to protest school violence and to lobby for gun reform.

Social media are particularly useful tools for engaging millennials. They allow young people to disseminate their views, mobilize like-minded others, and circumvent traditional gatekeepers of information.[7] Hashtags like *#MeToo* and #NEVERAGAIN became powerful symbols of strength for young women combating sexual assault and harassment and for young men and women combatting the scourge of gun violence. Millennials are also prone to register their political views through the marketplace; fully one-third have used their buying power expressly to reward or punish companies for social policies.[8] Members of racial and ethnic minorities display their own participatory strengths. For example, Hispanics are more likely than their white counterparts to attend political protests; African American youth are more likely than their non-black contemporaries to contact radio stations, TV stations, and newspapers to express political opinions.[9]

Yet, when it comes to electoral politics, a majority of millennials have been turned off by what they see and hear in the political arena. In one study, 60 percent said they believe elected officials are motivated by selfish reasons. Only 15 percent reported that they believe politicians are interested in helping people like themselves.[10] As a result, they actively avoid politics. Todd, a high school junior, responded to researchers asking if he had ever thought about running for political office this way: "It's about lying, cheating, getting nothing done. That's not how I want to spend my time."[11] Todd's views may seem unsurprising given the divisiveness of political dialogue in recent years and the negative images of political leaders portrayed in the media. This attitude might be changing, however, in the wake of dissatisfaction with recent government policies. Thousands of young people, particularly women, have expressed interest in running for offices at every level of government.

It is the millennials who will bear the brunt of political decisions made today. They face an uncertain future threatened by fiscal debt, rising levels of economic inequality, and environmental crisis. For that reason, it is more important than ever that millennials sustain active interest and participation in the political process and that we find ways to overcome disparities in income, education, ethnicity, and gender to ensure that all sectors of society get a fair hearing.

Now, as the largest voting bloc in the nation, it is your turn: your turn to make sense of our political choices, to formulate public policies, to run for office, to vote, and to serve in government. What will you make of this opportunity? Where will you take us?

Throughout this text, we will introduce you to young people already making a difference in the traditional political arena as well as through new forms of political participation. It is our hope that by learning about youth who are changing the face of American politics, you too will take a greater interest in exercising the powers you have as a citizen to effect change. In a democracy, citizenship is a two-sided coin: It confers rights and protections on members of the political community, but in return it requires allegiance and involvement. Each of us must weigh the costs and benefits of participation. The benefits may be policies we support; the costs involve our time and attention. Often, involvement is achieved only through the active encouragement of others.

As you will see throughout this book, citizenship today is in a precarious state. For much of the past half-century, voter turnout has remained well below that of other advanced democracies, and the level of trust between citizens and elected national leaders has reached historic lows.[12] We believe that citizenship today is at a crossroads: We can strengthen the reciprocal bonds of trust between citizen and government, or we can watch these bonds continue to fray. We can either work at finding solutions to the pressing problems that endanger our future or watch these problems worsen. There are signs that young people are ready to open a dialogue about how to construct a more vibrant democracy that works for all citizens. That is the central hope of this book. ∎

POLITICS, POWER, AND PARTICIPATION

We all live in communities in which we participate in a wide range of activities with our neighbors (see "Citizen Activities in a Democratic Society"). We attend school board meetings with some and go to church services with others. We play softball with neighborhood friends, and our siblings may attend scout meetings with others. These relationships make up **civic life**, the constellation of relationships that keep us connected with others and make our communities vital places to live and work. By voluntarily participating in civic life, we build what is called **social capital**, bonds of trust and reciprocity between citizens that form the glue holding societies together. No one forces us to attend a community meeting or to volunteer for environmental clean-up activities, or to contribute to a community foundation; but when we do, our communities are better for it and we feel a stronger connection to our neighbors.

Civic life includes institutions of **government**—the body or bodies charged with making official policies for citizens. Citizens participate in government by acts like voting, attending political meetings, and campaigning for candidates they support for office.

Politics is the process by which we choose government officials and make decisions about public policy. In a democracy, citizens play a primary role in this process, but—like being a good neighbor—it is a role they must choose to play. Americans are not forced to leave the pleasures and obligations of private life to engage in political or community service. Yet the vitality of our social and political institutions depends on our willingness as citizens to step outside of our private lives and to work with others voluntarily in making our neighborhoods safe, our communities strong, and our government work effectively for all.

If our engagement in voluntary associations with others builds social capital and gives rise to civic and political involvement, then is it better to be engaged in more voluntary associations? Some social scientists regard the number and kind of voluntary associations sustained in society as a sign of a nation's well-being.[13] That is why some of them, like Harvard's Robert Putnam, worry about what they see as a decline in civic activities ranging from attendance at school board meetings to meeting with one's neighbors to sitting down to dinner with our families. Putnam argues that a decline in civic life has led to falling interest in political activities from attending campaign rallies to voting. Some critics challenge Putnam's findings, noting that participation in new forms of civic activity like soccer leagues has replaced older associations and that young people have turned to electronic networking rather than face-to-face encounters in building social capital.[14] Still others claim that globalization and the pace of life are simply altering the ways citizens

civic life Participation in the collective life of the community.

social capital Bonds of trust and reciprocity between citizens that form the glue that holds modern societies together.

government The body (or bodies) charged with making official policies for citizens.

politics The process by which we choose government officials and make decisions about public policy.

Citizen Activities in a Democratic Society

PRIVATE LIFE	CIVIC LIFE	
Individual activities	**Civic engagement activities**	
	Nonpolitical activities	Political participation
Family School Work	Recycling Fellowship meetings Service activities	Voting Attending political meetings Political campaigning
Cultivates personal relationships, serves individual needs—e.g., getting an education, earning a living	Provides community services and acts as a training ground for political participation	Fulfills demands of democratic citizenship

Functions

Citizens have many opportunities to participate in the civic life of their communities.

direct democracy A form of government in which decisions about public policy extend to the entire citizenry.

representative democracy A form of government in which popular decision making is restricted to electing or appointing the public officials who make public policy.

majority rule The requirement that electoral majorities determine who is elected to office and that majorities in power determine our laws and how they are administered.

minority rights Protections beyond the reach of majority control guaranteed to all citizens.

The National Security Agency determined Facebook was used by foreign agents to influence the 2016 presidential election. Should the U.S. government mandate that Facebook report the source of political ads during political campaigns?

interact with government. Today's citizens, these critics claim, are more critical of traditional forms of participation like voting and supporting a political party, preferring instead more expressive and individualistic activities like boycotting companies that pollute the environment.[15] They are more prone to take advantage of new technologies to make their voices heard than to rely on older forms of political expression.

No matter which vision of civic health we choose to embrace, it still matters mightily who controls the levers of political power in government. Institutions of government affect almost every facet of our daily lives, from the quality of the water we drink to the type and quality of education we receive. Therefore, it is important that the choice of individuals controlling those levers be distributed widely and fairly. Democracy thrives when citizen participation is robust. But political and civic involvement is not evenly spread across the entire population. This has serious consequences for ensuring an equal voice for all citizens.

Your authors believe there is ample reason for optimism about the future of civic life in America, but there is vast room for improvement as well. We will highlight some promising avenues in the chapters that follow.

Types of Government

Governments may take a variety of forms, but a key distinction between them is how widely power is shared among the citizens. In a monarchy or dictatorship, a single person exercises absolute power. By contrast, in a **direct democracy**, political decision making extends to the entire citizenry. Some ancient Greek city-states, for example, made decisions about the use of power in open-air assemblies involving thousands of citizens. Only free males, however, were counted as citizens. Few modern nations employ direct democracy; most free nations prefer instead to restrict popular decision making to electing or appointing officials who make public policy. This type of government is properly called a **representative democracy**. Citizens in a representative democracy hold public officials accountable through periodic elections and the rule of law. America's representative democracy is characterized by **majority rule** and protections for **minority rights**. Electoral majorities determine who is elected to office, and majorities in power determine our laws and how they are administered. However, certain rights, like freedom of speech and religion, are beyond the reach of majority control. A majority of citizens may not deny to a minority those rights that are protected for all. We will discuss these features of our political system in more detail in Chapter 2.

Democratic societies also enshrine certain individual rights and place limits on the actions government officials can undertake. For example, our Constitution's Fourth Amendment outlaws unreasonable

searches and seizures. Of course, potential clashes between government authorities and individual rights are legion. Sometimes government actions presumably undertaken for our own protection may threaten individual rights. The National Security Agency, the Federal Intelligence Surveillance Court, and even local law enforcement agencies annually make thousands of requests to Facebook for information regarding users it suspects of terrorism or crime. These requests are made without the knowledge of users and include a nondisclosure agreement that prohibits Facebook from notifying its users of the government's action. Civil libertarians, and many Americans generally, believe such government actions threaten our privacy and our ability to protect ourselves from legal jeopardy. How best to balance the interests of personal freedom and national security is an important topic to which we will have many occasions to return throughout this text.

Political Power

The legitimate use of force and political power by a representative government rests on either explicit contracts establishing the relationship between governors and the governed—such as the U.S. Constitution—or on certain shared values and standards that citizens have come to accept over time. Although citizens may not agree with specific government policies, they will support as legitimate, or lawful, policies founded on accepted contracts and standards. For example, many Americans opposed the U.S. invasion of Iraq following the terrorist attacks of September 11, 2001, but few disputed the right of the president and Congress to wage war. Most Americans accept their duty to pay a fair share in taxes; but they would surely balk if the government tried to confiscate all of our wealth.

Even in democratic societies, questions frequently arise about who exercises real **political power** by influencing or controlling the institutions of government. One school of thought, the **ruling elite theory**, argues that wealthy and well-educated citizens exercise a disproportionate amount of influence over political decision making, despite the existence of institutions that encourage widespread participation. These individuals are more likely to have access to government officials or to become government officials themselves. They are also more informed about political issues and more interested in the outcome of these issues. The wealthy have a vested interest, for example, in reducing the amount of taxes they pay and creating favorable political and economic conditions for their investments. Some versions of ruling elite theory, however, suggest that elites actually are an important force for social advancement.[16] Empirical studies demonstrate that wealthier and better-educated citizens show a greater commitment to values such as fair play, diversity, and respect for civil liberties than those with less income or education. They are also more alert to threats to basic democratic values and more likely to insist on enforcement of individual rights.

A competing theory called **pluralism** asserts that various groups and coalitions constantly vie for government favor and the ability to exercise political power but none enjoys long-term dominance.[17] In this view, groups that get their way today may be on the losing end tomorrow. When a group of like-minded citizens is determined to change public policy or to fight a proposed policy that it finds threatening, it can organize into interest groups that employ a wide array of tactics, from supporting candidates who promise to advance their cause to developing sophisticated public relations campaigns and legal challenges to rally support (see Chapter 8). For example, for years opponents of same-sex marriage prevailed in outlawing the practice in most states. Over the years, lesbian, gay, bisexual, and transgender (LGBT) groups were able to mobilize support for their cause and to challenge these laws in court. In 2015, the U.S. Supreme Court, reflecting a swift change in political attitudes toward the LGBT community, legalized same-sex marriage nationwide. As long as the rules guiding interest group competition are fair and fairly enforced, pluralists claim, no one group is permanently disadvantaged.

A recent study testing these competing theories proposed a hybrid theory that its authors believe comes closest to describing the actual flow of power in America. Researchers concluded that economic elites and organized groups representing business interests have substantially greater independent impact on government policies than average citizens. Yet,

political power The ability to get things done by controlling or influencing the institutions of government.

ruling elite theory The view positing that wealthy and well-educated citizens exercise a disproportionate amount of influence over political decision making.

pluralism The view positing that various groups and coalitions constantly vie for government favor and the ability to exercise political power but none enjoys long-term dominance.

Opinions About Power and Influence

Most Americans Agree That They Do Not Have Enough Power And Influence in Washington

% Who Say Each Group has...

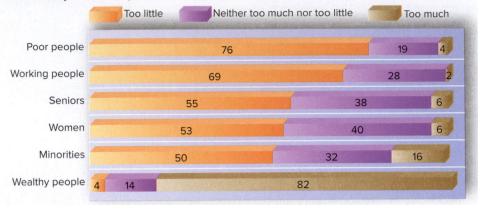

	Too little	Neither too much nor too little	Too much
Poor people	76	19	4
Working people	69	28	2
Seniors	55	38	6
Women	53	40	6
Minorities	50	32	16
Wealthy people	4	14	82

Most Americans are convinced that the wealthy exercise too much power in Washington while the poor and minorities are left behind.

---

biased pluralism The view positing that power and public policies tilt largely in the direction of the well-off.

the preferences of these economic elites and those of ordinary citizens often coincide. In such cases, both groups win when the policies favored by the elite are enacted. But when elite proposals and the interests of ordinary Americans conflict, it is often the economic elite who come out on top. The authors concluded that power in America—at least in recent years—is best characterized as a kind of **biased pluralism** in which the wealthy play a larger role in determining policies—especially economic policies—than do typical citizens, but that both wealthy and average Americans are well served when their interests intersect.[18] What is worrisome, however, is that income inequality is on the rise with wealth becoming concentrated into fewer and fewer hands. As a result, the interests of the wealthy and the average American may begin to diverge more sharply while the influence of the wealthy continues to rise. Opinion polls indicate the public is well aware of these disparities in power (see "Opinions About Power and Influence").

In this book, we are most concerned about increasing popular participation in ways that bring us closer to achieving genuinely pluralistic outcomes. Some sectors of the American population already participate at very high levels and can be sure their voices are heard, if not always heeded. Others are barely heard at all; throughout this book, we will identify ways to increase their volume.

Participation and Democracy

Active citizen participation is a cornerstone of democratic theory. The Greek philosopher Aristotle (384–322 B.C.E.) felt that citizens should not simply sit back and enjoy the benefits of society; they must also take responsibility for its operation. In Aristotle's time, policy decisions were formulated by assemblies of free citizens numbering in the thousands. Enlightenment thinkers who influenced the Framers of our Constitution generally agreed that democratic success depends on widespread participation. British philosopher John Locke (1632–1704) argued that the power of the government comes from the consent of its citizens and that consent is possible only when the citizenry is informed and engaged. Thomas Jefferson (1743–1826), in his more radical moments, called for periodic citizen uprisings to reinvigorate the spirit of democracy. Much of American history confirms the importance of citizen participation. Throughout our nation's history, many Americans fought long and hard to gain the opportunity to participate in democratic practices that were previously closed to them.

Many states provide expanded opportunities for citizen participation. A procedure called "initiative," available in twenty-six states, enables citizens to draft their own laws and propose constitutional amendments for voter approval if the sponsors of the measure gather enough signatures. There are two types of initiatives: **direct initiatives**, available in some states, allow proposals backed by a sufficient number of citizen signatures to go directly on the ballot; **indirect initiatives** are first submitted to lawmakers for approval before being submitted to the voters. Similarly, twenty-four states allow for **popular referendum**, which allows citizens to approve or repeal measures already on the books. **Legislative referendum** is another form of referendum, available in all fifty states, that requires legislative bodies to take some proposed measures directly to the voters for approval before taking

direct initiatives Procedure that enables citizens to place proposals for laws and amendments directly on the ballot for voter approval.

indirect initiatives Citizen-initiated procedure for placing proposals on the ballot, requiring legislative action before submission to voters.

popular referendum A device that allows citizens to approve or repeal measures already acted on by legislative bodies.

Legislative referendum Ballot measure aimed at securing voter approval for some legislative acts, such as changes to a state's constitution.

Declining Social Trust Around the World—Is This the Beginning of a New Generation of Critical Citizens?

Source: NASA/JPL

Many factors influence the bonds of trust between citizens and governments that are vital for effective governance. The chart shown here tracks levels of trust reported by adults ages 18 and older in ten nations representing some of the world's largest economies.

Most nations—especially in the West—have surprisingly low levels of trust in their national leaders. They seem to have experienced "a flight from politics, or what the Germans call *Politikverdrossenheit:* a weakness about its debates, disbelief about its claims, skepticism about its results, cynicism about its practitioners."* Political scientist Pippa Norris believes widespread cynicism about government signals the emergence of a new type of "critical citizen, dissatisfied democrats who adhere strongly to democratic values but who find existing structures of representative government invented in the eighteenth and nineteenth centuries to be wanting. . . ."† But these younger, well-educated citizens are not apathetic; they are more responsive to non-traditional means of participation like demonstrations or product boycotts than more traditional methods like voting because these alternative approaches promote a greater sense of social solidarity.

Questions:

1. What factors do you believe explain the generally low levels of trust in most of the world's richest nations?
2. What factors might account for the changes in trust levels in Western democracies between 2017 to 2018? Are these changes significant?
3. Does the graph support Pippa Norris's arguments? Why or why not?

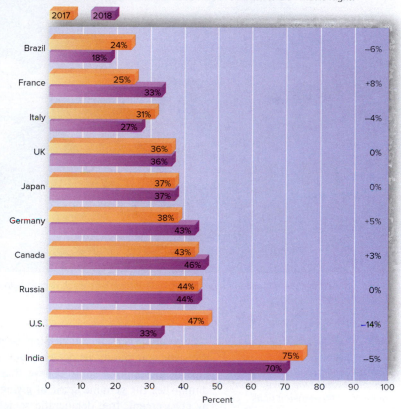

Trust in National Government
How Much Do You Trust the National Government to Do What Is Right?

Legend: 2017, 2018

Country	2017	2018	Change
Brazil	24%	18%	−6%
France	25%	33%	+8%
Italy	31%	27%	−4%
UK	36%	36%	0%
Japan	37%	37%	0%
Germany	38%	43%	+5%
Canada	43%	46%	+3%
Russia	44%	44%	0%
U.S.	47%	33%	−14%
India	75%	70%	−5%

Percent (x-axis: 0 10 20 30 40 50 60 70 80 90 100)

Source: 2018 Edelman Trust Baromoter https://www.edelman.com/trust-barometer.

*Norris, Pippa, "Introduction: The Growth of *Critical Citizens?" in Norris, Pippa, ed., Critical Citizens: Global Support for Democratic Government* (New york: Oxford University Press, 1999), 6; see also Ronald Inglehart, *Modernization and Postmodernization: Cultural, Economic, and Political Change in 43 Societies* (Princeton, NJ: Princeton University Press, 1997).

†Norris, 27.

---

effect. Changes in state constitutions usually fall into this category. Finally, nineteen states plus the District of Columbia permit **recall**, in which citizens can remove and replace a public official before the end of a term. Wisconsin held recall elections in 2012 for several legislators and the governor following an unpopular effort by these political leaders to limit collective bargaining rights for public employees.

A free society relies heavily on the voluntary activities of free individuals outside of government as well. Our nation accomplishes many of its social needs through the work of charitable organizations, religious congregations, and professional groups. Thousands of charities and foundations provide money and personnel for programs ranging from support for the arts to sheltering the homeless. Volunteers power these organizations by devoting their time and energy to improve the quality of life in our communities. As we will see, these organizations also serve as training grounds for developing the skills we need to become full and active participants in our nation's political system. Government can encourage

> **recall** Procedure whereby citizens can remove and replace a public official before the end of a term.

It is estimated that over 61 million Americans volunteer their time each year to help those less fortunate than themselves.

John Locke (1632–1704) argued that the power of the government comes from the consent of its citizens.

civic voluntarism by establishing networks of volunteers like AmeriCorps, the nation's domestic community service program. Though such programs have typically received strong bipartisan support, some believe that providing government incentives for volunteering diminishes the genuine spirit of giving. Whether or not volunteer activities are sponsored by government, free democratic societies depend on the readiness of individuals to take the time to get involved. They rely on the leadership skills of citizens to help find acceptable solutions to problems. They also require that a set of principles or ideals be adopted that extols the worth and contributions of citizens.

AMERICAN POLITICAL IDEALS

Ideas, values, and beliefs about how governments should operate are known as **ideologies**. Ideologies describe the basic principles political communities support and hope to advance (like democracy, equality, and freedom) as well as the extent of power governments should have in pursuing these ends. Some ideologies, like communism, for example, call for an expansive role of government in the everyday lives of citizens, one that may limit economic opportunities and freedom of expression. Other ideologies, like **liberal democracy**, the ideology that guided the Framers of our constitution, call for a more limited role for government.

In our liberal democracy, the primary role of government is to protect individual rights. It rests on three essential notions: natural rights, the formation of a social contract by consent of the governed, and majority rule. The most influential advocate of this ideology was John Locke. A physician by training, Locke became involved in the politics of Whig radicals who challenged the authority of the British Stuart monarchy in the late seventeenth century. These radicals, who favored placing more power into the hands of an elected Parliament, succeeded in pulling off a bloodless revolution in 1688.

Locke speculated that humans at one time probably had little need for authority because there was little competition for resources. Resources were plentiful, and most individuals found ways to avoid conflict. Each individual, to the extent possible, guarded his or her own life, liberty, and property to which he had a God-granted natural right. Over time, however, populations grew, creating competition for diminishing resources. Conflicts over ownership of property led to the need for a neutral arbiter to settle disputes peacefully. That arbiter was government. Locke believed that free and equal persons willingly entered into social contracts to establish governments in order to avoid the "incommodities" of war and conflict with others. On our own, we have a limited capacity to protect our life, liberty, and property. If we band together in government, we come to each other's aid in the protection of these natural rights.

In his *Second Treatise of Government,* Locke articulated the underlying philosophy of liberal democracy.[19] He argued that humans are born naturally free and equal; no one is born subject to another's will, and no one can control another without that person's consent. People place themselves under the control of a government because of the mutual advantages it offers its citizens. Under such an arrangement, majority rule provides a reasonable basis for making decisions. In this way, each member of the community has an equal voice in decision making, and decisions reflect the consensus of most citizens. Governments, however, derive authority from the consent of those who form them, and they hold our allegiance only if they protect our life, liberty, and property better than we could on our own. If government becomes a threat to citizens' rights, the social contract fails, and the people have the option of dissolving it and beginning anew.

The authors of our Declaration of Independence drew heavily on the ideas of Locke in drafting that document and making the case for independence from British rule. Ideas alone, however, do not make history; they must be advanced by proponents with the skills and determination to see them achieved. American history offers many examples of individuals like Susan B. Anthony and Martin Luther King, Jr., who worked tirelessly to bring opportunities for **political participation** like voting and running for office to a wider and more diverse population than originally envisioned by the Framers.

THE CHANGING FACE OF THE AMERICAN CITIZENRY

As we seek ways to increase the engagement of today's citizens, we must be aware that our citizenry is rapidly becoming older and more diverse. At the same time, the gap between those with substantial resources and those with few is increasing. Forces of globalization are intensifying these divisions.

When the U.S. Constitution was ratified at the end of the eighteenth century, more than four million white Europeans and their descendants lived in the United States. (This figure does not include Native Americans, whose population some researchers place at about 600,000,[20] although estimates vary greatly; nor does it include over a half-million black slaves and an estimated sixty thousand free blacks.) Today the U.S. population is over 325 million, drawn from all corners of the world. Hispanic Americans are the nation's fastest-growing minority group, now making up over 16 percent of the population. African Americans are a close second at about 13 percent, and Asian Americans represent about 5 percent of the population. A growing number represent multiethnic roots. Despite the progress these groups have made in securing civil rights, many are still not well integrated into American civic life.

The U.S. Census Bureau estimates that minorities from all backgrounds, now roughly one-third of the U.S. population, are expected to become the majority by 2044. The combined minority population in Texas, California, Hawaii, and New Mexico already exceeds the white non-Hispanic population in these states.

Fifty years ago, just over a third of all Americans lived in the suburbs; today that figure is about 55 percent. Once the preserve of mostly non-Hispanic whites, the suburbs today are growing increasingly racially and ethnically diverse (see "The People in Your Neighborhood Most Likely Look Like You"). According to a recent report, the number of diverse suburbs in the nation's fifty largest metropolitan areas increased to 1,376 in 2010, a 37 percent jump since 2000 with the greatest diversity found in the nation's older suburbs. During the same period, the share of metropolitan area residents who live in predominantly white suburbs (more than 80 percent white) slipped from 26 percent to 18 percent. However, the study also points out that diverse suburbs often have a hard time staying that way as populations continue to migrate. Many central cities remain racially divided with some minority groups facing apartheid levels of segregation and civic dysfunction.[21]

Although many neighborhoods may be experiencing greater racial diversity, these same neighborhoods may be becoming less diverse economically. Largely as a result of growing income inequality, the share of neighborhoods across the United States that are predominantly middle class or mixed income had fallen to 76 percent in 2010, down from 85 percent in 1980. At the same time, the share that are majority lower income had risen to 28 percent in 2010, up from 23 percent in 1980, and the share of majority upper income neighborhoods had grown from 9 percent in 1980 to 18 percent in 2010.[22] This pattern of growing income segregation can breed distrust, and it makes it harder to solve some of the social and economic problems facing our nation. There is also evidence that economic segregation depresses voter turnout in all but the wealthiest communities. Concentration of poverty in an area, for example, clusters together individuals with fewer political skills for addressing community issues and may lead residents to withdraw from engagement out of despair of ever changing conditions for the better.[23]

The past few decades have also witnessed a greater openness about sexual preferences that has produced a more politically active gay and lesbian community. In recent years, same-sex partners have pressed for the same rights as those afforded married couples, and the Supreme Court has legalized same-sex marriages in the United States. Still, many states continue to discriminate against LGBT individuals when it comes to employment, housing, and the use of public accommodations like access to public housing. The battle by the LGBT community for the right to the same protections as heterosexuals is likely to continue in a nation increasingly polarized over the role of government in personal choice. In general, young Americans are more accepting of racial, ethnic, and gender differences than are their elders.[24]

The People in Your Neighborhood Most Likely Look Like You

People Who Live in Your Neighborhood: More Racially Diverse, More Alike Economically (with Growing Income Segregation)			
	Living in Racially Diverse* Neighborhoods	People Living in Predominantly ** Lower-Income Neighborhoods	People Living in Predominantly** Upper-Income Neighborhoods
1980	NA	23%	9%
2000	26%	NA	NA
2010	30%	28%	18%

Neighborhood ethnic diversity is on the rise, but so is income segregation.

*Data from fifty largest metropolitan areas. Diverse defined as non-whites making up 20–60% of population.
Source: Myron Orfield and Thomas Luce, *America's Racially Diverse Suburbs: Opportunities and Challenges* (Minneapolis: Institute for Metropolitan Opportunity, University of Minnesota Law School, July 20, 2012), 2, http://www.law.umn.edu/uploads/e0/65/e065d82a1c1da0bfef7d86172ec5391e/Diverse_Suburbs_FINAL.pdf.

**Based on census tracts from 942 metropolitan and metropolitan statistical areas.
Source: Paul Taylor and Richard Fry, "The Rise of Residential Segregation by Income," Pew Research Center, August 1, 2012, http://www.pewsocialtrends.org/2012/08/01/the-rise-of-residential-segregation-by-income/.

Source: Taylor, Paul and Fry, Richard, "The Rise of Residential Segragation by Income," *Pew Research Center,* August 1, 2012, http://www.pewsocialtrends.org/2012/08/01/the-rise-of-residential-segregation-by-income/.

Growing Older

The elderly population is expected to double by 2050, when one in five Americans will be over age 65 (see "The Graying of America"). The aging of the population poses some special problems. The Social Security and Medicare Boards of Trustees project substantial shortfalls for Social

Security and Medicare as fewer able-bodied working-age adults work to support the needs of the growing number of elderly Americans. How will we meet this growing need for financial support and medical services? No doubt the elderly, who vote in much higher numbers than young people, will exert political pressure to keep or even increase their benefits. How will the younger generation respond? Given the scale of the coming elder boom, will young people still be willing to support generous government programs that provide for the needs of elderly Americans?

Growing Apart

When the U.S. Constitution was written, **social class** divisions among Americans were much more visible than they are today. They manifested themselves through distinctions in dress, social stature, and political power. For example, workmen wore functional clothing of washable unbleached linen; by contrast, gentlemen regularly sported wool coats and jackets, and donned powdered wigs on special occasions. More than two centuries later, class divisions are not so obvious. In a world in which even those with few resources own cell phones and the wealthy wear jeans and sweat suits, it is increasingly difficult to tell someone's status by looking at his or her clothes. During the boom years at the beginning of this century, easily available credit and the flattening of prices for technology gave many Americans access to high-end consumer items. Today, nearly three-quarters of Americans own smartphones[25] and the number of wireless devices in use in America actually exceeds our total population, with many people using more than one device.[26]

Yet the gap between rich and poor is growing. According to the Organization for Economic Co-operation and Development, income inequality in the United States is the fifth highest among the organization's 34 member nations.[27] (Only Turkey, Chile, Costa Rica, and South Africa have higher rates of income inequality.) Rich households in America are leaving behind both middle- and lower-income groups. The top 10 percent of income earners took home more than half of the nation's total income in 2012, with the top 1 percent alone taking in almost a quarter (24 percent) of all income, the highest levels recorded since 1913, when the government first started tracking such data. And although incomes among all Americans grew from 2013 to 2016, gains at the highest levels of income grew the fastest and the wealthy were able to recover much more quickly from the recent recession than were the middle or lower classes.[28] Moreover, the challenges to climbing the economic ladder are steeper than many people imagine. In a study comparing nine economically developed countries in Europe and America, the United States scored lowest on intergenerational upward mobility, with the possible exception of the United Kingdom.[29] One researcher concludes: "the chances of ending up rich if you were born to a low-income family [in the United States] are on the order of just one percent."[30] These are the types of concerns that helped fuel the Occupy Wall Street movement that started in 2011 and gave rise to support for candidates like Bernie Sanders in the 2016 presidential campaign.

Throughout much of the twentieth century, many working-class Americans could count on a career in one of the nation's skilled industries like steel or auto manufacturing. Labor unions organized workers in these fields, enhancing their job security and income and propelling them into the middle classes. Over the past thirty years, however, employers have transferred many of these jobs overseas where they can employ cheaper labor. Between 2000 and 2010 alone, the United States lost more than five million manufacturing jobs, amounting to nearly one-third of its manufacturing employment.[31] Although there are signs that the pace of job loss in manufacturing may be slowing, it is increasingly clear that the well-paying jobs of the future for American citizens will emphasize high levels of financial acumen, technological proficiency, and creativity. This shift places great emphasis on access to education for career advancement and financial security. At the same time, however, the cost of a college education is skyrocketing while government resources to help students cover those costs are shrinking. So the economically disadvantaged must choose debt or low wages, and unfortunately they sometimes end up with both.

The Graying of America

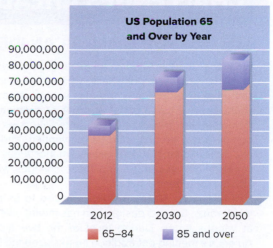

US Population 65 and Over by Year

Legend: 65–84 | 85 and over

Projections show Americans living longer and longer lives with fewer workers paying into the social programs that support them. The nation has not yet tackled how to address this challenge.

Source: An Aging Nation: The Older Population in the United States Population: Estimates and Projections. Current Population Reports, May 2014.

social class The perceived combination of wealth, income, education, and occupation that contributes to one's status and power in society.

THE CHANGING AMERICAN IDENTITY

What does it mean to be an American? The national identity, once defined by middle-class, white male standards has shifted dramatically over the past several decades. These changes have come about because of a variety of factors including immigration, changes in fertility rates for various demographic groups, cultural reinvention, and legislative and judicial changes. As a result, America today is more diverse than ever before, and these changes will continue into the foreseeable future.

The United States is often referred to as a nation of immigrants. But this designation has meant different things at various times. During most of the twentieth century, America's melting pot tradition emphasized the importance of cultural and social integration. While not completely ignoring some of the traditions of their native lands—especially in the enclaves in which they lived—immigrants were expected to speak English and to conform to the ways and traditions of the dominant culture. Today, it is not unusual to see public signposts in several different languages and, in some locales such as Los Angeles, voters can cast their ballots in any of seven different languages, including Khmer, Korean, and Tagalog.

Women's roles have changed substantially as well. Once expected to dutifully perform the chores of the household and to raise children, women emerged as a major economic force in the late twentieth century and, although their numerical strength is not yet reflected in corporate boardrooms and state capitols, they have changed the ways Americans view the relationship between family and work life.

In 1965, there were no blacks in the U.S. Senate, no black governors, and only a handful of black representatives and state legislators. Although blacks are still underrepresented in government, their numbers have expanded and 2008 witnessed the election of the first African American president, changing forever the aspirational ceiling for black leaders.

Gender stereotypes have also been shattered. Rulings like *Obergefell v. Hodges* opened the door to same-sex marriages, and transgender individuals have gained legal protections in some states and cities.

A survey taken after the 2016 presidential election showed most Americans have embraced these changes, with a majority believing American identity is tied to factors such as respect for American political institutions and laws, having American citizenship, and accepting people of

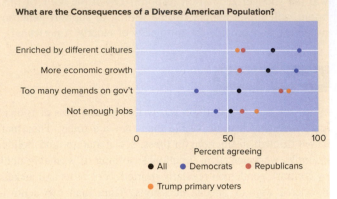

What are the Consequences of a Diverse American Population?

- Enriched by different cultures
- More economic growth
- Too many demands on gov't
- Not enough jobs

Percent agreeing

● All   ● Democrats   ● Republicans

● Trump primary voters

Perceptions of the impact of our quickly diversifying nation vary considerably by political party allegiances.

Source: Sides, John. *Democracy Fund 2016 Voter Study Group.*

diverse backgrounds. However, there were signs of resistance to these changes that broke along partisan lines. For example, 23 percent of Republicans and nearly one in three (30 percent) of Trump primary supporters said that European heritage is important to American identity; by contrast, only 16 percent of Democrats felt this way. Whereas 30 percent of Democrats considered Christianity to be important to American identity, 56 percent of Republicans and nearly two-thirds (63 percent) of Trump supporters said Christianity was part of what it means to be an American.*

Partisan differences also arise regarding what a more diverse citizenry means for the future of the American economy and government (see chart above). These differences may be related to the fact that Donald Trump attracted many lower-income, white males without a college degree, a demographic that has not fared very well economically in our increasingly global economy. (This is a topic to which we will return several times in this text.)

As America moves toward becoming a majority-minority nation, conflicts may continue to arise over the meaning of American identity. However, as in the past, American identity will continue to evolve.

*John Sides, *Race, Religion, and Immigration in 2016: How the Debate over American Identity Shaped the Election and What It Means for a Trump Presidency.* Democracy Fund2016 Voter Study Group, June 2017, https://www.voterstudygroup.org/publications/2016-elections/race-religion-immigration-2016.

Social class adds another dimension to our consideration of civic engagement. We will see in forthcoming chapters that political activity is not spread evenly across all social classes. Those who vote, run for office, contribute to political campaigns, and engage in a wide array of political and civic activities are disproportionately individuals with more wealth. As a result, the wealthy are more likely to be heard by political actors in the corridors of power.

THE FUTURE OF CITIZENSHIP

A number of ideas are surfacing about how we might alter and improve the civic engagement and political participation of American citizens today. Some states now require students to perform community service in order to graduate from high school. More colleges and universities are turning to student **service learning programs** as a legitimate educational experience. Will service learning eventually reconstruct the social capital that many believe will reinvigorate political participation? Or will it contribute to a growing sense that political solutions to social problems are futile? A recent poll found that Americans overwhelmingly support policies designed to support public or community service. But a majority—especially those younger than 30—felt the best way to make positive change was through community volunteerism

Freshman Class Survey: Essential or Very Important Personal Objectives

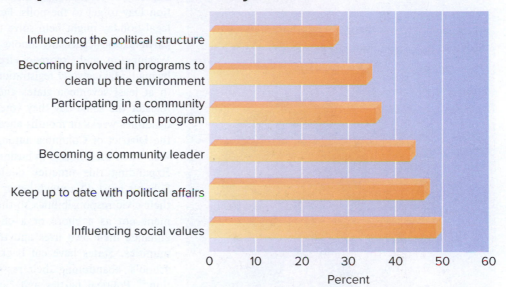

Young people continue to express more interest in community-building activities than direct political participation.

Source: UCLA Higher Education Research Institute, *The American Freshman National Norms Fall 2016.* Accessed at https://www.heri.ucla.edu/monographs/TheAmericanFreshman2016.pdf

rather than through engagement with the political process.[32] One study found that although students exposed to service learning experiences demonstrated increased political awareness, they did not increase their political engagement. Students gained little knowledge about how to bring about political change and remained skeptical about their ability to affect the political system itself.[33] Unlike **civic engagement**, which seeks to build community relationships, **political engagement** involves direct participation with the institutions and processes of the political system. Consequently, the two types of engagement require explicitly different types of education.[34] Although public service is laudatory, the fact that it might displace political participation is troubling. As some have said, young people seem to be running away from politics rather than running for office.

> **service learning programs** Agencies that help connect volunteers with organizations in need of help.
>
> **civic engagement** Involvement in any activity aimed at influencing the collective well-being of the community.
>
> **political engagement** Active interest and participation in political activities

citizenship Quiz

Can you pass the U.S. Citizenship Test? See how well you know the content in this chapter covered on the citizenship test required of foreign-born candidates for naturalization.

1. Name one *responsibility* that is only for U.S. citizens.
2. Name one *right* of only U.S. citizens.
3. Name *two rights* of everyone living in the United States.

(1) Serve on a jury, vote in a federal election. (2) Vote in a federal election, run for federal office. (3) Freedom of expression, speech, assembly, petition, and worship; right to bear arms.

Source: U.S. Citizenship and Immigration Services.

Perhaps the alienation many young people feel from politics can be eased by changes in our political system and in our electoral processes. Participation improves when government agencies become more open, when participation is made more accessible, and when a range of political and nonpolitical associations mobilize citizens to take action. For example, a majority of young people find they are simply too busy on Election Day to get to the polls. Perhaps, declaring Election Day a legal holiday might help solve this dilemma and increase voter participation—especially among the young. Or, like in Oregon, Washington, and Colorado, elections can be conducted entirely by mail. Making voter registration easier would also help. Citizens in at least seventeen states and the District of Columbia can register the same day they vote instead of meeting registration deadlines weeks or months ahead, and at least twelve states and the District of Columbia automatically register every citizen to vote when they engage in business with any government agency. Expanding this practice could boost turnout substantially. Schools must do a much better job of educating students about their civic responsibilities so that they will see political involvement not as a chore or a choice but as an opportunity to enhance their own lives and those of their families and communities. States have cut back on civics requirements in the schools, abandoning their responsibility to democratic education.[35] Political parties and candidates can help increase participation by speaking more directly to the issues that impact young voters and by extending their reach through the use of social media.

Technological change is altering the way we conduct politics in this country. For example, President Donald Trump has demonstrated how powerful Twitter can be in citizen engagement. The #MeToo movement has fostered real hope for change in the ways women are treated in the workplace. Most political leaders and candidates maintain Facebook pages and Twitter feeds. YouTube videos instantaneously record and magnify the actions of the candidates—sometimes to their chagrin. And the Web now has a proven track record as a fundraising tool.

We will discuss many of these ideas and more for enhancing civic and political involvement throughout this text. The most important ideas for improving civic engagement may not yet have been discovered. That is where you come in. As you consider your place in the social fabric of America, we hope you will share your ideas with your class, your community, and your political leaders. In the process, you will be helping to shape the way our democracy functions and fulfilling your role as citizen.

Summary

1. **What kinds of civic involvement fuel democracies?**
   - Citizens can contribute to the civic life of democracy by participating in voluntary associations that build social capital, or bonds of trust among citizens, and by participating in the political process that fuels our form of government.
   - Ours is a representative democracy that allows us to choose and hold accountable leaders who make our laws and policies, thereby enabling us to share in the exercise of political power. In some states, individuals are given additional powers like initiative, referendum, and recall, which permit a more direct exercise of democratic control.
   - There is debate about how power is dispersed in America. Some claim it is exercised almost exclusively by the wealthy; others believe it is widely dispersed among many competing groups with overlapping membership. What is clear is that since those who are well off are more knowledgeable about and more active in political life, their voices are more likely to be heard in the corridors of power than are those of average citizens.

2. **What ideals fuel American democracy?**
   - American democracy gets its inspiration from the liberal democratic views of John Locke and rests on three

essential notions: natural rights, the formulation of a social contract by the consent of the governed, and majority rule.
   - Natural rights include the right to life, liberty, and property. Because these rights are protected, they cannot be denied to any citizen by majority wishes.
   - Our Constitution embodies the notion of popular consent and works best when citizens are informed and actively involved in various forms of political participation, like voting and running for office.

3. **What are some changes and challenges facing America today?**
   - We are growing more diverse as racial and ethnic minorities constitute a larger proportion of our citizenry.
   - We are growing older, a challenge that will make it increasingly difficult to fund programs for the elderly from a smaller population of younger workers.
   - We continue to reflect the divisions of class as those with fewer resources and less education fall further behind economically.

Chapter 2

The Constitution
The Foundation of Citizens' Rights

The U.S. Constitution has endured for over 230 years and has been an inspiration for numerous nations around the world. Is all that changing?

©doublediamondphoto/E+/Getty Images

OUR CONSTITUTION: TIME FOR A CHANGE?

The 2016 presidential election was the fifth in which the candidate losing the popular vote became president. This occurred first in 1824 when, despite losing both the popular and Electoral College votes, John Quincy Adams was awarded the presidency when the matter was sent to the House of Representatives for resolution following the failure of any single candidate to procure the required majority of electoral votes. (The Electoral College vote was spread among four candidates.) The loser of the popular vote went on to become president with a majority of electoral votes in 1876, 1888, 2000, and again in 2016.

It is true that the Framers of our Constitution did not intend the president to be tied too closely to popular opinion; but the institution has evolved in a more democratic direction, causing some observers—and a near majority of the American people[1]—to believe that the way we elect presidents is obsolete. Under the current system, every state regardless of population gets two electoral votes on the basis of equal Senate representation. This arrangement gives small, mostly rural states an advantage over more urban and more

populous states in presidential elections. As a result, California gets one elector for every 713,637 people while a state like Wyoming gets one electoral vote for every 195,167 people. As some commentators have noted, "a Wyoming voter has more than *three-and-a-half times* the electoral power of a California voter" (emphasis in original).[2]

This is not the only feature of our Constitution that critics would like to see changed. The two-senators-per-state provision also gives smaller states more clout in the legislative chamber. The twenty-one smallest states combined hold fewer people than California (which has 39.9 million people), meaning that these smaller states outvote the much larger California by a margin of forty-two to two. What's more, a bill could pass out of the Senate with the support of senators representing just 16.2 percent of the population from the twenty-five smallest states and the vote of the vice president even if the remaining senators representing over 270 million people voted the other way.[3] Obviously, this population imbalance was not as extreme in 1787 when the Constitution was written.

As You READ

- **What factors contributed to the need for a Constitutional Convention?**
- **What are the basic principles that inform our Constitution?**
- **In what ways does constitutional change occur?**

Other changes critics would like to see include a ban on political contributions in our elections, an end to partisan redistricting in the House of Representatives, the addition of seats in the House for states with large populations, a rebalancing of the relative power of each branch of government so that the power of the president is more effectively checked, a requirement for balanced budgets, and other reforms. Some of the more extreme measures call for the replacement of the presidential form of government with a parliamentary form in which the winning party can more easily accomplish the goals it pledged to the electorate.[4]

Of course, the Framers already provide a mechanism for change—the amendment process. But critics believe the process is too onerous (described later in this chapter). Some scholars and jurists believe our Constitution, once seen as a model for the world, has become increasingly irrelevant in the modern world, where democracy and individual rights have become far more expansive than when the Framers met in Philadelphia. Today, emerging nations are more likely to look elsewhere for constitutional guidance. Legal scholars David Law and Mila Versteeg undertook a detailed study of world constitutions in 2012, analyzing provisions of 729 constitutions adopted by 188 countries. It seems that sometime in the late twentieth century, nations turned away from the U.S. model and toward models with more comprehensive rights' protections.[5] Anglo nations are now more likely to look to the Canadian Charter of Rights and Freedoms, which expanded and more firmly guaranteed individual rights during a period of constitutional reform in the late 1960s.

Still, a call for a convention to replace our current constitution is fraught with difficulty. Once convened, there is no way to limit proposals, no matter how fanciful or dangerous. The 1787 convention was originally called simply to revise the Articles of Confederation but led to a completely new form of government. Nevertheless, it may be useful to remind ourselves of Jefferson's admonition that every constitution "naturally expires at the end of 19 years" because "the earth belongs always to the living generation."

In this chapter, we will review the events that led to the adoption of our nation's founding document and examine the provisions that have made it the longest living constitution in the history of the world. We will also investigate those provisions of the over-230-year-old document that might cause it to be straining to meet the needs of twenty-first century America. ∎

THE FOUNDATIONS OF AMERICAN DEMOCRACY

During the first 150 years of English settlement in America, the colonists gave little thought to independence. They focused on survival, which included developing and nurturing institutions of local self-government. Only when the British government looked to the colonies for financial support did relations between the Crown and the colonies sour and, aided by the agitation of radicals, deteriorate to the point of revolution.

Early Colonization

House of Burgesses The first legislative assembly in the American colonies.

The first permanent British colony in North America was Jamestown, founded in 1607 by the Virginia Company of London for the purpose of developing trade and mining gold. In order to regulate and protect the colony, the settlers formed a government consisting of a president and a seven-member council. By 1619, colonists created an assembly known as the **House of Burgesses**, the nation's first legislative body. Composed of representatives elected from among the settlers, it imbued the settlers with an ardor for self-rule. Unfortunately for the company, there was no gold, and harsh conditions coupled with conflicts with native populations hampered trade. The Crown took control of the failing colony in 1624, replacing the president with a royal governor. The House of Burgesses, however, survived the king's efforts to abolish it.

A year after the House of Burgesses was created, forty-one religious dissenters called Puritans established a permanent settlement in the area of modern-day Plymouth, Massachusetts. The Puritans rejected attempts by both the Catholic pope and the king of England to

Jamestown, Virginia, founded in 1607, failed as a mining town but became a training ground for self-rule.

dictate religious doctrine or belief. Because of this stance, they found themselves barred from many professional positions that required membership in the official Church of England. Despairing of reform from within the church, they chose to establish foreign religious outposts of their own. En route to the New World, these dissenters entered into an agreement for self-government, known as the Mayflower Compact. Under this document, the settlers pledged to "constitute, and frame such just and equal laws, ordinances, acts, constitutions, and offices . . . as shall be thought most meet and convenient for the general good of the colony. . . ." The Compact served as a model for other colonies and gave early settlers a taste for self-government that went uncontested by the British for years.

Although they came to America to flee religious persecution, the Puritans themselves were intolerant of dissent. Soon, some settlers began to challenge Puritan orthodoxy. Faced with execution or expulsion, dissidents migrated to form their own colonies; Rhode Island, for example, grew from breakaway settlements founded by former Massachusetts residents. Roger Williams, the colony's founder, sought complete religious toleration and was banished from Massachusetts for proposing separation of church and state.

By 1732, thirteen British colonies dotted the eastern coast of North America, reflecting a variety of religious and political points of view as well as a wealth of nationalities. Each colony developed its own fledgling institutions of government, which despite their differences reflected a commitment to self-rule, popular consent, and respect for law.

The Colonists Respond to Economic Pressures

British policies limited economic progress in the colonies. The Crown saw its colonies primarily as suppliers of raw materials such as cotton, tobacco, and furs to manufacturers in Britain. There these resources were made into finished goods such as clothing, tools, and furniture, many of which were then exported back to the colonies for sale. The colonists were required to trade exclusively with Britain, which meant that all finished goods exported to the colonies—regardless of their source—first passed through England. The goods were loaded on British ships and taxed before sale, making non-British products more expensive for colonists and preventing genuine competition. For years, colonists skirted these limits through tactics such as smuggling and piracy. Colonial governors, whose salaries often depended on approval by local assemblies, largely ignored these widespread practices.

The Seven Years' War (1756–1763) brought home dramatically to Britain the costs of protecting their North American colonies from France and its Native American allies while maintaining a vast empire elsewhere in the world. The British sought to defray costs by imposing taxes on sugar and printed materials. New England merchants and distillers of rum were particularly disturbed by the sugar tax and objected that the taxes were imposed without their participation in their enactment, giving rise to the rally cry of "taxation without representation." The British responded paternalistically that colonial interests were taken into consideration by members of Parliament even if the colonists themselves did not have a direct say. More contentious than the sugar tax, the Stamp Act affected a far wider swath of colonists from all walks of life by requiring revenue stamps to be affixed to newspapers and pamphlets as well as all legal documents. Secret organizations known as the "Sons of Liberty" organized in several colonies to protest the act, often by resorting to violence against customs agents representing the Crown. The Virginia House of Burgesses denounced the tax and the Massachusetts Assembly invited delegates from all the colonies to attend a meeting dubbed the Stamp Act Congress in 1765. There, representatives from nine colonies adopted resolutions condemning the tax as a subversion of the rights of the colonists and asserting that no taxes could be levied on the colonies except by their own legislative bodies.

The British responded a year later by repealing the Stamp Act and easing restrictions on sugar. However, the British thirst for revenue as well as their eagerness to regain control over rebellious colonists led to a new round of taxes.

Minuteman statue in Concord, Massachusetts.

In 1767, the Townsend Acts were imposed, applying duties to a wide variety of important colonial staples. As dissent grew, many colonial legislatures urged a boycott of British goods. Pamphlets like Samuel Adams's *The Rights of Colonists* stoked the flames of popular anger. The British then inadvertently helped the dissenters' cause by passing several more increasingly hated duties, including a tax on tea. In 1773, Boston radicals protested by storming East India Company ships moored in Boston Harbor, dumping their cargoes of tea into the harbor. Parliament punished the city for the "Boston Tea Party" with actions that included blockading the harbor and forcing colonists to quarter British troops in their homes.

Colonists Mobilize for Action: The Continental Congress

Tensions between Britain and her colonies were reaching a breaking point. Seeking a way to address these tensions, representatives of every colony except Georgia met in Philadelphia in September 1774 for the first Continental Congress. They approved a declaration of grievances and urged a boycott of British goods. Although hopeful of restoring good relations with Britain, the colonists strengthened their local militias and left open the possibility of another meeting should tensions not ease. It was not long before relations worsened. In an effort to disrupt the colonial military buildup, British general Thomas Gage marched toward Concord, Massachusetts, in April 1775 to confiscate munitions that were being stored there. As they marched through Lexington, the British encountered a band of Minutemen—militiamen known for their readiness to fight. A skirmish led to shots, leaving eight dead and ten wounded. The British moved on to Concord, destroying the munitions that remained. Much of the firepower, however, was already in the hands of militiamen who pounded the British as they moved toward Boston, killing more than 250 of them.

In the shadow of Lexington's "shot heard 'round the world," a second Continental Congress assembled in Philadelphia on May 10, 1775. This gathering produced a more radical agenda that included marshaling military forces under General George Washington and planning to finance the war effort by borrowing funds and issuing bonds. The king soon declared the colonies in a state of rebellion and sent more troops to subdue local uprisings.

The Congress also produced the Articles of Confederation, a constitution of sorts that consolidated the colonies loosely under a common rule. Ongoing efforts to solve the confrontation between Britain and the colonies proved futile, and in 1776, Congress appointed a committee to prepare a formal declaration asserting independence. Largely the work of Thomas Jefferson, a draft of the Declaration was presented by committee members Jefferson, Benjamin Franklin, and John Adams to Congress on June 28, 1776. The final text was officially adopted on July 4.

The Declaration of Independence served not only to declare war against Britain but also to assert the equality of men and the right to "life, liberty, and the pursuit of happiness."

Declaration of Independence

Although the Declaration of Independence consists mainly of a list of grievances against England's King George III, it is most important for its embodiment of John Locke's philosophy of natural rights, discussed in Chapter 1. The Declaration forcefully asserts the equality of men and the inalienable rights to "life, liberty, and the pursuit of happiness," a phrase that euphemistically expresses an inherent right to own private property. It asserts that these rights are not granted by humans but by God, and that they must be defended by government for enjoyment by each of its members. When a government can no longer defend these rights—or when it actively threatens them—the people have the right to alter or abolish that government and replace it with another that is better able to do so.

The Declaration of Independence inspires awe and respect and has been admired by advocates of liberty the world over. It is not, however, a perfect affirmation of human rights; but we need to see it in the context of the times. Notice that it reserves these rights to *men*. That term was not then used as a surrogate for humanity; it referred specifically to males. Only property owners of sufficient means were allowed to participate in the political process, and very few female colonists owned enough property to qualify. The signers also clearly did not agree that *all* men were created equal. Many of the signers owned slaves, and some of those who helped draft the Declaration forced Jefferson to remove from the document language attacking the institution of slavery.

The Declaration of Independence served not only as a declaration of war with Britain but also as a tool to rally support from a population that lacked consensus about separation from Britain. About one-third of Americans chose to fight for independence from the Crown; another third, it is estimated, were loyal to the king and Parliament; the remainder were too busy scratching a living from the harsh frontier environment to take much interest in politics. Thomas Paine's pamphlet *Common Sense,* published the same year as the Declaration, was just as significant for mustering popular support for independence. The pamphlet sold a half-million copies, 120 thousand within the first three months of publication. By this time, however, the propaganda war had given way to a shooting war with the battles at Lexington and Concord the previous year.

THE BIRTH OF A NATION

Throughout the colonial experience, colonists acquired a taste for self-governance and respect for representative democracy. Most colonial governments included popularly elected lower houses with substantial ability to influence policy. Colonists also developed a fierce love of liberty reflected in the many charters they developed for local rule. When the king's agents sought to destroy the Fundamental Orders of Connecticut protecting individual rights, colonists hid the document in an oak tree to prevent their hard-won charter from being destroyed.

In the prelude to the War for Independence, the colonies reconstituted themselves as states and developed governing constitutions. However, no similar governing document existed for the new nation as a whole. The Second Continental Congress drafted the Articles of Confederation to serve that purpose, and it performed that function adequately during the Revolution. Shortly thereafter, however, the flaws of this document became apparent to colonial leaders, who made plans to replace it.

The Articles of Confederation: A Document Whose Time Had Come and Gone

The Articles of Confederation created a single national assembly, or Congress, in which each state possessed one vote. Congress and its various committees coordinated national affairs during the Revolution. This arrangement, however, was inadequate to address the country's myriad postwar economic and security problems. Consequently, colonial leaders began to search for a new national governing structure.

The Articles of Confederation recognized the colonies as **sovereign**, or independent, units. It created a Congress composed of delegates from every state, but its powers were quite limited. Congress was responsible for maintaining the army and navy, conducting foreign policy, and declaring war and peace. However, there was no president or judicial body, and Congress's power to enforce laws was quite limited. The Articles served as the organizing document for the new nation even while disputes over its ratification dragged on during the war years with final adoption assured only with Maryland's ratification in 1781. Despite its limitations, the Articles proved useful in helping the new nation settle state claims to western territories, establish a system of governance for the Northwest Territories, and ratify the Treaty of Paris, ending the war.

The problems created by a central government with limited powers to respond quickly and with a single voice to collective problems became increasingly apparent as the war

[**sovereign** Independent.

In 1786, Daniel Shays led debt-ridden farmers in armed insurrection in Massachusetts, prompting the nation's new leaders to question the viability of the Articles of Confederation as a governing document.

Thomas Jefferson and the members of the Declaration Committee present the Declaration of Independence to the Second Continental Congress.

drew to a close. Among these were three pressing economic concerns:

1. the lack of a common national currency;
2. a lack of coordination over interstate commerce; and
3. an inability to collect federal taxes.

The first two problems were closely linked. As a sovereign entity, each state issued its own currency while reserving the right to impose duties on goods imported from the others. Both of these practices hindered trade and limited the growth of interstate markets.

The government's inability to collect taxes concerned leaders who envisioned the new nation emerging as an international economic power. The Continental Congress planned to pay off the debt it amassed during the Revolution by assessing each colony a portion of the war's total cost. States would collect money to pay for the assessments by imposing taxes on their own subjects. Collection, however, proved slow and unreliable; no state fully met its obligations, and the nation's poor credit precipitated economic hardship for many. Higher interest rates prevented business expansion and increased the cost of foreign and domestic goods. Lack of financial capital also limited the national government's ability to defend its borders and to improve interstate commerce by building roads and canals. Strengthening of the powers of the central government seemed to be the solution to all three of these economic problems.

High prices for imported commodities, combined with increased taxes imposed by hard-pressed states, drove many people into debt. Small farmers were especially hard hit, and the number of people imprisoned for failure to pay debts burgeoned. In 1786, dissidents known as Regulators roamed western Massachusetts demanding debt relief for small farmers. In late summer, a group of Regulators led by Daniel Shays, himself a farmer, captured a cache of weapons from the Springfield armory. The state militia, sent to quell the disturbance, switched sides, adding fuel to the rebellion. The national government was powerless to intervene because it lacked the authority to raise or deploy a standing army. Eventually, representatives of the state's banking interests hired an army of mercenaries to attack the Regulators. Not until February 1787 was the rebellion quashed and Shays's followers dispersed into surrounding states. Incidents such as Shays's Rebellion shook colonial leaders to their core.

Concern over the vulnerability of the colonial governments to continued internal strife led state leaders to realize that they needed a stronger central government.

The Road to Philadelphia

Although state leaders recognized the need for a stronger central government, assembling a group to reform the Articles of Confederation took some doing. In September 1786, representatives from five states (Delaware, New Jersey, New York, Pennsylvania, and Virginia) met in Annapolis, Maryland, to discuss the weaknesses of the Articles. Alexander Hamilton and James Madison proposed a more inclusive meeting of delegates from every state to be held the following year in Philadelphia. Congress scheduled a meeting to commence May 14, 1787, for the "express purpose of revising the Articles of Confederation." Although calls for reform had been met by a lukewarm reception in the past, Shays's Rebellion gave the states a new sense of urgency.

It was not until May 25 that a sufficient number of delegates arrived to permit a formal discussion of reform. The fifty-five delegates represented every state except Rhode Island, which refused to send a delegation for fear that the assembly would ignore the plight of debtors who made up a substantial portion of the state's population. Judging from external appearances, Rhode Island had reason for concern. Of the fifty-five delegates, almost all were wealthy and well educated. All were white males, six owned plantations, and about a third owned slaves. More than half were lawyers, and most had held leadership positions in their states. Each represented the accepted notion of a politician in an age of deference, where wealth and community standing were understood to be requirements for leadership. Nowhere was this principle of elite deference demonstrated more clearly than in the selection of George Washington, the wealthy Virginia planter and Revolutionary War hero, as the convention's president.

The delegates, however, were by no means unified in their ideas about government or about advancing the interests of any particular economic group. All understood that citizens in their home states would closely scrutinize their actions. Each county had interests and concerns that it wanted the delegate from that state to champion. Producing a workable compromise in such a situation was an extremely difficult task, but the delegates were marked by outstanding political acumen. Grasping the sensitivity of the issues they had come to discuss, they pledged to conduct deliberations in secrecy—behind closed doors and windows—despite the sweltering heat and humidity of the Philadelphia summer. They also understood the art of compromise, and that the time had come to exercise it. The delegates were neither the demigods Jefferson called them nor a crafty elite plotting their own fortunes, as some historians have suggested.[6] Political scientist John P. Roche aptly describes them as a group of extremely talented democratic politicians seeking practical answers to practical problems confronting them.[7]

Constitutional Convention

Several delegates came prepared with their own plans for the shape of the national government. Edmund Randolph formally presented the **Virginia Plan**, largely a creation of his colleague James Madison, calling for a **bicameral**, or two-house, legislature. Members of the lower house proportionate to the number of free inhabitants would be chosen by popular election, and they would in turn select the members of the upper chamber from nominees proposed by state legislatures.[8] Lawmakers would serve limited but unspecified terms, and the legislative branch would have the power to nullify state laws that interfered with the powers of the national government. The plan included a single executive chosen by the legislative branch with the power to execute national laws. A judicial branch consisting of both inferior courts and a supreme body was proposed with members eligible to hold office unless impeached for bad conduct.

Talk of proportional representation in the legislative chambers made delegates from small states uncomfortable. They feared that more populous states such as Virginia, Pennsylvania, and Massachusetts would dominate the legislature. On June 15, William Paterson presented the **New Jersey Plan**, which was more to the liking of the small states. He proposed a

Virginia Plan Edmund Randolph's proposal at the Constitutional Convention for a strong central government comprising a two-house legislative body apportioned by population with the power to make and enforce laws and collect taxes.

bicameral Composed of two houses.

New Jersey Plan William Paterson's proposal for a national government consisting of a unicameral legislature in which every state had equal representation and a plural executive body chosen by the legislature.

James Madison (1751–1836) came to Philadelphia with a blueprint for change and is known as the Father of the Constitution.

©WDC Photos/Alamy Stock Photo

unicameral, or a single-body, legislature, maintaining the equal state representation established under the Articles of Confederation but granting Congress additional powers over trade and security. The plan would also establish a plural executive body chosen by Congress with the power to direct military operations, command troops, enforce national laws, and appoint federal officers. It provided that the executive was removable by the national legislature but added this could be initiated by a call of the executives of the states. A system of courts was authorized with judges of the supreme body appointed by the executive to serve for life or good behavior. Notably, the plan included a provision that national law was supreme and that states were bound to follow.

On June 19, delegates rejected the New Jersey Plan, signaling their desire to create a completely new form of government. By June 21, they settled on support for a bicameral legislature, but the debate—like the weather—was hot. Some delegates withdrew from the convention, never to return. On July 16, Roger Sherman from Connecticut found a solution to the question of congressional representation. His committee called for seats in the lower body to be allocated based on population, while in the upper chamber each state would have an equal vote. At first, both large- and small-state delegates continued to jockey for more favorable terms. The introduction of the requirement that money bills originate in the lower house secured passage of the agreement, known as the **Great Compromise**, by a single vote.

Great Compromise The agreement at the Constitutional Convention to split the legislature into two bodies—one apportioned by population, the other assigning each state two members.

Regional Tensions: Slavery and the Three-Fifths Compromise

Thorny issues remained, the most important of which touched on the institution of slavery. While the southern economy had become extremely dependent on slaves, the northern states were developing a commercial and manufacturing economy in which slave labor was not as profitable as paid labor. Many northerners opposed slavery on economic, as well as moral and religious, grounds. Some states, such as Rhode Island, had abolished slavery completely or enfranchised free blacks who owned property.

The immediate problem that concerned delegates was the question of how to count slaves for purposes of congressional representation. Should they be treated as inhabitants or simply as property? If they were inhabitants, each would count as a person for determining a state's representation in Congress. This would give southern states a disproportionate amount of political influence relative to the North. At the same time, however, the law required states to pay federal taxes based on population. Under this formula, counting slaves as inhabitants would require southerners to pay more in taxes.

Uncomfortable with either option, southern delegates resurrected an earlier proposal to base representation on the whole number of free citizens and three-fifths of all others, excluding Indians, who did not pay taxes. "All others" clearly referred to slaves. This accommodation, called the "three-fifths compromise," won the day and secured agreement among the delegates. A related issue dividing regional delegates was the return of runaway slaves. Southern delegates demanded and received a constitutional provision directing states to return fugitive slaves to their owners.

Trade also proved to be a source of friction between states. Delegates from colonies with large trade and mercantile interests insisted that Congress must have the power to regulate commerce in ways that made their goods more competitive with foreign markets. Meanwhile, delegates from agricultural states—particularly those employing slaves—feared that such power would result in Congress taxing agricultural exports to the detriment of their own economies. They also

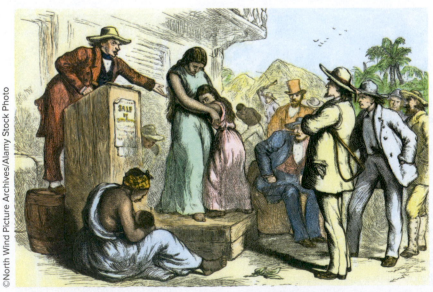

©North Wind Picture Archives/Alamy Stock Photo

Slavery was the most divisive issue at the Philadelphia Convention, and the compromise agreed upon planted the seeds for civil war.

feared that Congress would use its commerce power to halt the importation of slaves and moved to prohibit Congress from taking such action. Despite the moral objections to slavery from some delegates, a compromise was reached, permitting congressional regulation of commerce in principle but prohibiting taxes on exports and permitting the importation of slaves until 1808.

A number of unrelated issues that had arisen over the course of the summer had been assigned to committee for consideration. Among these was the provision that states would set their own requirements for voting since states disagreed about voter qualifications. Although land was considered the standard for southern states, property in northern states assumed a variety of forms. Delegates were wary about the impact any new government might have on property use and wanted to ensure that the dominant property interests in their states at the time would control the ballot box. Committees also wrangled with issues ranging from presidential selection to the jurisdiction of the courts.

Most of the delegates had doubts about various provisions in the final document; some doubted it would survive ratification. To bolster its chances of passage, the delegates determined that the document would take effect whenever nine colonies had ratified it. This decision was taken to ensure that Rhode Island—a fiercely independent colony—could not sabotage the committee's work by itself. One of the most ingenious features of the document was the incorporation of a process for change, allowing parts of the document to be altered while preserving the structure of government as a whole. Even with these precautions, delegates were reluctant to support the new agreement until Benjamin Franklin urged them to "doubt a little of their own infallibility and put their name to the instrument." Forty-two of the original fifty-five delegates remained at the closing of the convention on September 17, and thirty-nine signed the document. Three men who played prominent roles in the convention declined to sign, fearing adverse political reaction back home: George Mason and Edmund Randolph of Virginia and Elbridge Gerry of Massachusetts. Their reluctance to sign prefigured the coming battle over ratification.

The Framers considered Congress the centerpiece of the new government and gave it a prominent position as Article I in the Constitution.

Source: Carol M. Highsmith Archive, Library of Congress [LC-DIG-highsm-12945]

CONSTITUTIONAL PRINCIPLES

The U.S. Constitution has been called a patchwork document "sewn together under the pressure of time and events by a group of extremely talented democratic politicians,"[9] but this does not mean it lacks vision and principle. Most notably, the Constitution enshrines the principles of liberal democracy buttressed with protections achieved through the separation of powers, checks and balances, and federalism.

Liberal Democratic Principles

It is no accident that the Constitution begins with the words "We the People." This is a dramatic expression of citizen consent that expresses the principle at the heart of the document—the belief that humans create governments by their own consent and that, once created, governments must be compelled to limit their reach. Madison eloquently captured this philosophy in *The Federalist* No. 51:

> **"IN FRAMING A GOVERNMENT** which is to be administered by men over men, the great difficulty lies in this: you must first enable the government to control the governed; and in the next place, oblige it to control itself."[10]

"We the People" also expresses a dramatic shift in the locus of authority for the new government. While the states were the central players prior to the adoption of the Constitution, this phrase signaled a new national unity that transcended state loyalties.

Separation of Powers and Checks and Balances

To limit the reach of the government, the Framers incorporated into the Constitution the principles of separation of powers and checks and balances. The first principle stems from John Locke and the French philosopher Baron de Montesquieu (1689–1755). While Locke proposed separating government into a legislative branch that made law and an executive branch charged with implementing the law, Montesquieu added an independent judiciary to settle disputes that might arise between the two. Dividing the functions of government ensured that no one branch could consolidate power in its own hands. The difficulty of gaining control of all three branches also decreased the likelihood that a single group might threaten individual freedoms.

The Framers of the Constitution added a second layer of protection against excessive government power: a system of checks and balances (see "System of Checks and Balances"). This involved providing each branch with overlapping powers so that no one branch could exercise complete control of any function of government. For example, the Constitution grants Congress principal responsibility for making laws but allows the president to check this power by vetoing legislation. Congress, in turn, has the ability to override the veto of a president who stands in the way of needed legislative change. The courts can check the power of the other two branches by challenging the constitutionality of laws passed with the consent of the legislature and the executive branch. To balance the power of the courts, the president can attempt to alter their composition through his or her power of appointment. For its part, Congress can exercise power by withholding funds from the courts or by proposing legislative changes or amendments to circumvent court decisions.

Although this system may seem to be a prescription for stalemate, it is intended to prevent the arbitrary use of power and to give leaders sufficient time to forge consensus on divisive issues. Repeated disagreement between President Obama and the Republican-

System of Checks and Balances

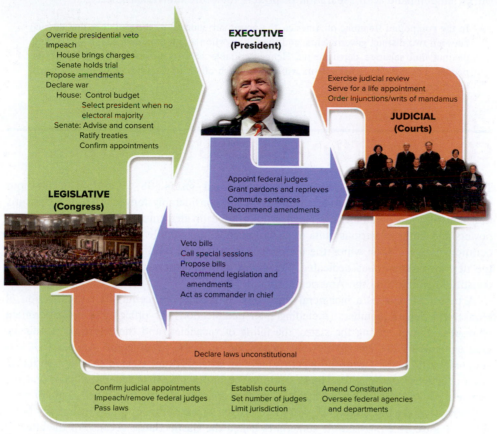

**EXECUTIVE
(President)**

**LEGISLATIVE
(Congress)**

**JUDICIAL
(Courts)**

Override presidential veto
Impeach
    House brings charges
    Senate holds trial
Propose amendments
Declare war
    House: Control budget
        Select president when no
        electoral majority
    Senate: Advise and consent
        Ratify treaties
        Confirm appointments

Exercise judicial review
Serve for a life appointment
Order injunctions/writs of mandamus

Appoint federal judges
Grant pardons and reprieves
Commute sentences
Recommend amendments

Veto bills
Call special sessions
Propose bills
Recommend legislation and
    amendments
Act as commander in chief

Declare laws unconstitutional

Confirm judicial appointments
Impeach/remove federal judges
Pass laws

Establish courts
Set number of judges
Limit jurisdiction

Amend Constitution
Oversee federal agencies
    and departments

This approach to governing was established so that no one branch of government would have too much power, but the Framers could not envision what divisiveness and gridlock might do to the system.

Top: ©Bastiaan Slabbers/Alamy Stock Photo; Right: ©Pablo Martinez Monsivais/AP Images; Left: ©Donaldson Collection/Michael Ochs Archive/Getty Images

controlled House of Representatives over the budget and health care reform resulted in stalemate and even a government shutdown in recent years. However, faced with a sense of urgency, the system can respond expeditiously, such as when Congress and the president (each branch controlled by different political parties) quickly approved a measure in 2008 to save troubled financial institutions involved in risky mortgages whose failure would have worsened an already faltering economy.

Federalism

Although the Framers acknowledged the problems of governing a confederation of autonomous states, they also were aware of the people's fear of putting political power in the hands of a remote national government. Debate over the role and power of the states was intense at the Constitutional Convention, spilling into ratification battles over what some saw as a capitulation of states to the power of the central government. To accommodate the conflicting need for a stronger national government while preserving state prerogatives, the Framers established a form of power sharing between the states and the national government called **federalism**. Under a federal system, some powers—such as the power to declare war—are properly controlled by the national government whereas others—such as the ability to create cities and towns—are reserved to the states. Yet, where state and federal laws clash, federal authority takes precedence (Article VI). We will see in Chapter 3 that the division of power is actually more fluid than this distinction would imply. Nevertheless,

federalism Power-sharing arrangement between the national and state governments in which some powers are granted to the national government alone, some powers are reserved to the states, some powers are held concurrently, and other powers are prohibited to either or both levels of government.

federalism was meant to protect citizens by preventing each level of government from exercising power outside its intended sphere. According to Madison, this division of power works hand-in-hand with separation of powers to secure individual liberty:

> In the compound Republic of America, the power surrendered by the people is first divided between two distinct governments, and then the portion allotted to each subdivided among distinct and separate departments. Hence a double security arises to the rights of the people. The different governments will control each other; at the same time that each will be controlled by itself.[11]

CONSTITUTIONAL CONSTRUCTION

The U.S. Constitution is a relatively brief document—just 4,608 words that occupy four sheets of parchment. Most state constitutions are considerably longer. The U.S. Constitution consists of a preamble and seven articles, each divided into sections, prescribing the powers and limits of various units of government. The preamble expresses the liberal democratic principles upon which the nation was founded and outlines the purposes to which the new government was dedicated. Preambles have become a typical feature of national constitutions following the American example.

Article I establishes a bicameral legislature. It specifies procedures for the election of House and Senate members (including their qualifications for office), the apportionment of representatives among the states, the filling of vacancies, and the selection of officers. House members are elected by the people, but until the Seventeenth Amendment was adopted in 1913, the Constitution provided that senators were elected by state legislative bodies. Article I outlines the House's role in the impeachment of federal officials and the Senate's role in their trial. The legislative powers of Congress are established, including the authority to make those laws necessary and proper for carrying out provisions of any other laws it passes. This provision is sometimes called the **elastic clause** because of the effect it has had on expanding or constraining congressional authority. Article I specifies that revenue bills must originate in the lower House and denies to the states many powers granted to the federal legislature, like the power to make war. The powers of Congress will be explored at length in Chapter 11.

Article II establishes the executive branch, including the offices of president and vice president. It deals with issues such as qualifications for the office of president, the method of election, succession of the vice president to the office of president in case of a vacancy, the president's salary, and the oath of office. It establishes the powers of the president as

elastic clause The provision of Article I of the Constitution authorizing Congress to make those laws necessary and proper for carrying out the other laws it passes.

Articles of the U.S. Constitution

Article I	Establishes Legislative Branch and Outlines Powers of Congress
Article II	Establishes Executive Branch: Powers and Limits
Article III	Establishes Judicial Branch and Creates Supreme Court
Article IV	Outlines Responsibilities and Duties of the States
Article V	Specifies Ways to Amend the Constitution
Article VI	Holds States to Debt Repayment and Establishes Supremacy of Federal Law
Article VII	Discusses Ratification Process

The Articles of the Constitution may seem brief, but legal scholars and lawyers have debated their application since their inception.

commander in chief, outlines his authority in negotiating treaties, grants him the power to fill vacancies when the Senate is not in session, and specifies additional duties of the office. One section provides for impeachment as the ultimate check on the authority of federal officials. Chapter 12 reviews these powers in detail.

Article III establishes the judicial branch, creating the Supreme Court and authorizing Congress to create additional federal courts. It sets the terms of appointment and removal of all federal judges. It specifies the types of cases to be heard in federal courts and how cases will come before the Supreme Court. One section also presents the legal definition of treason. The powers of the Supreme Court will be discussed in Chapter 13, although the impact of court decisions on the powers and functions of all levels of government will be found throughout the entire text.

Article IV guarantees every state a republican form of government derived from the consent of the people, and protection against invasion and domestic violence. It also compels states to recognize the laws of other states by granting them "full faith and credit." That is, each state court is compelled to respect the judgments of courts from other states. A judgment won in one state may be enforced in another. Article IV provides for extradition of persons charged with crimes and the return of runaway slaves—a provision abolished by passage of the Thirteenth Amendment ending slavery. It discusses the admission of new states and provides for federal jurisdiction over federal lands such as state parks.

The remaining articles deal with a variety of miscellaneous issues. Article V details provisions for amending the Constitution (see discussion of the amendment process in the section "Constitutional Change"). The federal government assumes responsibility for the federal debt in Article VI, which also contains the **supremacy clause** that gives federal law precedence over state law. This article also specifies that members of Congress shall swear allegiance to the U.S. Constitution without reference to religious affiliation. Article VII discusses ratification of the Constitution, a process that—as we will see in the next section—faced considerable hurdles.

> **supremacy clause** Provision of Article VI stipulating that the federal government, in exercising any of the powers enumerated in the Constitution, must prevail over any conflicting or inconsistent state exercise of power.

THE FIGHT FOR RATIFICATION

The delegates left Philadelphia hopeful that their work would bear fruit but by no means overconfident. Even before the convention adjourned on September 17, outside observers voiced suspicions about the motives of the delegates who had shrouded themselves in secrecy for so many months. Even some of those who had a hand in creating the document were disgruntled. Some delegates refused to sign the document because it lacked a bill of rights. This provision, common in most state constitutions, defined individual freedoms and protections that were beyond the reach of the government. Tired and impatient to return home, most of the delegates were unwilling to tackle yet another potentially divisive issue.

Supporters of the new constitution, called **Federalists**, believed the document sufficiently limited the power of federal bodies, making a bill of rights unnecessary. As it turned out, the delegates' failure to add specific protections for individual rights proved a major stumbling block to ratification.

> **Federalists** Supporters of the Constitution and its strong central government.

Antifederalist Opposition

Opponents of the document, known as **Antifederalists**, were drawn from various quarters and expressed concerns over a range of issues. Many farmers opposed creation of a new national currency, fearing that it might lower prices for their commodities or enable the very wealthy to buy up their land. Debtors saw the national government as a collection agency for wealthy lenders. Small-town residents distrusted the urban, legal, and commercial elite whose members had crafted the document. Others were angry that the delegates ignored their charge to reform the Articles of Confederation and instead created a whole new governing document. As one historian put it:

> **Antifederalists** Opponents of the ratification of the Constitution.

"[T]HE AVERAGE MAN ON THE STREET (or farm) . . . likened [the Constitutional Convention] to an instance where a group of carpenters had been called upon to add a dormer, a walk-in closet, and a pantry, and then, without permission of the absentee owner, decided to tear down the farmhouse and build a new one from scratch."[12]

Philosophically, Antifederalists worried that the new country was so large that only a strong central government could maintain order and unity, a prospect that threatened the very existence of the states. They reminded their opponents that ancient philosophers believed democracies were only possible in small states and that large nations required the rule of a monarch or even a despot. Antifederalists argued that senators served for too long and represented excessively large territories and worried that these factors would cause senators to lose touch with the electorate. They were concerned about the role a standing army would play in enforcing federal law (and collecting federal taxes) within the states. And they worried about the lack of a written bill of rights to protect the freedoms the revolutionaries fought to achieve. Patrick Henry, whose passionate oratory had advanced the revolutionary cause, spoke with equal passion about the lack of written protections:

> How does your trial by jury stand? In civil cases gone—not sufficiently secured in criminal—this best privilege is gone. But we are told that we need not fear; because those in power, being our representatives, will not abuse the power we put in their hands. . . . I am not well versed in history, but I will submit to your recollection, whether liberty has been destroyed most often by the licentiousness of the people, or by the tyranny of rulers. I imagine, sir, you will find the balance on the side of tyranny.[13]

The Battle in the States

The Constitution found support in commercial centers, in western territories that desired protection from foreign powers and Native Americans, among land speculators and plantation owners, and in the smaller states that gained equal representation with big states in the proposed Senate. Five states quickly ratified the document by unanimous or lopsided votes (see "Ratification of the Constitution"), albeit at times by the use of questionable procedures.

In Pennsylvania, for example, two Antifederalist delegates were forcibly removed from a local saloon and returned to the assembly hall in order to obtain a quorum, after which the convention ratified the document.

In Massachusetts, the nation's most populous state, a showdown loomed as legislators debated ratification for three weeks without resolution. When some Federalists floated the suggestion that Governor John Hancock might serve in the nation's first administration, Hancock swung his support in favor of ratification. To secure his support, however, he demanded that the final document include amendments protecting many of the individual rights guaranteed in Massachusetts's state constitution.

With Massachusetts on board, supporters of ratification turned their attention to two larger and more important states: Virginia

Trial by jury in criminal cases is guaranteed by the Sixth Amendment to the U.S. Constitution.

© Tim Pannell/Corbis via Getty Images

Ratification of the Constitution

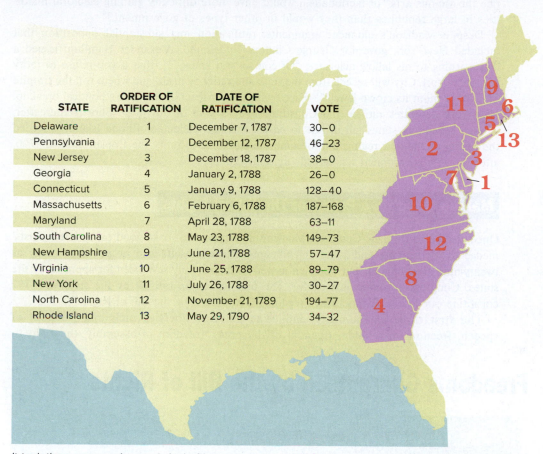

STATE	ORDER OF RATIFICATION	DATE OF RATIFICATION	VOTE
Delaware	1	December 7, 1787	30–0
Pennsylvania	2	December 12, 1787	46–23
New Jersey	3	December 18, 1787	38–0
Georgia	4	January 2, 1788	26–0
Connecticut	5	January 9, 1788	128–40
Massachusetts	6	February 6, 1788	187–168
Maryland	7	April 28, 1788	63–11
South Carolina	8	May 23, 1788	149–73
New Hampshire	9	June 21, 1788	57–47
Virginia	10	June 25, 1788	89–79
New York	11	July 26, 1788	30–27
North Carolina	12	November 21, 1789	194–77
Rhode Island	13	May 29, 1790	34–32

It took three years and a great deal of bargaining and political persuasion for all thirteen states to ratify the Constitution.

and New York. Although the Framers provided that the document could take effect with the adoption by as few as nine states, it was clear that union without the approval of two of the largest and most powerful states was practically out of the question. Virginia had a sizable Antifederalist contingent, but it also boasted supporters of the document who ranked among the most respected and influential figures in the nation, including Madison, Jefferson, and Washington. Despite a sometimes bitter debate, Madison's promise to amend the document to include a bill of rights was enough to secure Virginia's ratification by a ten-vote margin on June 25, 1788.

Winning ratification in New York proved more difficult, and Federalists exerted great energy there to sway public opinion. In October 1787, James Madison, Alexander Hamilton, and John Jay published the first in a series of eighty-five articles, which came to be known as *The Federalist,* in the New York press extolling the virtues of the new Constitution and attempting to quell opponents' anxieties about the proposed national government. Intended primarily as a propaganda weapon in the Federalist drive to secure ratification, modern scholars hail *The Federalist* for its insightful analysis of the principles of American government.

In *The Federalist* No. 10, Madison warned that **factions**—distinct groups most often driven by economic motives—threatened the unity of the new Republic by placing their own interests above those of the nation as a whole. The cure for factionalism, Madison claimed, was precisely the type of republican government found in the Constitution. He argued that the size of the new nation, rather than being a threat to citizens, actually served to protect them. A faction that dominated a single state would find it much more difficult to dominate national politics in a large union. Even large and influential factions would have difficulty controlling large districts such as those proposed in the new republic,

factions Groups—most often driven by economic motives—that place their own good above the good of the nation as a whole.

where elected representatives were under pressure to weigh the wishes of the diverse interests they represented. Madison also believed that "unworthy" candidates "who practice the vicious arts" of factionalism would have more difficulty gaining electoral majorities in large republics than they would in other types of government.[14]

Despite Madison's eloquent arguments, ratification met substantial opposition that included New York governor George Clinton. Undaunted, Alexander Hamilton issued a dire warning to his fellow delegates: "Of course, you know . . . that if you refuse to ratify then New York City will secede from the state and ratify by itself, and where will the Empire State be without its crown jewel?"[15] Faced with the prospect of the state's political breakup, New York delegates ratified the Constitution by a vote of 30 to 27. Shortly thereafter, enough remaining states fell in line to ensure passage. Reluctant Rhode Island conceded the reality of the new regime and became the last state to ratify the Constitution in 1790, after the new government was already up and running.

Making Good on a Promise: The Bill of Rights

Once elected to the new Congress, Madison determined to make good on the Federalists' pledge to incorporate additional amendments. Massachusetts had proposed as many as twenty-nine amendments, but Madison moved to submit only seventeen for approval by the states; Congress approved just twelve. The first ten to be ratified by the states in 1791 constitute our Bill of Rights (see "Freedoms Guaranteed by the Bill of Rights").

The first three amendments emphasize political liberties including freedom of speech, freedom of religion, freedom of the press, freedom of assembly, the right to

Freedoms Guaranteed by the Bill of Rights

First Amendment	Prohibits Congress from establishing religion and restricting its free exercise; also prohibits Congress from abridging freedoms of speech, press, assembly, and petition...
Second Amendment	Guarantees the people the right to bear arms
Third Amendment	Prohibits enforced quartering of soldiers in times of peace and allows for the regulation of such practices in times of war
Fourth Amendment	Protects against unreasonable searches and seizures...
Fifth Amendment	Prescribes the use of grand juries, protects against being tried in the same court twice for the same offense, protects against self-incrimination, prescribes due process and compensation for property taken for public use
Sixth Amendment	Guarantees speedy and public trial in criminal procedures, trial by impartial jury, the right to be informed of charges and the right to face accusers, the right to obtain witnesses and to secure counsel for defense
Seventh Amendment	Guarantees the right to a jury trial in civil cases...
Eighth Amendment	Prohibits excessive bail as well as cruel and unusual punishment
Ninth Amendment	Mandates that those rights not explicitly listed are reserved for the people
Tenth Amendment	Mandates that those powers not delegated to the national government are retained by states and the people

Originally a concession to secure support from opponents of ratification, the Bill of Rights embodies the freedoms Americans have come to consider essential.

bear arms, and protection against being forced to quarter troops in peacetime. The next five outline the basic rights that constitute due process of law, designed to protect innocent citizens accused of crimes. The Ninth and Tenth Amendments deal with federal–state relations and specify that rights and powers not explicitly granted to the federal government in the Constitution remain in the hands of the people and the states.

Although the Bill of Rights protected citizens from actions taken by the national government, it did not compel state governments to provide these same protections for their own citizens. As a result, citizens in many states did not enjoy protections against unreasonable state government searches or the right to an attorney or to a speedy trial in a state court. Even states that did recognize these rights did not apply them equally to all citizens. In many places, minority populations lacked these basic protections. In 1833, the Supreme Court affirmed that the Bill of Rights applied only to protections from the powers of the national government in the case *Barron v. Baltimore*. The Court argued that, since the Constitution was created "by the people of the United States" to apply only to the national government, the states were obliged only to provide their citizens with protections they themselves had adopted in their state constitutions. It was not until much later—in the wake of the Civil War—when the Fourteenth Amendment was ratified in 1868 that many of the protections found in the U.S. Constitution's Bill of Rights were made applicable to the states. You will learn more about the fight for "incorporating" these rights within the states in Chapter 4.

Madison proposed an Eleventh Amendment, which failed to gain approval at the time. It proposed that members of Congress be prohibited from receiving pay raises during the same session in which they are approved. The amendment failed to obtain the necessary state support for adoption during Madison's lifetime, but it was never really declared dead. In 1982, an undergraduate at The University of Texas at Austin, Gregory Watson, discovered that no time limit had been placed on the ratification of early amendments, so Madison's proposal was still eligible for adoption. Watson mounted a one-man ratification drive targeting strategic states whose ratification was not yet secured. In May 1992, the measure received legislative approval in Alabama, putting it over the top and making it the Twenty-Seventh Amendment—203 years after Madison originally proposed it. Another of Madison's unratified proposals limiting the size of Congress will experience no such revival, however. When Congress certified the ratification of the Twenty-Seventh Amendment, it canceled all other outstanding proposed amendments.

CONSTITUTIONAL CHANGE

One of the reasons the U.S. Constitution has endured for as long as it has is that the Framers made provisions for change. The amendment process is the most familiar way to effect change; but it is by no means the only means—in fact, it has been used sparingly. Changes in the ways constitutional powers are exercised also come about as our institutions of government adapt to social and technological developments that the Framers never envisioned. For example, environmental protection and regulation were not on the Framers' radar. Constitutional change is also effected by rulings made by the Supreme Court, which interprets the Constitution under its power of judicial review. In these ways, the document remains a flexible, living instrument.

Methods for Proposing and Ratifying Amendments

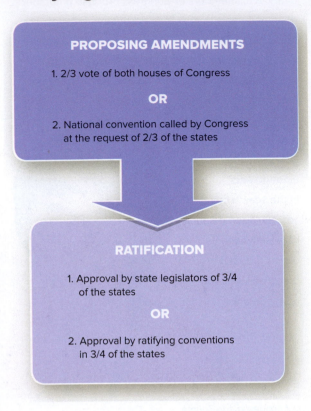

PROPOSING AMENDMENTS

1. 2/3 vote of both houses of Congress

OR

2. National convention called by Congress at the request of 2/3 of the states

RATIFICATION

1. Approval by state legislators of 3/4 of the states

OR

2. Approval by ratifying conventions in 3/4 of the states

Amending the Constitution

The Framers proposed two methods for submitting amendments (see "Methods for Proposing and Ratifying Amendments"). Under the first method, an amendment that is introduced to Congress and approved by a two-thirds vote of both houses may be submitted to the states for ratification. This method has been used to initiate every existing amendment. Alternately, if requested by two-thirds of the state legislatures, Congress may call a national convention at which amendments may be proposed. Individuals from a variety of ideological backgrounds have expressed interest in mounting a campaign for a new convention but without success so far. Some scholars worry that, like the original meeting in 1787, such a convention could wander beyond its original mandate. Presumably, the delegates could propose a whole series of changes—even a new form of government.

Amendments passed by the Congress must still be ratified by three-quarters of the states to become part of the Constitution. This can happen either by approval of the legislatures in those states or by ratifying conventions held in the states. State legislatures have ratified every amendment except the Twenty-first, which repealed the Eighteenth Amendment prohibiting the manufacture and sale of alcoholic beverages in the United States. The ratification process originally had no fixed time limit, which is why one of Madison's amendments remained viable for 203 years. In the early twentieth century, however, Congress began placing time limits on the ratification effort, usually seven years. Congress occasionally allows extensions, as it did in 1982 when it allotted an additional three years for states to consider the Equal Rights Amendment. Despite the extension, the amendment barring discrimination on the basis of sex fell three states short of ratification. Even though Illinois decided to add its support by ratifying the amendment in 2018, it remains two states shy of adoption and its viability remains uncertain.

Although the Framers designed the Constitution to be adaptable to change, they did not want change to come easily. They ensured that anyone who wished to amend the Constitution would need to build broad popular support for their proposals. The track record of amendment attempts illustrates the difficulty of the task. Of the more than ten thousand amendments proposed since 1789, only thirty-three made it to the states for ratification and only twenty-seven became part of the Constitution. See "Recent Unsuccessful Attempts to Amend the Constitution" for some recent proposed amendments that didn't make it—or at least, not so far.

Institutional Adaptation

For the Constitution to remain viable, it must be able to adapt to changing times and deal with matters that its authors could hardly have anticipated. The individuals who crafted the Fourth Amendment did not envision the government electronically monitoring the conversations of suspected terrorists, nor did they consider the need to regulate fundraising by political parties when they penned the First Amendment. Formal parties did not even exist at the time, and the Framers generally viewed them with disdain.

The Constitution is also flexible enough to survive the recurring power struggles among competing branches of government. For example, although the Constitution grants Congress the power to declare war, presidents have repeatedly asserted broad power over the military, greatly expanding the constitutional role of commander in chief. In fact, although the United States has been involved in hundreds of armed conflicts, Congress has formally declared war only five times.[16] This reflects, in part, the changing nature of warfare. Compared to the present day, eighteenth-century weapons were crude and communications were extremely slow; national leaders had more time to respond to military threats. The pace and destructiveness

Recent Unsuccessful Attempts to Amend the Constitution

**115th Congress
(2017–2018)**

- To confirm that money is not free speech and that corporations are not people for purposes of the First Amendment right to make campaign contributions by enacting a constitutional amendment overturning the decision of the Supreme Court in the case of *Citizens United v. Federal Election Commission.*
- To provide that the rights extended by the Constitution are the rights of natural persons only.
- To repeal the sixteenth amendment.
- To reform the Electoral College and establish a process for electing the President and Vice President by a national popular vote and [to] encourage individual States to continue to reform the Electoral College process through such steps as the formation of an interstate compact to award the majority of Electoral College votes to the national popular vote winner.
- To prohibit Congress and the States from abridging the right of citizens to affordable, quality health care.
- To clarify the presidential pardoning power.
- To require a balanced budget.
- To prohibit the physical desecration of the flag of the United States.
- To limit the number of terms an individual may serve as a Member of Congress.
- To protect the rights of crime victims.

The Framers of the Constitution constructed it in such a way that amending it would not be easy for future generations.

Source: Carol M. Highsmith Archive, Library of Congress [LC-DIG-highsm-16167]

of modern warfare has produced a tendency to defer to presidential authority in matters of war and peace, and presidents have not been shy about wielding such authority. Recent presidents have ordered drone strikes over sovereign territories sometimes without Congress's approval and without congressional authorization. We will discuss war powers in more depth in Chapters 11 and 12.

Congress, too, has expanded its powers by the way it has interpreted the language of the Constitution. For example, in the mid-twentieth century, Congress used its power to regulate interstate commerce in a way never imagined a century before to achieve a host of goals unrelated to trade or business. By prohibiting businesses that transport goods and services across state lines from practicing discrimination, Congress advanced the cause of racial integration. Prior to the Civil War, such use of this power was unthinkable.

The Constitution has also withstood substantial changes in the relationship between the states and the federal government. In 1787, the states were independent entities that jealously guarded their power from federal encroachment. Although states can still set policies for residents within their borders, the federal government often uses its budgetary power to coerce them to adopt national standards. In the 1980s, for example, Congress voted to withhold federal highway

©Saul Loeb/AFP/Getty Images

The president is commander in chief of the armed forces, but Congress is entrusted with the power to declare war.

funds from states that failed to adopt a minimum drinking age of 21. Every state soon fell in line. Again, these actions reflect adaptation to changing circumstances; variations in drinking ages may have made more sense before interstate highways essentially obliterated the borders between states.

Judicial Review

The decisions of the Supreme Court have effected greater changes to our system of government than any other actions save constitutional amendments. As cases work their way through trial and appeals courts in our state or federal judicial system (described in Chapter 14), they occasionally raise questions about the constitutionality of particular laws or acts of political institutions. When this happens, the Supreme Court renders a final verdict on whether or not these laws and actions pass constitutional muster. Most Americans take for granted the Court's role as final arbiter in interpreting the Constitution. However, the Constitution does not explicitly grant that power; instead, the Court assumed it in the 1803 case of *Marbury v. Madison*. In his opinion, Chief Justice John Marshall claimed for the Court authority for **judicial review**, the power to review the acts of other political institutions and declare them unconstitutional. Most scholars agree that the Framers assumed the Supreme Court would have this power, as did the British courts with which they were familiar. Alexander Hamilton even wrote in *The Federalist* No. 78:

judicial review The power of the U.S. Supreme Court to review the acts of other political institutions and declare them unconstitutional.

> The interpretation of the laws is the proper and peculiar province of the courts. A constitution is, in fact, and must be regarded by the judges as, a fundamental law. It therefore belongs to them to ascertain its meaning as well as the meaning of any particular act proceeding from the legislative body.[17]

Nevertheless, the Court sometimes endures severe criticism when it exercises this power. In its highly controversial ruling *Roe v. Wade* (1973), the Court ruled that state laws making abortions illegal violated a woman's constitutional right to privacy. Although privacy is not mentioned explicitly in the Constitution, the Court ruled it could be inferred from the Ninth Amendment and the due process clause of the Fourteenth Amendment. Justice Harry Blackmun wrote: "The right to privacy . . . is broad enough to encompass a woman's decision whether or not to terminate her pregnancy."[18] More than four decades later, the ruling still arouses heated emotional opposition and political debate. Abortion opponents have been successful in persuading state legislatures to place funding and consent restrictions on the right to obtain an abortion, and they continue to promote a constitutional amendment to reverse *Roe v. Wade*. You will learn more about this in Chapter 4.

Expanding the Franchise

At the time of its writing, the Constitution granted the vote only to propertied, white, adult males. Yet despite placing severe limits on the franchise, it offered a process for expanding individual rights and a structure that enabled citizens to effect change. Property qualifications for voting fell first in the western territories, repealed by settlers attracted by free land and eager to form new social and political networks.[19] This experience taught astute eastern politicians that they could increase their base of popular support by expanding the franchise to those without property. By the middle of the nineteenth century, property qualifications for voting had crumbled across the nation.

Women and African Americans found voting barriers much more difficult to overcome. Prominent women such as Abigail Adams spoke for women's rights from the time of the Revolution, but women secured the vote only with passage of the

A strong voice for equal rights, Abigail Adams (1744–1818) cautioned her husband, the second president of the United States, to "remember the ladies."

Current Controversy

An Arcane Provision Comes to Life

No Person holding any Office of Profit or Trust under [the United States], shall, without the Consent of the Congress, accept of any present, Emolument, Office, or Title, of any kind whatever, from any King, Prince, or foreign State. U.S. Const. art. I, § 9, cl. 8.

Charles Pinckney urged his colleagues at the Philadelphia Convention to accept this language, known as the emoluments clause in order to prevent foreign ministers and other officers of the United States from falling under the influence of foreign agents. A similar clause was found in the Articles of Confederation.

Despite this provision, our earliest presidents, including Washington and Jefferson, received gifts of value from foreign governments without consulting Congress and without raising the concern of the legislative branch. Although the meaning and applicability of this arcane stipulation continue to be debated by constitutional experts, most modern-era presidents placed their financial holdings in blind trusts designed to ensure they could not be certain what impact their policies would have on their future finances or they requested legal guidance before accepting gifts of value.*

Donald Trump's vast international holdings, however, have raised concerns among legislators and legal scholars alike. His failure to make his income tax returns public exacerbated these concerns since it was impossible to know how his policy decisions might affect his widespread foreign investments. Of

Donald Trump's failure to divest his holdings while serving as president has raised ethical and legal questions about whether he is in violation of the emoluments clause of the U.S. Constitution. Protesters projected these images onto the entrance of the Trump International Hotel in Washington, D.C.

particular concern was his failure to give up his interest in the Washington, D.C., Trump International Hotel, which had been leased to him under an agreement with the U.S. General Services Administration prior to his election. Might foreign governments frequent his hotel in order to curry favor?

In response to these concerns, President Trump handed over operation of his businesses to his sons and a trustee and has pledged to donate profits from the hotel to the Treasury Department. Moreover, his attorneys claim that the emoluments clause does not apply to presidents and that presidents are exempt from conflict-of-interest laws. The president has found support for his views among some legal scholars who claim that the emoluments clause

applies to appointed and not elected officials.

The failure of Trump to divest his holdings and the vagueness of the constitutional provision made this conflict ripe for judicial intervention. Soon after the 2016 election, a number of lawsuits were filed by state and local governments and by members of Congress alleging that Trump was in violation of the constitution. The courts have allowed these cases to proceed and will no doubt bring clarity to the meaning and applicability of this arcane provision.

*David J. Barron (Acting Assistant Attorney General), *Applicability of the Emoluments Clause and the Foreign Gifts and Decorations Act to the President's Receipt of the Nobel Peace Prize,* December 7, 2009, https://www.justice.gov/sites/default/files/olc/opinions/2009/12/31/emoluments-nobel-peace_0.pdf.

Nineteenth Amendment in 1920 after decades of political protest. The nation had to endure a civil war before African Americans won their freedom with the Thirteenth Amendment and black males won the franchise with the Fifteenth Amendment. It took African Americans another century of litigation, protest, and political campaigning to secure the full promise of the franchise through civil rights legislation in the 1960s. In 1971, the Twenty-Sixth Amendment broadened the franchise even further, granting 18-year-olds the vote.

Although most legal barriers to voting are gone, issues of motivation, mobilization, and resources, which disproportionately affect those at the lower end of the income spectrum, remain. We will examine these in later chapters.

THE CONSTITUTION AND CIVIC ENGAGEMENT TODAY

Congress designated September 17 as Constitution and Citizenship Day,[20] a day set aside to commemorate the legacy of our founding document. Yet, we celebrate the U.S. Constitution every day when we write our senators and representatives about some important issue, read press accounts of current events, attend religious services, donate money to a political cause or candidate, engage in political debate in the classroom, or make a donation to an interest group. All of these activities reflect fundamental rights enshrined in our Constitution.

But we should remember that rights are never totally secure. They face continuing challenges and must adapt to meet changing times. Since the 9/11 terrorist attacks, many rights have been curbed in the interest of security. In some cases, such as the baggage searches and other intrusions of personal privacy that air travelers must endure, Americans generally take these inconveniences in stride. Most feel that the need for security outweighs issues of personal privacy in such situations. Other measures the government has taken in the name of security are far more controversial. For example, Congress has given the executive branch the right to monitor international phone calls and Internet traffic without obtaining a warrant, and with less judicial oversight than was required in the past. The intelligence community can order Internet providers, phone companies, and online services like Facebook, Google, and Skype to turn over all communications that are reasonably believed to involve a non-American who is outside the country. Agencies do not have to name their targets or get prior court approval for the surveillance. Should the government assume such

©Drew Angerer/Getty Images

Numerous police shootings of unarmed black men have raised questions about whether our existing laws provide equal protection for the constitutional rights of all Americans.

broad powers and make them a permanent feature of the American political system? Does government need such powers to protect its citizens—or are such powers unwarranted intrusions into our personal lives that go beyond the requirements of genuine security?

The rights of some minorities have come under attack as well. New restrictions on voting, like voter ID laws, and techniques for drawing electoral boundaries to limit the representation of certain groups have been adopted by many states in recent years. The militarization of local police forces has also placed the lives of some minority groups in jeopardy. Such actions threaten the nation's long-standing commitment to equal rights and equal protection under the law.

These are concerns for citizens of your generation to face, just as the founding generation faced questions dealing with the right of government to quarter soldiers in their homes or to shut down town meetings held without the prior approval of royal governors. There are plenty of ways you can get involved in exploring such issues and making your voice heard. You can join one of the many interest groups that focus their efforts on this issue and that can offer detailed information and analysis. You can hold university or community forums to solicit the views of your classmates and neighbors. You can meet with law enforcement officials and legal scholars to get their views. These are rights that your generation has inherited, and they are yours to keep as long as you stay involved. Thomas Jefferson's famous aphorism "the price of freedom is eternal vigilance" applies no less today than it did in his own day.

citizenship Quiz

Can you pass the U.S. Citizenship Test? See how well you know the content in this chapter covered on the citizenship test required of foreign-born candidates for naturalization.

1. How many amendments does the Constitution have?

2. What stops *one* branch of government from becoming too powerful?

3. The House of Representatives has how many voting members?

4. There are four amendments to the Constitution about who can vote. Describe *one* of them.

5. The *Federalist* supported the passage of the U.S. Constitution. Name one of its writers.

6. Why does the flag have thirteen stripes?

(1) 27 (2) Checks and balances/separation of powers (3) 435 (4) Citizens 18 and older can vote [26]/You don't have to pay (a poll tax) to vote [24]/Women have the right to vote [19]/A male citizen of any race can vote [15] (5) James Madison/Alexander Hamilton/John Jay/Publius (6) Because there were thirteen original colonies/because the stripes represent the original colonies

Source: United States Citizenship and Immigration Services.

Thinking It Through ≫≫≫

Learning Objective: Explain how the Constitution was negotiated and ratified.

Review: Constitutional Principles

Discuss the reasons why the Framers constructed a government that divides powers among branches and incorporates checks and balances. What historical forces led them to design such a system? Discuss the continuing relevance, including advantages and disadvantages, of this system today.

Summary

1. **What factors contributed to the need for a Constitutional Convention?**

   - After the Revolution spawned by the desire for greater economic opportunity and self-rule, the colonies were administered by a Continental Congress created by the Articles of Confederation. Colonists soon found the Articles too weak to help them pay their war debt, control interstate commerce, and put down local rebellions like the one fomented by Daniel Shays in Massachusetts.

   - A call went out to convene a meeting to reform the Articles in Philadelphia, but the fifty-five delegates decided instead to create a new governing document. Disagreement over the apportionment of the legislature led to a key compromise, known as the Great Compromise, in which seats in the lower chamber were allocated on the basis of population, appeasing the larger states, whereas in the upper chamber, each state was granted equal representation (two seats), satisfying the interests of the small states. Concerns over the institution of slavery were resolved by the three-fifths compromise and by allowing the importation of slaves to continue for twenty years.

   - Once the document was released, it was not met with wide acceptance. Support was generated by a series of newspaper articles that came to be known as *The Federalist,* penned by James Madison, Alexander Hamilton, and John Jay.

2. **What are the basic principles that inform our Constitution?**

   - The basic principles of the Constitution are separation of powers, checks and balances, and a division of power between the states and the national government known as federalism.

   - The Constitution establishes a bicameral legislature, a single executive, and a federal court system that includes the Supreme Court. Powers of each branch overlap in ways that make it difficult for any one branch to exercise complete control. Powers are divided further between the national and state governments, providing for what Madison called "a double security" for the rights of the people.

   - Antifederalists who opposed the Constitution wanted even more individual protections and called for the adoption of a bill of rights. The Federalist supporters of the Constitution obliged by appending ten amendments during the first legislative session of Congress. The amendments, known as the Bill of Rights, guarantee free speech and freedom of religion and protect the rights of those accused of crimes, among other protections.

3. **In what ways does constitutional change occur?**

   - The Constitution can be changed through amendment; through the actions of political leaders who stretch its meaning to adapt to social, political, and economic change; and by court interpretation.

   - Amending the Constitution is a two-stage process. The first stage requires either the adoption of the measure by a two-thirds vote by both houses of Congress, a procedure used for all existing amendments, or by a national convention called by two-thirds of the states. Ratification, the second stage, requires either approval by the legislatures in three-quarters of the states or approval by ratifying conventions in three-quarters of the states. The latter method was used only to repeal Prohibition.

   - Political actors can also extend the meaning of the document as Congress sometimes does when it takes an expansive view of the "necessary and proper" clause.

   - The Supreme Court can effect change by exercising judicial review to interpret the document over time.

Chapter 3

Federalism
Citizenship and the Dispersal of Power

AT ODDS OVER IMMIGRATION

Oscar and Irma Sanchez were faced with a terrible decision. Their newborn baby was diagnosed with a serious condition that prevents food from being digested in the small intestine. The local hospital in Harlingen, Texas, did not have the resources to deal with the baby's condition and urged the parents to take the child to a better-equipped hospital in Corpus Christi. However, the Sanchez's were undocumented immigrants and the trip north

©John Moore/Getty Images

The federal government crackdown on undocumented immigrants is being met by resistance by state and local governments claiming sanctuary status.

would require them to pass through a Border Patrol checkpoint. While they pondered their options, a Border Patrol agent arrived—perhaps tipped off by a hospital employee—and placed the couple under arrest. They were permitted to take their American-born child to Corpus Christi for treatment, but they were informed that deportation proceedings would begin shortly thereafter.[1]

The story of the Sanchezes, a couple with no criminal record, is one of many that came to light in the aftermath of the Trump administration's crackdown on the undocumented in this country. Advocates for the undocumented say immigration police have turned up to arrest people at hospitals, homeless shelters, and courthouses. The administration went even further, pursuing a "zero tolerance" that resulted in the separation of children from their parents at the border until a courts ordered an end to the practice.

Inspired by stories like these, many cities—and several states like California—have adopted legislation pledging not to commit public resources to discovering and reporting undocumented immigrants with no criminal records to Immigration and Customs Enforcement (ICE) officials as required by federal statute. Responding to efforts by officials in these so-called "sanctuary cities," the Trump administration pledged to withhold federal grants to municipalities with similar provisions, claiming that compliance with federal law is essential for ensuring public safety and security. Federal courts have pushed back, blocking the administration from withholding federal funding for failure to aid in federal civil immigration enforcement.

As You READ

- **How is power dispersed in American federalism?**
- **How have the powers of the national and state governments evolved over the nation's history?**
- **What factors influence relations between national and state governments today?**

Sanctuary cities are not new. They date back in the United States at least to the time of slavery when some cities in the North acted to protect runaway slaves from enforcement of fugitive slave laws. In the modern era, sanctuary cities arose during 1980s protests against federal immigration policies that denied asylum to refugees from El Salvador and Guatemala. San Francisco was the first to assume this status but was quickly followed by numerous other cities.[2]

The Trump administration claims that sanctuary cities threaten public safety. Officials in these cities claim local participation in federal immigration enforcement against those with no criminal past will result in immigrant populations being less likely to report crime or assist with police investigations.

While these claims and counterclaims move through the judicial system, families of the undocumented like the Sanchezes are confronted with tough choices. Although local officials may be willing to ignore their immigration status, federal officials demand that cities and towns report their location for possible deportation.

Jurisdictional conflict over immigration is just one example of the tensions that can arise between our national and state governments as a result of a feature of the American political landscape known as **federalism**. Federalism disperses authority among different levels of government, providing citizens with different points of access for voicing their concerns as well as different units of authority with which to conform. This chapter focuses primarily on government at the national and state levels, but the nation's governmental structure is much more complex. In addition to the federal and state governments, the United States comprises 3,034 county governments, 19,429 municipal governments, 16,504 town and township governments, and over 45,000 special and school district governments.[3] Most of these governments have some taxing authority, and all conduct legal and fiscal transactions with other units of government. Relationships among these various levels of government evolve continually to reflect the changing political and financial currents of the day, potentially affecting the lives of millions of people like Oscar and Irma Sanchez. ■

federalism Power-sharing arrangement between the national and state governments in which some powers are granted to the national government alone, some powers are reserved to the states, some powers are held concurrently, and other powers are prohibited to either or both levels of government.

THE DIVISION OF POWER

Following the American Revolution, the nation's Framers faced the problem of organizing a rapidly growing nation whose citizens cherished local rule. Although history furnished ideas for power sharing within the national government—such as separation of powers and checks and balances—it offered few workable models for nation–state relations. The individuals who framed the Constitution were forced to devise their own solution—a historic innovation called federalism.

Prevailing Models for Dispersing Power

Prior to the Constitutional Convention, two models of intergovernmental relations predominated throughout the world: unitary and confederated (see "Unitary and Confederated Forms of Government"). Under a unitary form, all power resides in the central government, which makes the laws. State or local governments act primarily as vehicles to administer and enforce national laws. Many of the Framers found this kind of distant government unacceptable and considered it a threat to personal liberty. This form of government characterized the British system against which the colonies rebelled and persists in many nations today, including England and France.

By contrast, in a confederation, states and localities retain sovereign power over their own jurisdictions, yielding to the central government only limited authority as needed. This form of government—which characterized the government under the Articles of Confederation—was also clearly unacceptable to the Framers. It had led to many of the difficulties we discussed in Chapter 2. Confederations are, for the most part, relics of the past. Very few modern nations employ this form of government because it slows the central government's ability to act. A confederacy does, however, characterize some intergovernmental organizations that include nation-states as members, such as the United Nations.

Even opponents of a strong national government understood that only a more "energetic" central power could deal with the pressing national issues that were inadequately

Great Britain has a unitary form of government in which most authority is exercised by officials at the national level.

Unitary and Confederated Forms of Government

Unitary Government   ### Confederation

Arrows represent the flow of decisions and resources.

🔴 Central   🟡 State   🟣 Local

Unitary systems privilege central authority over state and local governments, whereas confederate systems place the locus of power in state and local units of government.

enumerated powers The list of specific powers granted to Congress by Article I, Section 8, of the Constitution.

implied powers Powers necessary to carry out constitutionally enumerated functions of government.

inherent powers Those powers that are part of the very nature of the institution and necessary for the institution to do the job for which it was created. For example, the president must have the power to use force as part of his duties as commander in chief.

reserved powers Powers constitutionally allocated to the states.

concurrent powers Powers shared by both state and national governments.

prohibited powers Powers denied one or both levels of government.

addressed under the arrangements of the Articles of Confederation. These included a lack of control over interstate commerce and the absence of a national currency, which seriously limited the development of national markets. Most significantly, however, the national government lacked central taxing power, making it impossible to raise money to repay the substantial debts it accumulated during the Revolution. The Continental Congress could assess each state for taxes, but it had no power to enforce collection. The delegates to the Constitutional Convention faced the problem of providing the central government with enough power to function effectively but not so much that it dominated the states. Federalism was their solution.

The Federalist Solution

In a federal system, four main attributes characterize power arrangements among levels of government:

1. **Enumerated powers** are those governmental powers specifically granted the national government by Article I, Section 8, of the U.S. Constitution. The power granted to Congress to declare war is one example. This section of the Constitution also includes the so-called elastic clause authorizing Congress to make "all laws which shall be necessary and proper for carrying into execution the foregoing powers." That is, if Congress has the power to do something, it must also have the authority to select reasonable means for doing it. For example, Congress can authorize the building of aircraft carriers as a means of carrying out its powers to provide for the common defense and to declare war. We call these powers of Congress to carry out constitutionally enumerated functions its **implied powers**. But Congress and the president also exercise **inherent powers**, those powers that are part of the very nature of each institution and necessary for the institution to do the job for which it was created. For example, the president must have the power to use force as part of his duties as commander in chief.

2. **Reserved powers** are those granted by the Constitution specifically to the states. The Constitution places certain limits upon national power, and the Tenth Amendment reserves to the states or to the people all powers not specifically granted to the national government. Many actions states take with regard to protecting the health and welfare of their residents issue from their reserved powers.

3. **Concurrent powers** are shared jointly by the federal and state governments. For example, both have the power to tax.

4. **Prohibited powers** are denied to either or both levels of government. For example, states may not declare war. Neither the national nor state governments may grant titles of nobility. See "Attributes of U.S. Federalism" for examples of major powers in each category.

Proponents of a federal system among our Framers felt federalism not only was a more practical solution to the sharing of powers but also served as an additional guarantee of individual freedoms. Madison argued that the federal system offered a dual protection of citizens' rights. In *The Federalist* No. 51, he wrote:

> In the compound Republic of America, the power surrendered by the people is first divided between two distinct governments, and then the portion allotted to each subdivided among separate departments. Hence a double security arises to the rights of the people. The different governments will control each other, at the same time that each will be controlled by itself.[4]

For Federalists such as Madison, federalism protected individual freedom, encouraged participation in national affairs, and enhanced public security.

Attributes of U.S. Federalism

Powers of National Government	Powers Reserved for State Governments	Concurrent Powers
Make war	Regulate intrastate commerce	Tax and spend
Coin money	Protect health and safety	Borrow money
Admit new states	Pass laws	Establish courts
Regulate interstate commerce	Charter local governments	Charter banks and corporations
Establish post offices	Regulate voting	
Raise army and navy	Establish schools	
Establish uniform naturalization laws		
Fix standard weights and measures		

Powers Prohibited— National Government	Powers Prohibited—States	Powers Prohibited— National and State
Capitation tax	Make treaties	Ex post facto laws
Tax state exports	Impair contracts	Bills of attainder
Preferential treatment for ports	Tax exports	
Grant titles of nobility	Make war	

The chart illustrates the powers primarily exercised by each respective level of government.

Antifederalists, however, remained suspicious of the power of the national government. They found particularly worrisome the supremacy clause in Article VI, which declared federal law supreme in instances when national and state laws collided. Despite the addition of the Bill of Rights, explicitly limiting the federal government's ability to encroach on the rights of individuals and states, Antifederalists remained uncomfortable with the federal arrangement well into the formative years of the new republic. They warned that the new federal system would unravel the bonds of citizenship that they believed flourished only in small, homogeneous communities. To some extent, the debate over which conditions best foster citizen participation—small, like-minded communities, or larger, more diverse ones—persists.[5] It seems clear, however, that a federal system is well suited to a country such as the United States, where regional interests must seek accommodation with broader national goals.

The town-meeting form of government, which permits local residents to act as legislative bodies, is largely a remnant of our colonial past; however, many New England towns still use them.

©Sandy Macys/Alamy Stock Photo

THE EVOLUTION OF INTERGOVERNMENTAL RELATIONS

Although the Constitution provides ground rules for the federal allocation of power, the balance of power among various levels of government has not remained static. It has ebbed and flowed over the course of the past two and a third centuries, making federalism a dynamic force in our nation's history. The nature of federalism has evolved as a result of changes in leadership, national crises, and ambiguity over the locus of authority granted by the Constitution. (We will explore this last item in more depth in the next section of this chapter.)

The National Government Asserts Itself: 1789–1832

In the early days of the new republic, former colonial allies disagreed heatedly about how much power the Constitution granted the federal government. The Constitution left unanswered all sorts of questions regarding national and state power, including the meaning of terms and phrases such as *commerce* or *necessary and proper*. It was left to the U.S. Supreme Court to determine the meaning of these terms and how they affected federal-state relations. One of the first cases in which the court was asked to deal with such matters regarded the formation of a national bank. Federalists in the new government, such as the treasury secretary, Alexander Hamilton, advocated exercising strong national authority in the arena of finance and commerce, urging President Washington to support his plans for a national bank that would finance the construction of canals and roads. Secretary of State Thomas Jefferson opposed Hamilton's plan, arguing that a national bank favored northern industry over southern farming and represented unfair competition for state financial institutions. Congress authorized a twenty-year charter for the bank in 1791, setting in motion a schism between supporters of Hamilton and supporters of Jefferson that led to the growth of the nation's first political parties.

Congress neglected to renew the charter of the First Bank of the United States, which expired in 1811. However, it established a Second Bank of the United States in 1816, once again raising the ire of state banking interests.

Maryland reacted by imposing a tax on the federal banks within its borders including the Baltimore branch where James McCulloch worked as a cashier. The tax was intended to drive business away from the federal institution. Believing the state's tax on the federal bank to be unlawful, McCulloch refused to pay the tax, arguing that a state could not tax an institution created by the national government. After losing his battle in state court, McCulloch appealed his case to the U.S. Supreme Court, where John Marshall, a longtime Federalist supporter, presided as chief justice.

Marshall's court was asked to decide two issues: (1) Did the national government have the authority to establish a national bank in the first place, and (2) if so, could a state tax the bank's operations within its borders? In his landmark decision, *McCulloch v. Maryland* (1819), Marshall ruled against state interests and in favor of the federal bank on both issues. He found congressional authority to establish the bank

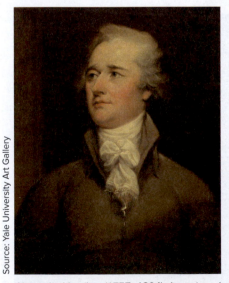

Alexander Hamilton (1757–1804) championed a strong federal government with the power to take the lead in the nation's economic development.

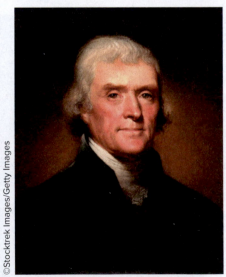

Thomas Jefferson (1743–1826) broke with Hamilton, arguing that a national bank favored northern industry over southern farming.

under the "necessary and proper clause" of Article I:

> The government which has a right to do an act, and has imposed on it the duty of performing that act, must, according to the dictates of reason, be allowed to select the means. . . . To its enumeration of powers is added that of making "all laws which shall be necessary and proper for carrying into execution the foregoing powers, and all other powers vested by this constitution, in the government of the United States, or in any department thereof."[6]

Marshall relied on the supremacy clause to deny states the power to tax a federal institution:

> The result is a conviction that the States have no power, by taxation or otherwise, to retard, impede, burden, or in any manner control, the operations of the constitutional laws enacted by Congress to carry into execution the powers vested in the general government. This is, we think, the unavoidable consequence of that supremacy which the constitution has declared.[7]

In 1798, President John Adams (1797–1801) pushed through Congress the Alien and Sedition Laws to stifle political opposition at a time when international tensions were on the rise.

Source: National Gallery of Art, Washington

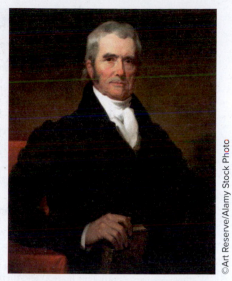

Chief Justice John Marshall (1801–1835) affirmed national supremacy in McCulloch v. Maryland and several other cases.

©Art Reserve/Alamy Stock Photo

Marshall argued that taxation by the states had the potential to destroy federal institutions and undermine the supremacy of national law.

Marshall's ruling set the stage for an expansion of national power at a time when economic production and commerce were burgeoning. Inevitably, questions soon arose regarding the national government's powers to regulate commerce. In 1824, the Marshall court heard its first case to test those powers, *Gibbons v. Ogden.* The case involved a conflict between two steamboat operators, Thomas Gibbons of New Jersey and Aaron Ogden of New York. Both men had received rights to operate off the coast of New York and New Jersey: Ogden from the state of New York and Gibbons by an act of Congress. A lower court upheld Ogden's claim, ruling that the state of New York had the right to regulate commerce with neighboring states, regardless of any concurrent national power over commerce. Gibbons appealed the case to the U.S. Supreme Court.

In *Gibbons v. Ogden,* the Marshall Court upheld the supremacy of the national government in regulating commerce, not simply in intercoastal waterways but also within states when commerce between or among states was involved. Marshall also defined the term *commerce* loosely, applying it to goods as well as to passengers. This definition significantly expanded the power of Congress and the president to oversee the economic development of the new nation in areas previously considered the preserve of states. Advocates for a strong federal role in matters ranging from education to welfare would later use the same logic to support their efforts.

Debate over the powers of the central government pitted some of the nation's most cherished leaders against each other in the early years of the Republic. In 1798, for example, John Adams pushed through Congress the Alien and Sedition Laws, intended to stifle political opposition to his foreign policy. In response, Thomas Jefferson, James Madison, and their allies developed the new philosophy of **nullification**, which proclaimed that states had the authority to declare national acts unenforceable within their borders. Virginia and Kentucky state legislatures passed resolutions affirming the doctrine of nullification in 1798. However, once he became president in 1800, Jefferson ignored this new doctrine he helped create as he sought to extend the reach of national power himself. Several decades later, southern secessionists resurrected the nullification philosophy as the nation moved toward civil war.[8]

nullification The doctrine that asserted the right of states to disregard federal actions with which they disagreed.

Negroes for Sale.

A Cargo of very fine stout Men and Women, in good order and fit for immediate service, just imported from the Windward Coast of Africa, in the Ship Two Brothers.—

Conditions are one half Cash or Produce, the other half payable the first of January next, giving Bond and Security if required.

The Sale to be opened at 10 o'Clock each Day, in Mr. Bourdeaux's Yard, at No, 48, on the Bay.

May 19, 1784.　　　JOHN MITCHELL.

Thirty Seasoned Negroes

To be Sold for Credit, at Private Sale.

AMONGST which is a Carpenter, none of whom are known to be dishonest.

Also, to be sold for Cash, a regular bred young Negroe Man-Cook, born in this Country, who served several Years under an exceeding good French Cook abroad, and his Wife a middle aged Washer-Woman, (both very honest) and their two Children. Likewise, a young Man a Carpenter.

For Terms apply to the Printer.

©MPI/Getty Images

In the 1830s and 1840s, abolitionists intensified their efforts to combat the institution of slavery.

dual federalism An approach to federal–state relationships that envisions each level of government as distinct and authoritative within its own sphere of action.

Dual Federalism, Disunion, and War: 1832–1865

Whereas the formative years of the Republic witnessed the extension of federal power over the states, nation–state relations in the period immediately preceding the Civil War were dominated by a philosophy of **dual federalism**. Dual federalism holds that the powers of the state and national governments are distinct and autonomous in their own domains. Levels of government are likened to layers in a cake that sit atop each other but do not intermingle. This viewpoint gave rise to disputes over the powers of each level of government, especially with regard to finances and the thorny issue of slavery.

Marshall's strong stance regarding the scope of federal power created resentment among southern farmers and financiers, who feared northern economic dominance. President Andrew Jackson's administration further inflamed these fears by enforcing a tariff on imported goods that protected northern manufacturers, causing some southerners to threaten secession. Jackson's vice president, South Carolinian John C. Calhoun, resigned over the matter in 1832 and justified his home state's opposition to the tariff by citing the Jeffersonian concept of nullification. Jackson adroitly solved the crisis by lowering the tariff, but talk of nullification continued as a debate over slavery took center stage in national politics.

While fear of northern dominance and support for the doctrine of nullification fueled southern passions, the Supreme Court's ruling in *Dred Scott v. Sandford* in 1857 inflamed abolitionist sentiment in the North.[9] Applying the perspective of dual federalism to bolster the power of the states, Chief Justice Roger B. Taney rejected the authority of Congress to outlaw slavery in the states and accelerated the momentum toward civil war. Republican candidate Abraham Lincoln's victory over a divided Democratic Party in the presidential election of 1860 brought the legal stalemate over slavery to an end as seven southern states seceded. Over the next four years, the United States and the Confederacy fought a bloody civil war to resolve not only the issue of slavery but also disputes over the future of our federal system that rhetoric alone did not settle.

After the Confederate surrender in 1865, Congress passed three new constitutional amendments as part of its proposed reconstruction program. The Thirteenth Amendment ended slavery. The Fourteenth Amendment guaranteed to former slaves basic rights under the U.S. Constitution. Further, it asserted that no state shall "deprive any person of life, liberty, or property, without due process of law; nor deny to any person within its jurisdiction the equal protection of the laws." The Fifteenth Amendment gave black males the vote. Of all the Civil War amendments, the Fourteenth has generated the most controversy and continues to define many debates surrounding federalism today.

Federalism in the Age of Commerce: 1865–1932

With the end of the Civil War and the principle of union firmly established, the nation moved into an era of unprecedented economic change and growth. Millions of rural farm workers joined large numbers of immigrants from foreign lands moving into the growing cities. The dangerous working conditions in many urban factories produced calls among reformers for government intervention to improve the lot of American workers. The Supreme Court consistently refused to allow the federal government to intervene in limiting the rights of states to issue licenses and to regulate commerce within their borders. It rejected limits on business practices in contracting for the services of employees.

In *Hammer v. Dagenhart* (1918), for example, the Supreme Court overturned federal efforts to end child labor. Associate Justice William R. Day, citing the Tenth Amendment, asserted that regulation of production was not a power expressly assigned to the national government and therefore was reserved to the states and to the people.[10]

The Court delivered a blow to federal efforts to restrain the growth of corporate trusts or monopolies in *U.S. v. E. C. Knight Co.* (1895).[11] In 1890, the federal government enacted the Sherman Antitrust Act in an effort to stop the tide of monopoly power in certain industries. One of these monopolies, the E. C. Knight Company, controlled over 98 percent of the sugar-refining business in the nation and sought authority for contracts to control even more. In *U.S. v. E. C. Knight Co.*, the Court was asked to determine whether the Sherman Antitrust Act applied to manufacturers like the Knight Company. A majority of the justices ruled that the act did not apply to Knight since the manufacturing of sugar or similar commodities is not commerce but an intrastate activity subject to state control. The Court argued that the activities of the company only incidentally and indirectly affected interstate commerce.

In an age when commerce was ascendant, the Court was even at times reluctant to uphold state power in limiting business activity within its own borders when it believed that it infringed on individual liberties. In *Lochner v. New York* (1905), the Court overturned a New York state law limiting the number of hours a baker could work. The state legislature had passed the bill on the grounds that extensive exposure to flour dust was detrimental to the health

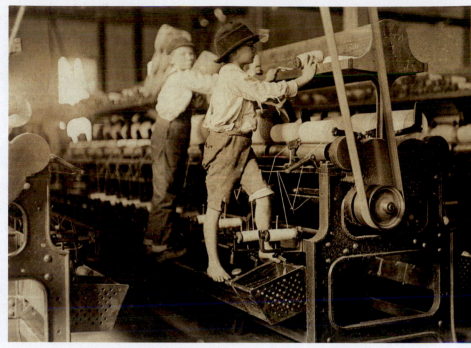

Failing to secure the help of the federal government, reformers during the Progressive Era turned to the states in their quest to end child labor.

Source: Library of Congress Prints and Photographs Division

of employees and that the state had the duty to protect the health of its citizens. The Supreme Court disagreed, arguing that the law interfered with the rights of both the employee and the employer to enter freely into a contract, a freedom guaranteed by the Fourteenth Amendment.[12] Justice Oliver Wendell Holmes, Jr., issued a stinging dissent that would later impact Court deliberations concerning the states' powers to protect worker safety.

As Progressives during this period fought unfavorable Court rulings by increasing pressure on lawmakers, the tide was about to change in favor of greater federal authority in protecting the rights of consumers and workers. Citizen reform groups, many headed by women such as labor rights advocate Mother Jones, conducted marches and confronted political leaders with demands to end child labor, to improve working conditions for women, and to limit the influence of big business on the political process. The success of interest groups at the state level put pressure on federal lawmakers, producing a number of reforms that again reshaped the face of federalism. Perhaps most significant among these changes were constitutional amendments permitting the federal government to tax personal income (Sixteenth Amendment), the direct election of senators (Seventeenth Amendment), and the expansion of the voting franchise to women (Nineteenth Amendment). These amendments focused attention on the powers of the national government as an agent of change.

The Progressive Movement helped swing the pendulum in the direction of increased federal power. President Theodore Roosevelt championed mine safety and meat inspection laws, signed the Pure Food and Drug Act into law in 1906, and expanded efforts to protect the nation's forests. Woodrow Wilson later extended federal powers over commerce by pushing for the Federal Trade Commission and the Clayton Antitrust Act of 1914. Although subsequent Court actions weakened some of these measures, by the time of the New Deal, the tide was clearly moving in the direction of greater federal authority.

The New Deal and the Growth of National Power: 1932–1937

Economic, not political, developments triggered the most dramatic increase in federal authority, as the prosperity of the early twentieth century gave way to the Great Depression of the 1930s. In response to the national crisis, President Franklin Roosevelt's administration created programs of economic regulation and development in areas that had previously been the states'

President Franklin D. Roosevelt (1933–1945) proposed a New Deal with numerous federal programs designed to address Depression Era insecurities.

domain, including health, welfare, labor relations, and agriculture. Programs for social and employment security, a federal works project, a national program for rural electrification, and regulation of the banking and securities industries all increased federal participation in American life. Although federally operated, many of these programs required state participation involving financial and human resources. The public reacted positively to Roosevelt's so-called New Deal initiatives, providing him with a landslide reelection victory in 1936. The Supreme Court's reaction was not as enthusiastic.

In a series of cases, the Court struck down key pieces of New Deal legislation, with Chief Justice Charles Evans Hughes and his conservative allies on the bench usually prevailing by a 5 to 4 vote. In 1935, the Court invalidated the National Industry Recovery Act in the case of *Schechter Poultry Co. v. U.S.*[13] The Court ruled that the act, which empowered the president to regulate the hours, wages, and minimum ages of industrial employees, was an unconstitutional delegation of legislative authority from Congress to the president. In *U.S. v. Butler* (1936), the Court invalidated portions of the Agricultural Adjustment Act, which rewarded some farmers for reducing production of certain commodities in order to reduce surpluses that drove down prices. The Court declared that such federal activities intruded into state and individual decisions protected by the Tenth Amendment.[14]

Anticipating more bad news from the Court, Roosevelt fought back by proposing a Court reorganization plan that would add one new judge for each sitting justice over the age of 70. Although Roosevelt pitched the plan as a way to lighten the workload of elderly justices, he actually intended to use it to pack the court with justices of his own choosing who would produce decisions more to his liking. The plan proved unnecessary, however, when the Court began to decide subsequent decisions in the president's favor. Many historians credit the Court's change in course to Justice Owen Roberts, who altered his previously hostile stance toward New Deal legislation. His "switch in time that saved nine" prevented a confrontation over possible expansion of the Court beyond nine members. With legal opposition blunted, the federal government proceeded to remake federalism by forever changing the role of the national government in the lives of every American. Today, we continue to see the legacy of Roosevelt's New Deal in the Social Security program and financial assistance for the unemployed and disabled as well as in the preservation of public parks and lands.

Cooperative Federalism: 1937–1960s

cooperative federalism The federal–state relationship characteristic of the post–New Deal era that stressed state and federal partnership in addressing social problems.

After 1937, Court opposition to New Deal legislation waned, states adjusted to the growing dominance of federal power in the areas of health and welfare, and **cooperative federalism** became the dominant model for federal–state relations. This approach emphasizes federal–state partnerships as the primary means for solving public policy problems. It marries the federal government's financial advantage in tax collection with the states' ability to target services to local populations. For example, the federal government typically sets minimum standards for benefits such as welfare or medical care and funds a portion of the costs. States have some flexibility in enhancing federal benefits and delivering services, but they must also contribute to funding the programs. Cooperative federalism still characterizes federal–state relations today in areas including health, welfare, the environment, education, and highway safety.

Such cooperative arrangements eased power struggles between federal and state governments and allowed the different units of government to reach mutual accommodations on a host of issues. Policies created by these arrangements were the result of a mix of federal and state authority much as a marble cake is the product of the mingling of distinctive ingredients. As a result, cooperative federalism during this era is sometimes referred to as *marble cake federalism* and it characterized much social policy from the 1930s to the early 1960s.

Creative Federalism: 1960s–1970s

Linda Brown of Topeka, Kansas, just wanted to be able to attend her local elementary school like African American children in other states such as New York or California. When the local school board denied her admission to the all-white school and shuttled Linda to a separate school for black children, her family sued for admission. When her case and several others found their way to the Supreme Court in 1954, Chief Justice Earl Warren found for a unanimous Court that the state of Kansas had denied Linda the equal protection of the law guaranteed by the Fourteenth Amendment.[15] The case reversed an earlier 1896 "separate but equal" ruling allowing the states to practice racial segregation as long as they provided relatively equal accommodations for each race. In *Brown v. Board of Education,* the Court insisted that separate "is inherently unequal" and, in subsequent cases, demanded that states tear down the barriers to equal citizenship with "all deliberate speed."

The decision sparked a revolution in citizen rights and federalism. It cast a spotlight on the sometimes parochial side of state and local politics, one that seemed to sacrifice the rights of those without a voice at the state capitols. It likewise gave hope to those who had been discriminated against by state law that the national government would insist that every state accord all of its citizens the same rights under the law. In a flurry of subsequent decisions, the Court made it clear that states must conform to national standards regarding citizen rights. It also affirmed that it would interpret the Fourteenth Amendment's "due process" and "equal protection" clauses to affect national standards in areas ranging from abortion[16] to criminal prosecution[17] to voting.[18]

The civil rights movement of the 1950s and 1960s produced not only new federal programs but also a model of **creative federalism** that sought to eradicate racial and economic injustice by targeting money directly at citizen groups and local governments. Some programs offered assistance directly to local populations, completely bypassing the states. Others allowed the federal government to take over certain operations in states that failed to adopt federal standards within a specific period of time.

creative federalism The federal–state relationship that sought to involve local populations and cities directly in addressing urban problems during the 1960s and 1970s.

Some federal initiatives expanded the social safety net initiated in the New Deal by extending health and welfare benefits to millions more Americans. Many of these programs required state financial participation, and this involvement has grown substantially over time. In 1965, for example, the federal government moved to ensure health-care coverage for the poor under a program known as Medicaid, which provides federal funding in return for guarantees from the states that they will supplement minimum coverage for the poor with their own funds. This program has expanded over time and some states sought to take advantage of increased medical coverage for the poor with the passage of health-care reform legislation passed in 2010. In some instances, the federal

Linda Brown of Topeka, Kansas, asked the Supreme Court to allow her to attend a local school that allowed only white children, helping to end segregation in Brown v. Board of Education.

government also places restrictions on who can get federal funds. To qualify for federal money to build roads and bridges, for example, states might be required to set aside funds to employ a certain percentage of minority contractors.

In 1972, President Richard Nixon sought to disentangle the federal government from aid to the states. He proposed a program called **revenue sharing** that allocated money directly to states and local governments on the basis of formulas that combined population figures with levels of demonstrated need. For a period the program was extremely popular, providing money directly to cities and towns for use as they saw fit and with few strings attached. However, by 1986, with the federal government seeking to rein in a growing budget deficit, President Ronald Reagan ended the program, saying the government could no longer afford a program that often provided large sums to even wealthy communities. With the end of revenue sharing, the nature of the federal-state partnership changed once again.

revenue sharing A grant program begun in 1972 and ended in 1987 that funneled money directly to states and local governments on the basis of formulas that combined population figures with levels of demonstrated need.

devolution A movement begun in the 1980s to grant states greater authority over the local operation of federal programs and local use of federal funds.

New Federalism and the Devolution of Power: 1980–Present

The election of Ronald Reagan in 1980 brought changes to federalism that limited the role of the federal government. Reagan favored a model of smaller government, known as **devolution**, which returned power to states, localities, and the private sector. To achieve this end, he called for more local discretion in the use of federal funds and a reduction in federal regulations that had made compliance with federal programs burdensome to state officials. He loosened restrictions on the banking and natural gas industries and lifted federally imposed ceilings on interest rates. He changed the way federal funds were distributed for a variety of social programs for the poor and disabled by giving each state a lump sum to spend and allowing them greater freedom in determining how to allocate the funds. However, with this increased local autonomy also came a reduction in funding.

Although pleased with reduced regulation, states soon felt the impact of reduced federal expenditures as they had to assume a greater share of the cost of government programs. This was particularly problematic for states because most of them, unlike the national government, are required to balance their budgets every year. To the added dismay of many state officials, devolution did not stop the federal government from imposing new national standards or from denying the states authority to develop their own policies in some areas. For example, despite his intention to allow states greater freedom, President Reagan signed into law a measure that required states to raise the minimum drinking age to 21 or face a reduction in federal funding.

The pace of devolution accelerated in the 1990s, as all three branches seemed willing to cede power to the states and weaken the authority of the federal government. In 1995, Congress passed legislation requiring the government to provide detailed justification for federal programs that require states to spend more than a certain amount of money. The following year, President Bill Clinton supported welfare reform legislation that reduced federal requirements and expanded the options available to states for administering welfare policy. In 1995, the Supreme Court signaled its willingness to put the brakes on federal authority by refusing to expand the interpretation of the commerce clause to allow the national government to restrict the possession of handguns within a thousand feet of a school. The Court said such activity had nothing to do with commerce.[19] The Court also strengthened state immunity from federal background checks for handgun buyers[20] and relaxed

President Ronald Reagan (1981–1989) sought a "devolution" of political power, with states playing a more active role in governing.

standards for compliance with federal antidiscrimination laws in such areas as age[21] and disability.[22]

Some observers of these trends fear a reversal of hard-won rights guaranteed by the Fourteenth Amendment. They worry that the nation will return to an era of patchwork rights where some jurisdictions offer more protections than others or, even worse, that the states will institute a more restrictive environment for individual rights that favors the wishes of legislative majorities over protecting the rights of minorities. Even with recent devolution activities, however, the national government's financial resources allow it to retain a strong hand in steering the future course of federalism by providing states with financial incentives to adopt uniform policies.

Despite the trend toward devolution, the current era has witnessed presidents and Congresses inclined to allow states authority and flexibility when those measures advance their own policy priorities but demand greater federal control when states move in a different direction. For example, President Obama allowed states to pursue their own paths when it came to matters like gay marriage, but he took advantage of the economic downturn to aggressively use federal stimulus monies to advance initiatives he championed at the federal level in the areas of health care, education, and energy policy. Similarly, President Trump wants to restrict federal regulations on health care, but he seeks to impose limits on the actions of local officials in protecting the undocumented from deportation and to promote so-called clean coal policies that several states have already rejected. In response, states have sought relief in the courts.

The future of federalism will continue to evolve, but it is likely to be clouded by financial uncertainty. States are finding that some federal programs are so burdensome that much of their state budgets are devoted to matching federal expenditures. This is particularly true of Medicaid, which, in some states, consumes 20 percent or more of state funds. To cope, some states have begun cutting benefits and freezing reimbursements to doctors and hospitals. No doubt federal–state relations will continue to evolve as both levels of government tussle over funding and their respective responsibilities in meeting the needs of the people they serve.

©Washington Post/Getty Images

The debate over health-care reform pitted supporters of a federal mandate against states' rights activists.

PORTRAIT
OF AN ACTIVIST

Climate Change Activists

Fifteen teen activists from across the state of Alaska told reporters they were getting impatient waiting for action on climate change, so they decided to take action on their own.

Working with environmental leaders in the state, they developed a proposal for a series of measures to reduce greenhouse gas emissions, with a goal of achieving safe atmospheric concentrations of carbon dioxide by 2100. The 100-page petition they submitted called upon the Alaska Department of Environmental Conservation to "promulgate rules leading to effective emissions reduction in order to protect the rights of present and future generations of all Alaskans, including Alaska Natives, to a healthy atmosphere and stable climate system, and to safeguard their inheritance of the legacy and heritage of the State of Alaska."*

The petitioners said they were already experiencing a host of alarming climate impacts, including, but not limited to, loss of important glacier ecosystems; changing availability of subsistence resources like shellfish, caribou, and seal; ocean acidification; increasing health impacts, including asthma; more frequent and severe heat waves and wildfires; loss of traditional knowledge due to the rapid change from environmental conditions experienced by previous generations; and an urgent need to relocate entire communities due to sea level rise, storm surges, and permafrost melt. These impacts are predicted to intensify if meaningful action is not taken soon to reduce carbon dioxide emissions.

"This winter we didn't get much snow," one of the young petitioners told the local news station. "We actually had it raining in the winter. I believe that maybe in, like, 30 years we will also have to relocate our village" and, he added, the nearby village of Hooper Bay might need to relocate a lot sooner than that.[†]

Their petition grew out of a 2011 lawsuit led by six Alaska youths who charged that the state had a duty to protect and preserve the atmosphere from the effects of climate change. The Alaska Supreme Court acknowledged that the youth had standing to bring the lawsuit but ultimately set aside their request for a court-ordered emissions reduction plan, saying this political question was better left to the legislature or state agencies.[**]

Larry Hartig, the state's environmental conservation commissioner, met with the petitioners, praising the group for its civic engagement, but he did not promise that the current administration would agree to their request. Still, this group of young people is determined to see their program enacted. Their position can be summed up by one of the signs they held as they met with Hartig: "There is no Plan B."[‡]

Fifteen young people in Alaska decided they couldn't wait any longer for the state to act on climate change, so they took matters into their own hands in order to protect the beauty of their native land.

©Natural Selection David Ponton/Design Pics

*"PETITION of Youth Petitioners and Alaska Youth for Environmental Action to the Alaska Department of Environmental Conservation", https://s3.amazonaws.com/arc-wordpress-client-up-loads/adn/wp-content/uploads/2017/08/29005449/ALASKA-PETITION.08-28-17-11.pdf

†Cotsririlos, T., "Teen Activists Urge State to Take Stronger Stance on Climate Change" KYUK TV, August 29, 2017, http://kyuk.org/post/teen-activists-urge-state-take-stronger-stance-climate-change

**Nathaniel Herz, "Alaska Youth Environmental Group Asks State to Start Regulating Greenhouse Gas Emissions," Alaska Dispatch News, August 29, 2017, https://www.adn.com/alaska-news/environment/2017/08/28/alaska-youth-environmental-group-asks-state-to-start-regulating-greenhouse-gas-emissions/.

‡Ibid.

FEDERAL–STATE RELATIONS

We have already discussed the broad outlines of federal–state relations from a historical perspective, noting the political currents that have characterized the relative powers of each level of government. We now turn our attention to the means by which these relationships continue to be redefined fiscally, politically, and legally.

Federal Grants to States and Localities (Estimated, Fiscal Year 2018)

Although national and state governments have concurrent powers to tax and spend, the federal government collects far more tax revenue than do the states—nearly three-fifths of all tax revenue—and spends almost twice as much as state and local governments combined. Much spending goes directly to individuals in the form of income security through programs such as Social Security and Medicare for the elderly. Many other programs, however, are funded through grants-in-aid, which account for about 17 percent of the federal budget. Nearly 90 percent of these grants go directly to state governments, accounting for almost 30 percent of all state revenues.[23] In turn, much of the money spent by local governments comes from state grants.

Grants-in-aid are as old as the Republic, but their use became more widespread during the middle of the nineteenth century. One of the most successful aid programs was the Morrill Act of 1862, which granted land to states for building public universities specializing in agriculture, mechanics, and military science. Early in the twentieth century, the federal government increased the amount it appropriated for grants to the states, as it assumed greater responsibility for interstate transportation as well as for the health and welfare of its citizens. Grants programs expanded further during the New Deal to address state needs arising from the Great Depression and again in the 1960s as the federal government earmarked more funding for local programs to revitalize urban life and to reduce poverty.[24]

The federal government employs a variety of grant programs to states and localities to carry out congressionally approved initiatives (see "Federal Grants to States and Localities"). The two most common are categorical and block grants. Some types of grants give the donor more authority in specifying how the money is spent. Other types provide the recipient with more choices.

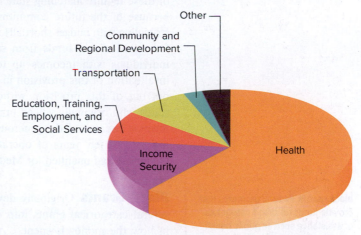

A large portion of federal grants cover health care for the poor, the sick, and the indigent. Grant-based programs like these can be found across the nation.

Source: U.S. Office of Management and Budget, *Budget of the United States Government, Fiscal Year 2016:* Historical Tables Table 12.3, Tool Outlays for Grants to State and Local Governments, http://www.whitehouse.gov/omb/budget/Historicals.

Categorical Grants The largest class of grants-in-aid is called **categorical grants**. These are reserved for special narrow purposes such as health care for the poor, highway safety, or flood assistance. These grants sometimes require the receiving government to provide matching funds. They provide extensive financial support to meet the need addressed but place restrictions on how the money is spent. Such funds, for example, cannot be allocated in a way that discriminates on the basis of race, ethnicity, or gender.

Some categorical grants are made available to all eligible jurisdictions on the basis of a formula, usually based on population and other factors. Medicaid is the largest such categorical grant to the states, providing half or more of the funds necessary to medically insure state residents who fall below a certain income level. The states are required to pick up the remaining costs and to provide a minimum level of assistance.

Categorical grants also fund specific projects targeted by Congress. These project grants are awarded on a competitive basis for a given period of time. In recent years, presidents have used this type of funding to entice states to participate in education reform. Under President Obama's Race to the Top program, the Department of Education made competitive grants to states that promise to advance more strenuous teacher evaluation and open new charter schools.

The federal government currently sponsors over 1,000 categorical grant programs designed to help states and local governments solve problems they cannot tackle with their own resources.[25] Critics claim that these programs impose burdensome application and reporting requirements on recipients and create a bewildering array of overlapping programs that lack coordination.

> **categorical grants** Federal assistance that provides funds for specific programs such as flood assistance.

The Patient Protection and Affordable Care Act (ACA) passed in 2010 added complexity to the grant-in-aid program. In addition to requiring state compliance with the overall provisions of health-care reform, the act makes dozens of new formula and project grants available to the states for programs such as community health, creation of high-risk insurance pools and health-exchange databases, HIV prevention, and quality measurement. Many of these require matching state funds, and some states had been reluctant to apply for them because of the future commitments they will incur. Of particular concern to many states struggling with budget shortfalls was the portion of the health-care law threatening to withhold federal Medicaid funds from states failing to expand Medicaid protection to nonelderly individuals with incomes up to 133 percent of the poverty line. The Supreme Court's invalidation of this provision in their landmark 2012 ruling on the health-care law let states opt out of this provision without penalty, although governors from several conservative states who originally voiced opposition to the ACA ended up accepting the new Medicaid formula because of the generous federal funding that accompanied its implementation during its first few years of operation. As of 2018, more than 30 states and the District of Columbia had qualified for Medicaid expansion in partnership with the federal government.

block grants Federal programs that provide funds for broad categories of assistance such as public health programs or law enforcement.

Block Grants Originally devised in 1966, **block grants** combine funding purposes of several categorical grants into one broader category, allowing recipients greater flexibility in how the money is spent.[26] A block grant for public health, for example, may combine previous grants that allocated funds for eradicating individual illnesses. Block grants allow the recipient government to decide how to spend its resources and relieve it of the need to apply for grants from several different agencies. Unlike many categorical grants, however, block grants place a cap on federal funds. Critics of block grants claim that federal policymakers often have no way of knowing how federal funds are spent or whether target programs meet the needs for which the money is allocated.[27]

Ronald Reagan combined seventy-seven categorical programs into just nine block grants in 1981 as part of his commitment to devolving federal power. Congress slowed the move toward block funding in subsequent years but embraced it as a centerpiece of welfare reform in 1996. Prior to the change in welfare funding, categorical grants provided assistance to families living in poverty, guaranteeing funding to recipients as long as they were in need. The new block grant approach allowed the states to vary the amount and time for which recipients qualified for assistance. This new approach allows states to adjust requirements to local needs but creates a degree of variation that is sometimes confusing to recipients and difficult for policymakers to monitor. The economic stagnation of recent years has resulted in an increased number of destitute families who have exhausted their benefits and are unable to find jobs in a weak economy (as we discuss in Chapter 15).

The Republican 115th Congress and President Trump sought to replace many of the components of the ACA with block grants giving more discretion to the states in how health-care spending is allocated. However, along with greater flexibility comes greater state responsibility for funding shortfalls if allocated federal funds are insufficient.

Political Relations

The interests of political actors at the national, state, and local levels are often at odds for a number of reasons. Policymakers at each level face a different

Source: White House Photo by Joyce N. Boghosian

President Trump wasted little time after entering office in signing executive orders designed to dismantle provisions of President Obama's signature legislation, the Affordable Care Act. The ACA increased the availability of health insurance for millions of Americans through a variety of federal grants in aid.

constellation of legal, social, and political pressures that can affect their fortunes at the polls. As a result, it is not unusual for them to differ over how best to fund government programs.

As noted, categorical grants give the federal government more authority over state and local recipients. They provide visible benefits, like health-care clinics, highways, and bridges. As a result, they give federal lawmakers the opportunity to take credit for creating programs that help people and for steering federal funds to their home districts or states. In addition, they provide strict accountability for the use of federal money. Such programs create grateful constituents who receive ongoing benefits that are protected by law.

By contrast, many state and local officials favor the decentralization, experimentation, and flexibility associated with block grants. They argue that local officials know best how to address local problems and that they should be free to experiment to find

Some programs, like President Obama's Race to the Top, establish federal mandates like school testing but do not supply all the money necessary to carry them out.

solutions that work best for their own citizens. Members of local government have a stake in maximizing the flow of federal dollars and minimizing the cost of compliance to taxpayers. With block grants, they may be able to subsidize purely state and local functions by the infusion of federal funds with few strings attached. State and local officials can take credit for innovative solutions they initiate with block grant funding, earning them electoral rewards. However, the administration of block grants is uneven. Studies show that although some states with a highly professional bureaucracy have successfully addressed social problems with block grants, other states have lagged behind.[28]

State and local officials are also concerned about the growing use of **federal mandates**—federally imposed requirements on state and local governments ranging from election reform to water treatment. They are especially anxious about **unfunded mandates**, which are requirements that Congress passes without providing funds to carry them out. In 1995, Congress passed the Unfunded Mandates Reform Act to stem the tide of such mandates. The act requires the Congressional Budget Office to flag legislation that costs state governments or private-sector bodies within the states more than $50 million for compliance. The bill's sponsors hoped that members of Congress would be unwilling to pass legislation that clearly increased the costs passed along to their home states. Although this tactic substantially reduced the growth of unfunded mandates, such mandates persist. It is estimated that between 2004 and 2013, Congress enacted 173 laws that imposed 322 mandates on states and local governments under both Republican and Democratic administrations alike.[29] The No Child Left Behind Act, for example, required states to adopt rigorous testing of students in a variety of subjects but failed to provide full funding for its implementation. The law was amended in 2015 to scale back federal authority over K–12 education, but testing requirements remain.

Debates over federal funding have spurred the growth of **intergovernmental lobbies** to advance the interests of various state and local governing bodies. The National Governors Association is perhaps the oldest of these, tracing its roots to the administration of Theodore Roosevelt. The U.S. Conference of Mayors also lobbies actively at the state and national levels for programs that address urban problems. Other lobbying groups represent professional bureaucrats and administrators responsible for the daily operation of government programs. Only a handful of such groups existed prior to 1900; by the mid-1980s, that number had mushroomed to more than one hundred.[30]

Some types of policies are more likely to be promoted and more likely to be successful if they are undertaken by one level of government rather than another.[31] For example, the national government is better equipped than state and local governments to address problems that spill across geographic boundaries, like air pollution, or that involve the infusion of substantial resources, like aid to the poor. State and local governments are better at addressing issues that require pinpoint targeting of resources, like economic development for cities or education reform.

federal mandates Federal requirements imposed on state and local governments, often as a condition for receiving grants.

unfunded mandates Requirements imposed on state and local governments for which the federal government provides no funds for compliance.

intergovernmental lobbies Professional advocacy groups representing various state and local governing bodies.

The past few years have been among the most consequential in the constitutional history of federalism. Particularly noteworthy have been cases involving same-sex marriage, immigration, the use of the commerce clause, and issues involving the 10th and 11th Amendments of the Constitution.

The 2013 decision in *United States v. Windsor* invalidated the 1996 Defense of Marriage Act, which declared marriage a union between one man and one woman. In the wake of this decision, at least thirteen states adopted laws permitting same-sex marriage. Because some states still refused to recognize the rights of couples married in other states, the Supreme Court took up the issue again in *Obergefell v. Hodges* in 2015.[32] In this landmark case, the Court ruled that the Fourteenth Amendment requires states to issue marriage licenses to same-sex couples and to recognize marital rights of those married in other states. The ruling angered conservative groups that believe marriage should be regulated by the states and reflect that state's prevailing views on homosexuality. Although all states must now permit same-sex marriages, many states still retain restrictions on the rights of the LGBTQ community in the areas of housing, employment, and public accommodation. The next battlefront for the LGBTQ community will be full civil rights protections regardless of sexual orientation or gender identity.

Immigration has traditionally been the province of the federal government, specifically the U.S. Congress. Arizona passed its own immigration law in 2010, claiming that Congress had failed to protect Arizona's borders by not providing sufficient resources to fully enforce its own immigration laws. Among other things, the Arizona law required law enforcement officers to determine immigration status during any lawful stop; created state crimes and penalties for failure to carry federally issued alien registration documents; made it unlawful for an unauthorized alien to knowingly apply for or perform work in Arizona; and permitted an officer to make a warrantless arrest if the officer had probable cause to believe the person had committed any public offense that made the person removable from the United States. The federal government claimed the law intruded into an arena of federal jurisdiction and sought to have the law overturned. In June 2012, the Supreme Court affirmed the federal government's "inherent sovereign power to control and conduct foreign relations."[33] It said the supremacy clause of the Constitution gives Congress the power to preempt state law where state law intrudes on federal authority. Nevertheless, the Court let stand a provision of the Arizona law that allows state and local authorities to require proof of citizenship from individuals police detain on suspicion of committing a crime. Those who cannot provide such proof can be handed over to federal authorities for possible deportation.

We have already seen in the opening vignette that state and local officials have sought to protect the undocumented from unwarranted detainment and that the Trump administration has sought to limit sanctuary protections. The courts will be asked to resolve any standoff between federal, state, and local authorities as immigration continues to be a hot-button issue. Although the federal government maintains its authority over immigration, the reserved powers provisions of the Tenth Amendment may provide a constitutional basis for challenging federal policies that interfere with the public safety procedures promulgated by local governments.

In recent years, the Court has sought to curb the use of the commerce clause as a vehicle for expanding the power of the federal government. The clause that allows Congress the right to regulate interstate commercial activities had been broadly interpreted since the New Deal to allow the regulation of activity within the states if those activities impacted interstate business and the national economy. In *Garcia v. San Antonio Metropolitan Transit Authority* (1985), for example, the Court held that Congress has the power under the commerce clause to extend the Fair Labor Standards Act to state and local governments by requiring employers to provide overtime pay to their employees.[34]

In 2008, the Supreme Court affirmed an individual citizen's Second Amendment right to bear arms, setting up future judicial challenges over the legality of gun bans in major cities across the country.

In 1995, however, the Court, in *United States v. Lopez,* signaled a new willingness to put the brakes on the expansion of federal powers granted under the commerce clause.[35] The case involved Alfonzo Lopez, Jr., who was charged with violating the 1990 Gun-Free School Zones Act for carrying a concealed firearm into his Texas high school. He argued that the law was unconstitutional because it relied on the commerce clause to regulate an activity that was not strictly economic. The Supreme Court agreed, arguing that carrying a firearm near a school was insufficiently related to commerce to justify regulation. The Court similarly limited Congress's reach in *United States v. Morrison* (2000), when it invalidated a provision of the federal Violence Against Women Act (VAWA).[36] The case involved a Virginia Tech freshman who claimed she was raped by two members of the football team. When the state did not bring an indictment, the federal government used the VAWA to intervene. The Court invalidated portions of the act, saying that the law outlawed criminal activity already regulated by the states and that it had no clear connection to commerce. The Court also said the federal government had overreached in applying the Fourteenth Amendment in this case because the amendment applies to regulating the behavior of states and does not directly apply to individuals.

The Court used the commerce clause again to reject the federal government's authority to deny funding to states unwilling to expand Medicaid under the Affordable Care Act (discussed earlier in the chapter). The denial of funds, the Court held, would constitute undue pressure on the states to accept policy changes with which they find it impossible to comply.[37]

The Court has also utilized the Tenth Amendment in recent years to limit congressional authority over the states. In the 1976 case *National League of Cities v. Usery,* the Supreme Court invalidated a federal law that extended the minimum wage to almost all state and local employees.[38] The Court's majority argued that the Tenth Amendment prohibited the national government from dictating what states can pay their employees. In 1992, the Court said Congress could not require the state of New York to dispose of low-level radioactive waste at its own expense in order to meet federal mandates just because the private party that generated it could not find suitable alternative means for disposal. Citing the Tenth Amendment, Justice Sandra Day O'Connor said the law "would 'commandeer' state governments into the service of federal regulatory purposes, and would for this reason be inconsistent with the Constitution's division of authority between federal and state governments."[39] Several years later, the Court invalidated a provision of the Brady Handgun Violence Prevention Act requiring the chief law-enforcing officers in the states to run background checks on handgun purchasers. The Court once again held it unconstitutional to enlist the state in enforcing federal law.[40] But the Court's decisions in granting states more power has not always been consistent. In 2005, the Court ruled against California in striking down a state law permitting the possession and use of marijuana for medical purposes, holding that Congress's authority to control the trafficking of controlled substances trumped the state's Tenth Amendment rights.[41]

Some states have proposed or passed resolutions of state sovereignty based on the claim that the Tenth Amendment gives them the authority to nullify federal laws with which their legislatures disagree. These resolutions, however, lack the force of law.

States been more successful in citing the Eleventh Amendment to uphold state sovereignty in cases where they have been sued to comply with federal statutes. In these cases, the state was found to be immune from lawsuits brought by its own citizens whether filed in federal court or within the state's own court system. For example, in *Alden v. Maine* (1999), probation officers sued the state for failure to pay overtime in violation of federal law. Citing the Eleventh Amendment, the court ruled the states are immune from such suits. Writing for the majority, Justice Anthony Kennedy held:

> Federalism requires that Congress accord States the respect and dignity due them as residuary sovereigns and joint participants in the Nation's governance. Immunity from suit in federal courts is not enough to preserve that dignity, for the indignity of subjecting a nonconsenting State to the coercive process of judicial tribunals at the instance of private parties exists regardless of the forum.[42]

More recently, the Court has issued mixed judgments on Eleventh Amendment protections for the states. While the Court upheld Florida's claim of immunity from lawsuits by rejecting a suit brought by state university employees claiming age discrimination,[43] it affirmed the right

A CLASH OF WILLS: CITIES PUSH BACK ON PREEMPTION

For the past few years, Republicans have controlled both legislative houses and the office of governor in roughly half of the states. At the same time, over 60 percent of the mayors in the nation's largest cities are Democrats. This partisan split has made for some interesting dynamics between state and local governments.*

Most cities derive their powers from the states. As a result, states have substantial authority over the policies cities must follow. Nevertheless, cities command respect as a result of their demographic and economic clout. Almost two-thirds of Americans live in cities and just three cities—New York City, Los Angeles, and Chicago—are responsible for more economic output than all but six states.†

Republicans in statehouses have pushed a conservative agenda reflecting the party's move to the right. Much of this agenda has been driven by American Legislative Exchange Council (ALEC), a consortium of conservative groups and more than 2,000 state legislators. Among the group's priorities are loosening pollution controls; expansion of school choice; adoption of right-to-work legislation that weakens labor unions; and, more recently, state preemption measures that override the authority of local governments to enact progressive policies.‡ Recent preemption efforts seek to enjoin cities from adopting gun control measures, from increasing minimum wages for workers, from regulating the controversial oil extraction method known as fracking, and from enacting LGBTQ protections.

Big-city mayors have responded to these initiatives aggressively. For example, in June 2016, mayors from 33 cities including Charlotte, Portland, and Pittsburgh issued a statement to state and federal legislators seeking greater local control over fracking. The statement reads, in part:

> we believe that all communities should have the right to decide whether, where, and how industrial fracking operations—including not only well pads, but waste disposal facilities and all related infrastructure—happen within their borders.**

Lawsuits were filed by mayors in Tallahassee and Philadelphia to prevent preemption of local firearms legislation. In Seattle, the Washington Supreme Court upheld Seattle's tax on firearms shops despite the state's attempt to prohibit the local regulation of guns and ammunition. Local efforts have met with mixed success when it comes to challenging LGBTQ preemptions. Particularly contentious are preemption measures aimed at limiting the authority of local governments and school districts to allow transgender individuals to use bathroom facilities that match their gender identity rather than their birth sex.

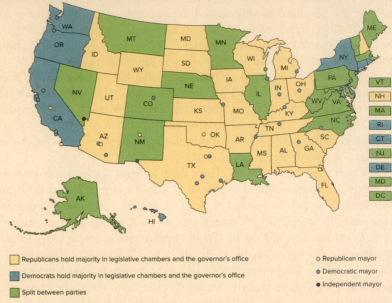

Republicans hold majority in legislative chambers and the governor's office

Democrats hold majority in legislative chambers and the governor's office

Split between parties

• Mayoral elections are nonpartisan

○ Republican mayor
● Democratic mayor
● Independent mayor

Republicans controlling most state governments have pushed for greater authority over policies that cities may implement. Democratically controlled cities have used a variety of tactics to push back.

Groups such as the American Civil Liberties Union, the U.S. Conference of Mayors, and the National League of Cities (NLC) are leading the way in addressing preemption efforts with lawsuits, lobbying efforts, and public information campaigns. A brochure published by the NLC presents the rationale for these countermeasures:

> Local control and city rights are priority number one. We know well that innovation happens in cities and then percolates upwards. This process should be celebrated, not stymied.‡‡

Conflicts like these between state and municipal governments are a reflection of our highly polarized society and are not likely to dissipate so long as partisan divisions between the two levels of government persist.

*"Partisanship in United States Municipal Elections," Ballotpedia. Retrieved October 22, 2017, from https://ballotpedia.org/Partisanship_in_United_States_municipal_elections#tab=Who_runs_the_cities_3F.

†Sophie Quinton, "Expect More Conflict Between Cities and States," Stateline, January 25, 2017, http://www.pewtrusts.org/en/research-and-analysis/blogs/stateline/2017/01/25/expect-more-conflict-between-cities-and-states?cid=email_TRUMPadelphia%20613.

‡Lisa Graves, "ALEC's 2016 Agenda Moving in the States: A Snapshot," Center for Media and Democracy PR Watch, May 5, 2016, https://www.prwatch.org/news/2016/05/13099/alec%27s-2016-agenda-snapshot.

**"Fracking Preemption Conflicts Between State and Local Governments,' Ballotpedia. Retrieved October 22, 2017, from https://ballotpedia.org/Fracking_preemption_conflicts_between_state_and_local_governments

‡‡National League of Cities, "City Rights in an Era of Preemption: A State-by-State Analysis 2017' nlc.org/sites/default/files/2017-02/NLC%20Preemption%20Report%202017.pdf

After the Supreme Court moved to legalize same-sex marriage, debate arose over the rights of transgender individuals to use public accommodations.

of a disabled man to sue the state of Tennessee for not complying with portions of the federal Americans with Disabilities Act by providing elevator access to a state courtroom.[44]

Clearly, the range of powers legitimately exercised by the national and state governments continues to undergo constitutional examination by the courts. Similarly, the range of powers exercised by local governments has not escaped Supreme Court scrutiny. In 2008, a divided Court in *District of Columbia v. Heller* rejected a strict gun control law in the District of Columbia, arguing that the U.S. Constitution provides federal protection for an individual's right to bear arms.[45] In 2010, the Court, in *McDonald v. City of Chicago,* extended the federal protection of the Second Amendment's right to keep and bear arms to every jurisdiction in the nation.

INTERSTATE RELATIONS

To function well, our federal system requires coordination not simply between national and state governments but also across state boundaries and even among localities within the states. The Framers provided some guidance for interstate relations in the Constitution, but the contours of interstate cooperation and competition continue to evolve.

Cooperation and Competition

The **full faith and credit** provision of the U.S. Constitution directs states to recognize legal judgments in lawsuits that are valid in another state. An individual who owes a sum of money to a creditor in Pennsylvania cannot escape his obligation by fleeing over the border into Delaware. Delaware is required to recognize the judgment and enforce it if the creditor pursues him. Similarly, every state is now required to recognize same-sex marriages performed in other states and receive all the benefits accorded any other married couple since the Supreme Court legalized same-sex marriages in *Obergefell v. Hodges.*[46]

But what if one state wants to sue another for actions it claims violates its interests? Recognizing that not all interstate relations would be amicable, the Framers provided that

full faith and credit The constitutional provision requiring each state to recognize legal transactions authorized in other states.

states with legal disputes may take their cases directly to the Supreme Court. Such cases are not all that common, but occasionally they do arise. For example, in 2003, the state of Virginia brought suit against the state of Maryland over the right to build a water intake pipe in the Potomac River, which Maryland claimed was given to its founder by King Charles I in 1632. The case was given original jurisdiction in the Supreme Court, meaning that it went directly to the nation's highest court. In this case, the Court ruled in favor of Virginia.[47]

Section 2 of Article IV provides that the citizens of each state shall be entitled to all the same **privileges and immunities** of citizens of the several states. This wording is ambiguous, however, and litigants often have asked the courts to interpret its meaning. The Supreme Court has ruled that states may not discriminate against nonresidents when it comes to fundamental rights like freedom to make a living and access to the political and legal processes of the state. However, states can treat nonresidents differently in a number of other areas. For example, nonresident workers may pay different tax rates than residents, and nonresident students may pay higher tuition and fees at state schools.[48]

Cooperation among states is often fostered by the use of **interstate compacts**, a device that must receive explicit approval "with the consent of Congress" according to the Constitution (Article I, Section 10). Such compacts may involve agreements to share environmental responsibility for waterways that cross their borders or to develop transportation authorities across borders with the power to collect fares and distribute revenues. Of course, not all states see eye to eye when it comes to the use of resources that cross borders, as we saw in the *Virginia v. Maryland* case described earlier.

privileges and immunities A constitutional phrase interpreted to refer to fundamental rights, such as freedom to make a living, and access to the political and legal processes of the state.

interstate compacts Cooperative agreements made between states, subject to congressional approval, to address mutual problems.

Innovation in the States

In his dissent in the case of *New State Ice Company v. Liebmann* (1932), Justice Louis Brandeis argued that the state of Oklahoma should have the authority to determine which businesses serve the public interest and therefore should be required to obtain state licenses. This was a legitimate way for the state, he felt, to protect public health and safety. His dissent is most famous, however, for his faith in the power of states to innovate within our federal system:

> To stay experimentation in things social and economic is a grave responsibility. Denial of the right to experiment may be fraught with serious consequences to the Nation. It is one of the happy incidents of the federal system that a single courageous State may, if its citizens choose, serve as a laboratory; and try novel social and economic experiments without risk to the rest of the country.[49]

©ginosphotos/Getty Images

Cross-state pollution of air and water creates conflicts between states, often leading to litigation.

American history is replete with examples of public policy innovation by states that served as a catalyst for widespread change. In 1898, South Dakota passed a law granting voters the right to initiate all forms of legislation. States throughout the Midwest quickly adopted the measure, as did many western states. More recently, welfare reform initiatives that originated in Wisconsin in the early 1990s served as a model for national legislation in 1996. Health care for low-income populations has also improved as a result of state initiatives in recent years. Massachusetts passed a law mandating the purchase of health-care insurance in 2006, and President Obama adopted a similar approach in his effort to promote universal health-care coverage in 2010. Oregon passed the first automatic voter registration law in 2015 making anyone who interacts with a government agency, like the Bureau of Motor Vehicles, instantly eligible to vote unless they specifically decline. Today, the practice had spread to include at least a dozen states and the District of Columbia.

Just how extensive are innovation and diffusion in the American federal system? The question is hard to answer because innovation is difficult to measure. Nevertheless, several studies cast light on the matter. In a pathbreaking study published in 1969, political scientist Jack L. Walker studied the spread of innovations in eighty-eight public policy areas ranging from corrections to welfare from 1870 to the mid-1960s.[50] Walker found that larger, wealthier states whose urban populations are well represented in the state legislature are most likely to innovate and to more rapidly adopt ideas pioneered in other states. New York, Massachusetts, and California consistently scored near the top in state innovation.

Political competition seems to have increased state innovation after 1930. Presumably, competition makes the political parties less complacent and more likely to innovate in order to bring new voters to their cause. Walker also found greater innovation in states with more professional full-time legislatures and state bureaucracies than among states with part-time citizen legislators.

A proliferation of policy innovation in the states in recent years has been driven, in part, by the inability of divided government at the national level to pass legislation addressing pressing policy needs but also by the diminished financial resources available for solving public problems. Of particular note have been policies that have redesigned government support programs for welfare and health and those that have increased state reliance on public–private partnerships designed to finance innovation. Often these changes are driven by individual policy entrepreneurs like governors or state legislators or by organized interests with a particular financial or ideological interest like the Chamber of Commerce or the conservative American Legislative Exchange Council. In his study of several health- and welfare-related policy innovations (see "Policy Innovations"), Andrew Karch found that **policy diffusion** frequently follows a two-stage pattern. In the first stage, word of successful pioneering programs percolates upward from the innovating state and receives national recognition by state and federal leaders who consider ways of extending and enhancing these innovations. In the second stage, national actors including elected officials, think tanks, and interest groups place their own stamp on the innovation and then use their leverage to mobilize constituencies in other states to adopt these changes. Adopting states then customize the innovation in ways that meet the specific

policy diffusion The spread of policy innovation across jurisdictions.

Policy Innovations

Policy Innovation	Policy Type	Diffusion Dates	Number of States
Senior prescription drug programs	Government support (expansion)	1975–2001	27
Welfare family caps	Government support (contraction)	1992–1998	23
Welfare time limits	Government support (contraction)	1993–1996	18
Medical savings accounts	Public–private partnership	1993–1997	28

Policy innovations may begin at a federal level, but the most successful implementation happens when the states fully integrate the programs to meet the specific characteristics of their populations.

Source: Adapted from Karch, A. *Democratic Laboratories: Policy Diffusion Among the American States* (Ann Arbor: University of Michigan Press, 2010), p. 18.

characteristics of their populations. In the case of widespread diffusion, the ability of state and national leaders to muster electoral support for the innovation is crucial.[51]

Walker and others have confirmed that federal grants-in-aid significantly shorten the time of diffusion, especially among states that typically are slower to embrace innovation.[52] Some states are willing to innovate consistently, but the federal government must prod others into action.

Just as some levels of government are better equipped to handle certain functions than others, each level of government also provides a unique combination of opportunities and challenges for citizen participation. Let us turn to this topic now.

FEDERALISM AND CIVIC ENGAGEMENT TODAY

Because federalism diffuses power across many competing power centers, it multiplies the number of opportunities for citizen political participation. Few of us may have the opportunity to shape national policies directly as members of the U.S. House or Senate, but many opportunities exist for citizen political involvement at the state and local levels as elected officials or as volunteer members of boards, associations, and neighborhood councils. These positions afford citizens the opportunity for intensive, direct participation in policymaking and implementation and serve as training grounds for those who wish to take the national political stage.

Participation at each level of government is also laden with its own pitfalls and challenges. It may be easier to devise solutions to problems in a small rural community than a highly urbanized one. Small-town residents who know each other may have an easier time agreeing on the design and location of a new school building for example than residents of a larger city with many competing points of view. Of course, entrenched local traditions that are difficult to overcome may also hinder growth. For example, a homogeneous local population may be less welcoming to newly arriving immigrants than a larger multicultural urban center.

©Sandy Huffaker/Getty Images

With over a half-million elective offices in the United States, 96 percent of which are at the local level of government, opportunities for political involvement abound.

Although participation in the national political arena requires patience in negotiating among many competing interests and respect for a wide diversity of values and traditions, measures calling for the expansion of rights are often more easily accommodated at the national level than at the local level of government. Interests that may be in the minority in an individual community or state may be able to obtain the critical collective mass at the national level necessary to overcome local or regional opposition. The civil rights movement demonstrated the strength numerical minorities can amass at the national level.

A group of political scientists studying the opportunities and challenges of federalism for civic engagement summarized the matter as follows:

> Active citizenship seems to flourish most naturally at the local level and in smaller communities. This does not mean that those who favor civic engagement should abandon wider and more inclusive goals or that those who favor diversity and inclusion should abandon local institutions. It does mean, however, that these two dilemmas—of scale and diversity—pose difficult political challenges.[53]

Our discussion in this section echoes the debate that raged between Federalists and Antifederalists during the ratification of the U.S. Constitution. Federalists argued for the benefits of combining local and regional interests in a national policy, whereas Antifederalists were concerned that national politics would lack the unity of purpose and intensity of citizen involvement present at the state and local levels. U.S. history shows that federalism is flexible enough to accommodate both perspectives, and both viewpoints often have been useful in charting our nation's course.

Although a federal system such as ours—with many layers of government—provides added security for citizen rights, it requires that we participate in governmental decisions at multiple levels and understand the importance of participating at each level. Alexis de Tocqueville took note of this when he toured America in the 1830s:

> But when one examines the Constitution of the United States, the best of all known federal constitutions, it is frightening to see how much diverse knowledge and discernment it assumes on the part of the governed. The government of the Union rests almost entirely on legal fictions. The Union is an ideal notion which exists, so to say, only in men's minds and whose extent and limits can only be discerned by the understanding.[54]

How much more daunting must it be for busy citizens to fulfill the obligations of citizenship in our federal republic today!

get involved!

Ballot initiatives have become increasingly popular devices for ensuring popular participation in setting the legislative agendas in many states. You can check on the most recent ballot initiatives in your state by examining the list maintained by Project Vote Smart at http://votesmart.org/elections/ballot-measures. If you are interested in placing an item on the ballot, you can contact your state's secretary of state for information about the requirements. Most states require a certain number of signatures on a petition and sometimes charge a nominal filing fee.

©Comstock/Getty Images

Thinking It Through »»»

Learning Objective: Analyze the benefits and drawbacks of U.S. federalism today.

Review: The Division of Power

What advantages and disadvantages are associated with a federal system that disperses power among various levels of government versus a unitary government that concentrates power at the national (or central) level? Explain how well these two types of power structures handle policy problems arising at the local, regional, and national levels.

Summary

1. **How is power dispersed in American federalism?**
   - The Constitution
     - Grants some powers, called enumerated, to the national government. The power to declare war is one example.
     - Grants reserved powers to the states. For example, state governments are empowered to create cities and towns.
     - Allows some powers, like taxing and spending, to be shared jointly.
     - Prohibits both federal and state levels of government from taking certain actions like passing ex post facto laws.

2. **How have the powers of the national and state governments evolved over the nation's history?**
   - Federalism has produced periodic shifts in the relative strength of the national and state governments, sometimes strengthening the national government and sometimes weakening it.
   - From our founding until about 1832, the national government asserted broad powers, particularly through court decisions that affirmed the supremacy of national law.
   - From 1832 until the Civil War, a period of dual federalism dominated in which national and state powers were kept fairly distinct, like the layers of a cake.
   - After the war, the courts gradually granted more powers to the states, particularly in the arena of economic regulation.
   - The New Deal produced dramatic growth in the powers of the national government despite resistance by the courts.
   - From about 1937 until the 1960s, the national and state governments forged cooperative partnerships in addressing social problems, with each partner contributing something to a mix sometimes described as a marble cake.
   - The 1960s and 1970s witnessed a period of creative federalism as the national government, in particular, experimented with new ways of addressing local problems directly.
   - Ronald Reagan initiated an era of devolution in which the national government turned more power and responsibility for programs over to the states and local governments.

3. **What factors influence relations between national and state governments today?**
   - The national government shares resources with the states by making available various types of grants:
     - Categorical grants provide funds for very specific programs and may come with a variety of strings attached. Some are distributed on the basis of predetermined formulae; some are awarded competitively for specific projects.
     - Block grants fold money for programs into broader categories and provide for more local discretion in spending.
   - Members of Congress often prefer to provide categorical grants over which they retain some control. State and local officials often prefer block grants that provide more local discretion in spending. State and local officials often complain about mandates that require states to provide services but do not provide necessary resources.
   - Conflicts over the powers of the state and national governments often revolve around legal issues raised by the Tenth Amendment, which reserves to the states powers not granted to the federal government; the Eleventh Amendment, which limits the legal liability of state governments; and the Fourteenth Amendment, which extends protections guaranteed at the federal level to the states.
   - Larger, wealthier states with substantial urban populations and policy entrepreneurs are more likely to innovate with the resources often provided by the federal government.

Chapter 4

Civil Liberties
Citizens' Rights Versus Security

CIVIL LIBERTIES VERSUS CIVIL RIGHTS: A SWEET DISPUTE

The case of *Masterpiece Cakeshop v. Colorado Civil Rights Commission* decided by the Supreme Court in 2018 highlighted tensions between civil liberties and civil rights. The litigation involved a same-sex wedding, a renowned baker of specialty wedding cakes, and a refusal of service. Chapter 4 discusses civil liberties, the basic rights and freedoms that Americans enjoy. Chapter 5 focuses on the civil rights of groups to be free from discrimination. When civil rights and civil liberties clash, we often look to the courts to resolve the issue.

Jack Phillips, custom wedding cake creator (pictured above), refused to bake a cake for the same sex marriage of Charlie Craig and David Mullins (pictured below).

Top: ©The Washington Post/Getty Images; Bottom: ©Chip Somodevilla/Getty Image

In the summer of 2012, Colorado couple Charlie Craig and David Mullins made plans to be legally married in Massachusetts, because their state did not yet recognize same-sex marriages, with a celebration in Denver to follow. Friends recommended the Masterpiece Cakeshop, located in the Denver suburb of Lakewood. The cake shop was run by master baker Jack Phillips, who specialized in making custom wedding cakes, some worth thousands of dollars. Craig and Mullins arrived at the bakery, with Craig's mother and a book of cake design ideas. Phillips cut the meeting short when he learned the cake was to celebrate the couple's wedding. He recalled saying, "Sorry guys, I don't bake cakes for same-sex weddings." Craig recalled, "We were so stunned he would say something like that it actually took a little time to sink in."[1]

As You READ

- Why was the incorporation of the Bill of Rights by the Supreme Court important?
- What are the First Amendment rights?
- What are some of the other important civil liberties guaranteed by the Constitution?

After learning that Colorado's public accommodations law specifically prohibited discrimination based on sexual orientation, the couple filed a complaint with the Colorado Civil Rights Commission and won. The Masterpiece Cakeshop was ordered not only to provide cakes for same-sex marriages, but to change its company's policies, provide comprehensive staff training regarding public accommodations discrimination, provide quarterly reports for the next two years regarding steps it has taken to come into compliance with state law, and indicate whether it has turned away any prospective clients. Instead of complying with the state's order, Phillips removed the cake shop from the wedding cake business and appealed the commission's decision to the Colorado Supreme Court, which upheld the ruling of the state's Civil Rights Commission. Phillips's appeals in the Colorado state court system also failed.

On the last day of the U.S. Supreme Court's session in 2017, the Court agreed to hear the case. Phillips's argument depicted his refusal to provide a wedding cake for a same-sex marriage as grounded in two fundamental civil liberties, the free exercise of religion and freedom of speech. He contended that he should not be forced by the government to provide a work of art, which is how he describes his custom cakes, supporting same-sex marriage, which conflicts with his Christian religious beliefs. He also contends that the government should not force his work of art to express a point of view that he finds abhorrent. He further contended that he would have sold the couple any item in the store that was already baked. Further, his lawyers argued that, as the same-sex couple was able to purchase a cake from another bakery shop, they suffered no real harm. The civil rights argument against Phillips's position was that the cake shop refused to serve customers based solely on their sexual orientation, which amounts to illegal discrimination.

The Supreme Court ultimately ruled for the baker but left open the core issue of whether a business can discriminate against gay and lesbian customers based on the First Amendment rights of freedom of religion and freedom of speech. The Court's 7 to 2 decision sidestepped the larger issue by holding that the Colorado Civil Rights Commission had exhibited hostility toward the baker's sincere religious beliefs that had motivated his objection in the first place. ■

HERITAGE OF RIGHTS AND LIBERTIES

Some of the first settlers in North America declared their dedication to individuality and freedom by setting forth their rights in public documents.[2] As early as 1641, the Massachusetts General Court adopted the "Body of Liberties," which defined the rights of citizens in the Massachusetts Colony. By the time of the American Revolution some 125 years later, each state had its own constitution containing a **Bill of Rights** that protected a variety of civil liberties. As discussed in Chapter 2, the delegates who met in Philadelphia in 1787 to create a new governing structure did not originally include a bill of rights in the new constitution.

Bill of Rights The freedoms listed in the first ten amendments to the U.S. Constitution.

The Constitution and Rights

Records of the 1787 deliberations show that the delegates soundly rejected a federal bill of rights on at least four separate occasions.[3] They did not, however, ignore the subject of individual freedoms. The new constitution forbade the legislature from passing ex post facto laws, which retroactively convict a person who committed a behavior before it was a crime, and bills of attainder, legislative pronouncements of guilt that should be left for a court to decide. The delegates also made it difficult for government to deny writs of habeas corpus to accused or convicted persons. Writs of habeas corpus allow individuals to petition judges to assess whether there is sufficient cause to hold an accused person for trial or to imprison a convicted person who may have received an unfair trial.

The Federalists opposed adding a bill of rights because they believed that a government founded on the principles of separation of powers and checks and balances would necessarily produce a political system free from tyranny. In addition, the Federalists felt that the states would wield enough power to safeguard the civil liberties of their citizens. Hamilton argued in *The Federalist* No. 84 that a bill of rights was not only unnecessary but also dangerous, because it was foolhardy to list things that the national government had no power to do.[4]

The Federalists found public opinion against them when the document went to the states for ratification. After the first five states ratified the document, momentum for a constitution that lacked a bill of rights slowed considerably. Swayed by Antifederalist rhetoric championing personal freedom, seven of the last eight states approved the document only on the condition that the Federalist-controlled Congress add amendments protecting individual liberties as soon as possible. The Antifederalist fear of the power of the new national government was thus responsible for the addition of a bill of rights to the constitutional document written by the Federalists.

The Bill of Rights

As discussed in Chapter 2, after winning a seat in the First Congress, Federalist leader James Madison drafted seventeen new amendments. The Senate rejected five of these, and the states ratified ten of the remaining twelve; these amendments became known as the Bill of Rights.[5]

Incorporation

From its adoption, the Bill of Rights stirred controversy concerning how widely it protected the rights it set forth. Did the Constitution protect these rights only from violation by the national government, or did they also protect citizens from the unjust actions of state governments? The Supreme Court first addressed this issue in 1833 in the case of *Barron v. Baltimore.*

John Barron had sued the city of Baltimore for damaging his wharf by dumping sand in the water during road construction. His lawyers argued that the Fifth Amendment's guarantee that "private property cannot be taken for public use, without just compensation"

The Bill of Rights

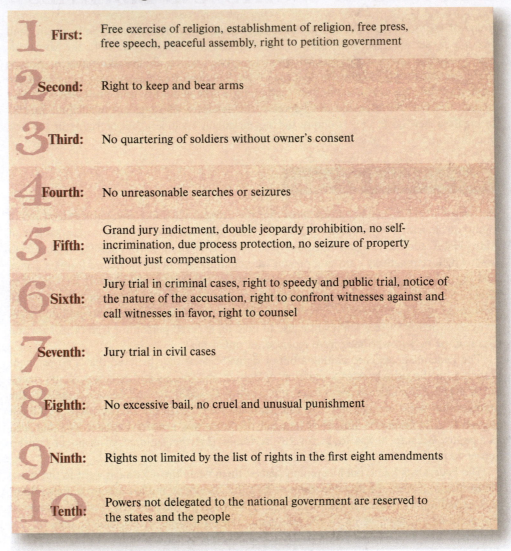

1	**First:**	Free exercise of religion, establishment of religion, free press, free speech, peaceful assembly, right to petition government
2	**Second:**	Right to keep and bear arms
3	**Third:**	No quartering of soldiers without owner's consent
4	**Fourth:**	No unreasonable searches or seizures
5	**Fifth:**	Grand jury indictment, double jeopardy prohibition, no self-incrimination, due process protection, no seizure of property without just compensation
6	**Sixth:**	Jury trial in criminal cases, right to speedy and public trial, notice of the nature of the accusation, right to confront witnesses against and call witnesses in favor, right to counsel
7	**Seventh:**	Jury trial in civil cases
8	**Eighth:**	No excessive bail, no cruel and unusual punishment
9	**Ninth:**	Rights not limited by the list of rights in the first eight amendments
10	**Tenth:**	Powers not delegated to the national government are reserved to the states and the people

should apply to the states as well as to the national government. Writing the opinion for a unanimous Court, Chief Justice John Marshall limited the application of the Bill of Rights to actions of the national government only.[6] He argued that the Antifederalists explicitly called for a bill of rights to protect citizens in their relations with the new national government. He also reasoned that Congress would have clearly stated its desire to have the amendments apply to the states if that had been the goal.

Passage of the Fourteenth Amendment after the Civil War reopened the question of the applicability of the Bill of Rights. That amendment includes the due process clause: "*No state . . . shall deprive a person of life, liberty, or property without due process of law.*"[7] Lawyers argued that if the rights enumerated in the due process clause—life, liberty, and property—were equivalent to the rights in the Bill of Rights, then the states would be bound by the first ten amendments to the U.S. Constitution. At first, proponents of this view met with little success. Ultimately, however, the Court used a process known as **selective incorporation** to conclude that most of the Bill of Rights should apply to the states. Only two of the first ten amendments remain entirely unincorporated: the Third and Seventh. In addition, the Fifth Amendment right to a grand jury hearing and the Eighth Amendment freedom from excessive bail and fines do not apply to the states. The provisions not incorporated were either rights that have never been violated, such as the quartering of soldiers without the homeowner's consent, or those considered less important to the protection of rights today, such as the right to a grand jury because defendants enjoy greater rights with the use of preliminary hearings in the states.

selective incorporation The process of applying some of the rights in the Bill of Rights to the states through the due process clause of the Fourteenth Amendment.

In 2017, more and more professional players began kneeling during the playing of the national anthem to protest the treatment of black citizens by the police.

Selective incorporation greatly enhanced the expansion of rights in the United States, as the vast majority of individual actions occur at the state level. Most people who exercise their rights of free speech and assembly, for instance, do so in one of the states, unless they carry their protests to Washington, D.C. The process of selective incorporation also created a uniform definition of our basic rights that is independent of geography. A criminal defendant has the same basic constitutional rights anywhere in the country.

The Modern Emphasis on Rights

Selective incorporation helped to usher in an era of greater emphasis on individual rights in which even the most humble citizens claim fundamental protections from government violation. Americans today confront questions of rights in a variety of settings. In 2017, the choice made by some professional football players to kneel during the national anthem to protest racial inequality in the United States revived a national conversation about the right to free speech. When President Trump indicated that such players should be fired, rights-conscious Americans disagreed (see "Opposition to Firing Kneeling NFL Players.").

Opposition to Firing Kneeling NFL Players

Do you think NFL teams should or should not fire players who protest racial discrimination by kneeling during the playing of the national anthem? %

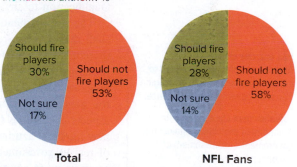

Total

Should fire players 30%
Should not fire players 53%
Not sure 17%

NFL Fans

Should fire players 28%
Should not fire players 58%
Not sure 14%

A majority of Americans disagreed with President Trump that professional football players should be fired for kneeling during the playing of the national anthem.

Source: YouGov.com, "Americans Disagree with Trump on Kneeling Football Players," October 9, 2017, https://today.yougov.com/news/2017/10/09/americans-disagree-trump-kneeling-football-players/.

FREEDOM OF RELIGION

The first two freedoms listed in the Bill of Rights pertain to the exercise of religion. This is not surprising; many of the early settlers left Europe to escape religious persecution and to establish communities where they could freely practice their own religions. Although many states placed the guarantee of religious freedom in their state constitutions, the delegates

The free exercise of religion clause of the First Amendment protects religious beliefs but not all religious activities, such as the handling of poisonous snakes.

who met in Philadelphia to consider a new federal constitution had differing ideas about the role of religion in the new country. At a particularly difficult point in the deliberations, Benjamin Franklin proposed that the delegates should pray "for the assistance of Heaven, and its blessings on our deliberations."[8] Nearly all the other delegates attacked Franklin's motion, arguing that a prayer session might offend some. The original text of the Constitution mentions the issue of religion only once. Article VI requires all government officials to take an oath to "support this Constitution; but no religious Test shall ever be required as a Qualification to any Office or public Trust under the United States."

The First Amendment contains two clauses dealing with religious freedom: "Congress shall make no law respecting an establishment of religion, or prohibiting the free exercise thereof." The second and least complicated provision is the **free exercise clause**, which prohibits the government from interfering with an individual's right to practice his or her religion.[9] The meaning of the **establishment clause** is less clear. At the very least, it prohibits the government from establishing a national religion. Although they address different aspects of religious freedom, the two clauses occasionally come into conflict. Some people may interpret actions such as providing military chaplains or setting aside Sunday as a day of rest as government attempts to establish religion, while the government may see them as attempts to create more freedom to practice religion.

free exercise clause The First Amendment provision intended to protect the practice of one's religion free from government interference.

establishment clause The First Amendment prohibition against the government's establishment of a national religion.

Free Exercise Clause

A literal interpretation of the free exercise clause suggests that a group may practice any religion it chooses, but is such an interpretation reasonable? What if the members engage in dangerous practices such as handling poisonous snakes or illegal ones such as taking hallucinogenic drugs? Should the government prohibit religious activities that are dangerous or offensive to a majority of the community?

Historically, American lawmakers and judges have adhered to the so-called belief–action distinction, articulated by President Thomas Jefferson in an 1802 letter to the Danbury Baptist Association: "Religion is a matter which lies solely between man and his God; that he owes account to none other for his faith or his worship; that the legislative powers of the Government reach actions only, and not opinion."[10] Jefferson believed that free exercise of religion is not absolute; government may regulate religious actions. The Supreme Court has supported this position, upholding the constitutionality of laws affecting religious practices as long as the legislation serves the nonreligious goal of safeguarding the peace, order, and comfort of the community and is not directed at any particular religion.[11] As a result, the Court has sustained laws prohibiting religiously sanctioned polygamy (the practice of taking multiple wives) and use of the drug peyote during religious services.[12] By contrast, the Court invalidated a law that forced a Seventh-Day Adventist to work on Saturday—her faith's Sabbath—in order to receive unemployment benefits.[13] The Court also upheld the right of the Amish to withdraw their children from public school before the age of 16.[14] The Amish believe the materialism, competition, and peer pressure that characterize secondary education would have a negative effect on their children's religious beliefs, Bible reading, and appreciation of a simple, spiritual life.

Congress and Religious Freedom

Congress does not always agree with the way the Court interprets the free exercise clause. In recent years, the legislative branch has shown greater support for freedom of religious expression than has its judicial counterpart. In 1986, for example, the Court ruled that an ordained rabbi, who was a captain in the U.S. Air Force, could not wear his yarmulke (skullcap) while in or out of uniform. Congress reacted by passing a 1987 law that allowed members of the armed forces to "wear an item of religious apparel while in uniform so long as the item is neat and conservative" and does not "interfere with the performance" of military duties.[15]

After the Court outlawed the use of peyote in religious ceremonies, Congress expressed renewed concern over the Court's reasoning in free exercise cases. Its Religious Freedom and Restoration Act (RFRA) urged the Court to use a more liberal judicial test in such cases but the Court ruled that part of the law unconstitutional, arguing that Congress had no power to tell the Court how to interpret the Constitution.[16] In 2014, however, a sharply divided Court ruled that the RFRA exempted closely held corporations, owned and controlled by members of a single family, from paying their employees' health-care costs that related to methods of contraception such as the "morning-after pill." In the joint cases of *Sebelius v. Hobby Lobby* and *Conestoga Wood v. Burwell*, the Court held that such companies cannot be forced to pay for medical methods that violated their religious beliefs even though such payments were mandated under the Affordable Care Act. The Court noted that the Obama administration had already made such exemptions for churches and accommodations for religious-based schools and hospitals.

In 2015, the Supreme Court continued its trend of supporting religious freedom claims by its interpretations of congressional statutes. In *Equal Employment Opportunity Commission v. Abercrombie & Fitch,* an 8 to 1 majority held that the trendy clothes store could not deny employment to a Muslim job applicant because her wearing of a headscarf violated their "Look Policy." The Court's reading of Title VII of the 1964 Civil Rights Act was that an employer cannot make an otherwise qualified applicant's religious practice a factor in employment decisions. In the same session, the Court ruled unanimously against an Arkansas prison policy banning prisoners from wearing beards that did not allow a religious exemption. The plaintiff in *Holt v. Hobbs* wanted to wear a half-inch beard in accordance with his religious beliefs. The justices held that their interpretation of the Religious Land Use and Institutionalized Persons Act allowed such a religious observance.

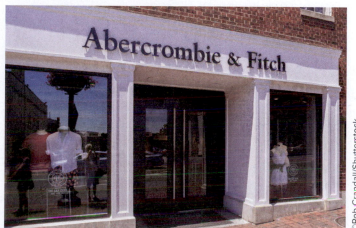

Abercrombie and Fitch faced a civil liberties case when they denied employment to a Muslim job applicant because wearing a headscarf violated the "Look Policy."

Establishment Clause

Whereas free exercise cases involve government intrusion into the practice of religion, establishment clause cases deal with the formal relationship between religion and government. We will see that the United States has usually followed a tradition of attempting to separate church from state, yet there also has been a strong inclination to mix

Importance of Religion

How important would you say religion is in your own life—very important, fairly important or not very important?

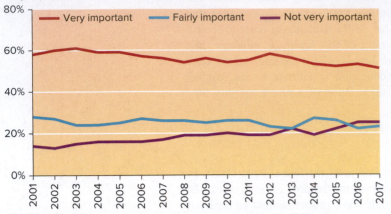

Although rates for those rating religion as "very important" have decreased somewhat in recent years, Americans remain very religious people.

Source: Religion survey, Gallup, http://news.gallup.com/poll/1690/religion.aspx

Public Support for Separation of Church and State

Most think religion should be separate from government policy

% who say . . .

	Government should support religious values, beliefs	Religion should be separate from government
Total	32	65
Rep/Lean Rep	43	54
Conservative	49	48
Mod/Liberal	31	67
Dem/Lean Dem	22	76
Conserv/Mod	30	69
Liberal	12	86
Protestant	43	54
White evangelical	54	43
White mainline	26	70
Black Protestant	44	55
Catholic	36	62
White Catholic	29	68
Hispanic Catholic	45	53
Unaffiliated	9	89
Religious attendance. . .		
Weekly or more	51	45
Less than weekly	22	76

Notes: Don't know responses not shown.

Two-thirds of all Americans believe religion should be separate from government policy.

Source: Pew Research Center, http://www.people-press.org/2017/10/05/5-homosexuality-gender-and-religion/5_7-4/

politics and religion. This is not surprising because Americans are a very religious people. Results from a 2017 poll indicate that 51 percent of Americans consider religion to be "very important" in their lives, with another 23 percent rating religion as "fairly important" (see "Importance of Religion"). However, another 2017 poll shows that two-thirds of Americans believe that religion should be separate from government (see "Public Support for Separation of Church and State"). The relationship between religion and party identification remains consistent.[17] In the United States, Protestants, white born-again/evangelical Christians, white Catholics, and Mormons tend to identify with the Republican Party; by contrast, the religiously unaffiliated, Hispanic Catholics, and members of the Jewish faith lean toward the Democrats in presidential elections (see "Presidential Vote by Religious Affiliation and Race").

Even the Founding Fathers disagreed about the relationship between church and state. Jefferson wrote that the First Amendment built "a wall of separation between Church and State." This is known as the separationist position because it prohibits most if not all forms of government support for religion.

Most scholars contend that a majority of the Founding Fathers disagreed with Jefferson and instead held accommodationist views. Accommodationists argue that the establishment clause forbids the government from showing preference to one religion with respect to another and prohibits the government from establishing a national religion.[18] However, they believe that government may constitutionally support religion as long as it does not discriminate against any particular faith. Today, the major argument between separationists and accommodationists is whether there should be a solid wall between government and religion. The former argues "yes" and the latter, "no."

The ambiguity of the establishment clause led the Supreme Court to develop a test for resolving establishment cases. According to the ***Lemon* test**, a law must meet three conditions in order not to violate the establishment clause:

1. The law must have a secular (nonreligious) purpose.
2. The primary effect of the law must be one that neither advances nor inhibits religion.
3. The law must not foster an excessive government entanglement with religion.

Using the test, the Court struck down a Pennsylvania law that provided direct state financial aid to pay teachers at a religiously affiliated school. The majority ruled that the law created an excessive entanglement between the state government and religion by requiring close government oversight of church matters.[19] Using similar reasoning, the Court upheld a state law granting property tax exemptions to religious organizations. The majority in that case argued that taxing the churches would create an extensive government entanglement.[20]

Presidential Vote by Religious Affiliation and Race

	2000		2004		2008		2012		2016		Dem change '12–'16
	Gore	Bush	Kerry	Bush	Obama	McCain	Obama	Romney	Clinton	Trump	
	%	%	%	%	%	%	%	%	%	%	
Protestant/other Christian	42	56	40	59	45	54	42	57	39	58	−3
Catholic	50	47	47	52	54	45	50	48	45	52	−5
White Catholic	45	52	43	56	47	52	40	59	37	60	−3
Hispanic Catholic	65	33	65	33	72	26	75	21	67	26	−8
Jewish	79	19	74	25	78	21	69	30	71	24	+2
Other faiths	62	28	74	23	73	22	74	23	62	29	−12
Religiously unaffiliated	61	30	67	31	75	23	70	26	68	26	−2
White, born-again/evangelical Christian	n/a	n/a	21	78	24	74	21	78	16	81	−5
Mormon	n/a	n/a	19	80	n/a	n/a	21	78	25	61	+4

In recent presidential elections, Republican candidates have been favored by Protestants, white Catholics, white born-again/evangelical Christians, and Mormons; whereas Hispanic Catholics, members of the Jewish faith, and the religiously unaffiliated favor Democratic candidates.

Note: "Protestant" refers to people who described themselves as "Protestant," "Mormon" or "other Christian" in exit polls; this categorization most closely approximates the exit poll data reported immediately after the election by media sources. The "white, born-again/evangelical Christian" row includes both Protestants and non-Protestants (e.g., Catholics, Mormons, etc.) who self-identify as born-again or evangelical Christians.
Source: Pew Research Centre analysis of exit poll data. 2004 Hispanic Catholic estimates come from aggregated state exit polls conducted by the National Election Pool. Other estimates come from Voter News Service/National Election Pool national exit polls. 2012 data come from reports at NBCnews.com and National Public Radio. 2016 data come from reports at NBCnews.com and CNN.com.

Source: Pew Research Centre analysis of exit poll data. 2004 Hispanic Catholic estimates come from aggregated state exit polls conducted by the Natioanl Election Pool. Other estimates come from Voter News Service/National Election Pool national exit polls. 2012 data come from reports at NBCnews.com and National Public Radio. 2016 data come from reports at NBCnews.com and CNN.com.

Most of the establishment clause cases that have reached the Supreme Court in recent years have involved issues such as the teaching of religion in public schools, religious use of public school facilities and funds, recitation of prayers in public schools, government aid to religiously affiliated schools, and official endorsement of religious displays such as a nativity scene or the Ten Commandments. Some observers see these disputes as examples of conservative Christians imposing their religious views on others. However, many of the nearly 70 percent of Americans who consider themselves to be Christians see in these conflicts government hostility toward religion, reflected in attempts to remove prayer from schools or religious displays from public buildings.

> **Lemon test** The three-part test for establishment clause cases that a law must pass before it is declared constitutional: It must have a secular purpose; it must neither advance nor inhibit religion; and it must not cause excessive entanglement with religion.

Religion and Public Schools

Since the Supreme Court ruled government-sponsored school prayer unconstitutional in the early 1960s, the nation's schools have been a leading battleground in the issue of establishment. Battles frequently have erupted over state laws that attempt to force the curriculum of secular subjects to reflect particular religious beliefs. Such laws often target subjects that discuss the origins of human life. In 1968, the Court struck down a 1928 Arkansas law that made it a crime for any university or public school instructor to "teach the theory or doctrine that mankind ascended or descended from a lower order of animals" or to "adopt or use . . . a textbook that teaches" evolutionary theory.[21] It has also invalidated a Louisiana law that prohibited public schools from teaching evolutionary principles unless theories of "creation science" were also taught.[22]

Today, opponents of evolution are advancing the same argument under the term *intelligent design*. This theory claims that some biological structures such as DNA codes are so complex that they could not have occurred because of evolution but must be the work of an intelligent designer. Proponents argue that intelligent design should be taught in schools alongside other scientific theories. Public leaders such as former president George W. Bush and former Senate majority leader Bill Frist have endorsed the idea. Opponents and the lower courts, however, have failed to see any differences from the earlier attempts to ban evolutionary theory from the schools.

Religious Use of Public School Facilities and Funds

As a matter of fairness and constitutional protection, do religious groups have the same right to use public school buildings as other groups? The Supreme Court answered the question "yes" with respect to public universities and later also ruled that religious groups should have access to secondary schools.[23] The Court also ruled that the establishment clause does not require schools to refuse religious groups the same right to free expression as secular groups. In the case of *Rosenberger v. University of Virginia* (1995), the Court struck down the University of Virginia's refusal to allow student religious groups access to funds collected by a mandatory fee of $14 from all full-time students. The Court held that the establishment clause did not mandate discrimination against religious expression.

Prayer in School

School prayer is probably the most controversial of the establishment clause issues. Reciting prayers and reading Bible passages have been commonplace practices in public schools throughout our nation's history. Separationists believed such practices violated the establishment clause and embarked on a plan to have the Supreme Court abolish them. In the case of *Engel v. Vitale* in 1962, the Court declared that compelling students to recite a twenty-two-word prayer written by the New York State Board of Regents violated the First Amendment.[24] Writing for the majority, Justice Hugo Black stated that "a union of government and religion tends to destroy government and degrade religion." The next year, the Court overturned a Pennsylvania law that required school officials to read at least ten verses from the Bible and the Lord's Prayer each day over the loudspeaker.[25]

The Pennsylvania decision was met with public disapproval; only 24 percent of those surveyed at the time agreed with the ruling, and by 2000, that figure still stood at just 38.8 percent.[26] Despite the decision, many school districts in the South continued the practice of reading the Bible in class. In response to public opinion, Congress members have made over 150 unsuccessful attempts to introduce constitutional amendments to return prayer to public classrooms. Supporters of school prayer have also continued to appeal cases to the Supreme Court, with no more success. Since 1992, the Court has struck down a silent prayer law,[27] the participation of clergy at high school graduation ceremonies,[28] and the traditional Texas practice of delivering a public prayer over a public address system before a high school football game.[29] In 2014, however, the Court held that a town's practice of beginning legislative sessions with prayers, unlike the school setting, does not violate the establishment clause because such an opening is consistent with tradition and it does not coerce participation by nonadherents.[30]

Aid to Religious Schools

The Supreme Court has also wrestled with the question of whether government may provide financial aid to religious schools and, if so, how much. In recent years, the Court has moved in an accommodationist direction on this question. Beginning in 1993, it held that a state may pay to provide a sign-language interpreter for a disabled student at a Roman Catholic high school without violating the establishment clause.[31] Four years later, the Court reversed two earlier cases and ruled that public school teachers may give remedial instruction to at-risk students who attend religious schools.[32] In *Mitchell v. Helms* (2000), the Court found federal aid to religious schools for computer resources, educational materials, and library holdings constitutional, again overruling two earlier cases.

In a landmark 2002 case, the Court upheld the constitutionality of providing government vouchers to attend religious schools. The Cleveland, Ohio, school system, reputedly one of the nation's worst, offered parents up to $2,250 in vouchers to attend private schools, either religious or nonreligious. Over 95 percent of the students who used vouchers to attend private schools enrolled in religious schools. In a 5 to 4 decision, the Court ruled that the program did not violate the establishment clause.[33] The majority argued that the program was neutral in nature and based on private choice rather than government endorsement of a religious school. In 2011, the Court continued to support the private school option by prohibiting Arizona taxpayers from challenging a state tax-credit system that permitted tax credits to be used for religious-school tuition scholarships. The five-member majority in *Arizona Christian School Tuition Organization v. Winn* ruled that the policy did not violate the establishment clause because the tax credits are donations of private money and not state money redirected to religious institutions.

Government Endorsement of Religion

How does placing the words "In God We Trust" on our coins and Federal Reserve notes square with the separation between government and religion mandated by the establishment clause? When does government tolerance of religious expression constitute active endorsement of religion? The Court recently has attempted to establish guidelines to determine what kinds of displays are permissible on government property. For example, it has revised the second part of the *Lemon* test to hold that public display of a nativity scene on government property is unconstitutional if its effect is to endorse religion. Using such a test, they found a nativity scene located in a government building with the words "Glory to God in the Highest" to be a Christian religious display that violated the establishment clause,[34] but not a government-sponsored nativity scene in a private park with a Santa Claus and a banner displaying the number of shopping days until Christmas.[35] Similarly, in a 2005 decision, the Court ruled a monument of the Ten Commandments on the grounds of the Texas Capitol permissible because it was part of a historical exhibit including forty other monuments such as tributes to the Alamo, Confederate veterans, and Korean War veterans.[36] The same year, however, it found the posting of the Ten Commandments inside two Kentucky courthouses an unconstitutional endorsement of religion.[37] In 2010, the Court ruled in *Salazar v. Buono* that Congress did not promote religion when it attempted to avoid an establishment clause issue by trading an acre of federal land containing a white, wooden cross approximately five feet tall for five privately owned acres elsewhere in the same Mojave Desert preserve.

FREEDOM OF SPEECH

Freedom of speech is essential to a democratic political system. Without the ability to speak about politics, citizens cannot make intelligent judgments about candidates, political parties, and public policies. Freedom of expression is also essential for the intellectual health of a society. John Stuart Mill wrote that freedom of speech was the only way to discover the truth. Mill saw a free society as one that traded in a "marketplace of ideas" that would either confirm previous beliefs or provide new perceptions of the truth.[38]

Speech takes several different forms, which are subject to different levels of protection. Sometimes speech consists of not spoken words but rather an act such as burning a flag or wearing a sign. As with freedom of religion, freedom of speech is not absolute in the United States. The Supreme Court has established boundaries for permissible speech by refusing to protect utterances that are obscene, defamatory, or that constitute what it calls "hate speech."

Political Speech

Political leaders often believe that freedom of speech is less important than considerations such as national security, public order, the right to a fair trial, and public decency. This sometimes produces legislation limiting freedom of speech to serve goals perceived as vital to the nation's interest. Popular opposition to U.S. participation in World War I led Congress to pass the 1917 Espionage Act, which made it a federal crime to obstruct military recruiting, to circulate false statements intending to interfere with the military, or to attempt to cause disloyalty in the military. The government later prosecuted Charles Schenck, the general secretary of the Socialist Party of Philadelphia, under the act for printing and mailing fifteen thousand pamphlets urging draftees to resist conscription. The Supreme Court upheld his conviction but, in doing so, left a broad scope for permissible speech.

clear and present danger test The free speech test that prohibits speech that produces a clear and immediate danger.

bad tendency test The free speech test that prohibits speech that could produce a bad outcome, such as violence, no matter how unlikely the possibility the speech could be the cause of such an outcome.

In articulating the **clear and present danger test** to determine free speech cases, Justice Oliver Wendell Holmes ruled that Schenck's writings would be constitutionally protected in ordinary times but "the character of every act depends upon the circumstances in which it is done." He compared writing such a pamphlet during wartime to falsely shouting fire in a crowded theater, stating that the context of a speech determines its permissibility. Only words that produce both a clear (obvious) and a present (immediate) danger are prohibited.[39] Justice Louis Brandeis supported Holmes, reasoning that prohibition is an appropriate remedy only for speech that threatens immediate harm. Given time to discover the facts through discussion and education, more speech serves the public interest better than enforced silence.[40]

Following World War I, fear of the new communist government in Russia and the spread of communism led to new limits on freedom of speech. At this time, the Supreme Court replaced the clear and present danger test with more restrictive tests such as the **bad tendency test**, which asked, "Do the words have a tendency to bring about something bad or evil?"[41] In 1969, the Court returned to the clear and present danger test to protect the right of a Ku Klux Klan leader to make a speech in Ohio.[42] Since that time, the Court has continued

Since 1969, even hate groups like the Ku Klux Klan enjoy the protection of free speech as interpreted by the clear and present danger test.

to use this more liberal test despite security concerns related to international terrorism and U.S. overseas military actions. Even with the liberal trend of protecting free speech, a closely divided Court in 2015 ruled that the state of Texas did not violate the free speech protection of the First Amendment when it refused to allow a specialty license plate bearing the Confederate battle flag. In *Walker v. Texas Division, Sons of Confederate Veterans*, the Court reasoned that messages on specialty license plates suggest that the government endorses such messages and thus should be considered the government's speech. As a result, government speech is immune from free speech attacks because the government cannot be charged with restricting its own speech. In 2018, the Court held that government workers who are represented by a union do not have to pay dues often referred to as "fair share fees" to support the costs of collective bargaining. The plaintiff in *Janus v. AFSCME* successfully argued that such payments violate the free speech rights of nonmembers by compelling them to subsidize private speech on matters of public concern like raising wages can lead to higher taxes.

Campaign Speech

Robust protection for political speech is necessary to maintain the open and public nature of our electoral system, but legitimate questions exist about what constitutes political speech, and the extent to which it is protected. The notion that money in the form of campaign contributions can be considered the equivalent of free speech has elevated the controversy regarding such contributions. Campaign contributions allow citizens and interest groups to express their views by supporting and influencing political candidates and parties. They also enable campaigns, candidates, political parties, and their supporters to present views to the electorate. However, are they equivalent to speech and thus deserving of constitutional protection?

Legal challenges to the 1974 Federal Election Campaign Act gave the U.S. Supreme Court the opportunity to answer those questions. Among its provisions, the act limited the amount of money that individuals and groups could contribute to federal campaigns in a calendar year. It also placed caps on total group and individual expenditures on behalf of a candidate, as well as the amount candidates could spend on their own campaigns. The Court upheld limits on contributions in order to prevent a political quid pro quo system in which government policies might be purchased by the highest bidder. At the same time, it ruled that restrictions on expenditures violated free speech guarantees because individuals, groups, and candidates alike had the right to vigorously advocate their positions.[43]

As a result, the Court's interpretation of the 1974 Federal Election Campaign Act allowed the limits on contributions to campaigns by individuals, groups, and even candidates themselves, but banned restrictions on campaign expenditures because such bans would be a restriction on free speech. Congress revisited the issue of campaign finance in 2002 when it passed the McCain-Feingold Act, formally known as the Bipartisan Campaign Reform Act of 2002, that placed further limits on interest group contributions and party expenditures. In 2014, however, the Court weakened limits on campaign contributions in the case of *McCutcheon v. Federal Election Commission*. The decision in the *McCutcheon* case invalidated the aggregate limits on contributions. As of this writing, there are no limits on the total amount of money a donor can give to all candidates, political party committees, and political action groups.

In 2010, the Court clarified its position with regard to speech in the form of broadcast ads in the case of *Citizens United v. Federal Election Commission*. The case involved the attempt of a conservative nonprofit group to broadcast commercials of their scathing documentary, *Hillary: The Movie,* and to run the movie on a cable video-on-demand service. In 2008, a federal district court had ruled that the attempt violated the provision of the McCain-Feingold law banning "electioneering communications" paid for by a corporation before a primary election.

In reversing that decision, the Supreme Court held that the government cannot restrict corporations from spending money to influence political campaigns. It based its decision on the argument that such censorship violated the freedom of speech guarantee of the First Amendment. The Court's opinion could soon open the door to direct contributions to candidates from corporations and unions that are still prohibited today. Conservative groups like the Center for Competitive Politics hailed the decision as a win for the political rights of small businesses and grassroots groups, whereas liberal groups like Common Cause feared the decision would now allow corporate profits to drown out the voices of the public, corrupting the political system. The bottom line is that after Congress attempted to impose a variety of limits on campaign spending, the Supreme Court overturned those limits using the argument that such limits curb freedom of speech.

The Court does view the issue of elections and campaign contributions differently, however, when applied to judicial elections. Thirty states have laws that prohibit judicial candidates from personally asking their supporters for campaign contributions. The Supreme Court faced this type of law in the 2015 case of *Williams-Yulee v. Florida Bar*. A five-member majority saw such laws as restricting free speech but nevertheless constitutional. They argued that such restrictions were required to protect the integrity of the judiciary and necessary to preserve public confidence in such courts. In 2018, the Supreme Court ruled on a Minnesota law that prohibited people from wearing political badges, political buttons, or other political insignia in polling places on election day. The Court agreed with the state concerning the importance of making polling places islands of calm where voters can peacefully contemplate their electoral choices. However, it held in *Minnesota Voters Alliance v. Mansky* that the law's definition of "politics" was too broad and the state's directive that banned issue-oriented material designed to influence voting raised more questions than it answered.

Commercial Speech

On an average day, people hear far more commercial speech than political speech. Companies are trying to sell us countless goods and services through every type of media outlet. In fact, studies show that Americans are more familiar with many advertising slogans than with First Amendment rights.

The courts traditionally have viewed commercial speech as being less worthy of free speech protection than political speech because the government has a legitimate interest in protecting consumers from deceptive advertising. If the advertising is not deceptive, however, the Court will protect it. The Supreme Court, for example, has invalidated a Virginia regulation making it unlawful for a pharmacy to advertise the prices of its prescription medications[44] and has supported the constitutional right of lawyers to advertise the prices of routine legal services.[45]

Symbolic Speech

At the time the Bill of Rights was written, political protesters expressed themselves through impassioned speeches and printed publications. Changing technology, however, has multiplied the channels for delivering and receiving political messages. Today, a protest march or a flag burning is more likely to receive media coverage than a forty-five-minute speech or a twenty-page pamphlet. When such activities convey a political message or viewpoint, courts may consider them to be **symbolic speech** worthy of First Amendment protection.

symbolic speech Ideas expressed by actions or symbols rather than words.

The Supreme Court has ruled that governments may suppress symbolic views if doing so serves an important purpose other than the suppression of unpopular speech. Using that reasoning, it has supported the federal government's authority to ban the burning of draft cards because the cards contain information necessary for the implementation of a military conscription system.[46] By contrast, in the *Tinker* case, the Court struck down a school ban on the wearing of black armbands to protest the Vietnam War, ruling that the symbolic speech did not negatively affect the school's educational mission.[47] The Court has even held that desecration of the American flag may be considered a form of protected speech. In 1989, the Court invalidated a Texas law that prohibited burning the American flag, arguing that the law's sole purpose was to suppress speech.[48] The decision motivated Congress to pass the Flag Protection Act of 1989, which penalizes anyone who "knowingly mutilates, defaces, physically defiles, burns, maintains on the floor or ground, or tramples upon any flag of the United States." Applying the same reasoning as the Texas case, the Court found that the federal law violated the guarantee of free speech.[49]

The Supreme Court has ruled that flag burning may be protected as symbolic free speech if the act does not produce violence or a serious disturbance.

Boundaries of Free Speech

The Supreme Court traditionally has not included certain forms of communication under the First Amendment protection given most speech. It has reasoned, for instance, that all thirteen states had laws against obscenity when they ratified the Bill of Rights. Thus, those citizens did not believe that laws against obscenity were inconsistent with the First Amendment's guarantee of free speech. In other words, certain utterances are so different from most speech that they fall outside of free speech considerations. In that sense, there are boundaries around what type of speech should be considered worthy of the free speech guarantee. The Court has also declined to grant First Amendment protection to utterances and writings that are defamatory. More recently, the Court has added hate speech to the category of unprotected expression outside the boundaries of free speech.

Obscenity

The Supreme Court has consistently held that obscenity falls outside the boundaries of free speech, but it has struggled to define the meaning of *obscene*. Justice Potter Stewart expressed the difficulty in his famous utterance: "I shall not today attempt to further define [obscenity]. . . . But I know it when I see it."[50] If Justice Stewart were alive today, would he view nudity on the Internet as obscene? The answer depends on the judicial test he used to determine obscenity. Today, the Supreme Court uses the *Miller* test, which asks three questions:

1. Does the average person, applying contemporary community standards, believe that the dominant theme of the material, taken as a whole, appeals to a prurient interest?
2. Is the material patently offensive?
3. Does the work, taken as a whole, lack serious literary, artistic, political, or scientific value?[51]

If the answer to any of the three questions is no, the Court considers the work not to be obscene.

Trying to regulate obscenity on the Internet has been difficult for Congress. In 1996, it passed the Communications Decency Act (CDA) that prohibited transmission of any obscene or indecent material over the Internet to anyone under the age of 18. In *Reno v. American Civil Liberties Union* (1997), the Supreme Court ruled the term *indecent* was too vague to prohibit speech.

In 1998, Congress tried again to limit the transmission of obscene materials in cyberspace with the Child Online Protection Act (COPA). Rather than prohibiting "obscene and indecent" materials, the statute banned any material "harmful to minors." The Supreme Court rejected this law as well with its argument that the "community standards" principle has no application to the Internet because of the unlimited geographic scope of online communications (*Ashcroft v. American Civil Liberties Union,* 2004). In 2011, the Court refused to create a new category of speech beyond the protection of the First Amendment. In *Brown v. Entertainment Merchants Association,* it struck down a California law that barred the sale of violent games to children. The issue of obscenity obviously involves questions of identification and definition that may change over time but what is clear legally is that once material is labeled as obscene, it is not protected by the free speech guarantee of the First Amendment.

Defamation

Free speech allows a vigorous exchange of ideas and criticisms that are sometimes hurtful and even mean-spirited. Legislative bodies have placed limits on such comments by allowing a person to sue anyone who makes false statements that injure his or her reputation. **Slander** is a false oral statement that causes injury, whereas **libel** is a written statement that has the same effect. Truth is an absolute defense in a slander or libel suit; a true statement cannot injure or defame.

The Court made it much more difficult for public officials and public figures to win defamation suits against their critics with its opinion in *New York Times Company v. Sullivan* (1964). In this case, the Court introduced the new *Sullivan* rule, which required that a public official in a libel or slander case not only prove the statements in question are false but also that the defendants wrote or spoke the words with malice. The Court defined *malice* as (1) knowledge the statements were false or (2) reckless disregard for whether the statements were false or not. The Court felt that this higher standard of proof was necessary to avoid self-censorship by critics of public officials, who may not have the ability to guarantee the truth of all their assertions.

slander Oral statements that are false and injure another's reputation.

libel Written statements that are false and injure another's reputation.

Sullivan rule The standard requiring public officials and public figures in defamation suits to prove that allegedly libelous or slanderous statements are both false and made with malice.

Hate Speech

Hate speech involves prejudicial and hostile statements concerning characteristics such as race, ethnicity, sex, sexual orientation, or religion. Many communities and college campuses have adopted laws and policies banning hate speech. Does your campus have such rules? Although they may be based on good intentions, do you believe they impede free speech in any way? In a related manner, are you comfortable discussing controversial topics in class? Does any reluctance to do so indicate a lack of support for free speech among you and your peers? The Supreme Court has been reluctant to ban hate speech. The justices voted 8 to 1 to allow members of the Westboro Baptist Church of Topeka, Kansas, to picket a military funeral with signs stating that God is punishing the

United States for its tolerance of homosexuality in the military. The Court ruled that such speech was permissible under the First Amendment even though the church's signs contained such hate messages as "Fag Troops," "God Hates You," and "Thank God for Dead Soldiers."[52]

FREEDOM OF THE PRESS

Because both freedom of speech and freedom of the press deal with expression, similar principles underlie each. Both forms of communication are essential to democracy due to their role in transmitting information. As we learned, the Founders knew and stressed the importance of an informed public in creating a successful democracy. The press protections they incorporated into the Constitution reflect those beliefs.

Prior Restraint

The authors of the Constitution and the Bill of Rights agreed with the famous English jurist William Blackstone, who wrote that authors and publishers may be tried for legitimate criminal violations only once their article is published and their words have entered into the marketplace of ideas. He rejected the notion that government had the right to exercise **prior restraint**, the ability to prevent publication of material to which it objected.[53] The U.S. Supreme Court embraced this position in the 1931 case of *Near v. Minnesota,* in which it invalidated a Minnesota law intended to prevent publication of material deemed to be malicious, scandalous, and defamatory.

> **prior restraint** The practice that would allow the government to censor a publication before anyone could read or view it.

The Court noted, however, that the government's interest in protecting national security, regulating obscenity, or preventing the incitement of violence may justify prior restraint in the most exceptional cases. The Nixon administration cited national security considerations in 1971, when it attempted to restrain *The New York Times* and *The Washington Post* from publishing the "Pentagon Papers," a series of articles about U.S. involvement in Vietnam based on government documents. The Court rejected the administration's argument, ruling that government may not prevent the press from exercising its right to criticize public officials and its duty to inform readers.

The "Pentagon Papers" case seems to have settled the matter of prior restraint, as the Court has heard no further cases of significance in this area. After the terrorist attacks on September 11, 2001, however, the Department of Defense requested that journalists refrain from publishing information that could harm the country's national security. The department also hinted that the government might demand to review stories before publication or broadcast. As of this time, however, the government has censored no articles.

Government Control of Media Content

Governments have sometimes attempted to exert control over the media's content by prohibiting the publication of certain information. For example, states often pass laws prohibiting the publication of certain criminal matters in order to protect the victim, the offender, or the fairness of the trial. In *Cox Broadcasting Corporation v. Cohn* (1975), however, the Court ruled that the press has a First Amendment right to report the names of rape victims obtained from judicial records that are open to the public. The Court has also invalidated a state law that prohibits the publication of the identity of juvenile offenders,[54] and it has struck down a trial judge's gag order that prohibited the press from covering a pretrial hearing for fear of prejudicial pretrial publicity.[55]

Governments have also attempted to control the print media by mandating the publication of certain information, but only with certain limits. In one case, the Court struck down a Florida statute that required newspapers under certain circumstances to print articles written by candidates for political office. In a unanimous decision, the Court ruled that the government has no constitutional authority to order the newspaper to publish an article. To allow such a law would limit the editorial decision-making power of the paper, increase its costs, and perhaps discourage political and electoral coverage.[56]

Traditionally, radio and television have not been as free from government control as the print media. As discussed in Chapter 10, the government decided to license radio and television stations and place more restrictions on them because of the scarcity of bandwidth. There simply were more persons who wanted to broadcast than there were frequencies to allocate. This scarcity led to the creation of the Federal Communications Commission (FCC) and imposition of such regulations as the fairness doctrine, which required broadcasters to discuss both sides of controversial public issues.

Special Rights

The media have argued for special legal rights to allow them to perform the important function of gathering and reporting the news—such as not disclosing the names of sources, gaining access to jailed inmates, and accompanying the police when they are executing a search or arrest warrant—but in most instances, the U.S. Supreme Court has looked unfavorably on these claims. It has not allowed reporters to maintain the confidentiality of their sources if the government can show compelling

©Robert Sullivan/AFP/Getty Images

Under the guarantee of freedom of the press, the media may disclose the names of juvenile offenders although they usually choose not to do so.

reasons for requesting their names, such as to advance a criminal investigation.[57] In 2005, the Court refused to review a lower court's decision to imprison *New York Times* reporter Judith Miller for failing to cooperate with a federal investigation. Miller, who wrote an article leaking the name of a CIA operative, refused to tell federal prosecutor Patrick Fitzgerald the name of the person who gave her that information. Miller spent eighty-five days in jail until her source released her from the promise of confidentiality.

Although the media frequently assert a special right of access, the Court has placed a variety of limits on reporters' ability to gather the news. It has found that reporters enjoy no access to county jail inmates that is denied to other individuals.[58] They also have no right to enter a home when police are executing a warrant.[59] The justices also failed to recognize a First Amendment right of the media to attend a closed pretrial hearing in a highly publicized case.[60] The Court ruled differently, however, with respect to a judge's attempt to close a trial to the media and the public. It held in *Richmond Newspapers v. Virginia* (1980) that the media's right to attend trials is implicit in the freedom of the press guarantee.

FREEDOM OF ASSEMBLY AND ASSOCIATION

The gathering and marching of groups such as neo-Nazis and racist organizations can strike fear and rage in observers. Yet, the First Amendment freedom of assembly is one of the cornerstones of American democracy, granting citizens the right to gather and engage in politics. It is the basis for the formation of interest groups and political parties that attempt to forge public policy and determine who will hold public office. Implied in the freedom of assembly is the right to associate by joining with like-minded individuals to pursue common goals. The freedoms of speech, press, and assembly would be nearly meaningless if one had to exercise them alone.

Freedom of Assembly

Freedom to peaceably assemble is critical for the survival of a democratic political system. Yet this does not mean that people can assemble to advance their own political agenda whenever and wherever they please. The government may have competing interests that override such freedoms, such as keeping the peace, maintaining order, and protecting the flow of commerce. As a result, governments have the authority to impose "time, place, and manner restrictions" on the conditions of a political gathering.

The freedom of assembly cases that come before the Court typically reflect debate about the significant controversies of the day. During the 1960s, such cases arose from the often emotionally charged civil rights demonstrations in southern cities. In one case, police arrested nearly two hundred African American student demonstrators in South Carolina for refusing orders to disperse after an hour of peaceful protest at the state capitol building. The Supreme Court reversed the conviction, holding that a peaceful demonstration at the seat of state government was the proper way "to petition government for a redress of grievances."[61] In later cases, however, the Court ruled that political assemblies in front of courthouses and jails were not constitutionally protected. The justices feared that protests in front of a courthouse to advocate a certain outcome for a trial could adversely affect the administration of justice and perceptions of the judicial system.[62] The Court ruled out peaceful demonstrations at a jail because jails, unlike state capitol buildings, are not typically open to the public.[63]

In the 1980s, the Court dealt with several cases stemming from confrontations between antiabortion protesters and supporters of a woman's constitutional right to have an abortion. Many states and communities have passed laws to regulate demonstrations outside abortion clinics. The Court upheld the enforcement of noise restrictions and buffer zones around the clinics' entrances and driveways, but not restrictions on signs or buffer zones to the backs and sides of the clinics.[64] The Court has also upheld a Colorado statute in 2000 that prohibited any person from approaching closer than eight feet to a clinic patient for the purpose of distributing literature, displaying a sign,[65] or engaging in oral protest, without the patient's consent. But the 2014 *McCullen v. Coakley* decision held that a 35-foot buffer zone around an abortion clinic bars traditional public forum communication and face-to-face communication in situations where there is no threat of violence or congestion.

Freedom of Association

The U.S. Supreme Court first recognized the implied right of freedom of association when southern states began to make laws regarding civil rights groups. In the 1958 case of *NAACP v. Alabama,* the civil rights group appealed a law mandating that it turn its membership list over to a state agency. The Court struck down the law, arguing that disclosure of the membership list could lead to economic reprisal, loss of employment, physical coercion, and public hostility against the individual members. Later, the Court recognized the right of the NAACP to use litigation to further its goals by stressing that the First Amendment supports the vigorous advocacy of a group's views.[66]

More recently, private organizations such as business clubs, fraternal organizations, and civic groups have tested their freedom to restrict membership on the basis of race, sex, or sexual orientation. Does freedom of association allow private groups to discriminate? Yes and no. In *Roberts v. United States Jaycees* (1984), the Court found that freedom of association is not an absolute right, nor does it pertain equally to all private organizations. It afforded smaller and more intimate groups—such as a married couple and families—as well as organizations espousing clear political and ideological views, the most protection. It ruled that the First Amendment's protection of larger national organizations such as the Jaycees, which do not express strong ideological views and do not have highly selective membership guidelines, is inferior to the state's interest in combating arbitrary discrimination. The Court reached similar decisions in cases involving the Rotary Club[67] and a private New York men's club.[68] It ruled that the right of a woman to belong and establish informal business contacts outweighs the right of the organization to associate with whomever they want.

The Trump candidacy and Trump presidency has emboldened white supremacists and neo-Nazis to march in cities such as Charlottesville, Virginia.

©Anadolu Agency/Getty Images

By contrast, the Court upheld the right of a private association to prevent gay rights groups from marching in a St. Patrick's Day parade in Boston.[69] The Court also upheld the right of the Boy Scouts of America to revoke the adult membership of an assistant scoutmaster who at college announced to others that he was gay. The five-person majority agreed with the organization that the retention of a gay member was inconsistent with the Boy Scout values represented by the phrase "morally straight and clean."[70]

RIGHT TO KEEP AND BEAR ARMS

The text of the Second Amendment—"A well regulated Militia, being necessary to the security of a free State, *the right of the people to keep and bear Arms, shall not be infringed*"—has generated significant disagreement and controversy among gun owners and those who favor limits on firearm ownership.[71] Gun control opponents such as the National Rifle Association emphasize the words that are italicized. They stress that the government owes citizens the right to own guns in order to secure their freedom. Those who favor restrictions on gun ownership stress the non-italicized words that imply that only persons who are members of a government militia have the right to own firearms. They believe the Second Amendment confers a collective right that conveys the right to possess a gun only to members of a military unit.

For years the meaning of the Second Amendment drew little attention from American courts. In 1939, the Supreme Court agreed with the collective right position when it decided a case that upheld the right of the federal government to require the registration of firearms.[72] By not incorporating the amendment, however, the Court left the states with a great deal of authority to restrict or protect gun ownership. In recent years, many states have tended to protect the rights of gun ownership with state constitutional guarantees.

Then in 2008, the Court dramatically changed the meaning of the amendment with its decision in *District of Columbia v. Heller.* Heller, an armed security guard, sued the District after it rejected his application to keep a handgun at home for protection. His application violated a strict 1976 D.C. ordinance that banned the private ownership of all handguns. Rifles and shotguns were allowed if they were kept disassembled or in a trigger lock or some similar device. By a 5 to 4 majority, the Court ruled that the Second Amendment confers an individual right for citizens to keep and bear arms to protect themselves.[73] The Court's decision has spurred a great deal of controversy as well as questions about its policy implications. The Court expanded its earlier decision in 2010 by ruling that an individual's right to bear arms applies also to state and local gun control laws (*McDonald v. Chicago*). The opinion emphasized, however, that the Court was not saying that the Second Amendment provided a right to "carry any weapon whatsoever in any manner whatsoever and for whatever purpose."[74]

In January 2011, in Tucson, Arizona, a disturbed young man with a Glock semiautomatic pistol gravely wounded U.S. representative Gabrielle Giffords (D-AZ) and then turned to fire on the crowd attending her outdoor political event. By the time he was subdued, six people were dead and many others were wounded. Despite the shock that ran through the nation, the incident failed to provoke a meaningful conversation about gun violence in the United States. The nation was again shocked in December 2012 when a lone gunman entered an elementary school in Newtown, Connecticut, and shot to death twenty-six persons, including twenty children between the ages of five and ten. Lobbying by the victims' parents in 2013 was unable to bring about any legislative changes by Congress despite a rash of other school and workplace shootings. Some states like Connecticut passed gun control legislation but without national change, guns can be transported across state lines from states allowing easier access to guns to those that do not.

Similar reactions of grief but no effective national political action occurred after mass shootings at Columbine High School, an army base at Fort Hood in Texas, a church in Charleston, South Carolina, a community college in Oregon, and all too many other acts of violence around the country. At the time, the nation's largest mass shooting in Orlando,

Florida, did lead to Senate votes on gun sale restrictions in 2016, but they were unsuccessful. Democrats in the House staged a sit-in to bring attention to the gun issue, but the result once again was no meaningful change. The following year, a lone gunman fired from a hotel room into a country-western concert in Las Vegas, killing a record number of people. Fifty-eight victims lost their lives, but there was no immediate response from Washington. President Trump ascribed the tragedy to mental illness, but some members of Congress pondered legislation that could make it more difficult for some people to acquire guns. In early 2018, 17 students and teachers were killed in a Parkland, Florida high school by a former student with a semi-automatic weapon. The surviving students soon became a political force by speaking out, travelling to the state capital, and planning a series of marches throughout the nation. The state of Florida passed some limits on gun purchases such as raising the age of eligible voters and were soon sued by the National Rifle Association. The new student-led movement strives to create meaningful change at the national level.

RIGHTS OF THE ACCUSED

The early Americans showed their unhappiness with the British criminal justice system by devoting four of the first eight amendments almost exclusively to rights granted to accused persons.[75] Remembering the treatment of colonial leaders by their British rulers, the Framers of the Bill of Rights were determined to provide procedural guarantees throughout the criminal justice system to ensure fairness and justice for the accused. Such protections are embodied in the Fourth, Fifth, Sixth, and Eighth Amendments. Yet with all these protections, incarceration rates are much higher in the United States than in European countries (see "Incarceration Rates Among Founding NATO Members").

Recent history has shown that not all accused persons are afforded the constitutional protections of the Bill of Rights that are discussed here. Chapter 12 details how President George W. Bush used presidential emergency powers after September 11, 2001, to curtail the rights of persons suspected of being enemy combatants in the war on terrorism. Detainees at the Guantanamo Bay prison were not allowed to know the charges against them, to

Incarceration Rates Among Founding NATO (Selected European) Members

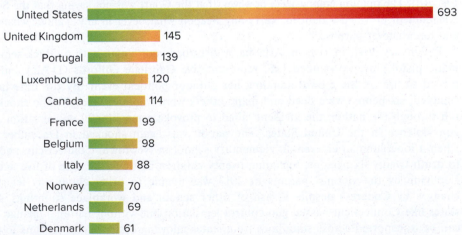

Incarceration rate (*per 100,000 population*)

The United States has a much higher incarceration rate than any of the selected European countries.

Source: Peter Wagner and Alison Walsh, States of Incarceration 2016, Prison Policy Initiative, https://www.prisonpolicy.org/global/2016.html.

have access to attorneys, to have evidence presented that was not hearsay or the fruits of coercion, nor to have access to federal courts to challenge their detention. Such rules were not only controversial but also led many to become concerned about the preservation of civil liberties in the United States. In *Boumediene v. Bush* (2008), the Supreme Court continued to reject most of these procedures, writing that the Constitution was meant to survive in extraordinary times and, therefore, that detainees have a right of habeas corpus in federal courts unless Congress explicitly exercises its constitutional authority to suspend the right.

The Fourth Amendment: Searches and Seizures

The Fourth Amendment guarantees freedom from "unreasonable searches and seizures," but the only type of search the Constitution mentions is one authorized by a search warrant. To obtain a warrant, police must present a neutral judge with an affidavit swearing there is reason to believe that a crime has been committed and that evidence can be found in a specific place. The judge then must determine whether **probable cause** exists to issue the search warrant. However, the Supreme Court ruled in 2012 that if mistakes are made and the police execute a search warrant without probable cause, they are entitled to immunity from any possible lawsuits (*Messerschmidt v. Millender*).[76] In 2013, the Court held in *Bailey v. United States* that police officers could not pick up and detain a person while they searched his premises for contraband if the individual had already left the premises before the execution of the search. Judges usually require the probable cause standard for wiretaps and electronic surveillance as well. Since the passage of the USA Patriot Act in 2001, however, federal agents investigating terrorism can trace e-mail messages with less than probable cause.

probable cause A practical and non-technical calculation of probabilities that is the basis for securing search warrants.

In two cases decided in 2014, *Riley v. California* and *United States v. Wurie,* a unanimous Supreme Court underscored the importance of the search warrant requirement in the digital age. It ruled that, without a warrant, police may not search the digital information on a cell phone seized from an individual who has been arrested.

The Constitution does not preclude the possibility of warrantless searches; it only requires that such searches be reasonable. But what is reasonable? The Supreme Court has recognized several categories of warrantless searches as reasonable:

- The police may conduct a search at the time of a valid arrest. They may search any area within the suspect's immediate control where he or she might obtain a weapon or conceal evidence.[77]

- The courts also recognize a search as valid if the police receive permission voluntarily from a person with the authority to give it. In 2001, the Supreme Court ruled that a person on probation must consent to have his or her property searched if the probation officer has a reasonable suspicion of wrongdoing.[78]

- Searches without warrants have also been justified when conducted in hot pursuit of a criminal who has just committed a crime, is considered dangerous, and may destroy evidence if the police must delay a search in order to obtain a warrant.[79]

- In the case of *Terry v. Ohio* (1968), the Supreme Court approved stop-and-frisk searches in which an experienced police officer believes a suspect is about to commit a crime. The Court reasoned that the police have the power to prevent crimes and that the frisk was necessary to protect the officer's safety. The Court held in a 2000 case that a young man running from a high-crime area when he saw uniformed police officers created sufficient suspicion to justify such a search.[80]

©Mario Villafuerte/Getty Images

The U.S. Supreme Court has upheld the validity of a dog sniff to establish the necessary probable cause to search an automobile.

- In 1973, the Supreme Court created a new category of warrantless searches known as "loss of evidence searches." In such cases, police may conduct a search if they reasonably suspect that a delay will result in the suspect destroying evidence.[81] In this instance, the Court allowed police to take fingernail scrapings of a murder suspect at the time of the interrogation and before an arrest because of the risk that the evidence could be easily destroyed at a later time.[82] The Court struck down a hospital-instituted drug-screening program for patients that gave results to the police as a requirement for receiving medical care. The Court does allow schools, however, to test students for drugs if only their eligibility for sports or extracurricular activities is at stake.[83]

- In considering the constitutionality of warrantless searches, the Court also has taken into account the place being searched and the means of the search. For example, it has ruled that the police may search a field for marijuana plants, even though the area is marked with No Trespassing signs.[84] Police may conduct an aerial search for marijuana plants growing in a greenhouse that is missing some of its roof panels.[85] They may not, however, point a thermal imager at a home to detect heat emanating from bulbs used to grow marijuana indoors.[86] In 2013, the Court in the case of *Florida v. Jardines* likened the use of a dog sniff at the front door of a marijuana grow house to the use of a thermal imaging device when it invalidated a search warrant obtained on the basis of a positive response by a trained police dog. The Court has generally given the police greater authority to search automobiles because of their ability to leave the jurisdiction of law enforcement officials, and because of the government's interest in regulating auto traffic and safety. In another 2013 dispute, *Florida v. Harris,* the Court upheld the validity of a dog sniff to establish probable cause for the search of a vehicle. Recently, however, it has not allowed officers at highway checkpoints to look for ordinary criminal wrongdoing such as the possession of illegal drugs.[87] In the related 2015 case of *Rodriguez v. United States,* the Court ruled that the police may not prolong traffic stops to wait for drug-sniffing dog searches. A police stop exceeding the time needed to handle the matter for which the stop was made violates the Fourth Amendment. The Court also widened its protection of motorists with its 2009 ruling in *Arizona v. Gant.* The majority held that the police may not search the interior of an auto if the occupant has been arrested and cannot gain access to the car. In *United States v. Jones,* the Supreme Court was presented the question as to whether a law enforcement task force could covertly install a GPS tracking device on a defendant's automobile without obtaining a search warrant that led to the discovery of incriminating evidence. In 2012, the Court held that the search was invalid because the government had to occupy private property, the defendant's car, for the purpose of obtaining information. In reaching the decision, the majority of the Court abandoned the expectation-of-privacy standard it had used in most search cases involving new technological applications and reverted to the old notion of a physical trespass. Finally, in 2013, the Court, in the matter of *Missouri v. McNeely,* refused to make an exception to the Fourth Amendment's warrant requirement when police ordered the forcible drawing of blood from an individual suspected of drunk driving.

exclusionary rule The judicial barring of illegally seized evidence from a trial.

The Supreme Court eventually adopted the **exclusionary rule**, which excludes from consideration at trial any evidence gathered illegally, thus removing the incentive for the police to make illegal searches.[88] The Court has allowed some exceptions to the exclusionary rule, for example, when it believes the police are acting in good faith.[89] The 2015 mass shooting in San Bernardino, California, raised a future issue of whether the government can compel a private company like Apple to help search the cell phone information of a criminal or suspect. Critics expressed concern that development of the software needed to access the locked phone could ultimately jeopardize the privacy of all consumers using the same type of device.

The Fifth Amendment: Self-Incrimination

The Fifth Amendment protects the accused against self-incrimination, a right that places limits on police interrogation of criminal suspects. Nevertheless, law enforcement officers frequently employed physical or psychological pressure during private interrogation sessions in order to gain confessions. To remedy this problem, the Court adopted the now familiar

Miranda **rights**, which require officials to remind suspects of their Fifth Amendment rights. In the 1966 case of *Miranda v. Arizona,* the Court ruled that "prior to any questioning, the person must be warned that he has a right to remain silent, that any statements he does make may be used against him, and that he has a right to the presence of an attorney, either retained or appointed." The warning of silence allows the suspect to make an intelligent constitutional choice concerning self-incrimination. The presence of an attorney guarantees that the right is protected under the intense pressure of a police interrogation. The Court will deny the admissibility of a confession if the police failed to notify the suspect of his or her *Miranda* rights. In 2000, the Court reaffirmed its support of the *Miranda* ruling by declaring unconstitutional a congressional statute mandating a return to a lesser confession standard.[90]

Miranda **rights** The warning police must administer to suspects so that the latter will be aware of their right not to incriminate themselves. The rights include the right to remain silent, the right to know statements will be used against them, and the right to have an attorney for the interrogation.

The Sixth Amendment: Right to Counsel

The Sixth Amendment guarantees the accused the right to counsel. At the time the Constitution was written, there were very few attorneys in the United States—most defendants handled their own cases—and criminal law was relatively uncomplicated. As American society became more complex, so did the laws needed to regulate and punish criminal behavior. By the twentieth century, criminal defendants increasingly began to hire attorneys to represent them. Because of the great complexity of modern criminal law, many observers now consider the right to counsel the most important of the rights possessed by the accused. Good legal advice is invaluable at every stage of the criminal justice process; it is no accident that the right to have an attorney is a key element of the *Miranda* warnings.

Although accused criminals had the right to an attorney, nearly 75 percent of them could not afford one. This put most defendants at a significant disadvantage when confronting a government prosecutor. The Supreme Court challenged the constitutionality of this situation under certain circumstances in *Powell v. Alabama* (1932). The year before, police in Alabama arrested nine African American youths, known as "the Scottsboro boys," for allegedly raping two white girls. The jury convicted eight of the nine suspects and sentenced them to death. Upon appeal, the Court ruled that in unusual situations such as these—the defendants were young and uneducated, they were facing the death penalty, and their fate was subject to intense public pressure—the accused were entitled to counsel at the government's expense.[91]

In 1963, the Court expanded the right to counsel for indigent defendants facing felony charges in response to the efforts of Clarence Gideon.[92] Tried and convicted in Florida without the aid of an attorney for the felony crime of breaking and entering, Gideon became a "jailhouse lawyer" by reading law books and filing legal briefs. After many attempts by Gideon, the Supreme Court agreed to hear his case in 1962, and voted that poor defendants did have the right to an attorney when confronting felony charges. Nine years later, the Court expanded its policy by ruling that indigent defendants facing even one day in jail are entitled to legal representation. Such cases may involve complex legal issues, and a guilty verdict leaves the defendant with the stigma of a criminal conviction.[93] Supplying attorneys for all cases can be an expensive proposition for state governments, however. Recognizing this fact, the Court ruled that the state need not supply counsel unless the defendant faces the possibility of jail time if convicted.[94] In a more recent case, however, the Court struck down a lower court ruling against a defendant without counsel who received a suspended sentence and two years' probation. The justices concluded that the state should have provided the defendant with counsel because he faced a possible deprivation of his freedom.[95]

In all of these cases, the rationale of the Court was that fairness to the defendant demands that accused persons have attorneys to safeguard their constitutional rights. A quite different issue related to right to counsel arises when the defendant has counsel that provides bad advice or fails to communicate. The Court addressed that issue in two cases in 2012. In *Lafler v. Cooper,* a criminal defendant, following his lawyer's advice, rejected a favorable plea bargain but was convicted and received a harsher sentence. The defendant in *Missouri v. Frye* was convicted and sentenced after his counsel failed to communicate the prosecution's plea offer. In both cases the defendants claimed that the ineffective assistance of counsel denied them their constitutional guarantee of a lawyer. The Court ruled that criminal defendants have a constitutional right to effective counsel during plea negotiations. Since approximately 95 percent of criminal convictions arise from guilty pleas, the Court's 5 to 4 decision represents

CELL PHONES AND CIVIL LIBERTIES: "CAN YOU HEAR ME NOW?"

We Americans love our cell phones. More than 95 percent of us own a cell phone of some kind.* Nearly 80 percent of us own smartphones. The numbers vary dramatically among age groups. Eighty-five percent of people over age 65 own a cell phone, but only half of them have a smartphone, whereas 100 percent of Americans ages 18 to 29 have a cell phone, 94 percent of which are smartphones.† We also use our cell phones extensively. The average American adult spends nearly three hours a day on a smartphone; for college-age adults, 18 to 24, the time spent is over four hours per day.‡

The great use of cell phones in our society can be a source of both instant connection and constant distraction. It also poses new challenges to the observance of civil liberties pertaining to the rights of accused persons, particularly the preservation of privacy. Such an issue was addressed by the U.S. Supreme Court in 2018 in the case of *Carpenter v. United States*.

©kanvag/Shutterstock

Cell phone towers can track our locations from the calls we make.

The case pertained to the arrest of Timothy Carpenter for a series of armed robberies that occurred in southeastern Michigan and northwestern Ohio in 2010 and 2011. Carpenter was not among the original four suspects arrested in April 2011. One of these four confessed that Carpenter was the

a vast expansion of judicial supervision over the criminal justice system. In the 2017 case of *Lee v. United States*, the Court continued this line of reasoning in saying that if defendants accept pleas based on ineffective counsel, they should have the opportunity to demonstrate that they would have gone to trial but for the errors of the lawyer.

A common law enforcement technique, is to hold a defendant's property traceable to the charged crime. In 2016, however, the Court further announced in *Luis v. U.S.* that the government's holding of a defendant's assets that were not traceable to a criminal offense violated the constitutional right to obtain counsel. In other words, withholding all of defendants' assets could impact their ability to choose the attorney they want.

The Sixth Amendment: Trial by Jury

The Sixth Amendment guarantees criminal defendants the right to a jury trial. (Parties in civil suits are also guaranteed jury trials in the Seventh Amendment.) Although 95 percent of all criminal cases are settled out of court by an informal process known as plea bargaining, the right to a jury trial remains a cornerstone of our criminal justice system. The courts select potential jurors—known as the jury pool, or *venire*—from government records such as voter registration lists or property tax assessment rolls. In two separate cases, the Supreme Court ruled that jury pools may not exclude blacks or leader of the group and that they had been helped by as many as fifteen other men who acted as getaway drivers and lookouts. The informant also provided the police with his personal cell phone number as well the numbers of the others involved in the robberies. Using this information, the FBI requested, pursuant to a disclosure order under the Stored Communications Act (SCA), more than five months of historical cell phone location records for several of the suspects, including Timothy Carpenter. The SCA allows the FBI to obtain records when there are reasonable grounds to believe that the information sought is relevant and material to an ongoing investigation. This standard is lower than the one used when the police request a search warrant. Using the cell phone location records, the FBI cross-referenced Carpenter's call detail records with cell tower locations and was able to deduce Carpenter's location and movements at multiple points each day. Specifically, they ascertained that his phone, and presumably Carpenter himself, were within a half-mile to two miles of each of the robberies around the time they occurred. Carpenter was ultimately found guilty of multiple federal crimes and sentenced to a prison term of 116 years.

On appeal, Carpenter's lawyers raised some interesting issues but nevertheless lost. The Sixth Circuit federal court of appeals recognized that the Supreme Court's interpretation of the search and seizure provision of the Fourth Amendment has long included the expectation of privacy that society considers reasonable. However, under the third-party doctrine, information voluntarily given to third parties such as cell phone companies or Internet service providers is not protected by the Fourth Amendment. In other words, although the Fourth Amendment protects the content of phone messages or e-mails, it does not protect metadata such as phone numbers or the sources of e-mails. Thus, in 1979 the Court allowed the government to use the dialed numbers of a defendant to prove he made threatening calls to a victim in the *Smith v. Maryland* case, but in 2014 it did not allow the use of the internal data of a smartphone to demonstrate a defendant's gang association in the *Riley v. California* case. The appeals court also distinguished Carpenter's case from the 2012 *United States v. Jones* case. In that case, the Supreme Court held that the government's installation of a GPS tracking device to monitor a suspect's automobile infringed on the suspect's expectations of privacy. The appeals court concluded that the Carpenter case was different because the FBI obtained the records from a third party and because cell-site data are less accurate than GPS data. The United States Supreme Court, however, reversed the lower court decisions and held for Carpenter noting that there are many complications when trying to apply Fourth Amendment standards to twenty-first century technology. Chief Justice Roberts joined with the four liberals in rejecting the third-party doctrine arguing that earlier courts could not have imagined a society in which a cell phone goes everywhere its owner goes providing a detailed and comprehensive record of the person's movements. The Court in responding to such a privacy threat to all persons not just criminals stressed that the police could still seek search warrants for such information and use constitutional surveillance techniques such as security cameras and the monitoring of cell phone location data in real time.

*Pew Research Center, "Mobile Fact Sheet," based on survey data collected Jan. 3–10, 2018, http://www.pewinternet.org/fact-sheet/mobile/.
†Ibid.
‡"How Much Time Do People Spend on Their Mobile Phones in 2017?" May 9, 2017, https://hackernoon.com/how-much-time-do-people-spend-on-their-mobile-phones-in-2017-e5f90a0b10a6.

women.[96] The Court has also ruled that defense attorneys may not exclude potential jurors on the basis of race or gender.[97]

At the time the Sixth Amendment was written, the United States employed English trial procedure, in which a twelve-member jury had to reach a unanimous verdict to convict a defendant. By the 1960s, however, many states had reduced the size of juries and made it easier to obtain a conviction. They reasoned that smaller juries and nonunanimous verdicts would save time and money, and result in fewer hung juries. In 1970, the Court upheld the constitutionality of smaller juries in noncapital (not involving the death penalty) cases.[98] Two years later, it held that nonunanimous verdicts in noncapital cases also were constitutional. The Court rejected the assertion that the disagreement of a minority of jurors raised questions of "reasonable doubt" about the verdict.[99]

The Eighth Amendment: Cruel and Unusual Punishment

The Eighth Amendment's ban on cruel and unusual punishment was probably motivated by the Framers' rejection of the barbarous methods of torture and execution practiced in medieval England, such as being stretched on the rack and/or disemboweled. Most of the debate over cruel and unusual punishment in the United States, however, has focused on the death penalty.

The issue received little attention from the Supreme Court until the 1970s. Then, in 1972, a deeply divided Court ruled that the Georgia death penalty was unconstitutional because it led to unacceptable disparities in executions. African Americans who murdered whites were much more likely to receive the death penalty than whites convicted of the same crime.[100] Only two of the justices, however, said the death penalty was unconstitutional in all circumstances.

Four years later, the Court clarified its position by upholding a new Georgia death penalty statute in **Gregg v. Georgia.**[101] The Court found the law constitutional because it contained adequate safeguards for the defendant. The law prescribed separate phases for trial and sentencing. The trial phase would determine the defendant's guilt or innocence; a verdict of guilty triggered a second phase to consider punishment. The law required jury or judge to consider both aggravating factors and mitigating factors in making a sentencing decision. An aggravating factor is any factor that makes the crime worse, such as murder for hire or felony murder, which is the commission of a murder while committing another felony such as robbery or rape. A mitigating factor is any factor that might excuse the crime to some extent, such as reduced mental capacity on the part of the defendant. The law also provided for an automatic appeal to the state's highest court. In 2017, in the case of *Moore v. Texas,* the Court strengthened the mitigating factor of reduced mental capacity by holding that the use of outdated medical standards regarding intellectual disability to determine whether a person is exempt from execution was cruel and unusual punishment. Opponents of the death penalty have also been encouraged by statistics and events in the past two decades. Public support for the death penalty has declined since 1992 and since 2005 continues to decline at an accelerated rate. (see "Public Support for the Death Penalty"), as have the number of executions and death penalty sentences, with the revelation that many innocent persons have been sentenced to death. The declining murder rate has also contributed to a decrease in executions (see "Executions in the United States").

In 2000, former governor George Ryan (R-IL) ordered a moratorium on all executions in his state after DNA tests led to the release of thirteen men on death row. Other states are now offering free DNA testing for death row inmates. In 2002, the Supreme Court ruled that the execution of mentally retarded defendants is cruel and unusual punishment; at the time, such executions were legal in twenty states.[102] Three years later, the Court prohibited the death penalty for any defendant who was under the age of 18 when he or she committed murder.[103] Before the decision, the United States was one of a handful of countries, including China, Pakistan, Iran, and Saudi Arabia, that executed juveniles. Despite these rulings, however, the national government and three-fourths of the states still have the death penalty, and the United States is now the only Western democracy that uses it (see "States Without the Death Penalty").

Opponents of the death penalty were cheered again when the Supreme Court agreed to hear a Kentucky case that challenged the state's administration of the lethal injection method of execution: which chemicals were administered, the training of the personnel, the adequacy of the medical supervision, and the risk of error. The prisoner's contention was that if the first drug, the barbiturate, was an insufficient anesthetic, the next two drugs that paralyzed the prisoner and stopped the heart could cause excruciating pain without the prisoner being able to move or cry out. Such pain, it was contended, would constitute cruel and unusual punishment. While the Court considered the case, it stayed the execution of prisoners from states with the lethal injection procedure, and some states voluntarily halted their executions until the Supreme Court rendered its decisions. As a result, only forty-two executions were carried out in 2007 and none in the early part of 2008 until the Court rendered its decision.

In April 2008, the Court upheld the Kentucky law.[104] For a 7 to 2 majority, Chief Justice John Roberts wrote: "Simply because an execution method may result in pain, either by accident or as an inescapable consequence of death, does not establish the sort of 'objectively intolerable risk of harm' that qualifies as cruel and unusual" punishment. Within days of the

Gregg v. Georgia The Supreme Court decision that upheld the death penalty in the United States.

Public Support for the Death Penalty

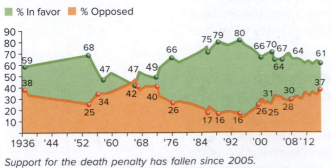

Support for the death penalty has fallen since 2005.

Source: Survey conducted Aug.23-Sept. 2, 2016. Pew Research Center.

opinion, states began lifting their execution bans and went on to execute thirty-seven persons in 2008 and fifty-two in 2009.

The Court ended its term in 2008 by rejecting the death penalty for those convicted of raping a child.[105] A closely divided Court held that with the exception of treason and espionage cases, the death penalty should not be applied when the life of the victim was not taken. Prior to the decision, only five states allowed for the execution of rapists whose victims were children, and the others except for Louisiana applied the penalty only in cases where the defendant had previously been convicted of raping a child. The fact that only five states had such laws and that no prisoner had been executed for the crime for a period of forty-four years led the Court to conclude that a national consensus had been formed on the issue. The following year the

Executions in the United States

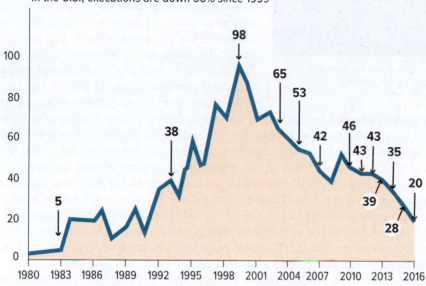

In the U.S., executions are down 56% since 1999

The number of executions in the United States continues to decline.

Source: Death Penalty Information Center

States Without the Death Penalty

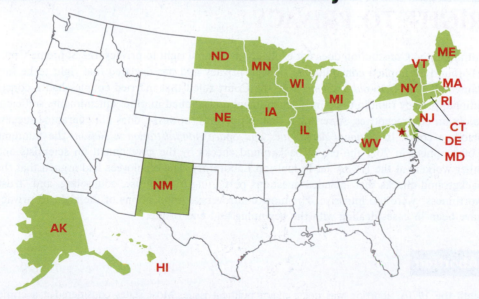

A majority of states still have the death penalty.

Source: Death Penalty Information Center

The Supreme Court has ruled that the death penalty is not the type of cruel and unusual punishment that is prohibited by the Eighth Amendment.

Supreme Court made it easier for death row inmates to sue for access to DNA evidence that could prove their innocence. In *Skinner v. Switzer,* the prosecutors in Texas had tested some but not all of the evidence from the crime scene. The justices ruled that the defendant could sue the prosecutor under a civil rights law for refusing to allow testing of all the DNA evidence.

In 2010, the Court extended the concept of cruel and unusual punishment to apply to sentences of life in prison without the possibility of parole for juveniles who commit violent crimes other than murder. It held in *Graham v. Florida* that such a sentence leaves a young defendant without hope and thus violates the Eighth Amendment provision. Then in the 2012 *Miller v. Alabama* ruling, it ruled that states may not use sentencing schemes for juvenile murders that result in automatic life sentences without the possibility of parole. According to a 2016 ruling in *Montgomery v. Louisiana,* the *Miller* ruling can be applied retroactively to inmates convicted earlier. In 2012, a 7 to 2 majority of the Court ruled that an Alabama death row prisoner should not be prevented from appealing because he missed a filing deadline after his lawyers dropped his case and failed to inform him. The majority in *Maples v. Thomas* wrote that the case amounted to abandonment by counsel rather than just ineffective counsel and that such an occurrence should not result in the defendant's execution without the opportunity to appeal. A 2013 ruling of the Court, *Ryan v. Gonzales,* held that a death row defendant who has exhausted all of his state remedies cannot delay his motion for federal relief on the grounds of mental incompetency or disease. Recently, the Court's death penalty cases have revolved around the method of execution, namely lethal injection. In 2015, the justices considered a challenge brought by Oklahoma death row inmates who alleged that the use of a sedative called midazolam poses a great risk that prisoners will suffer excruciating pain. A five-member majority in the 2015 case of *Glossip v. Gross* ruled against the prisoners, arguing that they failed to suggest an alternative to the drug. They also stated that the scarcity of more effective drugs could be traced to the anti-death-penalty movement and the pressure it has placed on pharmaceutical manufacturers to stop supplying drugs used for executions.

RIGHT TO PRIVACY

Although the Constitution does not explicitly mention a right to privacy, the Supreme Court has found an implied constitutional right to privacy and has declared that right to be fundamental.[106] In *Griswold v. Connecticut,* the Court ruled that married couples had a constitutional privacy right in the Ninth Amendment and implied in other amendments sufficient to obtain contraceptives. Asserting a claim of privacy, however, does not guarantee success before a court. In *National Aeronautics and Space Administration v. Nelson,* the Supreme Court upheld in 2011 the use of background checks by the government on scientists and other workers at the NASA Jet Propulsion Laboratory. The employees had argued that the background checks that included questions pertaining to drug use, counseling, and "trustworthiness" were too intrusive. The most controversial applications of the right to privacy have been in cases dealing with the beginning and end of life.

Abortion

Until the 1970s, abortion was not a major political issue. Most states considered it a crime, while including exceptions such as a pregnancy that threatened the health of the mother or one that resulted from rape or incest. That changed after an itinerant circus worker named Norma McCorvey challenged a Texas state law that criminalized abortion. The pregnant McCorvey already had a child in the care of her mother and did not want to have another; nor did she want to submit to an illegal back-alley abortion. Under the pseudonym Jane Roe, McCorvey ultimately appealed her case to the Supreme Court.[107] In *Roe v. Wade* (1973), the Court concluded that the constitutional right to privacy was broad enough to include the termination of a pregnancy. According to the majority ruling, a woman's right to privacy gives her an absolute right to terminate her pregnancy during the first trimester. In the second trimester, the government can regulate abortions only to protect the health of the mother. It is only in the third trimester that the government's interest in potential life outweighs the privacy interests of the mother, because at that point the fetus is viable and can live outside the womb. Since the passage of *Roe v. Wade,* an estimated one million abortions have been performed every year in the United States.

The *Roe* decision intensified the country's division over the issue of abortion.[108] Antiabortion groups have been unsuccessful in persuading Congress to propose a constitutional amendment banning abortions or the Supreme Court to overturn *Roe.* They have been successful, however, in getting state legislatures (and Congress, to a lesser extent) to adopt abortion restrictions. The Supreme Court has upheld state provisions requiring parental consent for abortions performed on minors, informed consent provisions, and a twenty-four-hour waiting period.[109] It also upheld state bans on the use of public facilities for abortions and has required viability testing at twenty weeks.[110] The justices have also validated the Hyde Amendment, which banned the use of Medicaid funds for poor women who wanted to secure abortions.[111] In the case of *Planned Parenthood of Southeastern Pennsylvania v. Casey* (1992), the Court declared it would not abandon a woman's right to an abortion first articulated in *Roe,* but the Court did dismantle the trimester system, since viability testing can be conducted in the second trimester. In 2007, the Court outlawed a later-term abortion method called intact dilation and extraction, which abortion opponents refer to as "partial birth abortion."[112]

Roe v. Wade The Supreme Court case that legalized abortions in the United States during the first two trimesters of a pregnancy.

In 2016, the Court decided its most important abortion case in over two decades, striking down a Texas law restricting access to abortions in *Whole Woman's Health v. Hellerstedt.* The law had placed two strict requirements on abortion providers in the state. First, all such clinics had to meet the state's standards for ambulatory surgical centers concerning buildings, equipment, and staffing. Second, the statute had required that doctors performing abortions must have admitting privileges at a nearby hospital. The effect of the 2013 law was the closing of half of the state's forty abortion clinics with the expectation that another ten would close if the law was upheld. The Court, however, decided by a vote of 5 to 3 that the law's provisions did not offer sufficient medical benefits to justify the burdens it placed on a woman's access. By its use of the "undue burden" test, the Court's decision meant that similar requirements in other states would likely be found unconstitutional as well. Public opinion on abortion is mixed, but nearly 80 percent of the U.S. population believes that abortion should be legal under at least some circumstances (see "Abortion and Public Opinion").

The Right to Die

Longer life expectancies, and modern medicine's ability to prolong the life of terminally ill or comatose patients, have increased Americans' concern with issues regarding the right to die. The Court has ruled that individuals have a

Abortion and Public Opinion

Do you think abortions should be legal under any circumstances, legal only under certain circumstances, or illegal in all circumstances?

■ % Legal under any circumstances ■ % Legal only under certain circumstances
■ % Illegal in all circumstances

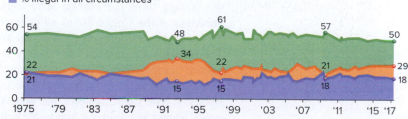

Only 18 percent of Americans believe that abortions should be illegal under all circumstances.

Source: Gallup, May 3–7, 2017

©Mark Meyer/The LIFE Images Collection/Getty Images

Current Controversy

More Than a Few Scraped Knees

Childhood memories of playing on a playground are typically carefree and joyful, devoid of adult responsibilities and concerns. Yet today we live in a time when even a playground can become the center of a conflict over civil liberties. As the case that follows illustrates, the articulation and protection of civil liberties is no longer an activity left solely to lawyers, politicians, and judges. Now any citizen can lay claim to being a champion of rights embedded in the nation's Bill of Rights. When they do so, however, they encounter competing claims for rights by others.

The Trinity Lutheran Church of Columbia, Missouri, operates a licensed preschool and daycare center called The Learning Center. It was originally opened as a nonprofit corporation but merged with the church in 1985. The preschool and daycare, which has an open admissions policy, incorporates Christian religious instruction into its programs. In 2012, the church applied for a grant from the Missouri Department of Natural Resources to purchase recycled tires to resurface its playground.

Children who had fun on this playground were unaware it was featured in an important Supreme Court case featuring clashing civil liberties.

The Natural Resources Department rejected Trinity Lutheran Church's application. The Department explained that according to Article I, Section 7, of the Missouri Constitution, no tax money may be granted to aid any church. The chairman of the church's board of trustees, Phil Glenn, contacted the Alliance Defending Freedom (ADF), an Arizona-based legal action group that provides resources to assist religious organizations in litigating freedom-of-religion cases. The ADF was involved in the 2014 *Hobby Lobby* suit in which the company's owners successfully argued that being forced to supply contraceptives

constitutional right to die that is derived from their constitutional right to privacy.[113] The problem occurs when patients have not made clear their wishes in a living will. In such situations, family members may disagree as to the patient's wishes, and in the most unusual of situations, politicians may get involved for a variety of altruistic and self-serving reasons. Such was the case in 2005 of Terri Schiavo, a Florida woman who had been in a vegetative state for over a decade when her husband went to court to have her feeding tube removed. Her parents opposed this decision and asked for custody. Before doctors eventually removed the feeding tube, the Florida state legislature, the Florida governor, Congress, and the president of the United States all attempted to intervene in this most private family issue.

Although the Court defends the right to die, it has not given its approval to assisted suicide. The Supreme Court ruled unanimously in *Washington v. Glucksberg* (1997) that no right to assisted suicide exists in the Constitution. Michigan physician Jack Kevorkian brought sympathetic national attention to the issue by helping terminally ill patients kill themselves quickly and painlessly. The Court, however, has upheld state laws criminalizing assisted suicide, citing the state's interest in preserving human life and protecting the vulnerable group of ill and predominantly elderly patients. A majority of the public is opposed to the practice as well. By 2018, seven states and the District of Columbia allowed physician- assisted suicide.

for employees under the Affordable Care Act infringed on their religious beliefs. ADF spokesman Erik Stanley said: "Phil reached out to us and said, 'This doesn't sound right'."[*]

What "didn't sound right" to the church was their belief that the grant denial placed them in the position of having to choose between being a church and receiving a government benefit. Their argument relied on a certain interpretation of the free exercise of religion clause of the First Amendment that prohibits the government from interfering with individuals' right to practice their religion. In the 1963 case of Sherbert v. Verner, the U.S. Supreme Court interpreted that clause to invalidate a law that forced a Seventh-Day Adventist to work on Saturday, her faith's Sabbath, in order to receive unemployment benefits. The First Amendment contains a second religion clause, however. The establishment of religion clause has been interpreted by the Supreme Court over the years to provide some degree of separation between church and state. As discussed in this chapter, the two religion clauses sometimes come into conflict.

Complicating the church's case in Missouri was a state constitutional provision similar to the establishment clause in the national constitution. This clause forbids direct government aid to educational institutions that have a religious affiliation, creating an even taller wall of separation than the federal establishment clause. The Missouri constitutional provision, Article I, Section 7, is similar to provisions known as Blaine Amendments in thirty-seven other state constitutions. These amendments were passed following a failed attempt in 1875 by Congress.[†]

After failing to win in the lower federal courts, the Trinity Lutheran Church was happy to have its case argued before the Supreme Court in April 2017 and even happier when it learned of its victory two months later. Writing for the majority, Chief Justice John Roberts concluded that denying a public benefit to an otherwise eligible recipient solely on account of their religious status violates the free exercise of religion clause even if the consequences are only "a few extra scraped knees." Roberts distinguished the case from a 2004 decision in Locke v. Davey that upheld Washington state's right to deny state scholarship money to a student choosing to pursue a theology degree. Roberts reasoned that the scholarship recipient was denied the money not because of who he was but rather because of what he proposed to do. Here, Trinity Lutheran was denied the funds because it was a church. The chief justice argued that the case more similarly resembled McDaniel v. Paty. In that 1978 case, the Court struck down a Tennessee provision that disqualified ministers from serving as delegates to the state's constitutional convention. In a strong dissenting opinion, Justice Sonia Sotomayor observed that the ruling weakened the nation's commitment to separation of church and state and for the first time required the government to provide public funds directly to a church. Scholars and advocates continue to argue whether this ruling invalidates the states' Blaine amendments.[§]

[*]Montgomery, R. "Columbia's Trinity Lutheran, victor in landmark case, back to being a 'little church'", July 2, 2017, http:///www.kansascity.com/news,politics-government/article159210004.html

[†]See Valerie Richardson, "Playground spat looms as key church-state separation case," January 20, 2016, http://www.washingtontimes.com/news/2016/jan/20/trinity-lutheran-church-v-pauley-looms-as-key-church/

[§]See Sarah Pulliam Bailey, "The Supreme Court sided with Trinity Lutheran Church, Here's why that matters." June 26, 2017, The Washington Post.

CIVIC LIBERTIES AND CIVIC ENGAGEMENT TODAY

Because so many of the political issues facing the nation are settled in the courts, organized interest groups inevitably have fought legal battles and sought judicial support for their views. Lawsuits are especially attractive political instruments for individuals or small groups whose size, limited financial resources, and lack of prestige reduce their influence in the electoral process. Although they may lack the ability to influence the outcome of elections, individuals and smaller groups can make persuasive constitutional and moral arguments to courts. The Jehovah's Witnesses, for instance, have won over 70 percent of their cases before the nation's highest court. As recently as 2002, their legal corporation, the Watchtower Bible and Tract Society, was successful in overturning a city permit requirement for door-to-door religious solicitation.[114]

The Jehovah's Witnesses traditionally go to court to defend the rights of their own members, but some groups sponsor cases on behalf of others. The American Civil Liberties Union (ACLU), for example, waits for a case to arise within its field of concern and then assumes

test case The practice by which a group deliberately brings a case to court in order to secure a judicial ruling on a constitutional issue.

amicus curiae brief Legal briefs filed by organized groups to influence the decision in a Supreme Court case.

all or part of the function of representing the litigant in court. Founded during the Progressive Era to combat growing militarism, the ACLU is the symbol of a new era of citizenship. It represents those people who believe one or more government policies violate their constitutional rights and takes on cases representing significant constitutional principles.

In some instances, a group may file a **test case** to challenge the constitutionality of a law. This involves deliberately bringing a case to court to secure a judicial ruling on a constitutional issue. In Chapter 5, we will see how the NAACP used this strategy to advance the cause of civil rights in the courts. The Supreme Court ruling in *Griswold v. Connecticut* (1965), regarding a state ban on advertising or selling contraceptives, was the result of a series of test cases. After a series of unsuccessful test cases, the director of the Connecticut Planned Parenthood League and a physician openly challenged the law by publicly advising married couples on how to use various contraceptive devices. After being arrested and convicted, they appealed the decision to the Supreme Court. The Court found the law unconstitutional because it violated a right to privacy.

Organized groups also try to influence the outcome of constitutional liberties cases by filing **amicus curiae briefs**, or "friend of the court" briefs. These are legal arguments that provide additional support to the arguments supplied by each side in the case. When a plaintiff challenges the constitutionality of a state policy before the U.S. Supreme Court, the state attorney general customarily seeks support from his or her counterparts in other states by asking them to file friend of the court briefs. This strategy backfired in the *Gideon* case, when the Florida attorney general received support from only two states but opposition from twenty-three others. In most constitutional liberties cases, groups from both sides of the issue submit amicus curiae briefs. The more such briefs are filed with the Supreme Court, the more likely it is to accept a case.[115]

In 1963, the Supreme Court recognized that the activities of interest groups in advancing civil liberties issues before the Court were themselves protected by the Bill of Rights. In *NAACP v. Button,* the Court rejected the state of Virginia's attempt to stop the NAACP and other groups from sponsoring lawsuits. The Court ruled that the First Amendment does more than protect abstract discussion; it also protects vigorous advocacy. The justices went on to recognize that the freedoms of speech and association encompass the right to advance issues through the legal system.

Thinking It Through ≫≫≫

Learning Objective: Apply knowledge of criminal due process rights provided by the Bill of Rights.

Review: Rights of the Accused

In a hypothetical scenario, the police receive an anonymous tip that the man who robbed the bank in Pleasantville was hiding in a red house two blocks from the bank. They entered the house without a search warrant, believing the suspect was armed and dangerous. It turned out that the owner of the house, Wally Williams, did not match the description of the bank robber, but a container of illegal drugs was found on his kitchen counter. After several minutes of police questioning Williams with their guns drawn, Williams admitted the drugs were his and that he was intending to sell some of them to his customers. The police then arrested Williams, and the next day he was taken before a judge. The judge told him that if he pleaded guilty, he would have to serve only two years in the state prison. Mr. Williams agreed to the judge's terms but did not realize his two years would be spent in solitary confinement. Which of the defendant's rights were violated?

Summary

1. **Why was the incorporation of the Bill of Rights by the Supreme Court so important?**
   - The addition of the Bill of Rights to the Constitution changed the landscape of civil liberties in the United States, but it only protected citizens from abuses by the national government.
   - Through the use of the incorporation doctrine, the Supreme Court interpreted the due process clause of the Fourteenth Amendment in such a way as to apply most of the Bill of Rights to abuses by state and local governments as well.
   - The policy of selective incorporation helped usher in an era of greater emphasis on individual rights.
   - Through use of the incorporation doctrine, the Supreme Court has become the key institution for interpreting citizens' basic rights.

2. **What are the First Amendment rights?**
   - The First Amendment rights include the establishment and freedom of religion clauses, freedom of speech, freedom of the press, freedom of assembly, freedom of association, and the right to petition the government.
   - The Court has developed the *Lemon* test to determine whether government policies violate the establishment clause.
   - To determine whether one's freedom of religion rights have been violated, the Court balances the importance of a government policy with the amount of burden placed on one's religious beliefs.
   - Today the Court uses the clear and present danger test to decide free speech cases, but in the past it used more restrictive tests.

   - The concept of prior restraint is the guiding principle in freedom of press cases.
   - The Court has balanced the freedom of assembly protection against the government's interest in preserving the peace, regulating the flow of traffic, jail security, and the administration of justice.
   - In freedom of association cases, the Court has recognized the implied privacy right inherent in an association with the competing right to be free from discrimination.

3. **What are some of the other important civil liberties guaranteed by the Constitution?**
   - The Second Amendment guarantees the right to keep and bear arms, and the Court is now interpreting this to be an important individual right that makes some laws banning guns unconstitutional.
   - The Constitution also provides rights for accused persons, such as the protection from unreasonable searches and seizures, protection against self-incrimination, the right to counsel, the right to a jury trial, and protection from cruel and unusual punishment.
   - In deciding cases regarding rights of the accused, the Court has established categories for which searches are legal, has produced guidelines for a constitutional death penalty law, and has constructed the *Miranda* rules to deter self-incrimination questions.
   - The Court has also recognized an implied right to privacy that has produced important decisions in abortion and right-to-die cases.

Chapter 5

Civil Rights
Toward a More Equal Citizenry

WHAT'S TO COME

SEXUAL ASSAULTS ON COLLEGE CAMPUSES

On April 4, 2011, then–vice president Joe Biden announced to a student audience at the University of New Hampshire that the Obama administration considered sexual assault not just a crime but also a violation of civil rights. On the same day, the Department of Education's Office of Civil Rights sent a nineteen-page document that would come to be known as the "Dear Colleague" letter to colleges and universities that receive federal funding. The letter interpreted Title IX, part of the 1972 Education Amendments to the 1964 Civil Rights Act, as requiring any institution of higher learning that knows or reasonably should know about student-on-student harassment, including sexual violence that creates a hostile environment, "to take immediate action to eliminate the harassment, prevent its recurrence, and address its effects."[1] The legal foundations for the letter can be traced to the 1977 case of *Alexander v. Yale,* in which female students sued Yale university over alleged sexual harassment by male employees. The students argued that sexual harassment was itself a form of sexual discrimination.

Dr. Martin Luther King, on the far right, leading the March on Washington for Jobs & Freedom in 1963. The struggle for civil rights has expanded to include many groups, including victims of campus assault.

©Robert W. Kelley/The LIFE Images Collection/Getty Images

Although the court dismissed the students' specific allegations, it did hold that sexual harassment equaled sexual discrimination.

The "Dear Colleague" letter included multiple best practices that colleges and universities should implement. School administrators should inform students reporting sexual assaults of their options, including allowing them to speak to the police. They should conclude investigations quickly, ideally within sixty days. Most important, schools should change the standard for deciding such cases from "beyond a reasonable doubt" to a "preponderance of the evidence" standard. In other words, hearing officers would not use the standard employed in criminal courts but rather a lesser standard that would allow them to rule in favor of the victim if they believed it more likely than not that the incident occurred. The Obama administration opted for the lower standard to help sexual assault victims and to increase the likelihood that they would report such incidents to their schools. It is often difficult to provide evidence of sexual assault "beyond a reasonable doubt" because such acts commonly occur away from third-party witnesses and produce trauma and embarrassment that can affect a clear reciting of the details. The ramifications of sexual assault can be severe. Victims often experience depression and post-traumatic stress. They are also at a higher risk for lowered academic achievement, chronic health conditions, and future sexual victimization.[2]

Then–vice president Joe Biden announced a new national plan for dealing with campus sexual assaults in 2011.

Source: State Department Photo by William Ng

As You READ

- How has the Supreme Court's attitude toward the civil rights of African Americans evolved?
- How have other minority groups benefited from the civil rights struggles of African Americans?
- What was unique in women's struggles for civil rights in the United States?

The "Dear Colleague" letter concluded with a critical warning. The Office of Civil Rights would seek voluntary compliance from the colleges and universities, but failure to come into full compliance could result in the withdrawal of federal funds and the referral of the matter to the Department of Justice for litigation. Colleges and universities soon began to change their procedures, particularly after the Office of Civil Rights announced over 300 investigations into the mishandling of reported sexual harassment and violence incidents on college campuses between 2011 and 2016.

Critics of the changes brought by the Obama administration argued that the new policy was an overcorrection that forced universities to trample on the rights of accused persons. In this view, the changes put the accused in the untenable position of having to prove that they did not commit a sexual assault. Some have

Universities and colleges must now recognize that acts of sexual violence on campus are viewed as a civil rights issue.

gone into hearings not knowing what they were accused of, who was accusing them, or when the supposed incident occurred. Often alcohol was involved, making it even more difficult to remember the details of an encounter that may have happened weeks or months earlier.[3] In many cases, the accused have been given no opportunity to have a hearing where they could question witnesses and mount a defense. At Harvard University, more than two dozen professors protested that the new rules presume the guilt of the accused and thereby abrogate the civil rights of men.

Criticism of the changes was strengthened following a few notable cases in which college men were found to have been falsely accused. In 2006, three members of the Duke University lacrosse team were accused of raping a black student who attended North Carolina Central University. A year later the attorney general of North Carolina dropped all charges, announcing that there had been a "tragic rush to judgement" by a rogue local prosecutor who, among other misdeeds, failed to share exculpatory DNA evidence. In 2014, *Rolling Stone* magazine published an article entitled "A Rape on Campus." Using only a single source—the victim, who was referred to as Jackie—the story described a brutal rape by multiple men at a fraternity party at the University of Virginia, along with the lack of support Jackie received from university officials. In 2015, the local Charlottesville police concluded that there was "no substantive basis" to conclude the rape had occurred. The magazine then commissioned a review of the article by the Columbia Graduate School of Journalism, which found that *Rolling Stone* had not followed routine journalistic practices to verify Jackie's story. The magazine retracted the story and later lost a defamation case brought by the fraternity.[4]

Always lurking at the fringes of any discussion of campus sexual assault is a degree of uncertainty concerning its prevalence. The conversation on the topic has revolved around the finding, from the 2007 Campus Sexual Assault Study, that one in five college coeds is a victim of campus assault. The study was based on a sample of senior undergraduate women at two large public universities, one in the South and one in the Midwest. The study used a Web-based survey with a relatively low response rate of 42 percent. The high nonresponse rate raised questions about whether victims were over- or underrepresented in the study and thus led to doubts about the one-in-five conclusion.[5] A more extensive study conducted in 2015 by the Association of American Universities, however, seems to confirm the findings of the earlier study. In this study, more than 150,000 students enrolled in twenty-seven universities completed online surveys. This study found that just over 23 percent of college-age females (18–24) reported having been the victim of rape or sexual assault. Over 50 percent of the women who reported serious incidents in the study had not reported them to authorities because they were embarrassed, ashamed, thought it would be too emotionally difficult, did not think anything would be done about it, or did not think the matter was serious enough.

The election of Donald Trump in 2016 altered the political response to the issue of campus assault. In September 2017, Trump's education secretary, Betsy DeVos, announced a reversal of the Obama policy on campus sexual assault investigations. Speaking on the campus of George Mason University, she charged that the system instituted by the previous president had failed too many students, and she promised to better protect students who are accused of such misconduct. She proclaimed that, from that point on, colleges would be free to abandon the "preponderance of the evidence" standard of proof and replace it with the higher standard of "clear and convincing proof." She also eliminated a requirement that investigations be completed within sixty days and announced that her department would allow mediation sessions in which an accuser and the accused hash out their differences, if both sides agree. The Obama administration did not permit mediation, believing that it would place undue pressure on the alleged victim. Critics believe the policy changes mark a return to the days when sexual assault victims were shamed, blamed, and abandoned.[6]

The issue of sexual assaults on campus is instructive with respect to civil rights. Many groups, including women, have historically faced great obstacles to achieving equality in the United States and have often turned to the law in search of justice. African Americans endured the degradations of slavery, segregation, and voting barriers before the Supreme Court ultimately responded positively to their legal arguments. This response, in turn, mobilized civil rights advocates who have fought for other disadvantaged groups, such as Native Americans, Hispanic Americans, Asian Americans, the disabled, seniors, the LGBTQ community, and women. The story of disadvantaged groups' struggle for equality, and the impact it has had on the nation, is the subject of this chapter. ■

AFRICAN AMERICANS AND CIVIL RIGHTS

Whereas civil liberties focus on the personal freedoms guaranteed individuals in the Bill of Rights, **civil rights** concern the protection of persons in historically disadvantaged groups from discriminatory actions. Civil rights constitute a positive action by government to guarantee that every person, regardless of his or her group identity, is treated as an equal member of society.[7] Yet despite espousing equality as one of the nation's core values, the United States has often failed to make equality a reality for millions of Americans. Many groups of Americans have had to struggle for equal rights.

> **civil rights** The protection of historically disadvantaged groups from infringement of their equality rights by discriminatory action.

Most people associate the quest for civil rights in the United States with the struggles of African Americans. American blacks were among the first groups to agitate for civil rights, and no other group has had to overcome comparable obstacles to equality: slavery; segregation; and discrimination in voting, housing, and employment. Their battle for equality has served as a road map for other mistreated groups in terms of both inspiration and tactics.

Slavery

When the delegates to the Constitutional Convention met in Philadelphia in 1787, slavery had existed in North America for nearly 170 years. The owners of large plantations in the south relied heavily on slave labor to produce their cash crops. Although some northern delegates, such as Gouverneur Morris, denounced slavery, powerful southern opposition prevented any attempt to abolish slavery via the new constitution. In the end, each state was left to decide for itself whether to permit slavery.

Attempts by the nation's early leaders to prevent the issue of slavery from dividing the country were short-lived. As the nation's population moved westward in the early 1800s, northern and southern representatives faced a dilemma regarding the admission of new states to the Union. Would such states have free or slave status? The issue came to a head in 1820, when Missouri applied for admission to the Union as a slave state.

Division of Free and Slave States After the Missouri Compromise

Legend:
- Free states and territories in 1820
- Slave states and territories in 1820
- Closed to slavery by the Missouri Compromise
- Missouri Compromise line (36°30')

Except for Missouri, new territories and states closed to slavery north of this line

Map labels: OREGON COUNTRY (occupied by United States and Britain); BRITISH AMERICA; MEXICO; UNORGANIZED TERRITORY; MICHIGAN TERRITORY; Missouri Compromise Line; 36°30'; Vermont (1791); Maine (1820); N.H.; Mass.; New York; R.I.; Conn.; Pennsylvania; N.J.; Illinois (1818); Indiana (1816); Ohio (1803); Del.; Missouri (1821); Kentucky (1792); Virginia; Maryland; Arkansas Territory; Tennessee (1796); North Carolina; Miss. (1817); Alabama (1819); Georgia; S.C.; La. (1812); FLORIDA TERRITORY

The Missouri Compromise was intended to settle the free states versus slave states debate for all future states admitted to the Union after Missouri's admission in 1821.

Source: Brinkley, A. *American History* (New York: McGraw-Hill, 2007).

Northern senators opposed Missouri's admission, which would give the states with slavery a majority of seats in the Senate. The Missouri Compromise temporarily settled this divisive issue by granting Missouri admission as a slave state while allowing Maine to enter the Union as a free state (see "The Division of Free and Slave States After the Missouri Compromise"). The compromise also banned the admission of any slave states from the Northwest Territory above 36 degrees, 30 minutes north latitude, with the exception of Missouri. Unfortunately, this compromise created only a temporary solution. The issue of slavery became even more volatile with the continued westward migration of settlers.

Dred Scott

With the nation split between free and salve states, the Supreme Court heard the *Dred Scott* case in 1857.[8] Scott was a slave whose owner held him in bondage while in the free state of Illinois and the free federal territory of Minnesota. Scott sued for his freedom, arguing that he was emancipated as soon as his owner took him into free territory. The Court, however, rejected Scott's argument, noting that African Americans had no rights and thus could justly be reduced to slavery to be bought and sold as ordinary articles of merchandise. Hence, slaves could never be citizens and bring lawsuits to the courts. Chief Justice Roger Taney went further, arguing that Congress lacked the authority to ban slavery in the western territories because doing so violated the due process rights of slave owners to own property under the Fifth Amendment. The decision dealt a swift blow to Scott's freedom and the country's antislavery forces. It invalidated the Missouri Compromise and helped set the stage for the Civil War by removing any possibility for Congress to resolve the divisive issue of slavery in a manner that satisfied all Americans.

The Civil War and Reconstruction

The Civil War and the Reconstruction period marked the end of slavery and the first great advance of civil rights in the United States. In 1862, at the height of the war, President Abraham Lincoln issued the Emancipation Proclamation. This executive order freed all the slaves in states that were still in rebellion as of January 1, 1863. Since the Emancipation Proclamation freed only those slaves living in the South, the complete abolition of slavery did not occur until the adoption of the **Thirteenth Amendment** in 1865. It provided that "neither slavery nor involuntary servitude" shall exist within the United States except as a punishment for the commission of a crime.

However, the passage of the Thirteenth Amendment did not ensure equality for African Americans. Most of the former states of the confederacy failed to ratify the **Fourteenth Amendment**, which provided all persons with the privileges and immunities of national citizenship, guaranteed equal protection under the laws of any state, and safeguarded due process to protect one's life, liberty, and property from state government interference. This led Congress to institute the Reconstruction program, which was designed to prevent the mistreatment of former slaves in the South. Reconstruction legislation dissolved the state governments in ten of the Southern states and partitioned them into five military districts. Tennessee avoided the military occupation by rejoining the union on July 24, 1866. These new governments enfranchised blacks and disqualified many white voters who had fought against the Union in the Civil War. Under such pressure, enough southern legislators ratified the Fourteenth Amendment that it was adopted in 1868. Two years later, the **Fifteenth Amendment** gave former slaves the right to vote.

Soon afterward, however, a partisan political deal at the highest levels of government dashed the hopes and aspirations of the former slaves. In the presidential election of 1876, electoral votes in three states were in dispute, making the election too close to call. Both Republican Rutherford B. Hayes and Democrat Samuel Tilden claimed victory. Congress established a bipartisan commission to determine the victor, but behind the scenes, the Republican Party forged a plan to retain control of the White House. It promised Democratic representatives from southern states that a Republican administration would withdraw federal troops from the South and provide funds to rebuild the area. The Democrats accepted the deal and the commission declared Hayes the winner, bringing the Reconstruction period to an end. The former slaves were once again at the mercy of their former oppressors.

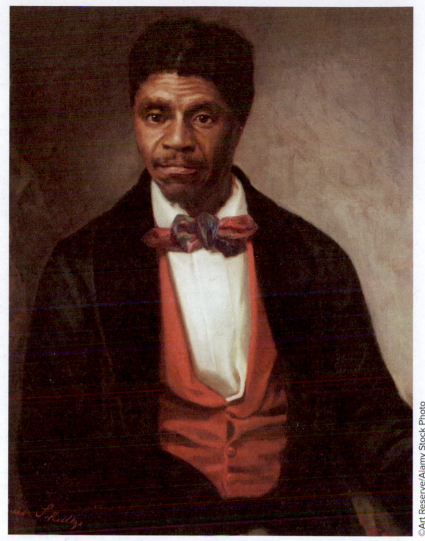

Dred Scott was a slave who asked for his freedom in the federal courts and lost when the Supreme Court in 1857 ruled that slaves had no constitutional rights.

Thirteenth Amendment The Civil War amendment that specifically prohibited slavery in the United States.

Fourteenth Amendment The Civil War amendment that provided all persons with the privileges and immunities of national citizenship; the guarantee of equal protection of the laws by any state; and the safeguard of due process to protect one's life, liberty, and property from state government interference.

Fifteenth Amendment The Civil War amendment that extended suffrage to former male slaves.

Segregation

The constitutional amendments and the various civil rights laws of the Civil War and Reconstruction era were of little value unless the federal government enforced them. Sadly, once federal troops pulled out of the South, most northern whites lost interest in civil rights, and the former slave states went back to business as usual. This included segregated living, enforced by **Jim Crow laws** that required whites and African Americans to use separate hotels, separate restrooms, separate drinking fountains, and even separate cemeteries.[9] The laws also prohibited interracial marriage. Any violation of the segregation code could lead to violent reprisals by the Ku Klux Klan.

Jim Crow laws Legislation in the South that mandated racial segregation in public facilities such as restaurants and restrooms.

On June 7, 1892, Homer Plessy bought a ticket in New Orleans and boarded a train headed for Covington, Louisiana. He took a seat in the white coach, even though he later described himself as "seven-eighths Caucasian and one-eighth African blood."[10] When Plessy refused to comply with the conductor's order to move, he was arrested for violating the state of Louisiana's new segregation law requiring railroads to carry blacks in separate cars. Plessy's arrest, however, was no accident, but the result of months of planning by the black community in New Orleans, in cooperation with railroad officials (who otherwise would not have known Plessy's race). That event would culminate in a U.S. Supreme Court ruling that defined the status of civil rights in the country for decades to come.

Plessy appealed his conviction to the Supreme Court, where his attorney argued that racial segregation on train cars perpetuated the notion of black inferiority that accompanied the institution of slavery. Since the law did not apply to "nurses attending the children of the other race," he reasoned that this legal exception was made because whites were willing to endure blacks who had a clearly dependent status. As a result, he concluded, the law violated the spirit and intent of the Thirteenth Amendment that ended slavery and the Fourteenth Amendment that promised equal protection under the law.

In May 1896, the Supreme Court handed down its decision supporting the Louisiana law and Plessy's conviction. This case established the "separate but equal" doctrine that would dominate U.S. Supreme Court decisions for another fifty-eight years. Under this doctrine, the government considered segregated facilities legal as long as they were equal. In reality, the Court tolerated segregation even when the facilities were clearly unequal. The *Plessy* decision ushered in the worst period of civil rights violations since the abolition of slavery. The case was used to justify continuation of separate facilities for the races, with African Americans always relegated to inferior facilities and, thus, opportunities.

In the twentieth century, segregation in the South included separate restrooms for both races. Now in the twenty-first century, public bathrooms have again become a civil rights issue involving transgender individuals.

©Bruce Roberts/Science Source

Voting Barriers

The end of Reconstruction led to pervasive attempts in the southern states to deny blacks their rights under the Fifteenth Amendment. Southern officials argued that the amendment did not guarantee African Americans the right to vote but, rather, prohibited states from denying the right to vote on the basis of race or color. This led them to construct so-called racially neutral laws to prevent African Americans from voting. Poll taxes, literacy tests, property qualifications, and even the notorious grandfather clause—a rule that someone could not vote if his grandfather had not voted—were used to exclude many potential voters.[11] In practice, these devices most often kept African Americans from voting; most African Americans were too poor to pay poll taxes or to own property, were not educated enough to pass a literacy test, and, as the descendants of slaves, did not have a grandfather who had been allowed to vote.

NAACP

African Americans watched with despair as the walls of segregation rose around them. Their hopes for equality, based on the Civil War amendments passed during the Reconstruction period and civil rights laws, were nearly gone. In 1909, the publisher of the *New York Evening Post*, who was the grandson of the famous abolitionist William Lloyd Garrison, called a conference to discuss the problem of "the Negro." The group soon evolved into the National Association for the Advancement of Colored People (NAACP).

In the 1930s, the leaders of the NAACP decided to test the constitutionality of *Plessy v. Ferguson* in the federal courts. Lacking the political clout to accomplish legislative change, they hoped the federal courts might rule that the separate but equal doctrine was a barrier to the possibility of equality for African Americans. The NAACP sponsored test cases as forums in which to present sociological data and statistics that provided the courts with evidence of discrimination. The organization concentrated on the field of education, beginning with cases of segregation in graduate and professional schools. Because so few African Americans had attained these advanced educational levels, the NAACP reasoned that whites would be less threatened by changes in these venues. They also reasoned that the courts would be more inclined to rule in their favor, because there was little chance that the government would have to implement the decision. Only later did they challenge the segregation of elementary and high schools, which would affect millions of students and the social mores of the country.[12]

The NAACP enjoyed several victories following this strategy of using test cases that would affect very limited populations, including successfully challenging the exclusion of an African American student from a state law school. This decision paved the way for the Court to deem unconstitutional the establishment of a segregated Texas law school for African Americans only.[13] In that case, the NAACP argued successfully that an African American student who was isolated in a segregated state graduate school was denied an equal education.[14]

Modern Era of Civil Rights

After 1950, the NAACP concluded it was time to change the plan of attack. It decided to pressure the Court to overrule the *Plessy* decision on the grounds that separate facilities, even if equal, were unconstitutional because segregation *itself* was unconstitutional under the equal protection clause of the Fourteenth Amendment. The organization was now ready to challenge legal segregation in the nation's primary and secondary public schools.

Brown v. Board of Education The 1954 *Brown* case actually related to five separate cases brought against local school districts in Delaware, South Carolina, Virginia, the District of Columbia, and Kansas. The Brown family in the Kansas case, for example, challenged the idea that their daughter could not attend the white school that was located close to their home. The new chief justice, Earl Warren, wrote the opinion for the unanimous Court striking down the separate but equal laws. Warren acknowledged that the original intent of the Framers of the Fourteenth Amendment was unclear but argued, "We must consider public education in the light of its full development and its present place in American life throughout the Nation." He reasoned that modern public education was essential for full political participation because it opens up life opportunities and provides the basis for intelligent citizenship. Warren's opinion also confirmed the wisdom of the NAACP's tactic of relying on psychological and sociological studies in its brief, given the lack of legal precedents to support its cause. The unanimous Court held that to separate children from others because of their race generates within them a feeling of inferiority "that may affect their hearts and minds in a way very unlikely ever to be undone."

Because the *Brown* case dealt only with **de jure segregation**—discrimination by law—it primarily affected the southern states that had passed Jim Crow laws. It did not address **de facto segregation**—racial separation based on factual realities such as segregated housing patterns—which existed throughout the United States. In 1955, the following year, the Court ruled in *Brown II* that the racially segregated school systems must be abandoned "with all deliberate speed."[15] They also determined that federal district judges, instead of state court judges who were more susceptible to local political pressure, would enforce the decision. Unfortunately, the phrase *with all deliberate speed* gave the southern states the opportunity to delay desegregation and ultimately to engage in massive resistance to the change. Nevertheless, *Brown v. Board of Education* is the landmark case that put an end to the legal doctrine of separate but equal.

Southern resistance to public school integration led to federal action on several occasions. In 1957, President Dwight D. Eisenhower sent federal troops to enforce the integration of the school system in Little Rock, Arkansas. Throughout the 1960s, Congress drafted major civil rights legislation to advance the cause of desegregation. Some federal judges ordered students bused to schools in other neighborhoods to achieve racially balanced school districts.[16] By 1995, however, support for direct federal intervention had declined, and the Court announced that it would not look favorably on continued federal control of school districts, like one in Kansas City that had spent millions of dollars under federal direction to attract white students from the suburbs.[17]

Civil Rights Mobilization

The *Brown* decisions sparked not only southern resistance but also a popular civil rights movement exemplified by people such as Rosa Parks. Parks was a petite woman who worked as a seamstress and served as the NAACP youth council advisor in Montgomery, Alabama. She had been active in NAACP activities such as voter registration drives, but she did not intend to launch a civil rights crusade on the December afternoon in 1955 when she refused to leave her seat in the front of the bus to make room for a white passenger. Parks later said she did not move because she thought she had the right to be treated the same way as any other passenger on the bus. Her act of defiance was not only illegal but also dangerous. Montgomery's buses were segregated by law, and African Americans had been beaten and even killed for not obeying bus drivers.

Police arrested Parks, who was later convicted of violating the state's segregation law and fined ten dollars. The NAACP responded by distributing handbills urging African Americans to boycott the Montgomery bus system to protest Parks's arrest. Martin Luther King, Jr., a recently arrived minister, emerged as a leader in the year-long boycott effort. When a lower federal court finally ordered the buses to integrate, the tactic of nonviolent protest had proved its value. Parks received the Congressional Gold Medal in 1999, and upon her death in 2005 political leaders across the nation praised her efforts and character.

The **civil rights movement** spawned groups in addition to the NAACP that pursued different strategies to secure equality for African Americans. King formed the Southern Christian Leadership Conference

©Bettmann/Getty Images

Federal troops were needed to support the Supreme Court's school integration decision in Brown v. Board of Education *by protecting the students who were integrating the formerly all-white schools.*

(SCLC), which spurned litigation as a major tactic and instead used nonviolent protest to achieve equality. Whereas the SCLC drew heavily on its base in the southern black community, other groups such as the Student Nonviolent Coordinating Committee (SNCC) recruited young people of all races. These new groups organized events (such as boycotts, sit-ins at segregated restaurants, and "freedom rides" pairing civil rights activists with college students) that were designed to draw attention to the segregation of public accommodations. Martin Luther King, Jr., became the most famous civil rights leader in the country with his eloquence and courage. He grabbed national attention in August 1963 when he organized a massive march on Washington, D.C., and delivered his famous "I Have a Dream" speech: "I have a dream that my four little children will one day live in a nation where they will not be judged by the color of their skin but by the content of their character." The march was planned to demonstrate widespread support for President John F. Kennedy's proposal to ban all discrimination in public accommodations and to argue for an end to discrimination against African Americans in all aspects of life. Other leaders, such as Stokely Carmichael, rallied followers with the call for "Black Power," which entailed a resurrection of black pride and a belief that integration with whites was not desirable.

Martin Luther King, Jr., drew national attention to the civil rights movement with his "I Have a Dream" speech in 1963.

The civil rights movement used nonviolent protests to draw attention to its cause.

Civil Rights Legislation

Senior southern Democrats in Congress, supported by conservative Republicans, opposed Kennedy's civil rights proposal. Because of their long tenure in Congress, these Democrats held key committee positions that allowed them to dominate both houses of Congress and frustrate the president's plans. Kennedy's assassination on November 22, 1963, changed the political landscape. His successor, Lyndon Johnson, was a Texan who had been a powerful majority leader in the Senate. He knew how to get legislation passed and how to talk to the southern members of Congress. Johnson's political skill, added to the wave of sympathy that accompanied the death of the young president, led Congress to pass the historic **Civil Rights Act of 1964**.[18]

The 1964 Civil Rights Act bars discrimination in public accommodations engaged in interstate commerce. For instance, a hotel that has customers from other states or that orders any products from other states cannot refuse to serve customers based on their race.[19] The act also prohibits discrimination in employment on the grounds of race, religion, national origin, or sex. The law established the Equal Employment Opportunity Commission (EEOC) to enforce and monitor bans on employment discrimination and to withhold federal funds from state and local government programs that discriminate against providers or consumers. A year later, Congress passed the **Voting Rights Act of 1965**, which increased voter protections by outlawing literacy tests and by allowing federal officials to enter southern states to register African American

Civil Rights Act of 1964 Historic legislation that prohibited racial segregation in public accommodations and racial discrimination in employment, education, and voting.

Voting Rights Act of 1965 Federal legislation that outlawed literacy tests and empowered federal officials to enter southern states to register African American voters; the act dismantled the most significant barriers to African Americans' suffrage rights.

Impact of the Great Recession

Median net worth of households, in 2016 dollars

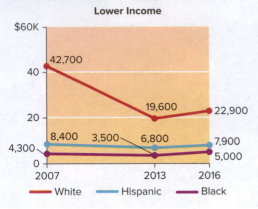

Lower Income

- White: 42,700 (2007), 19,600 (2013), 22,900 (2016)
- Hispanic: 8,400 (2007), 3,500 / 6,800 (2013), 7,900 (2016)
- Black: 4,300 (2007), (2013), 5,000 (2016)

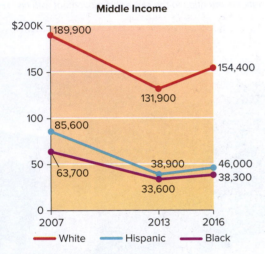

Middle Income

- White: 189,900 (2007), 131,900 (2013), 154,400 (2016)
- Hispanic: 85,600 (2007), 38,900 (2013), 46,000 (2016)
- Black: 63,700 (2007), 33,600 (2013), 38,300 (2016)

Note: Blacks and whites are single-race only and include only non-Hispanics.

The median net worth of black and Hispanic families continues to lag far behind that of white families.

voters. This provision enabled hundreds of thousands of African Americans to register to vote in southern states.

Retrospective

The efforts of those who participated in the civil rights movement dramatically changed the lives of African Americans and their role in civic life. The passage and enforcement of voting laws have resulted in substantial numbers of African Americans winning election to public office since the 1960s. Although still underrepresented at the national level, even considering the election of Barack Obama, African Americans have made considerable advances in state and local government. Today, it is not surprising to find an African American serving as a sheriff in Mississippi or as a mayor in Alabama. African Americans still have a long way to go, however, to achieve full equality in America.

The income of the average African American family today is barely two-thirds that of the average white family. In terms of median net worth, white families far surpass black and Hispanic families, although the Great Recession of 2008 nearly halved the wealth of lower-income white and middle-income black and Hispanic families (see "Impact of the Great Recession"). One study has shown that the race "opportunity gap" that separates African Americans and Hispanic Americans from whites is greatest in the Midwest and Northeast and lowest in the South and West. Opportunity gaps are composed of five factors: residential segregation, neighborhood affluence, public school quality, share of employment, and share of home ownership.[20]

African Americans are more likely to be convicted of crimes than whites and are more likely to receive harsher punishments, including the death penalty. Recent well-publicized incidents around the country in locations such as Ferguson, Missouri, Chicago, and Baltimore show that African American

Perceptions of Police Officers

*% who rate **police officers** on a 'feeling thermometer' from 0 (coldest rating) to 100 (warmest rating)*

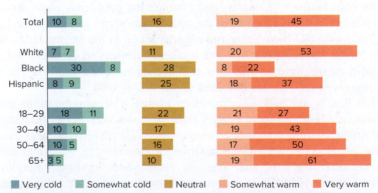

	Very cold	Somewhat cold	Neutral	Somewhat warm	Very warm
Total	10	8	16	19	45
White	7	7	11	20	53
Black	30	8	28	8	22
Hispanic	8	9	25	18	37
18–29	18	11	22	21	27
30–49	10	10	17	19	43
50–64	10	5	16	17	50
65+	3	5	10	19	61

Note: Feeling thermometer ratings: very cold (0 to 24), somewhat cold (25–49), neutral (50), somewhat warm (51–75), very warm (76–100). Whites and blacks include only those who are not Hispanic; Hispanics are of any race.

Blacks are four times more likely to have very cold views of the police than Whites or Hispanics.

Perceptions of Racial Advantage

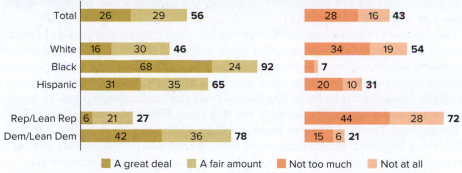

% who say white people benefit___from advantages in society that black people do not have

	A great deal	A fair amount		Not too much	Not at all	
Total	26	29	**56**	28	16	**43**
White	16	30	**46**	34	19	**54**
Black	68	24	**92**	7		
Hispanic	31	35	**65**	20	10	**31**
Rep/Lean Rep	6	21	**27**	44	28	**72**
Dem/Lean Dem	42	36	**78**	15	6	**21**

■ A great deal ■ A fair amount ■ Not too much ■ Not at all

Note: Whites and blacks include only those who are not Hispanic; Hispanics are of any race. Don't know responses not shown.

White and black Americans differ greatly in their beliefs concerning whether whites benefit from societal advantages. The view among white Democrats is closer to that of blacks than to that of white Republicans, who see little advantage for whites.

suspects are sometimes the victims of police violence that results in their death. Although each incident has to be examined on its own merits, videotape and photo evidence has too often shown that black suspects are treated harshly and unprofessionally. As a result, blacks are less likely than whites to view police in a positive way (see "Perceptions of Police Officers"). Such incidents led to the inception of the Black Lives Matter movement.

Given these realities, the races have very different perceptions as to the fairness of American society. Blacks and Hispanics are much more likely to believe that whites benefit from advantages they themselves do not have (see "Perceptions of Racial Advantage"). The struggle for civil rights is the struggle for equality. We have seen how Supreme Court decisions have both hindered and advanced the efforts of African Americans to achieve equality. In the next section, we will examine how the Supreme Court interprets equality by creating judicial tests and by determining how to evaluate affirmative action programs.

INTERPRETING EQUALITY

When a disadvantaged group takes a discrimination case to the U.S. Supreme Court, its success depends on how the Court interprets the word *equality.* The word *equality,* however, appears nowhere in the original Constitution or the Bill of Rights. The Court must, therefore, interpret the concept in the context of the Fourteenth Amendment, which guarantees that no state shall deny any person the "equal protection of the laws."

Judicial Tests

The Court has stated that it prohibits only "invidious discrimination"—that is, discriminatory acts that have no rational basis. Some acts of discrimination are necessary and reasonable. For example, we are all taught not to take candy from a stranger. But who decides what is rational or reasonable? When we are young, it is our parents. In civil rights law, it is the Supreme Court. When governments make laws, those laws might treat different groups differently. When the United states last had a military draft, it was deemed reasonable to treat males and females differently as to whom could be drafted. To treat males and females differently, however, in terms of who could go to college would be unreasonable. To determine which discriminating laws are reasonable and thus constitutional, the Supreme Court constructs judicial tests, specific standards that a government policy must meet in order to be ruled constitutionally permissible. These tests specify which party has the burden of proof. That is, must the party challenging the policy prove that the policy is unconstitutional, or must the government prove that the policy is constitutional? Since judicial tests are not part of the Constitution, the Supreme Court has great latitude to decide how and when to use them.

The Supreme Court has constructed three tests for cases arising under the equal protection clause of the Fourteenth Amendment. The oldest of these is known as the **rational basis test**. It considers whether a law that gives preference to one group over another is a reasonable means to achieve a legitimate government purpose. The rational basis test places a burden on the alleged wronged party by compelling them to prove that the legislature passed an unreasonable law. It is easier for the government to win such cases. With this in mind, Justices William O. Douglas and Thurgood Marshall began to ask for additional tests to protect litigants.[21] In 1976, Justice William J. Brennan authored a new test known as the **intermediate scrutiny test**. It places the burden of proof on the government, and its standards are considered more exacting. Even before Justice Brennan formulated the intermediate scrutiny test, the Supreme Court adopted the **strict scrutiny test** for racial discrimination cases. This test places the burden of proof on the government to prove that the law serves a compelling government end and that the racial classification law is the "least restrictive means" of achieving that end. There is a greater burden on the government to defend its law under the strict scrutiny test, less of a burden when the Court uses the intermediate test, and still less when the Court uses the rational basis test. Today, the Court uses the rational basis test for discrimination allegations based on economic status, sexual preference, or age; the intermediate scrutiny test for gender discrimination cases; and the strict scrutiny test for racial and ethnic discrimination cases.

Affirmative Action

The quest for civil rights has come to mean more than the elimination of biased behavior toward certain groups. It has also come to mean that government should provide remedies to promote equality. As early as the 1940s, presidents issued executive orders to attempt to expand federal government employment opportunities for African Americans. Since that time, both the government and the private sector have sponsored **affirmative action** programs to ensure equality for historically disadvantaged groups and to eliminate the effects of past discrimination. Affirmative action programs attempt to clear a path to the good life for those whose progress was blocked in the past. Their goals include helping members of disadvantaged groups gain admission to universities, secure employment in all occupational fields, and win promotions once hired.

Affirmative action programs move beyond the traditional notion of equality of opportunity to promote the goal of equality of outcome. Instead of aiming to ensure that everyone has the same chance to receive a good education or good job, they strive to ensure that every group in society has the same rate of success in attaining a good education and a good job. The concept of equality of opportunity would be satisfied if a prestigious college allowed students of all races and both genders to attend if they had an outstanding high school record. The concept of equality of result, however, wants to guarantee a proscribed number of enrollments for each race and gender. To secure equal results, affirmative action promotes preferential treatment for members of groups that have suffered from "invidious discrimination." Such programs typically create separate racial classifications and provide members of historically disadvantaged groups with preferential consideration for admission to universities or promotion in the workplace.

Racial Classifications

The Supreme Court responded to affirmative action for the first time in the case of *Regents of the University of California v. Bakke* (1978). To increase minority student enrollment, the University of California at Davis developed two admissions programs to fill the one hundred seats in its freshman medical school class. The regular admissions program evaluated candidates on the basis of undergraduate grades, standardized test scores, extracurricular activities, letters of recommendation, and an interview. The special admissions program was

rational basis test The equal protection test used by the Supreme Court that requires a complainant to prove that the use of a classification such as age, gender, or race is not a reasonable means of achieving a legitimate government objective.

intermediate scrutiny test The equal protection test used by the Supreme Court that requires the government to prove that the use of classifications such as age, gender, or race is substantially related to an important government objective.

strict scrutiny test The equal protection test used by the Supreme Court that places the greatest burden of proof on the government to prove that classifications such as age, gender, or race are the least restrictive means to achieve a compelling government goal.

affirmative action Programs that attempt to provide members of disadvantaged groups enhanced opportunities to secure jobs, promotions, and admission to educational institutions

Regents of the University of California v. Bakke The 1978 Supreme Court case that declared unconstitutional the use of racial quotas to achieve a diverse student body but allowed the use of race as one of many factors in admissions decisions.

reserved for applicants who indicated they were economically or educationally disadvantaged or who were African American, Chicano, Asian, or Native American. Those in the special admissions program were judged on the same factors as the other applicants, but they competed only against each other. Sixteen of the one hundred seats for the entering class were filled from the special admissions program.

In 1973, Allan Bakke, at the age of 33, applied for admission to the University of California at Davis medical school. Bakke is a white male who had graduated with honors from the engineering program at the University of Minnesota, had received a master's degree in engineering from Stanford, had worked for the National Aeronautics and Space Administration, and was a Vietnam veteran. He was denied admission in both 1973 and 1974. Arguing that his qualifications were higher than those admitted under the special admissions program, Bakke sued. He claimed that the university's dual admissions program violated the equal protection clause of the Fourteenth Amendment.

The Supreme Court was deeply divided over this case. Four justices had serious reservations about affirmative action programs, four strongly supported them, and Justice Lewis Powell was caught in the middle. Justice Powell sided with the first group in holding that the university had used race to discriminate against Bakke, who should be admitted to the medical school. Powell applied the strict scrutiny test to the university's admission program, concluding that even though a diverse student body is a compelling governmental interest, the use of racial quotas was an impermissible means of achieving that interest. However, he did align with the affirmative action supporters by stating that such programs were permissible if they did not include quotas and used race as just one of many factors in considering admission.

The *Bakke* case left many questions unanswered. Exactly how could racial classifications be used in university admissions programs? Could racial quotas be used to increase employment opportunities for racial minorities? Could gender classifications be used in affirmative action programs?

The Supreme Court has answered these questions over the past few decades. In 1979, the Court held that an apprenticeship training program at a Kaiser Aluminum and Chemical plant in Louisiana was legal, even though it contained racial quotas.[22] The Court stressed that the company and the United Steelworkers union voluntarily agreed to implement the program and that the plan was temporary in nature. Eight years later, it upheld the use of racial quotas to reverse the effects of long-standing discrimination in the Alabama Department of Public Safety.[23] The Court has also ordered quotas for minority union memberships and added gender as a category to be included in private affirmative action programs.[24] In 2009, in the case of *Ricci v. DeStefano,* however, the Supreme Court held that the city of New Haven, Connecticut, was wrong in throwing out a white firefighters' promotion exam because white applicants scored higher than African American or Hispanic American applicants. The ruling has the potential of changing employment practices nationwide and potentially limiting the liability of employers when there is no evidence of intentional discrimination.

Current Impact on Education

The Supreme Court had to consider how its affirmative action decisions in other fields affected education two decades after the *Bakke* case. When it decided that classifying people by race in the business field was unconstitutional, it opened the door to new issues involving education and affirmative action.[25] Soon, several states enacted legislation that banned the use of racial preferences in education. In *Hopwood v. Texas* (1996), the Fifth Circuit Court of Appeals held that preferential policies affecting admission to the state universities in Texas, Mississippi, and Louisiana violated the Fourteenth Amendment. The state of California dropped its affirmative action program in light of this ruling. The elimination of these affirmative action programs significantly decreased the proportion of African American and Hispanic American students in the California university system. The number of African American freshmen enrolled at the major state universities in Texas fell by 28 percent in the two years following the case and the number of Hispanic students was reduced by 14 percent.[26] In its 2014 ruling in *Schuette v. Coalition to Defend Affirmative Action,* the Supreme Court ruled that a state constitutional ban on race- and sex-based discrimination related to public university admissions did not violate the equal protection clause of the Fourteenth Amendment.

In 2004, the Supreme Court agreed to hear two appeals challenging affirmative action programs at the University of Michigan. Unlike the cases just described, these cases dealt with the constitutionality of programs already in existence. *Gratz v. Bollinger* (2003) challenged the university's undergraduate admissions policies, and *Grutter v. Bollinger* (2003) questioned the admissions policies for the University of Michigan law school. The *Gratz* case overturned the undergraduate admissions program, which utilized quotas, but the Court reached a different decision in the law school case. The University of Michigan Law School's admissions policy looked beyond test scores and grade point averages in order to admit a diverse student body. Its goal was to achieve a critical mass of minority students so that they would not feel isolated or feel the need to be spokespersons for their race. The policy did not set quotas for members of underrepresented groups, nor did it award points for minority status. The Court ruled that this admissions policy was allowed because it was narrowly tailored and permitted the individual review of applicants in a non-mechanical way.

In the 2013 *Fisher v. University of Texas* case, the Court did not invalidate that university's admissions plan, which accepts all students who graduate in the top 10 percent of their high school class, but does use race as a factor in the acceptance of all other students. In remanding the case to a lower court, the Supreme Court passed on the opportunity to overrule the *Grutter* opinion. The Court revisited the *Fisher v. University of Texas* case in 2016. In a surprise vote, Justice Kennedy joined the majority in upholding the university's affirmative action plan. Kennedy argued that universities must be given substantial leeway in designing their admissions policy in order to produce the student body diversity that is central to their identity and educational mission. Kennedy did warn, however, that universities must be careful to reconcile the pursuit of diversity with the constitutional promise of equality. Abigail Fisher, the white student who had brought the lawsuit, graduated from Louisiana State University by the time the Court reached its final determination. The Court's opinion left the *Grutter* decision intact.

The Court clarified its position regarding affirmative action in primary and secondary schools in 2007, when it held that public school systems could not use voluntary programs designed to integrate schools that take explicit account of a student's race. In outlawing the programs of Louisville, Kentucky, and Seattle, Washington, Chief Justice Roberts wrote for the five-person majority that "the way to stop discrimination on the basis of race is to stop discriminating on the basis of race."[27] The dissenting justices angrily denounced the decision—one that affects the assignment of students to schools in hundreds of school districts across the United States—as a break from the famous *Brown* decision of 1954.

The policy of affirmative action has led to protests of reverse discrimination.

Continuing Controversy

The constitutionality of affirmative action programs remains uncertain in many areas, and the debate about the wisdom of these policies continues. Opponents of affirmative action programs believe that merit is the only fair way to distribute the benefits of society.[28] They claim that affirmative action programs amount to **reverse discrimination** and argue that both the Fourteenth Amendment and the 1964 Civil Rights Act prohibit racial discrimination. They feel that keeping Allan Bakke out of medical school is an example of racial discrimination. Supporters, by contrast, argue that merit is not always self-evident and may include subjective considerations. They assert not only that affirmative action is necessary to compensate for the effects of past discrimination but also that it benefits the entire community by taking advantage of the talents of all citizens participating in a diverse social, economic, and political environment. Finally, they point to research that indicates that gains for disadvantaged groups come with only small costs to white males.[29] In summary, proponents of affirmative action argue that white males will not be hurt by such programs, that society will benefit as a whole from allowing opportunities for those from diverse backgrounds, and that the old way of making decisions based on "merit" may have been more subjective than people surmised. As we will see, disadvantaged groups include not only African Americans but also a wide range of other minorities, and even the largest single segment of the U.S. population—women.

OTHER MINORITY GROUPS

African Americans no longer represent the largest ethnic minority in the United States. The nation's Hispanic and Asian populations, in particular, have grown substantially since 1990 (see "Population Increases by Race and Ethnicity from 1990 to 2050"). Many of these other minority groups have benefited to varying degrees from the African American struggle to secure equal rights. The victories won by the black civil rights movement gave hope to other minorities that they, too, could work successfully to overcome historical discrimination.

Population Increases by Race and Ethnicity from 1990 to 2050

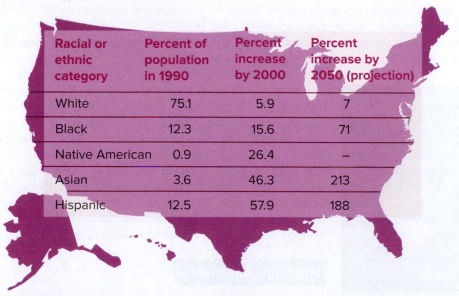

Racial or ethnic category	Percent of population in 1990	Percent increase by 2000	Percent increase by 2050 (projection)
White	75.1	5.9	7
Black	12.3	15.6	71
Native American	0.9	26.4	–
Asian	3.6	46.3	213
Hispanic	12.5	57.9	188

The United States is changing demographically with the number of whites growing far less rapidly than that of Hispanics, Asians, Native Americans, and blacks. This has to do with both birth rates and immigration.

Source: www.anthro.palomar.edu.

Native Americans

Government policy toward Native Americans has gone from genocide and isolation to forced assimilation, and finally to citizenship. Congress and the federal courts initially promoted westward expansion at the expense of Native American rights. One author has referred to Native American policy as "genocide-at-law" because it encouraged both land confiscation and the cultural extermination of the native population.[30] The government forcibly resettled the displaced Native Americans onto isolated reservations. In the 1880s, Congress adopted a new strategy of assimilating Native Americans into the mainstream of cultural life. Legislation banned native languages and rituals and required children to attend boarding schools located off the reservation. The federal government did not grant Native Americans citizenship and the right to vote until 1924. It took another twenty-two years after that for Congress to settle financial claims resulting from the confiscation of native lands. Native Americans have faced some of the harshest treatment of any minority group.

Despite their poor treatment at the hands of the government, Native Americans engaged in no formal social or political movements to protest their unequal status until the 1960s. At the height of the civil rights movement, however, Native Americans began to mobilize. Native American activists such as Dennis Banks and Russell Means of the American Indian Movement (AIM) drew attention to the plight of Native Americans. In 1969, Native American activists seized Alcatraz Island in San Francisco Bay to dramatize the loss of Native American lands. Two years later, Dee Brown published the best-selling book, *Bury My Heart at Wounded Knee*,[31] which focused on the 1890 massacre of nearly three hundred Sioux by the U.S. Cavalry in Wounded Knee, South Dakota. The book helped to mobilize public opinion against the poor treatment of Native Americans in much the same way that Harriet Beecher Stowe's *Uncle Tom's Cabin* did for African Americans a century earlier. In 1973, armed members of AIM held hostages at Wounded Knee for seventy-one days until the national government agreed to consider Native American treaty rights.

Like the NAACP, Native Americans began to use the courts to accomplish their goals, filing hundreds of test cases and forming the Native American Rights Fund (NARF) to finance them. Their victories include the securing of land, hunting and fishing rights, and access to ancient burial grounds and other sacred locations. The 1968 Civil Rights Act includes an Indian Bill of Rights, leading one author to conclude that Native Americans have now entered the self-determination phase of their history.[32] Nevertheless, Native Americans still suffer more than most Americans from ill health, poverty, and poor educational opportunities. Nearly half live on or near a reservation.

An ongoing area of controversy for Native Americans is the continued use of stereotypical and demeaning names and mascots by some professional and collegiate athletic teams. Native Americans have called upon the NFL's Washington Redskins and major league baseball's Atlanta Braves to change their team names. They have also complained about what they consider the offensive caricature of a Native American used as a mascot by baseball's Cleveland Indians. Those complaints have led to some change. The Cleveland baseball team agreed to remove the Chief Wahoo logo from their uniform in 2019. At the college level, the NCAA adopted a new restriction on the use of Native American nicknames, mascots, and logos. Thirty schools have been asked to explain their use of such items under a new appeals system. Some college teams, such as the Florida State Seminoles, the Utah Utes, and the Central Michigan Chippewas, have been allowed to keep their nicknames after deliberations with the NCAA. Other universities continue to appeal.

Despite calls for changing the team's name, the Washington Redskins, which is seen to be offensive to Native American culture, the owner of the National Football League's team deflected the pressure and has not yet changed the name.

Hispanic Americans

Hispanic Americans are currently the largest minority group in the United States, with a population of 57.5 million in 2016, a sixfold increase since 1970. They come primarily from Puerto Rico, Mexico, Cuba, El Salvador, and Honduras. Immigrants from Mexico make up the majority of Hispanics in California, Arizona, Texas, and New Mexico, and large numbers of Caribbean Hispanics populate the states of New York, New Jersey, and Florida.

As with Native Americans, the Hispanic American drive for civil rights began in earnest during the mid-1960s. Hispanic American leaders carefully observed African American groups and adopted many of the same tactics. Inspired by the NAACP's Legal Defense Fund, Hispanic Americans formed similar organizations, including the Mexican American Legal Defense and Educational Fund (MALDEF). They, too, brought test cases before the courts to realize goals such as implementing bilingual education, increased funding for schools in low-income minority districts, ending employment discrimination against Hispanic Americans, and challenging election rules that diluted Hispanic American voting power.

Like other minority groups, Hispanic Americans did not depend exclusively on litigation in their struggle for civil rights. Drawing again on the experiences of African Americans, they staged sit-ins, marches, boycotts, and other related activities to draw attention to their concerns. The best-known Hispanic American protest leader, César Chávez, organized strikes by farm workers in the late 1960s and 1970s to attain basic labor rights for migrant workers. Migrants worked long hours for little pay, lived in substandard housing that often lacked plumbing and electricity, and were unwelcome in the local schools. When farm owners refused to bargain with his group, Chávez launched a national boycott of California lettuce and grapes. The boycott was successful, with American consumers siding with the migrant workers. Responding to the pressure, California passed a law giving migrant workers the right to bargain collectively.

Hispanic Americans have clearly benefited from the 1964 Civil Rights Act and other important civil rights legislation first implemented to aid African Americans. For example, a 1968 amendment to the 1964 act funded public school programs that offer English instruction in the language of children for whom English is a second language. In addition, today there are more than five thousand elected Hispanic American officials across the United States. The high-profile victory of Antonio Villaraigosa in the 2005 Los Angeles mayoral race and his campaign for California governor in 2018, as well as the presidential campaign of Senator Marco Rubio (R-FL), signal that this trend is going to continue. In terms of education, college enrollment among Hispanics is rising faster than for any other group. In 2016, equal percentages of Hispanics and whites were attending college.

However, challenges continue. Many citizens believe that Hispanic Americans face more discrimination than other groups because they are at the center of the issue of illegal immigration. On the fundamental question of whether immigrants are viewed as a strength to society, or as a burden on it, a majority now view them as a strength. Since 2006, however, the partisan gap on the question has grown (see "Partisan Gap in Views of Immigrants' Impact "). Generational differences in attitudes, evident since the mid-1990s, have grown wider in recent years. Millennials have the most positive view of the role of immigrants (see "Generational Differences in Views About Immigration").

Asian Americans

The first Asian immigrants to this country were Chinese and Japanese laborers who came to the western United States during the late 1800s to build railroads and work in mines. When the need for railroad laborers declined, Congress passed legislation in 1882 to temporarily halt Chinese immigration. Over the next three decades, the country barred all but a few Asians through a series of informal agreements with Asian governments. In 1921, Congress began to set immigration quotas based on the country of origin. Western European nations were given large quotas and Asian countries very small ones. Only 150 persons of Japanese origin, for instance, could enter the United States annually. In 1930, Congress prohibited immigration from Japan altogether after the Japanese government protested a California law barring anyone of Japanese descent from buying property in the state. Discrimination against Asian immigration did not end until 1965, when Congress adjusted quotas to favor those groups who had previously been targets of discrimination.

World War II marked the darkest chapter in the history of Japanese American civil rights. The Japanese attack on Pearl Harbor that brought the United States into the war

Partisan Gap in Views of Immigrants' Impact

Which comes closer to your view? Immigrants today. . . (%)

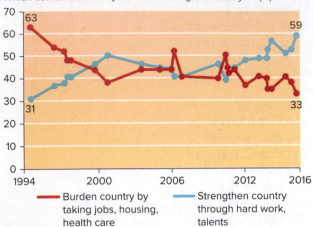

Legend:
— Burden country by taking jobs, housing, health care
— Strengthen country through hard work, talents

% who say immigrants today strengthen the country because of their hard work and talents . . .

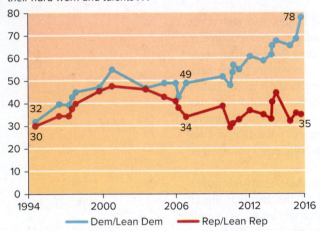

Legend:
— Dem/Lean Dem
— Rep/Lean Rep

A majority of Americans believe that immigrants strengthen the country. Seventy-eight percent of Democrats support the positive impact view of immigrants, compared to only 35 percent of Republicans.

©Buyenlarge/Getty Images

During World War II, more than a hundred thousand Japanese Americans living in the states of California, Oregon, and Washington were placed in internment camps.

Generational Differences in Views About Immigration

% who say immigrants today strengthen the country because of their hard work and talents ...

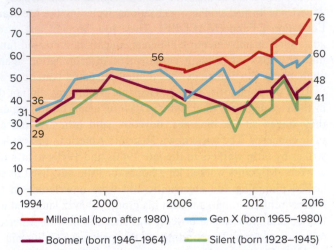

Legend:
— Millennial (born after 1980)
— Gen X (born 1965–1980)
— Boomer (born 1946–1964)
— Silent (born 1928–1945)

Millennials view immigration more positively than any previous generation.

made Japanese Americans the objects of fear and hatred, especially on the West Coast. Shortly after Pearl Harbor, Japanese Americans living on the West Coast were subject to nightly curfews. In February 1942, President Franklin D. Roosevelt issued an executive order removing more than a hundred thousand Japanese Americans from their homes in California, Oregon, and Washington and placing them in internment camps for the duration of the war. In *Korematsu v. United States* (1944), the U.S. Supreme Court ruled the internment was constitutional. Noting the law was based on a racial classification, the Court applied the strict scrutiny test. The Court held, however, that the security of the United States was a compelling governmental interest and that interning Japanese Americans was the least restrictive means to identify potentially disloyal members of the population. Concluding that war involved hardship, the Court ruled the treatment of Japanese Americans was not a civil rights violation. In the late 1980s, Congress expressed its disagreement with this view and granted benefits to former internees.

Asian Americans are the fastest-growing minority group in the United States today, growing from 11.9 million in 2000 to 20.4 million in 2015. Most of the increase comes from international migration. (See the figure entitled "Growth of Asian and Hispanic Populations.") No single country of origin dominates the U.S. Asian population, but the largest groups are of Chinese, Indian, or Filipino descent. They have gained prominent positions in American society and experienced notable academic success. However, Asian Americans' academic success has not yet been matched by corresponding positions in business management, the professions, or political office; nor have young Asian Americans exhibited high levels of political engagement.

Disabled Americans

After every war over the past century, disabled Americans have lobbied hard for antidiscrimination laws. World War I veterans were largely responsible for the first rehabilitation laws passed in the late 1920s. Following the civil rights campaigns of the 1960s, World War II, Korean War, and Vietnam War veterans began to work for greater protection for disabled Americans.[33] The 1973 Rehabilitation Act added people with disabilities to the list of Americans who were to be protected from discrimination. The 1975 Education of All Handicapped Children Act entitled all children to a free public education appropriate to their needs. Prior to the legislation, four million disabled students were receiving either no education or one that did not fit their needs.

The crowning piece of legislation for Americans with disabilities was the 1990 Americans with Disabilities Act (ADA). It guarantees all Americans access to public facilities, workplaces, and communication services. The statute requires schools, governments, and businesses to make existing facilities accessible. Wheelchair ramps leading to doors and grab bars in restrooms have become common sights on the American landscape since 1990. Yet a 2004 survey of disabled Americans conducted by *USA Today* reveals that a majority of them do not believe the law has made a difference in their lives and that four in ten do not expect their quality of life to improve.

Recent Supreme Court rulings have both extended and limited the impact of the ADA. In 1999, the Court ruled that students who require special care at school are entitled to it as long as they do not need a physician to deliver that care.[34] The year before, the Court added persons afflicted with acquired immune deficiency syndrome (AIDS) to the list of those persons protected by the ADA.[35] In contrast, the Court ruled that people with bad eyesight or high blood pressure were not protected, because they can function normally when they wear glasses or take their medicine.[36] Yet, disabled Americans have clearly benefited from the 1973 Rehabilitation Act, the 1975 Education of All Handicapped Children Act, and the 1990 Americans with Disabilities Act, which protect them from discrimination and increase opportunities. In early 2018, the House of Representatives passed a bill that would remove incentives to businesses to provide the handicapped with access to their facilities.

Growth of Asian and Hispanic Populations

Percent of total population change from 2012 to 2013 accounted for by ...

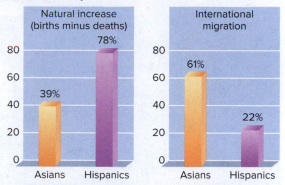

Note: Asians include mixed-race populations, regardless of Hispanic origin.

Hispanic growth in the United states is accounted for by a high birth rate, whereas Asian growth is the result of international migration.

Korematsu v. United States The 1944 Supreme Court decision that upheld the constitutionality of the U.S. government's internment of more than one hundred thousand Americans of Japanese descent during World War II.

American Seniors

Today, 38 million Americans are 65 years of age or older, and that number is likely to double by the year 2025. You will read later about the emergence of "gray power" in the political system. AARP, for example, has become one of the most powerful interest groups in Washington, D.C., advocating for seniors' rights. Nevertheless, elderly Americans still face various forms of age discrimination such as mandatory retirement rules and cost-cutting measures that target older, higher-paid workers for termination or layoffs. Some professional and graduate schools reject older applicants on the grounds that they will have fewer years to work in their professions upon graduation.

At the height of the civil rights movement in 1967, Congress passed the Age Discrimination in Employment Act (ADEA) that protected workers over the age of 40 from age discrimination unless an employer proved that age was a bona fide occupational qualification. The law even applied to an older worker who was replaced by a younger worker who also fell under the protection of ADEA.[37] In 1975, civil rights legislation denied federal funds to any institution discriminating against persons over 40 because of their age. Congress amended the ADEA in 1978 to raise the age of mandatory retirement from 65 to 70. In 1986, Congress phased out mandatory retirement for all but a few occupations, such as firefighting.

In dealing with cases of age discrimination, the Supreme Court uses the rational basis test. It has upheld a state law requiring police officers to retire at the age of 50.[38] In 2000, by contrast, the Court made it easier to win age discrimination cases with circumstantial evidence and inferences drawn from that evidence.[39] In the 2005 case of *Smith v. City of Jackson,*

Older Americans continue to work for material and social reasons, but they often face discrimination in the workplace.

homophobia Irrational fear and hatred directed toward persons who are homosexuals.

Mississippi, the Court may have also expanded the protection of the ADEA. The Court ruled that a person 40 years of age or older can sue if an employer's policies, practices, or other employment actions have a negative effect on older employees, even if unintentional. But in another ruling, the Court, on the basis of the doctrine of sovereign immunity, disallowed age discrimination suits by plaintiffs against any state and local government entities without their consent.[40] Seniors fared better in a 2008 Court decision regarding the federal government. A seven-member majority ruled that federal workers who file claims of age discrimination have the same protections from retaliation as they would in the private sector.[41]

Gay and Lesbian Americans

Some scholars argue that gay and lesbian Americans have had a more difficult time in achieving equality than other minority groups.[42] They must contend with negative stereotyping and **homophobia**. Fear and hatred of homosexuals is deeply rooted in our culture and sometimes finds violent expression. The death of political science student Matthew Shepard is a particularly poignant example. The 21-year-old University of Wyoming student was attacked after attending a meeting for Gay Awareness Week on his campus. After being hit repeatedly in the head with a pistol, and kicked repeatedly in the groin, he was left tied to a fence to die by himself.

Although exact numbers are difficult to obtain, millions of Americans identify themselves as homosexual. Homosexuals enjoy higher average incomes and educational levels than other minority groups, but until recently they were not able to convert these resources into an effective drive for equal rights. Overcoming cultural bias and the strong stance taken by many religious groups against homosexuality has proved to be a daunting task. By 2017, a majority of Americans disagreed with the statement that society should discourage homosexuality, but the gap between Republicans and Democrats on this proposition is growing (see "Should Society Discourage Homosexuality?").

The triggering event of the gay and lesbian rights movement in the United States was a police raid on the Stonewall Inn in New York City on June 27, 1969. The patrons of the popular gay and lesbian bar responded by throwing beer bottles and cans to protest what they viewed as constant police harassment. Stonewall had a galvanizing effect on the gay community. "Gay Power" signs appeared in the city, and gay and lesbian groups such as the Gay Activist Alliance and the Gay Liberation Front began to organize to combat invidious discrimination. Soon hundreds, and then thousands, of state and local organizations sprang up to exert pressure on legislatures, the media, churches, and schools to change laws and public attitudes toward homosexuals.

Gay and lesbian groups have achieved some significant political results at the state and local levels of government. Presently, several states and more than two hundred cities have statutes protecting gays and lesbians from discrimination in employment, credit, housing, and public accommodations. In 1996, the U.S. Supreme Court struck down an amendment to the Colorado state constitution that invalidated state and local laws protecting gays and lesbians. The Court held the Colorado amendment to be in violation of the equal protection clause of the U.S. Constitution.[43]

At the national level, the government lifted a ban on hiring gay men and lesbians and repealed a law that prohibited gay men and lesbians from immigrating to the United States. President Bill Clinton's attempt to lift the ban on gays in the armed services, however, met resistance from military leaders who viewed homosexuality as incompatible with

Should Society Discourage Homosexuality?

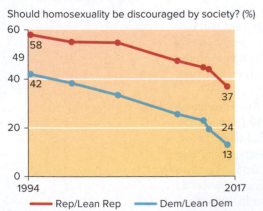

Should homosexuality be discouraged by society? (%)

A majority of Americans disagree with the statement that "Homosexuality should be discouraged by society." The disagreement is stronger among Democrats, but identifiers of both parties are more likely to reject this view than they were in 1994.

military service. The resulting "Don't ask, don't tell" compromise policy prevented the military from inquiring about soldiers' sexual orientation, but also barred gay and lesbian soldiers from revealing their homosexuality. The policy had not served gay and lesbian military personnel well. From the time the policy went into effect in 1993, more than 7,800 gay men and women were forced out of the military. In December 2010, President Obama signed legislation repealing the policy, but the implementation of a new open policy was delayed until the Pentagon ascertained its effect on recruiting. The following month, the U.S. Government Accountability Office reported that the "Don't ask, don't tell" policy had cost the military $193 million from 2004 until 2009. The repeal went into effect in September 2011.

Privacy has been an area of particular concern for gay and lesbian civil rights activists. In the 1970s and 1980s, they were successful in reducing the number of states with antisodomy laws from forty-nine to twenty-four, using both state legislative and judicial strategies. In 1986, however, the Supreme Court ruled that antisodomy legislation in the state of Georgia was constitutional. It held that homosexual sex acts were not a fundamental liberty that was protected by the right to privacy in the Fourteenth Amendment.[44] The Court reversed itself seventeen years later in the case of *Lawrence v. Texas* (2003), ruling that the Fourteenth Amendment protects consenting adults engaging in homosexual behavior in the privacy of their homes. By contrast, the same Court upheld the Boy Scouts' refusal to allow a gay man to serve as a troop leader, based on the premise that such a leader would undermine the organization's "morally straight" values.[45] In 2010, the Supreme Court ruled in favor of gay and lesbian groups in two different cases. It held that a state law school can refuse to recognize a religious student group—with student activity funding, meeting space, and other privileges—that discriminates against gay students in *Christian Legal Society College of Law v. Martinez* (2010). The Court also decided in *Doe v. Reed* (2010) that persons who signed a petition to have an antigay referendum on a state ballot did not have a general First Amendment right to keep their names secret.

One of the most sensitive and controversial issues regarding gay and lesbian rights has been the legalization of same-sex marriages. The issue gained heightened attention in 1993 when the Supreme Court of Hawaii ruled that denying marriage licenses to gay couples might violate the equal protection clause of their state constitution.[46] Many states reacted by prohibiting same-sex marriage. In 1996, Congress passed the Defense of Marriage Act, which prohibited federal recognition of gay and lesbian marriages and allowed state governments to ignore same-sex marriages performed in other states. In 2013, the Supreme Court invalidated the federal law in *United States v. Windsor*. Still the nation remained divided on the issue of same-sex marriage and in which states such marriages were allowed.

The Supreme Court finally brought a sense of uniformity to the issue when they decided the case of *Obergefell V. Hodges* in 2015. By that time, public opinion had shifted to support same-sex marriage; this support continues to grow, particularly among millennials (see "Support for Same-Sex Marriage"). The case was brought by fourteen same-sex

The civil rights of gays and lesbians have been debated within the U.S. judicial system at the local, state, and federal levels as well as within the Supreme Court. A major decision on same-sex marriage came in 2015 when the Supreme Court held that the Fourteenth Amendment requires a state to license same-sex marriages and to recognize same-sex marriages lawfully licensed and performed in another state.

Support for Same-Sex Marriage

% who favor allowing gays and lesbians to marry legally

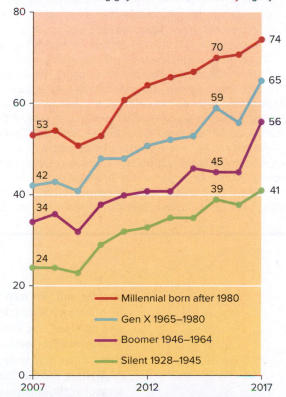

Note: Data for 2007–2015 based on yearly averages.

Support for same-sex marriage has risen among all generations; millennials are the most supportive and the silent generation is the least supportive.

VOTER SUPPRESSION AND THE 2016 ELECTION

In a democracy, the challenge of achieving equality is typically tied to the ability to vote. For African Americans, securing that right has been particularly burdensome. As slaves, they had no political or legal rights at all. Following the end of the Civil War, the Fifteenth Amendment removed race and previous condition of servitude as barriers to voting, but southern states still found ways to suppress the black vote with violence and massive election fraud. When Reconstruction and the federal military occupation of the South ended in 1877, states in the South legalized the disenfranchisement of black voters with poll taxes, literacy tests, property qualifications, and grandfather clauses. Meaningful change did not occur until nearly a century later when the federal government passed the Voting Rights Act in 1965. Section 5 of the statute mandated that any state or local government with a history of discriminatory election practices had to obtain approval of the U.S. attorney general or a panel of three federal judges before implementing any voting changes. Section 4 of the law contained the coverage formula that determined which state and local jurisdictions would be covered by the preclearance mandate. By June 2013, nine states as well as counties and townships in six other states were still required to get preclearance.

In 2008, Democrat Barack Obama became the first African American to win the presidency. His historic campaign drew more people to the polls than the nation had witnessed for forty years. Almost all of the increase came from African American, Hispanic, and young voters, who tend to vote for Democratic candidates. The surge in voting by these groups quickly led to a backlash, with state lawmakers across the country introducing hundreds of bills to restrict voting. Of the twenty-two states that passed new restrictions, eighteen were governed by entirely Republican-controlled bodies. In fact, voting restriction laws are more likely to pass as the proportion of Republicans in a state legislature increases or when a Republican governor is elected.* This suggests that partisanship plays a large part in the passage of such laws.

Of the eleven states with the largest black turnout in 2008, seven passed laws making it harder to vote. One popular type of voter suppression law restricted the opportunity for early voting. In the 2008 and 2012 presidential elections, one-third of Americans voted early and the early black vote was particularly heavy. Ten states made it more difficult for citizens to register to vote by requiring documentary proof of citizenship, eliminating same-day registration, or making it harder for people who move to stay registered. The states of Florida, Iowa, and South Dakota restricted the voting rights of people with past criminal convictions, disenfranchising 1.5 million people in Florida alone. Before 2011, only two states required voters to show government-issued photo IDs at the polls. During the next four years, nine states passed strict new ID laws. Citizens who do not possess driver's licenses or passports must assemble other documents, such as birth certificates, naturalization forms, and proof of residence, and take them to the appropriate election official. Such laws disproportionately affect blacks, Hispanics, the poor, the young, and the elderly.** Fewer people voted in the 2012 presidential election than did four years earlier. In fact, fewer people voted in 2012 than in 2004, even though the number of eligible voters had grown by eight million. Was it the result of apathy or voter suppression?

Amidst this flurry of state laws, in 2013 the Supreme Court invalidated Section 4 of the 1965 Voting Rights Act. In the 5 to 4 decision in *Shelby County v. Holder,* the majority argued that the preclearance requirement was no longer necessary, because the large gap between black and white voter registration numbers in the affected states no longer existed. The dissenting justices argued that the majority failed to recognize a second generation of barriers to ballot access, such as voter identification laws and restrictions on early voting. In the aftermath of the Court's decision, six of the states formerly covered by the federal law passed strict new voter identification laws. The Court's decision puts citizens in the position of having to prove that a new voting law is discriminatory, whereas before the ruling, states had to prove that such new voting laws were not discriminatory.† The 2016 presidential election was the first one in over fifty years to be waged without the full protection of the 1965 Voting Rights Act.

couples and two men whose same-sex partners were deceased. They challenged the laws in Michigan, Kentucky, Ohio, and Tennessee that defined marriage as a union between one man and one woman. When the Supreme Court decided the matter, it held that the Fourteenth Amendment requires a state to license same-sex marriages and to recognize them when they were lawfully licensed and performed in another state.

Writing for the five-person majority on the court, Justice Kennedy first stressed the transcendent importance of marriage in bringing dignity to people. It allows two people to pursue a life that could not be found alone. Second, Kennedy stated that the Fourteenth Amendment not only encompasses most of the rights in the Bill of Rights through the process of selective incorporation, but it also includes certain matters of personal choice that are central to individual dignity and autonomy. The majority went on to

Fourteen states passed new voting restrictions for the first time in 2016, including the crucial swing states of Wisconsin and Virginia. During the summer and early fall of 2016, as the election approached, a string of federal court rulings struck down, blocked, or loosened restrictive voting laws in key states across the nation. A federal court, for instance, blunted Wisconsin's strict new voter ID law, by requiring the state to make temporary voter IDs available on demand to any eligible voter who requested one. Lawyers for the state of Wisconsin pledged that any voter who went to a Department of Motor Vehicles office and presented identification documents would be mailed a temporary voter ID. The problem was that state officials did not keep their word. A voting rights group sent volunteers to DMV offices around the state and recorded their interactions with clerks. Many clerks did not even seem to be familiar with the changes mandated by the federal court, and volunteers were often given inaccurate information regarding how to obtain a temporary voter ID. The result was that many Wisconsin citizens, an estimated 300,000 potential voters, lacked the proper identification documents to vote in the 2016 presidential election. There were 60,000 fewer voters in the 2016 presidential election than in the election before. Donald Trump carried the state by less than 30,000 votes.

Other states resisted federal court rulings as well. When a federal court struck down North Carolina's strict voter ID law in 2016, stating that it targeted African American voters with "almost surgical precision," Republican-controlled county elections boards reduced the number of polling sites in the first week of early voting. In Guilford County, the number of polling sites was reduced from sixteen to one, resulting in voters having to wait hours in long lines. At the end of early voting, a North Carolina Republican memo boasted that African American voting turnout had dropped by 9 percent compared to 2012.[‡] On Election Day, the states of North Carolina, Texas, and Arizona had a total of 868 fewer polling places than in 2012. In Ohio, a federal appeals court blocked a state law that removed voters from the rolls if they had not voted for six years and ordered that the purged voters be restored. The Ohio secretary of state, however, failed to include those previously purged voters on the statewide absentee ballot mailing. In 2018, the Supreme Court ruled on the constitutionality of Ohio's voter purging law in the case of *Husted v. A. Philip Randolph*. A

©Jason Connolly/AFP/Getty Images

closely divided Court held that the Ohio practice which cancels the registration of voters who do not go to the polls and who then fail to respond to a notice does not violate federal law. More states are expected to adopt a similar policy to trim voter rolls.

We will never know precisely how many voters are turned away on Election Day and how many others are so discouraged by the restrictions placed on their voting rights that they opt not to vote.

See Ollstein, A. M. and Lerner, K. "Republicans Were Wildly Successful in Suppressing Voters in 2016," *ThinkProgress*, November 15, 2016, https://thinkprogress.org/2016-a-case-study-in-voter-suppression-258bf90ddcd/.

Source: Weiser, W. R. Weiser, "Voter Suppression: How Bad? (Pretty Bad)," *The American Prospect*, 2014 Fall issue; Keyssar, A. "Voter Suppression Returns," *Harvard Magazine*, July–August 2012; Brandeisky, K. and Tigas, M. "Everything That's Happened Since Supreme Court Ruled on Voting Rights Act," www.propublica.org/article/voting-rights-by-state-map.

*Wendy R. Weiser, "Voter Suppression: How Bad? (Pretty Bad)," *The American Prospect*, 2014 Fall issue.

**Alexander Keyssar, "Voter Suppression Returns," *Harvard Magazine*, July–August 2012.

†Kara Brandeisky and Mike Tigas, "Everything That's Happened Since Supreme Court Ruled on Voting Rights Act," www.propublica.org/article/voting-rights-by-state-map.

‡See Alice Marie Ollstein and Kara Lerner, "Republicans Were Wildly Successful in Suppressing Voters in 2016," ThinkProgress, November 15, 2016, https://thinkprogress.org/2016-a-case-study-in-voter-suppression-258bf90ddcd/.

observe that the generations who wrote and ratified the Bill of Rights and the Fourteenth Amendment entrusted to future generations the ability to expand the body of liberties, to include rights such as same-sex marriage, as current generations recognize them. The Court defended their right to make a decision affecting laws passed by the states by reasoning that, in a constitutional system, people do not have to wait for legislative action to assert a fundamental liberty. Those dissenting stated that the decision had no basis in the Constitution or any past decisions of the Court. They accused the majority of judicial policy making and stressed that the issue of same-sex marriage should have been left to the states. Following this decision, gays and lesbians can now be married in every state.

In 2017, in *Pavan v. Smith*, the Court struck down an Arkansas law that precluded a same-sex couple from being listed as the two parents on their child's birth certificate. Such an exclusion can affect a parent's ability to participate in activities that require proof of parentage. The Court noted that the state allowed a nonbiological father to be listed on a birth certificate if he was married to the biological mother. Then, in 2018, the Supreme Court handed down its decision for the baker in *Masterpiece Cakeshop v. Colorado Civil Rights Commission* while delaying to a future time the issue of whether a business can deny services to gays and lesbians on the grounds of religious beliefs. (The case is featured in the introduction to Chapter 4.)

WOMEN AND CIVIL RIGHTS

The fight for civil rights by women in America differs in many respects from the struggles of the previously discussed groups. First, women do not represent a minority in the United States; there are more women than men in the country. Their struggle for equal rights, therefore, is not based on their small numbers but rather on long-standing historical and cultural assumptions concerning their proper role in society.[47] Second, women began their struggle for civil rights as early as did African Americans, but were thwarted by the dominant male culture. In other words, the civil rights movement for African Americans was not so much a template for the women's movement as a parallel movement.

Historically there have been three high points of activity for the pursuit of women's civil rights, followed by years of little visible or public activity. Although women as early as Abigail Adams discussed the concept of political equality with their prominent husbands, the most active periods of female political mobilization occurred from 1840 to 1875, from 1890 to 1920, and from 1961 to the present.[48] This section examines those three periods of activity and features three issues of current concern: workplace equity, sexual harassment, and women's role in the military.

Early Women's Movement: 1840–1875

The seeds of the early women's movement were planted in 1840 when Lucretia Mott and Elizabeth Cady Stanton accompanied their husbands to London to attend a meeting of the World Anti-Slavery Society. After a long debate, the male participants denied the women the right to participate at the meeting and forced them to sit in the balcony as spectators. This rebuff strengthened Mott and Stanton's determination to work on behalf of women's rights in the United States. Their work was delayed for eight years, however, because both women were raising young children.

The early women's movement was linked with religious revivalism, as well as the abolition movement.[49] Women who were active in these movements established communication networks among themselves, laying the foundation for a movement focusing on women's rights. In 1848, Mott and Stanton organized the first women's rights convention in the small town of Seneca Falls, New York. Over the next twelve years, women's rights groups held seven conventions in different cities. With the outbreak of the Civil War, the movement temporarily suspended its activities to support the Union war effort. After the war, the early feminists learned a cruel political lesson. Despite the critical role they played in abolishing slavery, women were not granted the right to vote by the Fifteenth Amendment. In 1875, the U.S. Supreme Court upheld Missouri's denial of voting rights for women.[50]

The Suffrage Movement: 1890–1920

In 1890, women's rights advocates formed the National American Woman Suffrage Association (NAWSA), with Susan B. Anthony as its leader. Rather than seeking expanded social, legal, economic, and political rights for women, the new association concentrated primarily on securing the vote. Contemporary social trends such as the temperance movement and a concern for the working conditions of women aided the group in its efforts.[51] The tremendous growth of women's clubs in the 1880s and 1890s also invigorated the suffrage movement.[52] Enjoying more free time, white middle-class women joined self-improvement clubs such as reading societies. As women in these clubs became involved in social causes, they soon realized the inferior position shared by all women.

By 1917, the NAWSA boasted over two million members, and the suffrage movement had become a broad social movement. A coalition of groups led by NAWSA secured ratification of the Nineteenth Amendment in 1920, guaranteeing women the right to vote. This success can be credited to the NAWSA's strategies of using popular concern for better working conditions for women and temperance as rallying cries, and the growth of women's clubs that helped organize their efforts.

The suffrage initiative that led to women getting the right to vote in 1920 grew into a broad social movement pressing for such demands as better working conditions for women.

After this historic victory, the coalition that made up the suffrage movement soon disintegrated. Winning the vote was the only goal all the participating women's groups shared, and they failed to reach consensus on a post-suffrage agenda. There was little organized demand for women's rights until the 1960s.

The Second Women's Rights Movement: 1961–Present

The civil rights movement of the 1950s and 1960s attracted many female activists, just as the abolitionist movement had in the nineteenth century. Like their sisters of an earlier era, these activists encountered prejudice and were often treated as second-class citizens by their male activist counterparts. In 1961, the Supreme Court ruled that a jury selection system that virtually excluded women was constitutional because, as the center of home and family life, women should not be burdened with jury duty.[53] This case, and three events that followed in quick succession, initiated the second women's rights movement in the United States.

First, President John F. Kennedy created the President's Commission on the Status of Women in 1961. The commission's 1963 report, *American Women*, documented widespread discrimination against women in all walks of life. That same year, Betty Friedan published her best-selling book *The Feminine Mystique*. Friedan's book challenged women to assert their rights and question the traditional gender assumptions of society. Finally, the 1964 Civil Rights Act prohibited discrimination based not only on race but also on sex. It also created the Equal Employment Opportunity Commission (EEOC) to enforce antidiscrimination measures. When the EEOC failed to enforce sex discrimination laws, female activists formed the National Organization for Women (NOW). Like the NAACP, NOW pledged to work within the system by lobbying for a constitutional equal rights amendment and by using the courts to gain equality.

NOW initially focused on the passage of the **Equal Rights Amendment** (ERA), which was first introduced in Congress in 1923 but was never given a hearing. Its wording was simple and straightforward: "Equality of rights under the law shall not be denied or abridged by the United States or by any state on account of sex." Despite intense efforts by women's rights groups, only thirty-five states voted for ratification, three short of the required three-quarters majority. NOW and other allied groups have been more successful in bringing equal protection cases before the U.S. Supreme Court. Using the intermediate scrutiny test, the Court has prohibited laws that allow women but not men to receive alimony.[54] It has banned single-sex nursing schools.[55] It has also disallowed state prosecutors' use of preemptory challenges to reject either women or men in order to produce a more sympathetic jury.[56] At the same time, the Court has upheld statutory rape laws that apply only to female victims[57] and draft registration laws that apply only to males.[58]

Equal Rights Amendment The proposed constitutional amendment that would have prohibited national and state governments from denying equal rights on the basis of sex.

The modern women's movement has placed significant emphasis on involving women in politics. Although women vote more than men, the number of women holding political office is still significantly lower than their share of the population. Yet this trend seems to be changing: in 2006 Nancy Pelosi became the first female Speaker of the House, and

The initial focus of the second women's movement was passage of the Equal Rights Amendment, which ultimately failed.

Hillary Clinton emerged as the nation's first female presidential candidate to lead in national polls. Then, in 2008, Sarah Palin became the second woman to be chosen as a vice presidential candidate of a major party. During the Obama administration, women served as secretaries of state, health and human services, homeland security, and labor as well as Environmental Protection Agency administrator and the United Nations ambassador. In 2016, Hillary Clinton nearly became the first elected female president.

Female legislative candidates scored impressive victories in the 2018 mid-term elections. Women will hold at least 100 seats in the House of Representatives (pending a few races yet decided at the time of publication) and 24 seats in the Senate that will most likely expand to 25 after the Mississippi run-off election. Both totals represented the greatest number of women ever in each of the two houses of Congress. The number of first-time female House members in 2019 surpassed the previous record set in the 1992 "Year of the Woman" elections.

In terms of how women vote, they are more likely to vote for the Democrat presidential candidate than their male counterparts. this difference has produced a significant gender gap that reached its high mark in 2016. (See the figure entitled "The Gender Gap in Presidential Elections.")

Current Issues

By redefining their status in American society, women entered more fully into the public lives of their communities. This move into more public arenas of society gave rise to several issues that are particularly relevant to women's groups of today: workplace equity, sexual harassment, and women's role in the military.

Workplace Equity American life has changed dramatically since the first debates on the ERA. Very few modern women fit the traditional role of stay-at-home wife and mom. More than seventy million American women are in the workplace—some 60 percent of all adult females in the country—and a majority of those are married. Two-thirds of American mothers who have children under school age work outside the home. Women now constitute a majority of the American civilian workforce.

The Gender Gap in Presidential Elections

	Men	Women	Difference
1992	+4	+8	4 pts.
1996	+1	+15	14 pts.
2000	−7	+8	15 pts.
2004	−12	+4	16 pts.
2008	0	+14	14 pts.
2012	−8	+12	20 pts.
2016	−12	+12	24 pts.

Figures represent lead/deficit for Democratic candidates among men and women in each election, in percentage points.

Source: USA Today, November 9, 2016.

Congressional legislation to promote fairness in the workplace dates to the Equal Pay Act of 1963. The legislation requires equal pay for equal work, regardless of sex. It does not address the fact that some jobs traditionally filled by women (such as nurses and secretaries) pay less than jobs traditionally held by men (such as construction workers and truck drivers). In 1972, Congress gave the EEOC the power to sue employers suspected of illegal gender discrimination. The 1991 Civil Rights and Women's Equity in Employment Act shifted the burden of proof by requiring employers to demonstrate that their hiring and promotion practices are solely related to job performance. In 2009, Congress passed the "Lilly Ledbetter Fair Pay Act," which makes it easier to file a lawsuit claiming unfair wages based on gender.

Despite these efforts, women still earn less than men earn. When the Equal Pay Act was passed, a female earned, on average, 59 cents for every dollar earned by a male. By 2010, the figure increased to 82 percent of a man's pay for full-time working women in terms of median weekly earnings. However, the figure dropped to 79 percent for women in full-time management, professional, and related occupations.

By 2016, women's median annual earnings continued to lag behind those of men. Projections in one study predicted that pay equity could come by 2059, but a second projection predicted that such equity would have to wait until 2119 (see "Women's Median Annual Earnings as a Percentage of Men's for Full-Time, Year-Round Workers, 1960–2016 and Projections"). The pay equity gap in terms of median weekly earnings increases as women get older and have more education (see "Median Weekly Earnings, by Age and Gender, 2016" and "Median Weekly Earnings, by Level of Education and Gender, 2016"). Some authors suggest that wage justice can be secured only by adopting a **comparable worth** policy.[59] Such a policy attempts to compare dissimilar jobs in terms of knowledge, effort, skill, responsibility, and working conditions. Jobs that are equivalent in these terms should be compensated equally. Proponents of this approach argue that society historically has devalued jobs traditionally performed by women. Opponents argue that differing pay scales between jobs simply reflect free market economic forces and personal job preferences. In

comparable worth The notion that individuals performing different jobs that require the same amount of knowledge, effort, skill, responsibility, and working conditions should receive equal compensation; the proposal would elevate the pay structure of many jobs traditionally performed by women.

Women's Median Annual Earnings as a Percentage of Men's for Full-Time, Year-Round Workers, 1960 to 2016 and Projections

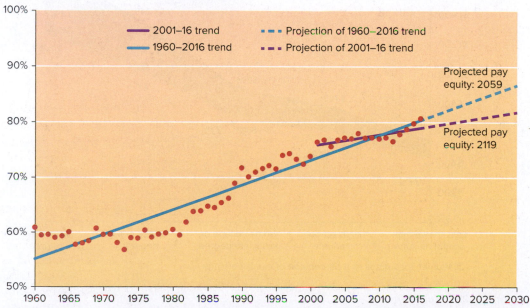

Women's median annual earnings continue to lag behind men's, and projections suggest they will continue to do so in the foreseeable future.

Source: *The Simple Truth About the Gender Pay Gap* Report (Spring 2018), American Association of University Women (AAUW).

Median Weekly Earning, by Age and Gender, 2016

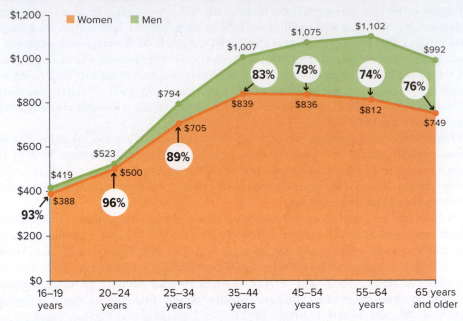

% Women's earnings as a percentage of men's earnings

Note: Based on median usual weekly earnings of full-time wage and salary workers, 2016 annual averages

Median weekly earnings show that as women get older, the pay equity gap increases.

Source: *The Simple Truth About the Gender Pay Gap* Report (Spring 2018), American Association of University Women (AAUW).

Median Weekly Earnings, by Level of Education and Gender, 2016

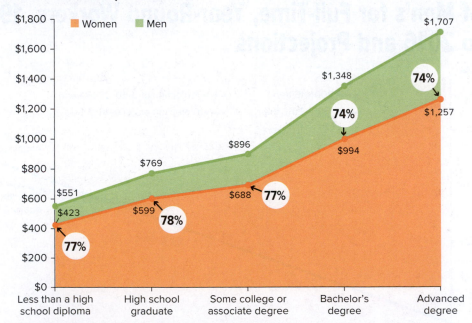

% Women's earnings as a percentage of men's earnings

Note: Based on median usual weekly earnings of full-time wage and salary workers, ages 25 and older.

Median weekly earnings show that pay equity for women gets slightly worse among women with more education.

Source: *The Simple Truth About the Gender Pay Gap* Report (Spring 2018), American Association of University Women (AAUW).

2011, the Supreme Court heard a case that had the potential to clarify workplace equity for women with respect to pay and promotion decisions. Approximately 1.6 million women brought a discrimination case against Wal-Mart seeking billions of dollars in back pay. Dividing along ideological lines, the five-member Court majority held that the case could not proceed as a class action suit because the female employees' claims did not have enough in common to form one lawsuit. The liberal dissenters in *Wal-Mart Stores, Inc. v. Dukes* argued that the common elements were Wal-Mart's uniform policy over pay and promotions.

Workplace equity may involve more than equal pay for equal work. In 2006, Peggy Young, a delivery driver for United Parcel Service (UPS), requested a leave of absence to undergo an *in vitro* fertilization procedure. The request was granted and Young became pregnant after the procedure. During her pregnancy, Young was told by her physicians not to lift more than 20 pounds. UPS, however, has a policy that their employees must be able to lift up to 70 pounds. Not being able to fulfill this work requirement, Young was forced to take an extended, unpaid leave of absence during which time she lost her medical coverage. She later sued the company arguing that she had been the victim of both gender- and disability- based discrimination under the Pregnancy Discrimination Act and the Americans with Disabilities Act. In 2015, the Court ruled in *Young v. United Parcel Service* that the Pregnancy Discrimination Act did allow a plaintiff to show that she faced different treatment from her employer more likely than not based on discriminatory motivation.

Although women continue to gain important jobs in the private and public sectors, a gap still exists between the salaries paid to women and men.

Sexual Harassment With men and women spending more time together in the workplace, **sexual harassment** has become an increasingly important issue for American women. The Supreme Court has ruled that sexual harassment qualifies as gender discrimination under Title VII of the 1964 Civil Rights Act if it is so pervasive as to create a hostile or abusive work environment.[60] In 1993, the Court reinforced its position in *Harris v. Forklift Systems*, in which a female employee complained that her boss made numerous offensive remarks and sexual innuendos, such as asking her to remove coins from his pockets. Under that ruling, plaintiffs are not required to prove the workplace is so hostile as to cause severe psychological injury or prevent them from performing their jobs. The Court emphasized that federal law protects a plaintiff up to the point at which the harassment leads to serious psychological difficulty.

In two 1998 cases, the Court addressed the employer's responsibility for sexual harassment committed by its managers. In *Faragher v. City of Boca Raton,* the Court ruled that an employer is responsible for a supervisor's sexual harassment of an employee even if the employer is unaware of the sexual harassment. The Supreme Court thus made it easier for employees to win such cases and placed a burden on employers to take reasonable steps to prevent harassing behavior at the work site. The Court also ruled in 1998 that an employer can be held liable for sexual harassment caused by a supervisor's actions, even though the employee suffered no job-related harm.[61]

In 1999, the Court turned its attention to sexual harassment in the public schools. The Court determined in *Davis v. Monroe County Board of Education* that a school district was liable for one student harassing another if the school had knowledge of the harassment or was deliberately indifferent to it. The harassment must be so severe, pervasive, and objectively offensive that it deprives the victims of access to the educational opportunities provided by the school. Sexual harassment and sexual abuse against female students at the military service academies have led to congressional and military inquiries, but the Supreme Court has yet to hear a case on the matter.

In 2017, the issue of sexual harassment became a central focus when reports of movie producer Harvey Weinstein's acts of sexual harassment and sexual assault became known. National exposure of the issue led to an outpouring of similar stories across all American industries and the dramatic firings of notable persons such as Matt Lauer and Charlie Rose

sexual harassment The practice of awarding jobs or job benefits in exchange for sexual favors, or the creation of a hostile work or education environment by unwarranted sexual advances or sexual conversation.

©Ryan McVay/Getty Images

and the resignation of Senator Al Franken. Women began the #MeToo movement to encourage other women to come forward and share their experiences. It remains to be seen how the movement will affect public policy in the future.

Women's Role in the Military Until 1948, women served the military in separate units such as the Women's Army Corps (WACs) and the Nurse Corps. Since that time, the sexes have served together in regular noncombat military units, and women currently make up about 15 percent of the American armed forces. The integration of women into the regular armed forces raises a variety of controversial issues, perhaps the most contentious of which involves women's role in combat.

The Obama administration took on that controversial issue when then–defense secretary Leon Panetta announced in 2013 that the Pentagon had lifted the military's ban on women in combat. The change in policy opened up potentially hundreds of thousands of additional front-line jobs. American public opinion has been supportive of the change

©Alliance Images/Alamy Stock Photo

Women serving in wars face the same dangers as their male counterparts.

(see "Americans' Support for Allowing Women to Serve in Combat"). By 2016, Congress was debating the inclusion of females in the registration process for a potential draft system.

CIVIL RIGHTS AND CIVIC ENGAGEMENT TODAY

We have seen in this chapter that the pursuit of civil rights is related to political mobilization. Political mobilization is the process by which candidates, parties, activists, interest groups, and social movements induce other people to engage in politics. As we discuss later in the book, people are more likely to engage in politics if they are asked. They are also more likely to participate if they possess resources such as time, skill, knowledge, and self-confidence. Mobilization for the civil rights goals of political, social, and economic equality creates a problem for activists because the people most affected lack many of the resources related to political participation. As a result, initial civil rights activity often involves attempts to influence judicial bodies, which requires relatively fewer resources. Federal court judges, in addition, are more insulated from political pressures than are members of Congress and the president. As a result, they are often more willing to make broad-reaching decisions regarding the social and political fabric of the country that, in the short run, may run afoul of public opinion but, ultimately, may gain public acceptance and result in a more just society.

Americans' Support for Allowing Women to Serve in Combat

Suppose that on election day you could vote on key issues as well as candidates. Would you vote for or against a law that would allow women to serve in combat?

	Would vote "for" allowing women in combat	Would vote "against" allowing women in combat	No Opinion
	%	%	%
Total	74	20	6
Men	73	22	5
Women	76	18	6
Democrat/Lean Democratic	83	14	3
Republican/Lean Republican	70	28	2
18 to 49 years	84	10	6
50 and older	63	32	5

Military policy leaders have followed the public's support for women in combat. The Defense Department lifted all gender-based restrictions on military service in January 2016.

Source: Gallup Poll, January 24, 2013.

Thinking It Through ≫≫

Learning Objective: Demonstrate knowledge of the civil rights movement for women.

Review: Women and Civil Rights

In the autumn of 2017, American film producer and former film studio executive Harvey Weinstein was fired by the board of his business amid scores of allegations that he committed acts of sexual assault, sexual harassment, and rape against women who were in the movie industry or wanted to become stars. As the story unfolded, it became clear the movie mogul's predatory behavior had gone on for decades without any negative consequences for Weinstein. Following the accusations against Weinstein, women made accusations against other prominent men, launching the #MeToo movement mentioned in the chapter. How does the #MeToo movement fit into the larger movement for equal rights for women? How does it differ from earlier efforts?

Summary

1. **How has the Supreme Court's attitude toward the civil rights of African Americans evolved?**
   - Civil rights issues concern the protection of all persons in historically disadvantaged groups from discriminatory action, but the struggle for civil rights in the United States is most often associated with African Americans.
   - The Supreme Court embraced the concept of slavery in the *Dred Scott* case.
   - The Court approved the doctrine of segregation in *Plessy v. Ferguson.*
   - The concept of de jure equality was recognized in the *Brown* decision.
   - Today, the Court struggles with the concept of affirmative action.

2. **How have other minority groups benefited from the civil rights struggles of African Americans?**
   - The civil rights struggles of African Americans have served as a road map for other groups in terms of tactics and inspiration.
   - Other disadvantaged groups such as Native Americans, Hispanic Americans, Asian Americans, disabled Americans, American seniors, and gay and lesbian Americans have used the civil rights tactics of litigation and social protest employed by African Americans as a template for their own struggles for equality.
   - The Court has used different interpretations of the equal protection clause of the Fourteenth Amendment to assess the unique problems faced by members of different groups, such as access for disabled persons, language and immigration issues for Hispanic groups, and homophobic attitudes faced by gays and lesbians.

3. **What was unique in women's struggles for civil rights in the United States?**
   - Women are the only other group besides African Americans whose struggles for equality led to massive social movements.
   - Their first movement led to disappointment when women were left out of the freedoms granted after the Civil War.
   - Decades later, a massive movement led to the Nineteenth Amendment granting the right to vote.
   - The most recent movement has included women under the protection of civil rights legislation and has opened up debates on workplace equity, sexual harassment, and military roles.

Chapter 6

Public Opinion

CHANGING TIDES OF PUBLIC OPINION

It seems paradoxical: Barack Obama voters voting for Donald Trump in 2016. How could support for a black progressive morph into

©Saul Loeb/AFP/Getty Images

Donald Trump tapped in to the economic anxieties of many Americans as well as their concerns about what it means to be an American.

support for a populist accused of racial insensitivity and sexual harassment? Shortly after the 2016 election, the *Atlantic* magazine asked Trump voters who reported they had previously voted for Obama to explain the reasons for their choice.

One reader complained about Hillary Clinton's support for globalism. A second was turned off by the Democrat's focus on political correctness, noting that those who question liberal ideas about multiculturalism are sometimes treated like bigots. "It creates a sense of shame and anger," he wrote. "Like other slurs, it shuts down the conversation immediately and creates a mutual distrust."[1]

A third reader, taking umbrage at the term *deplorables* that Hillary Clinton used to describe Trump voters, submitted a poem to anti-Trump protesters, reading, in part:

> I'm sorry you are hurt. I hurt too. In 2008 I voted for Obama. In 2012, I didn't vote at all. Either way, it didn't matter. Nothing changed . . . I still didn't have enough money to pay my mortgage, which had tripled. Neither did my family, my neighbors, my friends. And my job disappeared, over the Pacific, or the Atlantic. I forget . . . I looked in my refrigerator and then I stood in line at the food bank where they gave me rancid cake mix—did you know a cake mix can get rancid? I watched. I waited. Along with my family, my neighbors, and my friends. We held our breath as the Bail Out began.[2]

It is estimated that approximately 9 percent of Trump voters backed Obama in 2012. Although this is not a huge number, it should be remembered that the 2016 election was won by a combined 77,744 votes, coming from three key battleground states of Pennsylvania, Wisconsin, and Michigan.[3] Understanding why some voters switched from Obama to Trump is important not only to political candidates and their parties but also to students of public opinion trying to analyzing emerging trends. Some of the reasons for the switch may be idiosyncratic, but are there common elements that can help us understand the direction of American politics today?

As You READ

- **What is public opinion, and why is it important?**
- **How is opinion best measured, and how do we know these measures are reliable?**
- **What are some of the most basic features of American public opinion today?**

As researchers drill into the numbers, two factors seem particularly noteworthy in understanding Trump's success. Trump tapped in to a growing backlash against international trade deals that many Americans believe are responsible for a decline in good middle-class jobs and incomes.[4] Although both Trump and Clinton attempted to capitalize on this trend by opposing new trade deals, Donald Trump's rhetoric proved more convincing to many—especially those in Rustbelt regions of the upper Midwest.

Second—and perhaps more important—whites without a college degree continued to migrate away from the Democratic Party over issues of race and immigration. These voters had a less favorable opinion about immigration, black people, and Muslims than either Democrats or Republicans with a college degree, and they may have been more susceptible to appeals from the Trump campaign regarding a Muslim ban and building a wall between the United States and Mexico. They also may have been anxious about Clinton's "Better Together" theme, which seemed to embrace the nation's growing multiethnic population. In other words, divisions over race and immigration may have become more important in 2016 in part because the candidates put these issues front and center in the campaigns.[5]

Although these findings from the 2016 election raise questions about the future of race and immigration in America, they should not obscure the long-term continuities of American public opinion of a more inclusive nature. For example, most Americans continue to respect our political institutions and laws and accept people of diverse backgrounds. More agree that demographic change will likely produce cultural enrichment and economic growth than believe there will be too many demands on government services or not enough jobs.[6]

Understanding public opinion requires careful analysis. Short-term changes may obscure long-term trends. Yet, abrupt changes may also signal new directions. Public opinion is not uniform but must be understood in light of the views of various subpopulations. Public opinion must be interpreted in light of the intensity with which individuals hold particular views. Those for whom an issue is most salient are more likely to act on their beliefs and make their voices heard. Meanwhile, political actors may be attuned only to some voices while filtering out others.

In this chapter, we will investigate the nature of public opinion: how it is formed, how it is shaped, how it is measured, and how and why it motivates some people to take action. We will also identify some of the prominent and enduring contours of American public opinion as well as ways in which it continues to change. ■

UNDERSTANDING PUBLIC OPINION IN THE CONTEXT OF AMERICAN POLITICS

It seems logical that a nation founded on the consent of the governed should recognize and respect the opinions of the people. However, what is less clear is exactly what opinions policymakers should pay attention to, how these opinions are to be gauged, and how political leaders should accommodate them. Should policymakers be more responsive to the opinions of a majority of their constituents, even if ill informed, or to a minority of knowledgeable and better educated civic and business leaders, or **elites**? Some political leaders believe that policies should principally be fashioned by the will of the people; others find popular opinions must be tempered by a consideration of the potential problems popular opinions might pose. For example, although many Americans want to limit free trade, believing that it costs jobs at home, policymakers need to take into consideration the potential for trade wars that might leave their constituents even worse off. Over the years, the ways in which opinion has been valued, measured, and utilized have changed dramatically.

elites Individuals in a position of authority, often those with a higher level education than the population at large.

The Nature of Public Opinion

Political scientist V. O. Key, Jr., once defined **public opinion** as "those opinions held by private persons which governments find it prudent to heed."[7] Key's definition points out certain essential aspects of public opinion. First, public opinion attaches itself to issues of public, rather than private, concern. Of course, the dividing line between private and public life is fluid and often contentious. Most Americans view sexual behavior as a private matter, but public debate over issues like abortion and transgender rights continues unabated.

public opinion Opinions held by private individuals that governments find it prudent to heed.

political culture The dominant values and beliefs of a political community.

Second, public opinion sets boundaries on the type and expanse of policy proposals that citizens find acceptable. These boundaries reflect a respect for historical precedent and institutional arrangements, as well as for the political culture that informs our democratic republic.[8] A people's **political culture** is its historically rooted values and beliefs about government. Our political culture emphasizes support for the values of liberty, individualism, equality of opportunity, and private property.[9] Although policy boundaries are flexible, these values structure the types of solutions that Americans are most willing to support. For example, unlike societies such as Sweden that provide extensive "cradle-to-grave" government services, American political culture supports a far more limited government role in meeting individual needs such as health care and income security. As a result, we provide limited support for those who demonstrate need, rather than blanket coverage for all citizens.

Third, Key's definition suggests that it might be more important for the government to heed the opinions of some citizens rather than those of others. The public comprises various groups of individuals, some of whom are more visible to political leaders or more attentive to certain issues at particular times. When considering health-care reform, for example, political leaders are especially attentive to the views of health-care professionals, such as doctors. Physicians not only have expertise in this matter but also are likely to react intensely to changes that adversely affect their practice, and they can mount substantial opposition

Public figures seldom pass up the opportunity to "press the flesh" to gain firsthand knowledge of public opinion.

© Jessica McGowan/Getty Images

to measures they deem ill conceived. Similarly, the elderly, who consume more health-care dollars, are more likely to be attentive to changes in health care than are young people, who are more concerned about other issues.

Finally, opinion is different from judgment. Opinions can sometimes reflect momentary feelings based on little reflection. Judgments form slowly over time with the infusion of information and thought. That is why there sometimes appears to be a difference between "overnight polls" that are taken by media outlets in response to events such as mass shootings and long-term support for policies about gun control. Political leaders understand this difference and are more likely to react to settled judgments than to momentary bursts of opinion.

Changes in Assessing and Using Public Opinion

The Framers felt that the opinions of common people were best limited to expression at the ballot box. In *The Federalist* No. 71, Alexander Hamilton wrote:

> The republican principle demands that the deliberative sense of the community should guide the conduct of those to whom they entrust the management of their affairs; but it does not require an unqualified complaisance to every sudden breeze of passion, or to every transient impulse which the people may receive from the arts of men, who flatter their prejudices to betray their interest. . . .[10]

Fear of faction and mob rule caused colonial leaders to be suspicious of popular attitudes. Nevertheless, political leaders were never indifferent to public attitudes. George Washington corresponded with a friend in Virginia, David Stuart, whom he relied on to mingle with ordinary people in order to find out what they thought about presidential actions.[11] And presidents have always spent time "pressing flesh" to engender support and good feelings.

Before the era of scientific polling, political leaders attempted to gauge popular support from a variety of sources. Newspaper reports and editorials provided officials with some measure of information regarding popular attitudes. In the era of the party press (see Chapter 10), however, few reports were objective. From Jackson through Lincoln, it was common for presidents to curry favor with journalists and editors by appointing them to government offices.[12] When the partisan press gave way to the commercial press in the second half of the nineteenth century, politicians paid close attention to opinions conveyed in newspapers printed in their home districts. They also often attempted to influence press coverage of their campaigns. Members of Congress sent newsletters to constituents extolling their skills at representation, and these were often reprinted verbatim in local newspapers.

Party leaders in wards and precincts could sometimes predict election results with uncanny accuracy—a result of both their proximity to average citizens and their ability to turn out those who supported their candidate. In some cases, informal polls were conducted by party leaders at political rallies among partisan supporters with predictable results duly reported to cheering crowds.

A variety of ad hoc methods of sampling also produced often surprisingly accurate portraits of public opinion. Tavern owners placed "poll books" in their establishments, where townspeople could register their preferences. **Straw polls**, which sampled opinions from lists of experts, journalists, or subscribers to particular newspapers or consumer services, became popular at the turn of the twentieth century.[13] The *Literary Digest* magazine conducted perhaps the most famous of these polls, mailing millions of ballots to people from across the country from lists generated by automobile registration records and telephone directories. Despite the unscientific nature of its poll, the *Digest* accurately picked presidential winners in 1924, 1928, and 1932. In 1936, the magazine's luck ran out when it predicted an electoral victory for Alf Landon; it went out of the polling business shortly thereafter.[14]

That same year, George Gallup issued his first scientifically designed presidential election poll, based on emerging marketing research techniques. After accurately predicting Franklin D. Roosevelt's win, Gallup's newly created American Institute of Public Opinion quickly became a world leader in survey research, conducting weekly polls for a number of newspapers across the country. Gallup did not intend that politicians should slavishly follow survey results, however, and many did not. In the decades that followed, many political leaders advanced policies well beyond the mainstream of public opinion by advocating bold

straw poll An unscientific survey of popular views.

initiatives in areas such as race relations and civil liberties. For these public opinion leaders, polls provided not so much a road map for political success as a way of gauging how far they could advance reforms before facing serious resistance.

Today, survey research is ubiquitous. Hardly a day goes by when we do not hear about one poll or another regarding almost every aspect of life, from health care to fashion to politics. Survey research can aid in making life more enjoyable and bringing public policies more in line with public sentiment. However, it can also be used to manipulate preferences and behavior. More than ever, citizens must be able to navigate their way through polls and to understand the nature and limits of public opinion in a democracy.

HOW POLITICAL OPINIONS ARE FORMED

Individuals develop opinions about the political world from a host of sources, including family, friends, schools, and the media. We form many of the enduring attitudes, values, and beliefs that shape our opinions early in life through a process called **political socialization**. Even so, we constantly form new opinions and revise old ones as we confront new issues, new people, and new technologies.

> **political socialization** The process by which individuals come to adopt the attitudes, values, beliefs, and opinions of their political culture.

The Process of Socialization

Pioneering studies in the 1950s and 1960s demonstrated that children begin forming impressions about the political communities in which they live as early as preschool age.[15] They embrace national symbols, such as the flag, and associate authority figures like police and firefighters with the protective functions of government. Impressions at this stage are fairly positive, although the strength of these sentiments may vary among subcultures and minority populations.[16] Children also develop an awareness of national, racial, and gender differences in early grade school, along with friendly or hostile feelings toward specific groups. Even at this early stage, gender differences seem to appear regarding issues of war and peace, with boys more likely than girls to support aggression.[17]

As children approach adolescence, they become more skeptical of political authority, begin differentiating leaders they like from those they dislike, and learn to distinguish between the major political parties. Much of their awareness remains impressionistic at this stage. It is only with late adolescent maturity that we come to associate issue and party positions with particular ideological viewpoints, such as liberalism or conservatism. Many of the political opinions we develop in youth have sticking power. This is especially true for party identification, but less so concerning specific issues, which are more subject to reformulation over time.[18]

Civic education has a strong impact on increasing knowledge and interest in politics among young adults.[19] Young people who take courses in government, or who engage in student government opportunities in high school, are more likely to be politically active as adults.[20] Students who take one college civics course typically see a significant rise in civic literacy.[21]

Political outlook and behavior can change as we age. Some of the age differences in politics are the result of **life cycle effects**, changes in our life circumstances. These changes are fairly uniform and predictable, and they are largely related to the aging process. As people age, they accumulate more property and political knowledge. They settle into community life and become more aware of their material self-interest. As a result, they are more likely to participate in the political system.

Other age-related differences are not as predictable. Known as **generational effects**, they result from unique issues and events confronting each **cohort**, or generation, at a time when its political identity is being forged.[22] For the generation that grew up in the 1950s and 1960s, the civil rights movement served as a catalyst for civic activism and spurred support for the expansion of individual rights and freedoms. Growing toleration is even more evident

> **life cycle effects** The impact of age-related factors in the formation of political attitudes, opinions, and beliefs.
>
> **generational effects** The impact of events experienced by a generational cohort on the formation of common political orientations.
>
> **cohort** The members of one's own generation.

for the generation that came of age politically during the administration of the first African American president in the nation's history. Studies show, for example, that millennials are far less interested than their elders in "'identity politics' that distinguishes one group from another (by race, gender, religion, sexual orientation) and more interested in making room for everyone in a broad American middle."[23]

Agents of Political Socialization

A number of cultural and institutional forces shape and mold our opinions over a lifetime. Their relative impact on our political maturation depends on when, how long, and how strongly we are exposed to them. Families, for instance, have the greatest impact on political socialization because of our intense interactions with family members during our formative years.[24]

Family Families help to shape our interest in politics, our party affiliation, and the attitudes we hold toward others in society. Our first memories of political events often come from family members expressing their own political viewpoints. For example, many who grew up in Democratic households during Barack Obama's administration recall hearing about measures taken to make health care more affordable and accessible. Children of Republicans at that time are more likely to recall discussions of trade imbalance and policy gridlock. These early memories carry an emotional weight that we often express in adulthood by adopting the party preferences of our parents.

Parental influence reaches far wider than partisan affiliation alone. Children are likely to follow their parents' lead when it comes to political activism and voting. According to a recent study, young people whose parents discuss politics regularly in the home are more likely to exhibit trust in government, feel more empowered about making a difference in their communities, are more likely to believe in the importance of voting, and are more likely to volunteer their time.[25] Three-quarters of young people who grew up with political discussion in the home are registered to vote, compared with only 57 percent of those who grew up in households without political discussion. Children who accompany their parents to the polling place on Election Day are far more likely to develop the habit of voting themselves. And young people who are encouraged by their parents to consider a political career are five times more likely to be interested in running for office in the future than those who grew up in households with no such encouragement.[26] It is no wonder that children of politically active families often follow in the footsteps of their parents.

Educational Institutions Early experiences in school tend to encourage support for our political system and its underlying values. Tales about George Washington and the cherry tree, and daily recitation of the Pledge of Allegiance, are intended to build positive feelings toward the government and its leaders. Middle- and high-school education fills in a little

Voting, like any habit, is most enduring if developed early.

more detail of American history; but it is only in college, when most students are exposed to extensive study of our nation's past, warts and all, that they form their own opinions about our Republic. To a greater degree than many others around the world, the U.S. educational system emphasizes egalitarian themes and encourages support for equal opportunities. Unlike some European countries, such as Germany, that provide different educational tracks for the college and noncollege bound, American schools tend to provide similar educational paths for all students.

Variations in political attitudes between those who attend college and those who do not reveal important differences that higher education can make. Compared to peers who have some college experience, young adults who do not attend college—or do not intend to go to college—express less trust in government, are more likely to see politics as the business of elites rather than average citizens, are less likely to believe their votes count, and are less likely to believe that political leaders are interested in their problems. In the 2016 presidential election, those without a college degree broke for Donald Trump, who appealed to their economic insecurities and distrust of Washington politicians; college graduates preferred Clinton.

Race complicates the education picture. African Americans at all levels of education express more pessimism than whites about politics in general and about their ability to bring about meaningful change.[27] This may change as more black leaders overcome obstacles to seeking high office.

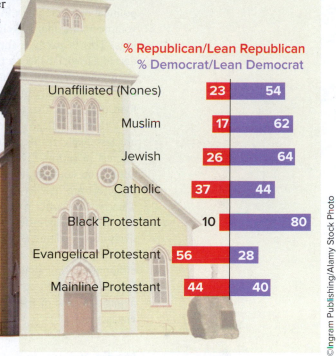

Party Affiliation Among Religious Groups

% Republican/Lean Republican
% Democrat/Lean Democrat

Group	% Republican/Lean Republican	% Democrat/Lean Democrat
Unaffiliated (Nones)	23	54
Muslim	17	62
Jewish	26	64
Catholic	37	44
Black Protestant	10	80
Evangelical Protestant	56	28
Mainline Protestant	44	40

As the chart shows, religious and partisan affiliation are closely related.

Source: Pew Research Center, "Party Affiliation,"Religious Landscape Study, 2014, http://www.pewforum.org/religious-landscape-study/party-affiliation/.

Religious Institutions Americans are among the most religious people in the world, as measured by expressed belief in God and attendance at church services. America's religious preferences are also more diverse than those of any other nation. Eighty-four percent of Americans claim affiliation in one of twenty-one major denominations or in one of the scores of minor church assemblies across the nation. In recent years, increasing numbers of Americans have described themselves as non-Christians or claimed no particular religious belief.[28] Still, the number of those who consider themselves religious and who attend services is quite high. Slightly more females than males consider themselves religious and attend services regularly.

There is little racial integration within denominations. Only nine of the twenty-one largest denominations have black membership of 10 percent or higher, demonstrating the familiar refrain that "Sunday morning service is the most segregated hour in America." Hispanics, by contrast, attend services with white Catholics.

Religious affiliation is closely associated with partisan preference (see "Party Affiliation Among Religious Groups"). Some religions stress traditional values that more closely align with the positions advanced by the Republican Party; others express acceptance of more diverse moral points of view, aligning more closely with the tenets of the Democratic Party. For example, Mormons and evangelical Protestant congregations, including Southern Baptists and Pentecostals, heavily favor the Republican Party. Mainline Protestants such as Episcopalians and Presbyterians are more evenly dispersed across both political parties. Latino Protestants trend Democratic, whereas black Protestants are overwhelmingly in the Democratic camp. Although Catholics have drifted away from the Democratic Party, a plurality still calls itself Democrat. This is largely a function of the growing number of black and Latino Catholics with strong Democratic leanings. Smaller Christian congregations skew Republican, while Jews and members of minority religions continue a long tradition of support for the Democrats. Among the growing number of those expressing no particular religious affiliations,

Democrats far outnumber Republicans. On the flip side, frequent church attendance is highly correlated with Republican Party identification.

Churches are important training grounds for learning civic skills, as we will see in Chapter 7. They provide opportunities to learn organizing and management skills that can be useful in the political realm. Organizing a church outing or social gathering is not much different from helping to plan a political meeting or rally. For the poor and for minorities, churches provide a venue for acquiring civic skills that is often unavailable elsewhere due to limited educational and workplace opportunities.[29]

Voluntary Associations There is also a close connection between volunteerism and political engagement, although it is not uniform across all groups. Older and more religious volunteers are more likely to involve themselves in politics and have strong political opinions. This is partly a function of the fact that older Americans are more likely to have developed social ties to their communities than younger and newer residents. Those who attend church regularly may also be more attuned to political issues impacted by their faith and they are easily mobilized by their churches not only to assist community members in food drives but also to vote on Election Day.

Although college students support voluntarism in their churches and communities, they are less likely regularly to discuss politics than their elders and they often express little interest in getting involved politically, with the possible exception of voting. Often, young adults see community activism and political activism as separate domains. Those who volunteer are half as likely to be registered to vote or to take part in political activities.[30] They would sooner participate in a 5K Breast Cancer Run sponsored by their sorority than attend a candidate debate for political office. Those who are active politically may be less likely to do volunteer work but more likely to conduct voter registration drives. As one scholar puts it, civic engagement is more "duty-driven" whereas political engagement entails either promoting a particular policy or defending a personal political interest or right.[31] This lack of close connection between volunteering and political participation raises questions about the value of service learning programs offered by many schools for fostering political engagement.

Media Because we hold preexisting opinions and points of view, it is difficult to disentangle the effects of media messages from the impact of other socializing agents. Although the media pervade every facet of our lives, most researchers believe that media choice is guided by existing preferences and not the other way around.[32] The source of one's political information, however, does seem to determine how politically informed one is. It should come as no surprise that those who get their news from news magazines and newspapers (or newspaper websites) seem to be better informed than the almost two-thirds of the American public who rely on television as their major news source.[33] Newspapers provide longer, more detailed coverage of events and issues. Nevertheless, a large percentage of highly knowledgeable Americans turned to NPR, *The Daily Show, The Rachel Maddow Show, The Sean Hannity Show*, and the *PBS NewsHour* for their news.[34] Of course, it is hard to know whether they are knowledgeable because of these sources or whether they turn to these sources because they are knowledgeable. Young people are much more likely to turn to the Internet for news than their elders. With the explosion in media outlets, we also see more self-selection based on one's political point of view. Conservative viewers are more likely to tune to Fox, liberals to CNN and PBS. Conservatives log on to *Breitbart* or *Drudge Report*, liberals to *Daily Kos* and *Alternet*. And young people are more likely to share news they find of interest with those they know through social media like Facebook, Twitter, and Tumblr. In fact, about six in ten online millennials (61 percent) report getting political news on Facebook in a given week, a much larger percentage than turn to any other news source.[35]

The media, however, may influence our political beliefs and attitudes in more subtle ways. News and entertainment shows alike, for example, often communicate negative stereotypes about the political process, making it seem inherently corrupt and portraying political leaders as untrustworthy. News programs afford political scandals an inordinate amount of coverage, and late-night comics incessantly poke fun at national leaders. Our

views about other races may be influenced by the way television news portrays them. For example, one study found that white viewers exposed to local news coverage of crime on television had more negative attitudes toward African Americans and expressed greater support for punitive measures against those convicted of crime.[36]

GROUP DIFFERENCES IN POLITICAL OPINIONS

We all go through life assembling a variety of group identifications that make a difference in the views we hold. While we can decide to join a fraternity or sorority or play on a softball team, we cannot make choices regarding other aspects of our identity, including race, ethnic background, gender, and area of the country where we are born. The life experiences associated with given group identities generate interesting political differences across America's diverse population.

Racial and Ethnic Identity

African Americans, who make up about 13 percent of the U.S. population, generally are more liberal on domestic political issues than whites. They express much stronger support for government enforcement of civil rights and government action to aid the poor. They favor affirmative action in the workplace and for university admission by a six to one margin over white respondents. They also show much greater support than whites for government efforts to reduce income inequality; but blacks are somewhat more traditional when it comes to moral issues, registering less support for same-sex marriage than whites.[37]

Most Hispanic Americans are Catholics and are strongly opposed to abortion. They also desire to preserve their cultural heritage, which is reflected in their support for bilingual education in the public schools. The Hispanic American population is itself quite diverse, however, with each subgroup reflecting the strong influence of its country of origin. Cuban Americans have long expressed distrust of the communist regime in

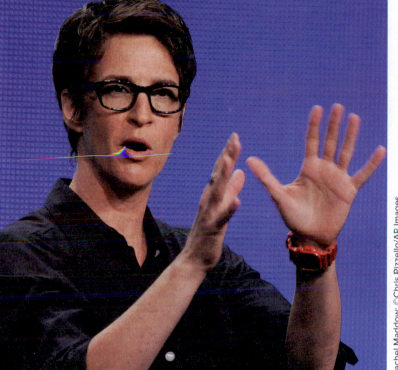

Trevor Noah: ©Evan Agostini/Invision/AP Images

Rachel Maddow: ©Chris Pizzello/AP Images

Sean Hannity: ©Paul Zimmerman/Getty Images

Cuba because many families fled to the United States after Fidel Castro assumed power in 1959. This attitude is changing somewhat among younger Cuban Americans, however, as diplomatic relations between the United States and Cuba thaw. Puerto Ricans and Mexican Americans hold opinions similar to African Americans, especially in support of social welfare and anti-discrimination policies. As a whole, Hispanic Americans skew Democratic, but Republican support is growing and 2016 witnessed two Cuban Americans, Ted Cruz (R-TX) and Marco Rubio (R-FL), running for the Republican Party presidential nomination.

Asian Americans are the fastest growing racial group in America, although they represent a diverse assortment of nationalities from the Far East, Southeast Asia, and the Indian subcontinent. They are highly educated, satisfied with their financial success, and place a high value on family life. As a group, they skew Democratic in party orientation and liberal ideologically, especially younger Asians.[38] Native Americans are in many ways the least visible ethnic group in America because nearly half live in enclaves known as reservations. A long history of displacement, discrimination, and broken promises and treaties by federal authorities has produced high levels of cynicism and distrust of government among Native Americans.

Gender

gender gap The systematic variation in political opinions that exists between males and females.

For many years, social scientists claimed that there were few differences in political attitudes and opinions between males and females. That viewpoint changed when researchers discovered a significant **gender gap** in the 1980 presidential election. Women voted about equally for Ronald Reagan and Jimmy Carter, but men favored Reagan by 19 percentage points. As discussed in other chapters, this gender gap has persisted nearly unabated in both voting behavior and party preference ever since. In 2016, women favored Hillary Clinton by 13 points (54 percent to 41 percent).[39]

Gender Differences in Political Opinions

Opinion Force, Violence, and Aggression	Male	Female Percent	Difference
Make it more difficult to buy gun	46.6	60.1	13.5
Oppose/Strongly oppose death penalty	50.8	56.8	6.0
Very willing to use force to settle international problems	18.7	15.0	3.7
Use troops to Fight ISIS	55.8	50.0	5.8
Compassion and Opportunity			
Govt. should provide many more services and increase services	37.0	52.6	15.6
Increase govt. spending on healthcare for those who cannot afford	61.3	67.7	6.4
Govt. should increase spending on aid to the poor	38.9	45.8	6.9
Gender and Environment			
Importance of women being elected to office	37.3	49.5	12.2
Govt. should do more to reduce rising temperatures	46.6	53.4	6.8

Opinion polls reveal gender differences on issues involving force, compassion, and aggression.

Source: American National Election Studies 2016.

Gender differences arise when we examine opinions on specific issues as well. As "Gender Differences in Political Opinions" indicates, women are less likely than men to support policies involving force, violence, and aggression. They are more likely to oppose the death penalty, much more likely to favor stricter gun control laws, and less likely to favor military action over diplomacy. Gender differences also exist concerning attitudes toward health care, helping the poor, and environmental protection. Compared to men, women express more support for government programs in all of these areas. These attitudes may well stem from differences in early socialization. For example, studies reveal that adults accept or even encourage aggression as part of the socialization of young boys, whereas they discourage such behavior in young girls.[40]

Women also exhibit somewhat less interest in and engagement with politics than their male counterparts, although the gap is narrowing.[41] A study by Verba, Burns, and Schlozman found that these differences persisted even after controlling for occupation, education, and access to political resources.[42] A more recent study confirmed this finding, illustrating that gender differences may have more to do with socialization factors during one's lifetime than with the intergenerational benefits conferred by parental income or education.[43] As a result, political ambition is generally lower among women than men, with one study showing men are approximately 60 percent more likely than women to consider running for office.[44] There is one interesting exception to this pattern: Political engagement among women is higher in states having a female U.S. senator or a female governor than in states where women do not hold these visible elective offices. Some observers conclude that the lack of political interest among women may be tied to the scarcity of role models. The unprecedented number of women running for elective office in 2018 signals important changes in female political engagement.

Geography

Geography also plays a part in explaining differences in political opinions. Southerners, for example, tend to be somewhat more conservative, are more supportive of our military, and—along with Midwesterners—express greater pride in being an American than those who live in the Northeast or on the West Coast.[45]

Some of this variation may be traced to early settlement patterns as Americans moved westward, giving rise to lasting differences in state and regional political cultures.[46] One can argue, however, that changes in communications and transportation have created a more uniform national culture today. We all tend to watch the same TV shows, listen to the same music, and eat at the same fast-food outlets, no matter where we live. Nevertheless, regional variation, as evidenced by differences in ideology and party identification, is very real. As we will see in coming chapters, southern and Midwestern states have become increasingly conservative and Republican, while the Northeast and West have become more liberal and Democratic.

Some political scientists, demographers, and journalists have argued that geographic differences are intensifying as Americans sort themselves into distinct ideological enclaves.[47] There is some evidence that for at least the past quarter-century Americans have increasingly chosen to live in states—and even local communities—with people who identify with the same ideology and political party as themselves. As a result, liberals and conservatives, Democrats and Republicans, have become more geographically isolated. Studies show, for example, growing political homogeneity in state and congressional districts where one party's candidates win consistently in overwhelming numbers.[48] "Partisan Clustering: 2016 Presidential Election Results by County" illustrates how each county in the nation voted for president in 2016. You can see that counties that voted for the Democratic candidate, shaded in blue, predominate along the coasts whereas red-colored Republican-voting counties prevail elsewhere.

Geographic differences are even more stark when we examine the political divide between urban and rural dwellers. An analysis by *The Washington Post* shows that, between 2004 and 2016, voters in a majority of counties with populations greater than 500,000—mostly urban, where roughly half of Americans live—increased their support for Democratic presidential candidates over Republican rivals. "In counties with fewer than 100,000 people—which make up 80 percent of counties in the country but contain only about 20 percent of the population—9 out of 10 voted more Republican [in 2016] than they did in 2004."[49] This partisan clustering along geographic lines means Americans are less likely to be exposed to individuals with differing points of view and may be less willing to seek compromise.

Partisan Clustering: 2016 Presidential Election Results by County

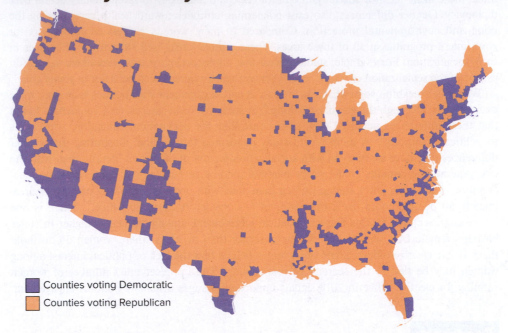

■ Counties voting Democratic
■ Counties voting Republican

An examination of the 2016 presidential vote by county illustrates the partisan sorting of the population.

Source: Newman, M. Department of Physics and Center for the Study of Complex Systems, University of Michigan. Accessed on November 18, 2017 at http://www-personal.umich.edu/~mejn/election/2016/.

MEASURING PUBLIC OPINION

Making meaningful assessments about public opinion requires an understanding of the dimensions around which opinions form as well as accurate ways of measuring them. Simply knowing that an individual prefers one candidate over another tells us little about the individual's probable behavior in an upcoming election or the person's reasons for holding that view. Only when pollsters apply rigorous methods to measure and sample opinions can the results of a poll give us some measure of confidence about what the public is thinking.

Dimensions of Public Opinion

When legitimate pollsters ask for our views, they usually attempt to peer beneath the surface of our opinions. They seek to know not only what we believe but also how strongly we believe it, how long we have held that view, the grounds on which we base that belief, how important that belief is to us, and what we might be prepared to do about it. Together, these elements make up the various dimensions of public opinion.

The term **direction** refers to an individual's preference with respect to a particular issue. Does the respondent favor the Democrat or the Republican for president? Does he or she favor or oppose gay marriage? This is the dimension of an opinion that the sponsor of the poll reports most often. **Salience** is the importance we attach to an issue or topic about which we are asked. Conservation may be an issue we are prepared actively to lobby and work to promote, or we may think about the matter only when a pollster asks about it. **Intensity** consists of how strongly an individual holds a particular preference on an issue. This dimension is important because people are more likely to act on opinions they hold intensely.

The term **stability** refers to how consistently an individual maintains a particular preference over time. Americans have had stable views about the death penalty but unstable opinions about foreign policy issues. This is understandable because beliefs about crime and punishment change slowly; our views about foreign policy are tied to changing world events. The dimension of

direction The attribute of an individual's opinion that indicates a preference for or against a particular issue.

salience The attribute of an individual's opinion that indicates how central it is to her or his daily concerns.

intensity The attribute of an individual's opinion that measures how strongly it is held.

stability The attribute of an individual's opinion that measures how consistently it is held.

informational support tells us how well-informed the respondent is regarding an opinion. When a person responds to a multiple-choice question, we have no way of knowing whether he or she is reacting to the question from a basis of knowledge or ignorance. For example, many individuals incorrectly believe that it is a crime to burn the American flag.

Psychologists and social scientists are beginning to learn more about **opinion persistence**, the failure of individuals holding views based on faulty information to correct their views when given more accurate information. As discussed in this chapter's Current Controversy box, individuals often don perceptual blinders when confronted with opinions that don't conform to their previously held beliefs. Often, attempts to correct their viewpoints backfire, resulting in even more strongly held belief in the misperception.[50] Some studies link this behavior to emotional centers in the brain that reinforce our identities. Attempts to correct misperceptions with "new facts" challenge our identities and cause emotional resistance.[51]

Types of Polls

Political campaigns employ a wide variety of polls and surveys. Campaigns often conduct **benchmark surveys** at the time a candidate enters a political race. These surveys measure the public's knowledge and assessment of the candidate at that point in time. **Trial heat surveys** pair competing candidates and ask citizens whom they would vote for in such a contest. **Tracking polls** supply the most current information on a race by polling on a daily basis. These polls allow campaigns to change their strategies on a moment's notice to respond to the latest changes in public sentiment. Such polls often interview one hundred people a day for four days and then report the totals. On the fifth day, pollsters interview an additional one hundred people whose responses become part of the total, while the one hundred responses from the first day are dropped. Respondents are subsequently added and dropped on a rotating basis for the length of the poll.

A **push poll**, the most notorious of campaign polls, is really a campaign tactic disguised as a poll. Campaign workers contact voters to provide them with negative information about their opponent and then ask the voters questions about that candidate. The goal is not to secure accurate information but to influence attitudes. Finally, **exit polls** survey voters as they leave polling places. These polls help campaign professionals and academic scholars to analyze demographic factors that influence election outcomes. These types of polls generally are accurate but do experience occasional problems. In the 2000 presidential election, for example, the major media networks initially cited misleading exit poll results that awarded the state of Florida to Al Gore rather than to the eventual victor, George W. Bush.

informational support The attribute of an individual's opinion that measures his or her amount of knowledge concerning the issue.

opinion persistence The failure of individuals holding views based on faulty information to correct their views when given more accurate information.

benchmark survey A campaign poll that measures a candidate's strength at the time of entrance into the electoral race.

trial heat survey A campaign poll that measures the popularity of competing candidates in a particular electoral race.

tracking polls Campaign polls that measure candidates' relative strength on a daily basis.

push poll A campaign tactic that attacks an opponent while pretending to be a poll.

exit poll Interviews of voters as they leave the polling place.

POLLING TECHNIQUES

You will be excused if you have lost confidence in opinion polls following the failure of most polls to accurately predict the results of the 2016 presidential election. Believe it or not, however, most national polls were fairly accurate regarding the final outcome of the popular vote.[52] State polls—which are crucial given our Electoral College system of electing presidents—were a different story. Many of these consistently missed their marks. The variation in poll results makes it even more important for each of us to be an informed consumer of polls. We need to understand what makes a poll scientific and which techniques differentiate good polls from bad. What makes a poll reliable? What are some of the most common flaws and how can we spot them? What information should we be looking for in order to evaluate poll results? To avoid being misled, we need to know how the poll was conducted, who was surveyed, and what questions respondents were asked.

©Bettmann/Getty Images

One of the most embarrassing moments for election pollsters came in 1948 when they predicted Republican Thomas E. Dewey would defeat President Harry Truman. Truman won, but newspapers giving the victory to Dewey had already been printed. Here Truman holds an example.

Don't Confuse Me with Facts

In a famous experiment, three Stanford researchers assembled subjects with opposing views on capital punishment. Half the students were in favor of capital punishment and thought that it deterred crime; the other half were against it and thought that it had no effect on crime. They were then presented with information that either confirmed or refuted their preexisting opinions. Did the "facts" change their opinions?

As the researchers report, detailed information supporting or refuting each side's beliefs simply caused participants to hold on to their preexisting beliefs more firmly. Information supporting the deterrent effect of capital punishment "caused proponents to favor capital punishment more and believe in its deterrent efficacy more, but caused opponents to oppose capital punishment more and believe in its deterrent efficacy less." Similarly, evidence that capital punishment did not deter crime failed to persuade its supporters. In short, "Subjects' decisions about whether to accept a study's findings at face value or to search for flaws and entertain alternative interpretations seemed to depend . . . on whether the study's results coincided with their existing beliefs."*

This result is an example of what psychologists call "confirmation bias" or opinion persistence and has been reproduced many times in both experimental and naturalistic settings. Researchers have also found that we are even more likely to hold on to preexisting beliefs—even if they are false—when our views are confirmed by others who think like us. For example: "If your position on, say, the Affordable Care Act is baseless, and I rely on it, then my opinion is also baseless. When I talk to Tom and he decides he agrees with me, his opinion is also baseless, but now that the three of us concur, we feel that much more smug about our views."** Social confirmation of

©gremlin/iStock/Getty Images

false information we receive from friends or sources we follow on the Internet allows us to hold on to our beliefs even more solidly and bolsters our confidence in our position.

It should be clear that this is an important feature in politics. For example, even after President Obama made public his birth certificate from Hawaii in 2011, a large portion of his Republican Party opposition continued to hold on to the belief that he was born outside the United States. As late as 2016, one poll found that 41 percent of Republicans disagreed with the statement that Obama was born in America and another 31 percent expressed doubts. Pollsters then probed to see whether disbelief was a result of a lack of political knowledge. They asked respondents three factual questions about politics and compared the beliefs of those correctly answering at least two of the three questions to those who did not. There were virtually no differences between low-knowledge and high-knowledge respondents.†

So, is it futile to try to bridge political differences if facts don't count? Psychologists suggest techniques that may be more effective than simply spouting facts. Scott Geller, director of Virginia

Tech's Center for Applied Behavior Systems gives the following advice:‡

1. Ask questions: Start out by asking for the other person's opinion—"Can you explain *why* you feel that way?" *Then* give your own opinion in response.
2. Acknowledge the other person's view and show some empathy. Admitting that everyone has their own biases may help the other person see your side as well.
3. Be circumspect about what you say in person or online. Don't say or post something that ratchets up conflict.
4. Be reflective and considerate.

*Lord, C. G., Ross, L. and Lepper, M. R. "Biased Assimilation and Attitude Polarization: The Effects of Prior Theories on Subsequently Considered Evidence," *Journal of Personality and Social Psychology 37:11* (1979): 2105.

**Kolbert, E. "Why Facts Don't Change Our Minds," *The New Yorker,* February 27, 2017, https://www. newyorker.com/magazine/2017/02/27/why-facts-dont-change-our-minds.

†Josh Clinton and Carrie Roush, "Persistent Partisan Divide over Birther Question," NBC News, August 10, 2016, https://www.nbcnews.com/politics/2016-election/poll-persistent-partisan-divide-over-birther-question-n627446.

‡Amanda Macmillan, "How to Disagree About Politics Without Losing Friends," Real Simple, https://www. realsimple.com/health/mind-mood/emotional-health/political-frenemies-social-media.

Who Is Asked? Selecting the Sample

Scientific polls use the mathematical laws of probability to ensure accuracy. These laws specify that we don't need to count every member of a population as long as we count a representative group within that population in a manner that isn't biased. For example, we don't need to count every green and red marble in a large container to know their relative proportions. So long as we select marbles in a random manner, a small sample can yield a very close approximation of the proportions in the entire container.

The individuals whose opinions pollsters measure constitute the **sample**. In a national presidential preference poll, the sample is likely to include between 1,000 and 1,200 respondents. The **population** consists of the larger group of people whose opinions the poll attempts to estimate. In the case of a presidential preference poll, for example, the population might be all citizens of voting age, just registered voters, or those considered most likely to vote in an upcoming election.

In measuring our opinions, pollsters try to select samples that accurately represent the broader population from which they are drawn. All good sampling designs use **probability sampling**, in which each individual in the population has a known probability of being selected. One type of probability sampling, **simple random sampling**, gives everyone in a population an equal chance of being interviewed. In a purely random sample of Americans, each person interviewed would have roughly one chance out of more than 250 million adults of being selected. Probability sampling avoids the kind of selection bias that affected the 1936 *Literary Digest* presidential poll. The sample for that poll included only people with automobiles or telephones at a time when a large percentage of potential voters possessed neither. Without using probability sampling, it is impossible for the pollster to know how closely the sample mirrors the overall population.

Simple random sampling, however, is not feasible in a country as vast as the United States. Even census data do not contain a complete and current list of all Americans. As a result, national pollsters use **systematic sampling** as a means of approximating the ideal. They begin with a universe of known telephone numbers, names, or locations. After picking the first number or name at random, they might make additional picks in a predetermined sequence. For example, researchers might randomly pick the number 21 from a universe of 100 possible respondents. They also randomly pick an interval, say, six. They then will interview every sixth person from the number 21 onward.

Some polls randomly select the initial portions of a telephone exchange and append randomly selected digits to complete the number. This is a procedure known as **random digit dialing**. It ensures that even those holding unlisted phone numbers have an equal chance of being selected for interview. As in pure random sampling, the goal is to approximate an equal chance of selection for every individual or household in the population.

Sampling error refers to a poll's degree of accuracy, usually expressed as a percentage. For example, in a population in which every individual has the same chance of being selected, a poll of between 1,000 and 1,200 respondents yields a sampling error of about ± 3 percent. That is, the results will deviate no more than three percentage points in either direction from results that would be obtained if every person in the entire population were surveyed. Suppose, for example, that a poll of 1,000 people shows Candidate A leading Candidate B by a margin of 46 percent to 42 percent. This means that Candidate A's margin among the entire voting population is anywhere from 43 percent to 49 percent, and Candidate B's is anywhere from 39 percent to 45 percent. From that information, the pollster would be wise to conclude that the race is too close to call. Polls that survey fewer individuals have a higher sampling error rate. Polls of just a few hundred are sometimes used when the sponsor lacks the money or time to conduct a larger survey, or when there is an interest in the gross dimensions of opinion and the poll sponsor is willing to accept greater uncertainty about the results.

Until now, pollsters have usually conducted polls in person or on the telephone. This could change with the advent of Internet polling, which is extremely inexpensive and can be conducted by virtually anyone with access to the Web and some simple software. These polls, however, pose significant risks regarding accuracy. Many Internet surveys reflect the views of a highly selective portion of the population, since respondents must choose to log

scientific polls Any poll using proper sampling designs.

sample The individuals whose opinions are actually measured.

population The people whose opinions are being estimated through interviews with samples of group members.

probability sampling A sample design showing that each individual in the population has a known probability of being included in the sample.

simple random sampling The technique of drawing a sample for interview in which all members of the targeted population have the same probability of being selected for interview.

systematic sampling A sample design to ensure that each individual in the population has an equal chance of being chosen after the first name or number is chosen at random.

random digit dialing A procedure whereby pollsters select the initial portions of a telephone exchange and append randomly selected digits to complete the number. The procedure ensures that even those holding unlisted numbers have an equal chance of being selected for interview.

sampling error The measure of the degree of accuracy of a poll based on the size of the sample.

IS POLLING IN CRISIS?

Shortly after the 2016 presidential election, a number of polling firms and professional associations, including the American Association for Public Opinion Research (AAPOR), began a months' long investigation into why the polls seemed to perform so poorly in predicting the election result. Some of their findings seemed unremarkable; others, potentially foreseeable in retrospect; and still others pose greater concerns for the profession as it goes forward.

First, it should be noted that national polls were not that far off from the final result. Clinton won the popular vote by almost three million votes, or 2.1 percent. The aggregated average of reputable national polls put her victory at 3.2 percent, a difference of just over 1 percent, well within the margin of error, especially in a close election.[†] In fact, national polls in 2016 tended to be more accurate than 2012 national polls.

But the presidency does not hinge on the popular vote. It is won or lost in the Electoral College, where each state's electoral votes are cast. As a result, we must look to state polls for an answer to what went wrong. Here, according to the AAPOR report, state polls "had a historically bad year."[‡] They were plagued by several problems:

- *Nonresponse bias.* This occurs when certain groups in the population do not respond to survey calls. Despite repeated attempts to reach every individual

selected at random, it is possible that Trump voters failed to answer the call—possibly due to their skepticism about polling in general.

- *Under sampling of non-college-educated whites.* All pollsters weight surveys based on their predictions about the makeup of the electorate. Historically non-college-educated whites had lower turnout than those with higher education levels. As a result, these polls underestimated the turnout of a group that was highly motivated by the Trump campaign.

- *Late deciders breaking for Trump by a significant margin.* According to Pew, "In the battleground of Wisconsin, for example, 14% of voters told exit pollsters that they had made up their minds only in the final week; they ultimately favored Trump by nearly two-to-one." Polls taken earlier in the campaign might have missed this trend entirely.

[†]John Gramlich, *Q and A: Pew Research Center's President on Key Issues in U.S. Polling,* Pew Research Center, June 16, 2017, http://www.pewresearch.org/fact-tank/2017/06/16/qa-pew-research-centers-president-on-key-issues-in-u-s-polling/.

[‡]American Association For Public Opinion Research, An Evaluation of 2016 Election Polls in the U.S. Accessed on November 9, 2017 at https://www.aapor.org/Education-Resources/Reports/An-Evaluation-of-2016-Election-Polls-in-the-U-S.aspx.

on to a particular site to participate. Although the jury is still out about the future of Internet polling, recent successes show promise. For example, YouGov, founded in 2000, demonstrated an accuracy rate as good as or better than traditional polls in predicting a number of election outcomes in Europe and the United States. In his postelection analysis of the polls, polling guru Nate Silver concluded that some of the most accurate polls in the 2012 election were those conducted online. YouGov fared well in this analysis, and particularly noteworthy was Google Consumer Surveys, which was only 0.3 percent off the final winning percentage for President Obama in its final 2012 Internet poll. In 2016, YouGov came in about middle of the pack in terms of accuracy.[53] Academics have increasingly turned to Internet polling because it is less expensive than telephone polling and because scholars can return to reinterview the same individuals over time to see how their views have changed.

Perhaps a more daunting challenge confronting pollsters is the growing number of people—especially young people—who no longer have landlines and do not list their cell phone numbers. Most good polls today include a majority of cell phones in their samples, but call screening technology helps individuals avoid the sometimes prying questions of pollsters. Pollsters are currently testing new techniques to avoid systematically excluding the views of these individuals by, for example, adjusting the sample to reflect the known proportion of various groups in the general population before analyzing the results. The samples are "weighted" by region, party, age, race, religion, and gender. In other words, pollsters know the number of men and women in the population, for example, and use that information to adjust the sample if too many or too few women are in the sample. Getting the weighting right in predicting who will show up on Election Day is important and the failure to predict the large number of whites with less than a college education who voted in 2016 is one reason why so many state polls failed to get it right.

A reliable poll must not only use good sampling techniques but also ask the kinds of questions that will accurately capture the respondent's true opinions. It should avoid asking **leading questions**, which are phrased in such a way as to produce a predetermined response. In the 1982 Democratic primary race for governor of Ohio, candidate Jerry Springer—who went on to become a television personality—was the target of a classic example of a leading question:

> As you may know, in 1974, Jerry Springer, who had gotten married six months earlier, was arrested on a morals charge with three women in a hotel room. He also used a bad check to pay for the women's services and subsequently resigned as mayor of his city. Does this make you much more likely, somewhat more likely, somewhat less likely, or much less likely to support Jerry Springer for governor this year?

Few persons responding to a survey want to admit that they are uninformed about an important or timely subject. As a result, they sometimes respond with **nonattitudes**, or uninformed responses to which they have given little thought. Nonattitudes are considered artificial opinions created by the poll.[54] A poll can at least partially avoid the problem of nonattitudes by screening for the respondent's level of knowledge or interest, and by making it socially acceptable for respondents to say they are unfamiliar with a particular issue or question. Question order is also important. It is easy to imagine that your initial response to a question that asks whether you favor free speech might be affected if it were preceded by a question asking whether you believe the government has a role in limiting the spread of child pornography.

> **leading question** A question worded to suggest a particular answer desired by the pollster.
>
> **nonattitudes** Uninformed responses triggered by requiring survey respondents to answer whether or not they know about the subject in question.

THE CONTENT OF AMERICAN PUBLIC OPINION

How knowledgeable are Americans about political issues? Do Americans develop their opinions out of confidence and trust in government institutions? Do citizens believe that their opinions matter? Do Americans really believe in the implementation of democratic principles we often uncritically espouse? Let's take a closer look at the content of Americans' attitudes and beliefs.

Political Knowledge

For years, surveys have shown that Americans' political information levels have fallen short of the democratic ideal. In general, Americans display a lack of familiarity with political leaders and issues of the day. In a recent poll, only 26 percent of respondents could accurately name all three branches of the U.S. government and 37 percent were unable to name any of the freedoms associated with the First Amendment.[55] As expected, however, this characterization does not hold for all Americans: Those who are well educated, those with higher incomes, and those who are older are quite knowledgeable about our political system and even about world politics. Generational differences are not great as far as knowledge of current events goes, but young adults are slightly less likely than the elderly to display knowledge across a broad range of political issues (see "Modest Generational Differences in News Knowledge"). Education is the strongest single predictor of political knowledge; better informed citizens "hold more opinions, have more stable opinions that are resistant to irrelevant or biased information . . . and have opinions that are more internally consistent with each other and with basic ideological alignments that define American politics."[56]

Leading questions skew poll results, as was the case when current TV host Jerry Springer ran for governor in Ohio.

Modest Generational Differences in News Knowledge

% answering each question correctly	18–29 %	30–49 %	50–64 %	65+ %
Paul Ryan is Speaker of House	56	59	69	60
Lead found in Flint, MI water supply	69	70	77	71
Emmanuel Macron current French President	41	36	38	34
Neil Gorsuch is Trump's first Supreme Court appointee	37	43	52	49
Zika carrier is mosquito	87	88	88	82
United Kingdom leaving European Union	62	55	62	60
Freedom Caucus is conservative Republican group in Congress	42	42	52	43

There are only modest generational differences in knowledge of current events.

Source: Pew Research Center. Accessed on November 18, 2017 at http://www.pewresearch.org/quiz/the-news-iq-quiz/ July 25, 2017.

get involved!

Compare survey results on the same topic from a variety of sources—for example, presidential approval ratings. Select a sample of three or four national polls from such sources as *The New York Times*/CBS News, *The Washington Post*/ABC News, or *USA Today*. Keep track of the differences in percentages reported and try to account for such differences by examining the number of persons sampled, the time period during which the poll was executed, and the wording and context of the questions asked.

©OJO Images/Image Source

Some types of political knowledge are more widespread than others. Americans are better informed about institutions and processes of government than they are about people and players in the political arena. For example, they are more likely to know that the Speaker of the House is the individual who presides over floor debate in the House of Representatives than the name of the current House Speaker. This makes intuitive sense because political personnel change more frequently, and often with less fanfare, than political institutions.

Americans are generally poorly informed about global affairs. The Council on Foreign Relations found, for example, that only 29 percent of college-age students could identify Indonesia on a map and only 34 percent knew that the United States was bound by treaty to defend South Korea if attacked.[57]

The pattern of limited political knowledge has been found to be quite stable over the last fifty years of survey research. The fact that educational levels have increased significantly over that period gives cause for concern since we would expect a more educated populace to be more politically sophisticated. However, Americans are able to acquire needed information when national or international crises focus their attention. For example, interest in world affairs spiked upward immediately following the September 11, 2001, terrorist attacks. A majority of Americans could identify the Muslim nations cooperating with the American war on terrorism, could name the countries sharing a border with Afghanistan, and knew the name of the new cabinet office, Homeland Security, created in the wake of the attacks. What's more, attention spurred by the attacks increased the level of interest in politics more generally for most Americans.[58] These results illustrate the fact that political learning is instrumental and reflects self-interest. Americans are able and willing to pay attention and to learn about government when they consider events to be important and when they are presented with a clear and steady stream of reliable information. Of course, political bias can also act as a filter that is sometimes impervious to correction by factual information. For example, many critics of President Obama continued to profess their doubts about his American citizenship even after he released his birth certificate as they had demanded.

Confidence in Government Institutions

In 1966, a majority of the American public had a great deal of confidence in the people running major companies, the field of medicine, the military, the Supreme Court, and our educational system. More than 40 percent had a great deal of confidence in organized religion, Congress, and the executive branch of the federal government. Then, a crisis of confidence in the leadership of major American institutions took place, blamed variously on political scandals, increased partisanship, or negative media coverage of politics.[59] No matter what the cause, confidence in U.S. institutions has never returned to its pre-1966 levels, with the exception of a short-term surge after the 9/11 attacks. Today, fewer than half of all Americans express confidence in the Supreme Court and the president; confidence in Congress is near a record low (see "Americans' Level of Confidence in the Three Branches of Government").

Trust in government, just like confidence in American institutions, has fallen since the late 1960s. Trust consists of the belief that the people who run government genuinely have the best interests of the public in mind. Lack of trust is expressed as **political cynicism**, the view that government officials mostly look out for themselves. Trust in government declined significantly in the wake of the Watergate scandal, in which President Richard Nixon was accused of covering up a break-in at the Democratic Party headquarters during his 1972 reelection campaign. Nixon subsequently resigned from office rather than face possible impeachment. Public support for the congenial Ronald Reagan lifted trust briefly and modestly in the 1980s, and trust rose temporarily once again following the 9/11 terrorist attacks. Recent years have seen trust in the federal government plummet to historic lows, contributing to a toxic attitude about politics in general.

The decline in trust in government cuts across all demographic groups and ages, but levels of trust in government vary among partisans depending on which party is in power. Democrats express less trust when Republicans are in office, and the reverse is true as well.

Although young people exemplified somewhat more confidence in government shortly after 9/11, by 2006, their levels of trust in government have fallen. Today only about a quarter of young adults ages 18 to 24 express a high level of trust in government.[60] Perhaps more disturbing is the fact that young people are growing more distrustful of others in general. In a recent study, only 19 percent of millennials agreed that "most people can be trusted." Minorities and low-income adults had even lower levels of social trust than other groups.[61] Scholars have linked this decrease in trust to a decline in our willingness to volunteer to help others.[62] As troublesome as this trend appears, however, we should not consider it a purely American phenomenon. Scholars have found similar declines in trust in other industrialized countries.[63]

Americans' Level of Confidence in the Three Branches of Government

Confidence in U.S. Institutions

Over the last quarter-century, confidence in all three branches of government has declined.

Source: Gallup Organization. Confidence in Institutions. Accessed on November 18, 2017 at http://news.gallup.com/poll/1597/Confidence-Institutions.aspx.

political cynicism The view that government officials look out mostly for themselves.

political efficacy The belief that an individual can understand and influence political affairs.

internal political efficacy An individual's self-confidence in his or her ability to understand and participate in politics.

external political efficacy An individual's belief that his or her activities will influence what the government will do or who will win an election.

Political efficacy measures citizens' perceptions about their capacity to understand and influence political affairs (see "Political Efficacy: Can the Average Citizen Influence Politics"). It combines measures of a citizen's level of confidence in his or her own ability to understand and navigate the political landscape, called **internal political efficacy**, and the belief that the government is responsive to our demands, **external political efficacy**.[64] External political efficacy is especially important to well-functioning democracies, which are predicated on the notion that citizens exercise control of their governments.

The long-term trend in external political efficacy is down, but there is much variation in this measure over time. External efficacy seems more closely tied to political events and issues than are confidence and trust. Levels of efficacy do not substantially differ by party affiliation. However, as with other measures of attitudes and opinions, differences surface when we look at education and income. Those

Political Efficacy: Can the Average Citizen Influence Politics?

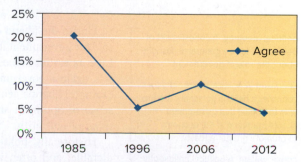

A declining number of Americans believe they have the power to influence the course of political events.

Source: General Social Survey (various years).

Public Tolerance for Advocates of Unpopular Positions

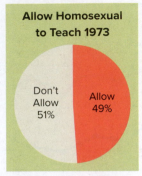

Allow Homosexual to Teach 1973

Don't Allow 51%

Allow 49%

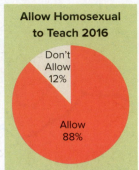

Allow Homosexual to Teach 2016

Don't Allow 12%

Allow 88%

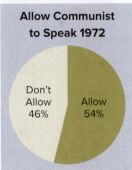

Allow Communist to Speak 1972

Don't Allow 46%

Allow 54%

Allow Communist to Speak 2016

Don't Allow 29%

Allow 71%

Remove Anti-Religionist Book 2016

Remove 23%

Don't Remove 77%

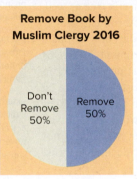

Remove Book by Muslim Clergy 2016

Don't Remove 50%

Remove 50%

The level of tolerance Americans display for those expressing opinions different from their own has increased in recent years. However, many Americans continue to display high levels of intolerance towards some subgroups within society.

Source: General Social Survey (various years)

---

political ideology A cohesive set of beliefs that form a general philosophy about the role of government.

liberalism A political philosophy that combines a belief in personal freedoms with the belief that government should intervene in the economy to promote greater equality.

conservatism A political philosophy that rests on the belief in traditional institutions and a minimal role for government in economic activity.

---

with more of both of these resources exhibit vastly higher levels of efficacy than do those with less.

Support for Democratic Values

Our democracy emphasizes not only support for majority rule but also support for the rights of minorities. Tolerance for diverse viewpoints and lifestyles is necessary for the preservation of liberty and equality of opportunity. Nevertheless, pioneering studies on political toleration just following World War II suggested that general support for civil liberties was surprisingly low among average Americans.[65] Of course, this was a period characterized by fear of the threat of communism and a greater willingness to sacrifice liberties for security.[66] Toward the end of the Cold War, tolerance among the general public seemed to have improved. Even today, however, Americans are not as supportive of democratic norms as one might hope, given our long tradition of liberty and diversity. The charts titled "Public Tolerance for Advocates of Unpopular Positions" illustrate the trend toward greater tolerance toward homosexuals and communists over the period from 1972 to the present. However, even today Americans are more reluctant to grant the same freedoms to members of some religious groups, like Muslims, than we are to members of other religious denominations. For example, the lower two charts show we are more willing to retain in our public libraries a book written by someone who opposes all religions than one written by a Muslim cleric.

Many political scientists blame institutional factors for a lack of tolerance and support for political liberties. They criticize politicians for exploiting public fears to win votes, as well as the media's failure to engage citizens in a manner that encourages thoughtful consideration of often conflicting national goals.[67] Timely events also have an impact on support for basic freedoms. In 1987 and 1988, only 29 percent of Americans surveyed believed that it "will be necessary to give up civil liberties to curb terrorism." Following the terrorist attacks in 2001, that number jumped to 44 percent.[68] By 2005, however, the number had fallen again to 33 percent.[69]

Political Ideologies

A **political ideology** is an ordered set of political beliefs.[70] These beliefs usually stem from an individual's philosophy about the nature of society and the role of government. In Chapter 2, we discussed the liberal democratic ideology that informed the origins of our nation. That ideology emphasizes liberty, equal opportunity, private property, and individualism. The dominant ideologies today in America are **liberalism** and **conservatism**. Each borrows elements from our founding values.

Unlike the liberal democracy extolled by the Framers, liberalism today embraces a larger role for government in protecting and ensuring equal opportunity, such as affirmative action. Like its earlier namesake, however, liberalism places a premium on civil liberties and counsels against government intrusion in private matters of personal and moral choice. For example, liberals generally support a woman's right to obtain an abortion. Liberals have a sense of optimism about our ability to improve our lives by changing institutions and patterns of authority.

Historically, political conservatives have believed that human nature is complex, unpredictable, and often immoral. As a result, conservatives tend to be suspicious of change. They place their trust in institutions such as the church and the family and traditional values that have demonstrated a capacity for constraining the excesses of human conduct. Conservatives today support a limited role for government in the private economy and faith

Conservative evangelicals have made support for school prayer a cornerstone of their ideology.

in free market mechanisms, both of which are consistent with the values of the Framers. However, conservatives today also support a more interventionist role for government in ensuring the preservation of traditional values and institutions. For example, many conservatives support prayer in public schools.

But ideology is more complex than the simple liberal–conservative dichotomy usually presented in popular culture and the media. Individuals can be liberal on some dimensions, such as support for government programs to help the poor, but conservative on other dimensions, like support for school prayer. Similarly, individuals can express liberal positions on social issues but reject government regulation in the economy, a position usually favored by conservatives.

The figure in "A Two-Dimensional View of Ideology" presents a more sophisticated model of ideological differences across two dimensions. The first dimension is economic, ranging from support for greater equality, even if government intervention is necessary to achieve it, to support for economic liberty where government plays a minor role. The other dimension deals with views on social issues. On this dimension, views range from progressive—for example, support for gay marriage—to traditional, such as the view that marriage should take place only between a man and a woman. Those in the upper left quadrant are generally considered liberals, and those in the lower right quadrant are conservatives. Those who support greater economic equality but hold traditional views on social issues are generally known as **populists** (lower left quadrant); those who stress economic liberty and progressive social views follow a political philosophy called **libertarianism**.

Although the number of Americans who identify themselves as populist and libertarian is quite small,[71] their partisan choices can be quite varied. For example, in 2016, both Republican Donald Trump and Democrat Bernie Sanders found followers among those we describe as populists. There has been somewhat of a recent rise in support for this orientation worldwide as evidenced by the British vote to exit from the European Union. The movement was driven both by the concerns of the working class that they were being left out of the benefits from international trade and by fear of the rising tide of immigration. Libertarians have found support in many elections across the nation, but the magnitude of this support is small.

On social issues, about a third of Americans self-identify as liberal or leaning liberal, similar to the number who call themselves conservatives; on economic issues, more Americans identify as leaning conservative.[72]

populist A political philosophy expressing support for greater equality and for traditional social values.

libertarianism A political philosophy that espouses strong support for individual liberty in both social and economic areas of life.

A Two-Dimensional View of Ideology

	Economic issues	
	Equality	Liberty
Progressive	Liberal	Libertarian
Traditional	Populist	Conservative

Social issues

When examining the ways in which economic and social issues interact, we find at least four different ideological types.

Ideological Leanings by Generation

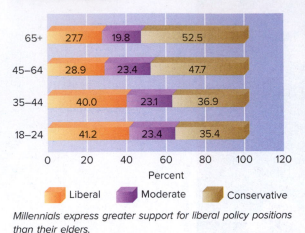

Age	Liberal	Moderate	Conservative
65+	27.7	19.8	52.5
45–64	28.9	23.4	47.7
35–44	40.0	23.1	36.9
18–24	41.2	23.4	35.4

Millennials express greater support for liberal policy positions than their elders.

Source: American National Election Studies, 2016.

ideologue One who thinks about politics almost exclusively through the prism of his or her ideological perspective.

These numbers are somewhat volatile, however, and often fluctuate in response to the actions of those in power. The number of Americans identifying themselves as somewhat liberal rose during the tail end of the George W. Bush administration as dissatisfaction with his Iraq policies rose. Similarly, the percentage calling themselves conservative rose in the latter years of the Obama administration as Americans reacted negatively to his handling of world events. Millennials under age 30 are more likely to self-identify at the liberal end of the political spectrum (see "Ideological Leanings by Generation"). They demonstrate greater tolerance on social and cultural issues than their elders and more support for government-sponsored programs to aid the economy.[73]

Most Americans, however, avoid ideological extremes. There are very few **ideologues**, those who think about politics almost exclusively in ideological terms. For example, only about 3 percent say they are very liberal, with a similar percentage calling themselves very conservative.[74] For the most part, Americans take a pragmatic view of politics; they are more interested in finding solutions to problems than in enforcing ideological purity. This does not mean that ideological divisions do not exist. Studies show that northeastern and West Coast states are growing more liberal while the South and the Midwest are more conservative; the cities and suburbs are more liberal than the rural areas; and those who have not attended college are more populist and progressive on economic policy but more conservative on cultural and national security policy than their college-educated counterparts.

In fact, ideological divisions between those who hold consistently liberal positions and those who hold consistently conservative views have been widening and hardening in recent years. These differences are evident across a wide array of policy areas including immigration, LGBTQ rights, abortion, the economy, and foreign policy. As the authors of one study note: "[C]onsistent liberals and conservatives approach the give-and-take of politics very differently than do those with mixed ideological views. Ideologically consistent Americans generally believe the other side—not their own—should do the giving. Those in the middle, by contrast, think both sides should give ground."[75]

There is disagreement among experts as to the reasons for this growing ideological gap. Alan Abramowitz holds that these ideological divisions reflect genuine differences among the American electorate over simmering issues that are mirrored in the heated rhetoric of our elected representatives. By contrast, Morris Fiorina and Samuel Abrams do not believe public opinion as a whole is growing more extreme; rather, our political parties, driven by those in leadership positions, have generated more ideologically consistent policy prescriptions and forced Americans to sort themselves into one or the other competing camps. They call this phenomenon "party sorting."[76] Both sets of scholars agree, however, that those holding ideological positions in the middle of the political spectrum have fewer political choices in today's highly polarized environment. We will discuss this trend more thoroughly in Chapter 9.

PUBLIC OPINION AND PUBLIC POLICY

Democratic theory posits a close relationship between public opinion and the policies generated by the political system. In a well-functioning democracy, we would expect elected leaders to act on the preferences of voters by providing policy solutions acceptable to a majority of citizens.

A number of uncertainties arise in this process, however. First, voters may simply not have clear preferences on a number of issues. For example, although there is widespread support for reducing carbon emissions, there is no consensus on how best to achieve it. Should we outlaw new coal-burning plants, adopt a carbon tax, or simply increase conservation? In an environment of uncertainty, public opinion is subject to influence by a variety of forces that frame issues in ways that benefit more narrow interests. In lieu of public mandates, minority interests attempting to control the agenda often subject policymakers to intense political pressure (see Chapter 8).

Second, many policies are the product of extraordinary events, like 9/11. Few Americans could foresee the possibility of terrorist attacks on our shores, nor could they imagine the set of security policies that would follow in the aftermath.

Third, many policies are initiated by enterprising policymakers, not the public at large. The success of their ideas becoming policy, however, hangs importantly on their ability to secure public recognition of the problem the policy is meant to address, support for the proposed solution, and consistency of the solution within broad political and cultural traditions.[77]

A final problem complicating the straightforward conversion of public opinion into policy is majority tyranny. What if majority opinion supports policies detrimental to the rights of minorities? The Framers believed that a representative government would act as a filter for public opinion, channeling it in ways that were not destructive to fundamental freedoms and rights. These concerns are not simply hypothetical; elected and appointed leaders sometimes find it necessary to act contrary to public opinion to preserve more fundamental principles. During the 1950s, for example, many southern states refused to abide by Supreme Court opinions ordering the integration of public schools. The Court was attempting to secure minority rights in an atmosphere superheated by opposing public sentiment. In this tense atmosphere, the federal government sent troops to public schools in the South to protect African American students against hostile crowds.

Despite these potential problems, studies reveal a high degree of correspondence between public opinion and public policy. Studies of policymaking from the Progressive Era through the late twentieth century show that changes in public opinion generate responsive policies. Political scientist Eileen Lorenzi McDonagh found that when voters expressed popular support in state referenda for labor reform, women's rights, and prohibition, Congress responded by passing legislation accordingly.[78]

Benjamin I. Page and Robert Y. Shapiro, in a famous political science study, found similar results when they examined hundreds of national policies between 1935 and 1979. Substantial changes in opinion, they found, were almost always followed by policy change in the same direction: "When there is opinion change of 20 percentage points or more, policy change is congruent an overwhelming 90 percent of the time."[79] This pattern is especially impressive when the population considers the policy in question to be important. Policy change is less certain when the percentage of opinion change in one direction or the other is small and when there is a high degree of uncertainty among the public about which policy is preferable. These and other studies suggest that policymakers do heed public opinion in forging policy, even though such congruence is not, and need not be, universal in a democratic republic.[80]

More recently, we have seen that swift changes in public attitudes toward the gay and lesbian community have led to anti-discrimination policies like the legalization of same sex marriages. Although there are still pockets of resistance, the speed with which major change in this policy area has occurred is testimony to the potency of public opinion.

But exactly how much direct impact do average Americans have on policy outcomes? New research testing the direct policy impact of average Americans, wealthy Americans, and interest groups found that the latter two groups have substantial direct influence on policy outcomes, whereas average Americans may have far less.[81] But this doesn't mean that average Americans don't get policies that are beneficial. That is because, the authors found, the interests of average Americans are often aligned with the policy preferences pushed by wealthy Americans. The result is what the authors call "democracy by coincidence." This is further evidence that public opinion matters, but the opinions of some may matter more than others.

PUBLIC OPINION AND CIVIC ENGAGEMENT TODAY

The role that public opinion should play in a democracy remains as highly controversial today as it was when the Framers penned our Constitution. The consent of the governed is the centerpiece of liberal democracy, but how closely should public officials track it?

As we have seen, public opinion is often based on low levels of information and little understanding of the complexities of policy options. It is sometimes prone to manipulation by political consultants who seek to frame issues in self-serving ways. Some political scientists believe that public policy is best left in the hands of elites who are better informed, are more knowledgeable about government, and often are more committed to ideals of tolerance and fair play than the population at large. Some even believe that citizens themselves are more comfortable leaving policy decisions in the hands of experts.[82]

There are others, however, who believe that citizens are fully capable of making informed decisions if they are given the tools. Professors James Fishkin and Robert Lushkin have pioneered a new kind of opinion research that could yet prove an informed and engaged citizenry not only is possible but may be the essential foundation for successful and thoughtful decision making. Called *deliberative polling,* the process begins with a baseline poll of a random, representative sample of the population. It then invites a small group of individuals with characteristics similar to those of the larger sample to a forum where they are given carefully balanced briefing materials on issues to discuss in small, moderated groups. Often participants come up with novel solutions to problems that defy positions based on stereotypical ideologies alone. "I think it's fair to say that the public, in aggregate if you give them a chance, is very wise," Fishkin said. "Policymakers and experts are always surprised at how smart the results are when people get together and focus on an issue."[83]

Fishkin and his colleagues piloted a large-scale deliberative poll in California in 2011 in which over 400 participants spent a weekend deliberating thirty different policy proposals related to political reform. Knowledge levels about the issues were tested before and after the event and compared with a control group that did not attend the session. Fishkin reports that information levels about the issues increased significantly among the participants and they managed to agree on a series of six reforms, which became part of Proposition 31 on the ballot that year. Although the proposition failed to gain enough votes to pass, Fishkin believes that the experience shows the potential of this approach for citizen engagement even in large states and provides valuable lessons that could lead to electoral successes in the future.[84]

Deliberative polling has also been tried in other countries. In Denmark, a party that ran on issues formulated by one such deliberating group picked up ten seats in the Danish Parliament.[85] Many political scientists remain skeptical about deliberative polling, and it surely is no panacea for our highly polarized political environment. Yet, as one advocate of the approach notes: "The great promise of a well designed deliberative process may not always be better policy, but its potential to change the participants themselves. It can teach people to be better citizens by entrusting them with responsibility and pushing them to talk—and listen—to people who look and think differently."[86]

Thinking It Through ≫≫≫

Learning Objective: Summarize demographic characteristics that influence public opinion.

Review: The Content of American Public Opinion

What impact does education have on our beliefs and our confidence in our ability to affect political change? Discuss the reasons why higher education and increased levels of political information can increase efficacy. How might differences in educational opportunities influence the likelihood that voices of rich and poor alike will be heard by those in power?

Summary

1. **What is public opinion, and why is it important?**
   - Public opinion consists of those opinions held by private persons that governments find it prudent to heed.
   - In a democracy, public opinion gives elected officials a sense of what citizens want and what they are willing to accept.
   - The Framers felt the opinions of common people were best expressed by voting; nevertheless, political leaders were never indifferent to public attitudes and could access them through a variety of ad hoc methods.
   - Individuals develop their political opinions through a process of political socialization.
   - The agents of political socialization that shape opinions include family, educational institutions, religious institutions, voluntary associations, and the media.
   - The life experiences associated with racial and ethnic identity, gender, and geography generate political differences across America's diverse population.

2. **How is opinion best measured, and how do we know these measures are reliable?**
   - The measurement of public opinion can be divided into the dimensions of an opinion: direction, salience, intensity, stability, and informational support.
   - A variety of polls are used to measure public opinion: benchmark surveys, trial heat surveys, tracking polls, and exit polls.
   - Opinion is best measured by scientific surveys using random samples in which every member of the population has about the same probability of being selected for an interview.
   - The reliability of surveys depends on how well the sample is drawn and on the quality of the questions. Leading questions, for instance, can lead to nonattitudes.
   - Opinion persistence is a phenomenon whereby individuals resist changing opinions based on faulty evidence even when presented with correct information.

3. **What are some of the most basic features of American public opinion today?**
   - Americans are not very trusting of their government.
   - Americans have lost confidence in elected leaders and institutions.
   - Most consider themselves neither too liberal nor too conservative, but ideology is not evenly spread throughout the country. For example, urban areas, the Northeast, and the West Coast tend to be more liberal; rural areas, the Midwest, and the South, more conservative.
   - The political knowledge of most Americans is lower than many political theorists would desire.
   - Studies reveal a high degree of correspondence between public opinion and public policy decisions, but the opinions of those with higher incomes and education seem more likely to be heeded by policymakers.

Chapter 7

Political Participation
Equal Opportunities and Unequal Voices

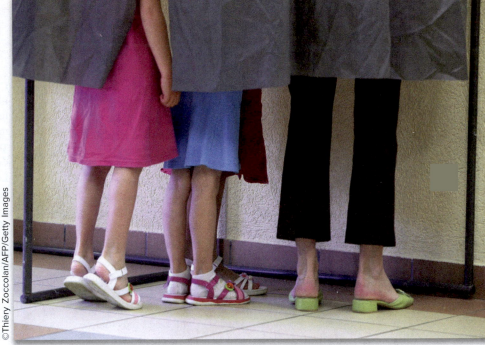

©Thiery Zoccolan/AFP/Getty Images

Although voting is the most notable form of political participation, its capacity for bringing change is relatively weak compared to running for office, as some millennials are finding out.

MILLENNIALS RISING

Stockton, California, is the first city in the nation to offer universal basic income, a program that provides residents facing hard economic times with sufficient money to cover basic living expenses without conditions or restrictions.[1] The program, also operated experimentally in Finland, aims to provide basic financial support to the most needy in an area that has seen stubbornly high unemployment rates. What makes the Stockton program especially unique is that it is funded entirely by private funds, some donated by major charitable foundations and some raised through crowd sourcing.[2]

The basic income program is the brainchild of Michael Tubbs, the first African American mayor of Stockton, California, and the youngest mayor in American history of a city of more than 100,000 people. He is the youngest elected official in Stockton's history and one of the youngest elected officials in the nation.

A lifelong resident of the city, Tubbs attended Stanford University, where he distinguished himself as a Truman Scholar en route to earning a master's degree in public policy. While in college, he advocated for increased access to higher education for underrepresented students and founded the Phoenix Scholars and the Summer Success and Leadership Academy at the University of the Pacific.[3]

He turned his attention to public service in 2010, when his cousin was murdered at a Halloween party. "I decided it would be cowardly for me to continue to do research and write essays about all of Stockton's problems and not try to do something about them," Stubbs told reporters.[4] After serving as a member of the Stockton City Council, he ran for mayor in 2016 and won.

Tubbs is one of a growing number of millennials seeking and winning elective office in local governments around the country. Some are like Brandon Paulin,

Michael Tubbs, mayor of Stockton, California, is the youngest mayor of a major American city.

©Andrew Burton/The New York Times/Redux

elected at age 19 as mayor of Indian Head, Maryland, a town of 4,000 residents located on the Potomac River, about twenty-five miles south of Alexandria, Virginia, where he serves while completing his college degree. Aja Brown, the youngest mayor ever elected in Compton, California, is working to change the town's image from being a haven for street gangs to a business-friendly community and home to software developers. Alex Morse, the mayor of Holyoke, Massachusetts, is transforming a former paper mill town into a high-tech center with the opening of the Massachusetts Green High Performance Computing Center. And in Ithaca, New York, 28-year-old Svante Myrick, the town's first mayor of color, has developed plans for a mixed-income housing project along with sidewalks and bike lanes in an effort to make Ithaca a more affordable, livable, and sustainable city.[5]

As You READ

- What is the nature of political participation in America?
- What are the major forms of political participation, and what resources do they require?
- What is the nature of voting in the United States?
- How do Americans decide how to vote?

It is not difficult to find common threads in the stories of these young leaders. Each was supported by family, friends, or teachers who encouraged political activity from an early age. Their schools provided access to political organizations where they could gain experience. And they share a sense of optimism about the future and their ability to shape events.

In this chapter, we will probe the nature of political participation, the types of opportunities open to Americans to take part in the political process, and the factors generally associated with the likelihood that people will become involved. We will pay special attention to what motivates citizens to vote and to the reasons many choose not to do so. We will examine the economic and social backgrounds of those who are most likely to participate and how these factors affect the kinds of policies enacted by our elected leaders. Finally, we will explore potential ways to increase citizen participation in the political process. ■

POLITICAL PARTICIPATION: OPPORTUNITIES, COSTS, AND BENEFITS

Free societies thrive on the active participation of citizens in the civic and political life of their communities. They also require equal access to the nation's civic and political institutions so that all who desire to contribute may do so. America, however, did not realize the promise of equal access all at once.

Civic-minded reformers, working outside the formal channels of government, led the effort to remove obstacles to participation. Nineteenth-century abolitionists raised political consciousness about the evils of slavery and paved the way for its eventual elimination after the Civil War. At the end of the century, civic-minded Americans who joined the suffrage movement broke down further barriers to participation, as did civil rights groups in the twentieth century.

Opportunities for Americans to participate in government and civic life have never been greater. Political activities open to us range from voting to attending local school board meetings to running for office to campaigning for candidates to signing petitions. Outside of the arena of government, we can work for changes in our communities by joining with other residents to pressure polluters into conforming with emission-control standards or by boycotting manufacturers who don't pay their workforce a living wage or by **buycotting**—that is, intentionally supporting with our purchases the products of environmentally friendly companies. Opportunities alone, however, do not guarantee participation. Personal factors such as income, age, and political socialization play a large part in determining our inclination to participate.

All political and civic activities involve trade-offs between the cost of involvement and the perceived benefits. Not everyone believes they can afford the costs of participation,

buycotting Using purchasing decisions to support the policies of businesses that make these products.

©Underwood & Underwood/Corbis Historical/Getty Images

Civic-minded reformers can work outside government channels to bring about change. The suffragists staged protests to raise popular support for the right of women to vote.

and many don't believe the cost is worth the effort. The perspective that choices are based on our individual assessment of costs and benefits is called the **rational actor theory**. From this perspective, it is difficult to account for people taking part in some types of political participation at all—voting, for example. One vote in a national election has an infinitesimal chance of affecting the election outcome and requires the effort of registering and getting to the polls—effort an individual could have spent on something more personally satisfying. Those who enjoy the benefits from an activity, democratic elections for example, without paying the costs of participation are known as **free riders**. In a society that does not require participation, free riders abdicate their own civic responsibilities and rely on others to expend their resources to carry on the functions of government.

Perhaps surprisingly, large numbers of citizens defy this logic every Election Day. For them, preserving democratic opportunities for engagement outweighs the cost of gathering information about issues or candidates and going to the polls. Activists report that they receive more psychological gratification from voting than from any other political activity.[6] Still, not everyone believes political participation is worth the price. Perhaps they lack the resources to get involved, feel they are not knowledgeable enough to make an informed decision, don't believe the candidates offer them a meaningful choice, or perhaps, no one has asked them for their vote. We will see next that the availability of resources, psychological motivation, and the invitation to get involved all play a part in our calculations of costs and benefits.

> **rational actor theory** The theory that choices are based on our individual assessment of costs and benefits.
>
> **free riders** Those who enjoy the benefits from activities without paying the costs of participation.

CHARACTERISTICS OF POLITICAL PARTICIPATION

Distinctions between political participation and other forms of civic engagement are not always clear-cut. For example, organizing a charity walk to raise money for autism research may not seem like a political activity, yet it raises public awareness of the issue and may pressure political leaders to devote more public funds to the cause. The skills learned in organizing such events are good preparation for political action such as running for office or becoming an advocate for a cause. Alexis de Tocqueville long ago recognized the close relationship between civic and political activity, noting that civic associations pave the way for political ones.[7]

Political participation differs most clearly from civic voluntarism, however, in at least two ways. First, people undertake political activities with the intent of directly or indirectly influencing government policy.[8] This includes a wide array of actions, such as voting in elections, working for a party or candidate, or writing a letter to a congressperson in support of specific legislation. Second, political activities have broad legal, social, or economic consequences for the entire community, not merely for members of a private group or organization. When individuals engage in political activities to raise the minimum wage, their actions, if successful, impact a host of workers, business owners, and consumers throughout the country.

Not all forms of political participation are identical. Some types convey more *information* than others. A letter to a political leader can describe exactly what the voter thinks about an issue. Some types of participation communicate with greater *volume*, i.e., more loudly than others. For example, a mass protest can garner a lot more attention than the individual act of voting alone. Participatory acts also vary in *frequency*. We can contact our leaders as many times as we want, but can only vote once. Some forms of participation give all citizens an equal voice, like voting; others give certain members of the community more clout than others, like when a wealthy individual makes a huge donation to a political campaign. The table "Attributes of Political Activities" categorizes the types of political participation open to American citizens according to the amount of information they convey and the amount of variation they permit.[9]

Attributes of Political Activities

Activity	Capacity for Conveying Information	Variation in Frequency and Strength of Messages Conveyed
Voting	Low	Low
Working on a campaign	Mixed	High
Contributing to a campaign	Mixed	High
Contacting an official	High	Intermediate
Participating in a protest	High	Intermediate
Performing informal community work (e.g., taking part in a neighborhood watch)	High	High
Serving on a local board	High	High
Being affiliated with a political organization	Mixed	High
Contributing to a political cause	Mixed	High

Americans can use many channels for transmitting their views, but each channel is distinctive in terms of information conveyed and the frequency and effort expended to transmit.

Source: Adapted from Verba, S., Schlozman, K. L. and Brady, H. E. *Voice and Equality: Civic Voluntarism in American Politics* (Cambridge, MA: Harvard University Press, 1995), 48.

Amount of Information Conveyed

Voting is the hallmark of democratic systems and the most-studied form of political participation, yet it conveys very limited information. Voters support a political candidate for a variety of reasons, including party affiliation, agreement on issues, personal characteristics, and advertising. Their choices usually depend on a combination of these factors. With such a wide variety of potential motivations, there is no clear way for the winner of the election to know precisely whether the voters supported her because of her stand on the issues or because they didn't like the views of her opponent, For the same reason, voters cannot be sure how the winner will interpret the message they sent at the ballot box.

Other types of political participation convey more explicit messages. A well-written letter lets a member of Congress know exactly what the writer thinks about a particular bill or policy. It conveys a unique message that lets the elected member know exactly how the policy affects the writer and how he or she wishes the member to vote. Similarly, working for candidates or contributing money to campaigns lets the candidates know how strongly we support them. Running for office is the most direct and clear expression of our beliefs. All these activities, however, may also involve higher costs for participants in terms of their time or money.

Variation in Frequency and Strength of Messages Conveyed

Political messages can vary in frequency and volume. Some messages can be delivered only once; their variability is low. For example, each citizen may vote once and only once in an election. Other activities permit greater variation in frequency, making involvement possible as often as time and resources allow. For example, campaign donors can contribute at various levels and at several points during a political campaign, up to the limits allowed by law. Citizens can write as many letters as they wish to their elected leaders.

Similarly, some acts of participation speak more loudly to leaders than others. Political leaders ordinarily pay a great deal of attention to the issues affecting donors who finance their campaigns. They are inclined to pay less attention to protesters, although the size and timing of the protest may have an impact on their actions. Protests following police shootings of Michael Brown and Philando Castile, for example, caught the attention of civil rights leaders who urged the U.S. Justice Department to initiate investigations into the shootings.

Public officials and candidates are more likely to pay attention to actions that convey more information, more often, and more loudly. As we will see, the frequency and strength of such messages are strongly related to the resources individuals possess.

INGREDIENTS FOR INVOLVEMENT

Why do some citizens become politically active while others remain on the sidelines? Three conditions are necessary for political participation. First, citizens must have the resources to participate. Some types of political activity require time; some require money; many require skill. These resources are not evenly distributed and their acquisition is tied to several factors, as we shall see. Second, participants must be interested in the political process and believe that their actions will make a difference. They must not only see political events as important to their lives but also believe that they can somehow influence the course of those events. Finally, people must be asked to participate. Much as in sports, those not recruited to play the game end up sitting on the sidelines.

Access to Resources

All acts of participation require the expenditure of resources: Voting requires time; making cash contributions requires money; organizing a political rally requires time and skill. The type and amount of resources required vary according to the type of political activity. Writing to a member of Congress, for example, requires only basic literacy. For highly educated Americans, this is a relatively simple task, but many Americans lack the confidence in their communication skills to undertake it. Non-native speakers have an even higher bar to clear. Running for elective office requires a combination of resources including the ability to communicate, organize, strategize, and work with others to raise and expend campaign funds.

The resources necessary for effective participation are not distributed equitably. Factors like wealth, education, race, and gender all have an impact on one's likelihood to participate in the political process. Money is a prime example of a resource that is not equally distributed among citizens. Some individuals can and do donate to a large number of causes and candidates up to the limits permitted by law. For citizens with little income, this form of participation is not open to them.

Family Wealth You have probably noticed that the same family names crop up time and time again in positions of political authority. The Bush, Kennedy, and Rockefeller families are legendary not only for

Resources Necessary for Various Types of Political Activities

Activity	Required Resources
Vote	Time
Campaign work	Time, Skills
Campaign contributions	Money
Contact an official	Time, Skills
Protest	Time
Informal community work	Time, Skills
Member of local board	Time, Skills
Affiliation with political organization	Time, Skills, Money
Contribute to a political cause	Money

Time · Money · Skills

Every form of political participation entails some combination of time, money, and skill.

Source: Adapted from Verba, S., Schlozman, K. L. and Brady, H. E. *Voice and Equality: Civic Voluntarism in American Politics* (Cambridge, MA: Harvard University Press, 1995), 48.

Political Activity Among High- and Low-Income Groups

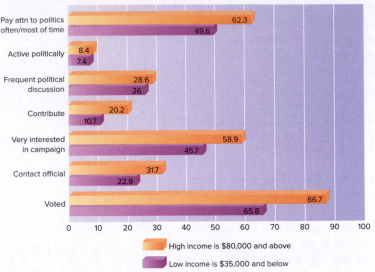

Bar chart:

Activity	High income is $80,000 and above	Low income is $35,000 and below
Pay attn to politics often/most of time	62.3	49.6
Active politically	8.4	7.4
Frequent political discussion	28.6	26
Contribute	20.2	10.7
Very interested in campaign	58.9	45.7
Contact official	31.7	22.9
Voted	86.7	65.8

Upper-income individuals are more likely to engage in virtually all types of political participation at higher rates than those with incomes of $35,000 a year or less.

Source: American National Election Studies, 2016.

their wealth but also for their intergenerational commitment to public service. This is no accident; family wealth confers opportunities that make a difference in the ability to participate in political life. Wealth directly affects the ability to contribute to political fundraising, and it is indirectly related to the possession of other resources, such as the time and skill necessary to engage effectively in other types of political activity. Many upper-income professionals have flexible schedules that allow them time to take part in community and civic projects, whereas few blue-collar workers can take time out of their workday to attend such functions. Family wealth often provides access to other high-status individuals who can help promote one's political aspirations.

As the figure "Political Activity Among High- and Low-Income Groups" illustrates, the wealthy are more likely than those in low-income groups to take part in a wide range of political activities, from talking with others about political issues and candidates to voting in elections. The effect of this imbalance can be felt in policies pursued by those with more money. The more affluent tend to be more liberal on social issues than those with less wealth; but political contributors, especially those who give large amounts, are significantly more conservative than the average citizen on economic matters, including redistribution to benefit those less well-off.[10] Wealth also opens doors to educational opportunities that train individuals in skills involving communication and organization necessary for effective participation in civic life.

Education No resource predicts political activity better than education.[11] The better educated are more likely to engage in political activities, including voting and working for political campaigns, and to participate in community activities such as charity fundraising. Education also has transgenerational effects; parents with high levels of education are more likely to expose their children to social networks that inform them about politics and reward political action.[12] Children from wealthy backgrounds are more likely to hear their parents talking with acquaintances about political issues and to be encouraged to take part in political activities. As a consequence, they are more likely to develop habits of civic involvement than are children of parents with less formal education. Involvement in student government activities also enhances the likelihood of participation in politics, as does exposure to classroom teachers who encourage debate and open discussion.[13]

Religious Affiliation There are other arenas that prepare the less affluent with skills necessary for political participation. Some acquire civic skills from the places where they worship. Religious institutions, particularly those that allow a great deal of local control of church events, open leadership positions to a large number of members and provide opportunities to learn civic skills that are transferable to the political world. For example, some churches and synagogues provide opportunities to practice public speaking skills during services and to organize group activities like picnics, clothing drives, and mission trips to help those less fortunate.[14]

Workplace The workplace also provides opportunities to develop resources such as analytic and communication skills that are useful for political life. Upper-income jobs, however, typically provide more such opportunities than those that pay considerably less. High-paying jobs often stress human-relations skills and provide many opportunities for exercising the organizational talent necessary to engage in politics. They also place individuals within a network of acquaintances who are likely themselves to be well-off and politically active, expanding opportunities for political alliances.

Participation Rates by Race and Gender

Activity	Male	Female	Whites	Blacks	Hispanics
			Percent		
Voted in 2016	53.8	58.1	58.2	55.9	32.5
Campaign activity (at least one act)	39.9	40.5	53.7	48.7	48.5
Make a campaign contribution	16.6	13.4	15.9	11.1	11.0
Contact a public official	28.5	24.0	28.2	19.2	19.3
Community work and attend political meeting	20.7	24.3	22.7	24.8	20.7
Have political discussions (1-2/wk)	23.9	22.7	23.0	24.8	23.2

Women and blacks participate at comparable levels as whites with regard to a number of political activities but notably lag behind on some others. Hispanic Americans have made great progress in catching up with other groups on most measures of participation but lag behind in voting.

Source: Vote source is U.S. Census Bureau. All others: ANES 2016.

By contrast, low-skill jobs that require little formal education provide fewer opportunities for making decisions or exercising leadership. However, labor unions—where they exist—provide an alternative forum for civic learning. Union forepersons, for example, must learn to resolve disputes and represent the rank and file to the management. Unions also promote civic activism by educating members about political issues and urging them to become active in their communities. Steep declines in union jobs over the past half-century, however, have severely undercut such opportunities for many workers.

Race and Gender Access to resources varies according to race and gender (see "Participation Rates by Race and Gender"). Past patterns of discrimination as well as differences in educational and economic opportunities are all factors. Whites, on average, have traditionally participated in political activities in greater numbers than African Americans or Hispanic Americans. However, participation by minority racial and ethnic groups has risen in recent years. Since the election of Barack Obama, blacks have caught up to or surpassed white participation rates on a number of measures like working on a campaign or having political discussions. The rise in voter turnout among African American youth and women has been especially impressive.[15]

Traditionally, women have had lower political participation rates than men, but that is changing, too, especially with regard to the act of voting. Women now vote at higher levels than men, whereas men contribute significantly more money to political leaders and contact political leaders more frequently than do women.[16] Women's political contributions have increased in recent years, but a gap remains, perhaps because women receive lower pay than men with similar jobs. Women may also be somewhat more reluctant to contact political leaders and attend rallies for candidates because far fewer leaders are female.

Political Engagement

Personal resources supply the necessary ingredients to take part in government, but they alone cannot explain why some people get involved while others do not. Some people become politically active because they see it as their civic duty or because politics is a vocational interest. These persons exhibit an interest in politics that motivates them to get involved, a

Top 10 Reasons for Inactivity

	%
I don't have enough time	39
I should take care of myself and my family before I worry about the community or nation	34
The important things of my life have nothing to do with politics	20
I never thought of being involved	19
Politics is uninteresting and boring	17
Politics can't help with my personal or family problems	17
Politics is too complicated	15
As one individual, I don't feel I can have an impact	15
For what I would get out of it, politics is not worth what I would have to put into it	14
Politics is a dirty business	13

There are many reasons Americans give for lack of involvement in the political process.

Source: Verba, S., Schlozman, K. L. and Brady, H. E. *Voice and Equality: Civic Voluntarism in American Politics* (Cambridge, MA: Harvard University Press, 1995), 129.

political engagement Active interest and participation in political activities

political interest An attribute of political participation that measures one's concern for an election outcome and the positions of the candidates on the issues.

political efficacy The belief that an individual can understand and influence political affairs.

political information A measure of the amount of political knowledge an individual possesses concerning political issues, political figures, and the workings of the political system.

strength of party identification The degree of loyalty that an individual feels toward a particular political party.

characteristic called **political engagement**. Others participate only when they feel political issues touch directly on their vital interests, such as when a community threatens to close one of its schools. Many simply feel politics has no relevance to their day-to-day lives and are unlikely to have any motivation to participate. Cross-cultural studies show that political engagement is also affected by the overall level of income inequality within the nation. Where greater income inequality prevails, individuals at the bottom of the income ladder are far less likely to demonstrate an interest in politics, to discuss politics, or to vote.[17] The table "Top Ten Reasons for Inactivity" lists several reasons people choose not to get involved in politics.

We can measure political engagement along four dimensions: political interest, political efficacy, political information, and strength of party identification.[18] **Political interest** is the level of concern that a politically engaged person has about an election outcome and the candidates' positions on the issues. Politically interested individuals care which candidate will win an election and which position on an issue the government will adopt. As a result, they tend to be more politically active. As discussed in Chapter 6, **political efficacy** is the sense of empowerment or satisfaction created by our understanding of the political system and our belief that the system will respond to our concerns.[19] People who lack a sense of political efficacy often regard political activity as intimidating and wasteful.

The third dimension of political engagement is **political information**, the amount of knowledge a person has about political issues, figures, and the workings of the political system. Citizens with more knowledge about the Constitution, political leaders, and the issues of the day are more likely to participate while those who know little may shy away. A final dimension of political engagement is **strength of party identification**. We will see in Chapter 9 that identification with either the Democratic or Republican Party can predict not only the direction of a person's vote but also whether he or she is likely to vote at all.

Such persons are more likely to participate because they feel they belong to an organized body that represents their interests.

It is unclear whether political engagement causes one to become active politically or whether participating in political activity increases one's sense of political engagement. The causal relationship probably runs both ways.

Mobilization

Even an individual with the necessary resources, a high level of interest, and confidence in his or her ability to make a difference is unlikely to get involved unless invited to do so and told what is expected of them. **Political mobilization** is the process by which citizens are alerted to opportunities to participate and encouraged to do so. The agents of political mobilization include political parties, elected officials, interest groups, candidates for political office, voluntary associations, friends, and neighbors.

Direct mobilization involves candidate and party organizations contacting citizens personally to invite them to take part in political activities. Examples include door-to-door canvassing, direct mail or e-mail solicitation, circulation of petitions, requests for money, and letter-writing campaigns. Political parties traditionally played the principal role in mobilizing voters by informing voters about when elections were being held and which candidates were running. Turnout was as high as 80 percent or more at the turn of the twentieth century partly because of party efforts to touch voters directly. Political parties energized communities with parades and picnics to generate support and sought the visible loyalty of citizens by providing their constituents with jobs, government contracts, and other tangible benefits. Today, however, the mobilizing role of parties has weakened as other institutions, such as the mass media, began delivering information about candidates and elections without the personal inducements from party leaders.

Candidates and parties still engage the public, but it is done in a far more selective manner than in days of yore. Parties today utilize what is called **microtargeting**, the practice of mining databases containing information about consumer interests and behaviors in an effort to design personal appeals to voters that are delivered to desktops and mailboxes before Election Day. Millions of voters now receive regular social media solicitations from candidates appealing to their individual interests and tastes. Supporters of gun control are likely to get a far different message than members of the National Rifle Association.

Indirect mobilization occurs when leaders use networks of friends, acquaintances, and organizations to persuade others to participate. Political leaders know that citizens are far more likely to respond to appeals from a member of their own religious congregation or a professional colleague, for example, than from a politician they do not know. They use these contacts to spread enthusiasm for a candidate or a cause. Think about your own situation. Are you more likely to heed the call to vote because of a message on TV or because your friends are tweeting about it or posting on Snapchat and encouraging you to join them at the polls?

Several factors affect the timing, targets, and method of mobilization. First, political actors—whether through direct or indirect mobilization—are likely to target their efforts at strategic times to enhance the success of their cause. For example, political parties concentrate their activities around elections. That is why the number of telephone solicitations, television ads, and tweets from candidates rises exponentially just before Election Day.

Second, political actors are more likely to target individuals and groups they believe are most likely to respond positively to their message and whose backgrounds or political leanings make them likely targets for mobilization. Democratic Party candidates will want to make sure they have secured support from voters of their own party before they go after Republicans and independents. Political actors are also more likely to appeal to upper-income, highly educated individuals who have the resources to support them with money, letter-writing, and campaign involvement.

Finally, the cost of the political action being requested affects mobilization success. Signing a petition involves little effort. Voting requires a bit more. Writing a thoughtful letter to a member of Congress can require still more time, energy, and skill. People are likely to consider responding to invitations to get involved in politics or a cause if the requests do not come too often, if there is a realistic chance of success, if they consider the outcome important, and if participation does not conflict with other important demands on their time.

political mobilization The process whereby citizens are alerted to participatory opportunities and encouraged to become involved.

direct mobilization The process by which citizens are contacted personally by candidate and party organizations to take part in political activities.

microtargeting The practice of mining databases containing information about consumer interests and behaviors to design personal appeals to voters.

indirect mobilization The process by which political leaders use networks of friends and acquaintances to activate political participation.

VOTING

Voting is a unique political activity for a variety of reasons. As we noted earlier, a rational actor may well see very little reason to vote, based on the perceived costs and benefits. And because voting conveys little information, even those who vote have no idea whether a candidate will respond to their needs. Nevertheless, tens of millions of Americans vote regularly in national elections. For many of them, voting confers the psychological benefit of satisfying their civic responsibilities and promoting candidates and issues important to their interests. Who votes? What factors influence turnout? And when we do vote, how do we decide for whom to cast a ballot?

Who Votes?

There are several ways of measuring voter turnout. We can measure turnout as a percentage of all persons who are of voting age (voting-age population, or VAP), or we can measure it as a percentage of only those who are eligible to vote (voter-eligible population, or VEP). Some people are not eligible because they are nonresidents, they are not citizens, or they have not registered to vote. Some states prohibit convicted felons from voting. Measuring voter turnout among those who are actually eligible to vote (VEP) is considered the more sound measurement.

No matter how it is measured, there are clear differences in turnout rates depending on the nature and timing of the elections. Presidential contests bring out between 55 percent and 60 percent of eligible voters every four years, whereas midterm congressional races regularly draw 20 percent fewer voters. Local government contests and special elections draw even fewer voters.

Clearly, resources make a difference in determining who votes. Voter turnout increases directly with employment status and wealth, level of education, and age (see "Who Votes"). Regional differences also exist; both coasts have traditionally voted at higher rates than the interior of the country or the South, although some regions, like the northern Midwest, are given a boost by high turnout in states such as Minnesota and Wisconsin, which recorded some of the highest participation rates in the nation in 2016.[20] Some scholars believe these regional differences may be tied to differences in political culture. For example, Minnesota has long been known for a civic culture that encourages an active citizenry. Some states have higher voting rates because they make voting easier. For example, voters in Oregon and Colorado vote entirely by mail, making it very convenient.

Although white males have traditionally voted at higher levels than minorities and women, the electoral landscape is changing. In 2016, turnout by African Americans was somewhat

Who Votes?

Total Voting

60.2%

Percentage who report having voted in the 2016 election

Region	
Northeast	61.6%
Midwest	64.3%
South	60%
West	60.7%

Age	
18 to 24 years	43
25 to 34 years	53.1
35 to 44 years	60.2
45 to 54 years	65.3
55 to 64 years	67.9
65 to 74 years	72.6

Race and Ethnicity	
White	58.2
Black	55.9
Hispanic (of any race)	32.5
Asian	33.9

Education	
9th to 12th grade, no diploma	35.3
High school graduate	51.5
Some college or associate's degree	63.3
Bachelor's degree	74.2
Advanced degree	80.3

Source: Michael McDonald, "2016 General Election VEP Turnout," United States Election Project, www.electproject. org; all other figures from U.S. Census Bureau, Current Population Survey, 2017.

©PhotoDisc/Getty Images

lower than the record numbers that turned out for Barack Obama in 2008 and 2012. Nevertheless, the trend for African Americans has been upward, driven by an increase in young and female black voters.[21] Although turnout rates for Asian Americans and Hispanics are lower than those for blacks and whites, their rates are rising. These two groups are the fastest growing minorities in America, and their impact on elections will become more important in future years as their numbers grow. Over 60 percent of whites voted in 2016, but their overall share of the voting population has been declining in recent years compared with increases in the vote share of minority communities. These changes are a harbinger of a more diverse electorate in coming years as the population diversifies. Female voting participation now outpaces male voting. This may be related to the increasing number of females attaining higher levels of education.

Turnout generally increases with age. Usually this is associated with the growing responsibilities one assumes as one ages, with an increase in resources like education and time, and with growing ties to one's community. Young people are more mobile, often moving out of their home towns for college or jobs. Older adults are more settled and more likely attuned to political issues in their communities. Many young people fail to vote because they are turned off by a political system mired in partisan gridlock. One study reports that more young people aspire to be a mechanic or a salesperson than president of the United States.[22] However, the right issues, inspiring candidates, easier registration procedures, and the use of youth-friendly technologies can all play a part in reigniting interest in politics among the young.

Turnout rates for young people between the ages of 18 and 29 declined in 2012 after peaking in 2008 at the highest rate recorded since 18-year-olds were first eligible to vote in 1972.[23] Youth turnout in 2016 was slightly below 50 percent, about the same mark achieved in 2012. However, young voters were the only age group to see somewhat higher turnout in 2016 over the previous presidential election.[24] Voting, like all forms of political participation, also increases with level of education. Young people with college experience generally turn out at a rate almost 30 percent higher than youth with no college experience.[25]

Who Doesn't? And Why?

From about 1960 to 1992, turnout in presidential elections declined, with the greatest declines occurring between 1960 and 1972. After a spike in 1992, it dipped again, only to rebound in 2004 and 2008. Overall turnout again dipped by about 5 percentage points in 2012, although some groups, such as African Americans, continued to show strong turnout numbers that year. Another dip in turnout appeared in 2016 during a contentious election that turned off many voters. Several factors help explain low turnout in American elections (see "Demographic Profile of Nonvoters"). Let's turn to these now.

Registration Americans must register to vote either in person or by mail, and they must reregister if they move or fail to vote in a certain number of consecutive elections. First-time voters must present forms of identification that may not be easily accessible, like a birth certificate. And, in most states, registration must be completed a certain number of days in advance of the election. These requirements, while not unreasonable, place additional burdens on the voter and cost more in terms of time. By contrast, some countries make qualifying to vote easier by using a civil registry system that automatically registers every eligible resident. Denmark, for example, uses a computerized national civil registry to produce a voter list. The government issues each citizen a number, somewhat like our Social Security numbers,

Demographic Profile of Nonvoters

	Percentage of all nonvoters who are:
Gender	**%**
Men	51
Women	49
Race	
White	55
Black	13
Hispanic	23
Age	
18 to 29 years	34
30 to 49 years	36
50 to 64 years	19
65 and older	10
Education	
Post grad	5
College grad	12
Some college	28
High school or less	54
Income	
$75,000 or more	18
$30,000–$74,000	27
Under $30,000	46
Religion	
Protestant	41
Catholic	23
Other	7
Unaffiliated	27

Younger, low-income individuals without a college education are among those most likely to be nonvoters.

Source: Pew Research Center, *The Party of Non-Voters: Younger, More Racially Diverse, More Financially Strapped,* October 31, 2014, http://www.people-press.org/2014/10/31/the-party-of-nonvoters-2/.

citizenship Quiz

Can you pass the U.S. Citizenship Test? See how well you know the content in this chapter covered on the citizenship test required of foreign-born candidates for naturalization.

1. What are two ways that Americans can participate in their democracy?
2. Four amendments to the Constitution address who can vote. Describe one of them.
3. What is one promise you make when you become a United States citizen?

(1) Vote, join a political party, help with a campaign, join a civic group, join a community group, give an elected official your opinion on an issue, call senators and representatives, publicly support or oppose an issue or policy, run for office, write to a newspaper (2) 15th, giving franchise to black men; 19th, securing right to vote for women; 24th, outlawing the use of poll taxes; 27th, lowering the voting age to 18 (3) Give up loyalty to other countries, defend the Constitution of the United States, obey the laws of the United States, serve in the U.S. military (if needed), serve (do important work for) the nation (if needed), be loyal to the United States

Source: United States Citizenship and Immigration Services.

for the delivery of all government services and the payment of taxes. Voters can present the number for identification at the polls throughout the country, no matter where they live. Some countries require registration only once in a lifetime so that voters remain permanently eligible no matter where or how often they move within the country.

Seventeen states and the District of Columbia have taken measures to make voting easier by allowing voters to register the same day they vote. Voter turnout in these states is generally higher than in others requiring registration at some earlier date.[26] Young people who are more mobile are more likely to turn out to vote in states with same-day registration.[27] In 2012, seven out of the top ten youth turnout states had laws that eased registration pressures, including Election Day registration, voting by mail (Oregon), or not requiring registration to vote (North Dakota).[28]

Thirteen states and the District of Columbia made registration even easier by adopting automatic voter registration. In these states, applicants for a driver's license or other public document are automatically registered to vote. They then have a number of weeks to

Voter Turnout

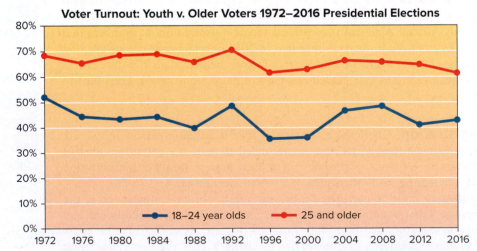

Voter Turnout: Youth v. Older Voters 1972–2016 Presidential Elections

Legend: 18–24 year olds; 25 and older

Young people between the ages of 18 and 24 have traditionally voted at lower levels than older Americans ever since first exercising their right to vote in 1972.

Source: Center for Information and Research on Civic Learning and Education.

"opt out" if they do not wish to remain registered. If they do not opt out, they remain registered to vote in future elections.

However, some measures have been instituted that make voting more difficult. Several states have imposed strict voter ID laws that require individuals to show proof of residence. In most cases, this is not difficult; but the poor, minorities, and the elderly sometimes have difficulties providing documents like birth certificates that cost time and money to procure in lieu of drivers' licences. Recently, the Supreme Court (*Husted, Ohio Secretary of State v. A. Philip Randolph Institute, et al,* 2018) allowed states to purge voters from the registration rolls if they fail to vote in successive elections or fail to respond to a notice from election officials. The ruling could result in thousands of voters finding themselves ineligible to vote when they show up at the polls.

Timing The timing and scheduling of elections also affects turnout. Voting in the United States often takes place on a Tuesday, which means that most Americans must adjust their workday schedules to go to the polls. By contrast, some European countries schedule elections on a national holiday to make it easier for voters to show up at the polls. Other nations, including Norway, Japan, Switzerland, and New Zealand, hold elections on weekends. This lack of convenience is one reason U.S. turnout lags behind turnout in other democratic nations (see "Voter Turnout Across the Globe").

More recently, Americans have been offered the choice of voting early, in some places up to a month before the election. This option is becoming much more popular. It is estimated that as many as a third of all voters in the 2016 presidential election voted prior to Election Day.[29] Most studies show that increased turnout in early-voting states may be short lived and that turnout decreases after a few years of use. Others, however, show marginal increases with the potential benefit that early voting may attract new voters.[30] There are differences of opinion over the advisability of early voting and voting by mail, however. Some argue that it artificially cuts the campaign short for some voters and destroys the sense of shared civic responsibility that accompanies a uniform day of voting for all Americans. Others claim that the benefits in convenience and potential for an increase in turnout are worth the costs.

Two-Party System Our two-party system also helps explain low turnout in the United States. Most other Western democracies have multiparty parliamentary systems that generally represent the interests of particular economic groups within the nation. In Great Britain, for example, the Labour Party has a long tradition of appealing to the working class; the Conservatives (popularly called the Tories), by contrast, make their appeals to the more affluent. The economic orientation of political parties can exert a powerful influence on getting out the vote by convincing voters that their economic interests are taken seriously by political leaders. In America, the major political parties rarely structure their messages primarily around economic divisions, preferring to appeal to the vast middle of the economic and ideological spectrum. (We will discuss this characteristic of American parties at greater length in Chapter 9.) Some researchers believe that the centrist appeal of American parties is partly responsible for the poor turnout of lower-income groups because citizens in these brackets fail to hear candidates addressing their concerns.[31]

Frequency of Elections The number and frequency of elections is another factor depressing turnout in the United States. The United States holds more primary and general elections at the national, state, and local levels than any other democracy. Unlike many European voters, who go to the polls once every three, four, or five years, American voters

Voter Turnout Across the Globe

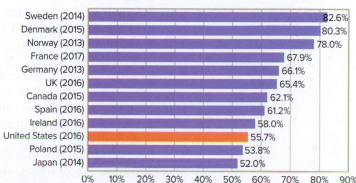

Voter Turnout Across the Globe

Country	Turnout
Sweden (2014)	82.6%
Denmark (2015)	80.3%
Norway (2013)	78.0%
France (2017)	67.9%
Germany (2013)	66.1%
UK (2016)	65.4%
Canada (2015)	62.1%
Spain (2016)	61.2%
Ireland (2016)	58.0%
United States (2016)	55.7%
Poland (2015)	53.8%
Japan (2014)	52.0%

VAP Turnout in Presidential Elections in Most Recent Election Year for Selected Advanced Western Democracies

Source Data: International Institute for Democracy and Electoral Assistance.

voter fatigue A tendency to tire of the process of voting as a result of frequent elections.

in most states are asked to vote in primary and general elections every year, and often more frequently. Special elections may be called to replace candidates who resign or are removed from office. Some states also ask citizens to vote on referenda to approve or reject particular measures ranging from tax increases to special funding for public schools. Many analysts believe the frequency with which Americans are called to vote creates **voter fatigue**, a tendency to tire of the process and refrain from going to the polls. It costs time and effort to go to the polls; and, although voting is important, it is often inconvenient. If elections were consolidated so that voters were called to the polls less often, more people might make the effort.

Lack of Competitive Races Finally, the competitiveness of the race affects turnout: The more competitive the race, the more interest it draws. Voters are less likely to show up if the result is clearly predictable. Although competitive races attract more interest and participation, only about half of the presidential contests since 1952 have been close right up to Election Day, and congressional elections today are rarely competitive.[32] As we will see in Chapter 11, upwards of 90 percent of incumbents are reelected to Congress. They come from districts that are so free of genuine party competitiveness that it often seems futile for supporters of the minority-party candidate to even show up on Election Day.

VOTERS IN THE ELECTORAL PROCESS: HOW AMERICANS DECIDE

When George Washington ran for the House of Burgesses in Virginia in 1758, voters took their cues from the voice votes of the town's most respected property holders. They were also offered material inducements. Washington provided twenty-eight gallons of rum, fifty gallons and one hogshead of rum punch, thirty-four gallons of wine, forty-six gallons of "strong beer," and two gallons of cider royal to be served to the 391 voters in his district.[33] When party strength was at its peak near the beginning of the twentieth century, voters were encouraged to cast highly visible color-coded ballots in plain view of party bosses and were entertained by parades and pageants.[34] Today, in the era of secret ballots, voters are left on their own to navigate electoral decisions on the basis of party affiliation, candidate characteristics, and issue positions.

Party Choice

As we saw in Chapter 6, early socialization generally shapes party identification. These early influences are strong and have considerable staying power. Over time, we come to view political personalities and events through a perceptional screen colored by partisan cues. For committed partisans, party affiliation is a powerful predictor of choice of candidate.[35] Democrats draw strongly from those with lower levels of income and education, although those with postgraduate degrees have gravitated to the Democratic camp in recent years. Minorities, single women, and those who never or infrequently attend religious services are among the strongest Democratic supporters. Higher-income and college-educated voters are more likely to be Republicans, as are white men (particularly southern whites), married women, and those who attend religious services regularly.

Voter dissatisfaction with the major political parties has increased the percentage of self-identified independents, especially among younger voters. However, although about a third of voters call themselves independents, most of these "lean" more toward one or the other party and behave more like partisans when election time rolls around (see "Party Identification").

As we will discuss in more detail in Chapter 9, the political parties have become more ideologically unified today than they were for much of the past fifty years. Democrats more consistently tout liberal policy options, while Republicans are more reliably conservative. Partisan voters have likewise been drawn to more polarized positions, leaving fewer voters who are likely to split their votes, or cross party lines, by voting Democrat for some offices and Republican for others on the same ballot. In fact, many partisans today wear their party allegiance as a badge of personal identity, sticking with their partisan choices despite disagreement with some of the issues positions taken by party leaders. Despite the strength of partisan affiliation, there are a number of weak partisans on both sides who are considered **swing voters**. These voters may switch parties from election to election depending on issues or candidates. These swing voters can mean the difference between victory or defeat for one or the other major-party candidates in a highly polarized and closely divided electorate.

Party Identification

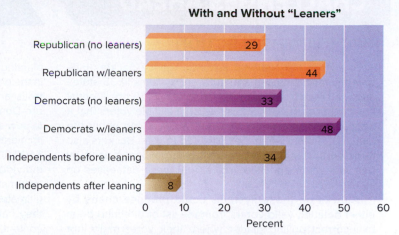

With and Without "Leaners"

Republican (no leaners)	29
Republican w/leaners	44
Democrats (no leaners)	33
Democrats w/leaners	48
Independents before leaning	34
Independents after leaning	8

Percent (0, 10, 20, 30, 40, 50, 60)

Although about a third of Americans self-identify as independents, that number shrinks to just 8 percent when asked which way they lean.

Source: Data from Pew Research Center, September 13, 2016

Not every political campaign follows a script dictated by traditional party ties, however. When party affiliation fails to provide reliable guidance for voters, they turn to short-term factors like issues and the personal characteristics of the candidates.

> **swing voter** A voter lacking strong attachment to one party or another and who likely votes across party lines.

Issues

Especially for independent voters who show little attachment to party labels, issues may be an important factor in voting decisions.[36] Issue voters try to match their own views on issues they believe to be most salient with the views each candidate presents. They are less concerned with party than those voters who consider themselves strong Democrats or strong Republicans. If addressing global warming is your top priority, you are more likely to pay attention to candidates' views on this issue than to party labels. Strong partisans, by comparison, may be less bothered by a candidate's ambiguity on the issues because it is their partisan attachment that drives their voting choice.[37] That doesn't mean that issues are entirely irrelevant to partisan voters. Even the staunchest party supporter will cross over to another party's candidate if she disagrees with the stance her own party's candidate has taken on an issue she considers very important. Notable Republicans voiced their opposition to Donald Trump in 2016 because they disagreed with his issue positions on trade and immigration.

Since much attention during the campaign focuses on the candidate's promises, we would expect **prospective voting**, in which voters make their choices primarily with an eye toward what the candidate says he or she will do if elected, to be quite high. However, voters understand that many factors may prevent the candidate from fulfilling campaign pledges. As a result, **retrospective voting**, holding politicians accountable for past performance, is more often the norm.

One of the most important ways voters judge a president or a party is by the way the economy performs during their tenure in office. Rightly or wrongly, voters attribute the state of the economy to elected leaders, particularly presidents, and hold them accountable. But voters do not simply make choices on the basis of their own financial condition. They make judgments about the direction and strength of the economy as a whole. Does it seem that the country is experiencing growth? Is unemployment shrinking? Are prices stable?

Economic considerations are so important to elections that many economists and political scientists have created models that predict outcomes on the basis of macroeconomic factors alone.[38] The direction in which the national economy is heading early in an election year

> **prospective voting** Voting choice made on the basis of anticipated results if the candidate of choice is elected.
>
> **retrospective voting** Voting on the basis of the candidate's or party's record in office.

HACKING THE ELECTION

According to the National Security Agency, hackers infiltrated voter databases and software systems in 35 states and the District of Columbia during the 2016 presidential election. Each state maintains a list of eligible voters that it periodically updates so that poll workers can verify the identity of voters when they show up to vote. Hackers also targeted software used in electronic pollbooks used by poll workers to check-in voters from these databases on election day.*

Attacks on these systems could produce chaos by either deleting valid voters from the list or directing them to incorrect polling places where their votes might not count. An attempt to delete or alter voter information was confirmed in at least one state—Illinois. Fortunately, the states were able to verify voter registrations with backup data they maintained.

Attacks on voting systems themselves are harder to pull-off since virtually none of the current systems currently in use can be accessed via the Internet. Voting systems are self-contained and voting in America is decentralized, meaning that anyone who wanted to alter an election would have to coordinate attacks at hundreds of local polling places across the state or nation. They would have to physically access the machines and tamper with their operation. Nevertheless, some of the machines currently in use are quite old and tampering might not require much sophistication in order to defeat their security capabilities.

Voting specialists have recommended a number of measures to shore-up security, including the use of paper ballots so audits and recounts can be performed to confirm vote counts, enhanced security of voter databases and mandatory frequent backups, and the replacement of older voting systems with more modern ones with better security features.[†]

The more difficult problem comes in trying to prevent foreign powers from attempting to sway the election by planting false information about the election or candidates in the press and on social media. We now know that Russian trolls and automated bots not only promoted explicitly pro-Donald Trump messaging, but also used social media to sow social divisions around controversial topics such as immigration and Islamophobia.[‡] With the purchase of about $100,000 of ads on Facebook, Russia was able to target individuals who might react with alarm to the planted information and then spread it to their friends and contacts, ultimately reaching millions of users.[¶] Facebook officials say they have implemented a series of steps to combat fake content, including recruiting outside reviewers to check out and flag dubious articles. However, they are reluctant to become the arbiters of fact and fiction.

Russia denies allegations of planting false information, but U.S. Intelligence officials believe the evidence is incontrovertible. Federal law prohibits foreign governments, companies, and citizens from spending money to influence American elections. In planning for the future, U.S. officials have warned that both government and social media companies must do more to root out foreign influence in our elections. The only certainty, they say, is that it will happen again if we don't find ways to prevent it.

*Sweeney L, Yoo J, Zang J. Voter Identity Theft: Submitting Changes to Voter Registrations Online to Disrupt Elections. Technology Science. 2017090601. September 6, 2017. Accessed on November 22, 2017 at http://techscience.org/a/2017090601.

[†]Brennan Center for Justice, "Voting System Security and Reliability Risks," August 30, 2016. Accessed on November 22, 2017 at https://www.brennancenter.org/analysis/fact-sheet-voting-system-security-and-reliability-risks.

[‡]Tom McArthur, "How Russia used social media to divide Americans." *The Guardian,* October 14, 2017. Accessed on November 22, 2017 at https://www.theguardian.com/us-news/2017/oct/14/russia-us-politics-social-media-facebook.

[¶]Scott Shane and Vindu Goel, "Fake Russian Facebook Accounts Bought $100,000 in Political Ads, *The New York Times,* September 6, 2017. Accessed on November at https://www.nytimes.com/2017/09/06/technology/facebook-russian-political-ads.html?_r=0.

Top Issues for Voters in 2016 Election

All Adults	Adults 18-30
Economy	Education
Terrorism	Economy
Foreign Policy	Terrorism
Healthcare	Healthcare
Gun Policy	Income Inequality

Though similar, the political agendas of younger and older voters differed as they headed to the polls on Election Day in 2016.

Source: All adults: Pew Research Center, "Top Voting Issues in 2016 Election," July 7, 2016, http://www.people-press.org/2016/07/07/4-top-voting-issues-in-2016-election/. Associated Press-NORC Center for Public Affairs Research, GenForward 2016 Toplines, June 16, 2016, http://genforwardsurvey.com/assets/uploads/2016/07/GenForward-June-2016-Toplines-1.pdf.

appears to be a particularly potent harbinger of Election Day results. Though these models have impressive records of success, they are not infallible. Modelers who predicted a Democratic victory in 2016 on the basis of a steadily improving economy under the sitting Democrat, Barack Obama, were proven wrong.[39] Of course, that was an unusual election because Hillary Clinton won the popular vote by nearly three million votes but narrowly lost in the Electoral College.

In 2016, the economy continued to be important for voters, but voters also said the government itself was a problem because of its seeming inability to get anything done. (See "Top Issues for Voters in 2016 Election.") This hostility toward government helps explain the level of support for insurgent candidates like Donald Trump and Bernie Sanders, who rejected the government's way of doing "business as usual." Some voters also gravitated to Donald Trump because of his strong stands on immigration and trade.

Candidate Characteristics

A candidate's personal characteristics have always mattered to American voters. Colonial voters saw attributes of leadership and wealth in George Washington that set him apart from others. In the glory days of party politics, however, personal characteristics took a backseat to party loyalty. In today's candidate-centered campaigns, voters once again are looking for those indefinable qualities associated with leadership.

Voters usually feel more comfortable with candidates with whom they can personally relate. During the 2016 campaign, Donald Trump became a magnet for voters feeling that establishment candidates had let them down. His straightforward bombastic style of voicing frustrations that resonated with some of the working class seemed a refreshing change from the stilted and guarded style of the other candidates. But Trump's off-the-cuff approach may have lost him as many supporters as his frankness gained. Many potential voters were dismayed by his remarks about Hispanics and his call to bar Muslims from entering the country. Bernie Sanders held personal appeal for liberal voters who believed the Democratic Party had grown too conservative. Young voters, especially, were drawn to his idealism and authenticity.

Voters are often more likely to cast ballots for members of their own race, ethnic group, or even gender, although evidence for this is not always consistent.[40] The 2008 election demonstrated that these characteristics can be extremely powerful in generating support for a candidate. Barack Obama won 96 percent of the African American vote in the general election. Of course, these characteristics can work against a candidate as well. Some observers feared that white Americans were giving pollsters erroneous yet socially acceptable responses when they said they supported the Obama candidacy. Pollsters were leery of these results as they had been caught off guard by inaccurate responses in previous elections involving black candidates such as the 1982 campaign of Tom Bradley for governor of California. It is hard to estimate the effect of racial bias in recent presidential campaigns; however, some political scientists believe racial prejudice denied Obama an electoral landslide in 2008.[41]

To tarnish the personal appeal of candidates, opponents sometimes use **opposition research** to find and exploit weaknesses in their rivals' backgrounds. The line between how much of this information is useful data that voters should know in evaluating the candidate (such as voting records) and how much is designed to smear the opposition (such as marital infidelity) is often a fine one. With party support closely divided and candidates scrambling for just a few more votes than the opposition, the temptation to uncover and use negative information about a candidate's past can be overwhelming. The public, however, has shown some impatience with such tactics, and it is unclear how much negative campaigning they are willing to tolerate. Some observers fear that attacks on candidates' characters may further alienate voters.

opposition research The practice of searching for events in candidates' records or personal lives that can be used to attack them during elections.

The election of 2016 was unusual in many ways. One of the most significant factors was the very high unfavorable ratings each candidate received from the electorate, in some cases approaching 70 percent. Donald Trump turned off many voters with his bombast; Hillary Clinton was believed to be untrustworthy by voters concerned about her handling of e-mails during her service as secretary of state. For many voters motivated by candidate appeal, the choice boiled down to whom they perceived as the least objectionable.

OTHER FORMS OF POLITICAL PARTICIPATION

Many forms of political participation require citizens to expend more resources than the simple act of voting. Some, like volunteering to work in a political campaign, require the additional expenditure of time. Some, like writing a letter to an elected official, require more skill. Others, such as contributing to a candidate or cause, require additional financial resources.

Although U.S. voter turnout compares poorly to that in other democracies, Americans show greater levels of participation in more time-consuming political activities. One study comparing the United States to Austria, the Netherlands, the United Kingdom, and Germany found that Americans ranked first in the amount of time they devoted to campaign work, contact with public officials, and community volunteering.[42] Unlike voting, there is no limit to the number of times one can perform such acts or the amount of time one can devote to them. Some stalwart activists find themselves limited only by the number of hours in the day. Activities that require more time also vary in the amount of information they convey and the level of skill necessary to perform them. Writing a thoughtful letter to a member of Congress and working a candidate's phone bank or Twitter feed during a political campaign are two examples of time-intensive activities that convey a high level of information and require a level of skill and knowledge not all may possess.

Because time-intensive activities demand a greater level of commitment than voting, we would expect these acts to hold the potential for greater benefits to the individuals who perform them. (See "Political Participation by Age") Some of the benefits may be material. Taking the time to perform door-to-door canvassing for a candidate may be worth the effort if the candidate manages to save your job at a local plant that was previously scheduled to close. Participation also provides psychological rewards such as the opportunity to meet and work with others who share similar views. Activists feel gratified when their work results in the implementation of policies they support.[43]

conventional participation Traditional forms of participation like voting that citizens have relied upon to make their voices heard and to impact governmental decisions.

unconventional participation Less common forms of participation that often challenge or defy authority.

Unconventional Forms of Participation For the most part, we have been discussing forms of participation that are **conventional**, that is, they are traditional practices like voting that Americans have relied upon to make their voices heard and to impact governmental decisions. There are also **unconventional** forms of participation like protesting that are not as common as other forms and that often defy or challenge those in authority. The number of Americans taking part in protests and rallies has increased in recent years in response to both events like police shootings of black men and the election of Donald Trump. Women's marches and the Black Lives Matter, Occupy Wall Street, and Tea Party movements are but four recent examples. Some researchers believe these actions represent an emerging pathway to more meaningful citizen engagement—a pathway that needs further scholarly exploration.[44]

Political Participation by Age

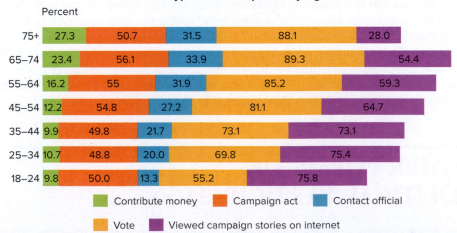

Types of Participation by Age

Percent

Age	Contribute money	Campaign act	Contact official	Vote	Viewed campaign stories on internet
75+	27.3	50.7	31.5	88.1	28.0
65–74	23.4	56.1	33.9	89.3	54.4
55–64	16.2	55	31.9	85.2	59.3
45–54	12.2	54.8	27.2	81.1	64.7
35–44	9.9	49.8	21.7	73.1	73.1
25–34	10.7	48.8	20.0	69.8	75.4
18–24	9.8	50.0	13.3	55.2	75.8

- Contribute money
- Campaign act
- Contact official
- Vote
- Viewed campaign stories on internet

Older voters are most likely to remain with traditional forms of participation, while younger voters turn to newer formats like social media to support political causes.

Source: American National Election Studies, 2016.

©baldyrgan/Shutterstock

Changing Patterns of Political Participation

In today's world, where identity politics and direct action are seen as being more important than simply voting with one's pocketbook, many citizens appear less interested in traditional political activities like voting or joining organizations and more interested in finding new modes of political self-expression. The table shows the types of unconventional political activities individuals from several nations say they have taken or are willing to undertake to register their voices. These activities range from signing a petition to boycotting a product to demonstrating, striking, and even occupying buildings to advance their cause.

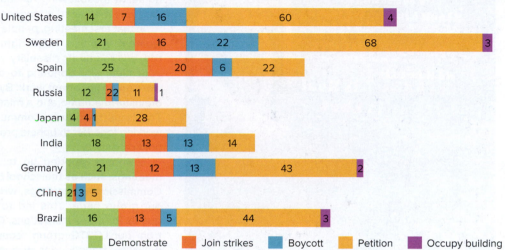

Unconventional Participation Around the World
(Percent saying they have engaged in or are willing to engage in these activities)

Country	Demonstrate	Join strikes	Boycott	Petition	Occupy building
United States	14	7	16	60	4
Sweden	21	16	22	68	3
Spain	25	20	6	22	
Russia	12	2	2	11	1
Japan	4	4	1	28	
India	18	13	13	14	
Germany	21	12	13	43	2
China	2	1	3	5	
Brazil	16	13	5	44	3

Source: World Values Survey, Wave 6: 2010-2014 Except Occupy Buildings 1995-2000 World Values Survey

A dramatic increase in unconventional political behavior was noticed several years ago by Ronald Inglehart and Gabriella Catterberg.[†] The authors claim the rise in these forms of participation reflects the interest people—especially the young—have in methods of expression that are more direct than the simple act of voting. They believe that it represents a new reality in the international political landscape. The authors reject the notion that citizens in advanced democracies are withdrawing from civic action. Instead, they insist, citizens in today's world are increasingly critical of elite decision making and unwilling to join elite institutions, and they are increasingly ready to intervene actively to influence specific decisions. In short, "the nature of citizen politics in advanced democracies has changed."[‡]

Since these authors first published their study, unconventional participation has only increased—and it has surfaced not only in advanced democracies where it was first noticed, but in a number of authoritarian counties as well.

Questions:

1. Why do you believe some types of unconventional participation are more popular than others, and what features distinguish those activities that are more popular from those that attract fewer participants?
2. Explain regional differences in participation rates evident in the table above.
3. What factors might explain the numbers of people willing to participate in unconventional acts even in repressive regimes?

[†] Ronald Inglehart and Gabriella Catterberg, "Trends in Political Action and the Post Honeymoon Decline," *International Journal of Comparative Sociology*, 43 (2002): 300–316.
[‡] Ibid., 314

Some unconventional forms of participation are personal and **expressive** in nature. Individuals across all age brackets take time to participate in many of these activities, but young people are somewhat more inclined to participate in expressive forms. These are tools often used by individuals who reject traditional forms of participation like voting and who feel they can find no other way to make their voices heard. These individuals do not have to rely on public figures to take action for them; they can take action on their own. One example is **hashtag activism**, the use of social media to draw attention to a cause. This type of activism can have a real impact on public policies. The #MeToo movement drew needed attention to sexual harassment and sexual assault leading to the ouster of

> **expressive participation** Engaging the political world by expressing to others one's views by words or actions. Common forms include the use of social media to promote one's stance, boycotting, and buycotting.
>
> **hashtag activism** Using social media to draw attention to a cause.

Source: Allie Armstrong

Allie Armstrong finds success organizing moms to improve lives in her community.

PORTRAIT
OF AN ACTIVIST

Meet Allie Armstrong and H-CAN Community Moms

After ten years working in child welfare, domestic violence, community mental health, and HIV care I became disillusioned with our political system and endlessly frustrated with grinding generational poverty, racism, and sexism. So when I had my children I opted out: I took "the personal is political" to heart and focused on being a mother and became president of my local Moms Club—providing social support and connection to other moms in my community.

Then I made a decision to stand up for my own progressive vision of the future for my daughters. So, I made a simple post to Facebook looking for anyone interested in organizing for a better future.

Friends began to post that they were interested, and I created a small Facebook group with about a dozen folks. It grew exponentially to 200 people. By the third day I decided we should meet in person and a fellow mom opened her home. By the following Tuesday we had our first meeting with forty-one motivated attendees, forty women and one man.

In that first meeting, people raised a number of concerns—women's rights, LGBTQ rights, racial justice, immigration, the environment, disability rights, civic engagement and education, and donating to other groups that we thought were doing important work. By the following week, we met to brainstorm a name and a mission statement. We settled on The Havertown-Area Community Action Network—a group working together to uphold progressive values and encourage political action.

Members stepped up to start attending regular local meetings, such as the school board and township's Board of Commissioners meetings, writing up notes, and sharing on our group page. This led to some groups organizing requests for these institutions. Our first media coverage came from our LGBTQ group requesting a standalone inclusive policy for transgender students, which was followed up by the district hiring an expert consultant and developing a new policy along with a plan for implementing it across the district. Members of our civic engagement group also organized and addressed the township Board of Commissioners about gerrymandering in the state of Pennsylvania and asked that they sign off on a resolution in support of the end of gerrymandering, developed by Fair Districts, PA. Their request was granted.

H-CAN has worked on understanding how our government functions on a township, county, and state level; hosted many speakers and workshops on topics such as racism, Islamophobia, women's self-defense, and disabilities; held candidate forums; held a vigil for a community member detained by ICE; and assisted in voter education and mobilization. We also hosted the first LGBTQ Pride Picnic in our community and a panel discussing moms running for office.

None of this would have been possible on my own, but with the enthusiasm and collaboration of so many inspiring and determined members of our community, we have started to make an impact in our community. We have become stronger by working together and know that when we raise our voice, others will stand with us.

political officials from office and the short-circuiting of careers. Online petitions helped short-circuit Internet antipiracy legislation pending in Congress in 2012, and it helped turn around a proposed funding ban for Planned Parenthood. Other expressive forms of participation include boycotting, refusing to make purchases from a merchant or company whose policies we reject; and buycotting, making purchases exclusively from dealers who promote the causes we favor.

Beyond Voting: Activities That Require More Skill

Voting is a fairly simple act. So is donating money. But some acts of political participation require more sophisticated skills. Political campaigns in America are fueled by thousands of unpaid average citizens who staff phone banks, contact donors, serve as financial consultants or liaisons with the press, coordinate activities with political parties, and organize rallies. Even writing a letter to one's congressperson requires confidence in one's ability to communicate effectively. These activities put us in close contact with our elected leaders, giving us an opportunity to express our views more clearly than the act of voting alone.

Citizens who engage in these activities are not equally drawn from all segments of the political community. The more affluent are more likely to write letters, volunteer for political campaigning, make political contact with elected officials, and work on solving community problems. The affluent often have training in the skills necessary for these more demanding tasks. Nevertheless, as we have seen, religious organizations and labor unions can provide those with fewer resources opportunities to develop these same skills. Often, lower levels of participation by the poor are traceable not to lack of skill but to lower levels of interest or a lack of confidence in their political efficacy. When political activities require financial commitment, however, the discrepancy in participation between rich and poor is not only greater, it is more difficult to overcome.[45]

Beyond Voting: Activities That Require Money

Contributing money is the political act that has the greatest capacity for variation from individual to individual. Within the limits of the law, contributors can donate as little or as much as they want. However, the clarity of the message conveyed by political donations can vary depending on the identity of the recipient. Contributing to a narrow political cause sends a clear message that one supports the goals established by the group. By comparison, contributing money to a presidential campaign may signal support for a candidate's position on Social Security reform or for his or her personal leadership abilities. The actual motivation for giving is ambiguous for the recipient.

Campaign contributions continue to come largely from those with greater resources, but the Obama campaign in 2008 demonstrated the potential of the Internet for widening the base of financial support. His campaign raised $1 million dollars a day or more, mostly from donors contributing $250 or less. Bernie Sanders set a new record of over two million individual donations in his 2016 run for the White House. However, we have also recently seen the emergence of donors with huge financial assets whose influence had been largely absent in American politics since campaign finance laws were passed in the wake of the Watergate scandal in the 1970s. Supreme Court rulings in recent years striking down limits on certain types of political contribution have opened the floodgates, with some individual donors contributing millions to political action committees (PACs) and super PACs in support of presidential candidates. It was not unusual to find some wealthy donors investing $10 million or more in presidential candidates and their campaign organizations in 2016. In cases in which wealthy individuals donate large sums, it would seem the potential for corruption is great. Nevertheless, the Court in *Citizens United* (2010) and *SpeechNOW.org v. FEC* (2010) vastly expanded the ability of

Although some people worry about the corrupting effects of money in politics, others see political donations simply as a First Amendment right.

©Nicholas Kamm/Getty Images

wealthy individuals, corporations, and labor unions to make political contributions, as we will discuss in more detail in later chapters.

Money is also an important asset for advocacy groups that promote a political agenda outside of the electoral arena. For example, the American Civil Liberties Union (ACLU) solicits donations to promote free speech. They take court cases on behalf of individuals who cannot afford to pay for their own defense. The Sierra Club solicits funds to promote environmental protection policies. These groups, too, receive most of their support from those with more wealth.

Some advocacy groups combine citizen action with cash contributions. They alert contributors and noncontributors alike to measures that threaten their interests and mobilize them to take action by contacting elected officials by letter or phone or over the Internet. Many advocacy groups facilitate citizen communication with political leaders by providing contact information or even direct access through the association's telecommunications network.

Another type of financial activism is on the rise as well: consumer activism, the practice of making a political or social statement with one's buying power. Commerce today is dominated by global corporations that reach beyond single continents. Their activities often escape regulation by individual nations. Except for shareholders with major stakes in these companies, individuals have little control over their operation. Nevertheless, some consumers find it useful to make a personal statement about the behavior of these companies or their products through their buying habits. Consumers can register their disapproval for the acts of certain businesses by boycotting their products; they can reward companies they believe are exemplary by buycotting. Consumer activism of this sort is surprisingly widespread. Roughly half of the adult population in the United States reports having used their buying power to either punish or reward companies or products in the past twelve months. These activities seem to be spread across all age levels, although they are more likely to be practiced by Americans with higher incomes and among those who are most attentive to politics.[46]

THE IMPACT OF PARTICIPATION PATTERNS ON POLICY

Does it matter that those at the upper end of the socioeconomic spectrum participate more and have greater contact with political elites than the less-advantaged? If the concerns and issues that mobilize the well-off are the same as those important to the rest of the population, there should be little cause for concern. However, if the concerns of the two groups differ, then there is reason to believe that politicians are more likely to pay attention to the needs of the wealthy while ignoring those of the poor.

Voting data seem to indicate that candidate preferences of voters and nonvoters are substantially similar.[47] With the possible exception of extremely close elections, increased turnout by the less-advantaged would probably not affect the outcome of most elections.[48] However, since voters are drawn disproportionately from those with more income and education, it is likely that their policy preferences are somewhat different from those of nonvoters. These differences are likely to be reflected in the policies that candidates advance, particularly those dealing with income redistribution.[49]

Participation that conveys more information to leaders displays a larger gap between the concerns of those who participate most and those who are least politically active. Citizens who depend on government assistance programs such as welfare, food stamps, and income support are far less likely to write letters, take part in community activities, contact political leaders, protest, or contribute time or money to a political campaign. When they do communicate with leaders, they are twice as likely as the advantaged to refer to their basic needs—food, housing, health care, and the like. By contrast, wealthier citizens—who are three times as likely as the disadvantaged to contact elected officials—are more likely to voice concerns about taxes, government spending, and the budget.[50] As a result, leaders hear more from their constituents about taxes and budgets than they hear about government programs that are vital to a large segment of the population.

Economic inequality not only affects the kind of issues political leaders are likely to take up. It also, as one researcher concludes, "stacks the deck of democracy in favor of the richest citizens and, as a result, most everyone else is more likely to conclude that politics is simply not a game worth playing."[51] Differences in access to resources, interest, and mobilization create patterns of political participation in America that result in a much louder voice for those already advantaged. In a study of Senate roll call votes, Larry Bartels found "senators appear to be considerably more responsive to the opinions of affluent constituents than to the opinions of middle-class constituents, while the opinions of constituents in the bottom third of the income distribution have *no* apparent statistical effect on their senators' roll call votes."[52] Another political scientist, Sidney Verba, describes the process this way: "Socioeconomic inequality produces inequality in political voice; this in turn fosters policies that favor the already advantaged; and these policies reinforce socioeconomic inequality."[53]

Some observers might argue that this imbalance in political participation is not all bad. After all, the affluent are often better informed and more tolerant of divergent beliefs than are the less well-off. One might argue that domination of political discourse by the more affluent will result in more enlightened policies.[54] Democratic governments, however, are supposed to balance the interests of different groups. The balancing act is made more difficult when our political leaders hear disproportionately from one segment of the population.

PARTICIPATION AND CIVIC ENGAGEMENT TODAY

We have witnessed a recent resurgence in political participation that is encouraging. Particularly encouraging is the increase in voting by formerly underrepresented groups such as minorities and women. Young people are joining the ranks of political candidates, marching in the streets for causes they hold dear, and using social media to effect change. There is no guarantee, however, that rates of participation will continue to rise or even stabilize. If we want participation rates to improve—and if we ever hope to achieve voting rates comparable with much of the rest of the developed world—we must make participation less costly in terms of time and money, two of the biggest constraints on participation.

Several proposed reforms could greatly reduce the inconvenience associated with the act of voting. First, keeping polls open longer on Election Day could encourage more people to vote. In some states, the polls close as early as 6 p.m., disenfranchising many working people and discouraging many young adults—a group that reports the need for greater flexibility in polling hours to accommodate their work and school schedules.[55] Second, many nonvoters say they would be more likely to vote if Election Day were a national holiday or held on a weekend. Making Election Day a holiday would also heighten social awareness of the importance of the activity. The recent trend of early voting, with poll centers open for several days before the election, including Saturdays, may prove to be a reliable way to increase voter turnout. Third, all states could adopt same-day registration. This would reduce the burden on citizens who move frequently or who want to participate but either are unaware of registration requirements or learn about them too late to comply with cutoff dates. As we have seen, several states with same-day registration or automatic registration have some of the highest levels of voter turnout in the country. Unfortunately, other states are actually making the process of voting even more onerous by requiring the presentation of official voter identification, such as a state driver's license, at the polls. Although this may discourage voter fraud (a practice that most researchers believe is negligible), it also has the unintended consequence of discouraging those without official IDs from voting. In 2008, the U.S. Supreme Court upheld Indiana's stringent voter ID requirement (*Crawford v. Marion County Election Board*). States like Texas, North Carolina, and Wisconsin proposed even

Voter Turnout in Advanced Industrialized Countries with Compulsory Voting

Country	Under 30	30–44	45–64	65 and Older
	Percent			
Australia (2004)	97	98	98	99
Belgium (2004)	89	98	97	92
Greece (2000)	90	93	95	93
Luxemburg (1999)	91	93	95	86

Compulsory voting increases turnout; but how many Americans would support such a system?

Source: Wattenberg, M. P. *Is Voting for Young People?* (New York: Pearson Education, 2007), 168.

Ranked Choice Voting A form of voting where voters can rank order their choice of candidates and those failing to achieve high levels of support are eliminated until one candidate is determined to have secured a majority.

more stringent voter ID measures until the courts intervened prior to the 2016 presidential election to prevent them from doing so. States have also won Supreme Court approval for removing thousands of voters from the voting lists if they don't vote in successive elections or fail to respond to notices from election officials (*Husted, Ohio Secretary of State v. A. Philip Randolph Institute, et al.*, 2018).

Some scholars suggest that voting rates have dipped too low for such piecemeal solutions. They recommend adopting compulsory voting as a means of reigniting the voting habit.[56] Compulsory voting laws would require eligible citizens to show up at the polls on Election Day or pay a small fine. Data show that such laws in other countries result in high turnout among every age category (see "Voter Turnout in Advanced Industrialized Countries with Compulsory Voting"). However, the idea of making voting a compulsory activity seems utterly out of sync with America's reliance on volunteerism. As a result, this is one solution that may have little future in this country.

Instead, reformers in the United States have focused on reducing the costs of voting by using some of the measures we discussed earlier to make the act more convenient. Some jurisdictions are experimenting with new approaches to voting like **ranked choice voting.** Voters can rank order their choice of candidates and those failing to achieve high levels of support are eliminated until one candidate is determined to have secured a majority. Research has clearly shown, however, that these approaches can get us only so far. Lack of interest and lack of trust in the political process are not easily corrected by making voting more accessible. Such reforms might be necessary but not sufficient to improve civic involvement. We must also enhance civic learning and the distribution of skills necessary for participation. In this area, educational institutions may be in the best position to help.

Over the last generation, high schools have reduced by two-thirds the median number of civics and government courses they offer. This represents an abandonment of one of the traditional functions of public schools: training students in the skills necessary to take part in their democratic heritage.[57] Schools should provide more intensive—and more interesting—courses in government. Students show more excitement and interest in politics when they are asked to get involved rather than merely to study a subject from a textbook or listen to lectures. Many schools already offer opportunities in participatory learning by encouraging or requiring students to attend public meetings, talk to government officials, and engage in service learning activities to assist community members in solving local problems. Schools can do more to encourage voting as well. Colleges can hold voter registration drives, help students locate polling places, and assist in disseminating absentee ballots.

In future chapters we will examine how institutional factors like our system of elections (Chapter 9), difficulties in establishing third-party alternatives (Chapter 9), the purposeful drawing of noncompetitive districts (Chapter 11), partisan stalemate in Congress (Chapter 11), and the Electoral College (Chapter 12) all contribute to voter disillusionment and diminish interest in participation. These factors alienate many voters, making them feel that their vote is unnecessary or useless. Rosenstone and Hansen conclude from their comprehensive study of voting that the "blame" for the long-term decline in citizen involvement rests as much with failures of the political system as with citizens themselves. The authors state the case bluntly: "Citizens did not fail the political system; if anything, the political system failed them."[58] This need not be the case, and in subsequent chapters, we will discuss what changes can be made to reverse this situation.

Thinking It Through >>>

Learning Objective: Analyze factors in political participation.

Review: Ingredients for Involvement

According to Jennifer L. Lawless and Richard L. Fox *(Running From Office,* Oxford Press, 2015), young Americans are alienated by our political system and are not very interested in running for office. What measures would you propose to generate greater interest in politics among today's youth? How might social media be used to engage young people and encourage them to consider running for a political office?

Summary

1. What is the nature of political participation in America?

- Americans can participate in politics in a variety of ways. Some activities like voting are widespread; others, like running for office, attract very few participants.
- Many Americans are willing to pay the costs of political participation even when the benefits might seem to be minimal.
- Different political activities vary in the amount of information conveyed, in the frequency with which they can be conducted, and in the strength of the message conveyed.
- Political involvement requires access to resources like time, skills, and money that are the result of factors such as family wealth, education, religious affiliation, type of employment, and one's race and gender.
- Political involvement also requires the desire to be politically engaged. Political engagement involves the dimensions of political interest, political efficacy, political information, and strength of party identification.
- Political involvement often hinges on an invitation to take part in political activities by a process of direct or indirect mobilization.

2. What are the major forms of political participation, and what resources do they require?

- Voting is the most common form of political participation in a democracy, requiring time and some skill but not money.
- Many forms of political participation require citizens to expend more resources than does the act of voting.
- Some political activities such as writing a member of Congress or participating in a campaign are more time-intensive than voting.
- Some political activities like organizing a political meeting or making a speech require more skill than does the act of voting.
- Other political activities such as contributing to campaigns or joining advocacy groups require money or time, resources that are not required for the act of voting.

3. What is the nature of voting in the United States?

- For many Americans, voting confers the psychological benefit of satisfying one's civic responsibility and promotes candidates and issues important to one's interests.
- Compared to other political activities, voting conveys little information, is limited in frequency, and is low in the strength of the message conveyed.
- Voters differ from nonvoters in resources such as wealth, employment status, and level of education. Gender, race, region of the country, and age are related to the likelihood of voting. However, women and African Americans have begun eclipsing whites in voter turnout and some other forms of participation.
- Voter turnout in the United States is affected by the registration requirement, the timing and scheduling of elections, the existence of the two-party system, and the number and frequency of elections.
- Compared to Western European democracies, voter turnout in the United States is low.

4. How do Americans decide how to vote?

- Many voters cast their ballots on the basis of party affiliation, but the strength of support among committed partisans varies.
- When party affiliation fails to provide reliable guidance for voters, they turn to other factors such as the issues. Holding politicians accountable for past performance is "retrospective voting" and voting for what candidates promise to do in the future is "prospective voting." The former is the more common type of issue voting.
- Voters also may turn to factors like the personal characteristics of the candidates as a basis for their preference in an election. Voters often feel more comfortable with candidates with whom they can personally relate or whose leadership characteristics they admire.

Chapter 8

Interest Groups in America

WHAT'S TO COME

Las Vegas concert goers comfort each other after the 2017 mass killing.

©David Becker/Getty Images

THE NATIONAL RIFLE ASSOCIATION AND THE STATUS QUO

On October 1, 2017, a lone gunman opened fire on a crowd of country music concert attendees from a thirty-second-floor hotel suite at the Mandalay Bay Casino in Las Vegas, Nevada. Twelve of the twenty-three guns at the killer's disposal were equipped with a "bump stock" that converts a semiautomatic weapon into an automatic one that can fire four hundred rounds per minute. Over a horrific period of nine to eleven minutes, the shooter rained down hundreds of bullets on the crowd, killing fifty-eight and wounding hundreds of others, until he took his own life as police approached his room. The carnage constituted the largest mass killing event at that time in American history. Such instances of senseless death have created "an image of an unstoppable national slaughter."[1] One journalist has noted that following mass killings a familiar pattern emerges: (1) full media coverage, consisting of initial shock followed by politicians' promises of change; (2) statements of regret or legal parsing from the gun lobby; and (3) mobilization of the NRA to resist political change.[2] After the Las Vegas massacre, however, leading Republican politicians did not even promise change with regard to gun laws. Both President Donald Trump and Speaker of the House Paul Ryan spoke of the need to address mental

health care, and Senate majority leader Mitch McConnell expressed the view that it is premature to address change immediately after a mass shooting.

The last major piece of successful gun control legislation was the ban on assault weapons, part of a larger crime-related bill in 1994 passed by Congress and signed by President Bill Clinton. The law applied to nineteen models of semiautomatic firearms and other guns that had similar features. The law expired in 2004, and repeated attempts to renew it have failed due to the efforts of the gun lobby. The primary interest group making up the gun lobby is the National Rifle Association (NRA). The powerful role of the NRA in today's debate over guns and violence raises questions about who constitutes the organization and why it is so powerful. The NRA was founded in the state of New York in 1871 and its first president was Civil War general Ambrose Burnside. The group did not begin lobbying the national government until 1934 and until the 1970s downplayed issues of gun control. By 1977, however, the NRA began to focus heavily on political issues, forming coalitions with conservative politicians, primarily Republicans.[3] Today, in its legislative battles, it opposes almost all gun control measures, using the argument that it is protecting the Second Amendment rights of all gun owners.

As You READ

- **What are interest groups, and what types of interests do they represent?**
- **Why might someone join an interest group?**
- **What do interest groups do?**

The NRA is very effective at using the interest group tactics of grassroots mobilization, financing campaigns, and lobbying the government. It is very effective, even masterful, in gathering support from its four million members to back congressional gun rights legislation and oppose gun control bills. One congressperson reflected that the organization's power is so evident that it is rarely challenged. Jan Schakowsky (D-IL) said: "If word gets spread around the floor that this is an NRA-scored bill, in the past anyway, that has been that. It is palpable on the floor when the message that is spread around is that the NRA is scoring this. It's like a wave."[4] Members of Congress fear a primary or general election challenge by a candidate supported by the NRA. The NRA spends millions of dollars attempting to elect their supporters and defeat their opponents. In 2016, the organization was so opposed to the Clinton candidacy that it spent over $30 million to assist the Trump campaign. In Ohio, for instance, one in eight ads was on gun rights, a state that Trump won. Overall, the NRA spent over $54.3 million in outside expenditures (money not given directly to the candidate or party, but used to affect the outcome of an election) on both the presidential election and congressional races.[5] Their contributions to congressional campaigns go primarily to Republicans. The average contribution to Senate candidates was $30,000 and just over $10,000 to House candidates.[6] Overall, in 2016, the NRA contributed $5.9 million to Republicans and $106,000 to Democrats.[7] Additionally, it spends money lobbying government officials to oppose all gun control measures. In 2013, for instance, right after the Sandy Hook shooting that killed twenty grade school students, the NRA and other gun rights groups spent $15.3 million arguing its case in Washington. In 2016, the gun rights lobby spent $10.6 million in lobbying efforts, with the NRA as the largest contributor.[8]

After the Las Vegas shooting, the NRA stated it might consider supporting legislation to outlaw bump stocks but later displayed no evidence it was doing so. The legalization of such devices was not even a policy that the gun lobby had pursued. In 2010, a gun parts manufacturer asked the Federal Bureau of Alcohol, Tobacco, Firearms, and Explosives for permission to market a bump stock for the benefit of handicapped gun enthusiasts, and the bureau consented, even though machine guns had been strictly controlled since the 1930s. In early 2018, the Department of Justice suggested it might institute such a ban rather than wait for Congress to act.

Public Opinion on Gun Laws

In general, do you feel that the laws covering the sale of firearms should be made more strict, less strict or kept as they are now?

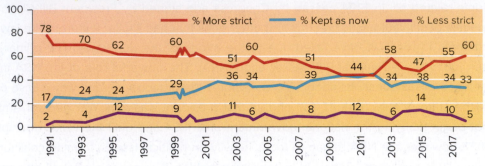

Sixty percent of American respondents believe laws covering the sale of firearms should be stricter.

Source: GALLUP, 2017.

The NRA exercises its vast influence over political decision makers, even though its position seems to run counter to most public opinion polls. Sixty percent of the American public believe the laws covering the sale of firearms should be stricter (see "Public Opinion on Gun Laws"). However, it is only Democrats and independents who overwhelmingly support gun control. A majority of Republicans oppose such measures. Similarly, only Republicans believe the United States would be safer if more people carried guns. Views on gun control also differ based on gun ownership. Guns are popular in our country: It is estimated that over 265 million of them exist in our society.[9] Forty-two percent of Americans have a gun in their homes (see "Gun Ownership at the Household Level"). Polls suggest that guns make the owners feel safer.[10] However, there appears to be agreement among respondents from both parties, and between both gun owners and those who do not own any guns, that gun violence will increase in the United States over the next ten years. In a recent poll, 47 percent of respondents predicted an increase in gun violence, whereas only 14 percent think gun violence will decrease.[11]

As discussed in Chapter 4, the activism displayed by the surviving students in the 2018 Parkland, Florida school shooting with respect to nationwide marches for gun control legislation and call outs of politicians supporting the status quo placed new challenges on the NRA. The organization, however, did not concede its role to block new policies supported by the students and public opinion.

A great many interest groups, including the NRA, exist in the United States to exert pressure on the political system to advance their collective interests. In this chapter we will examine the genesis of all interest groups, the way they have evolved and adapted to historic change, the kinds of people who join them, the reasons people support them, the strategies and tactics they employ, and their impact on civic engagement and public policy. ■

Gun Ownership at the Household Level

Do you have a gun in your home?

Fewer Americans have a gun in their home as compared to the 1960s, but 42 percent of homes still contain guns.

Source: GALLUP, 2017.

ORGANIZED INTERESTS: WHO ARE THEY?

Accomplishing broad yet shared goals is always easier when a number of people pitch in to help. Joining with neighbors to clean up a community after a storm and banding together with friends to convince your college cafeteria to purchase "free trade" coffee are both examples of cooperative action. Group activity is a hallmark of America's volunteer ethic. The same is true in politics. Organized groups are nearly always more effective in attaining common goals than are individuals acting alone. The term **interest group** refers to those formally organized associations that seek to influence public policy.[12] In America, it applies to a dizzying array of diverse organizations reflecting the broad spectrum of interests that make up our pluralistic society. Interest groups include corporations, labor unions, civil rights groups, professional and trade associations, and probably some of the groups with which you are associated as well.

interest group Any formally organized association that seeks to influence public policy.

political movement An organized constellation of groups seeking wide-ranging social change.

Neighbors or Adversaries?

Theorists from Alexis de Tocqueville to Robert Putnam have praised voluntary associations as training grounds for citizen involvement. De Tocqueville saw collective action as evidence of democracy at work. Putnam extols organized interests for creating social capital, the glue that binds together the citizenry so that they can achieve collective goals. Not all political theorists, however, share these views. In *The Federalist* No. 10, James Madison warned against factions—groups of individuals, "whether amounting to a majority or minority of the whole, who are united by some common impulse of passion, or of interest, adverse to the rights of other citizens, or to the permanent and aggregate interests of the community."[13] Although opposed to factions, believing they often act in a selfish manner, Madison felt that they could not be eliminated because they expressed the innately human drive for self-interest. Instead, he argued, the government must dilute their influence by filtering their views through elected officials and submerging their interests in a sea of competing interests. Only by countering the ambition of such groups with the ambition of others, he believed, could government fashion the compromises necessary to accommodate interests common to all.

Interest groups usually do not intend to work against their communities, but the benefits they seek may result in costs for others. Whether a particular group represents a "good neighbor" or an adversary is often in the eye of the beholder. We will see that organized interests play an important role in American politics in their attempts to promote policies beneficial to their particular members.

Distinctive Features

Like **political movements** of the past and present that advance causes such as abolition or civil rights, interest groups seek to use the power of government to protect their concerns. However, whereas political movements promote wide-ranging social change, interest groups are more narrowly focused on achieving success with regard to specific policies. For example, the women's movement of the 1960s sought to change Americans' views about the role of women at home and in the workplace, whereas interest groups like the National Organization for Women (NOW) focus on solving specific problems faced by women in a world that has already grown more accepting of the diverse roles women play.

Interest group causes may be purely economic, as in the case of a business seeking tax breaks or a union seeking negotiating

Organized Interests

Think you don't belong to an organized interest or advocacy group? Think again. Are you a member of any of these groups?

- ☐ American Automobile Association (AAA)
- ☐ Amnesty International
- ☐ Defenders of Wildlife
- ☐ 4-H
- ☐ Future Farmers of America
- ☐ Interfaith Alliance
- ☐ Mothers Against Drunk Driving (MADD)
- ☐ National Council of Churches of Christ in the USA
- ☐ National Organization for Women (NOW)
- ☐ National Rifle Association (NRA)
- ☐ Ocean Conservancy
- ☐ Parent Teacher Association (PTA)
- ☐ Sierra Club
- ☐ United Students Against Sweatshops (USAS)
- ☐ Veterans of Foreign Wars (VFW)

clout; they may be ideological, as in the case of those favoring or opposing abortion rights. Some, known as **public interest groups**, advocate policies they believe promote the good of all Americans, not merely the economic or ideological interests of a few. Environmental groups such as the Sierra Club fall into this category. Some interest groups, such as trade associations and labor unions, have mass memberships; others represent institutions and have no individual membership at all. One example of the latter is the American Council on Education (ACE), a collection of institutions of higher education that promotes policies that benefit colleges and universities.

As with other forms of participation, those who are better educated and better off financially are more active in interest group politics. The wealthy and well educated belong to more associations, are more likely to be active in these interest groups, and give more money to political causes than those with less education and income. Highly educated professionals are many times more likely to belong to one or more interest groups than those who lack a high school degree. Interest group activity has exploded since the mid-1970s, even while our nation has experienced a long-term decline in voter turnout. This reflects the fact that interest groups multiply the opportunities for participation by those who are already politically active.[14]

THE ROOTS OF INTEREST GROUP POLITICS IN AMERICA

Political scientists offer a number of reasons for the growth of interest groups. First, there is the ever-present reality that Americans are joiners. Echoing de Tocqueville, historian Arthur M. Schlesinger wrote that our "instinctive resort to collective action" is "one of the strongest taproots of the nation's well-being."[15] Beyond this, interest group growth is tied to forces of change such as technological innovation, war, and the expansion of the role of government.

Interest Groups on the Rise

By the time Alexis de Tocqueville traveled across America in 1831, voluntary associations—including those with explicitly political goals—were already well established. Women, who were excluded from leadership positions in government, organized many groups that provided humanitarian relief to the poor, sick, and disabled. These "auxiliary societies," as they were sometimes called, were formed to combat perceived evils like drunkenness and prostitution.[16] Abolitionist societies were perhaps the most politically influential associations, and many of them organized across class and racial lines to advocate an end to slavery. Women also organized for the right to vote, meeting in Seneca Falls in 1848 to issue a *Declaration of Rights and Sentiments.*

By the mid-nineteenth century, economic change and advances in transportation brought rapid growth in the number of voluntary and political organizations. The development of a national railroad system led the Central Pacific Railroad to send its own representative to Washington in 1861 to protect railroad subsidies and land grants. A number of rural associations arose in reaction to these changes. For example, the Grange, an association of rural farmers, formed in opposition to high rates set by rail carriers for hauling their produce to the nation's largest markets. The origin of the term **lobbying** to describe the practice of influencing public decisions for private purposes dates back to this period. It seems that businessmen often approached President Ulysses S. Grant (1869–1877) to seek favors as he indulged in brandy and cigars while relaxing in the lobby of the Willard Hotel.

By the end of the nineteenth century, the pace of economic development displaced many rural workers, who migrated to cities to compete for dangerous, low-wage jobs in the new industrial economy. Labor organizations, charitable associations, and reform groups arose to lobby for better working conditions, an end to child labor, and safe food and medicines.

As the organizing strength of political parties began to decline, interest groups emerged as the great hope for participatory democracy. They became the principal means for expressing popular views and mobilizing support for reform.[17]

World War I created a large pool of veterans who organized to petition the government for benefits in compensation for their service to country. In 1932, more than thirty thousand World War I veterans and their families and supporters marched on Washington, D.C., and set up makeshift camps in the capital, demanding redemption of government certificates issued after the war. Although federal troops routed the so-called Bonus Army out of their camps, veterans eventually received the cash payments they sought. Their actions paved the way for more generous benefits for future generations of soldiers.

The New Deal spawned hundreds of groups with a stake in federal policies, as did the explosion of government regulation of business and the environment in the 1960s and 1970s. The period following World War II brought increased specialization and professionalization to the workforce at the same time that it saw increases in union affiliation. Membership in the American Bar Association quadrupled between 1945 and 1965. Union membership rose in the postwar period from about 12 percent of the nonagricultural workforce in 1930 to over 30 percent in the 1950s, before cascading downward in the last quarter of the twentieth century.[18]

The Advocacy Explosion

In the 1950s and 1960s, the nation experienced a "rights revolution" that had important implications for the evolution of interest group politics in the United States.[19] African Americans led the way as they sought to dismantle segregationist policies in the South by lobbying the national government to enforce constitutional guarantees. Other groups followed, insisting that government help tear down the barriers of racial, ethnic, and gender exclusion that characterized associational life in earlier eras. Soon, even mainstream interests like those of consumers joined the "rights revolution." The national focus of these reform efforts made it imperative for rights advocates to establish a presence in Washington.

The period witnessed an explosion in Washington-based **advocacy groups**, associations asserting broad public goals but without local chapters and often without any formal membership.[20] Only about one-eighth of the organizations active in national politics are classic voluntary membership associations of individuals.[21] Leaders of these groups, often self-appointed and aided by philanthropic organizations and think tanks that supplied financial and intellectual capital, helped forge a new relationship between citizen and leadership. Citizens no longer needed to organize locally, meet with one another, or choose neighborhood leaders. Instead, national leaders would set the agenda, formulate strategies, and lobby public officials for them. Citizens were asked to send money and write an occasional letter to a public officeholder. Political engagement, some observers believe, became more passive as citizens had their interests managed for them.[22]

The impact of the explosion in advocacy has been mixed. On the one hand, these groups are instrumental in protecting individual rights and in making the products we use safer and more effective. On the other hand, they may have contributed to a more passive role for citizens. The period that witnessed a rise in Washington-based advocacy groups also witnessed an overall decline in civic voluntarism. We will return to assess these changes at the end of this chapter.

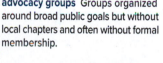

advocacy groups Groups organized around broad public goals but without local chapters and often without formal membership.

Businessmen often sought favors from President Ulysses S. Grant as he indulged in brandy and cigars in the Willard Hotel lobby in Washington, D.C.

©Bettmann/Corbis via Getty Images

WHOSE INTERESTS ARE REPRESENTED?

The array of interest groups active in American politics is large and wide ranging. Some groups boast large numbers, others have financial heft, and some are led by the well-connected who have access to power brokers. Each employs the resources it has at its disposal to advance its cause.

Who Has the Numbers?

Of all organizations active in Washington, more than half (53 percent) represent business in one way or another. Of these, corporations are by far the most numerous. Entire industries also make their presence in Washington felt. The pharmaceutical and health products industry, for instance, which includes not only drug manufacturers but also dealers of medical products and nutritional and dietary supplements, has spent nearly $250 million in recent years to influence federal legislators and bureaucrats (see "Lobbying Expenditures by the Pharmaceuticals and Health Products Industry"). Such industry groups are known as trade associations and make up most of the remainder of the business sector.[23] The U.S. Chamber of Commerce, for example, represents thousands of small and medium-sized businesses throughout the country, and the National Association of Manufacturers advances the interests of major manufacturing companies. In contrast, blue-collar and service workers, along with those out of the workforce, are substantially underrepresented.[24]

Professional associations such as the American Chemical Society represent the next largest sector of the Washington interest group community. Labor unions also maintain a strong presence, although union members represent a dwindling portion of the labor force. Education is a fast-growing sector, with more than a thousand individual lobbyists and organized groups, such as the American Federation of Teachers, practicing in the nation's capital today.

Advocacy groups represent a growing portion of the interest group community.[25] A few of these, including the Children's Defense Fund, promote the interests of those who don't have the resources to advocate for themselves. But an increasing array, such as Common Cause (dedicated to government reform) and Public Citizen (organized to safeguard consumers), cater to more wealthy contributors on whom they rely for support. Numerous single-issue groups have also organized around specific legislative concerns, such as banning handguns or outlawing abortion. The overwhelming majority of organized interests founded since 1960 have been advocacy groups,[26] but they have a high rate of attrition. Only 33 percent of advocacy organizations active in 1960 existed two decades later. The

Lobbying Expenditures by the Pharmaceuticals and Health Products Industry

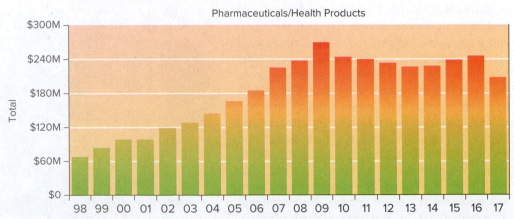

Lobbying expenditures by the pharmaceuticals and health products industry has exceeded $200 million in recent years.

Source: Open secrets.org, Center for Responsive Politics, October 21, 2017.

most successful of the survivors deal with environmental and consumer issues.[27]

Governments themselves also organize for representation in Washington. Virtually every nation in the world maintains a Washington office to oversee its relations with American leaders. So, too, do state and local governments, whose policies are often impacted by federal law. The National Association of Counties, the National League of Cities, and the U.S. Conference of Mayors are three examples. Even executive branch agencies in the U.S. government hire legislative liaisons to communicate their needs to members of Congress.

The business holdings of President Trump have created new settings for lobbying activities and raised new ethical concerns. This is particularly evident in the influence pursuits of foreign governments. The Trump International Hotel, formerly the Old Post Office Pavilion, is the second tallest building in Washington, D.C.

Education is a fast-growing and powerful sector of the interest group community. Together the American Federation of Teachers (AFT) and the National Education Association (NEA) boast 4.6 million members.

It is a place where lobbyists began to congregate in 2017. "Foreign governments seem particularly keen to patronize Trump's property."[28] For example, while lobbyists for the kingdom of Saudi Arabia were arguing against legislation that would allow victims of terrorist attacks to sue foreign governments, they spent $270,000 at the Trump Hotel for rooms, catering, and parking, according to foreign lobbying disclosures.[29]

Who Has the Money?

Another way to evaluate which interests are best represented is to examine the resources groups expend. The figure "Which Interests Are Best Represented?" provides information on the number of paid professionals—either from within the organization or from outside firms—representing various sectors of the interest group community in Washington. It also lists the total expenditures each made in pleading its case before government. Business groups employ the largest number of paid professionals and spend more than half of all the money spent on lobbying. Over 50 percent of all Washington lobbyists, whether in-house or working as consultants, represent business interests. Combined with trade associations, business interests employ 63 percent of the direct lobbyists and 58 percent of the outside lobbying firms and account for 78 percent of all lobbying expenditures. Unions, by contrast, employ 2 percent of the direct lobbyists and less than 1 percent of outside lobbying firms, and their share of the total lobbying expenditures in Washington is 2 percent.

Whose Interests Are Not Represented?

Clearly, interest group politics in the United States has a distinctively upper-class tilt. Many interests at the bottom of the economic spectrum receive minimal or no representation at all. There are no lobbyists for the homeless or groups representing Americans without health insurance. Interest group politics, however, is quite fluid; new groups often arise to meet emerging challenges.[30] For example, the northern migration of blacks from the South spawned the birth of organizations like the National Association for the Advancement of Colored People (NAACP) and the National Urban League to champion the cause of equal rights. Similarly, the environmental movement in the 1960s led to the expansion of groups advocating the protection of air and water quality. In addition, existing groups often expand to adopt causes tangential to their mission. For example, several philanthropic and health advocacy organizations joined forces in 2007 to push for the adoption of wider health insurance coverage for America's uninsured children.

Which Interests Are Best Represented?

Percentage of all lobbying
expenditures by organization

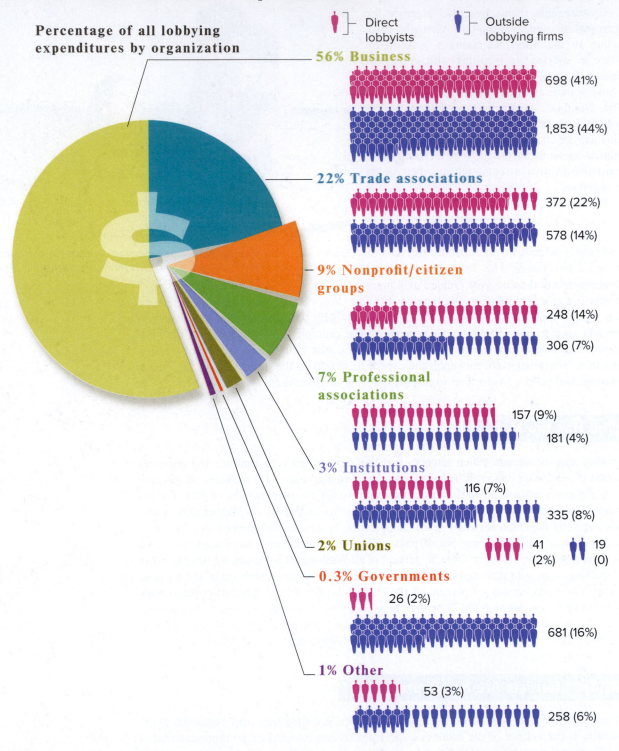

Direct lobbyists · Outside lobbying firms

56% Business
698 (41%)
1,853 (44%)

22% Trade associations
372 (22%)
578 (14%)

9% Nonprofit/citizen groups
248 (14%)
306 (7%)

7% Professional associations
157 (9%)
181 (4%)

3% Institutions
116 (7%)
335 (8%)

2% Unions
41 (2%)   19 (0)

0.3% Governments
26 (2%)
681 (16%)

1% Other
53 (3%)
258 (6%)

The findings of this study show that business interests bring greater resources to lobbying than all the other groups combined.

Source: Compiled from Baumgartner, F. and Leech, B. L. "Interest Niches and Policy Bandwagons: Patterns of Interest Group Involvement in National Politics," *Journal of Politics* 63, no. 4 (2001): Table 1, 1195, and Table 3, 1197.

WHY JOIN?

Political strength comes from assembling the resources and voices of many individuals. Any student who has tried to effect changes in university policy recognizes that administrators are more likely to listen if many students work collectively to voice their concerns. Still, the job of bringing students together, getting them to agree to a uniform set of proposals, and having them follow through with letters or petitions or marches is not an easy task. Students who agree with proposed changes may prefer to have others do the hard work of organizing and going to meetings. After all, if proposed changes are successful, even students who don't lift a finger will reap the benefits. Fortunately for the leaders of organized interests, many people are highly motivated to join a group that fights for a cause they support, and others can be enticed by various incentives. A group can also employ various incentives to sustain membership and active commitment, and it can add or change incentives as the organization matures.[31]

Monetary Incentives

Monetary or material benefits include anything that can be measured in terms of money, such as goods, special services, and financial incentives. AARP, originally known as the American Association of Retired Persons, for instance, began with the goal of providing affordable health care for the elderly but now offers its members discounts in a variety of establishments, guidance in avoiding consumer fraud, organized travel opportunities, auto insurance, low-interest credit cards, and a discounted mail-order pharmacy. Offering these material benefits has helped AARP recruit more than 35 million members and become the most powerful organization in America representing the interests of the elderly. Political leaders who seek to change Social Security or Medicare policies recognize the importance of courting this organization if their proposals are to have any chance of passage.

Few organizations can match AARP's clout, but many business associations and unions offer material incentives as well. For example, the U.S. Chamber of Commerce offers member businesses access to health care plans that are cheaper than plans they could buy on their own. Although the power of unions has waned in recent years, many can still provide members with higher negotiated wages than workers could obtain without a union card.

Social Incentives

Human beings are social creatures who enjoy the company of others. Membership in a group whose participants share a common interest can be very pleasurable. It provides the joiner with the likely possibility of friendship and an opportunity for "networking." Again, this is a selective benefit reserved to the members of the group that nonmembers cannot easily share. Members of professional organizations, such as the American Medical Association (AMA), look forward to annual meetings where they can renew friendships, share new ideas, and network. Often, members attending these conventions vote on resolutions outlining the political agendas the organization will pursue over the coming year.

©Bettmann/Corbis via Getty Images

Environmental activists in the 1960s dramatized their concerns about the nation's unhealthful air quality at public protest rallies.

Idealist Incentives

For organizations that depend heavily on idealistic or purposive incentives, interest groups offer their members more than discounts and social outings. They offer the opportunity to pursue policy goals that members genuinely support. Members gain a measure of inner satisfaction from knowing that they are trying to change the world rather than just complaining about it. Despite the cynicism that sometimes pervades media reports about those engaged in public life, millions of Americans devote countless hours volunteering in big and small ways to promote causes in which they believe.

For organizations that depend heavily on idealistic or purposive incentives, the role of the **political entrepreneur** is particularly important in mobilizing support among those who sympathize with the group's goals.[32] Political entrepreneurs develop support for latent causes or projects that have not yet gained widespread popularity. Even groups with passionate views, such as those on both sides of the abortion issue, rely on strong and enterprising leaders to recruit members and to sustain interest and activity.

political entrepreneur An individual who develops support for latent causes or projects that have not yet gained widespread popularity.

collective goods Goods that are not owned privately but benefit all citizens equally, such as clean air.

Assessing Motives

Economist Mancur Olson argued that it is irrational for individuals to join most groups. It is more rational, he wrote, to be a free rider who receives benefits without doing the work or paying dues. We can all enjoy clean air without being a member of an environmental group, and we can earn the latest increase in the minimum wage without carrying a union card. We can remain rationally uninvolved and spend our free time pursuing leisure activities or working at a second job to earn extra money.[33] Olson believes that providing incentives is the only way for membership in interest groups to flourish.

Despite the seeming logic of Olson's view, people often do not make what appears to be the rational choice. Political scientist Jack Walker conducted a study in which interest group leaders ranked the benefit of each type of incentive as an inducement for attracting members. Contrary to rational choice theory, the leaders of all types of groups ranked material benefits to be the least important of all the incentives. The study also found that most groups do not even use such inducements. Instead, leaders of all kinds of groups ranked idealist incentives highest, with social incentives close behind.[34] Additional studies have confirmed high levels of purposeful joining, especially among interest group activists.[35] This finding should be surprising only to those who have paid insufficient attention to our history as a "nation of joiners." There is an additional consideration for free riders to ponder. If everyone acted as a free rider, **collective goods**—goods that are not owned privately but benefit all citizens equally, such as clean air—would have no champions, and all of us would suffer the consequences.

INTEREST GROUP STRATEGIES

To get what they want, interest groups must develop a plan and execute it with a series of specific actions. The overall plan is their **strategy**; the specific actions they undertake are **tactics**. Strategies and tactics employed by an interest group vary with the nature of the issue under consideration and the kinds of resources the group has available to it.

strategy A group's overall plan for achieving its goals.

tactics Specific actions that groups take to implement strategies.

Generally speaking, strategies can be categorized as inside or outside. Inside strategies emphasize direct personal encounters with public officials to present information or resources that might influence the course of policy. Tactics useful to implement this strategy include lobbying and contributing money to support the election of political candidates favorably disposed to the group's viewpoint. Outside strategies are activities intended to show popular support for one's cause and indirectly to create public pressure on elected officials. Outsiders usually adopt grassroots tactics that include letter writing, shaping public opinion, and orchestrating protests. Interest groups attempt to influence decision makers face-to-face (inside) or use popular pressure (outside) to get their policy preferences enacted.

Groups adopt strategies based on the types of issues involved and the resources the group can bring to bear. Some groups have wide-ranging interests that are likely to attract the attention of a large number of Americans. For example, military intervention is an issue that affects almost everyone—from those who fight or lose family members in battle to those who simply oppose the use of their tax dollars in this manner. Both supporters and opponents of the use of military force are likely to employ outside strategies to demonstrate to lawmakers the depth and breadth of public sentiment for their position. Changes in the tax code, by contrast, are likely to provoke the use of inside strategies by groups whose immediate but narrow interests are most directly affected. The arcane and complicated features of our tax code rarely draw widespread attention, enabling those with an immediate interest and expertise to fashion changes to their liking through direct interaction with lawmakers.

There are times when it makes sense for groups to employ both inside and outside strategies at once. For example, both proponents (for example, labor unions) and opponents (such as health insurers) of President Obama's health care overhaul worked closely with members of Congress and the administration to fashion changes in his reform proposals—an insider's approach. At the same time, however, they helped organize workers and employees to attend rallies and town meetings to demonstrate widespread support for their positions, and they spent lavishly on television ads to influence public opinion—outside strategies.

Resources useful in advancing a group's cause include money, numbers, prestige, and leadership. Businesses, for example, can generally count on accumulating money to communicate their message, but they cannot often count on large numbers of individuals supporting their cause. Labor unions, by contrast, try to exert influence by the number of votes they can muster for particular candidates and parties. To be effective, however, a group's members must be dispersed geographically across areas that key lawmakers represent. Sometimes, groups with smaller numbers have an easier time organizing politically because they can maintain greater intensity and cohesiveness. Strong intensity is a characteristic of groups on both sides of the abortion issue in recent years. Prestige is also an important resource; when the American Medical Association speaks on matters of health care, for example, it can be particularly persuasive. Leadership from a variety of sources—scholars, celebrities, political entrepreneurs, and public officials themselves—can generate momentum around issues previously ignored by the political system. Rachel Carson's controversial 1962 book *Silent Spring* is credited with almost single-handedly launching the environmental movement. More recently, Irish rock star Bono mobilized global support to fight AIDS and to provide debt relief for poor and developing countries.

Because few interest groups have sufficient quantities of all of these resources to dispense at will, each group must carefully assess how best to deploy the strengths it possesses.

©Jeff Fusco/Getty Images

Celebrities like Bono have been effective in mobilizing support for increasing aid to developing nations.

LOBBYING AND OTHER TACTICS

Interest groups use many tactics to advance their positions, such as testifying at congressional hearings, helping to draft administrative rules and regulations, and mounting grassroots lobbying efforts. In recent years, spending on these tactics has exceeded $3 billion, with the number of registered lobbyists ranging from 10,404 to 14,827 (see "Total Lobbying Spending and Number of Lobbyists"). In this section, we will review some of the most notable lobbying tactics.

Lobbying

revolving door A term referring to the back-and-forth movement of individuals between government and interest group employment.

In the early years of our republic, members of Congress had no offices; most lived alone in boardinghouses or hotels. The only way to contact them was to wait outside their offices, or in the lobbies of the places where they were staying, in hopes of having a word with them as they came and went. Modern-day lobbyists continue to ply their trade in the hallways of the Capitol, but interest groups have found far more sophisticated ways to increase their clout.

Total Lobbying Spending and Number of Lobbyists*

Year	Spending		Year	Lobbyists
1998	$ 1.45 Billion		1998	10,404
1999	$ 1.44 Billion		1999	12,924
2000	$ 1.57 Billion		2000	12,543
2001	$ 1.63 Billion		2001	11,853
2002	$ 1.83 Billion		2002	12,150
2003	$ 2.06 Billion		2003	12,959
2004	$ 2.18 Billion		2004	13,201
2005	$ 2.44 Billion		2005	14,098
2006	$ 2.63 Billion		2006	14,493
2007	$ 2.87 Billion		2007	14,827
2008	$ 3.31 Billion		2008	14,141
2009	$ 3.50 Billion		2009	13,730
2010	$ 3.51 Billion		2010	12,917
2011	$ 3.32 Billion		2011	12,617
2012	$ 3.30 Billion		2012	12,235
2013	$ 3.24 Billion		2013	12,127
2014	$ 3.26 Billion		2014	11,843
2016	$ 3.22 Billion		2016	11,545
2016	$ 3.15 Billion		2016	11,169
2017	$ 3.34 Billion		2017	11,444

Note: Figures on this page are calculations by the Center for Responsive Politics based on data from the Senate Office of Public Records. Data for the most recent year was downloaded on January 24, 2018.

*The number of unique, registered lobbyists who have actively lobbied.

The total amount of lobbying spending has surpassed $3 billion since 2008, whereas the total number of lobbyists has declined.

Source: OpenSecrets.org, Center for Responsive Politics, October 21, 2017.

Who Lobbies? Average citizens lobby on behalf of issues they support by writing or calling elected leaders, but lobbying is increasingly the province of permanent and salaried professionals. Sometimes these are interest group staffers who work in Washington or a state capital directly on behalf of the group's membership. Increasingly, they are "hired guns" whose services groups purchase from professional firms specializing in government relations. Nearly twelve thousand people work as lobbyists in Washington, D.C., and many are quite well paid.

A good lobbyist needs to be a specialist in a policy area and needs to have thorough knowledge of the political process. For this reason, former government workers are well suited for the job. Individuals who have worked as congressional staff members or in administrative agencies have the kind of policy and political knowledge useful for lobbying. One study reported that forty-six former staffers from the powerful House Appropriations Committee, thirty-six from the Ways and Means Committee, and thirty-four from the House Energy and Commerce Committee have left their congressional jobs between 1998 and 2006.[36] Former members of Congress also make formidable lobbyists, sometimes maintaining virtually unlimited access to the chambers and the congressional gym. In January of 2017, 14 of the 61 retiring members of Congress had already secured jobs as lobbyists[37]

Some observers refer to the movement between government service and interest group employment as a **revolving door**. The door swings in both directions. Not only do retiring lawmakers and staffers join firms that lobbied them when they were in government, but government agencies often recruit issue specialists from fields that they regulate. Defenders of this practice claim that the revolving door keeps good and knowledgeable people involved in the policy process. It develops a cadre of experts, many of whom have spent their lives studying issues under government scrutiny. Critics believe the practice raises ethical concerns, especially when a person leaves a federal government position to join an interest group he or she once helped to regulate. Rep. Billy Tauzin (R-LA), for example, left the House of Representatives in 2004 to become the president of the Pharmaceutical Research and Manufacturers of America shortly after writing the Medicare Drug Benefit law that is widely seen as protecting the interests of drug companies that he went on to represent. Former Senate majority leader Tom Daschle (D-SD) became a lobbyist with ties to the health care industry once he left office, and he nearly became secretary of Health and Human Services under President Obama until his candidacy was sidetracked by the revelation that he failed to pay a portion of his back taxes. There are laws limiting the kind of access former officials may have once they leave office. Obama expanded restrictions on the revolving door by curtailing executive agency hiring of individuals who had recently lobbied and by prohibiting those who left his administration from lobbying agencies for which they had worked for a period lasting until the end of his administration or for two years after their departure. President Trump weakened Obama's lobbying rules by allowing lobbyists to join the executive branch without a waiting period, as long as they do not work on anything they specifically lobbied on for two years, and by allowing former executives to work immediately on lobbying activities except with respect to the agency they just left.

One study identifies two types of lobbying, one that involves issues that are not highly salient to the public and that occur at the periphery of the interest group system; and one at the system's core dealing with highly visible issues.[38] Some groups strategically narrow their policy focus and establish themselves in an issue niche with little competition from other groups and little public attention. Such groups are more likely to hire lobbying firms than use in-house lobbyists. These lobbyist firms specialize in narrowly defined policy domains where they almost always prevail. Other interest groups operate at the core of the system where there is much competition, diversity, and media attention. In recent years, the policy domains at the core have included health care, taxes, trade, and the federal budget and appropriations.[39] Due to their advantage in gaining access to the decision makers in the legislative and executive branches, interest groups often hire former government officials and employees to lobby around these core issues.[40]

Lobbying Congress Despite lobbyists' sometimes unsavory reputation, most members of Congress see them as possessors of valuable resources. Two of the most valuable of those resources are information and electoral support, often in the form of campaign contributions.

Members of Congress need information because they must vote on many highly technical pieces of legislation during the course of a legislative session. Except for the policy areas they know well because of their committee assignments, congresspersons are policy generalists who lack the kind of detailed information that lobbyists can supply. Such information is crucial to legislators because they never know which vote on a bill could become an issue in the next campaign.[41]

To maintain a good relationship with a legislator, the lobbyist must supply credible and reliable information based on accurate research. Overworked legislators welcome help from interest group advocates in assessing and sometimes even drafting legislation. Lobbyists also contribute political information, letting legislators know how a particular piece of legislation will sit with important constituencies back home. Lobbyists may communicate information by testifying at congressional committee hearings. By testifying openly, the interest group can impress its members back home with its status as a Washington player. Such visibility can increase membership and, in turn, the group's potential clout.

Lobbyists might slant information in order to "make the sale," but they dare not lie. A good lobbyist will even include information damaging to his or her cause from time to time in order to maintain credibility. As one lobbyist put it, "You can't ever afford to lie to a member of Congress because if you lose access to him, you've had it."[42]

Lobbyists need access to members of Congress in order to obtain policy results for their members. Opportunities for access in the policymaking process have increased in recent years since the powers granted committee chairs have been weakened, making individual members more important. Greater turnover, occasioned by term limits for committee chairs and self-imposed term limits by some individual legislators, has elevated the status of

THE PAYOFF OF LOBBYING

Politics in Washington, D.C., is almost synonymous with the work of lobbyists. Lobbyists spent $3.34 billion in 2017 to influence public policy.

Yet the question remains as to the extent of the lobbyists' influence. In his book, *Capitol Punishment,* Jack Abramoff, the once powerful and now disgraced lobbyist, discussed the payoff for himself and the clients he represented: "We worked long and hard for the tribes we represented and in return, the law firm and Scanlon's company were making a lot of money. Millions. Our efforts were saving the tribes hundreds of millions, if not billions."[†] Abramoff's figures appear to be consistent with the perception held by interest groups, the media, and the general public that lobbying is a powerful means for affecting public policy.

Until recently, academic studies found inconclusive results when attempting to quantify the rate of return on political lobbying expenditures. A recent study, however, examined the effect of lobbying on a tax law, quantifying lobbying returns by comparing a taxpayer's tax liabilities prior to and after a tax law change. The study of the American Jobs Creation Act of 2004 was a unique opportunity for such an inquiry because the tax benefits were limited to a single taxable year and the benefits were publicly disclosed in financial statements. The findings were astounding. The companies lobbying for the tax provision had a return in excess of $220 for every $1 spent on lobbying. In other

©Alex Wong/Getty Images

Lobbying can result in great material benefits.

words, the rate of return was 22,000 percent! The average tax savings for each of the companies was over $1 billion.[‡] Any attempts to regulate lobbying will certainly be opposed by interests gaining such a high rate of return on their lobbying investment.

[†]Abramoff, J. *Capitol Punishment* (New York: WND Books, 2011), 191.

[‡]Raquel Alexander, Stephen W. Mazza, and Susan Scholz, "Measuring Rates of Return for Lobbying Expenditures: An Empirical Case Study of Tax Breaks for Multinational Corporations," *Journal of Law and Politics* 25:401 (2009), http://ssrn.com?abstract=1375082.

---

congressional staff members, whose cultivation can be useful in communicating a group's message to lawmakers. Staff contacts are particularly important in the smaller Senate, whose members have greater responsibilities and time commitments.[43]

Even the White House lobbies Congress in order to secure legislation it deems important. The Office of Legislative Affairs in the White House acts as the president's liaison with Congress. This office gives the White House a very powerful means of influencing legislator behavior. For example, the White House may release information beneficial to the cause of members whose support they seek, or the president can accept an invitation to a fundraising event for a member who is up for reelection. Some presidents pay more attention to congressional relations than others. Usually, those who work hard at nurturing support with key members are the ones most likely to gain support for their legislative agendas.

Lobbyists employ several generally recognized rules of thumb to maximize their effectiveness with Congress. They are aware that it is rarely effective to lobby opponents to one's cause in an effort to convert them. It is better to deploy one's resources working with allies in high places, especially members of key committees with jurisdiction in the area of one's interests. It is generally easier to avoid conflicts on big issues and concentrate instead on writing the details to one's advantage. It is easier to defeat a measure than to pass new ones.

Lobbying the Executive Branch Since the beginning of the twentieth century, the federal government has greatly expanded its authority over a wide range of private activities, from regulating pollutants emitted by industries to overseeing fair employment practices. This has provided interest groups with fertile ground for lobbying the cabinet departments and independent agencies of the federal bureaucracy that oversee these activities. Agency administrators and personnel are policymakers just as much as members of Congress. Their task is to write the rules that implement federal legislation. These rules involve a great deal of technical detail, take considerable time to draft, and often are the result of negotiations between bureaucrats and lobbyists for the organizations affected. Some of the rules implementing the Clean Air Act of 1991, for example, took twelve years to draft. Through the Federal Register, a daily compilation of federal regulations and legal notices, executive agencies invite public comment and reactions to proposed rules. This allows organized interests to draft written responses and appear before hearings to present their arguments.

Of course, lobbyists who have established good relationships with agency staff members can get an early start on the process by learning, in advance of public disclosure, what new rules are being considered,[44] or even helping to write these rules themselves. Sometimes members of the executive branch will actively court lobbyists in order to secure support for proposals they intend to initiate. President Obama actively courted members of the pharmaceutical and hospital industries in support of health-care reform, managing to secure promises from them to reduce costs.

If they fail to influence the rule makers, interest groups can pursue a number of alternative approaches. They can challenge rules they believe to be unfair in the courts. They can also seek favorable treatment by influencing the appointment of agency officials with whom they must deal. This is generally easier if the organization has good contacts with the administration and with key senators who must confirm the appointments of top administrators. Finally, interest group representatives can serve on advisory commissions and boards that meet with executive agencies to provide advice and guidance in areas of agency jurisdiction.[45]

Critics of executive-branch lobbying worry that businesses and groups that are regulated by a particular agency often manage to "capture" the agency by exercising too much influence over the rules it writes and implements. For years, many observers believed the airline industry exercised undue influence over the Federal Aviation Administration, which resulted in overly favorable treatment regarding fee arrangements and travel routes. Research into agency capture produced no firm or universal findings, however, and the recent trend to deregulate and open business activity to market forces has weakened support for this viewpoint.[46]

Some critics also worry about what has been described as an **iron triangle**, a decision-making process dominated by interest groups, congressional committees, and executive agencies. In this arrangement, the parties cooperate by advancing each other's goals: Interest groups benefit by winning policy concessions or contracts; members of Congress benefit from electoral support supplied by the interest group; and federal agencies benefit from congressional approval for their administrative proposals.[47] In 1961, President Eisenhower warned about an overly cozy relationship between defense-industry lobbyists, the Pentagon, and members of congressional appropriation committees. Most policy observers today agree, however, that the threat from potential "iron triangles" is on the wane,[48] especially because of inroads made by advocacy groups in gaining access to policymakers and in opening records of meetings.[49]

Still, it is not uncommon for small groups of experts to dominate policy creation and implementation. These groups, sometimes called **issue networks**, include lobbyists, members of Congress, bureaucrats, and policy specialists from think tanks and universities. These expert groupings are more open, less formal, and less permanent than iron triangles. Actors come together around immediate issues and disband once the issue is settled. Rather than having a permanent and reciprocally beneficial relationship, their only link is shared interest and expertise in a particular policy area. Issue networks often are open to groups with opposing interests and viewpoints, unlike the iron triangles, in which policy interests are more uniform.

iron triangle A decision-making structure dominated by interest groups, congressional committees, and executive agency personnel who create policies that are mutually beneficial.

issue networks Decision-making structures consisting of policy experts, including lobbyists, members of Congress, bureaucrats, and policy specialists from think tanks and universities.

Iron Triangle

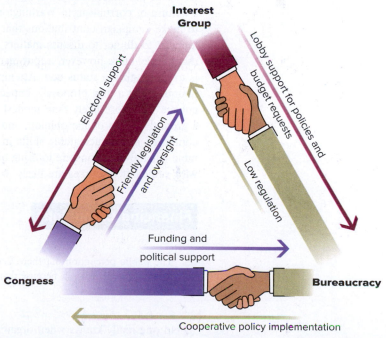

The iron triangle refers to the decision-making structure dominated by interest groups, congressional committees, and bureaucratic agencies for their mutual benefit.

Regulating Lobbying Activity Concerns about inappropriate lobbying activity date back to the nineteenth century, when bribery in Washington was not uncommon. In 1946, Congress passed the Federal Regulation of Lobbying Act, which attempted to deter the excesses of lobbying through the concept of disclosure. The law required lobbyists to register with the clerk of the House and the secretary of the Senate if they received money used principally to influence legislation before Congress. Despite these provisions, the act did not regulate the *practices* employed by lobbyists to any great extent, and it lacked enforcement. In 1995, Congress passed a new Lobbying Disclosure Act that defined lobbyists more broadly and included those seeking access to the executive branch. It also adopted new rules on gifts and sponsored travel.

A series of high-profile scandals that erupted in 2005 raised corruption as a major issue in the congressional elections of 2006. Superlobbyist Jack Abramoff went to prison for bilking his Native American clients out of millions of dollars while lobbying on behalf of their gaming interests. (See Current Controversy later in the chapter.) So, too, did former congressman Bob Ney (R-OH), who was convicted of accepting illegal gifts from Abramoff. In unrelated scandals, Rep. Randy "Duke" Cunningham (R-CA) was forced to resign and serve prison time for accepting bribes from defense contractors who sought favors from the Defense Appropriations Subcommittee on which he served, and Rep. William Jefferson (D-LA) was forced to relinquish his position on the House Ways and Means Committee amid reports of bribes after the FBI found $90,000 in cash in his freezer. Jefferson also served time in prison. Reacting to these events, the 110th Congress passed a new round of reforms, the 2007 Honest Leadership and Open Government Act, which included a ban on accepting gifts, meals, or trips from lobbyists. The bill also ended the practice of accepting free or reduced-fare trips on corporate jets, mandated greater disclosure about special pet projects (known as earmarks) that legislators insert into bills on behalf of special interests, and required greater disclosure and tracking of the source of campaign funds exceeding $15,000 that come in "bundles" from members of the same organization. It also required senators and members of the executive branch to wait two years after leaving government service before lobbying Congress; House members must wait one year.

These changes have by no means leveled the playing field for political access; lobbying Congress is a very expensive game that only the best-financed interests can play effectively. According to the Center for Responsive Politics, for example, the pharmaceuticals and health products lobby spent over $200 million on lobbying in 2017 (see the figure "Lobbying Expenditures by the Pharmaceuticals and Health Products Industry" earlier in this chapter). Nor are these changes likely to allay the suspicions of many Americans who perceive a culture of corruption in Washington. The reforms include loopholes that permit lobbyists to make campaign contributions that the representative or senator can then use to take the lobbyist to dinner to discuss matters of mutual interest. It is difficult to assess just what all this money buys; however, a four-year study found that the most likely outcome of lobbying is to maintain the status quo. Attempts to bring change are often easily defeated by sowing doubts about a new proposal's impact. Where change did occur, however, significant policy change was more likely than modest change. A variety of forces, including new leadership, a groundswell of public opinion, and events that brought attention to unresolved problems, combined to produce stable shifts in the policy environment.[50] Thus, it is vital to be at the table when events conspire to bring big change. As we have seen, however, only those groups with sufficient resources are likely to stick around for the long haul.

Financing Campaigns

> The public perception out there that someone who gives a thousand dollars has influence is laughable. It really is, because that's such chump change today that it doesn't even register on the scale.
>
> *Wright Andrews, lobbyist*[51]

No one really knows when organized interests started taking over the financing of political campaigns. An early milestone was Marcus A. Hanna's success in raising more than $3.5 million for the campaign of Republican William McKinley in 1896 by assessing corporations and banks predetermined amounts to finance the campaign.[52] Since then, it seems incumbent on organizations that want an elected official's ear to "pony up." For the average individual, $1,000 is hardly "chump change," but some U.S. Senate races cost more than $30 million to run. In light of extravagant campaign costs, candidates are in a continuous search for funds, and interest groups stand ready to help.

Financing elections takes place within a web of legal restrictions that have become more complicated and contentious over time. The first regulations date to 1907, when the Tillman Act outlawed contributions directly from corporations. The act was fraught with loopholes, however, and enjoyed little genuine enforcement. It was not until the 1970s that Congress seriously revisited the issue of campaign finance regulation. The Federal Election Campaign Act of 1971 required candidates to disclose the sources of contributions but did little to reform campaign financing beyond reporting. Congress passed more sweeping legislation in 1974 in the wake of the Watergate scandal. The legislation provided for public financing for presidential elections and the creation of the Federal Election Commission to monitor election finances and place limits on contributions by individuals, political parties, and **political action committees (PACs)**. PACs are organized financial arms of interest groups that collect and distribute money to candidates for elective office.

Interest groups challenged the law's limits on political contributions by individuals and PACs as a violation of their First Amendment right to free speech. In *Buckley v. Valeo* (1976), the Supreme Court struck down some of the bill's provisions but allowed continued limits on individual and PAC contributions. With caps on the contributions allowed by any given PAC, the number of PACs increased dramatically. PAC growth represents a wide spectrum of political and economic interests, including business, labor, and citizens' groups. Even elected officials maintain so-called **leadership PACs** as a means of financing the campaigns of political allies who they believe will reciprocate with support for their own political ambitions.

Congress revisited the issue of campaign finance in 2002, passing the so-called McCain-Feingold Bill, named for its two vocal Senate sponsors, John McCain (R-AZ) and Russell Feingold (D-WI). Although interest groups challenged these reforms in 2003 and again in 2007,[53] the Supreme Court upheld most of the new law's provisions. Yet interest group members and lobbyists can still contribute to a candidate and again to PACs that support the candidate. Lobbyists also sometimes serve as treasurers of campaign committees for candidates, thereby elevating the visibility of their group.[54]

In the 2010 case *Citizens United v. Federal Election Commission,* the Supreme Court ruled that the portion of the McCain-Feingold law that restricted corporations and unions from spending money to influence political campaigns violated the First Amendment. The Court's slim majority wrote that political contributions represent free speech, and as such, the government has no business in regulating the amount of money spent on independent ads for or against candidates. Later that year, in *SpeechNow.org v. Federal Election Commission,* the U.S. Court of Appeals for the D.C. Circuit lifted the donation limits on groups running such ads. The Federal Election Commission subsequently issued advisory opinions affirming the legal right of groups and individuals to give unlimited sums of money to independent committees. First labeled "super PACs" by reporter Eliza Newlin Carney, these independent-expenditure-only committees have been permitted to accept unlimited contributions and make unlimited expenditures aimed at electing or defeating federal candidates.[55] **Super PACs** may not contribute funds directly to federal candidates or parties.

Despite their recent origin, super PACs have played a major role in federal elections. In 2010, nearly eighty super PACs emerged and spent over $60 million attempting to elect or defeat federal candidates. By 2012, the number of these groups had grown to 1,300. At the presidential level, super PACs played a major role in financing both the Obama and Romney campaigns. For the 2014 midterm elections, the number of super PACs was slightly larger than in 2012; they raised nearly $700 million and spent about half that total in key Senate and House races.

The race for the White House in 2016 revealed the increasing importance of these new kind of PACs. All of the announced candidates had ties to super PACs, except Democrats Bernie Sanders and Jim Webb and Republican Donald Trump, although the super PAC "Make America Great Again" was backed by Trump's daughters-in-law. For candidates Jeb Bush, Ben Carson, Hillary Clinton, Ted Cruz, Marco Rubio, Carly Fiorina, and Rand Paul, donations from super PACs represented critical components of their campaign budgets. Knowing that federal law requires these organizations to be independent of the campaign itself, the presidential candidates found creative ways to work in concert with their independent allies. Super PACs like Bush's

political action committees (PACs) Organized financial arms of interest groups used to collect and distribute money to candidates for elective office.

leadership PACs Political action committees set up by political leaders as a means to finance the campaigns of political allies who they believe will reciprocate with support for their own political ambitions.

Super PACs Independent expenditure-only committees that are permitted to accept unlimited contributions and make unlimited expenditures to help elect or defeat federal candidates.

"Right to Rise USA" and Cruz's "Keep the Promise" were run by close allies. In fact, all the candidates were aided by independent organizations run by friends, allies, or former strategists.

One loophole in the system set up to regulate super PACs is related to the question of when a candidate becomes a candidate under federal law. The Federal Election Commission reached no decision on this question, and candidates are free to coordinate with independent groups before formally announcing their candidacy. In the six months before officially announcing his candidacy, Jeb Bush raised $100 million for his "Right to Rise USA" super PAC, provided it with staff, and sat in on strategy sessions. Even after declaring their candidacy, candidates can attend super PAC fundraising events as long as they do not ask any individual for money beyond the individual contribution level. If the candidate's appearance, however, persuades a donor to give much greater amounts to the organization when the candidate is not present, that is acceptable. Advertisements by a super PAC must be independent of the candidate's campaign, but the organization can use raw footage of the candidate that was shot before the formal declaration of candidacy, as did Ted Cruz's "Keep the Promise" super PAC. Hillary Clinton's campaign collaborated directly with one of her super PACs, "Correct the Record," to provide her campaign with opposition research.[56]

Congress appears to have as little appetite for changing the election laws as the Federal Election Committee has to enforce the current laws in a way that would close the loopholes. Representative David E. Price (D-NC) expressed his dismay, saying, "The rules of affiliation are just about as porous as they can be, and it amounts to a joke that there's no coordination between these individual super PACs and the candidates."[57] An editorial in the *The New York Times* argued that the corrupting influence of money "is not limited to bribery; the broader problem is the ability to put into office those who support their political agendas or financial interests."[58]

outside spending Political expenditures made by organizations and individuals other than the candidate campaigns themselves.

Despite such criticism, super PACs continue to increase the amount of **outside spending** in American elections. In 2016, the total reached over $1.4 billion with super PACs being the largest contributor to the outside spending figure (see "Outside Spending in the 2016 Elections"). This increase in outside group spending helped to make the 2016 presidential election the most expensive election in American history, surpassing the $6 billion mark (see "Total Election Costs, 1998–2016").

Even before the advent of super PACs, interest groups had effectively played the money game in Washington, D.C. Business interests used to dominate the process, but in recent years issue groups have increased their footprint. The number of issue groups, such as the National Rifle Association or the National Organization for Women, has increased dramatically in recent years, and so have their contributions. According to one study, citizen groups constitute five of the fastest growing sources of campaign funds when individual contributions and PAC funds are combined.[59] The growth of this sector clearly suggests that civic groups, sometimes responding to requests by entrepreneurial leaders, are not shrinking from engaging in the high-stakes arena of campaign finance in order to advance the interests they espouse.

Corporate interests are also major players. Corporate interests may be represented by multiple PACs—once through a company PAC itself and then through several additional professional

Outside Spending in the 2016 Elections

Super PACs	$1,117,746,826
Parties	$252,892,106
Social Welfare 501 (c)(4)	$146,891,771
Other*	$130,089,154
Trade Assns 501 (c)(6)	$30,653,327
Unions 501 (c)(5)	$19,049,178

Spending in U.S. dollars

Outside spending by super PACs alone surpassed $ 1 billion in the 2016 elections.

Source: OpenSecrets.org, Center for Responsive Politics, October 21, 2017.

and trade PACs. Business PACs historically have given the largest proportion of their dollars to incumbents. Although interests such as energy and pharmaceuticals generally favor Republicans, and others (such as labor and trial lawyers) generally favor Democrats,[60] party loyalty is not the exclusive hallmark of PAC giving. All but the most ideologically committed groups commonly adjust their spending when party control changes hands.[61] In the 2016 elections, organizations representing labor, lawyers, and lobbyists favored Democrat candidates, whereas construction, agribusiness, transportation, and defense interests favored Republicans (see "Contributions to Parties by Sector, 2016").

Two new patterns of political financing have emerged with the advent of super PACs. First, there has been an increase in the outsized influence of a small number of donors. The top 100 family donors gave over 11 percent of the total money raised in the 2016 elections. The top ten individual donors are listed in the table "Top Ten Contributors." Second, there has been a dramatic increase in the amount of **dark money** spent in political campaigns. Organizations set up by interest groups as nonprofit organizations can receive unlimited donations from corporations, unions, and individuals and spend those funds to influence elections. The funds these tax-exempt organizations can collect and disperse are often referred to as "dark money" because the organizations are not required to disclose their donors. Super PACs in some circumstances can also be considered dark money groups. Although they are legally required to disclose their donors, they can accept unlimited contributions from political nonprofit organizations and "shell" corporations that may not have disclosed their donors.

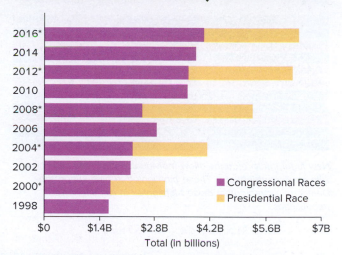

Total Election Costs, 1998–2016

The total cost of the presidential and congressional elections surpassed $6 billion in 2012 and 2016.

Source: OpenSecrets.org, Center for Responsive Politics, 2016.

dark money Spending by a group that is meant to influence the decision of voters, where the donor is not disclosed and the source of the money is unknown.

Contributions to Parties by Sector, 2016

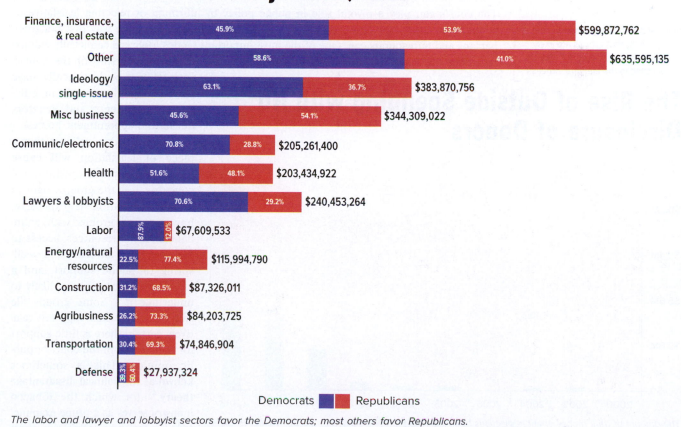

The labor and lawyer and lobbyist sectors favor the Democrats; most others favor Republicans.

Source: Center for Responsive Politics, "Totals by Sector," 2016, https://www.opensecrets.org/overview/sectors.php?cycle=2016.

Top Ten Contributors

Donor	Organization	Total
Thomas & Kathryn Steyer	Fahr LLC	$57,271,342
Sheldon & Miriam Adelson	Sands	$47,342,600
Donald Sussman	Trust Asset Management	$34,459,000
Robert & Diana Mercer	Renaissance Technologies	$23,545,700
Paul & Linda Singer	Elliott Management	$22,488,296
Fred Eychaner	Newsweb Inc	$22,262,291
Michael Bloomberg	Bloomberg LP	$20,145,178
Richard & Elizabeth Uihlein	Uline Shipping Supplies	$19,743,400
George Soros	Soros Fund Management	$17,689,038
James & Mary Pritzker	Pritzker Group	$16,256,648

New legal interpretations allow individuals to influence elections with large contributions. Those highlighted in blue supported Democratic candidates; those highlighted in red supported Republicans.

Source: Center for Responsive Politics, OpenSecrets.org.

The largest and most complex network of dark money groups is funded by the conservative business magnates David and Charles Koch. One study has referred to their network as a private political machine.[62] Their network accounted for about 25 percent of the dark money spent in 2012.[63] The year 2014 marked "the greatest wave of secret, special interest money ever."[64] In the Senate elections, most of the dark money was concentrated in the most competitive states: North Carolina, Colorado, Iowa, Kentucky, Arkansas, Georgia, Alaska, and Kansas. In these states, dark money as a percentage of nonparty outside spending was at least 63 percent and dark money expenditures surpassed those of super PACs and traditional PACs. In 2016, dark money reached $6 million and is projected to be over $13 million for the 2018 election cycle (see "The Rise of Outside Spending with No Disclosure of Donors"). The Federal Election Commission has been unable to control this phenomenon because of an overtaxed staff and disagreement between its three Democratic and three Republican commissioners.[65]

In summary, very few restrictions were placed on the financing of campaigns by interest groups until the 1970s. In 1971, federal law required candidates to report the sources of their contributions but did little to reform campaign practices beyond reporting. Legislation in 1974 created the Federal Election Commission and placed limits on the amount of contributions given by individuals, political parties, and PACs. Additional limits were imposed in 2002, but subsequent court decisions that interpreted limits on groups' outside spending as a violation of free speech led to ever more expensive elections and the troubling rise of dark money.

Accessing the Courts

The courts can play a pivotal role in public policy by affirming or rejecting legislative or administrative actions. However, judges cannot be lobbied in the same way that congresspersons and bureaucrats can. One of the most important tactics lobbyists can legally employ regarding the legislative branch is to attempt to control the membership of the courts. Interest groups historically have played a significant role in influencing presidents and senators during the appointment process.

When a group believes that a piece of legislation will cause them harm or raises constitutional concerns, it is the group's right to litigate. Litigation is expensive, however, and groups with abundant financial resources, access to full-time staff attorneys, a wellspring of public support, and a clear issue focus are most likely to undertake it.[66] Some groups file suit in court when they are relatively certain there is little support for their cause in the court of public opinion. This is sometimes known as the **political disadvantage theory**,[67] for which the tobacco industry serves as a prime example. It is far easier to convince a court to reject an industry regulation

political disadvantage theory The view positing that groups are likely to seek remedies in courts if they do not succeed in the electoral process.

The Rise of Outside Spending with No Disclosure of Donors

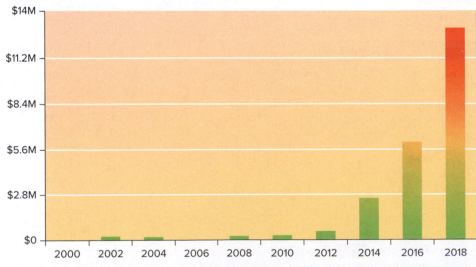

The amount of dark money spent in elections began growing exponentially with the 2014 election cycle.

Source: OpenSecrets.org, Center for Responsive Politics, 2017.

on legal grounds than to expect sympathy from a public that is increasingly turned off by smoking. Instead of bringing suit themselves, many interest groups file *amicus curiae,* or "friend of the court," briefs outlining their support for the claims of others, especially when the case holds promise to advance their own interests.

Most of the important constitutional cases with broad policy implications decided by the Supreme Court in recent years have taken the form of test cases. These are cases brought by organized interests in an attempt to set new precedents.[68] In the 1950s, for example, the Legal Defense Fund of the National Association for the Advancement of Colored People (NAACP) won numerous court cases supporting equal rights for African Americans.[69] More recently, advocacy groups that agree with the legal claims of environmentalists, women, civil libertarians, or fundamentalist Christians have supported their cases before the Supreme Court.[70] We will return to discuss the role of advocacy groups in the courts in Chapter 14.

Grassroots Mobilization

Grassroots mobilization is the practice of organizing citizens to exert direct pressure on public officials in support of a group's policy preferences. Lawmakers want to be reelected, and they know constituents retain the power to reward or punish them at the polls. As a result, organizations with large member bases and with members spread across a broad swath of congressional districts can be especially effective.[71] The National Education Association (NEA) is one of the larger membership-based grassroots organizations, representing more than three million educators. The Christian Coalition is another, with an estimated 1.9 million members. The strength of large organizations like these comes from their ability to mobilize large numbers of citizens into action quickly. Such groups can rouse members to write or call their lawmakers, to work on political campaigns, and to get out the vote on Election Day. Organized groups can provide workers to bring a candidate's message door-to-door, distribute campaign literature, and staff telephone banks. The electioneering efforts of the Christian Coalition helped the Republicans gain control of Congress in 1994, and the strong efforts by organized labor provided Democratic gains in both houses in 2006 and again in 2008.

Modern technology is making it easier than ever for interest groups to deliver constituents' messages to their elected officials. A survey by the Congressional Management Foundation, a nonpartisan group that helps train legislative staff, reported that 44 percent of Americans had been in contact with their House members or senators in the previous five years. Not unexpectedly, "84 percent of citizens contacting lawmakers had been prompted by a third party, mostly lobbying and advocacy groups."[72]

As we know from Chapter 7, those who are better educated and more affluent are more readily mobilized, and their communications are more highly prized by political leaders. Because of this, some public relations firms specialize in mining databases for high-status community leaders to contact legislators in key districts to support the sponsoring group's position. This practice, known as **mobilizing the grass tops**, earns these firms hefty fees for setting up meetings between high-profile constituents and members of Congress.[73] The National Federation of Independent Business (NFIB), for example, regularly communicates by Internet and e-mail with its members to educate and mobilize them.[74] The group maintains contact information for its members and data about members' types of businesses, issue positions, political backgrounds, and legislative districts. This kind of data makes it easy for the NFIB to target its message to those members who are most likely to respond to calls for quick mobilization.

grassroots mobilization The practice of organizing citizen support for a group's policy or candidate preferences.

mobilizing the grass tops Mining databases for high-status community leaders for purposes of contacting legislators in key districts regarding sponsoring a group's position.

get involved!

In addition to their constituents, what interests do your U.S. representative and senators represent? How much money did they raise in the last election cycle, and where did it come from? You can search financial records that reveal this information easily at www.opensecrets.org. The site provides access to the source of both individual and PAC funds. Once you have the data, you can check voting records to discover whether or not they voted for issues supported by major backers.

©Peter Dazeley/Getty Images

Another tactic, known as **astroturf lobbying**, uses deceptive practices and lack of transparency to manufacture grassroots support for an issue important to a particular set of unidentified interests. For example, in 2009 the American Coalition for Clean Coal Electricity, an organization funded by coal producers, allegedly hired a lobbying firm to drum up what appeared to be widespread public opposition to a proposed climate change bill in the U.S. House. The group's plans were thwarted, however, when a dozen letters supposedly written by average citizens were discovered to have been forged. Astroturf lobbying was also a popular tactic employed in the recent health-care debate by organizations representing both sides of the issue.

Many interest groups build grassroots support for their causes by supplying voters with ratings or scorecards to guide their electoral choices. The Christian Coalition has been particularly adept at this practice, issuing ratings for candidates to member churches for distribution on the Sunday prior to Election Day. The liberal group Americans for Democratic Action (ADA) uses a similar rating scheme. The group gives each legislator a score based on the percentage of times he or she voted in favor of the group's position. Generally, Democrats receive average scores much higher than Republicans from this liberal interest group. The ADA also publishes a list of House and Senate "heroes" (100 percent agreement with the group) and "zeros" (0 percent agreement with the group). (See the figure "Americans for Democratic Action Ratings for Senators in the 114th Congress, 2015.")

Coalition Formation

The rapid growth in the number and variety of interest groups since the mid-1980s has created a strong incentive for groups to act in concert by forging coalitions. Organized groups benefit from alliances by expanding their access to resources and information, increasing their visibility, and enlarging the scope of their influence. Members of Congress and federal bureaucrats often seek out coalitions because they provide a means for reconciling intergroup differences in a way that facilitates compromise in policy formation.

Coalitions are not always easy to build because there are risks in joining. Some of the views of coalition partners may be at odds with those of other partners, and smaller groups may fear that their priorities will be submerged beneath those of larger partners. Each group must evaluate the trade-offs of joining a coalition on an issue-by-issue basis.[75] Sometimes, however, issues bring together coalitions of highly unlikely partners. For example, groups as disparate as the liberal American Civil Liberties Union (ACLU) and the conservative Rutherford Institute found common ground in opposing restrictions on civil liberties proposed in the USA Patriot Act following the 9/11 attacks. Health-care reform has also fostered coalition building. A number of organizations representing insurers, hospitals, and health-care workers—groups that had worked in opposite directions during the Clinton administration to scuttle reform—combined forces to support President Obama and ensure that each of them got a say in the Patient Protection and Affordable Care Act passed in 2010.

Americans for Democratic Action Ratings for Senators in the 114th Congress, 2015

HERO
100% Agreement with ADA positions

Warren (D-MA)
Durbin (D-IL)
Gillibrand (D-NY)

ZERO

Grassley (R-IA)
Rubio (R-FL)
Blunt (R-MO)

0% Agreement with ADA positions

Many interest groups build grassroots support for their causes by supplying voters with legislator ratings to guide their electoral choices.

Source: Americans for Democratic Action Ratings for Senators in the 114th Congress, 2015, retrieved October 6, 2016, from http://www.adaction.org/pages/publications/voting-records.php.

Current Controversy

Abramoff and Lobby Reform

At the turn of the twenty-first century, Jack Abramoff was the most powerful lobbyist on Capitol Hill. By 2006, however, he was serving time in federal prison for a variety of illegal activities. Adopting a "winning at all costs" philosophy, his lobbying activities included many legal and ethical violations. He had not always followed the legal registration requirements for lobbyists, so that he could submerge his tactics regarding a particular legislative bill. He had constructed nonprofit entities to hide some of his vast earnings, to avoid paying taxes. He constantly violated the ban on gifts to congresspersons and their staff. Nobody knew how to game the lobbying system in Washington better than Abramoff, and his 2011 book *Capitol Punishment: The Hard Truth About Washington Corruption from America's Most Notorious Lobbyist* offers some valuable insights for reforming the system and protecting it from the type of predator he was.

Aware that "reform can be an illusion,"[*] Abramoff recommends four measures "that would bring real reform to our political system."[†] First, he would break the connection between money and politics, not by limiting the size of any American's campaign contribution, but by entirely eliminating any contribution by those lobbying the government, participating in a federal contract, or in any way financially benefiting from the public treasury.

Second, he believes lobbyists should be banned from giving gifts to members of Congress and their staffs. He wants to eliminate the practice entirely in order to remove all temptation. In his days as a lobbyist, Abramoff provided gifts to congressional offices ranging from donuts in the morning, to sandwiches at lunch, meals at posh restaurants for dinner, rounds of golf at prestigious golf courses, and visits to resorts. His firm spent in excess of $1.5 million annually purchasing event tickets. During football season, for instance, they had seventy-two tickets each week to give away for Redskins games. He saw it as a great way to build relationships with congresspersons and staff.

His third prescription for reform is to completely remove the lure of post–public service lobbying. He believes the "revolving door" is one of the greatest sources of corruption in government because he used it so effectively in his career. He described the process:

> Once I found a congressional office that was vital to our clients—usually because they were incredibly helpful and supportive—I would often become close to the chief of staff of the office. In almost every congressional office, the chief of staff is the center of power. Nothing gets done without the direct or indirect action on his or her part. After a number of meetings with them, possibly including meals or rounds of golf, I would say a few magic words: "When you are done working for the Congressman, you should come work for me at my firm."[**]

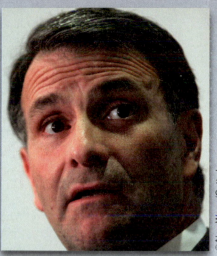

Jack Abramoff came to personify the inappropriate excesses of lobbying by his tactics.

Abramoff believed that after such an offer, he owned the chief of staff because 90 percent of them have an interest in leaving their position for a more lucrative position as a lobbyist. All future moves made by the chief of staff were made with his or her future plans in mind. To Abramoff, "It was a perfect—and perfectly corrupt—arrangement."[††]

Finally, Abramoff favors term limits for senators and House members. He believes it is too easy for lobbyists to build relationships with members who stay in Washington for long periods of time.

[*]Jack Abramoff, *Capitol Punishment* (New York: WND Books, 2011), 272.
[†]Ibid., 273.
[**]Abramoff, J. *Capitol Punishment* (New York: WND Books, 2011), 95.
[††]Ibid., 95.

Protests

Protests have always been a part of the American political landscape. They include nonviolent techniques such as picketing or marches and sit-ins like those used by the civil rights movement under the leadership of Dr. Martin Luther King, Jr. They may also involve violence, as in Shays's Rebellion shortly after the American Revolution. Protest is the ultimate form of grassroots activity because members are asked to be willing to sacrifice their lives and their freedom for the cause. As a result, protest usually accompanies issues that are highly charged emotionally. The 1973 *Roe v. Wade* decision, for example, triggered a significant increase in protest activity that continues to surround the abortion issue to this day.

Although it is protected by the First Amendment, many observers see protest as being outside the mainstream of political activism. As a result, it is a common tactic among those with few resources and little direct access to the centers of power. Protesting might be considered the ultimate outside strategy, reserved for groups with few other visible means for making their voices heard. This does not mean, however, that protesters themselves are poor and uneducated. Some studies show that protesters disproportionately come from those with higher levels of income and education.[76] Many of the people who attended town hall meetings held by their senators and congresspersons in 2017 were well educated and articulate. The students who organized the 2018 March for Our Lives all around the country and their followers provided a most dramatic example of protests as the ultimate outside strategy against the powerful gun lobby and the members of Congress who do their bidding.

INTEREST GROUPS AND CIVIC ENGAGEMENT TODAY

Whereas voluntary associations of earlier eras emphasized local organization and citizen training, interest group politics today is often run by professionals in Washington. This development is the result of important structural changes in the nature of our political system. As Matthew A. Crenson and Benjamin Ginsberg note, "Beginning with the development of its regulatory capacity at the start of the twentieth century, American government multiplied the mechanisms by which organized interests could achieve their ends without mobilizing their grassroots constituents."[77] Petitioning of executive-branch agencies and litigation necessitate the work of skilled professionals, not average citizens. Government and philanthropic foundations multiplied the opportunities for groups to support themselves without relying exclusively on membership contributions. As a result, interest groups increasingly seem to manage interests from above rather than fully involving the citizens they are supposed to represent.[78]

Some observers warn that these changes in patterns of interest group activity are transforming citizens from "participants" to "mailing lists." Today, entrepreneurial advocacy groups launch campaigns from Washington seeking direct access to lawmakers and the courts without first investing much effort in generating popular support for their positions in towns and neighborhoods.[79] AARP, for example, has the largest membership base of any American interest group. Yet their 35 million members do not gather in conventions to determine their political agenda. Their leaders contact them by mail. Participation is limited to contributions; the leadership sets the agendas, and groups often bring their issues before courts or administrative boards without needing to demonstrate any broad support for the actions they undertake. Interest groups demand little from members but much from government.

However, interest groups have *always* depended on strong national leadership willing to employ new techniques in mobilizing popular support. Some of the largest grassroots organizations today, such as the NAACP, began as national organizations and later cultivated local chapters for support. Advocacy groups continue to play an important role in opening new avenues of expression and preserving constitutional rights for millions of previously disaffected minorities. To a large extent, interest groups have simply adapted their methods to reflect changes in the lifestyles of most Americans. Most Americans have little time to meet with neighborhood associations after a long day of work and after-dinner soccer practice with their children. They cannot monitor the fine points of legislation that may threaten their interests. Organized groups recognize this reality by offering citizens a variety of participatory options; for instance, they encourage check writing and provide help in contacting local representatives. They are even developing hybrid techniques that combine national activation with local action. For example, some groups use the Internet not merely to inform citizens of legislative threats or to solicit funds but also to help local citizens organize meetings in their own communities. These "meetups" hold the promise of reigniting community activism in the Internet age.

United Students Against Sweatshops and other organizations have mounted effective grassroots campaigns to stop retailers from carrying clothing made by manufacturers employing unfair and unsafe labor conditions.

Finally, there is growing interest in global issues that defy national borders and traditional interest group activities. Young Americans are especially interested in global organizations like Greenpeace and Oxfam, and in expanding the frontiers of political action. Many of the organizations that address international issues, such as United Students Against Sweatshops (USAS) and the Global Fund to Fight AIDS, Tuberculosis and Malaria, employ innovative approaches to political participation that include boycotting manufacturers who use sweatshop labor or buycotting—selectively purchasing from merchants who donate a portion of their receipts to a good cause.

Nevertheless, interest group politics continues to pose challenges to our voluntaristic ethic. Although citizens are indeed writing more letters and checks, boycotting, and buycotting, these actions continue to be taken disproportionately by those who are well off. As a result, groups reflecting the interests of the upper reaches of society are better represented when political decisions are rendered. The pluralism that thrives in a community characterized by numerous interest groups is at risk when the majority of those groups speak with what one political scientist calls "an upper class accent."[80]

> # Thinking It Through »»»
>
> **Learning Objective:** Define the patterns of membership in interest groups.
>
> **Review:** Why Join?
>
> Your college roommate tells you she has joined the campus organization known as PIRG, a state public interest research group. You later learn that such campus groups across the nation advocate for policies such as new voter registration, improved mass transit, global warming awareness education, and cheaper college textbooks. Give at least two motivations that your roommate may have had for becoming affiliated with this interest group.

Summary

1. **What are interest groups, and what types of interests do they represent?**
   - Interest groups are formally organized associations that seek to influence public policy.
   - Unlike political movements that promote wide-ranging social change, interest groups are more narrowly focused on specific policies.
   - Interest groups may organize for specific economic or ideological goals, or they may be public groups that advocate for the good of all Americans.
   - There have always been interest groups in America, but they experienced their greatest growth in the 1960s and 1970s.
   - Those groups representing the wealthy and the better educated are the most numerous.
   - Many interests at the bottom of the economic spectrum receive minimal or no representation at all.

2. **Why might someone join an interest group?**
   - Someone might join an interest group for material incentives such as discounts for products or services or higher wages.
   - Someone might join an interest group for social incentives, the social support from others with similar backgrounds or interests.
   - Someone might join an interest group for the purposive intent to advance a cause in which she or he believes.
   - Studies have found that material incentives are the least important for joining groups, particularly among the young.

3. **What do interest groups do?**
   - Interest groups seek to advance the public policy interests of the people they represent.
   - Groups develop an overall plan or strategy based on the type of issue involved and the resources the group can bring to bear.
   - Strategies can be categorized as inside, direct personal encounters with public officials, and outside, activities showing popular support for the group's cause.
   - Tactics are the specific actions taken by a group.
   - Interest group tactics include lobbying, financing campaigns, filing suits in court, working to create grassroots support, forming alliances with others to advance their cause, and protesting.

Chapter 9

Parties and Political Campaigns
Putting Democracy into Action

WHAT'S TO COME

The political seems to have gotten a lot more personal in recent years with partisans preferring the company of like-minded partners.

SEPARATE TABLES, PLEASE

"If you are a Trump supporter, I'm not even going to consider meeting you for coffee," the fifty-year-old single woman confessed to a reporter, clarifying her views on dating these days.[1]

Trump-supporting singles are just as adamant about not dating partisan rivals, even screening them on websites like TrumpSingles.com.

Whole families have been torn apart by partisan differences in recent years, adding new tensions and stresses to family gatherings. The media have taken to giving advice about how to avoid political conversations with loved ones when sitting down to holiday dinners.[2]

The phenomenon of avoiding individuals whose partisan choices are different from our own is not new, but its incidence is growing, and scholars have begun studying the phenomenon. In one study, using in part a sample from online dating communities, researchers concluded, "People do seem to construct their social lives around politics, and such sorting appears substantively consequential in explaining which relationships form. We also find that political homophily [bonding with others like ourselves] is more than the result of restricted partner markets or selecting on other demographic and social characteristics, explanations previous work cannot easily and definitively reject."[3]

As You READ

- What are political parties, and why do we have just two major parties?
- How are parties organized, and how has our party system adapted to change?
- What is the relationship between candidates and parties in our electoral system?
- Why are the parties so divided today, and what, if anything, should be done about it?

There is even experimental evidence that partisanship affects our ability to make mathematical judgments. According to one study, when presented with problems dealing with noncontroversial issues like assessing the effectiveness of a skin cream, individuals with good mathematical skills could make correct inferences. However, when presented with political issues like gun control, even those who were good at math couldn't help shading results based on their ideological preferences.[4]

Political parties have become closely bound up with our individual identities. They are part of how we define ourselves. But, they are far more. They help citizens make choices about the nation's future direction and help us organize our political world. They have not always been as polarizing as they are today, but they have always been forums for political battle.

In this chapter, we will learn about political parties, the role they play in guiding our political choices, the ways in which they shape our elections, and how they organize our government. We will study the ways in which political parties have grown and developed over time. We will examine the coalitions that constitute each party's base and how these coalitions occasionally shift over time as they adapt to social and economic change. And we will see that, despite the dysfunction they sometimes appear to display, political parties are vital to our democratic process. ∎

POLITICAL PARTIES AND ELECTORAL POLITICS

Without political parties, our system of government would seem even more fragmented than it is now. Individuals would have to run for office without benefit of an identifying label. Once elected, they would be on their own to forge alliances to get anything done in legislative chambers. Turnover would likely be frequent, and it would leave lobbyists and special interest groups the primary agents of institutional memory and know-how. Presidents would have to build new coalitions to support each and every new initiative. And there would be no established organization representing citizen interests with the power to take collective action on the citizens' behalf once elected and to take responsibility for success or failure. Although it is true that parties sometimes complicate the process of finding solutions to pressing problems, it is probably also true that matters could be much worse without them. As political scientist E. E. Schattschneider once said, "Modern democracy is unthinkable save in terms of the parties."[5]

political party An organization created for the purpose of winning elections and governing once in office.

Political parties are organizations created for the purpose of winning elections and governing once in office.[6] They perform a variety of functions for candidates, for voters, and for the government the parties serve. These functions include the following:

- Parties carry candidates' messages to voters and summon voters to the polls on Election Day.
- They help broker differences among groups they represent, developing policies that satisfy diverse viewpoints.
- They attempt to construct voting majorities in legislative bodies to enact laws.
- They organize governing bodies in order to create and administer public policy.

Traditionally, they have also been a source of political talent, finding and grooming candidates to run for office. Parties have also played a vital role in the expansion of the voting franchise by reaching out to new voters as a means of amplifying citizen voices as well as enhancing their own strength.

The Nature of Parties in America

In some countries, political parties are membership organizations. That is, citizens pay dues to belong to the party and in return have a direct say in the policies it promotes and the leaders it selects. Parties in America are much more loosely organized. They connect interest group activists, elected leaders, and voters in an effort to promote policies they all support. However, these parts are far less tightly integrated and far more fluid than membership parties.

Parties fulfill different roles for different actors. For voters, parties are useful devices for simplifying electoral choices. They signal political viewpoints or philosophies that serve as a guide in choosing candidates. Like brand names, they are both a means of personal expression and a guide to decision making. Since the New Deal, voters have typically seen the Democrats as the party of the working and middle classes and Republicans as the party of business. The Republican Party is associated with conservatism; the Democrats, with liberalism.

The use of the elephant and donkey to represent our two political parties traces back to the work of political cartoonist Thomas Nast in the 1870s.

For candidates, parties are organizations that help them gain political power.[7] Unlike interest groups, which focus more on advancing policies than politicians, parties concentrate on getting their candidates elected to office. They are the only organizations that run candidates under their "brand" names. To do this, they must mobilize support by building coalitions among many groups to produce winning margins. As political scientist E. E. Schattschneider put it, they *mobilize the bias* of voters by appealing to their common interests.[8]

For interest groups and activists, political parties are vehicles they use to capture government to advance their particular goals, whether these be materially self-interested or high minded.[9] For example, businesses may seek to promote candidates who advocate lower taxes. Environmentalists look for candidates who advance policies aimed at combating climate change. For any interest group to win popular support, it must combine with other groups to develop mutually acceptable agendas and work to elect candidates committed to their purposes.

Finally, for elected officials, a party provides a common set of principles that help them govern. Under the party label, officials can devise, pass, and implement policies that express their common viewpoint. Voters can benefit as well by assigning to party leaders collective responsibility—for success if the party's policies succeed and for failure if they do not.[10] Since parties, unlike any other political organizations, are held accountable in elections, it is in their interest to build wide support for the positions and candidates they promote. In this chapter, our discussion will focus on the role of parties in elections, that is, the way they function as guides for individual voters and as organizations that promote candidates to elective office. In other chapters, we will discuss their continuing and important role in governing once their members are in office.

Why Two Parties?

Although we have come to associate political parties with electoral and governing activities, you will search the U.S. Constitution in vain for a description of their nature or function. In fact, the Framers opposed political parties, fearing that they would split the nation into factions more focused on narrow interests than on the interests of the country as a whole. Alexis de Tocqueville captured the spirit of the Framers' sentiments when he called parties an evil—even if sometimes necessary—inherent in free governments.[11]

Of course, even as the Framers warned against factions, they were themselves dividing into factional groups that quickly assumed the function of parties. It is easy to see how disagreements over how to run the nation would generate party competition. It is more difficult to explain why the development of the American party system took the course it did. In particular, why have we developed a dual-party system instead of a system with multiple parties? After all, most European democracies have systems in which many parties, representing diverse points of view, compete for political power. There are several reasons why our system differs from theirs. These include election rules, the tendency of American voters to shy away from ideological extremes, state laws, and the way our elections are financed.

Election Rules The manner in which elections are conducted has an impact on the number of viable parties representing the electorate. In some countries, voters cast ballots for a slate of candidates representing the party of their choice and seats in the national legislature are awarded on the basis of the percentage of the popular votes received by each party. This method is known as **proportional representation**. For example, if one party receives 40 percent of the popular vote to fill a 100-member parliament, it is entitled to forty seats. Another party winning 20 percent will send twenty members, and so on. Even minor parties that reach some threshold of votes are entitled to some number of seats. In Finland's 2015 election, the Finnish Center Party received approximately one-fifth of the popular vote, which translated into forty-nine seats in the 200-member Parliament. However, even a small party, the Åland Coalition, received enough votes to qualify for one seat in the Parliament. This type of system tends to reward even small parties by assuring them a place in the legislative assembly even if they received a small number of votes overall.

By contrast, the United States employs a winner-take-all approach. Voters cast ballots for individual candidates based on where they live rather than for a whole slate of candidates chosen by the party to represent the entire nation. The candidate who secures more popular votes than any other candidate is the sole victor and represents the entire district. There is no reward for losing candidates representing minor parties as in proportional systems. This type of election rule is called the **single-member district** or winner-take-all system. We use it to conduct elections for Congress and most state legislatures.

The single-member district system tends to limit the number of competitive parties over time. Attempts to unseat candidates from a party that has long dominated a district usually depend on minority political forces joining together into one viable opposition party. The result over the long run is electoral contests between just two larger competitive parties. Smaller parties are absorbed by one of the larger parties or they may vanish altogether. The principle that single-member district elections generally lead to stable two-party systems is sometimes referred to as **Duverger's law**, named for the French sociologist who first proposed it.[12]

Critics complain that the rules governing our elections make it difficult for minority candidates, or anyone whose point of view varies from those represented by the two major parties, to gain a foothold in elective offices. It is true that the single-member district system does discourage minority-party and independent candidates from running and may reduce voter turnout by discouraging voters who do not support either major-party candidate.[13] However, our electoral system also simplifies leadership once the election is over. In the Finnish example presented earlier, what if no one party wins majority control of the chamber? That would mean that several parties would need to form coalitions to get anything done. Such coalitions are fragile and may lead either to inaction or frequent calls for new elections. By contrast, two-party systems like ours provide more stability once the election is over. One party likely will control the legislative body and the positions of leadership within it until the next regularly scheduled election, even if its majority is slim. In any case, it should be noted that the winner-take-all approach used to conduct our elections is by far the most important reason why only two parties dominate American politics.

Another set of rules that has the effect of limiting the number of competitive parties in our country involves the **Electoral College**, the assemblage of state electors constitutionally charged with casting the deciding votes in presidential elections. As we will see in Chapter 12, when we vote for president, we are actually choosing a slate of electors who represent the entire state. With the exceptions of Maine and Nebraska, states award all their electoral votes as a bloc to the candidate who has won the most popular votes in the state. Since victory in presidential contests requires an absolute majority of the electoral votes from all the states and the District of Columbia (270 out of 538), one of the two established major

proportional representation A system of representation in which seats for office are awarded on the basis of the proportion of votes received by candidates or parties.

single-member district An electoral system in which the candidate receiving a plurality of votes wins the election to represent the district.

Duverger's law The principle that asserts single-member district elections lead to two-party systems.

Electoral College The assemblage of state electors constitutionally charged with casting the deciding votes in presidential elections. With the exception of Maine and Nebraska, the candidate who wins the popular vote in a state is entitled to all the electoral votes from that state (with some exceptions). It takes the vote of 270 of these electors to declare a president the winner.

parties is most likely to have amassed enough votes in enough states to win. Minor parties that have a difficult time gaining traction in a large number of states stand almost no chance of winning the White House.

Ideological Centrism In some countries, long-standing economic, regional, and ethnic divisions give rise to political parties with narrow agendas. They seek to represent minority interests in the national government and often pursue narrow ideological agendas. Labor parties seeking worker control of the workplace, conservative parties seeking more free market competition for business interests, and ethnic and nationalistic parties of liberation seeking independence from foreign rule are just some examples. These parties are sustained partly because the proportional parliamentary systems in which they compete can reward even small parties by giving them a place in the legislative body.

By contrast, Americans historically have downplayed differences based on class or ethnic identity. There has traditionally been little support for a "workers' party" or a party for Americans who trace their roots to the Puritans. This reduces the attraction of parties that target specific groups or classes. Since most Americans are neither extreme liberals nor extreme conservatives (see Chapter 6), parties that stray too far from a "middle of the road" or centrist position are unlikely to fare well in elections. Given these features of American life, two parties seem to capture the viewpoints of a majority of voters.

Still, ideological differences between the parties seem to grow at times and contract at other times. In the current era, divisions between a largely liberal Democratic Party and a largely conservative Republican Party are particularly striking. Politics in times like these can be extremely volatile.

State Laws The U.S. Constitution does not mention political parties, so regulating them is largely the job of the states. Each state sets its own requirements for running candidates in elections, and the two major parties in these states usually set rules that make it difficult for minor parties or candidates to compete. For example, although both major parties in Alabama must simply demonstrate that each received at least 20 percent of the statewide vote in the last race for governor (something the Democrats and Republicans can easily demonstrate), a third-party or statewide independent candidate for all offices (except president) must obtain signatures from 3 percent of the number of people who voted in the last governor's race to qualify. Since almost 1.2 million voted in that race in 2014, the bar for gathering signatures is very high indeed. And the deadlines for gathering those signatures is early in the election cycle. Meeting state requirements such as these is expensive and time consuming and a challenge for third parties or independent candidates to regularly satisfy.

Financing Running for office is an expensive proposition. Although some states provide limited support to candidates regardless of party,[14] most states place fundraising responsibilities squarely on the shoulders of the candidates who must seek funds from private donors. Many of the largest and most reliable contributors give to candidates and parties with a track record for victory. They are less inclined to give to untested candidates and third parties with limited chances of success. Since few third-party or independent candidates can sustain the costs of a competitive campaign during the long months of the contest, they are at a decided disadvantage against well-funded major-party competitors.

GROWTH AND DEVELOPMENT OF OUR TWO-PARTY SYSTEM

Parties were born in America from the desire to produce lasting governing coalitions on issues that divided our leaders. No coalition, however, is permanent, and the history of our two-party system demonstrates that individual parties rise and fall over time for a number of reasons, including competition, failure to adapt policy or ideological positions to changing times, and internal struggles among factions. Over the course of our history, at least five distinct party systems have emerged, giving rise to the partisan landscape we see today.

The Evolution of American Political Parties: Five Party Systems

We saw in Chapter 2 that some members of the Framers' generation, like Alexander Hamilton, envisioned a national government with broad authority in financing undertakings necessary to make the new country a commercial force in the world. Supporters of this position became known as Federalists. Others, including Thomas Jefferson, believed Hamilton's vision took power away from states and localities and called for greater local autonomy. Followers of Jefferson became known as Democratic-Republicans. On a number of issues, these two sides fought by proxy in Congress, assembling makeshift majorities either to advance or to thwart the Hamiltonian vision. Those aligned with Jefferson, with the help of a rudimentary campaign organization and powerful partisan press, had won a majority of House seats by 1800. When national political figures lined up behind Hamilton's Federalists and Jefferson's Democratic-Republicans, the rudiments of the **first party system** in America came into existence. These partisan divisions were mostly confined to political leaders struggling to create stable voting coalitions within the government's legislative body.[15]

Andrew Jackson, aided by New York senator Martin Van Buren, later built a new organization that mobilized average voters in cities and towns across the nation; that achievement helped transform Jefferson's elite party into the first mass-based political party known simply as the Democrats. With the use of parades, speech making, rallies, and bonfires, often fueled by monies raised in Washington or New York and funneled to local political clubs across the nation, Democrats boosted popular participation substantially. Although only 30 percent of those eligible voted for a presidential candidate in 1824, voter turnout surged to 50 percent by 1828.[16] Structural changes, such as the popular election of presidential electors (who had in earlier elections been selected by legislative leaders), also helped spark voter interest by giving them a larger role in the election process.

By 1836, opponents copied the pattern of organizational success pioneered by Jefferson and Jackson, ushering in the **second party system**, one that pitted the Democrats against a new opposition party championed by Henry Clay, the Whigs. The parties differed on a number of issues, including the size and scope of the national government and the use of tariffs to protect native industries. As the issue of slavery gained prominence, internal divisions among the Whigs on this and a number of other issues led to the party's demise. From its ruins, a new Republican Party (unrelated to Jefferson's Democratic-Republicans) emerged, drawing support largely from the North and the new northwestern states. By 1860, the Democrats also had split over slavery, with northern and southern factions nominating different presidential candidates. Democratic feuding opened the way for Republican Abraham Lincoln to win the presidency in 1860 and set the stage for a showdown over slavery.

Following the Civil War, the **third party system** emerged, lasting for nearly half a century, from 1854 to the late 1890s. During this period, both parties competed vigorously, but Republicans controlled the presidency and Congress more often than the opposition. Democrats, torn by division after the Civil War, still managed to dominate big cities such as New York in the North, and held the loyalty of the white population in the South and portions of the Midwest. Southern blacks stayed loyal to Lincoln's Republican Party, and Republicans gained in areas of the Northeast and Upper Midwest where industry was flourishing. Westward expansion and migration to the cities served to keep the politics of the era fluid, but this period also witnessed the virtually uninhibited growth of big business and the susceptibility of the nation to wild swings in economic fortune.

Economic displacement, the growth of organized labor, and waves of immigrants contributed to growing discontent, but they also proved fertile ground for parties competing vigorously for voters' allegiances. Party bosses sought out these votes by assembling **political machines**, strong party organizations providing services to the needy and to new immigrants in return for their votes. Often, votes were exchanged for government jobs, a practice known as **patronage**. Difficult economic times combined with factional strife inspired violence

first party system The period from the founding until about 1824 that gave birth to the Federalist Party and the Democratic-Republican Party (later known simply as the Democrats).

second party system The period from the late 1820s until about 1854 in which the Democrats dominated American politics and in which the Whig Party became ascendant.

third party system The period from about 1854 to the late 1890s in which the newly formed Republican Party gained prominence while the Democrats split into factions. This period was marked by very high levels of voter turnout and corruption.

political machine A strong party organization that maintained control by giving favors in return for votes.

patronage The practice of providing jobs or favors in exchange for political loyalty.

between immigrants and domestic laborers who viewed political success as a surrogate for personal fortune. Nevertheless, the intensity of political conflict during this "golden age of electoral politics" produced voter turnout rates higher than ever before or since.[17]

Just before the turn of the twentieth century, discontent with the corruption of big city political machines as well as an economic depression led to the emergence of a number of independent third-party movements. Most prominent among these parties was the Populist Party, which drew support from various politically active farmers' alliances and from displaced urban workers. Although Democrats made inroads among Populist followers, their party was weakened by internal discord and support was largely confined to the South and portions of the West. At the same time, Republicans experienced growth in the burgeoning metropolitan areas of the North where they had strong support from industrial leaders and business interests. The period from about 1896 until 1932 is known as the **fourth party system**, during which the Republican party came to dominate national politics. This era saw a number of reforms in government that had been championed by progressives, including the growth of the **civil service**, a merit-based system of employment and personnel management that replaced patronage.

The Great Depression allowed the Democrats to recapture the northern electorate. At the peak of the Depression, one worker out of four was unemployed and more than five thousand banks had failed. By 1932, the nation was poised for a major party switch as Democrats swept the White House and both houses of Congress. This signaled the beginning of the **fifth party system**, a time of Democratic dominance that lasted until the late 1960s. Franklin D. Roosevelt's political legacy was the forging of a **New Deal**

Populist leader William Jennings Bryan gave more than 500 speeches in a twenty-nine-state tour during his vigorous 1896 campaign for president.

The Great Depression created the conditions that helped Franklin Roosevelt forge the New Deal coalition, enabling the Democrats to dominate national politics for forty years.

coalition of Democratic supporters, including southern whites, northern industrial workers, immigrants, urban dwellers, Catholics, Jews, and African Americans who gravitated toward the Democrats despite continued discrimination in southern Democratic enclaves. This unlikely coalition proved remarkably resilient as a result of strong leadership, a willingness to ignore potentially divisive issues like race, and mobilization of voters by newly empowered groups, especially organized labor. Although Republicans were the minority party during this period, they also put together a stable coalition of upper-income whites, Protestants, growing numbers of suburbanites, and small business owners.

fourth party system The period from about 1896 until 1932 in which the Republican Party dominated American politics.

civil service A merit-based system of employment and personnel management that replaced patronage.

Major Developments in the History of U.S. Political Parties

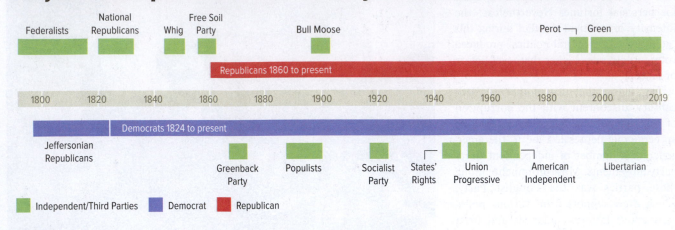

fifth party system The period, beginning in 1932 and continuing at least until the mid-1960s, characterized by the dominance of the Democratic Party and its New Deal coalition.

New Deal coalition The constellation of social groups that became the core base of support for the Democratic Party after the election of Franklin D. Roosevelt.

Shifting Tides: 1968 to Present

Democratic support for civil rights for minorities created deep fissures in the party as early as the 1940s, but these grew more serious in the 1960s. Southern whites distanced themselves from the national Democratic Party on racial issues and ran alternative candidates for president in 1948 (States' Rights Party) and 1968 (American Independent Party). By the mid-1960s, Democrats were straining to maintain the coalition that had made them the dominant party since 1932. Republicans capitalized on this disenchantment, recruiting new members in the rapidly growing South. Their "southern strategy" appealed to social conservatives who believed the federal government had overstepped its bounds in promoting racial equality in the states and over-extended its reach into the economy. From the 1960s onward, Republican gains in the once "solid Democratic South" have been dramatic. By 2016, the Republican Party controlled the governors' offices and both houses of the state legislatures in almost all of the old South.

A resurgent Republican Party regained the White House in 1968 and in subsequent years built national support as the Democratic coalition weakened. Drawing upon southern whites, conservatives, evangelical Christians, and upper-income businesspersons and professionals, Ronald Reagan built a coalition that attained parity with Democrats among the national electorate in 1980. Under Reagan, Republicans made inroads into several formerly Democratic constituencies, including middle-income and blue-collar voters as well as union members. The Republican share of votes among southerners, housewives, and conservatives has been impressive. White Catholics have gravitated to the Republican Party in recent years, primarily because of the party's more conservative stance on social and cultural issues like abortion and homosexuality.[18] By 2002, Republicans achieved control of the White House and both houses of Congress.

Meanwhile, the Democratic Party has undergone demographic change as well. Democrats have done better in recent years among professionals with higher incomes and education—especially those with advanced degrees. African Americans continue to be a loyal constituency, as have Hispanic American Catholics. Since the 1980s, a gender gap has developed between the parties, with men moving decidedly in the direction of the Republicans and women fairly consistently preferring Democrats.[19] This gap hides important subgroup differences, however. For example, although single women are much more likely to vote Democratic, housewives prefer the Republicans. Democrats have increased their share of younger voters and voters in northeastern and far western states. They do better among the rising number of Americans who seldom or never attend religious services. As a group, Democrats appear to be more consistently liberal on a number of issues ranging from abortion to gun control.

Overall, demographic and political changes have resulted in a regional reassortment of partisan divisions, with southern and lower midwestern states growing more securely Republican, coastal states more Democratic, and the number of closely divided states shrinking. Despite fluctuations in overall levels of party support as a result of short-term events, the major parties today maintain rough parity among voters.

By 2016, both major parties were again showing signs of strain. Donald Trump and Jeb Bush exposed the tension within the Republican coalition between social conservatives seeking to restrict immigration and mainstream forces in the party attempting to welcome growing numbers of Hispanics to their ranks. Bernie Sanders threatened to undo the coalition between organized labor and the professional classes that helped fuel electoral successes for Democrats. As these events demonstrate, party systems are fluid and dynamic and continue in flux.

Senator Bernie Sanders captured some of the populist fervor of the 2016 presidential campaign causing at least a temporary rift in the Democratic coalition.

© Trevor Collens/Shutterstock

Party Realignment

As we have seen, parties undergo periodic changes in strength, composition, and direction. Such changes, known as **realignments**, scramble party composition and political fortunes. Supporters of each party re-assort themselves, forming new coalitions and sometimes reversing the relative positions of strength previously held by each party in the electorate. For example, African Americans were steadfast supporters of Lincoln's Republican Party following the Civil War. However, following the Great Depression, most blacks switched allegiance to the Democrats.

Political scientists have offered various accounts about how and why these changes occur. Some scholars claim realignments reflect generational changes occurring every twenty-eight to thirty-six years,[20] although other scholars look to a longer time frame.[21] Major events like the Civil War and the Great Depression have also been linked to realignments. Such events can increase voter interest and party competition, upsetting the electoral balance that defined the era before the event. Realignments can be signaled by one or more **critical elections**, in which the opposition party sweeps dramatically into national power by winning the presidency and both houses of Congress, and then begins building on its new voter coalition. For example, scholars cite the elections of 1932 and 1936 as critical in transforming the political landscape in favor of the Democrats after a long period of Republican control.

More recently, scholars have voiced skepticism about the notion of critical election realignments and predictable cycles of party control. Instead, they prefer to rely on careful historical analysis of major transforming events such as the Great Depression and on the impact of strong leadership in individual election match-ups. These factors contribute to what has been called **equilibration**, periodic rotation in party control of the White House and Congress.[22] Even a party that wins control of both the White House and Congress as impressively as the Democrats did in 1932 has a tendency to run out of steam, finding its support eroding in subsequent elections. Another recent theory focuses on **issue evolution**.[23] According to this viewpoint, the electorate reacts to salient issues brought to its attention by political elites who compete for electoral dominance. Partisan change occurs incrementally over long periods of time as the electorate reacts to these issue positions and responds by altering political allegiance. Recent examples include civil rights, abortion, and gay marriage. Changes initiated by interest groups and political leaders in these areas have sparked reactions that have scrambled party loyalties among the electorate.

Although the causes may be debated, the fact remains that major changes have taken place in party composition over the past few years. The once solid Democratic South is now a Republican stronghold; the once viable and strongly Democratic blue-collar vote is now splintered, more volatile, and less unified because of a drop in union membership. Donald Trump made inroads into this group in 2016 by promising to renegotiate international trade deals, which he blamed for a drop in employment opportunities for these workers. Moderate Republicans, particularly in the northeastern states, are a disappearing

realignments Periodic changes in party strength, composition, and direction.

critical elections Elections signaling realignments, often sweeping the opposition party into control of the presidency and Congress.

equilibration The tendency toward periodic alterations in party control of the White House and Congress.

issue evolution The theory that partisan change occurs incrementally as the electorate reacts to salient issues advanced by party elites.

breed. The Democratic Party is much more consistently liberal in orientation and membership; the Republicans, more conservative. And the nation has become more ideologically and politically divided. Still, some elements of the old alignment remain. Democrats continue to attract a disproportionate number of minorities and low-income voters; Republicans attract upper-income whites and business owners. Yet neither party in recent years has been able to dominate the national government for a sustained period of time. In fact, much of the past fifty-year period has been characterized by **divided government**, with one party controlling the White House while the other controls one or both houses of Congress. Partisan identification has been closely divided throughout much of this period, and national elections have been extremely competitive.

Some scholars—although in the minority, to be sure—believe we have undergone a **dealignment**, in which both parties began to lose their relevance for the American voter.[24] More voters seem to reject both major parties, increasingly identifying as independents or nonpartisans. This seems to be especially true among younger voters. Donald Trump and Bernie Sanders did particularly well among voters who express disdain for both dominant political parties in 2016. But political parties are not dead. Party identification is still a powerful predictor of how voters will cast their ballots and whether they will vote at all.[25] Most who call themselves independents reveal reliable partisan preferences for one or the other major party.

divided government Control of the White House by one party while the opposition party controls one or both houses of Congress.

dealignment A falloff in electoral support for both major political parties.

partisan polarization The term used to describe the growing ideological divide separating our two major political parties.

Parties Today: Poles Apart

Parties today serve to define the issues that drive political discourse in America, and they do so in ideologically distinctive ways. Although political scientists may have worried in the mid-twentieth century that the parties did not offer voters distinct choices, they need not have such fears today. From the standpoint of ideology and behavior of elected lawmakers, the gulf between the parties is wide. We call this growing divide between an increasingly liberal Democratic Party and an increasingly conservative Republican Party **partisan polarization**. To be sure, periodic polarization of America's normally centrist parties is not a new phenomenon. Particularly intense were conflicts between Federalists and Antifederalists over the U.S. Bank in the early days of the Republic; Democrats and Whigs over tariffs and banking policy prior to the Civil War; and Democrats and Republicans in the late nineteenth century over industrial policy. Yet these periods gave way to longer stretches in which internal disagreements within the parties necessitated at least a measure of bipartisan cooperation to get anything done. Ideology eventually gave way to pragmatism. This was the case over a long period from the 1940s to the 1970s.[26]

How did we get to this point? Quite a few factors have been implicated, although experts disagree about the relative impact of each.[27] Clearly, demographic factors playing out over the past half-century play a part. The South attracted more conservative and elderly residents who identify as Republicans; younger, liberal, more affluent populations moved to urban regions, particularly on the coasts, identifying with the Democrats. These movements helped change the political landscape of the regions and the ideological orientation of the leaders they sent to Washington.

It is also true that party leaders and interest group elites sometimes advance issues that drive the parties further apart. For example, Democrats' support for same-sex marriage sparked a backlash from many conservatives in the Republican Party and reinforced partisan divisions over cultural issues. But partisan divisions are not merely a reflection of differences among party leaders. Recent polls have shown that voters in each party have drifted further apart on a number of issues, with rank-and-file Democrats holding more consistently liberal positions on issues and Republican voters hewing more closely to conservative views.[28] The graph in "Democrats and Republicans More Ideologically Divided Than in the Past" illustrates how far apart Democrats and Republicans have moved from each other since the 1990s. Divisions are exacerbated by the fact that for many voters party affiliation has become a badge of personal identity with all of the emotional heat that can bring.[29]

We will discuss the implications of partisan polarization for our political system and what, if anything, should be done about it in the concluding section of this chapter.

Democrats and Republicans More Ideologically Divided Than in the Past

Distribution of Democrats and Republicans on a 10-item scale of political values

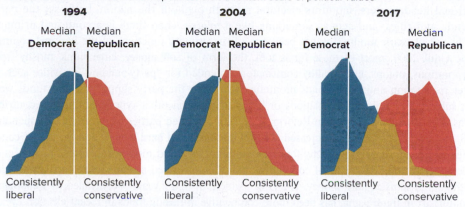

1994

Median **Democrat**   Median **Republican**

2004

Median **Democrat**   Median **Republican**

2017

Median **Democrat**   Median **Republican**

Consistently liberal   Consistently conservative

Consistently liberal   Consistently conservative

Consistently liberal   Consistently conservative

Notes: Ideological consistency based on a scale of 10 political values questions. The blue area represents Democrats and Democratic-leaning independents; the red area represents Republicans and Republican-leaning independents.

As Democrats and Republicans have become more ideologically divided, the overlap between the two groups has grown considerably smaller.

Source: Pew Research Center, *The Partisan Divide on Political Values Grows Ever Wider,* October 5, 2017.

BUILT TO WIN: PARTY STRUCTURE

During the first half of the twentieth century, parties ran campaigns for candidates they selected and groomed for offices at every level of government. They relied on local party workers who could look forward to rewards for getting out the vote. Today, candidates have taken a more active role in running their own campaigns. Nevertheless, political parties remain a major electoral force, and they are organized in ways that maximize their opportunities for winning elections.

Because we elect candidates to multiple levels of government, from local school board to president of the United States, parties must also organize on multiple levels. Each level is responsible for nominating candidates, amassing resources such as money and volunteer support, and getting out the vote to ensure their candidate wins election. Although each layer is primarily concerned with electing candidates for those offices for which it is responsible, there is an ongoing exchange of communication and resources among all levels of operation and their allies, including interests groups and donors.[30] In the discussion that follows, we will highlight the various functions and operations of each level of party organization.

National Committees

Atop the organizational chart of each political party sits the national committees. Their primary responsibility is to nominate and elect their party's candidates for president and vice president of the United States.

The national committees are populated by a mix of national leaders and representatives from the various state party organizations that sit lower on the organizational chart. The Republican National Committee (RNC) consists of more than 150 members, including one male and one female representative chosen from each state and U.S. territory, together with the chairs of party organizations in each state. The Democratic National Committee (DNC) is larger, consisting of the chairs and vice chairs of each state Democratic Party Committee and over two hundred members elected by Democrats in all fifty states and the territories. The national committees of each party make policy recommendations

National Committees

Congressional and Senatorial Campaign Committees

State Committees

Local Government Committees

Each level of the party is organized so as to maximize the electoral chances of candidates seeking office at that level.

about the issues each will pursue, and they organize and run the presidential nominating conventions, which occur every four years.

The national committee membership of each party formally elects a national party chair, although, in practice, the membership usually approves the nominee selected by the party's candidate for president. The national party chair presides over everyday operations of the national headquarters, monitors electoral races throughout the nation, helps set the party agenda and rules, and acts as something like a referee when there is a contested primary.

In recent years, fundraising has been one of the primary functions of the national committees. Until 2002, most of these funds took the form of **soft money**, large sums, mostly from corporations, unions, and wealthy contributors, intended for "party-building" activities such as voter registration and running ads promoting the issues the party supports. These funds were not subject to the federal regulations or limits that govern other types of campaign contributions. The Bipartisan Campaign Reform Act of 2002 banned parties from raising and spending soft money. Instead, the act increased contribution limits on **hard money**, donations that candidates and parties can use directly for electoral activities. Hard money donations are subject to federal regulation. The national committees have demonstrated an impressive capacity for collecting large sums of hard money. The DNC, which for many years badly trailed its Republican counterpart in fundraising, has been more competitive in raising funds in recent election cycles, achieving parity with Republicans and sometimes outraising them. There are other sources of campaign contributions, however, which have become even more important in the wake of recent court rulings. We will return to this topic when we discuss campaigning later in this chapter.

The national committee provides a variety of additional services to candidates as well as to state and local party organizations to help them win elections. Candidates can tap national committees for the latest polling results and can secure advice from campaign

soft money Unlimited sums of money raised from corporations, unions, and wealthy individuals used to support party activities. Political parties are no longer able to raise this type of funds.

hard money Campaign money received by candidates or parties that can be used for any purpose and is subject to federal limits and regulations.

National party conventions galvanize the support of partisans and help catapult the party's nominee into the general election campaign.

consultants. The national committee also places candidates in contact with interest groups that will raise additional funds and provide volunteers and campaign workers.

A close working relationship with interest groups that help raise funds for the parties has transformed national parties into "networks of issue-oriented activists," as one political scientist puts it.[31] These groups have pressured the parties to adopt specific positions on divisive issues like abortion, civil rights, and gun control. Liberal interest groups have moved the DNC more to the left of the ideological spectrum, while social conservatives have helped move the Republican Party to the right. The result has been greater ideological differentiation between the parties.

Each party's national committee is responsible for running a **national convention**, the quadrennial gathering of party members who formally nominate their party's presidential candidate (see Chapter 12 for details). Each party has its own rules that govern how these delegates are selected and how many delegates each state is allotted.

Democrats elect delegates to the national convention during presidential primary elections in each state or through state nominating conventions, depending on state rules. In primary election states, delegates are selected proportionally on the basis of the popular vote received by each presidential candidate. For example, in a state where Hillary Clinton received 60 percent of the vote, she would be allotted 60 percent of the delegates from that state, each pledging to vote for her nomination. Democratic conventions also include a number of **superdelegates** (mostly elected officials) appointed by the national committee and who are unpledged, allowing them to vote for the candidate of their choice. Controversy over the role of these superdelegates has caused the party to plan to scale back their independence and influence in the future. The 2016 Democratic convention hosted 4,765 delegates; 2,383 votes (or just over half) were required by a candidate for nomination.

Delegates to the Republican national convention are also selected in primaries and caucuses, though the total number (2,472 in 2016) was about half the number of delegates seated by Democrats. Some Republican states choose delegates on a winner-take-all basis rather than proportionately. For example, if Donald Trump received 51 percent of the popular vote, he would receive all of the delegates allotted to that state. The Republicans do not have unpledged superdelegates.

Prior to officially nominating the presidential candidate, delegates in each party draft and approve the party **platform**, or statement of issue positions that will nominally guide the party's course for the next four years. These positions often reflect more closely the views of party loyalists and interest groups supporting the candidates than those of the general public (see "How Closely Do Platforms Mirror the Views of Party Supporters and the Electorate?").

Republicans in 2016 strayed from the usual party convention playbook. Donald Trump was an insurgent who played little role in Republican party politics in the years preceding his nomination. He ran a primary campaign often at odds with establishment party regulars who control the reins of the party apparatus. Evidence of the rift between Trump and establishment Republicans was his threat to remove House Speaker Paul Ryan (R-WI) as chairman of the convention because Ryan expressed doubts about the Trump candidacy. Trump also insisted on molding parts of the party platform to suit his own preferences, often at odds with Republican orthodoxy—most notably on planks dealing with immigration and trade.

Insurgent Bernie Sanders left his mark on a similarly fractured Democratic Party. After garnering 45 percent

national convention An event held every four years by each political party to formally anoint its presidential candidate and to signal the initiation of the general election campaign.

superdelegates The term used to refer to Democratic Party leaders and elected officials attending the party convention. The independent influence they played in the nominating process in the past as been recently curbed by changes in party rules.

platform The statement of political principles and campaign promises generated by each party at its national convention.

How Closely Do Platforms Mirror the Views of Party Supporters and the Electorate?

2016 Republican Party Platform Planks	Republicans	All voters
Oppose same-sex marriage*	54%	37%
Favor building wall at Mexican border*	67%	38%
Oppose ban on assault weapons†	48%	40%

2016 Democratic Party Platform Planks	Democrats	All voters
Require employers to provide paid family leave‡	88%	80%
Support nationwide $15 minimum wage**	73%	48%
Favor ban on assault weapons†	70%	57%

Party platforms are more reflective of the views of party activists than of the general electorate.

*Pew Research Center, *Campaign Exposes Fissures Over Issues*, March 17–27, 2016, http://www.people-press.org/2016/03/31/campaign-exposes-fissures-over-issues-values-and-how-life-has-changed-in-the-u-s/.

†Pew Research Center, *Continued Bipartisan Support for Background Checks*, August 13, 2015, at http://www.people-press.org/2015/08/13/continued-bipartisan-support-for-expanded-background-checks-on-gun-sales/.

‡New York Times Poll, *Americans' Views on Income Inequality and Workers' Rights*, June 3, 2015, http://www.nytimes.com/interactive/2015/06/03/business/income-inequality-workers-rights-international-trade-poll.html.

**YouGov, *Poll Results: Minimum Wage*, April 2016, https://today.yougov.com/topics/politics/articles-reports/2016/04/13/poll-results-minimum-wage.

of pledged delegates during the primary season, Sanders sought to use his delegate strength to mold the party platform. The Clinton campaign yielded to changes in the allocation of superdelegates in future elections and support for a $15 national minimum wage as well as a plan to provide free tuition for most college students. Still, Sanders's supporters jeered during some speeches at the convention and walked out in protest. Sanders ultimately asked the convention to make Hillary Clinton's nomination unanimous.

Congressional and Senatorial Campaign Committees

safe seats Legislative districts that regularly remain in the hands of the same candidate or party.

leadership PACs Political action committees set up by political leaders as a means to finance the campaigns of political allies who they believe will reciprocate with support for their own political ambitions.

A second tier of party organization is devoted primarily to helping party members win election or reelection to the U.S. House and Senate. These committees—the National Republican Congressional Committee (NRCC), the National Republican Senatorial Committee (NRSC), and their Democratic counterparts, the Democratic Congressional Campaign Committee (DCCC) and the Democratic Senatorial Campaign Committee (DSCC)—work with other tiers in the party organization as well as with interest groups and individual candidates to raise and distribute funds, share polling data, and offer expertise about running campaigns for Congress.

Not every candidate can count on help from these committees, however. Because resources are limited, Democratic and Republican committee staffs make strategic choices about which candidates are most likely to benefit from assistance.

The national party organizations (top tier of the party organization) can give up to $5,000 to individual House candidates and $47,400 to Senate candidates (as of FEC rules for the 2017-18 election cycle) to spend directly on their campaigns. But candidates running for Congress can tap other sources of money. Members from **safe seats**, in which the incumbent faces only limited or token opposition, often make some of their own campaign contributions available to more needy candidates through what are called **leadership PACs**. Affiliated with party leaders in each chamber, these donations may be instrumental in providing the margin of victory for recipients, and they generate a substantial amount of goodwill for the legislative donor.

get involved!

Become a delegate to your party's state or national political convention. If you are eighteen and registered to vote, you probably qualify. Hundreds of young people under the age of twenty-four have attended the Democratic and Republican national conventions in recent times. Contact your precinct leader or your party's local office. In some states, you can become a delegate by working directly for a candidate if he or she wins the primary election. In others, delegates have to file their own nominating petitions and are elected directly by the voters. In most states, you can also work closely with your local party to be considered as a delegate from your district. As a delegate, you'll attend the convention in the city selected for the event and have a voice in forging your party's platform as well as in selecting official party candidates for the general election.

©Jack Hollingsworth/Getty Images

State Committees

State party committees stand as the third tier of the party structure. Every state has party organizations designed to recruit candidates, fund campaigns, and get out the vote for candidates running for statewide office. Each state organization has its own peculiarities, but most state parties are headed by state central committees composed of members drawn from smaller units of government like municipalities and legislative districts, and led by a state party chair. State party officers, together with their staffs, concentrate on statewide elective offices such as governor and key state executive branch positions. In some states, party conventions similar to those held at the national level and composed of delegates selected in local primary elections or by party officials meet to select nominees for statewide office. Some states use a combination of conventions and primaries to select their nominees. Day-to-day activities of state committees remain in the hands of the chairperson.

There is quite a bit of integration of party activities between national and state organizations. For example, national and state parties may share campaign costs for joint appearances and coordinate their advertising efforts. State parties often team up with interest groups to organize voter registration drives around the state. For example, liberal groups such as the Service Employees International Union (SEIU) and conservative groups like Club for Growth were actively involved in voter mobilization and issue-ad sponsorship at the state level during recent election cycles.

State parties have become adept in recent years at raising money, communicating with voters, and using polling data to improve electoral prospects for their candidates.[32] State parties have developed clearly targeted mailing lists for use in both fundraising and communicating with constituents about pressing issues. The bulk of their expenditures include contributions to candidates; funding for consultants, polling, and advertising; and funds for administrative expenses such as salaries, rent, equipment, and travel. State committees also spend money on media such as direct mail for the entire ticket.

Local Party Organizations

Finally, local party committees constitute the bottom tier of the party pyramid. These committees help field and run candidates for offices in counties, cities, and towns across the country. Local parties are usually organized around geographic units called **precincts**. Precincts are the geographic areas served by a polling place and can vary markedly in size, depending on population dispersion. Precinct leaders can be elected or appointed. Because precinct leaders are our neighbors, they can exert a powerful influence on our voting behavior. They knock on our doors to alert us about local issues and inform us about voting procedures, poll locations, approaching registration deadlines, and candidates running for office. They remind us of our civic duty and even drive us to the polls on Election Day. Although much of the energy at the local party level comes from volunteers, some precinct leaders hold government positions. As a result, they work hard to bring their party's supporters to the polls since their own jobs may be tied to the fate of their party's at the ballot box.

precinct The geographic area served by a polling place and organized by local party units.

Nevertheless, local party units are not the powerhouses they were in the days of big city machine politics. Many factors contributed to this decline, including party reform, the replacement of patronage employees by a professionalized government workforce, the growth of government welfare services to replace favors once performed by local party bosses, the development of candidate-centered campaigns (which we will discuss shortly), and the rise of the mass media as an independent source for voter information. Where local party organization is weak, party offices sometimes remain vacant, requiring party functions to be handled by higher-level county and state party officials.[33]

Working Together

Electoral success depends on all levels of the party organization working together and deploying the latest tools for locating voters and communicating their message. Local government officials such as mayors can sometimes boost their party's electoral chances by working with higher-level officeholders of the same party to secure special projects and grants to aid their communities. Higher-level officeholders are often anxious to help since mayors and local party workers play an important part in getting out the vote on Election Day.

Parties are actively experimenting with new technologies and new methods that combine information gleaned from large databases operated by the national party organization with canvassing provided by local party activists in order to get out the vote. Political parties are not shy about investigating consumer habits of voters and using this information to identify potential supporters. Armed with this information, precinct workers, along with local candidate supporters and interest group volunteers, can design individualized messages to bring to voters' doorsteps. Text messaging, social networking, and peer-to-peer appeals are proving especially useful in mobilizing younger voters. These techniques are reinvigorating local party activity, and their use will continue to be studied to see if they can sustain increased voter turnout. We will describe additional efforts to attract young voters later in this chapter.

THIRD PARTIES AND INDEPENDENT CANDIDACIES

Our nation has witnessed important third-party challenges, even if most were short lived. Usually, third parties and significant independent candidacies arise in periods of great change or crisis. They attract the attention of many who had not previously voted and those who perceive a lack of genuine difference between the major parties. Often they reflect a desire for change in the political direction of the nation.

Some **third parties** have been around for a long time. They frequently run candidates but their share of the vote is usually small. These include the Libertarians, the Socialist Workers, and the Green Party. Some third parties arise for a year or two and then disappear. For example, Henry Wallace ran for president under the banner of the Progressive Party in 1948, promoting universal health care and an end to the Cold War. However, the party's fate was short lived and Wallace soon came under attack by lawmakers for his alleged ties to communism. The Tea Party movement, whose goal is to reduce the role of government in American life, ran a small number of candidates for Congress in 2010, but made much greater inroads by throwing its weight behind Republican candidates, helping the GOP recapture the House, and moving Republicans in a more conservative direction.

There are several varieties of third parties. Some third parties are **splinter parties**,[34] parties that break away from one of the major parties. The Republicans began as a splinter party, breaking away from the Whigs over the issue of slavery in 1852 and eventually supplanting them as the major competitor to the Democrats. Other notable splinter parties included the Populists, who emerged as an offshoot of Democratic politics in 1892; the Bull Moose Party, which nominated former president Theodore Roosevelt in 1912 after he broke with Republicans; the States' Rights and Progressive Parties, which split in different ideological directions from the Democrats in 1948; and the American Independent Party, which broke off from the Democrats over civil rights policy in 1968 by nominating Alabama governor George Wallace for president.

Some third parties are **ideological parties** that reflect a commitment to an ideological position different from that of most voters. Socialists committed to government ownership

third party A minor party that runs a slate of its own candidates in opposition to major-party organizations in an election.

splinter parties Political parties that are formed as offshoots of major political parties, usually by dissenters.

ideological parties Minor parties organized around distinct ideological principles.

single issue or candidate Minor parties arising in electoral response to important issues not addressed by major-party candidates or around a strong personality.

©AP Photo

Theodore Roosevelt led the most successful third-party movement in American history, receiving 27 percent of the popular vote and 88 electoral votes while running under the mantle of the Bull Moose Party in 1912.

of factories and businesses gathered limited support for their cause during the early twentieth century. Libertarians, who call for smaller government and the privatization of many government services, have gathered sporadic support more recently, especially among younger voters.

Finally, some independent campaigns outside of the major parties arise around a **single issue or candidate**. Ross Perot's impressive showing in 1992 revealed the potential strength of personal appeal coupled with a compelling issue: fiscal responsibility in the face of mushrooming budget deficits. The Green Party, which advocates environmental reform, has also fielded successful candidates in a number of state and local elections across the country.

Faced with the substantial obstacles involved in getting on the ballot and the difficulties involved in organizing supporters and amassing sufficient funds to mount a credible campaign—all the while lacking incumbent officeholders to promote its programs—it is no wonder that most third-party and independent candidacies fail to persist. Third parties generally face one of three possible fates: they disappear after a short burst of enthusiasm as their issue or candidate fades from memory; they persist as minor players; or the issues (sometimes the candidates themselves) are absorbed by a major party that takes up their cause.

Many candidates emerge for one or two election cycles and then disappear because of a lack of resources. Ralph Nader's independent candidacy, for example, fizzled in 2004 after gaining almost 3 percent of the popular vote in 2000.

Some independent and third parties, such as Libertarians and the Greens, continue on as perennial minor players. In some years, they may even attract substantial support, as in 2016 when many voters turned to them as an alternative to major -party nominees they did not trust. Yet, neither Libertarian Gary Johnson nor Green Party nominee Jill Stein met the polling threshold necessary for inclusion in the presidential debates. Johnson ended up with just over 3 percent of the popular vote; Stein, with just over 1 percent. Neither candidate secured any electoral votes.

Still other third parties are absorbed by a larger party that heeds their message or adopts their ideology or policy prescriptions. For example, Republicans have moved to absorb the ideological orientation of Tea Partiers after their success in congressional elections in 2010.

Although third-party and independent candidacies generally fail to persist in American politics, they are by no means inconsequential. They can have several effects on the future direction of the parties and politics in general. By advancing and getting support for positions that differ from those of the established parties, third parties can signal voter discontent with politics as usual. They alert leaders of the two major parties that voters want change and, by threatening to take votes away from the major parties, third parties can motivate them to change their policies. Ross Perot's third-party entry in 1992 raised the issue of budget deficits and led the Democrats and Republicans to take action to reduce the nation's debt. Occasionally, third parties act as "spoilers" by taking enough votes away from one candidate to swing the election to another. Some observers speculate that Jill Stein's Green Party and Gary Johnson's Libertarian Party candidacies may have siphoned enough votes away from Hillary Clinton in 2016 to cost her victory in a few key states.[35]

Significant Third Parties and Independent Candidacies in Presidential Elections

Third party	Year	% Popular vote	Electoral votes	Fate in next elections
Anti-Masons	1832	7.8	7	Endorsed Whig candidate
Free Soil	1848	10.1	0	Received 5% of vote; provided base of Republican supporters
Whig-American	1856	21.5	8	Party dissolved
Southern Democrat	1860	18.1	72	Party dissolved
Constitutional Union	1860	12.6	39	Party dissolved
Populist	1892	8.5	22	Endorsed Democratic candidate
Progressive (T. Roosevelt)	1912	27.5	88	Returned to Republican Party
Socialist	1912	6.0	0	Received 3.2% of vote
Progressive (LaFollette)	1924	16.6	13	Returned to Republican Party
States' Rights Democrat	1948	2.4	39	Party dissolved
Progressive (H. Wallace)	1948	2.4	0	Received 1.4% of vote
American Independent (G. Wallace)	1968	13.5	46	Received 1.4% of vote
John B. Anderson	1980	7.1	0	Did not run in 1984
H. Ross Perot	1992	18.9	0	Formed the Reform Party and ran again in 1996
Reform Party (H. Ross Perot)	1996	8.4	0	Perot engaged in struggle for control of Reform Party
Reform/ Independent (Pat Buchanan)	2000	.42	0	Little impact in 2004
Green Party (Ralph Nader)	2000	2.74	0	Refused to slate Nader in 2004

Source: Adapted from Bibby, J. F. *Political Parties in the United States*, U.S. Department of State Information Programs, http://usinfo.state.gov/products/pubs/archive/elect00/table.htm.

CANDIDATES AND ELECTORAL POLITICS

In the heyday of political parties, campaigns were about electing a team of candidates, for whom voters felt considerable emotional allegiance, to multiple offices. Parties groomed candidates and rewarded them for being "team players." Candidates often worked hard and long at the lower levels of the party pyramid to demonstrate their loyalty, waiting their turn to run for office themselves. Today's candidates need not have extensive experience within political parties; they need not have worked on previous campaigns at all. Their allegiance to party creed or philosophy may be minimal. Instead, they are entrepreneurial self-starters who carry a substantial portion of the burden of campaigning themselves. Some candidates are promoted by party elites; others by interest groups, each believing their candidate to be both electable and sympathetic to the issues they espouse. We will discuss campaigns for specific offices in the chapters dealing with Congress and the presidency. Here, we will discuss the general features of today's campaigns for virtually all political offices.

Show Me the Money

One of the most important burdens for a candidate is raising money. The cost of campaigns keeps escalating at all levels of government. You may not be surprised that running for the U.S. Senate involves millions of dollars. But it is sobering to consider that running for a state legislative seat in a moderate-size state such as Indiana may cost more than $200,000, for a part-time job that pays little more than $24,000 a year. In many cases, parties look for candidates with enough personal resources to front most of the campaign expenses themselves or extensive ties to donors and organized groups that can offer financial backing. When raising and spending funds, candidates must play by the state and federal rules regarding the offices they seek.

Candidates devote a large part of their campaign day to raising money, often thousands of dollars a day. Phone calls, personal appearances, chicken dinners, and fish frys are all part of the fundraising effort, and they require both stamina and boldness. Candidates usually bear the entire cost of primary campaigns but can usually count on substantial financial help from their party once the primary is over. The rules governing the raising and spending of campaign cash are complicated and, in light of recent court rulings, increasingly porous.

Limits and Transparency State campaign laws regulate the activities of candidates for state and local offices. Many states still allow soft-money contributions that candidates can use in a number of ways—including advertising and get-out-the-vote drives—to advance their campaigns. Some states provide partial public funding for elections; others impose regulations on the ways campaigns can obtain financing.

Candidates for federal office, as we learned in Chapter 8, must conform to campaign finance rules passed in the wake of the Watergate scandal to stem the influence of big donors and to provide transparency so that voters could know exactly which donors and interest groups were supporting each candidate. However, recent court decisions dramatically altered the campaign finance landscape. Donors today can contribute almost unlimited sums through a variety of channels, and in some cases disclosure can be avoided.

In *SpeechNow.org v. Federal Election Commission* (2010) and *Citizens United v. Federal Election Commission* (2010), federal courts ruled that individuals, corporations, trade associations, unions, and nonprofit organizations may spend unlimited amounts of money as *independent* advocates for or against political candidates or causes.[36] These rulings opened the way for so-called super PACs. In 2016, super PACs funneled over $1.1 billion into independent campaign activities for presidential and congressional candidates,[37] bypassing candidate committees, the political parties, and traditional PACs. Although super PACs are prohibited from coordinating their expenditures with parties or candidates, close ties between super PAC fundraisers and political candidates raise questions about the genuine independence of these groups. Super PACs can also extend the life of a candidate with little electoral support by continuing to fund her or his candidacy past the point when it is clear the individual stands little chance of victory. The end result is to prolong primary battles and to make running for office that much more expensive. Super PACs are required to report their donors.

527 groups provide individuals with another vehicle for making campaign contributions. These are tax-exempt organizations that can raise and spend unlimited amounts, but they cannot directly support or oppose an individual candidate. Instead, they are permitted to advocate for specific issues and to fund the mobilization of voters during elections. Like super PACs, they must disclose their donors. But the line between issue advocacy and candidate support is a fine one, especially when a candidate is well known for a particular stand on the issue the 527 group supports. Examples of 527s are the liberal-oriented Moveon.org and the conservative Americans United to Preserve Marriage. Some 527s are even connected to national party organizations like the Democratic Governors Association.

Yet another group that can raise and spend unlimited amounts is known by the number of the tax code that applies to it. These **501(c) groups** are considered advocacy groups whose primary purpose is to promote "social welfare." They are allowed to engage in campaigns so long as they spend less than 50 percent of their money on politics. Their political ambitions are often difficult to disentangle from the social welfare they advocate, however, especially because they do not have to disclose the identity of their donors. The lack of transparency has prompted some observers to call this type of funding dark money. Examples include Americans for Prosperity, affiliated with the conservative Koch brothers and the liberal-leaning Planned Parenthood Action Fund.

Impact of Funding Rule Changes Despite an escalation in the number of large donors with now almost unlimited opportunities to influence politics, some of the largest contributors have been disappointed with the results of their investments. Some billionaire donors in the last few presidential elections poured money into organizations that backed losing candidates such as Jeb Bush, Newt Gingrich, and Rick Santorum.

At the other end of the spectrum are candidates who increasingly rely on contributions from small donors in the amounts of $200 or less. Barack Obama raised millions of dollars from small donors, much of it over the Internet, in 2008 and again in 2012. On the Republican side, Rand Paul raised substantial sums from small donors during his 2016 primary campaign, using both the Internet and direct mail. Bernie Sanders outdid them all in 2016, raising over $228 million from small donors who averaged $27 per contribution.[38] Donald Trump, too, late in the general election campaign demonstrated the ability to collect tens of millions of dollars from small donations. Available evidence suggests that while small donors resemble large donors in some demographics, such as race and income (they are more likely to be white and wealthy), a growing number of individuals of more moderate means are contributing to elections as well. Moreover, Internet contributors represent more diverse interests than large cash contributors, who are typically drawn from industry, the professions, and trade organizations.[39]

Finally, there are a few self-funded candidates. Donald Trump won favor with some voters by claiming that by self-funding his campaign he was free from special interest ties. In fact, however, he loaned his campaign much of the money, which he expected would be recouped from "unsolicited donations." During the primary campaign, Trump was able to keep costs down by using free media effectively. During the general election, however, Trump turned to the party's fundraising apparatus and to a surprising number of small donors to fuel his campaign.

527 groups Tax-exempt organizations set up by interest groups to engage in political activities.

501(c) groups Tax-exempt organizations considered advocacy groups whose primary purpose is to promote "social welfare."

TAMPING DOWN THE COST OF ELECTIONS

Polls show that Americans agree that money has too much influence on elections and that candidates who win office promote policies that help their donors. One *New York Times* poll showed that 84 percent of Americans believe that money has too much influence on politics. That number includes 90 percent who identify as Democrats and 80 percent who identify as Republicans. Large bipartisan majorities also believe campaign financing should be reformed or overhauled, and a majority believes that campaign contributions are not a form of free speech, despite the Supreme Court's ruling in *Citizens United v. Federal Election Commission*.[†]

So what's the future of campaign finance reform? With Washington awash in money from special interests, many Americans are looking to the states to take the lead in campaign finance reform. Currently, more than a dozen states provide some kind of public financing for campaigns for major state-level offices.[*]

Some states, such as Florida and Hawaii, provide matching funds to candidates who agree to limit expenditures to a certain amount and abide by other contribution limits. Hawaii governor David Ige used matching funds in his 2014 gubernatorial win against a challenger who decided to finance his own campaign in a sign that this type of program can be successful.

Some states, such as Arizona, Connecticut, and Maine, operate what are known as clean elections programs. These programs provide candidates with a sum of money equal to the expenditure limit for that race once the candidate raises a certain number of small (no more than $5) contributions. In return, the candidate promises to abide by limits on how much she or he spends.

State-level initiatives like these might be on the rise if the chorus for campaign finance reform continues to grow.

[†]"Americans' Views on Money in Politics," *The New York Times,* June 2, 2015, https://www.nytimes.com/interactive/2015/06/02/us/politics/money-in-politics-poll.html.

[*]A variety of state initiatives dealing with campaign finance reform can be found at National Council of State Legislatures, "Overview of State Laws on Public Financing," http://www.ncsl.org/research/elections-and-campaigns/public-financing-of-campaigns-overview.aspx.

The weakening of spending limits and the emergence of super PACs, 527s, and 501(c) organizations has opened the floodgates to virtually unlimited spending by megadonors. The campaign finance reforms put in place after the Watergate scandal in the 1970s have now been all but abandoned.

Where Does All the Money Go?

Hillary Clinton, her party, and the super PACs backing her candidacy raised over $1.4 billion to finance her 2016 presidential run. Donald Trump, together with his party and super PACs, raised just over $950 million. Where does all this money go?

APPROVED BY HILLARY CLINTON. PAID FOR BY HILLARY FOR AMERICA.

WCredit

Donald J. Trump Verified account @realDonaldTrump
FollowFollow @realDonaldTrump
More

Crooked Hillary Clinton deleted 33,000 e-mails AFTER they were subpoenaed by the United States Congress. Guilty – cannot run. Rigged system!
5:47 AM - 2 Nov 2016

Source: Hillary For America

Source: Twitter

Hillary Clinton outspent Donald Trump on paid advertising in 2016, while Trump was able to garner free media attention from his controversial tweets.

National and statewide elections require large expenditures on mass media advertising. The amount varies with the size of the media market in which the candidate lives. A candidate campaigning for a U.S. House seat in San Francisco will spend more on television, for example, than one in Muncie, Indiana. In some campaigns, the largest advertising costs may be direct mail that targets potential supporters with the candidate's message. Radio is also an important advertising medium, especially in rural areas.

Media costs in presidential elections are especially large. Hillary Clinton spent over $250 million on TV ads alone in 2016. Donald Trump spent only about $90 million, in part because of the free publicity he received due to his notoriety as a former TV star and his penchant for controversy.[40] TV expenses have actually declined in recent years, while digital media costs have grown. In 2016, both presidential campaigns combined to spend about $81 million on Facebook posts alone.[41]

Campaigning also requires a staff that includes a press secretary, a scheduler, and consultants. This last category may include issue experts and political strategists who analyze precinct returns to ensure that the candidate focuses his or her effort on areas that will produce the most votes. Candidates and their strategists rely on polls that they commission to learn how they are faring among potential voters. Candidates also need printed materials for volunteers to hand out as they canvass neighborhoods. As well, they need some way to identify likely supporters. Here, market research is increasingly important; even a small expenditure for mailing lists targeting products purchased by likely supporters can yield big rewards by giving campaign workers an idea of which households are likely to vote for their candidate. The candidate choices of beer drinkers are likely to differ from those of voters who prefer white wine.

Candidates must also rent campaign headquarters and install phone banks so that volunteers can follow up with voters as the election nears. Finally, there are administrative costs associated with simply filing the paperwork to run, including fees and the preparation of financial statements. Candidates can share some of these expenses with the state party, especially those involving office and equipment rental and the production of printed materials that encourage voter registration and turnout. However, virtually all of the burden for raising and spending money prior to the primaries—and most of it afterward—rests with the candidate, who acts much like an entrepreneur for a small business, one in which he or she is the product. Obviously, presidential campaigns are the most expensive, but major categories of expenditure are similar for those running for any office.

Candidates and the Parties

Once candidates have demonstrated that they have both the necessary financial resources and the backing of key constituent groups required to be viable, they must still fend off party rivals to establish themselves as the party's official nominee. In most cases, this involves running against challengers in **primary elections**.

There are several types of primary election. Some states employ **closed primary** elections in which voters can choose candidates only from the party for which they are registered. The idea behind the closed primary is that only party members should be able to determine who will lead them in the general election. Most states that utilize this type of primary also exclude voters registered as independent from voting. **Open primaries** allow voters of both parties, and usually independents, to select candidates in whichever party's primary they choose. **Blanket primaries** allow voters to choose freely from among all candidates for an office from any party on the ballot. However, this kind of balloting was struck down by the U.S. Supreme Court as an unconstitutional infringement on the association rights of parties.[42] Some states employ the **caucus**, a gathering that functions much like a primary where voters meet in local venues to debate and vote on nominating the candidates of their choice.

California voters recently approved a new primary measure, the **top-two primary**, that allows them to choose candidates of either party from a single ballot. The top two vote-getters proceed to the general election regardless of party affiliation. This produces some contests in which candidates from the same party face off against each other in the

primary election An election in which voters choose candidates to represent the political parties in the general election.

closed primary An election in which voters can choose from potential nominees only within their own party.

open primary An election in which voters can choose from among potential nominees from their own party or those from the other major political party.

blanket primary An election in which voters can choose from among potential nominees in both parties; currently outlawed by the U.S. Supreme Court.

caucus A voter gathering used to select party candidates to run in the general election.

top-two primary A primary election in which voters choose from a list of all candidates regardless of party, with the top two facing off in the general election.

Jessica Sena works closely with elected leaders like former Montana congressman Denny Rehberg in her leadership position with the Young Republican National Federation.

PORTRAIT
OF AN ACTIVIST

Meet Jessica Sena

I caught the "bug" at a young age, and always answered the question "What do you want to do when you grow up?" with one word: politics.

I grew up surrounded by God-fearing people who worked hard for everything they earned. My grandparents on both sides, as is true with most of my generation, were immigrants. Their success stories helped to shape many of my political views; namely, that *any* person can achieve the quality of life they desire if they're willing to work diligently and are afforded the freedom and opportunity to do so.

After college, certain changes in our nation's leadership compelled me to take action on important issues: specifically, government spending, government land ownership, government jobs, government regulations, and government subsidies and entitlements.

I sought out town-hall meetings. It took less than a month of networking before I was elected as state committeewoman for my hometown's central committee in rural Montana and asked to manage a state House race, which resulted in victory for the candidate I was employed by.

The same year I was hired as the communications aide to the Senate leadership for the 2011 legislative session and, by then, was also appointed as the national committeewoman for the Montana Young Republicans.

At the close of the session, I took a job on a gubernatorial campaign for the presumptive Republican nominee. About the same time I started on that campaign, I ran for an executive position with the Young Republican National Federation and won the title of Western Regional Vice Chair (RVC).

In the capacity of RVC, I facilitate communication among Young Republican groups in the West, which collectively build resources to get out the vote for Republican candidates. We, the Young Republicans, promote the Republican Party platform in hopes of securing greater prosperity, opportunity, freedom, and liberty for our generation and the next.

My goal is to maintain activist status as a professional working within various groups to educate voters, especially future voters, about Republican ideals. I firmly believe that conservative values are good for all people. At the end of the day, limited government affords *everyone* the ultimate opportunity to achieve that nostalgic "American Dream," the same dream that brought many of our ancestors to this, the greatest country on Earth, the shining city on the hill, as Reagan put it.

---

runoff elections A second election between the top two vote-getters in a race that did not produce a majority winner.

general election. In 2010, the Supreme Court upheld the constitutionality of a top-two primary system in Washington. As of 2018, at least four states had approved the use of some form of top two primary. Some states require **runoff elections** between the top vote-getters if no one candidate receives a majority of the votes the first time around. Finally, some states employ a combination of primaries and party conventions, much like the process employed by national parties in the presidential election process, which we will discuss in Chapter 12.

Officials within the party are expected to remain neutral during the primary campaign. Their job is simply to make sure that party rules are observed and that all candidates vying for their party's nomination have a level playing field. In reality, this is not always the case. In 2016, leaked emails from the Democratic National Committee showed that party insiders discussed derailing the campaign of Bernie Sanders in order to improve Hillary Clinton's chance of victory. The revelations led to the resignation of Debbie Wasserman Schultz, the DNC chair, and the removal of several other top party officials. Only after the party has settled on its nominee through the primary process is the party establishment expected to close ranks and throw its full support behind the victor.

Even with the party support, the volunteer help, the expert consultants, and the money that comes with a primary victory, nominees cannot count on party loyalty alone to win the general election. Most decisions about strategic use of resources, such as the targeting of media, personal appearances, deployment of ground volunteers, and crafting of policy proposals, rest with the inner circle of the candidate's staff. Although party and candidate may work in tandem in a well-coordinated campaign, candidates rely more heavily on their own organizations because they have more control over them. When party leaders and candidates do not see eye to eye on issues, they may go their separate ways. More than ever before, the candidates must sell their own policies and personalities to voters. Party identification alone is often not enough to carry most candidates to victory.[43]

Candidate Communications To get elected, a candidate needs to be known. This is far easier for **incumbents** who have developed name recognition in earlier campaigns and who garner ongoing publicity associated with the offices they hold. In local elections, candidates sometimes walk through neighborhoods to introduce themselves to voters and to ask for support. Something close to this occurs at the presidential level in the early caucus and primary states of Iowa and New Hampshire, where candidates sometimes show up years before the election to engage in highly personal **retail politics**. This is a time-intensive undertaking, however, and is feasible in only a limited number of campaigns, such as those in small districts or far from major media markets.

A more economical and efficient way of getting one's name and message across is by securing **earned media**, that is, free social media, television, radio, and newspaper coverage devoted to a candidate because of some action or position he or she has taken. To encourage press coverage, candidates must demonstrate newsworthiness, which they often accomplish by calling news conferences at locations that provide interesting visual backdrops. For example, a candidate speaking about clean water policies may summon the media to a water treatment plant. Social media provide a new and far less expensive way for getting the word out. Donald Trump used his Twitter account effectively to keep his name in the news. Political conventions and candidate debates are also a rich source of free media coverage. Studies of voter attention to campaign activities show that, at least in presidential campaigns, voter interest in some of these events is quite high.[44]

Of course, candidates must also employ **paid media**, which includes television, radio, and newspaper ads, along with Internet ads and printed brochures, as discussed earlier. Candidates use paid media to emphasize their good character and their positions on important issues. Of increasing use in recent election cycles have been both **contrast ads** and **negative advertising**. Contrast ads are used to draw distinctions between the candidates with regard to issue positions or elements of style and character. For the most part, they tend to be substantive, concentrating on real differences the sponsoring candidate or group hopes the voters will keep in mind as they weigh their choices. Negative ads are more personal, attacking the opponent with the intent of arousing

incumbent The current occupant of an office.

retail politics A campaign style emphasizing close personal contact between the candidate and voters.

earned media Media attention for which candidates do not pay; associated with major events like debates.

paid media Media access for which candidates or the party must pay a fee; advertisements.

contrast ad Advertising that draws attention to differences that clearly distinguish each candidate.

negative advertising Advertising that attacks one's opponents, usually on the basis of issue stance or character.

Attack ads often focus on unattractive personal characteristics of one's opponents. In 2016, presidential candidate John Kasich used Trump's depiction of a reporter with disabilities to question the candidate's character.

©Richard Ellis/Alamy Stock Photo

anger among voters. For example, whereas a contrast ad might compare one candidate's voting record on climate change with her opponent's, a negative ad would question the opponent's motives in taking money from an oil company executive.

A recent study found that political advertising has become distinctly more negative over the past few election cycles.[45] This increased negativity is due in part to the role played by outside groups, which sponsor most of these types of ads. By and large, researchers have found that both contrast and attack ads convey information that some voters find useful in making up their minds.[46] They disagree, however, about the long-term impact of attack ads on the political process. In their study of the 2012 presidential race, John Sides and Lynn Vavreck found that the impact of negative ads decayed very quickly, having very little long-term effect on the election outcome.[47] Some researchers have found that negative ads depress turnout, especially among independent and undecided voters.[48] Others conclude that any discouraging effect is minimal and that negative ads may actually stimulate the interest of voters who might not otherwise have participated in an election.[49] Over the long haul, however, negative ads may take their toll on political interest, reducing feelings of political efficacy. Negative politics tends to wear down some voters to the point where they simply want to avoid politics completely.[50]

Voter Mobilization The goal of candidate communication is, of course, to win support and secure election. But communication may not be enough. Voters may be convinced that the candidate has the right message. They may be convinced he or she will make an excellent officeholder. But they still may prefer to stay home on Election Day and let others do the voting. It is the job of the candidate and the party to get supporters to the polls.

Each election, the campaign staffs their headquarters with volunteers who make last-minute calls to potential voters checking to see if they have yet voted and urging those who did not to get to the polls. They will offer rides to those in need of assistance. Staff will also check with precinct leaders with knowledge of voting habits in their districts to monitor the flow of voters from areas where they believe support is strong. Low turnout from crucial districts will spur last-minute get-out-the-vote efforts with urgent calls from friends and neighbors. Personal contact has been shown to be the most effective way to mobilize voters. Facebook posts and tweets from friends who have voted and implore their friends to do the same are also proving effective.[51]

early voting A practice used in some states in which voters are allowed to cast votes days before Election Day. The practice was begun to enhance voter access and convenience.

Voter mobilization became more complicated with the advent of **early voting**. Early voting increases the convenience and accessibility of voting by allowing voters who may be unable to get to the polls on Election Day to cast their ballot up to a month in advance at satellite voting locations, including shopping malls, even on weekends. About one-third of all votes in early voting states are cast prior to Election Day. Of course, this means voter mobilization must be moved up earlier into the election cycle. In most jurisdictions, election officials provide daily reports on how many voters from each party have voted. Campaign officials don't know exactly how these individuals have voted, but the figures they receive give them enough information so that they know where to concentrate their efforts in getting out supporters in subsequent days. In states where people do not register by party, daily totals still provide sufficient information about neighborhoods and voter characteristics to allow estimates to be generated about the number of likely supporters who have already cast ballots. Steve Schale, a Democratic strategist in Florida, described the winnowing process to one reporter: "On Election Day campaigns will know exactly who is left out there."[52]

Information about early voting is fed back to campaign headquarters, where staff will factor the progress of early turnout into their messaging. A candidate who is behind may need to step up the attack. A candidate who perceives he or she is ahead may continue a soft sell. Ads can also be targeted to low-turnout areas while high-turnout regions see reduced media buys. A fair amount is already known about early voters. They tend to be more partisan and older than those who wait until Election Day. This information is also important in strategizing.

©Daniel Acker/Getty Images

Personal contact by phone or door-to-door is still one of the most effective ways to get out the vote.

Political scientist Paul Gronke notes, "The smart campaign will not launch all of its artillery 'early,' and will focus early ads on the demographic groups (older, wealthier, more partisan, more ideological people) that tend to vote early. Later ads will remind voters of the salient points in the earlier ads."[53]

PARTIES, POLITICAL CAMPAIGNS, AND CIVIC ENGAGEMENT TODAY

The electoral landscape today is beset by contradictory forces. On the one hand, both candidates and political parties have become experts at reaching out to voters, often using new techniques and technologies, to engage them more fully in the political process. Using tools and techniques from Internet fundraising to online contests with a chance to win a dinner with the candidate to online blogs and interactive campaign chat rooms, campaigns have reinvented political campaigns for a new generation. Along with highly competitive races, the result has been higher-than-average turnout in some recent presidential election cycles. The same cannot be said for non-presidential elections where turnout has been substantially lower. In the case of these "off-year" elections, parties and candidates need to follow the lead of the national parties in getting more voters to the polls.

Although we both encourage and applaud the outreach efforts of parties and candidates to turn out voters in greater numbers, we worry about the ability of parties to govern once in office. Big money and partisan polarization threaten to undermine the kind of meaningful and widespread political dialogue necessary for addressing the problems voters care about most by reducing the ability of lawmakers to reach consensus. In coming chapters, we will discuss the various ways in which hyperpartisanship can create gridlock and the inability of our governing institutions to get things done.

In a parliamentary system in which the winning party is virtually assured of implementing its agenda, partisan polarization might actually be less of a concern. Voters could always signal their objection at the next election by replacing one party's control of Parliament with another's. What worries some observers about partisan polarization in America is that our system requires parties to work together much more closely to get anything done. For example, there are many points in the legislative process at which a minority party can completely stymie the majority's attempts to accomplish its goals. If compromise is not possible, the business of government may come to a halt.

Clearly, a certain amount of conflict and party competition is healthy, and no one believes that there are magic bullets to alleviate the excesses of partisanship. We should also note that, in the past, short-term polarization has not prevented Americans from nudging the parties back in line with the policy wishes of the majority.[54] But sometimes it is necessary to tweak the system in ways that make it more responsive. What might be done to enhance civic engagement while dialing down the political rhetoric? Let us highlight a few ideas that are promising.

First, improve the financing of elections in order to reduce the influence of big-money donors with ideological agendas. More than a dozen states provide public financing of some sort to candidates. Several others provide matching funds to candidates who promise to abide by spending limits.[55] There is evidence that public financing in these states contributes to greater competition without sacrificing candidate quality.[56] It limits the amount of time lawmakers spend scrambling for money, increases candidate diversity, and encourages closer ties between would-be representatives and those they seek to serve, thus reducing the impact of special interest donors. Most important, perhaps, public financing increases the perceived legitimacy of elections for the public.[57] A promising proposal for enhancing public financing was offered by a group of scholars in a report titled "Reform in the Age of Networked Campaigns." Among their recommendations: provide tax credits or rebates to small donors to fund the system and offer a four-to-one or five-to-one match for small donors to encourage candidates to spend more time chasing small donors than trolling for large ones.[58] In 2015, Seattle voters approved a measure called Democracy Vouchers, providing every voter in the city with a taxpayer-funded $100 voucher to be used by voters as campaign contributions to candidates in city races. Candidates who agree to accept the voucher money agree to participate in a number of debates and to observe lower campaign spending and contribution limits.[59] Efforts like these bear watching.

Second, a more far-reaching proposal for reducing partisan polarization is the elimination of the closed primary. Primary elections produce lower turnout and attract ideologically more extreme voters. Elections in which independents can vote, and in which voters can choose on Election Day the party's ballot they wish to take, produce somewhat higher turnout and attract a more ideologically diverse electorate. There is some limited evidence that the top-two primary systems used in states like Washington and California may have the effect of producing more moderate lawmakers, helping to steer the parties away from the extremes that fuel partisan polarization.[60] These reforms also bear watching.

As we have seen, political parties are an essential ingredient of our democracy. It was just a half-century ago that political scientists were complaining that the parties were not ideological enough, not offering voters clear choices. That is not the case today. The parties do represent different values and viewpoints, and they bring voters to the polls to register their support for one set of ideas or another. The problem today is that neither party is willing to bridge the ideological divide once in office in the interest of fixing some of our most pressing problems—like deficits and growing income inequality. Instead, in a country that is narrowly divided by party, each side focuses on winning the next election and defeating the opposition. The job for the next generation of leaders will be to preserve the ability of parties to offer viable alternatives while taking responsibility when elected for finding solutions that a majority of Americans, regardless of party, can support.

Thinking It Through >>>

Learning Objective: Discuss candidate-centered campaigns.

Review: Candidates and Electoral Politics

Outline your plan to run for a seat in your state legislature. Which political party will you seek to represent and what groups within the party will you target as your key supporters? Ascertain how much money it will take to win (check online expenditure records available in most states) and how you plan to raise those funds. Finally, present a media plan including how you will seek to obtain free media and how you will use social media to mobilize your key supporters.

Summary

1. **What are political parties, and why do we have just two major parties?**

   - Political parties are organizations created for the purpose of winning elections and governing once they are in office.
   - For voters, parties are useful for simplifying electoral choices; for candidates, parties help them gain political power; and for elected officials, parties provide a common set of principles that help them govern.
   - Constitutional election procedures like single-member districts and the Electoral College, the centrist ideology of most Americans, state laws, and the financial hurdles of mounting a campaign while not holding office all help to explain why just two major parties have come to dominate our political system.

   - American political parties today emerged as a result of a series of changes producing five party systems:
     - The first party system gave birth to the Federalists and Democratic-Republicans (later known simply as Democrats) during the period from the founding until about 1824.
     - The second party system, from late 1820s until about 1854, saw the Democrats dominate American politics with token Whig opposition until Lincoln's successful Republican challenge.
     - During the third party system, from about 1854 to the late 1890s, the newly formed Republican Party gained prominence while the Democrats split into

factions. This period was marked by very high levels of turnout and corruption.

- In the fourth party system, Republicans dominated politics at the national level during the era of Progressive reform.
- The fifth party system was characterized by the New Deal realignment and extended Democratic dominance until the 1960s.

- Since the 1960s, there has been relative parity among the two parties with a substantial minority not identifying with either.

2. **How are parties organized, and how has our party system adapted to change?**

- To win elections, parties are organized into national committees, congressional and senatorial campaign committees, state committees, and local government committees. Each level of the party is organized so as to maximize the electoral chances of candidates seeking office at that level. For example, the national committees run the presidential nominating conventions, develop rules for running primaries and caucuses, and raise significant amounts of money primarily for the purpose of winning the presidency.

- Throughout American history, parties have undergone periodic changes in strength, composition, and direction known as "realignments."

- Despite the dominance of the two-party system, there have been major third parties. These splinter parties, ideological parties, and single-issue or single-candidate parties can influence the outcome of specific elections by affecting election results or by influencing the future direction of the major parties.

3. **What is the relationship between candidates and parties in our electoral system?**

- Candidates vie for party support through primary elections, conventions, or a combination of both.

- During the nomination period, candidates assume the bulk of the responsibilities for running their own campaigns.

- Once candidates become official party nominees, the party will provide financial and personnel support throughout the general election campaign, although individual candidates are still in charge of their own campaigns.

- Throughout the election process, candidates devote a large part of their campaign day to raising money, much of which is spent on campaign advertising.

- Although individuals who contribute directly to a candidate's campaign must still abide by spending limits, super PACs and other financial entities that can spend unlimited funds to influence elections have become a powerful, potentially independent, force in campaigns.

4. **Why are the parties so divided today, and what, if anything, should be done about it?**

- America's parties today have become much more ideologically distinct, with Republicans moving to the right and Democrats to the left of the ideological spectrum.

- Influential interest groups and party elites are probably most responsible for the drift to the extremes; however, demographic change, redistricting, and fragmentation of the mass media have also played a part.

- Although ideological parties can present viable alternatives to voters, they can also contribute to gridlock in a non-parliamentary system like ours when elected members are unwilling to compromise with opponents.

Chapter 10

Media
Tuning in or Tuning Out

HOW TO RESTORE CONFIDENCE

In recent decades, the public has grown increasingly skeptical of the media. In 2017, a Gallup poll revealed that only 27 percent of respondents had "a great deal" or "quite a lot" of confidence in newspapers. Confidence in television news was 24 percent, and just 16 percent had confidence in news gathered on the Internet.[1] In comparison, only one other institution had a confidence rating lower than 20 percent—Congress, at 12 percent. The challenges facing the media have been increased by the antagonism the Trump administration has expressed toward them. The president has repeatedly charged that the media deal in "fake news" and that members of the media are the "worst people in the world." Trump's

©Robert Emerson/Alamy Stock Photo

Walter Cronkite was the anchorman for the CBS Evening News from 1962 to 1981. During that period, he was often referred to as "the most trusted man in America."

attorney general, Jeff Sessions, expressed the view that some members of the media should be in jail. (See the "Current Controversy" section at the end of the chapter.)

To navigate this troubling environment, the media need to polish their image. A recent study from the Media Insight Project, a collaboration of the American Press Institute and the Associated Press–NORC Center for Public Affairs Research, suggests that news organizations need to work on establishing trust, both to succeed as businesses and to effectively serve the role of keeping citizens informed in a democracy. Audiences need to know that they can rely on the news.

As You READ

- **How have the media and media consumption changed over the years?**
- **What are the major characteristics of mass media in America?**
- **How do the media cover political campaigns and government actions?**

Using both survey research and focus groups, the study indicated that American audiences valued accuracy and completeness as the two most important principles of trust in a news source (see "Principles of Trust in a News Source"). Nearly 70 percent of respondents also rated the principles of transparency and balance as "extremely important" or "very important."[2] The research broke "trust" into five components—accuracy, completeness, transparency, balance, and presentation—linked to twelve specific behaviors. That a news organization should get the facts straight was the behavior rated most vital in securing trust. Respondents placed the second highest importance on a news source always having the latest news and information. A majority of those surveyed also sought trusted journalists, transparency on how news sources gather information, expert sources and data, in-depth reporting, easy-to-find news, and news with diverse points of view (see "Factors Linked to Components of Trust").

Consumers of news rely on many different types of sources: national TV stations or programs; local TV stations or programs; radio stations or programs; specialty publications; local, national, or international newspapers; and/or online-only news sources or blogs. For all news media, respondents stressed the importance of sources getting the facts right, always having the latest news, and making it easy to find information. Viewers of television news place special emphasis on a source covering all the day's events and providing in-depth reporting. Americans rate trust components differently depending on the news topic. People are significantly more likely to cite expert sources and data and in-depth reporting as reasons why they rely on a source for national politics, while reporting that they seek out sources for lifestyle news that are "entertaining."

Those relying on digital platforms and social media for their news rated factors specific to that medium. This audience stressed the importance of ads not interfering with stories

Principles of Trust in a News Source

Accuracy and completeness are the most important principles of trust in a news source to Americans.

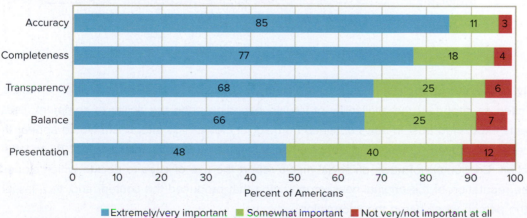

Americans want accuracy, completeness, transparency, and balance from their news source.

Source: The Media Insight Project, "A New Understanding: What Makes People Trust and Rely on News" (April 2016).

Factors Linked to Components of Trust

Americans place the most importance on specific factors linked to accuracy, completeness, and presentation

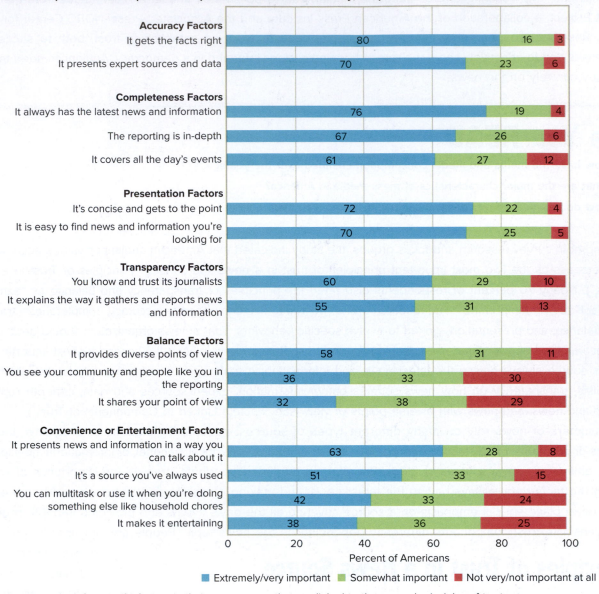

Accuracy Factors

It gets the facts right — 80 | 16 | 3

It presents expert sources and data — 70 | 23 | 6

Completeness Factors

It always has the latest news and information — 76 | 19 | 4

The reporting is in-depth — 67 | 26 | 6

It covers all the day's events — 61 | 27 | 12

Presentation Factors

It's concise and gets to the point — 72 | 22 | 4

It is easy to find news and information you're looking for — 70 | 25 | 5

Transparency Factors

You know and trust its journalists — 60 | 29 | 10

It explains the way it gathers and reports news and information — 55 | 31 | 13

Balance Factors

It provides diverse points of view — 58 | 31 | 11

You see your community and people like you in the reporting — 36 | 33 | 30

It shares your point of view — 32 | 38 | 29

Convenience or Entertainment Factors

It presents news and information in a way you can talk about it — 63 | 28 | 8

It's a source you've always used — 51 | 33 | 15

You can multitask or use it when you're doing something else like household chores — 42 | 33 | 24

It makes it entertaining — 38 | 36 | 25

Percent of Americans

■ Extremely/very important ■ Somewhat important ■ Not very/not important at all

Americans look for specific factors in their news source that are linked to the general principles of trust.

Source: The Media Insight Project, "A New Understanding: What Makes People Trust and Rely on News" (April 2016).

and information, the ability of the site or application to load fast, and whether the source works well on a mobile phone. Some users also cited as important the availability of visuals, hyperlinks, and the ability to comment. Less than one in four respondents expressed trust in news obtained from social media. This skepticism would appear to be justified given the placement of advertisements and stories on social media by Russian interests in 2016 to influence the presidential election. Consumers of news on social media report the use of cues to decide which stories to trust, assessing both the reputation of the original news organization that produced the content and, to a lesser extent, the reputation of the person who shared the information.

The Media Insight Project study provides the media with some useful suggestions on building trust with American consumers of news. The media's ability to exercise significant influence in the realm of politics and government seems to be dependent on such trust. The importance of the media in today's democracy is vast. The media determine what stories are newsworthy, they often influence what issues should be placed on the national agenda, and they interpret the motives of political officials.

Lack of trust in the media, when applied to politics and government, has an impact on civic engagement. To some extent, citizens are disengaging from the political system as they tune out the media's information about it. As you read the chapter, assess how the changing behavior and characteristics of the media—for example, narrowcasting, Internet news, social media, economic concentration, an emphasis on entertainment, and adversarial journalism—have affected the public's view of the media. ■

EVOLVING CIVIC LIFE AND MEDIA CHANGES

In the early days of the United States, politics was essentially an oral art conducted in taverns, boardinghouses, legislative chambers, and private parlors.[3] As the nation matured, a mass media developed—first newspapers and then the broadcast media—to keep citizens informed about local and national politics. The changes that the media have undergone over time have had an important influence on how the American people view their government and how that government connects to its citizens.

Early Days

Newspapers in colonial America did not get off to an auspicious start. The first newspaper published in America, *Publick Occurences, Both Foreign and Domestick,* appeared in Boston in 1690 and included an article on the alleged immoralities of the king of France. Offended by the article, the Massachusetts Bay Colony authorities ordered that no person could print a newspaper without first applying for a license from the government, resulting in the first American newspaper ending publication after just one edition. America's first regularly published newspaper, *The Boston News-Letter,* debuted in 1704 and appeared weekly until 1776. The paper's local and intercolonial articles included political speeches, official proclamations, crime stories, weather, and obituaries.[4]

By 1775, on the eve of the American Revolution, the colonies boasted forty newspapers, which played an important role in promoting discussion of the issues of the day. Such discussion would ultimately threaten the deferential politics that had flourished in the hierarchical society of colonial America.[5]

Partisan Press

After ratification of the U.S. Constitution, political leaders such as John Adams and Thomas Jefferson quickly saw the advantage of having newspapers promote their points of view. By granting newspapers lucrative contracts to print government documents, politicians could ensure wide dissemination of their words and deeds and secure friendly coverage of their ideas. As political parties formed, this mutual relationship between printers and government officials led to the development of the partisan press. Andrew Jackson further enhanced this relationship by appointing loyal gentlemen of the press to government positions. "These appointments rewarded journalists for their role in writing positive stories."[6]

Penny Press

In the 1830s, a commercial revolution swept a segment of the country's newspapers.[7] The invention of the rotary press dramatically increased the speed and volume in printing, while driving down costs. Observers of the day coined the term *penny press* to describe the cheaper, more widely available papers. Around the same time, the telegraph revolutionized

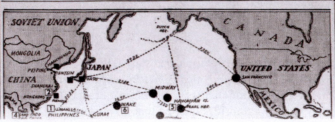

New York World-Telegram

LATEST
WALL ST.
PRICES
Real Estate, Page 31
PRICE THREE CENTS

Local Forecast: Light rains tonight, somewhat higher temperatures than last night; tomorrow cloudy followed by clearing, cooler than today.

VOL. 74.—NO. 135.—IN TWO SECTIONS—SECTION ONE   NEW YORK, MONDAY, DECEMBER 8, 1941.

1500 DEAD IN HAWAII
CONGRESS VOTES WAR

Tally in Senate Is 82 to 0, In House 388 to 1, with Miss Rankin Sole Objector

By LYLE C. WILSON.
United Press Staff Correspondent.

WASHINGTON, Dec. 8.—Congress today proclaimed existence of a state of war between the United States and the Japanese Empire 33 minutes after President Roosevelt stood before a joint session to ask such action and pledge that we will triumph—"so help us, God."

Democracy was proving its right to a place in the

100 to 200 Soldiers Killed in Japanese Raid On Luzon in Philippines

BULLETIN.
By the United Press.

MANILA, Dec. 8.—Press dispatches reported that 100 to 200 troops, 60 of them Americans, were killed or injured today when Japanese warplanes raided Iba, on the west coast of the island of Luzon, north of the Olangapo naval base.

BULLETIN.

Yellow journalists like Joseph Pulitzer made newspapers more sensational with bold headlines.

Journalist Edward R. Murrow had an unparalleled impact on both radio and television news, covering World War II and exposing political phonies.

newspaper journalism by enabling reporters and editors to send stories instantly over immense distances. These technological advances gave publishers access to a much wider audience, making newspaper advertising more enticing to merchants eager to reach a large base of consumers. The revenues generated from advertising freed newspapers from their previous financial dependence on government contracts and political parties.

Yellow Journalism

As the nineteenth century came to an end, a new kind of journalism took hold of America's burgeoning—and increasingly immigrant—population. Known as yellow journalism, it featured sensationalized stories, pictures, and bold headlines to grab the reader's attention. The name *yellow journalism* came from "The Yellow Kid," an extremely popular comic strip, and the first to be mass published in color.

One of the leaders in the field of yellow journalism was *New York World* publisher Joseph Pulitzer. The *World* added stories concerning scandal, gossip, sex, disasters, and sports to the usual fare of crime news. Large red or black headlines virtually "screamed excitement, often about comparatively unimportant news, thus giving a shrill falsity to the entire makeup."[8] Pulitzer's policy was to write stories that directly engaged his potential reading audience.[9] His stories often included the new technique of interviewing, or conversations between reporters and public persons that were designed to attract readers.[10] Pulitzer made his paper easy to read in order to attract immigrants, who made up 40 percent of New York City's population.[11]

By 1900, about one-third of the metropolitan papers practiced yellow journalism. Sympathy for the plight of ordinary citizens gave rise to a more aggressive form of investigative journalism known as *muckraking* in the early twentieth century. President Theodore Roosevelt was the first to use the term, comparing the process of news gathering to using a rake specifically designed to collect manure. Journalists such as Upton Sinclair and David Graham Phillips wrote about real and apparent misdeeds by government and business in order to stimulate reform.[12] Muckraking helped to expose corruption, but it often included publishing gossip and rumor without sufficient verification.

In the early decades of the twentieth century, the press changed direction in reaction to the excesses of yellow journalism. Newspapers made a commitment to objective journalism. New schools of journalism taught that newspapers should only print statements that followed established rules, such as using at least two independent sources to corroborate any claim made in print. The growth of national news agencies, including the Associated Press, United Press International, and the International News Service, also contributed to the development of objective journalism by concentrating on reporting bare facts with little interpretation.

Internet Grows as Campaign News Source

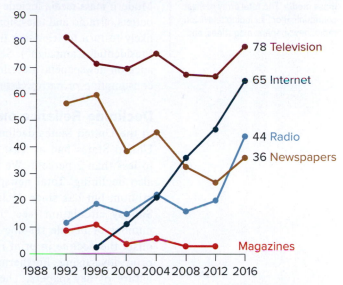

The Internet is gaining rapidly as a major source of campaign news.

Source: Pew Research Center, 2012 and 2016.

Broadcast Media

The first commercial radio program in the United States, aired in November 1920, reported the results of the presidential election between Warren G. Harding and James M. Cox. By the time of the next presidential election in 1924, nearly 1,400 radio stations were operating in the United States. By the mid-1930s, almost every household in America owned a radio. For the next twenty years, radio provided a popular source of news and entertainment. With broadcasts from the scenes of historic events, such as presidential inaugurals, royal coronations, and the fields of battle, radio provided listeners an immediacy that newspapers couldn't rival.

By the 1950s, television antennas had begun to appear on the roofs of American homes. At first, television stressed entertainment and advertising; the three networks—NBC, CBS, and ABC—initially produced just one fifteen-minute news program apiece, five evenings a week. That changed after all three networks decided to broadcast the 1960 presidential debates between John F. Kennedy and Richard M. Nixon. When those debates garnered an audience in excess of sixty million viewers, television executives realized that news programming could bring profits. The networks subsequently expanded their nightly news programs to thirty minutes and competed to produce the most highly rated news shows. Up to and including the 2016 presidential election, television continued to be the most used medium for campaign news, with the Internet as the fastest growing source (see "Internet Grows as Campaign News Source"). The 2016 election clearly demonstrated the impact of social media, websites, and apps on campaigns.

get involved!

Interview the news director of a local television station or the editor of your local paper. Find out what criteria he or she uses to determine what makes the headlines and what is left out. Would you make the same choices?

mass media The total array of mass communication, including television, radio, newspapers, magazines, and the Internet.

Citizens today have more sources for news of politics and government than ever before. Modern **mass media** include print outlets such as newspapers and magazines, the broadcast outlets of radio and television, and computerized information services, but citizens are more likely to turn to television than any other single source (see "Media Sources for the 2016 Presidential Campaign"). Several trends characterize media usage today: a decline in reliance on newspapers, a decline in news consumption among the young, and a growth in the consumption of narrowcasting.

Declining Reliance on Newspapers By 2016, the number of daily newspapers in the United States declined to 1,286.[13] In 1880, 61 percent of the major cities in the United States had at least two competing daily papers; today, that number has fallen to less than 2 percent. We have seen that circulation numbers for daily newspapers are also declining. Total newspaper circulation reached its zenith in 1985, surpassing 62 million, but has since declined to below 40 million, both for weekday circulation and Sunday circulation (see "Newspaper Circulation Continues to Fall"). Although the number of people reading newspapers online is growing rapidly, that growth has not offset the decline in print readership. The decline in readership is also reflected in less print advertising. Furthermore, declining newspaper print readership has changed the nature of newspapers. The papers are thinner and the stories shorter. There is less foreign, national, and business news. These trends raise questions about whether today's citizens are well enough informed to exercise the responsibilities of citizenship.

Media Sources for the 2016 Presidential Campaign

*Among those who learned about the election, % who name each source type as **most helpful***

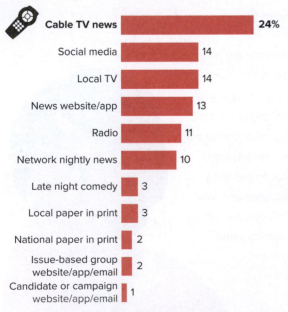

Cable TV news	**24%**
Social media	14
Local TV	14
News website/app	13
Radio	11
Network nightly news	10
Late night comedy	3
Local paper in print	3
National paper in print	2
Issue-based group website/app/email	2
Candidate or campaign website/app/email	1

Survey respondents found cable television to be the most helpful source for learning about the election in 2016.

Source: Pew Research Center Project for Excellence in Journalism, 2016.

Newspaper Circulation Continues to Fall

Total circulation for U.S. daily newspapers

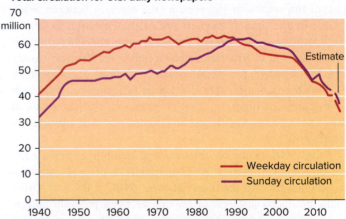

Weekday circulation
Sunday circulation

Note: Break in line indicates switch to estimated circulation. No data for 1941–1944 and 2010. To determine totals for 2015 onward, researchers analyzed the year-over-year change in total weekday and Sunday circulation using AAM data and applied these percent changes to the previous year's total. Only those daily U.S. newspapers that report to AAM are included. Affiliated publications are not included in the analysis. Weekday circulation only includes those publications reporting a Monday-Friday average. For each year, the comparison is for all newspapers meeting these criteria for the three-month period ending Dec. 31 of the given year. Comparisons are between the three-month averages for the period ending Dec. 31 of the given year and the same period of the previous year.

Newspaper circulation in the United States continues to decline.

Source: Pew Research Center.

Declining Interest in News Among the Young Americans between the ages of 18 and 31 are much less attentive to traditional news sources than are members of any other generation. Data show that millennials are less interested in politics and talk about it less than other generations.[14] This has created a special civic concern about millennials because they do not watch television news, read newspapers, or seek out the news in great numbers. Some observers fear that millennials' news-gathering habits result in a narrow view of the world that is insufficient for the exercise of citizenship duties in a democratic society.

Instead of newspapers, young people report using social media to gather information. This age group is more likely to use the Internet generally and has not experienced a time when consumers of the news had access only to the traditional media of newspapers, magazines, radio, and television. They report observing social media postings at a higher rate than any other age group. They are more likely to get their news from Facebook, YouTube, and Twitter than from any other news source.[15] These are more subjective postings than what one might find on a newspaper or magazine website, so the vetting process is up to the consumer in most cases. Overall, the online consumption of campaign political news has grown dramatically over the past two presidential election cycles. If you add up the social media, website, app, and email access to presidential election news shown in the figure "Media Sources for the 2016 Presidential Campaign," 30 percent of people learned about the campaign via these means, a greater percentage than cable news.

A study by the Media Insight Project revealed how the news habits of millennials differ from previous generations. They are more likely to get their weekly news about politics and government from Facebook than from television. Eighty-two percent get most of their news from online sources. Sixty-seven percent of Internet users under the age of 30 have a social networking profile, and half of these profile owners used social network sites to get or share information about the candidates and the campaign.[16] The study also found, however, that this newest generation of American adults is anything but newsless, uninterested, or disengaged from the world around them. Unlike earlier generations, they do not consume news at certain times of the day but rather acquire it as part of the "social flow" as they go online to see what is new among their network of friends.[17] The study indicated, moreover, that seeking out the news was the third most likely reason this younger generation went online and that a majority of them stated that the most important reason for being aware of the news was to be a better citizen.[18]

Increased Consumption of Narrowcasting A third trend evident today is the public's affinity for **narrowcasting**, programming directed to a small, specific segment of the population. In the early days of radio and television, news was broadcast to millions of Americans at the same time, which meant that most Americans shared the same news experiences; this is no longer the case. If you have access to cable or satellite television, you know about the great variety of channels available to viewers with specific and narrow interests. The Internet also provides a variety of news sources. Today, social media, news websites, and apps for tablets and smartphones are popular sources of news.

> **narrowcasting** Programming targeted to one small sector of the population, made possible by the emergence of cable television and the Internet.

In 2016, Trump supporters and Clinton supporters turned to different sources for coverage of their favored candidates' campaigns (see "Sources for 2016 Campaign Coverage"). Republicans preferred watching Fox News because of its conservative slant. Democrats, by contrast, preferred the CNN or the liberal MSNBC.

The way these cable stations choose to present the parties' national conventions to their viewing audiences is revealing. Fox News, CNN, and MSNBC all used their primary on-air personalities as hosts. Coverage of the conventions followed a talk show format as the hosts chatted with pundits, politicians, other journalists, and entertainers. They devoted less than 10 percent of their coverage to reporting what was going on at the podium or where the candidates or the parties stood on specific issues.

The liberal media outlets criticized the Republican convention as dark, pessimistic, and attended by less-than-enthusiastic delegates wary of their party's standard-bearer, whereas the conservative media proclaimed that the convention had made a strong case for change within the political system given the economic and national security concerns facing the nation. The Democrats held their convention the following week. Most media observers reported that the Democrats put on a nearly flawless convention with remarkable and effective speeches by the Obamas, Vice President Biden, and former president Bill Clinton. The

Sources for 2016 Campaign Coverage

% of voters who named__as their "main source" for news about the 2016 campaign

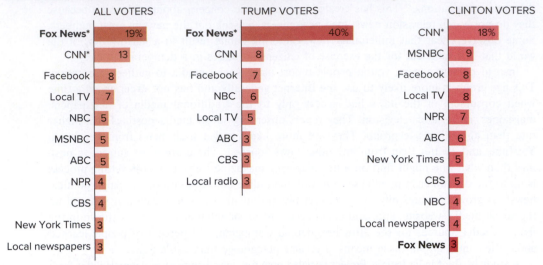

ALL VOTERS		TRUMP VOTERS		CLINTON VOTERS	
Fox News*	19%	Fox News*	40%	CNN*	18%
CNN*	13	CNN	8	MSNBC	9
Facebook	8	Facebook	7	Facebook	8
Local TV	7	NBC	6	Local TV	8
NBC	5	Local TV	5	NPR	7
MSNBC	5	ABC	3	ABC	6
ABC	5	CBS	3	New York Times	5
NPR	4	Local radio	3	CBS	5
CBS	4			NBC	4
New York Times	3			Local newspapers	4
Local newspapers	3			Fox News	3

*Among this group of voters, this source was named at significantly higher rates than the source below it. Significance of any other relationships provided upon request.

Note: Sources shown are only those that were named by at least 3% of each group. Results are based on responses to open-ended questions; respondents could write in any source they chose.

The American voting population is polarized with regard to the news sources they follow.

Source: Pew Research Center.

liberal media outlets proclaimed that the speakers effectively made the case that Donald Trump lacked the temperament to be commander-in-chief. The conservative media outlets said the Democratic convention did nothing to justify another four years of the Obama presidency led by Hillary Clinton or to reverse the public's reservations concerning her trustworthiness.

Narrowcasting has changed the way citizens receive messages from political leaders. Commenting on the trend of narrowcasting, one author concludes that "the effect of the fragmentation in the audience will be a reduction in the commonality of Americans' political experiences."[19] Another way to look at it is that specialized programming may provide a better fit between public messages and audience needs.

Jeff Bezos, the founder of Amazon, bought The Washington Post in 2013.

THE MEDIA ENVIRONMENT IN AMERICA

Today's American mass media environment is characterized by several trends that shape the messages we receive about government and, in turn, affect the kinds of citizens we become. These trends include private ownership that is becoming more highly concentrated; some government regulation, particularly of broadcast media outlets; an expansion of entertainment content at the expense of news content; an adversarial style of journalism that attacks politicians and their motives; and a belief by some that the media exhibit political bias.

Private Ownership

Private individuals have always owned the nation's media outlets; most modern Americans would consider any other ownership arrangement odd or even threatening. Yet the United States is the only advanced industrial nation in the world in which virtually all the major media outlets are privately owned.[20] The only exceptions are the Public Broadcasting System, National Public Radio, and public access channels. In other Western democracies such as France and Denmark, the government owns the media.[21]

Ownership of U.S. media outlets is highly concentrated, with a handful of huge corporations controlling hundreds of daily newspapers and local television channels. The years 2011–2012 were volatile for media ownership. Many traditional owners sold their interests in newspapers to hedge funds and private equity firms. In May 2012, Warren Buffett's Berkshire Hathaway Company purchased sixty-three newspapers from former news titan Media General Company, which now owns not a single newspaper.[22] Critics contend that an emphasis on profits has led to an excess of negative coverage, a rush to be the first to present breaking news without carefully checking for possible mistakes, and a tendency to make the news more entertaining than informative. Reporters also share this belief.[23]

This trend toward private ownership of the media continues, demonstrated by the sale of *The Washington Post* in 2013 to Jeff Bezos. As chief executive of Amazon, Bezos made billions of dollars transforming the book publishing business before buying one of the country's oldest and most respected newspapers. Admitting the newspaper was never something he wanted to buy, Bezos said: "I didn't know anything about the newspaper business, but I did know something about the Internet. That combined with the financial runway that I can provide, is the reason I bought the *Post*."[24] Bezos is working to modernize the publication by creating a new app for the paper to be used with Amazon devices. The paper has committed to posting all its articles on various social media sites like Facebook Instant Articles, Apple News, and Twitter Moments.[25] Some media critics worry that media owners are more interested in producing good consumers than good citizens and that recent trends threaten civic engagement by fostering citizens who are politically passive.[26]

Government Regulation

As discussed in Chapter 4, the First Amendment and its interpretation by the courts provide extensive protections for newspapers. The general rule is that government can exercise no prior restraint or censorship over the press. A court may waive these restrictions if it finds that a story raises real national security concerns or violates public decency.[27] Print outlets can also be sued for stories that constitute libel, but today the print media enjoy relative protection from such suits as a result of the Supreme Court's decision in *New York Times v. Sullivan* (1964).[28]

Electronic media are subject to the same restrictions as print media, as well as several others. Because only a limited number of frequencies are available for broadcasting, the government declared the airwaves public property during the early days of radio broadcasting. This allowed Congress to regulate use of the airwaves, both to prevent signals from interfering with each other and to ensure that no one person or group could monopolize broadcast frequencies. In 1934, Congress created the Federal Communications Commission (FCC) to regulate the electronic media of radio and television.

Ownership Limits

The FCC sets rules for private ownership of broadcast stations. Under the old "7-7-7 Rule" of the 1950s, a single owner could own no more than seven AM radio stations, seven FM radio stations, and seven television stations throughout the nation. In the 1990s, the FCC increased that number to twelve television stations and twenty of each kind of radio station. Then, in June 2003, the FCC announced new rules permitting a single company to own the leading newspaper as well as multiple television and radio outlets in a single market. This lessening of government regulation has encouraged even greater concentration of media ownership. This trend continued in 2017 when the FCC once again lowered media limits, allowing one company to own two television stations in one market and coordinate operations with stations owned by others.

Content Regulation

The FCC also fashions rules affecting the content of radio and television broadcasts. In 1934, it instituted the **equal time rule** to promote equity in broadcasting. The rule requires a broadcast station to provide airtime equally to all candidates if it provides airtime to any. The rule applies to free airtime as well as to paid advertising. If a station, for instance, interviews a Republican candidate for the U.S. Senate on the morning news or runs a commercial for the candidate, the Democrat candidate must be provided the same opportunities.

In 1949, the FCC issued the controversial **fairness doctrine**, designed to ensure that broadcasters reported on news events and public issues fairly by presenting all points of view. Many broadcasters complained that the rule was difficult to define and claimed that it discouraged them from covering controversial subjects. They argued that the rule produced what courts call a "chilling effect" on political communication. In 1985, the FCC abolished the fairness doctrine, stating that the growth in the number of electronic outlets assured balance and fairness in the presentation of political topics without government oversight.

Anyone who watched the 2004 Super Bowl is probably aware of another content function of the FCC: fining stations for indecent broadcasts. In September of that year, the FCC fined CBS a record $550,000 for Janet Jackson's "wardrobe malfunction," in which the singer exposed her breast during the Super Bowl halftime show. In 2009, the Supreme Court ruled in *Federal Communications Commission v. Fox Television Stations* that the use of the f-word by Cher in 2002 and the use of the same word by Paris Hilton and Nicole Richie in 2003, both of which occurred during the telecast of the Billboard Music Awards, empowered the FCC to punish broadcasters. The Court considered the question again in the 2012 *FCC v. Fox Television Stations* case. In the later case, the court ruled unanimously that the FCC had not given Fox or ABC fair notice regarding a new indecency policy that banned even the fleeting use of four-letter words or momentary glimpses of nudity. The Court also overturned a $500,000 fine CBS was charged that same year. It left for future cases the question as to whether the indecency policy violates the First Amendment.

Another issue for the FCC to contend with surrounds "technological advances" in media and the fact that FCC regulations apply to radio and broadcast TV, but not cable television or the Internet. What might *Game of Thrones* have been like if cable television stations could be fined for what the FCC considered indecent broadcasts? Chapter 13 discusses how the FCC's abandonment of the net neutrality policy may change people's Internet experiences.

Emphasis on Entertainment

As a private enterprise, the various media have always existed to make money. Yellow journalism and muckraking are two prominent examples of how publishers have sought to increase the bottom line by making the news more entertaining. Today, television programs such as *48 Hours, Dateline NBC,* and *20/20* blend news and entertainment programming to produce *infotainment.* The networks' evening news broadcasts feature an emphasis on celebrities, lifestyle issues, and human-interest stories. Some observers fear that the news has become a form of amusement rather than a public service.[29] As we will see, this aspect of the media environment has contributed to a reduction in the number of people who follow the news and an increase in those who just desire entertainment, thus widening the knowledge gap among citizens. It has also polarized those who do follow the news by encouraging them to choose the media outlets that most conform to their beliefs.

As the news has become more of a spectacle over the past twenty-five years, newsreaders and reporters have become media stars. The more "face time" they garner on television, the more famous they become. Many of today's journalists make millions of dollars a year on the lecture circuit. Journalist James Fallows has written that this "gravy train" may be good for individual journalists but is detrimental for journalism.[30] Fallows believes that such

equal time rule The rule that requires that all broadcasters provide airtime equally to all candidates if they choose to provide it to any.

fairness doctrine The law that formerly required broadcasters to present contrasting views on important public issues.

"buckraking" reinforces the idea that journalists are just performers who will put on a show for a price.[31] This star system also makes the coverage of politics more difficult: "By the 1980s, journalism's leading lights were millionaires with household names, whose fame equaled that of movie stars and sports heroes, and whose celebrity outshone the politicians they covered."[32]

Local television, whose format is increasingly oriented toward entertainment, has now become more popular than national news programming. Local news broadcasts feature a large number of crime stories (as the saying goes, in local news, "If it bleeds, it leads"), human-interest stories, weather, entertainment, and sports. Local stations place great emphasis on the appearance and personalities of the broadcasters. The anchors must be attractive, stylish, and well groomed, and the female anchor, in particular, must be young. Above all, local newscasters must engage in lively, happy banter in order to be invited back into viewers' homes; there is little emphasis on hard news. Such a trend does not encourage citizens to think deeply about important issues that confront them at the ballot box; instead, it urges them to sit back and be entertained.

Adversarial Journalism

During the past three decades, the national media has embraced **adversarial or attack journalism**, which adopts a hostile position toward government, political processes, and political figures. Some scholars trace this development to growing public distrust of government in the late 1960s and early 1970s.[33] After the Vietnam War and the Watergate scandal, citizens began to believe that their political leaders had been lying to them. Young journalists, inspired by the media's role in uncovering the scheme that drove President Nixon from office in 1974, did not want to miss the next big political scandal that might catapult them to fame.

> **adversarial or attack journalism** A form of interpretive journalism that adopts a hostile position toward government, politics, and political figures.

Following Watergate, the major networks poured a considerable amount of money into building investigative units that turned out stories focusing on the shortcomings of government officials, political candidates, and government programs. Reporters came to view their role as one of exposing the misstatements and misdeeds of political officials. As a result, the media inundated the American public with negative news. Citizens heard a daily drumbeat of inflammatory news about government officials, from politicians having sex with their interns to candidates misusing campaign funds.

Although some scholars worry that negative news may adversely affect the behavior of citizens, Americans are interested in negative news and eagerly tune in to hear about it. Coverage of President Bill Clinton's impeachment trial, for example, drew large audiences. In the long run, however, a steady diet of news about official wrongdoings turns citizens away from government and makes them less likely to fulfill their roles as citizens because they see the system as hopelessly corrupt. Negative news is causing citizens to tune out the political system.

More recently, some observers have complained that news reporters are now too easy on popular political leaders. When President George W. Bush's approval ratings skyrocketed after the terrorist attacks of September 11, 2001, some media outlets relaxed their scrutiny of information coming from the White House. Few, for example, seriously questioned the president's plans to attack Iraq because that country allegedly possessed weapons of mass destruction. When U.S. military forces discovered that no such weapons existed, *The New York Times* took the unprecedented action of publishing something of an apology to its readers for its one-sided reporting and its failure to aggressively investigate the administration's claims.[34] However, as the war in Iraq dragged on and the president suffered a series of setbacks in his handling of the hurricane-devastated South in 2005, the media provided daily coverage of the administration's missteps. Critics had a harder time sustaining the charge that the media were giving the president a "pass" on negative coverage. During the Obama administration, conservative talk show hosts like Rush Limbaugh believed the media were giving a pass to the president. No such charges have been claimed during the Trump years because the media has had no dearth of critical stories concerning the president's competence and honesty despite the favorable coverage he receives from Fox News.

Background studies have found that journalists are not representative of the general public. They are more likely to identify themselves as liberals and either Democrats or independents; very few describe themselves as Republicans or conservatives.[35] This is particularly true of journalists who work for large newspapers and television networks. Studies indicate, however, that these background characteristics do not translate into bias against Republican and conservative candidates. The classic study of presidential campaigns from 1948–2000 found no evidence of significant political bias in newspapers, news magazines, and television.[36] Journalists try hard to keep political bias out of their stories because of their adherence to the professional norm of objectivity, because of their need not to offend their more conservative employers, and because they are more interested in telling a good story than espousing a particular ideology.[37]

Despite studies to the contrary, an overwhelming number of people today see bias in the news. In fact, only 24 percent in 2016 thought that the news media try to report on news without bias. That proportion increased slightly, to 28 percent, in 2017 (see "Public Opinion About News Media Bias"). However, this still represents a 17-point drop from 2014. It is possible that negative news stories questioning the credibility of high-profile news media personalities, such as former NBC anchor Brian Williams, have influenced overall news media credibility among Americans. It is also possible that the public is reacting negatively to media coverage of high-profile and racially charged events in places such as Ferguson, Missouri, Baltimore, Maryland, and Charlottesville, Virginia. Republicans are much more likely than Democrats (87 percent to 53 percent) to believe that news organizations tend to favor one side (see "Partisan Gap in Perceptions of News Media Bias").

Republican mistrust of the news media has resulted in the proliferation of news and commentary shows with an admittedly conservative orientation. Talk show hosts such as Rush Limbaugh and Tucker Carlson believe they are serving as a needed counterpoint to the liberal slant of the media establishment. Fox News, which hosts many conservative commentators, proclaims itself "fair and balanced" in order to convey the notion that it is different from other, more liberal news organizations.

As we shall see, bias does turn up in almost all reports from the campaign trail and in the coverage of government. But the bias is largely commercial and sensational in nature, not political. Despite claims to the contrary, the American news media provide generally balanced coverage, while an increasing variety of specialized outlets are available for those seeking a particular point of view. It is within this environment that the various media outlets bring political campaigns to their audiences and provide the public with their competing views of the political process.

Perceptions of political bias can be embedded in other low evaluations of the media. A 2013 study revealed that only 26 percent of Americans believed the media got the facts straight, 20 percent saw the media as pretty independent, and only 19 percent thought it was fair to all sides.[38] However, nearly 80 percent of respondents believed the media play an important watchdog role by preventing political leaders from perpetrating misdeeds. Support for the media's watchdog role fell to 70 percent, however, by 2017 (see "Public Support for the Media's Watchdog Role"). However, the partisan divide on support for the media's watchdog role recently reached its greatest difference, with 89 percent of Democrats but only 42 percent of Republicans in favor of such a role (see "Partisan Divide on the Media's Watchdog Role"). The media's coverage in 2017 of the possible conspiracy between the Trump campaign and Russia in order to influence the 2016 presidential election

Public Opinion About News Media Bias

% of U.S. adults who think news organizations__when presenting the news on political and social issues

	Deal fairly with all sides	Tend to favor one side
2017	28%	72%
2016	24	74

Nearly 75 percent of Americans believe the media favor one side over another.

Source: Pew Research Center.

Partisan Gap in Perceptions of News Media Bias

% of U.S. adults who think news organizations *tend to favor one side* when presenting the news on political and social issues

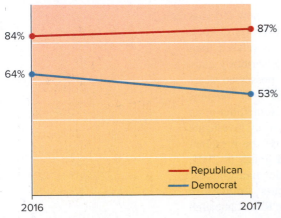

Republicans see more bias in the media than Democrats do.

Source: Pew Research Center.

Public Support for the Media's Watchdog Role

% of U.S. adults who think that criticism from news organizations ...

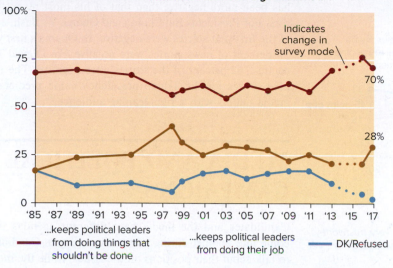

...keeps political leaders from doing things that shouldn't be done

...keeps political leaders from doing their job

DK/Refused

Source: Pew Research Center.

Partisan Divide on the Media's Watchdog Role

% of U.S. adults who think that criticism from news organizations *keeps political leaders from doing things that shouldn't be done*

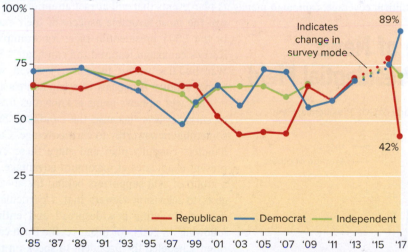

Republican Democrat Independent

Note: Dotted line indicates a change in mode. Polls from 1985–2013 were conducted via phone. In 2016 and 2017, the polls were conducted on the American Trends Panel, which is online.

Democrats are more approving of the media's watchdog role than are Republicans.

Source: Pew Research Center.

no doubt contributed to that widening partisan divide.[39] There is also a smaller but widening partisan gap concerning the perception that information from national news organizations is very trustworthy and does very well at keeping the public informed (see "Partisan Attitudes About News Media").

Partisan Attitudes About News Media

% of U.S. adults who say ...

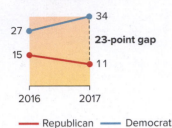

Information from national news organizations is very trustworthy

27
34
23-point gap
15
11

2016   2017

National news media do very well at keeping them informed

28
24
33
15-point gap
18

2016   2017

— Republican   — Democrat

Note: Independents not shown.

Democrats are more likely to rate the media as very trustworthy and as doing a good job of keeping them very well informed, yet neither party gives strong support in these areas.

Source: Pew Research Center.

As we note throughout this chapter, the relationship between the Trump administration and the media has been difficult. One study showed that the early coverage of the Trump presidency has been more negative than that of his most recent predecessors. For Presidents Bill Clinton and George W. Bush, 28 percent of the first-year stories were negative. In Obama's first year, only 20 percent of news stories were negative. For Donald Trump, by contrast, 62 percent of the stories were negative. The most positive stories for the Trump presidency came predictably from media outlets with a right-leaning audience.[40]

MEDIA AND POLITICAL CAMPAIGNS

Candidates and the media have different agendas that often come into conflict during political campaigns. Candidates want to talk about their positions on the issues, while the media often want to discuss campaign strategies and a candidate's standing in the polls. Although candidates and the media attempt to use each other for their own purposes, they also need each other to achieve their ends: victory for the candidate, access to the newsmakers for the media. In this section, we will examine how the media and presidential candidates interact in the course of political campaigns and the implication of those interactions for our democracy.

Free Media

Political campaigns need to be newsworthy to survive. Knowing that the media are selective about political coverage, campaign managers plan events that will attract attention and emphasize the most favorable aspects of their candidate. In the 2004 presidential race, for example, John Kerry's campaign featured the candidate's Vietnam War buddies whose lives Kerry saved with his heroic actions. Broadcast of a candidate's activities or messages as news items is known as *free media,* or *earned media,* because the candidate has done something newsworthy to earn coverage. Campaign handlers carefully plan and stage these events to present candidates at maximum advantage. Putting a group of avid supporters behind the speaker suggests to television viewers that a particular candidate is attracting a widespread and enthusiastic following. In 2004, for instance, the Bush campaign often scheduled the president to speak on the issue of terrorism before supportive crowds who had been prescreened for attendance. In 2008, candidate Obama was placed on stage before large audiences where his oratorical skills were used.

In 2015 and 2016, Donald Trump's campaign style landed him an inordinate amount of free media. Trump's often controversial and even outrageous statements attracted audiences, and the media kept him in their news cycles, attracted by the lure of high ratings.[41] (See the figure "Donald Trump's Share of News Coverage of the GOP Presidential Field.") Using his promotional skills

Donald Trump's Share of News Coverage of the GOP Presidential Field

Donald Trump's Share of News Coverage of GOP Presidential Field

40%

— Trump
— Average of others

20%

0%

Announcement of candidacy

30 days later

Data are generated using social analytic tools provided by Crimson Hexagon. Other candidates are Christie, Bush, Perry, Santorum, Walker, and Cruz. Graph by John Sides.

Donald Trump dominated his Republican rivals in gaining media attention during his drive for the Republican nomination.

from years in business and time on the show *The Apprentice*, Trump worked the media to his best advantage, using Twitter, talk show appearances, and squabbles with news commentators and other candidates to keep the spotlight on his campaign.

A campaign can also "stroke" members of the media by granting them exclusive interviews. Campaigns that utilize this strategy hope that giving a particular journalist or news outlet a momentary competitive advantage will ultimately earn the candidate more positive coverage from that source.

Candidates and campaign managers also attempt to **spin** the news, that is, convince the media to apply a particular interpretation to a story. This is why members of campaign press staffs are sometimes known as **spin doctors**. They spin by placing the most favorable interpretation on their own activities, and the most negative one on their opponent's activities. In 2004, the Bush campaign extolled the virtues of the war in Iraq and questioned Kerry's criticism of the war effort. In turn, Kerry interpreted every setback of the war as evidence of the administration's poor planning.

Since the 1992 presidential campaign, candidates have increasingly used alternative media such as entertainment programs or local news shows to spread their messages. Given the negative emphasis of the stories written and aired by the traveling press corps, candidates often prefer to appear on national talk shows or a local news program. There, the atmosphere is not adversarial and candidates can often speak at length. On mainstream news programs, the viewer hears only **sound bites**, small edited snippets of a candidate's statement that often last no longer than a few seconds. A reporter selects and frames a short clip, which typically shows a candidate speaking for less than an average of ten seconds, and then speculates on why the candidate has uttered those particular words. Sound bite coverage makes it difficult for a candidate to communicate a message in any depth.

spin A campaign's favorable interpretation of their campaign and unfavorable view of their opponent's activities.

spin doctors Political campaign operatives who interpret campaign events in the most favorable light to their candidate.

sound bites News programs' short video clips of politicians' statements.

Presidential Debates

The presidential debates offer one of the few opportunities for the American public to compare candidates side by side. The first televised debate in 1960, between Richard M. Nixon and John F. Kennedy, demonstrated how important such events could be for changing the momentum of a campaign. On television, the handsome and virile Kennedy appeared relaxed and informed; Nixon appeared pale, tired, and thin. He had spent the previous week in the hospital with a leg infection, and the shirt he wore was too large for him. That was not his only wardrobe problem, however. His staff had not investigated the debate site, so they did not realize that the gray suit he wore to the debate would blend in with the gray background of the stage. His appearance gave a whole new meaning to being "washed out." Nixon, however, was well informed on the issues and spoke with a resonant voice that sounded confident. Audiences listening on the radio believed Nixon won the debate, whereas the larger television audience saw the charismatic Kennedy as the clear winner. Television remains the favorite means for Americans to experience political debates.

Politicians and their advisors learned two important lessons from that first televised debate. First, television is a visual medium; candidates must look presidential as well as sound presidential. Second, challengers

The presidential debates give the candidates an opportunity to persuade millions of voters. Their importance has been recognized ever since the 1960 Kennedy–Nixon race. In 2016, Hillary Clinton was considered the clear winner in the first presidential debate.

©Rick Wilking/AFP/Getty Images

have more to gain from debating than do incumbents. Kennedy gained instant credibility just by appearing on the stage with his better-known rival, Vice President Nixon.

The 1976 U.S. presidential debate revealed yet another characteristic of televised debates: The media will pounce on any mistake or gaffe. In response to a reporter's question, President Gerald R. Ford stated that eastern Europe was no longer under the influence of the Soviet Union—which, of course, was not the case. At first, the public did not attach much significance to the statement. Polls taken immediately after the debate indicated that Ford won the debate over challenger Jimmy Carter by a margin of 44 to 33 percent. For the next twenty-four hours, however, the media stressed Ford's misstatement about eastern Europe. After the public was inundated with this type of coverage, the next polls gave Carter the victory by a margin of 63 to 17 percent![42]

Another key to success in televised debates is passing the "living room test"—that is, coming across as someone the audience would like to invite into their homes. Michael Dukakis in 1988 and Al Gore in 2000 flunked the living room test. Media critics faulted Dukakis for appearing cold and impersonal and suggested that Gore projected the image of a know-it-all.

The 2008 debates produced no gaffes or failures to pass the "living room test," and Senator Obama's performance in all three debates was rated superior by the viewing audience. In 2012, Governor Romney scored a big victory in the first debate against President Obama by being respectfully aggressive in challenging the president's record and by moderating his own conservative positions. Obama, by contrast, seemed tired, passive, and disengaged. Obama rebounded by winning the next two debates, but Romney's momentum from their first encounter pulled him even in the national polls during the final weeks of the campaign.

In 2016, most of debate attention during the primary season was focused on the Republicans. They had sixteen announced candidates and many more debate events. The early debates were dominated by the oversized presence of Donald Trump. Short on specifics but grandiose in language and gestures, Trump often seemed to dominate the stage while all of the other candidates had to compete for attention. Trump made further news when he boycotted the last debate prior to the Iowa caucus over a feud with *Fox News*. After Iowa, the debates turned especially combative and personal. Governor Chris Christie observed that Senator Marco Rubio repeated memorized statements, at which point the young senator did just that and created serious doubt concerning his campaign. Further Republican debates degenerated into the politics of spectacle when the three leading candidates, Trump, Cruz, and Rubio, hurled personal insults at each other. The Democrats had only three candidates and fewer debates that were less watched in part because a number of them were held on weekends. This led to controversy, because the number and timing of the debates by the Democratic National Committee were viewed as favoring the early favorite, Hillary Clinton.

The first presidential debate between Hillary Clinton and Donald Trump was viewed by over 80 million people, the most in American history. It was a much anticipated confrontation between the unorthodox Trump, who bragged about his lack of formal debate practice, and the traditional Clinton, who took days off from the campaign trail to practice with mock debates. After the first twenty minutes of the debate, Trump became less coherent in his responses, particularly about the use of nuclear weapons. Rather than giving complete and thoughtful answers to the questions posed, he constantly interrupted Secretary Clinton and the moderator and strayed off topic. Scientific polls reflected a big victory for Clinton. Presidential debate outcomes are also scored by the tenor of the post-debate news cycles. Trump lost the first debate by this measure as well.

Secretary Clinton also won the next two debates with her grasp of the issues, steady performance, and the ability to rattle Trump. The events leading up to the second debate further added to the unusual nature of the 2016 election. The release of a decade-old *Access Hollywood* tape featuring Donald Trump discussing how he used his star power to kiss and grope women dominated the news. Trump responded by inviting women to the debate who had in the past accused former president Bill Clinton of unwanted sexual advances. In the final debate, Trump made headlines by refusing to say that he would accept the results of the election. After the completion of the debates, Clinton held a growing lead in the polls. Despite winning the three debates, Clinton lost the electoral vote and thus the presidency. She was unable to join the other debate winners who went on to win the presidency: John Kennedy, Jimmy Carter, Ronald Reagan, George H. W. Bush, Bill Clinton, George W. Bush, and Barack Obama. When they ran for reelection, however, Carter and Bush Sr.

lost the presidential debates and the presidency. George W. Bush also lost the debates in his run for a second term but won a close race against John Kerry.

Paid Media

Because American media are privately owned, candidates who want significant public exposure must buy advertising on the various media outlets. Campaigns see advertising as the most effective way to capture the attention of the voters and to control their messages. Television commercials are also the most expensive way for candidates and campaigns to attempt to reach voters. In 2016, candidates spent $4 billion on TV commercials (i.e., candidates vs. PACs). Determining the effectiveness of advertising is not easy. So many factors determine the outcome of an election that it is difficult to isolate the impact of any single factor.[43] Nevertheless, television advertising has been a staple of every modern presidential campaign. Donald Trump's capture of the Republican nomination in 2016 with little paid advertising, however, has raised doubts about the relative importance of paid advertising going forward. Online display ads have become an important element in presidential campaigns, complementing broader paid-media strategies including TV, direct mail, video, social media, search, email, and more.[44] But more voting audiences, especially millennials, are blocking ads. There are now around 45 million monthly ad-blocking users.[45] Not all democracies allow political advertising; some believe that allowing candidates with greater financial resources to dominate political discourse threatens democracy. Scandinavian countries, for example, provide candidates with free access to publicly owned media.

Political advertising may be either positive or negative. Positive messages focus on a candidate's performance in office, issue positions, and character, without reference to the opposition. Negative messages focus exclusively on an opponent's weaknesses. A softer type of negative message is the comparative message, which contrasts the record of the candidate buying the ad with that of the opponent. By and large, researchers have found that attack ads can affect voter attitudes and behavior in specific elections. Voters find the information and message conveyed by the ads useful in making up their minds.[46] Scholars disagree about the long-term impact of negative ads on the political process, however. Some researchers have found that negative ads have a depressing effect on turnout, especially among independent and undecided voters.[47] Others conclude that any discouraging effect is minimal and that negative ads may actually stimulate the interest of voters who may not otherwise participate.[48]

The Internet

Since its debut as a political medium in the 1996 presidential elections, the Internet has become an increasingly important part of political campaigns. In 1996, the presidential candidates created fairly simple home pages containing their profiles, issue positions, campaign strategies, slogans, and email addresses. By 2000, the World Wide Web had become a major campaign tool for identifying potential supporters. In 2004, the campaign for Democratic contender Howard Dean used the Internet to raise millions of dollars, and the Kerry campaign later used the technology to overcome the early financial advantage President Bush enjoyed. The funds raised online by the presidential candidates in 2008 dwarfed the figures from 2004. By 2008, candidates were using the Internet to create virtual town meetings and to share ideas and coordinate campaign events with **bloggers**—average citizens who create online diaries and forums for the posting of opinions and personal viewpoints.

bloggers Citizens who create online diaries and forums for the posting of opinions and personal viewpoints.

The traditional media have had to react to the emergence of the Internet. All major media outlets now have their own websites, where they post breaking news stories to avoid being scooped by nontraditional journalist-bloggers like Matt Drudge. Drudge first broke the Clinton–Lewinsky story on his website after he learned *Newsweek* was considering the story. The traditional media disparage self-proclaimed journalists like Drudge as "those guys in pajamas" who lack credentials and do not follow conventional journalistic rules like requiring confirmation by independent sources. (See "Challenges Ahead: 2019 and Beyond" for more on Matt Drudge.)

BLOGGING: MATT DRUDGE

Matt Drudge, the first influential political blogger in the era of citizen journalists, is still around today. Nearly twenty years after breaking the President Bill Clinton–Monica Lewinsky scandal, Drudge remains a major and sometimes controversial figure in the world of Internet journalism. His website is ranked third among the most popular political websites (see "Top 15 Most Popular Political Websites, July 2017).

Drudge, born in Takoma Park, Maryland, in 1966, was considered a "loner" in high school, graduating near the bottom of his class academically. After high school, he worked in a variety of odd jobs. In 1989, he moved to Los Angeles and found work in a gift shop at CBS Studios. Inspired by the gossip he was hearing at work, Drudge decided to share the information. Drudge Report began as an email sent out to friends, and it included gossip and opinions. By 1996, the report evolved from entertainment gossip to political gossip, and it was transmitted via the Web. Drudge began actively reading and collecting news stories and then posting the news in real time to Usenet newsgroups.

Matt Drudge, who has no formal training as a journalist, has "a gift for plugging into the rumor and gossip mill," and that led him to some scoops, such as the news that Bob Dole had picked Jack Kemp to be his running mate in the 1996 presidential election.[†] Drudge has described himself as a "conservative populist," and he rose to prominence at approximately the same time that the Fox News Channel emerged as a media force. Drudge's rise to national prominence began when his 1998 report was the first to expose that then-president Bill Clinton had had extramarital sexual encounters with Monica Lewinsky, a White House intern. This breakthrough scoop for Drudge Report was not the result of arduous investigative journalism. The story had originated with *Newsweek*'s Michael Isikoff, who had been investigating the story for some time. *Newsweek* editors delayed running the story until they got more verification. When Drudge learned of the matter from one of his *Newsweek* sources, he posted the story online.[‡] *Newsweek* ran its story soon after, but Drudge got credit for breaking the story first.

Since the Lewinsky story in 1998, Drudge Report has been spectacularly popular. It continues to attract between 1.5 million and 2.3 million daily visitors.[§] Despite its popularity and income-producing ability, the site retains a low-tech look without flashy graphics or streaming video. Drudge does use tabloid-style headlines to link to news stories on other websites.

Drudge's influence and popularity as a citizen journalist has led to a variety of reactions concerning his journalistic contributions. He has been described as "a modern Tom Paine, a possible precursor to millions of town criers using the Internet to invade the turf of big-foot journalists."[¶] Others say he is "the kind of bold, entrepreneurial, free-wheeling, information-oriented outsider we need far more in this country."[**] At the same time, Drudge has been labeled as "the country's reigning mischief-maker,"[††] and according to journalist Michael Isikoff: "Drudge is a menace to honest, responsible journalism. And to the extent that he's read and people believe what they read, he's dangerous."[‡‡]

Matt Drudge is a pioneer in political blogging.

©Lawrence Lucier/FilmMagic/Getty Images

Today Matt Drudge lives as a reclusive millionaire in the Miami area and continues to wield political influence. During the 2012 Republican presidential campaign, candidate Fred Thompson and others complained that Drudge was slanting his coverage to favor Mitt Romney.[§§] The claims of bias continued into the 2016 presidential campaign. Conservative opponent Glenn Beck accused Drudge of bias against Hillary Clinton, citing Drudge Report's posting of a dated picture of Clinton with Bill Cosby, the once-beloved entertainer, who has been charged in a sexual assault case.[¶¶] Does the fact that Drudge Report is privately owned and ostensibly made up of "citizen journalists" make it any less bound to adhere to the professional norm of objectivity that professional journalists live by?

[†]Rogers, T. "Website Profile: The Drudge Report: A Pioneering Site Known for Conservative Politics and Rumor-Mongering," http://journalism.about.com/od/webjournalism/a/drudge.htm.

[‡]Ibid.

[§]The Drudge Report Network. Retrieved May 27, 2016, from http://www.drudgereport.com/.

[¶]McClintick, D. "Town Crier for the New Age," www.brillscontent.com/1998/11.

[**]Camille Paglia, "Ask Camille," http://archive.salon.com/col/pagl/1998/09/01pag.12.html.

[††]Todd Purdum, "The Dangers of Dishing Dirt in Cyberspace," http;//select.nytimes.com/1997/08/17/gst/abstract.

[‡‡]"Drudging Up News on the Web," CNN, May 6, 2002, http://edition.cnn.com/2002/ALLPOLITICS/05/06/cf.crossfire/index.html.

[§§]Jennifer Epstein, "Thompson: Mitt Campaign Has Drudge in Their Back Pocket," *Politico*, January 29, 2012, www.politico.com/blogs/politicolive/2012/01/fred-thompson-attacks-romney-campaign-for-having-drudge-112714.html.

[¶¶]Rebecca Mansour, "Glenn Beck Blasts Matt Drudge for Bias Against Hillary: 'How Can We Complain to Facebook About Bias?'" *Breitbart*, May 24, 2016, http://www.breitbart.com/2016-presidential-race/2016/05/24/glenn-beck-blasts-matt-drudge-bias-hillary-can-complain-facebook-bias/.

Political blogs have become quite common today. Some are ideological and some are journalistic. Leading the list of the fifteen favorite sites are Huffington Post, Breitbart, and Drudge Report (see the figure "Top 15 Most Popular Political Websites, July 2017").[49] One of them, Huffington Post, ran the Off the Bus project in 2007. The project paid the expenses to allow 2,500 ordinary persons to cover the 2008 presidential campaign. Arianna Huffington, founder of Huffington Post, was quoted as saying: "At Off the Bus, because they're not part of the professional gaggle, they can come up with their own views of what's happening, which may be different from what the conventional wisdom is saying."[50] One of these ordinary persons was Mayhill Fowler, who made audiotapes of both Bill Clinton's angry tirade concerning a magazine article criticizing him and Barack Obama's comments at a closed fundraising meeting that "bitter" small-town Americans

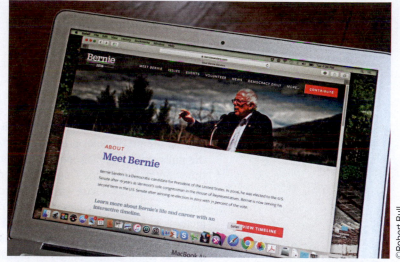

The Bernie Sanders candidacy in 2016 did a phenomenal job raising money online, with average donations of $27.

©Robert Bull

"cling to guns and religion." Governor Romney's 2012 campaign was also hurt when a Democratic opposition researcher (James Carter IV, the grandson of former Democratic president Jimmy Carter) found damaging video on the Internet shot by a bartender at a Florida fundraiser. The clip captured Romney's now-infamous comments concerning "the 47 percent of Americans who are dependent on government." Blogs also played an important role in the 2016 election, sharing views about the stolen and published emails from the Clinton campaign, the *Access Hollywood* tape of candidate Trump discussing ways he groped women, and the overheard Clinton comment that Trump supporters were deplorable.

Practitioners and supporters of blogging argue that it democratizes the media by allowing individuals to communicate to mass audiences. At the same time, however, it fails to provide any mechanism for distinguishing fact from fiction. It is assumed that bloggers exercise less than due diligence in researching their stories and often possess clear and stated political biases. Furthermore, unlike the traditional media, which can retract stories they get wrong, blogging often provides no formal recourse for those who have been treated unfairly. One critic points out that bloggers who attacked CBS for its faulty coverage of George W. Bush's fulfillment of National Guard obligations put out lots of inaccurate information themselves.[51] The bloggers had alleged, for example, that font and print styles used in the document secured by CBS were not available in the year the document was created. Further research by CBS revealed, however, that these options were available on some typewriter models. In sum, blogging allows more people to become involved in media-type activities but without the journalistic norms and traditions of the media.

As the Internet claims its position as a major media outlet, particularly with social media sites like Facebook and Twitter, new problems have arisen. In 2016, Facebook played a major role in the presidential election. In fact, Facebook executives have had to answer questions before Congress as to why they allowed political advertisements paid for by Russian entities as well as untrue articles. One research study has found that Facebook was the most common site for factually dubious articles known as "fake news." These were actually false stories, as opposed to President Trump's use of the "fake news" label to disparage real media outlets with which he disagrees. In a six-week period in 2016, one in four Americans visited a fake news website, but most of the visits were from 10 percent of the users who exhibited the most conservative online diets.[52]

Top 15 Most Popular Political Websites, July 2017

Site	Estimated Unique Monthly Visitors
Huffington Post	80,000,000
Breitbart	60,000,000
Drudge Report	30,000,000
Politico	25,000,000
The Hill	20,000,000
Slate	18,000,000
Daily Kos	15,000,000
InfoWars	9,000,000
Salon	8,000,000
The Blaze	7,700,000
Daily Caller	7,600,000
WND	6,000,000
NewsMax	5,750,000
Washington Time	5,600,000
Mother Jones	5,000,000

Huffington Post and Breitbart led the list of top political websites in 2017. These sites represent an interesting mix of liberal and conservative viewpoints.

Source: eBiz MBA Rank, July 2017.

Game Coverage

The media cover political campaigns much as they cover sports, as if campaigns were a game. They stress winning and losing, with strategy and tactics meriting more attention than a candidate's policy positions, past performance, or potential for future leadership.[53]

The favorite game reference in political coverage is the "horse race." Journalists focusing on horse race coverage rely on four scripts or story ideas: the candidate is leading; the candidate is trailing; the candidate is gaining ground; the candidate is losing ground.[54] During the presidential primaries, horse race coverage compares the candidates' standing in the polls and how much money they have raised. From those comparisons, the media predict the winners and losers. During the Republican nomination battle during the first months of 2012, the media's focus was on the soaring and crashing of the various candidates' front-runner status. The media's coverage of the general election continued to be the horse race analysis consisting of Obama's bounce after the Democratic national convention, Romney's surge after the first debate, and the resulting nearly tied race until Election Day. The coverage also featured the charges of partisans that claimed flawed and dishonest polls and the "doctoring" of government reports that showed decreasing unemployment figures and an improving economy.

In 2016, the media continued to stress the horse race aspect of a presidential campaign. They emphasized Clinton's lead in the polls after having a more successful political convention and victories in the debates. They publicized a crisis in the Trump campaign after the release of the *Access Hollywood* tape. As the campaign continued, the media noted lagging support for Clinton after her near collapse at the 9/11 ceremony due to a case of the flu and her declining numbers when the FBI director announced in late October, just weeks before the election, that the agency was going to examine some Clinton emails that were found on the computer of the estranged husband of one of Clinton's closest aides. The estranged husband, former congressman Anthony Weiner, was part of an ongoing FBI investigation.

The game approach used by journalists in their campaign coverage fits with their cynical and negative approach to politics generally. It also supplies them with an endless series of stories. Every event can be analyzed from the perspective of strategies, motivations, winners, and losers. It is relatively easy for reporters to use this approach. Reporting on complex issues such as nuclear proliferation and health-care reforms requires knowledge and training. The game format requires little familiarity with complex issues.

However, applying the game format to political campaigns can trivialize the democratic process, and when voters lose respect for the process, they are less likely to participate. American journalist James Fallows has written that the media have given us a view of public life that is similar to pro wrestling: "To judge by the coverage, everything is a sham. Conflicts are built up and then they blow over, and no one is sincere. . . ."[55]

Character Issues: Probing Personal Lives

Framing election campaigns as games, with players devising strategies to win at all costs, has in recent decades led the media to increase their probing of candidates' personal lives. After the decline of the partisan press in the early twentieth century, reporters tended to avoid excessive intrusion into politicians' personal affairs. For example, the media never published a photograph of President Franklin D. Roosevelt in a wheelchair, believing that his polio was unrelated to his performance as president. Nor did the media report on the infidelities of President John F. Kennedy, even though they occurred in the White House under the collective noses of the press corps. They evidently concluded that it was a personal matter. Times have changed! The playing of the *Access Hollywood* tape, in which Donald Trump talked about how he could grab women by the genitals because of his fame, is indicative of the new era of political coverage.

In the age of adversarial reporting and "gotcha" journalism, the private lives and personal failures of candidates are now considered fair game. Scholars have cited several reasons for this trend, including media anger at political deception and wrongdoing after the Vietnam War and the Watergate scandal; Supreme Court decisions making it more difficult to sue the media for libel; and television's role in constructing new rules for political coverage. One communications scholar believes this shift in focus from substantive issues to character is the result of the shift from newspaper to television news. Television is a visual medium, and voters who get their news from this source are more likely to be interested in facial reactions and personal traits than in issue positions.[56] Still others, including journalist Cokie Roberts, believe that the addition of women to the press corps has expanded the boundaries of what the media consider relevant to report.[57] As a result of these forces coming together, sex lives, military records, divorce decrees, physical ailments, and tax returns have become fair game for media coverage of elections.

Election Night Coverage

Election night coverage of voting results was once a relatively simple affair; newspapers waited for precincts to count the votes and then reported the results. The emergence of **exit polls** created a new dynamic for election night reporting, because the media would often know in advance which candidate the polls projected to win. Media outlets, eager to be the first to report the story, were tempted to predict the winners based on the poll numbers rather than waiting for the tabulation of actual votes. Calling a presidential election early, however, can discourage people from voting, because the outcome is already known. Thus, the media have agreed not to report any election outcome that would have an impact on races in a state where the polls are still open.

> **exit poll** Interviews of voters as they leave the polling place.

In 2000, under severe budget pressures, the broadcast networks agreed to hire a single firm, Voter News Service, to serve as a common source of exit poll data. The decision to rely on a single source of data proved disastrous. The networks first called Florida's electoral votes for Vice President Al Gore early in the evening, only to retract that call ninety minutes later when the actual vote count indicated that George W. Bush was running ahead of exit poll predictions. Fox then called Florida—and the presidency—for Bush at 2:16 a.m. Eastern Standard Time, followed soon after by the other networks. Less than an hour later, these results came into question when votes from Florida's heavily Democratic Broward County virtually wiped away Bush's lead. By morning, all the networks announced Florida was "too close to call."

The reliance on faulty exit polls was a colossal embarrassment. NBC anchor Tom Brokaw exclaimed that NBC did not have "egg on its face" but rather an "omelet." The networks built new safeguards into their use of exit polling in 2004, but once again the exit polls were inaccurate. They showed Senator Kerry winning both Ohio and Florida, which would have given him enough electoral votes to win the presidency. This time, the networks waited for the actual votes to be counted, and the voters of Ohio and Florida provided enough votes to put President Bush over the top. The networks did not proclaim a winner until the following morning, but at least they got it right. By contrast, some bloggers who had seen early and incomplete exit poll reports had proclaimed Kerry the winner earlier in the day.

The election night coverage for the past four presidential elections was free of mistakes. In 2016, the media continued to be cautious in announcing a winner, but they did almost universally express surprise over the Trump victory. The networks were aware that Trump was behind in nearly all the polls on election eve and that his path to an electoral vote majority was very narrow.

GOVERNMENT COVERAGE IN THE MEDIA

The dynamic that exists between the media and political candidates during campaigns also characterizes media relationships once candidates are elected leaders. Government officials need the public forum the media provide to persuade their constituents to support their policies. Journalists need information from these officials in the form of reports, news releases, speeches, and interviews. Interactions benefit both parties, but relationships sometimes get testy. As the media have become more cynical in their depiction of public life, officials have increased their effort to manage the news by trying to get the media to focus on the issues that portray officials in the best light. Presidents realize that events do not speak for themselves, and therefore a president's success often depends on the interpretations placed on events by the media.

Covering the President

The relationship between the media and the president has always contained some acrimony. During the era of the partisan press, George Washington fumed at the harsh treatment from rival newspapers.[58] His successor, John Adams, became one of the greatest media-bashers in the nation's history. By the time Abraham Lincoln was elected president, the press had become more independent of partisan influence. Although Lincoln attempted to woo editors by giving them exclusive information and interviews, such tactics rarely worked, especially in the crisis atmosphere of the Civil War. Lincoln later censored war-related news and even had editors jailed if he believed their stories gave away military secrets or threatened Northern morale.

As the press became more independent and professional, presidents became more sophisticated in their dealings with reporters. Theodore Roosevelt added a press room to the White House, spawning a permanent White House press corps that would become dependent on the White House as a source of news. He treated the reporters with respect and hired a press secretary to act as a liaison between the president and the White House press corps. Press secretaries are accountable to the president, but if they lose credibility with the media for not telling the truth, the president can suffer from skeptical media coverage. Woodrow Wilson was the first president to conduct regular press conferences, at least one per week for two and a half years. He later came to detest the press corps, because he did not enjoy answering all of the probing questions.[59] The presidency of Franklin D. Roosevelt entailed a dramatic increase in the power of the presidency, as his

©Bettmann/Corbis via Getty Images

By holding frequent news conferences in the White House, President Franklin D. Roosevelt enjoyed positive media coverage longer than any modern president.

administration responded to the dual crises of the Great Depression and World War II. Reporters now sought assignment to the White House because that was where the power resided. Once they arrived, they were flattered when the president greeted them personally. Roosevelt held numerous press conferences and enjoyed the longest media honeymoon of any president in history.[60]

The atmosphere between the media and Presidents Harry Truman, Dwight Eisenhower, and John Kennedy remained friendly, like that of a men's club. Conditions turned more adversarial with the Lyndon Johnson administration. As criticism of the Vietnam War increased, the president became more secretive. The relationship between the media and the president remained very strained during the Nixon years. As the media pursued the Watergate scandal, Nixon became surly and ordered the Internal Revenue Service to audit some of the journalists.

Ronald Reagan's skill at dealing with the media earned him the nickname "The Great Communicator." Reagan's experience as a former actor served him well in the age of television, when the smallest facial gesture or delivery of a phrase could be displayed on an evening news sound bite. His administration planned every day around a "message of the day." Reagan's staff structured his public events each day to emphasize a single theme, with the president visible in a variety of situations though not really accessible to the media. When Reagan's vice president, George H. W. Bush became president, he lacked his predecessor's ease with the media and was unable to communicate his vision for the country.[61] As a result, he appeared in the news less often than Reagan, even though he was personally more accessible. Bush held more press conferences in his four years as president than Reagan did in eight years.

The Clinton administration got off to a bad start with the White House press corps because of its attempts to limit journalists' access to key staff members. The media's coverage of the Clintons' Whitewater land deal, Clinton's involvement with Monica Lewinsky, and his impeachment further soured the administration's relationship with the media.

President George W. Bush ran a tight ship with respect to sharing information with the media. No member of his staff could appear on television or in print without prior approval. The president's visit to New York City in the wake of the 9/11 terrorist attacks catapulted his approval ratings and garnered positive coverage from even formerly critical outlets such as *The New York Times*. The long-running war in Iraq, and the administration's botched response to a series of hurricanes along the nation's Gulf Coast in 2005, changed the climate of coverage. The glowing coverage Bush previously enjoyed soon dissipated. Party identification plays a large role in determining whether one feels that critical coverage does more good than harm. Democrats were more likely to believe criticism of Bush was good for the country; during the Clinton presidency, Republicans were more likely to see criticism of the president as beneficial.

President Obama received generally favorable coverage by the media, with calls for more press conferences and occasionally respectful discussions concerning his foreign policy objectives. The same could not be concluded about the media's relationship with President Trump. Trump continued his war of words with the media after being sworn in as president, by labeling as "fake news" stories he disagreed with and pronouncing many journalists to be "terrible people." The very first press conference of the Trump administration set the stage for the escalating hostility when Press Secretary Sean Spicer clashed with reporters concerning the number of people attending Trump's presidential inauguration. His daily meetings with the press became fodder for *Saturday Night Live* sketches in which Melissa McCarthy played the soon-to-be fired Spicer.

Because favorable media coverage is vital to their success, presidents have increasingly sought to manage it in a number of ways. At press briefings, the president's press secretary exercises some control over the topics discussed and the flow of the questioning. Some members of the press can always be counted on to throw "softball" questions that deflect criticism away from administration policies. The administration exercises even tighter control at background, or restricted, sessions between a presidential aide and the media, at which no questions are taken. Even at live TV press conferences, the president is well briefed about the questions likely to arise and has practiced set responses. Reporters may ask only one follow-up question, and the president decides which reporters to call on for questions.

The administration is especially careful when its lower-level officials speak to the media. It arms them with talking points—prepared arguments supporting administration policies and positions. Talking points are meant to ensure that officials stay "on message" by repeating the same themes the president articulates. The administration also controls its message through press releases, carefully worded official statements that reporters can cite in their articles. When the administration is unsure of the public's reaction to one of its policy options, it might send up a trial balloon—a hypothetical proposal it can back away from if public reaction is negative.

The corps of journalists in Washington, D.C., during the Obama and Trump administrations was somewhat smaller and dramatically transformed from its predecessors some twenty years ago. The traditional media serving the general public have shrunk, but new niche media offering specialized and detailed information to smaller elite audiences with targeted financial and lobbying interests have grown dramatically.

To sum up, there has always been some tension and acrimony between presidents and the media. Modern presidents have tried to control their relationship with the media by having a message of the day, conducting exclusive interviews with certain reporters, and by supplying administration spokespersons with talking points for all interviews. Some presidents like Franklin Roosevelt and Obama have been able to forge mostly positive relations with the media, whereas others like Nixon, Lyndon Johnson, and Trump have had very strained relationships.

Covering Congress

The media cannot possibly pay as much attention to 535 members of Congress as they can to one president. Sometimes, White House pets receive more national media coverage than does the average member of Congress. In addition, Congress lacks a single leader who can speak authoritatively for the entire institution. The majority and minority leaders often have a hard time keeping their own members from breaking ranks. Nevertheless, there are more than three thousand members of the congressional media corps. The Capitol houses four separate press galleries—one each for daily publications, periodicals, photographers, and the electronic media.[62] The number of newspapers and periodicals covering Congress has declined since the 1980s.

The congressional press corps deals with the size and fragmentation of power within Congress by concentrating on three groups of members. First, they cover the Republican and Democratic Party leaders in both the House of Representatives and the Senate, because these members can speak for a majority of their party colleagues. Second, they report on the House and Senate committee chairs whose work deals with an important topic of the day. The media are particularly interested in committee chairs who head up investigations into volatile topics such as the State Department's actions leading up to the attack on Benghazi in Libya and the investigation of the Trump campaign's possible collusion with Russia and Russia's hacking activities related to the 2016 election. Third, local newspapers and broadcast stations like to cover their local legislators. Members of Congress have their own press secretaries and can use the Capitol's recording studios for their interviews. Individual members of Congress get considerable coverage in the local media outlets in their districts and states.

Although members of Congress often get favorable coverage from local media, the same is not true of national press coverage. As with coverage of the president, the national media treat Congress with great cynicism. Media coverage emphasizes partisan conflict, gridlock, and scandal. The media often trivialize congressional policy accomplishments, framing them as partisan victories or defeats. They portray debates over policy questions as power struggles, rather than as principled discussions of reasonable alternatives. Some scholars believe that citizens form negative perceptions of Congress based on such journalism.[63]

Members of Congress make use of news sources to communicate with constituents in the digital age. One study showed that their sharing habits on Facebook revealed the polarized partisan nature of Congress.[64] Nearly 50 percent of the legislators on Facebook used links to national news outlets that are predominantly shared by one party (see "Patterns in Lawmakers' Sharing of Facebook Links"). Republicans relied on such sources as The Daily Signal, Breitbart, *National Review,* and The Daily Caller, whereas Democrats shared posts from ThinkProgress, Vox, Huffington Post, and *The New York Times.* Members of both parties shared with constituents news stories from sources such as *USA Today*, CBS News, and *Roll Call.*

Patterns in Lawmakers' Sharing of Facebook Links

Congressional sharing score, by news outlet

◄ Shared by more liberal members   Shared by more conserv. members ►

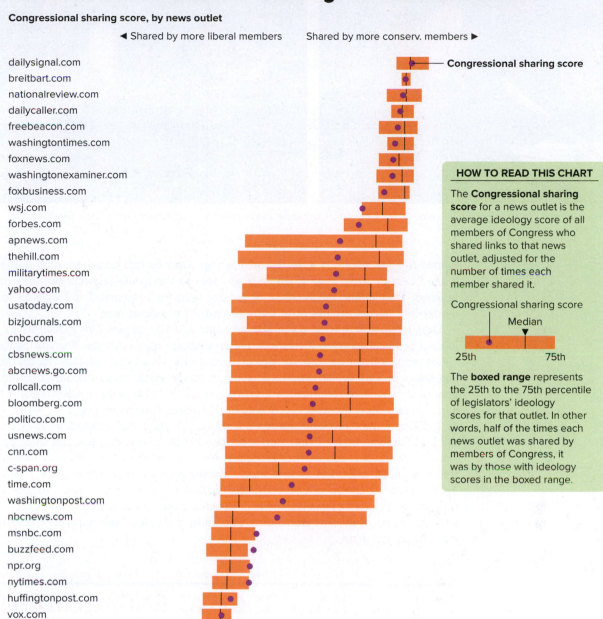

HOW TO READ THIS CHART

The **Congressional sharing score** for a news outlet is the average ideology score of all members of Congress who shared links to that news outlet, adjusted for the number of times each member shared it.

Congressional sharing score

Median

25th   75th

The **boxed range** represents the 25th to the 75th percentile of legislators' ideology scores for that outlet. In other words, half of the times each news outlet was shared by members of Congress, it was by those with ideology scores in the boxed range.

Members of Congress exhibit polarization in the news articles they share with colleagues.

Source: Pew Research Center.

Covering the Supreme Court

Institutional characteristics of the Supreme Court limit its coverage in the media. The key activities of the Court are cloaked in secrecy, and most judicial decisions receive little coverage. The public does not have access to the justices' discussions of the issues, nor their votes on the cases that take place in the conferences, until the judicial opinions are printed and distributed to the media. The justices let their formal opinions speak for themselves; they do not hold press conferences or grant interviews to explain their decisions. Although oral arguments in a case are open to the media and the public, the Court has

Due to a lack of media coverage of the Supreme Court, more Americans know Judge Judy than know Justice Ruth Bader Ginsburg.

refused to allow television to record the hearings. Only on rare occasions, such as the *Bush v. Gore* case in 2000, does it release audiotapes to the media immediately following the hearings. In addition, the language of judicial opinions is technical and difficult to summarize in a few paragraphs or in thirty seconds of broadcast time.

Despite these obstacles, the major networks and newspapers hire specialists to cover judicial proceedings, even if they give the proceedings little coverage. The stories that the media report often deal with ideological splits on the Court and speculate on the winners and losers in a particular judicial outcome. In recent years, the media have become quite interested in judicial confirmation hearings, especially in the wake of allegations of sexual harassment against Supreme Court nominee Clarence Thomas in 1991.

In many ways, Americans are more familiar with state trial courts than they are with the U.S. Supreme Court. Crime stories permeate local news broadcasts, and some criminal trials reach national audiences. Americans were fascinated with the Michael Jackson and Casey Anthony trials, just as they were a decade earlier with the trial of O. J. Simpson. TruTV, formerly known as Court TV, has made it possible for Americans to follow such trials in depth. Court drama is a staple of late-afternoon television programming on network affiliates. More Americans are familiar with Judge Judy than with Supreme Court Justice Ruth Bader Ginsburg.

THE MEDIA AND CIVIC ENGAGEMENT TODAY

Scholars such as Joseph Cappella and Kathleen Hall Jamieson believe modern media culture in America is increasingly fragmented, prone to emphasize negative aspects of our political system, and steeped in cynicism. They argue that it causes people to shun not only political coverage but news in general. We saw earlier that newspaper readership has declined steeply in recent decades, and the decline in network news viewership has been equally drastic. As one network news executive stated: "Network news is basically a corpse that hasn't been pronounced [dead] yet."[65]

There has been a concern that younger generations follow the news substantially less than older generations. Specifically, there is the worry that the millennial generation spend less time following the news on a daily basis. By contrast, older generations such as the silent generation (67- to 84-year-olds) devote more time per day in their daily pursuit of the news.[66]

There is some evidence that adversarial reporting and game coverage of politics cause citizens to lose confidence in political leaders and institutions and to become increasingly cynical.[67] This cynicism extends to the media as well. Americans today are much less likely to believe the media protects democracy than they were in 1985. Only in the first few months after September 11, 2001, did views concerning the media improve temporarily.[68] Ironically, in today's information age, people have become less trusting of the information they receive.

Some observers cite the rise of alternative media, cable, and Internet news as a cause of the decline in news consumption. The wide selection of media outlets today means that many people can avoid news programming altogether. The greater choice among different media has also widened the knowledge gap between people who like news and those who prefer entertainment. Stephen Macedo and his coauthors have concluded, "Those motivated enough to follow the news despite greater availability of other media content are more partisan. The audience that remains for the news is, therefore, more ideologically polarized than in the past."[69] Conservative news consumers turn to Fox for their information; liberals turn to MSNBC or National Public Radio. With all the choices available, citizens who live side by side may have entirely different views of the political world in which they live because of the media choices they make.

Although the trends discussed here are troublesome, particularly in a democracy that depends on informed citizens to make collective judgments on the basis of common information, there are clear signs that Americans—especially the young—are adapting to the new media age. Americans consume news in a completely different way than they did in previous generations. Because news is available twenty-four hours a day, they set their own schedules for getting the news. In this digital age, news consumers can be divided into two broad categories. There are news seekers who actively search out the news and news bumpers who are more likely to discover the news by accident as they are doing other things.[70] Nearly 40 percent of millennials consider themselves news seekers, compared to 65 percent of the total population. However, the desire to become an informed citizen was the number one reason millennials cited for consuming the news (see "Millennials' Reasons for Consuming the News").

Millennials' Reasons for Consuming the News

Becoming an informed citizen is the number one reason Millennials cite for using news and information

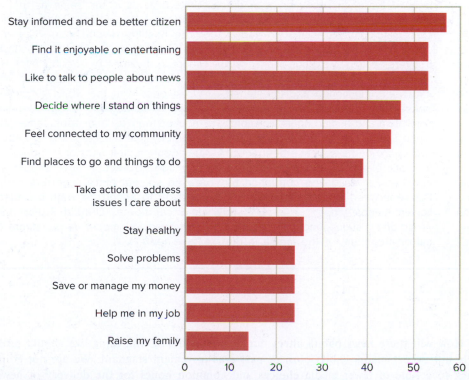

Millennials believe that staying informed makes them better citizens.

Source: Associated Press, NORC Center for Public Affairs Research, and American Press Institute, "How Millennials Get News: Inside the Habits of America's First Digital Generation" page 8, March, 2015.

Attacks on Journalists and Journalism

On July 7, 2017, U.S. president Donald Trump and Russian president Vladimir Putin were chatting with each other at the opening of the G20 summit in Hamburg, Germany. As the two-hour meeting was about to begin and the press were asked to leave, Putin gestured toward the exiting reporters and reportedly asked Trump, "These are the ones who insulted you?" according to a translation from CNN's Jim Sciutto.* Trump broke into a chuckle, and the two leaders continued talking. Placed in the context of Putin's alleged behavior toward Russian journalists and the political and personal attacks on American journalists made by Trump, this moment can be seen to have ominous overtones.

Ten years earlier, internationally acclaimed Russian journalist Anna Politkovskaya was gunned down on the ground floor of her apartment building in what appeared to be a contract killing.† She had worked as a special correspondent for a small liberal newspaper, and many of her stories featured the terror that pervaded the southern republic of Chechnya. Her last story had reported on repeated acts of torture carried out by squads loyal to the pro-Russian prime minister. In the West, Politkovskaya's work brought fame and awards, but in Russia she was isolated, harassed, threatened, and ultimately murdered. At first, Putin tried to ignore her murder and refused to make any gesture of sympathy. At a press conference in Germany, he finally addressed the matter, saying she was "too radical" to have a very strong influence on Russian political life.‡

NBC journalist Katy Tur faced threats of violence as she covered the Trump campaign.

In 2017, less than three months before Putin and Trump shared their chuckle concerning journalists, another well-known critic of Putin died in St. Peterburg, after a severe beating by a group of unknown attackers. Nikolai Andrushchenko, who had been imprisoned and threatened before, had reported on government corruption and human rights violations. Since Putin came to power in Russia, twenty-six journalists have been killed for work-related reasons. Many of them had been investigating corruption by Putin-appointed officials and Putin's billionaire friends.**

No one is suggesting that the political environment for the media in the United States is the same as that in Russia. Yet, Donald Trump has directed more hostility toward journalists and the media generally than any political figure in decades or possibly ever. He has called members of the media "the worst people in the world," accusing them of constantly lying. He has mocked them for their appearance and even physical afflictions. Trump's attorney general, Jeff Sessions, suggested that libel protection laws should be eased so that more reporters could be sent to prison. As both president and candidate, Donald Trump has portrayed the media as purveyors of "fake news."

How will these news habits affect our democracy? For one thing, we should probably not expect media habits born of past eras to remain stagnant. We are not going back to a time of fewer media choices and common hours for the delivery of news. Citizens are finding alternative ways to use the media in constructive ways, and new media hold the promise of reconnecting citizens to their government. It is possible that the multiple ways citizens have today to gather the news may still provide the opportunity

In her recent book, *Unbelievable*, NBC and MSNBC reporter Katy Tur describes how the new Trump environment can impact an individual journalist. She was assigned to the Trump campaign because she happened to be in New York when he announced his candidacy. That assignment began a roller-coaster ride with the candidate, who called her out at campaign events for not looking at him and for being a "little liar." With the unruly atmosphere of many of the Trump rallies, such "call outs" created a dangerous situation for Tur. The situation became so frightening that Secret Service agents had to escort her to her car after a rally. With her new notoriety, she began to receive death threats. One New Yorker confronted her on the street, voiced his complaints about her coverage of the Trump campaign, and then spit in her face.[§]

It is not only journalists who are concerned about the present attacks on the media. In early 2018, Senator Jeff Flake (R-AZ) took to the Senate floor to publicly criticize his fellow Republican, President Trump, on the issue. The senator cited the president's use of the phrase "the enemy of the people" to describe the media, reminding his audience that the phrase was a well-known label used by Russian dictator Joseph Stalin for his enemies. The phrase became so infamous that subsequent Soviet leader Nikita Khrushchev banned its use. Flake stated that the president had the relationship backward: Despotism is the "enemy of the people" and the free press is the enemy of despotism, making it the "guardian of democracy." The senator also criticized the president's use of the term "fake news," because it belittled

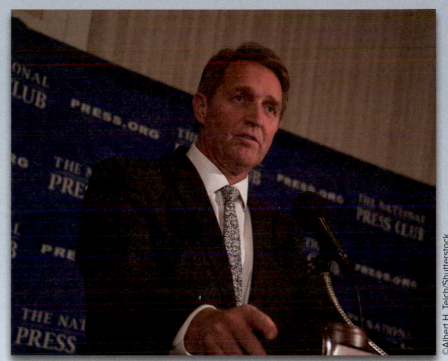

In 2018, Senator Jeff Flake criticized President Trump's attacks on the media.

the sacrifices made by journalists to report the truth. Flake pointed out that, worldwide, eighty journalists were killed in 2017 and a record 262 imprisoned. Flake went on to state that the president's unproven claims about rigged elections and voter fraud, combined with the well-established fact of Russian interference with the 2016 election, undermine the people's trust in public institutions, including the media. Finally, he reminded the president that the values of free expression and reverence for the free press have been global hallmarks of the United States' political system, keeping the government honest and the people free.[¶]

*See Mark Abadi, "Putin Appears to Joke with Trump About Reporters in Front of Them," *Business Insider*, July 2017.

**Leonid Bershidsky, "Commentary: Is It Fair to Call Putin a Killer?", *Chicago Tribune*, February 7, 2017. The author argues that it has not been proven that President Putin has been responsible for the murders.

†See Michael Specter, "Why Are Vladimir Putin's Opponents Dying?" *The New Yorker*, January 29, 2007.

‡ Ibid.

§See Katy Tur, *Unbelievable* (New York: Harper Collins, 2017).

¶A transcript of former senator Jeff Flake's speech can be read in Rachel Wolfe, "Jeff Flake Just Compared Trump's Treatment of the Press to Stalin's," Vox, January 17, 2018, https://www.vox.com/policy-and-politics/2018/1/17/16901130/jeff-flake-senate-speech-fake-news-trump-stalin.

for citizens to reach collective decisions based on information from a variety of news sources.

The traditional media can help their cause by working to correct some of the deficiencies cited by large numbers of news consumers. They can pay more attention to issues than to personalities; make issue coverage more comprehensible to average citizens; examine the impact of policies on the lives of Americans from diverse backgrounds; help remind citizens of their electoral duties and of the times and places they vote; spend less time covering sensational news stories and more on politics; and stop treating politics as a game or spectator sport. Finally, they need to follow those actions in gathering and reporting the news to make themselves more deserving of the public's trust. Educators must do better as well. They must spend more time teaching students how to be selective and critical consumers of media.

Thinking It Through >>>

Learning Objective: Describe the media, and identify their political functions.

Review: Media and Political Campaigns

Studies have shown that Donald Trump won the Republican nomination in 2016 in part because he received more media coverage than all of his Republican opponents combined. Assess how much influence the media has over the outcome of a presidential election.

Summary

1. **How have the media and media consumption changed over the years?**
   - Newspapers were partisan in nature, and their partisanship was rewarded with government jobs and contracts.
   - Technological advances led to cheaper papers, greater circulation, and increased advertising revenues, thus allowing these papers to become politically independent.
   - Near the end of the nineteenth century, many metropolitan newspapers practiced a type of sensationalist journalism known as yellow journalism, but reaction to it led to a more professional press in the twentieth century that would soon be augmented by the broadcast media of radio and television.
   - Today, Americans' consumption of the news has been characterized by a steady decline in the use of newspapers, a decline in news consumption by young persons, and increased fragmentation of audiences due to narrowcasting.

2. **What are the major characteristics of mass media in America?**
   - The mass media in America are privately owned, and that ownership is becoming more concentrated economically.

   - The government regulates the electronic media by setting ownership limits and regulating content.
   - The media emphasize presenting the news in an entertaining fashion.
   - The media during the past three decades have adopted an adversarial approach to the news that leads many Americans to believe the coverage is biased.

3. **How do the media cover political campaigns and government actions?**
   - The media focus on the polls, campaign strategy, and the character of the candidates rather than on the issues.
   - The televised presidential debates offer the candidates an opportunity to speak to the voters in an unfiltered manner.
   - National candidates spend the majority of their funds on paid media advertising that is often negative in tone.
   - Once the elections are over, the media cover the winners, spending more time on the president than the more fragmented Congress and more secretive Supreme Court.
   - The relationship between the media and government is both symbiotic and adversarial.

Chapter 11

Congress
Doing the People's Business

LAST MAN STANDING?

"Serving in the United States Senate has been the great honor of my life," Senator Al Franken (D-MN) told his colleagues from the well of the Senate floor as he announced his resignation from the body following allegations by several women of improper sexual conduct. As the Senate Ethics Committee prepared to investigate the

Senator Al Franken (D-MN) announced he was stepping down from his seat after several women came forward and accused him of sexual misconduct. Franken was one of several members accused of harassment or misconduct during the 115th session of Congress (2017–2019).

Source: Senate TV via AP

charges against him, his Democratic colleagues urged him to step down. Heeding their call, Franken admitted "it's become clear that I can't both pursue the Ethics Committee process and at the same time remain an effective senator."[1] The governor of Minnesota quickly moved to appoint the state's lieutenant governor, a woman, as Franken's replacement.

Following Franken's resignation, the dominoes began to fall as allegations against other members of Congress surfaced. One by one, congressmen from Michigan, Texas, Arizona, and Nevada decided to end their legislative careers in the face of charges of harassment or other charges of sexual wrongdoing. Clearly, this was a reckoning for Congress and a signal that women would no longer sit passively by while men abused their authority. Within

As You READ

- What powers does Congress have?
- What are some factors affecting election to Congress?
- What are the keys to political power in Congress?

a short period of time, new measures were adopted in the House to deal with charges of sexual harassment against members and to protect those filing complaints.

What made these revelations so salient is the fact that women are vastly underrepresented in the halls of Congress. Although women make up over 50 percent of the U.S. population,[2] the percentage of women in Congress is just slightly more than 20 percent.[3] It can be argued that the lack of women in Congress contributes to the hostile environment faced by female staffers and interns. More important, however, it means that the views of women are less likely to be heard on matters ranging from health care to warfare. And there is evidence that women legislators have a more collaborative work style than men, enabling them to more effectively work together to get things done.[4] As more and more women seek congressional office, we may witness a change in how the institution functions.

In this chapter, we will examine the complex forces at work in the current legislative process, one that is slow, deliberative, often driven by arcane rules—and sometimes riven with partisan division and factional strife. It is a process that sometimes resembles a chess match, in which each side attempts to entrap the opponent and win control of the board, frequently resulting in stalemate. It is a game, however, with high stakes—for the political interests with a stake in the outcome; for the members who face continual electoral scrutiny; for **constituents**, the citizens these elected officials represent; and for future generations that will have to live with the consequences of congressional action or inaction. ∎

constituents The citizens from a state or district that an elected official represents.

ORIGIN AND POWERS OF CONGRESS

bicameral Composed of two houses.

Great Compromise The agreement at the Constitutional Convention to split the legislature into two bodies—one apportioned by population, the other assigning each state two members.

When the Framers met in Philadelphia to devise a new system of government, they turned their attention first to the body that would make laws. Although some delegates called for a single body to represent all citizens—called a unicameral form—most colonists were more familiar with **bicameral**, or two-chamber, legislatures. In most colonies, the upper house represented the interests of the Crown and its colonial governors, and the lower body represented the interests of freemen. Not only were the Framers more familiar with the bicameral form, but a two-chamber legislature also resonated with their belief that legislative authority itself should be subject to checks, with the lower house reflecting the will of the common man while the upper chamber protected the interests of the wealthy and well-educated elite in the states.

Some delegates to the Constitutional Convention called for proportional representation in both houses of Congress. Under such an arrangement, the three most populous states—Virginia, Pennsylvania, and Massachusetts—would have commanded almost half the seats in both the upper house (the Senate) and the lower house (the House of Representatives). Luther Martin of Maryland reflected the views of many small-state delegates when he called the plan a "system of slavery which bound hand and foot ten states of the Union and placed them at the mercy of the other three."[5]

After nearly two months of deliberation, the delegates finally reached what scholars refer to as the **Great Compromise**. They agreed to give each state two seats in the

Senate, while apportioning seats in the House according to population. This satisfied the demands of smaller states by giving them an equal voice with larger states in at least one chamber.

The delegates carved out a number of differences between the two houses. The House of Representatives was the "people's house" with its members elected directly by the people. The Senate, however, was designed to safeguard the rights of the states and minorities against mass opinion. As a result, state legislatures elected senators until 1913, when ratification of the Seventeenth Amendment provided for the direct popular election of senators. Most of the delegates favored short terms of office and frequent elections to keep lawmakers on a short leash. James Madison, however, debated that members of Congress needed time to learn and ply the legislative art. A compromise fixed a two-year term for members of the House and a staggered six-year term for senators, with one-third of the Senate coming up for election every two years.

The specific powers granted to Congress by Article I, Section 8, of the Constitution are known as **enumerated powers**. The chart "Enumerated Powers by Function" lists some of the most important of these. Most notably, Congress has the power to make laws, including those that are "necessary and proper" for carrying out other duties. Over time, Congress has used this phrase, sometimes known as the **elastic clause**, to expand the reach of the federal government. It gives Congress the ability to adapt to changing circumstances unforeseen at the time the Constitution was written. For example, Congress today makes laws establishing agencies and procedures to protect the environment, a consideration that was hardly a worry for the Framers.

Enumerated Powers by Function*

Financial & Economic Powers

Power to levy and collect taxes and duties (expanded by the Sixteenth Amendment in 1913 to include taxing income)
Power to borrow money
Power to regulate commerce with foreign nations and among states
Power to coin money
Power to fix standards of weights and measures
Power to punish counterfeiters
Power to grant patents and copyrights
Power to establish uniform laws on bankruptcy
Power to establish post office and post roads

Defense-Related Powers

Power to declare war
Power to raise and support armies
Power to create and maintain the navy
Power to regulate the armed forces
Power to organize the militia (today's National Guard) and to call the militia into national service to defend against rebellion

Checks & Balances

Power to impeach federal officials
Power to establish lower federal courts along with specifying (with some exceptions in the case of the Supreme Court) the kinds of cases each can hear
Power to override presidential veto

Legislative Power

Power to make all laws necessary and proper for carrying out foregoing powers
Power to govern the District of Columbia

Article I of the Constitution spells out the powers specifically granted to Congress.

*Congress also has a role in the process of succession to the Office of President should a vacancy occur, a procedure that was clarified and strengthened with the adoption of the Twenty-Fifth Amendment in 1967.

Although both houses have a hand in making laws, each house has its own distinctive powers as well. For example, all revenue bills must start in the House of Representatives, an acknowledgement from the Framers that taxation requires the consent of the common people. The lower House also initiates impeachment of federal officials (as will be discussed later). The Senate has the additional authority to ratify treaties and confirm presidential appointments. It also acts as the trial court for impeachments. Whereas the House chooses the president in the case of an electoral vote tie, the Senate chooses the vice president in such cases. The qualifications for holding office are also somewhat different for the House and the Senate, as noted in the chart "Major House and Senate Differences".

The delegates to the Constitutional Convention also debated which powers to accord to Congress and which to **reserve** to the states. For example, the powers to regulate trade within a state and to establish local governments are powers the states are granted, as was discussed in Chapter 3.

Article I of the Constitution also explicitly denies Congress certain powers, including granting of titles of nobility, imposing certain types of taxes, and suspending certain categories of individual rights. Of course, the actions of other branches also limit congressional power. The balance of power between Congress and the executive branch has changed throughout history as each has jockeyed for control over the nation's political

enumerated powers The list of specific powers granted to Congress by Article I, Section 8, of the Constitution.

elastic clause The provision of Article I of the Constitution authorizing Congress to make those laws necessary and proper for carrying out the other laws it passes.

reserved powers Powers constitutionally allocated to the states.

Major House and Senate Differences

House	Senate
Apportioned on basis of population	Equal representation (2) from each state
Fixed (since 1911) at 435 members	100 members
Two-year terms	Six-year terms (one-third elected every two years)
Members must be at least 25 years of age, 7 years a citizen, and reside in the state from which chosen	Members must be at least 30 years of age, 9 years a citizen, and reside in the state from which chosen
Power to impeach federal officeholders	Power to try federal office-holders who have been impeached
Initiate bills raising revenue	Approve treaties, cabinet-level appointments, and appointments to the Supreme Court
Choose president in case of electoral vote tie (Article II). In case no presidential candidate receives a majority, the House chooses from the top three vote getters.	Choose the vice president in case of tie (Article II)*

The qualifications for election to the House and the Senate differ, as do several of the powers granted each chamber.

*Originally, the Constitution accorded the vice presidency to the runner-up in the presidential election, provided the presidential candidate received a majority of electoral votes. This procedure was altered by the Twelfth Amendment (1804), which provided for separate ballots in the selection of the president and the vice president.

agenda. In Chapter 14, we will see how the judicial branch can limit the power of Congress by challenging the constitutionality of congressional actions.

CIVIC LIFE AND CONGRESSIONAL CHANGE

Congress has responded to changes in American civic life by becoming more open and hospitable to involvement by an increasingly diverse citizenry. Minorities and women, once denied a formal role, are a growing presence in the halls of Congress. Today, Americans enjoy unprecedented access to their representatives and senators through websites, email, phone calls, letters, Facebook, and Twitter. Thousands of groups representing almost every conceivable interest give citizens the opportunity to amplify their individual voices in pressuring members of Congress to respond to their concerns. Access and openness did not come easily or all at once, however. Powerful interests, strong and obstinate leaders in control of legislative procedures, and clashes with other branches of government have all stymied change at one time or another. And the power of Congress itself has waxed and waned over time as our institutions of government have responded to changing times.

Building the Institution

When the first session of the U.S. Congress met in New York City in 1789, many of the members knew each other personally from serving together on other governing bodies, including colonial legislatures. The new Congress moved quickly to create committees, prescribe the powers of leadership, and place limits on floor debate, but most policy initiatives in these early days, including the call for a national bank and the funding of canals for commerce, came from the office of the president.

The elimination of property qualifications for voting led political leaders to mobilize newly enfranchised citizens into political parties. Control of Congress soon became a political contest with the strongest party in each chamber assuming the leadership positions. President Andrew Jackson (1829–1837) used his popularity with voters to assert authority over members of his own party in Congress by rewarding those members who supported his proposed legislation and punishing those who opposed him. Few presidents in subsequent decades would enjoy such power at the expense of Congress.

As Congress admitted additional states to the Union, the Senate became the preeminent forum for debate on the issues dividing the Union, eclipsing the presidency as the hub for policy formation. Floor debates could be intense—and violent. In 1856, Congressman Preston Brooks of South Carolina assaulted Senator Charles Sumner, an antislavery advocate from Massachusetts, on the Senate floor. Brooks beat Sumner senseless with a walking stick over Sumner's opposition to admitting Kansas to the Union as a slave state.[6] Debate and compromise, it seemed, could not bridge the growing divide over slavery. By the time Abraham Lincoln was elected president in 1860, hope for avoiding dissolution of the Union had all but faded. A bloody civil war ended slavery in the United States and opened the way for greater citizen participation by enfranchising all former male slaves. Southern states elected the first black members of Congress, including thirteen ex-slaves.

In the years that followed the Civil War, Congress dominated national affairs as attention shifted from regional concerns to those that were more national in scope, like completion of the transcontinental railroad and the development of a national economy. Serving in Congress became a profession and turnover less frequent.

Control of the legislative process by party leaders was also on the rise. At the beginning of the twentieth century, Republican Speaker of the House Joseph "Uncle Joe" Cannon gained enormous influence, controlling the timing and content of bills brought to the floor, effectively rewarding or punishing fellow members in exchange for their votes. Partisan power was just as strong in the Senate, which many Americans considered a "millionaire's club" that represented only the interests of party bosses and big business trusts.

The Era of Reform

The **Progressive Era** (1890–1920) brought significant reforms to the nation that chipped away at the autocratic power of leaders like Cannon. The era saw passage of pure food and drug laws, restrictions on child labor, and anti-trust laws designed to outlaw monopoly business practices—all over the objections of Speaker Cannon. The reforms were made possible by a coalition of Democrats and "insurgent" Republicans reacting to widespread public support for these measures. Eventually, the reformers wrested control of the House from Speaker Cannon in 1910 and brought the chamber more in line with the public's growing demand for greater openness and transparency in government.

Progressive Era The period of social activism from roughly the 1890s to the 1920s, resulting in widespread political reform.

The Seventeenth Amendment (1913) gave voters the power to elect senators directly, taking it out of the hands of local and state party bosses who had dominated the process for decades. Rule changes in both the House and the Senate further curtailed the power of party leaders. Another landmark change came in 1917, when Jeannette Rankin became the first female House member after spearheading a successful drive for women's suffrage in her home state of Montana.

The Resurgent Executive Branch

A shift in power away from Congress became increasingly apparent during the presidencies of Theodore Roosevelt and Woodrow Wilson. With the election of Franklin D. Roosevelt in 1932, the shift became a central fact of American political life. With commanding Democratic majorities in both houses, FDR rushed through Congress numerous emergency measures to spur economic recovery during the Great Depression of the 1930s. The first one hundred days of Roosevelt's administration were some of the most prolific in legislative history.

By 1937, however, disputes over the constitutionality of Roosevelt's New Deal legislation led conservative southern Democrats in the House

In 1917, Jeannette Rankin (R-MT) became the first woman to serve in Congress, even before women were granted suffrage by the Nineteenth Amendment.

to defect and form an alliance with Republicans. This conservative group created new rules designed to slow or block presidential initiatives. Southern Democrats gained control of powerful committees, which became the key power centers, and they were able to stymie progressive legislation. However, cracks in Democratic solidarity also led to brief periods of Republican control of Congress after World War II. Republicans took control of the House from 1947 to 1949, and both the House and the Senate briefly from 1953 to 1955.

The Rights Revolution and Partisan Polarization

The civil rights movement of the 1950s and 1960s opened a rights revolution in which many groups sought protective legislation for various causes. Women, minority groups, environmentalists, government reform advocates, as well as organized interests opposing these causes, streamed to Washington in a new wave of activism. At the same time, Congress itself became more diverse. The Senate welcomed its first Asian American, Hiram Fong, in 1959; its first Native American, Ben Nighthorse Campbell, in 1993; and its first African American woman, Carol Moseley Braun, in 1993.

Newly elected representatives sought not only new legislation but also changes in the way Congress operated. They helped wrest control from chairmen of powerful committees who had come to dominate the legislative process and opened committee meetings to the public. By the late 1970s, the baronial congressional system in which key committee chairs controlled the substance and flow of legislation faded as rank-and-file party members demanded and received a more significant role in the legislative process.

To be effective, however, party members had to be team players. Legislative success required party leaders to settle internal party differences and develop strategies for passing legislation.[7] It became increasingly important for party members to unite over priorities and to trust their leaders to use chamber rules to achieve legislative victory, a feat more easily accomplished if their party held a majority of seats in the chamber. Members of the party holding a minority of seats also found it necessary to unite in opposition in the hopes of stalling legislation they opposed.[8] The result today is a highly polarized Congress in which partisan divisions have become more prominent and party leaders have become more important in the legislative process.

Polarization in Congress: Ideological Differences Between Parties in the House and the Senate (114th Congress, 2015–2017)

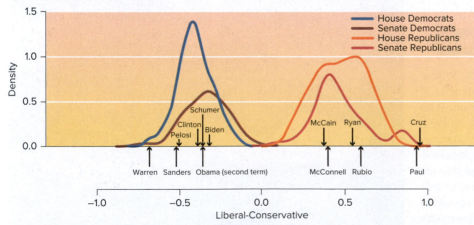

The ideological divide between the parties is growing in both the House and the Senate, with Democrats clustering around the liberal end of the policy spectrum and Republicans, around the conservative end. Names of party leaders most closely associated with these positions are listed for reference.

Source: https://voteviewblog.com.

The gap between conservative Republican members on one side of the aisle and liberal Democratic members on the other is wider today than it has been since the period following the Civil War.[9] The result is a contentious partisan atmosphere, tending toward dysfunction, gridlock, and stalemate as each party struggles to control the legislative agenda, often with razor-thin margins (see the figure "Polarization in Congress"). We will return to the ways in which extreme partisanship impacts legislative outcomes.

Understanding how Congress operates within this political atmosphere means knowing the roles played by party, position, and procedure—the keys to getting legislation passed. Before we examine these keys, however, we need to understand how congressional elections are conducted and how our electoral system affects the quality of representation we receive.

GETTING ELECTED

The challenges facing those wishing to serve in Congress are steep. Individuals who decide to run must muster significant resources on their own to secure their party's nomination. Even after winning a party primary, candidates continue to be largely responsible for their own campaigns, having to commit both the substantial blocks of time necessary for campaigning and the money needed to hire professional consultants and advertising. Challengers face greater obstacles than incumbents, who enjoy advantages like name recognition. Candidates for the House rarely stop campaigning because they must face the voters every two years. They also face the challenge of running in districts whose geographic boundaries shift with population changes.

Resources

The average congressional district contains about 710,700 people. Imagine trying to get a message out to that many voters! Few people can afford to spend the countless hours necessary to greet voters, solicit funds from individuals and interest groups, and make campaign appearances while maintaining a full-time job. This is one reason Congress includes few Americans from blue-collar occupations. Wealthy individuals may be able to take enough time away from their jobs to run for office, but most Americans don't have this flexibility.

Money is another critical resource for congressional candidates, because getting a message out to voters requires lots of it. In 2016, candidates for House seats spent an average of $735,576 running for office. Senate candidates spent an average of $3,120,057. The expenses of high-profile races, however, dwarf these average figures. Over $188 million was spent by candidates and outside groups in the hotly contested Pennsylvania senate race in 2016.[10] Candidates—especially challengers and those running in close races—must continuously solicit funds from individual contributors and PACs (political action committees—see Chapter 9). Even candidates from **safe districts**, those in which the candidate from the dominant party consistently wins 55 percent of the vote or more, are almost continuously raising large sums of money, much of which they share with party members in more competitive districts. One congressman describes the time devoted to fundraising this way:

> When I was here in Washington, I would go over to the NRCC [National Republican Congressional Committee] or the Senatorial Committee offices to make telephone calls (for) an hour, two hours every day. When I was home in Florida, which was a good portion of the time, that's the bulk of what I did. It's a very time-consuming process, on the telephone mostly, organizing fundraisers or getting individual people to contribute.[11]

Because candidates spend so much time soliciting funds from organized interests and wealthy donors, they may be better versed in the needs of these groups than in the wishes of the average voter. Of course, Congress itself is composed largely of the wealthy and near wealthy. The median wealth for a senator in 2015 was around $3 million; for a member of the House it was nearly $1 million.[12]

safe district An electoral district in which the candidate from the dominant party usually wins by 55 percent or more.

The Incumbency Factor

Even in years that witness historic electoral change, incumbents generally have a big advantage over challengers. In fact, incumbency is the single biggest advantage in congressional elections. The chart "The Power of Incumbency" shows the level of success House incumbents have enjoyed since 1994. After a dip in 2010, when Democrats were ousted in large numbers by a Republican wave, retention rates for incumbents returned to historic high levels in recent years with 93 percent of House members seeking reelection returned to office in 2018. (More than 60 members resigned, retired, or preferred to run for other offices in 2018–the most since 1992.) Turnover in the Senate has been slightly higher in recent years with incumbent Democrats losing a number of highly competitive seats in 2018 in an environment that favored the opposition.

The Power of Incumbency

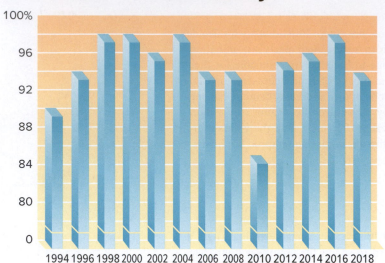

Excludes those resigning, retiring, running for other offices, and incumbents running against incumbents. Compiled from *Congressional Quarterly*, *various years*, and various news reports in 2018. Although Americans complain about the poor performance of Congress, we regularly return a high percentage of incumbents to office.

Money and Incumbency: Senate and House Fundraising by Type of Seat

Senate

Type of Candidate	Total Raised	Number of Cands	Avg Raised
Incumbent	$368,532,005	29	$12,708,000
Challenger	$203,163,709	127	$1,599,714
Open Seat	$114,716,739	64	$1,792,449
Grand Total	**$686,412,453**	**220**	**$3,120,057**

House

Type of Candidate	Total Raised	Number of Cands	Avg Raised
Incumbent	$664,873,622	418	$1,590,607
Challenger	$149,000,679	643	$231,727
Open Seat	$214,460,277	337	$636,381
Grand Total	**$1,028,334,578**	**1,398**	**$735,576**

One reason for incumbent success is the ability to attract more campaign funds than challengers. Figures include all candidates who have filed reports.

Source: Center for Responsive Politics, "Incumbent Advantage," https://www.opensecrets.org/overview/incumbs.php. Based on data released by the FEC on May 18, 2017.

One reason incumbents are so hard to unseat is the advantage they hold in raising money. Donors are more likely to give to candidates they believe will win; because donors know that incumbents are more likely to be successful, they give more to incumbents. This circular logic creates a self-fulfilling prophecy that reinforces and helps sustain the power of incumbency. In 2016, House and Senate incumbents far outspent challengers (see the chart "Money and Incumbency"). Business and labor PACs give overwhelmingly to incumbents, whereas ideological groups are more likely to take a chance on challengers whose views they support.[13] The party holding the majority of seats in Congress also typically enjoys a fundraising advantage because it controls a majority of the positions of power in the body, as we will see.

Incumbents, unlike challengers, also enjoy the advantage of visibility, that is, the ability to keep their names and faces in front of the public. For example, sitting members have limited use of **franking privileges** that allow them to send newsletters, questionnaires, and letters to constituents at the government's expense, except in the last days of a campaign. Challengers must finance their own mailings. Incumbents can also get free news exposure by announcing new programs for their local communities and talking with the local media about legislation before Congress. Such exposure reinforces name recognition among voters. Finally, incumbents can offer constituents help in securing assistance from government agencies, a practice known as **casework**. For example, an Iraq War veteran may ask her congressperson for help in securing educational benefits. Voters are likely to reward a member of Congress who makes the effort to help them navigate the bureaucratic maze to resolve problems with government personnel or agencies. This helps to explain why most constituents believe their representative is doing a good job despite the disdain most have for Congress as a whole.

Midterm Elections

Midterm elections—those contested in years between presidential elections—draw an average of 20 percent fewer voters than do presidential elections. In 2018, voter turnout is estimated to have have topped 49%, the highest midterm turnout in 104 years.

Turnout this high is unusual in midterms and reflected an electorate energized by issues including healthcare and immigration. Scholars have advanced many theories to explain voter drop-off in midterm elections, including election fatigue (that is, a sense of political exhaustion after the sometimes bruising politics of presidential elections), less media coverage of political contests below the level of the presidency, and voter apathy.

Candidates in midterm elections confront an electoral environment that is somewhat different from that of presidential election years. First, only the most committed partisans are likely to vote in midterm races. Voters with weak or no partisan ties are harder to mobilize; only the visibility and media focus of a presidential contest will draw their active involvement. Second, the issues that motivate strong partisans often work against members of the president's party. Midterm voters sometimes use their ballots to register dissatisfaction with the president by voting against members of the same party in congressional races.

As a rule, the president's party usually loses seats in midterm elections, as the honeymoon between voters and the president wears off. Even if a sitting president is popular, candidates from the president's party rarely benefit from their partisan ties to the president when he is not on the ballot or when he fails to campaign vigorously for congressional members of his own party. The figure "Gains and Losses of Congressional Seats for the Party of the President in Midterm Elections" illustrates wide variation in the pattern of midterm losses for the president's party in the House. The elections of 2010 proved particularly painful for Democrats, who, stung by criticism of the Affordable Care Act and the slow pace of economic recovery, lost more than sixty seats in the House and with them their majority status. The loss was the largest for a sitting president since 1938 and erased virtually all of the gains the Democrats had made in the previous two congressional elections. Occasionally, however, voters reward the president's party with a bonus, as they did in 1998, reflecting satisfaction with the economy under Bill Clinton's administration, and in 2002, when they signaled their support for George W. Bush's handling of the "War on Terror" following the 9/11 attacks. In 2018, the Republican party lost the most seats in the House since 1974 but far below Democratic losses in previous years. In the Senate, the president's party has lost seats six of the last ten midterm elections but added a number of seats in 2018.

Gains and Losses of Congressional Seats for the Party of the President in Midterm Elections

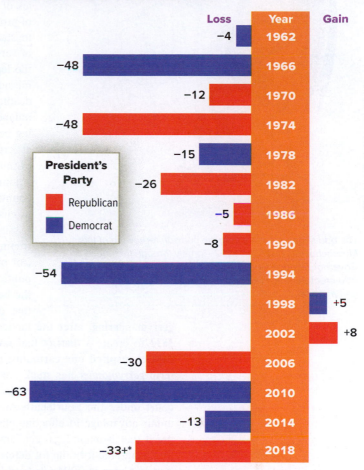

Loss	Year	Gain
−4	1962	
−48	1966	
−12	1970	
−48	1974	
−15	1978	
−26	1982	
−5	1986	
−8	1990	
−54	1994	
	1998	+5
	2002	+8
−30	2006	
−63	2010	
−13	2014	
−33+*	2018	

President's Party
■ Republican
■ Democrat

The party of the sitting president generally loses seats in midterm elections.

Source: *Congressional Quarterly* various years and news reports at time of publication for 2018. *Republican losses at time of publication not including races too early to call and recounts.

Redistricting

Senators represent states whose boundaries do not change despite fluctuations in population. House members, however, represent districts whose populations are constantly in flux. To ensure equal representation despite population shifts, the Constitution prescribes that the boundaries of congressional districts be redrawn every ten years on the basis of Census data. The change in district boundaries is called **redistricting**. Supreme Court rulings in the 1960s made it clear that the size of the population within each district must be relatively equal.[14] The Supreme Court has also ruled that redistricting may take place more often.[15] Because Congress permanently fixed the total number of seats in the House at 435 in 1911, the number of seats allocated to some states will increase as their populations grow while the number allocated to others will decrease as their populations fall. This reallocation of seats among states is called **reapportionment**. Over the past few decades, states in

franking privilege Free postage for members of Congress to communicate with constituents.

casework The practice of finding solutions to constituent problems, usually involving government agencies.

redistricting The practice of drawing congressional district boundaries to accord with population changes.

reapportionment The periodic reallocation of 435 House seats among and within the states as population shifts from one region to another.

THE GERRY-MANDER.

The odd shape resulting from the partisan redrawing of this Massachusetts district in 1812—largely through the efforts of Governor Elbridge Gerry—inspired one cartoonist to depict it as a creature much like a salamander, giving rise to the term gerrymander.

the Northeast and Midwest generally have lost seats, while southern and western states have made gains. For example, New York lost two seats after the 2010 reapportionment due to population loss, and Texas picked up four seats as its population grew.

When states gain or lose seats, they must redraw the boundaries of each congressional district. States have adopted a variety of procedures to redraw district boundaries. Most give this power to state legislatures; some states employ advisory commissions of various sorts that may include members of the public though the legislators have final approval. Still others use backup commissions composed of elected officials in case the legislature deadlocks. Finally, some states, like Arizona and California, use independent commissions with primary responsibility for redrawing boundary lines with members largely drawn from the public at large. In all cases, states are expected to follow several rules of thumb: boundaries should be compact, be contiguous (that is, adjoining or bordering one another), avoid splitting cities or counties, and balance the size of the population in each district to ensure the principle of "one person, one vote."

Since political bodies control the process in most states, redistricting is subject to partisan manipulation. Party leaders in control of state legislative chambers work with demographers and political consultants to fashion districts that give their own party the best chance for controlling the majority of seats. This practice of drawing boundaries for partisan advantage is called **gerrymandering**, after the tactics employed by Massachusetts governor Elbridge Gerry in 1812 to create a district that favored Republicans over Federalists. The odd shape of the district inspired one cartoonist to depict it as a creature much like a salamander, and the term *gerrymander* has stuck ever since.

The Supreme Court ruled in 1986 that partisan gerrymandering could be challenged in court under the Fourteenth Amendment if it could be shown that it gives one group an unfair advantage in affecting election outcomes.[16] However, it set such a high standard of proof that it made legal challenges of such districts extremely difficult. The court failed to find a suitable formula for determining when partisan gerrymandering violated the constitution in a case in 2004 (*Richard Vieth, Norma Jean Vieth, and Susan Furey, v. Robert Jubelirer, President of the Pennsylvania Senate, et al.* No. 02–1580). In 2018, the Supreme Court declined once again to settle the issue by, in one case, sending the matter back to the state where the appellants would be allowed to present more compelling evidence that partisan redistricting in Wisconsin had an adverse impact on the voters in that state; (*Gill v. Whitford*, No. 16-1161); and, in the other, by upholding a lower court's refusal to block Maryland's redistricting map because of legal uncertainty surrounding the issue (*Benisek v. Lamone*, No. 17-333).

Some critics of Congress blame partisan gerrymandering for reducing competitiveness in House races. Reformers have called for more widespread use of nonpartisan commissions like those already employed in some states to take over the job from politicians with a vested interest in the outcome. Studies show, however, that partisan redistricting is not entirely to blame for high levels of reelection of incumbents.[17] Demographic changes have led some districts and states to become more politically homogeneous,[18] potentially increasing the number of safe seats for one party. We will revisit this issue at the end of the chapter.

Because some states had a history of racial discrimination, the 1965 Voting Rights Act outlawed **racial gerrymandering**, the practice of redrawing legislative districts in a manner that minimizes the influence of racial minorities. Prior to this law, residents in regions with large black populations were spread across many different voting districts so as to dilute their impact on the election outcome in any given district. To counter this practice, the Voting Rights Act required the federal government to grant prior approval or "preclearance" of election practices and district boundaries in some, mostly southern, states where the practices had been most egregious. In 2013, however, the U.S. Supreme Court held that conditions in these states had sufficiently improved so that preclearance was no longer

gerrymandering The practice of drawing congressional boundaries to the advantage of one party.

racial gerrymandering The practice of redrawing legislative districts in a manner that minimizes the likelihood that minorities will be able to elect their preferred candidate.

©Bettmann/Corbis via Getty Images

necessary.[19] In 2018 (*Abbot v Perez*), the court ruled that individuals or groups alleging racial discrimination in redistricting must demonstrate intent on the part of the state, making it more difficult to bring similar claims in the future.

However, under certain circumstances, the Court has permitted the creation of so-called **majority-minority districts**. These are districts where a language or racial minority is consolidated to create a voting majority where the group's preferred candidate has a better chance of success—just the opposite of what happened with racial gerrymanders. At one time, the Justice Department encouraged the creation of such districts to combat the legacy of past discrimination. More recently, the Court has tightened the rules applying to such districts, ruling for example that the minority population in the district must constitute at least 50 percent of the population while remaining geographically compact. The court has approved some of these districts and disallowed others.[20]

Scholars are still debating the impact of majority-minority districts. There is some evidence that majority-minority districts increase participation by African Americans and Hispanic Americans without diminishing turnout among whites. Districts where African Americans and Hispanic Americans together constitute a majority report higher turnout among both groups.[21] Nevertheless, by compressing minorities into fewer districts, this form of gerrymandering may also increase the number of districts that elect white majority representatives who may be less sympathetic to the needs of minority populations.[22] As a result, majority-minority districts may actually work against achieving the policies that many minorities support, even as they ensure a higher number of minority members in Congress.

> **majority-minority district** A district in which minority members are clustered together, producing a majority of minority voters in the district.

DOING THE JOB: RESPONSIBILITIES AND BENEFITS

Once elected, members of the House of Representatives and the Senate face a variety of tasks besides their primary function of making laws. They must deal with constituents and represent their interests in government; meet with lobbyists and interest groups; consult with fellow members; and work with policy experts on their staffs. Members receive substantial resources to help them carry out these functions.

Representing the People

One of the oldest issues facing members of Congress is how to interpret their roles as representatives. Should representatives mirror the views of their constituents on all votes, or should they exercise their own judgment on behalf of the citizens who have elected them to make such decisions? A more recent debate has arisen around the question of whether the makeup of Congress should reflect the socioeconomic, gender, and racial composition of the nation. If not, is our national legislature truly representative?

Styles of Representation If you found yourself elected to Congress, how would you go about representing your constituents? Would you adopt a **delegate** style, attempting to mirror the views of your constituents on each and every issue coming up for a vote? Or, would you act as their **trustee**, exercising your own judgment on behalf of those you serve? A moment's thought will show the difficulty in adhering strictly to either course. For one thing, it is difficult to know exactly what your constituents think about every issue among the hundreds of issues upon which you will be expected to vote. For another, you may be privy to classified information that changes your views about what your constituents are demanding. For example, voters in your district may oppose stricter screening regulations at airports but you may have information about potential terrorism threats that convinces you the measures are needed despite the inconvenience they may cause your constituents. At the same time, you don't want to stray so far from your constituents that you sacrifice reelection. Neither do you want to ignore the wishes of your party leaders for fear of finding your own priorities shelved by the leadership.

> **delegate style** A style of representation stressing the lawmaker's role as a tribune of the people who reflects their views on issues of the day.
>
> **trustee style** A style of representation stressing the lawmaker's own judgment in legislative decision making.
>
> **politico** A style of representation in which the lawmaker attempts to balance the views of constituents, interest groups, and party leaders with his or her own ideological leanings.

TO DIVERSIFY CONGRESS, EXPAND THE PIPELINE

Today's Congress is more diverse than ever before. Yet, women hold only 20 percent of the seats in Congress while making up almost 51 percent of the U.S. population. African Americans constitute 13 percent of the U.S. population but occupy just 8 percent of congressional seats. The same disproportion holds for Hispanics and Latinos, who make up 17 percent of the population but occupy only 6 percent of the seats in Congress. And America's fastest growing ethnic group, Asian Americans, hold only 2 percent of the seats in Congress while constituting 5.4 percent of the U.S. population and growing. Why are women and racial and ethnic minorities still so far behind their white male counterparts?

Scholars note a variety of reasons. For one, it takes time for people who have not seen many members of their own gender or ethnic or racial minority in positions of authority to come to think of themselves as candidates for such positions. For another, it takes significant resources to mount a run for Congress. Women have now achieved parity with men in fundraising, but ethnic and racial minority group members still struggle to amass the cash necessary to mount credible campaigns. There is another important reason: failure to recruit minority candidates to lower-level political posts that serve as a pipeline to Congress.

State legislatures serve as incubators for developing legislative skills and a good source for the recruitment of congressional candidates. About half of all members of Congress served as state legislators before running for the House or the Senate.* This has been the case traditionally for women as well as for men[†] and increasingly for members of other minority groups as well. So, if we want to increase the diversity of Congress, we should start with state legislative bodies.

The New American Leadership Project suggests a number of steps to promote diversity in political recruitment:

- Invest in community organizations since these are a rich source of potential minority recruits.
- Cultivate community leaders and provide a path for fundraising.

Group	Percentage of All State Legislators	Percentage of U.S. Population
Women	24%	51%
African Americans	9%	13%
Hispanic/Latino	5%	17%
Asian/Pacific Islander	1%	5%
Whites	86%	76%

Women and minorities are underrepresented in state legislatures around the country.

Source: National Conference of State Legislatures, "Women and Minority Legislators Compared to U.S. Population." Retrieved January 3, 2018, from http://www.ncsl.org/research/about-state-legislatures/who-we-elect-an-interactive-graphic.aspx#.

- Ask new Americans to run and assist minority communities in opening a dialogue about the importance of running for office.
- Train potential candidates in the nuts and bolts of running campaigns.
- Change the perception of public office as a profession for only the elite.
- Create a stronger sense that public service is an effective and achievable venue for minorities.
- Focus on state legislatures as venues for policy change and pipeline development.

*National Conference of State Legislatures, "Former State Legislators in Congress and White House." Retrieved February 20, 2016, from http://www.ncsl.org/ncsl-in-dc/publications-and-resources/former-state-legislators-in-congress.aspx.

[†]Kira Sanbonmatsu, Susan J. Carroll, and Debbie Walsh, "Poised to Run: Women's Pathways to the State Legislatures," Center for American Women and Politics, Eagleton Institute of Politics, Rutgers University, 2009.

Because of the various pressures faced by elected lawmakers, most members of Congress find themselves balancing the interests of voters, interest groups, and party leaders along with the tug of their own ideological leanings, a representative style known as **politico**.[23] In some matters, representatives can ill afford to navigate too far from constituent wishes. For example, representatives with a substantial number of senior citizens in their districts will not likely vote for cuts in Social Security—at least not for current recipients or those approaching retirement age. Similarly, representatives whose party leaders are seeking to present a united front on some issue will have to weigh the cost of party loyalty against diminished influence if they decide to buck the party position.

descriptive representation The idea that our representatives should reflect the demographic makeup of the population and not just our political interests.

How Representative Are Our Representatives?
Should the makeup of a "representative" political body reflect the demographic diversity of the population as supporters of **descriptive representation** suggest? If so, then the U.S. Congress is hardly representative. The

membership is older, much better educated, more well off financially, and much less ethnically and racially diverse than the U.S. population at large. Some observers have referred to the members of Congress as primarily "pale, male, and stale." Minorities have far fewer members than their numerical strength in the overall population would warrant, and women are grossly underrepresented. (See "Challenges Ahead" for a discussion of increasing diversity in Congress.) Members are more likely to belong to one of the many Protestant religious denominations, but Catholics make the second largest showing, with over 160 in both chambers. There are far fewer Jews or members of minority religions represented. But membership is slowly growing more diverse. The 116th Congress is younger, more female, and more racially diverse than any in the past. It includes the first two Native American women to serve in Congress as well as its first two Muslim women. Tammy Baldwin, the first openly gay member elected to the Senate in 2012, was re-elected to a second term. With Democrats retaking control of the House, Nancy Pelosi, who became the body's first female Speaker in 2007, was slated to return to that position though she faced opposition by some younger members of her party.

Tammy Baldwin (D-WI) became the nation's first openly gay member of the Senate in 2012.

©Scott Olson/Getty Images

Although the electoral qualifications for Congress outlined in the Constitution are very broad and inclusive, the elite historically have made up the bulk of the membership. This long-standing trend reflects past patterns of discrimination, disparities in educational attainment, and difficulty in obtaining the financial resources necessary to make the long and costly run for office. Fortunately, these gaps are closing.

Pay and Perks

Benjamin Franklin proposed that elected government officials go unpaid for their service, but his views did not carry the day. Instead, the Framers provided compensation to be paid from the federal treasury. From 1789 to 1815, members of Congress received $6 per day while Congress was in session. Members began receiving a salary in 1815, when they were paid $1,500 per year. Today, the members' annual salary is $174,000; salaries for party leaders are somewhat higher. All members receive retirement and health benefits under the same plans available to other federal employees. Additional benefits of holding office are listed in "Perks Aplenty: Benefits for Members of Congress."

citizenship Quiz

Can you pass the U.S. Citizenship Test? See how well you know the content in this chapter covered on the citizenship test required of foreign-born candidates for naturalization.

1. We elect a U.S. senator for how many years?
2. The House of Representatives has how many voting members?
3. Name your U.S. representative.

(1) Six (2) 435 (3) See the complete list at www.house.gov. Just type in your ZIP code.

Source: United States Citizenship and Immigration Services.

Perks Aplenty: Benefits for Members of Congress

- Free office space in Washington, D.C. and in the home district.

- A staff allowance (2014) of $994,671 for each House member and from $2,361,820 to $3,753,614 for clerical/administrative staff for senators (depending on the population of the state and its distance from the Capitol). In addition, each senator is authorized $477,874 to appoint up to three legislative assistants.

- An expense account for telephone, stationery, and other office expenses.

- Reimbursed travel to and from home district based on a formula using distance from Washington.

- Travel allowance and free travel to foreign lands on congressional inquiries.

- Limited franking privileges.

- Free access to video and film studios to record messages for constituents.

- Free reserved parking at Reagan Washington National and Dulles Airports.

- Discounted use of congressional gym.

- Free assistance in preparation of income taxes.

- Generous pension benefits.

- Up to $3,000 tax deduction for living expenses while away from their districts or states.

- Participation in Federal Employees Group Life Insurance Program.

Members of Congress reap generous benefits for their service to the country.

Source: Congressional Research Service, Congressional Salaries and Allowances, 7-5700, July 14, 2016.

home style Those actions that link members of Congress to their constituents. These include mail, the use of electronic communication, visits to the district, and town hall meetings.

credit claiming The practice of personally taking credit for some action of government, like announcing the award of federal funds to one's constituents, in order to receive acclaim.

Keeping in Touch with Voters: Home-Style Politics

Keeping in touch with constituents is vital both for members' electoral prospects and for the health of representative government. Members pursue a variety of activities to gauge the pulse of the community, such as holding town meetings in their districts, making themselves available to local press for interviews, and keeping close tabs on mail from back home. These "**home-style**" activities enable members to present themselves to the voters and to explain their actions in Washington.[24]

Representatives often first become aware of important issues confronting constituents through a personal communication such as a letter, an email, or a phone call. These communications first pass through the hands of staff members, who sift through correspondence, tally support for issues coming up for a vote, and respond to constituents who wrote or called. They also select individual messages for the lawmaker's personal attention. Often, the letters the lawmaker sees come from high-profile constituents whose electoral support is important. Sometimes they reflect a representative sample of opinion or simply provide a well-articulated perspective. Staff also carefully track mass mailings organized by interest groups—especially those that are active in election-year politics—although these generally have less impact than more personalized communications. Email correspondence has increased the workload of staffers, and email correspondence has quickly replaced mail as the primary vehicle for communication between constituents and Congress. Postal mail has dropped to just 7 percent of overall correspondence, and the number of emails received grew to over 90 million by 2011.[25] Changes in modes of communication have created challenges for the member and staff. With a large volume of email, it is impossible to know (even with the use of special filters) whether the messages are coming from the home district. This makes filtering constituent interests from outside-the-district interests much more difficult, especially in an era in which interest groups mobilize mass email campaigns. Electronic communication has, in effect, nationalized a member's mail and may distort the member's perspective of district opinion.[26]

Much of the mail a member receives involves a direct request for assistance in dealing with a particular government agency or program. Staffers in the member's home district are most often responsible for fulfilling such requests. These requests provide the lawmaker with the opportunity to serve as a constituent ombudsman, or personal liaison between citizens and government agencies, and filling these requests builds support for reelection. Constituent service can turn congressional offices into reelection machines that specialize in cultivating good will between constituents and representatives.[27]

Today, members of Congress are also reaching out on social networking sites such as Facebook and Twitter to keep constituents apprised of their activities. They are especially adept at informing constituents of federal funding or grants they have won for their district, a practice known as **credit claiming**.[28]

WORKING WITH OTHERS

Meeting the demands of the office requires legislators to keep up with the workload, meet with diverse interests, and get along with colleagues. To handle these demands, legislators must rely on many other people for support. Success requires a mix of personal and administrative skills and a willingness to adapt to the ways business is conducted in the chamber.

Dealing with Organized Interests

Members of Congress interact frequently with lobbyists, or representatives from interest groups, to their mutual benefit. Because of the help these groups provide in campaigns and elections, they often gain favored access to Congress members and greater support for their causes. In addition to campaign contributions and voter mobilization, lobbyists and interest groups help members by supplying detailed information about the impact of legislation that only groups close to the policy may be in a position to offer. G. William Whitehurst, who represented Virginia for eighteen years as a Republican member of the House, recalls "many instances when I emerged from a meeting with an industry lobbyist better informed and therefore better prepared to vote on legislation that was pending."[29] Whitehurst warned, however, about the volatile situation that results from the ever-increasing number and stridency of groups seeking access to lawmakers who, in turn, rely on these groups for money and reelection support: "The result is a cacophony that leads to an unstable legislative arena, where calm, dispassionate, and reasonable discussion is made more difficult."[30]

Lobbyists are especially interested in gaining access to members in key positions of authority like party leaders and chairpersons of committees with jurisdiction over issues important to their clients. Most often, lobbyists serve as information gatherers for members of Congress who may not have enough time or staff to research an issue on their own. They present testimony before committees and often supply research generated by think tanks they fund. Although information provided by lobbyists is often useful, members of Congress are wise to consider diverse and independent sources of information as well.

The sometimes cozy relation between lobbyists and Congress carries with it the potential for corruption. Enticements like free travel or jobs for family members are sometimes difficult for even well-intentioned members to resist. The House forced Randy "Duke" Cunningham (R-CA) to resign in 2005 after he pleaded guilty to accepting millions of dollars from defense contractors in return for using his position on the Defense Appropriations Subcommittee to steer lucrative contracts to these firms. In the face of public consternation, Congress passed a reform act in 2007 that restricts the amount and kind of gifts and travel lobbyists can provide to members of Congress, requires greater disclosure of lobbyist contributions, and lengthens the period of time for which former members of Congress, staffers, or certain members of the executive branch must refrain from lobbying their former colleagues.

The Office of Congressional Ethics in the House and the Select Committee on Ethics in the Senate were created to investigate charges of ethical violations. Types of punishment include expulsion, suspension, censure (a formal statement of disapproval), reprimand, and admonishment (a less serious form of disapproval). Few members of Congress have been expelled, but several have been censured or admonished, including Senator Robert Menendez (D-NJ) who received a letter of admonishment from the Senate Ethics Committee in 2018 for accepting unreported gifts from a friend. The committee ordered him to pay back the gifts he received.

Recently, charges of sexual harassment and inappropriate sexual behavior have been referred to ethics committees in respective houses for investigation. The House passed additional measures to streamline the processing of complaints of sexual harassment and to protect those filing charges. In most recent cases of sexual harassment and wrongdoing, accused members have either resigned or decided not to run for reelection.

©Bill Clark/CQ Roll Call/Getty Images

Rep. Blake Farenthold (R-TX) resigned from the House when it was learned that he used taxpayer money to settle a sexual harassment claim brought against him by a female aide.

Personal Staff

Members of Congress receive an allowance, based on the size of their districts and their role in leadership, to hire personal staff both in Washington, D.C., and in their district offices back home. On average, about thirty people work for each senator—about half that number are employed by House members.

The Washington, D.C., staff generally tackle policy questions dealing with legislation. An administrative assistant or chief of staff runs the Washington, D.C., office and monitors demands on the member's time. A legislative director keeps the lawmaker informed about the issues coming up for a vote and provides assessments of the merits of bills outside the lawmaker's expertise. The office likely also includes a press secretary to deal with media inquiries, an appointment secretary to schedule the lawmaker's limited time, and a number of interns and office assistants who monitor constituent requests and handle mail.

Back home, the district office handles mostly casework or personal requests for help from constituents. Administrative assistants and caseworkers make up the bulk of the staff in home district offices.

Staffers in both Washington and the district offices are an important link for citizens with their government. Members of Congress, whose time is severely limited, rarely meet directly with citizen advocates. Instead, citizens meet with staffers who are trained to be responsive. Citizen requests range from seeking help in receiving government benefits to petitioning for legislative change. In most cases, staffers diligently share the messages of constituents and work hard to help them receive the help they request.

Professional Congressional Committee and Agency Staff

Lawmakers also work closely with staff specialists attached to the committees or subcommittees on which the members hold assignments. Committee staffers are highly trained professionals with rich expertise in policy and procedure; they provide detailed assessments of policy problems and options for members to consider in drafting legislation. Many are lawyers or hold advanced degrees, and they are generally older and more experienced than members of lawmakers' personal staffs. The size of a committee's staff varies according to the committee's size and jurisdiction. In the House, the average size of a committee staff is about sixty-five, with a range from around twenty to over two hundred on the Appropriations Committee; in the Senate, the average size is about fifty, with some of the largest committees, such as Government Affairs and Homeland Security, employing over one hundred staffers. Staff composition is split between majority- and minority-party appointees, with the majority party always enjoying more appointments.

Congress also uses professional staff to maintain specialized service agencies like the **Congressional Budget Office**, which provides detailed assessments of budget proposals; the **Government Accountability Office**, which supplies agency audits; and the **Congressional Research Service**, which produces specialized reports on a variety of topics at the request of members.

Committee staffers, who often have more knowledge of the details of legislation than lawmakers, frequently assume responsibility for drafting bills, negotiating with opponents, and forging legislative agreements. This has led critics to warn about the possible influence these unelected individuals have on legislative outcomes. Some have called for reductions in staff to minimize the role of staff in legislative matters. Others warn that without adequate committee staff, members of Congress would be even more beholden to lobbyists for the information they receive about pending legislation. In any case, the size of professional congressional committee and agency staff has shrunk in recent years. Partly, this is a cost-saving measure by congressional leaders worried about government deficits; but partly it is a result of the difficulty Congress has in attracting and retaining professionals who can earn twice as much or more in the private sector.[31]

Congressional Budget Office The nonpartisan agency created by Congress to review and assess the impact of proposed budget items.

Government Accountability Office The congressional agency that investigates how the federal government spends taxpayer dollars and the performance of agencies funded by the government.

Congressional Research Service A congressional agency providing nonpartisan policy and legal analysis to committees and members of both the House and the Senate.

Colleagues

Of course, lawmakers must also work closely with other lawmakers. Legislators meet formally with members of their own party and informally with like-minded members

PORTRAIT
OF AN ACTIVIST

Meet Jonathan Castañeda

Two role models shaped my understanding of activism in public service: Senator Robert Menendez and Congressman Albio Sires. Both grew up in the same working-class, majority-minority community of West New York/New Jersey as I did. I was in awe that people who looked like me, who shared my narrative, could make it to the most prestigious legislative bodies in the world, and I was inspired by the work they were doing on behalf of the residents of our community.

During my collegiate studies at Seton Hall, I interned at and eventually was hired by the Office of Congressman Sires. Shortly after, I was selected to be one of fourteen policy fellows with the Congressional Hispanic Caucus Institute in Washington, D.C. There, I had the honor to work in the Office of Senator Menendez on Hispanic affairs. I was disturbed by conditions in the marginalized outskirts of D.C. They closely resembled, almost paralleled, the conditions faced by people in my hometown: lack of opportunity, housing instability as a result of gentrification, and lack of security.

I debated whether to stay in Washington and work on policy or go back home and try to make a difference at the grassroots level. I decided to return home, where I worked on rehousing homeless veterans with a local nonprofit. I also enrolled at the Bloustein School at Rutgers to pursue a master's degree in city and regional planning, with the goal of helping to shape the environment for my community and the youth who will inherit it.

Currently, I serve my community as chief of staff for the Town of West New York and as an elected trustee on the

Courtesy of Jonathan Castaneda

West New York Board of Education. My work includes overseeing municipal operations, partaking in discussions about our education system, organizing and managing political events and campaigns, and leading efforts to build affordable housing.

I encourage everyone to get involved in the political process—and I do not mean sharing your views on social media. Instead, research candidates, participate in thoughtful conversation with friends and family about the impact of every election, volunteer at a local political or civic organization that aligns with your interests, and consider running for public office yourself!

---

sharing their own legislative goals and interests. These groups are known as **congressional caucuses**. There are several types. One type is the **party caucus**. These are meetings of party members to work out sometimes contentious issues of leadership and policy in order to promote party unity. Democrats and Republicans each have their own party caucus. Independent members, and those from third parties, must choose to meet with one or the other major political party in order to have a voice in setting legislative priorities. For example, Senator Bernie Sanders, an independent from Vermont, meets with the Democrats. Non-party caucuses include the Congressional Black Caucus and the Congressional Caucus for Women's Issues, in which colleagues from both parties concerned about issues of race or gender can meet to discuss mutual concerns.

Another type of informal meeting ground is called a study group, usually led by some of the party's most ideological members, who attempt to steer the party leadership in their direction. The Democratic Study Group begun in the 1970s was influential in moving the party's agenda in a liberal direction, whereas the Republican Study Committee, now consisting of over 150 members, has pushed the party in a more conservative direction.

congressional caucuses Unofficial party or special interest groups formed by like-minded members of Congress to confer on issues of mutual concern.

party caucus A meeting of party members in closed sessions for the purposes of setting legislative agendas, selecting committee members, and holding elections to choose various floor leaders.

Most members of Congress hire student interns to work in their offices both in Washington, D.C., and in their home districts. To apply, contact the office of your representative or senator or log on to their websites, where internship opportunities are usually posted. Interns perform such tasks as answering telephones, running errands, helping to answer mail, scheduling meetings, and researching constituent problems. Most internships are unpaid positions, so they are not for everybody. Nevertheless, they are a valuable source of knowledge and provide great contacts for career advancement.

©Comstock/Getty Images

norms Informal standards about what constitutes acceptable social behavior.

Getting Along

Political scientists have long observed a number of **norms**, or informal standards about what constitutes acceptable social behavior, that members rely on to minimize personal conflict with colleagues. In the past, members often demonstrated courtesy or cordiality by the ways in which they would refer to one another during floor debates. Even during heated arguments, members usually addressed each other as "colleagues" or "friends." For years, newcomers refrained from grandstanding to advance their personal careers. Instead, they deferred to more senior members, relying on their expertise and guidance before asserting their own legislative independence. They often sought to bridge differences with members of the opposition party in order to achieve common ends.

The increasing partisan and ideological polarization of Congress in recent years has substantially weakened many of these norms.[32] Newcomers are no longer shy about challenging their elders. Comity across party lines is not always respected. This was seen shortly after the 2010 midterm elections when newly arrived Tea Party Republicans insisted that their party refrain from compromise with Democrats on important tax and budget issues, leading to protracted stalemate and a downgrading of the U.S. credit rating. Floor debates have become shrill with members even attacking others from their same party, as when Senator Ted Cruz (R-TX) in 2015 attacked his own majority leader as autocratic. Intense debate and heated rhetoric are not new to Congress by any means, but it appears the current super-heated political environment has taken a toll on social accord and the norms of respect that prevailed in an earlier era.

KEYS TO POLITICAL POWER: PARTY, POSITION, PROCEDURES

Navigating a bill through Congress or performing any other congressional duty requires an understanding of the role of political parties in controlling the flow of business, identification of the key positions of authority within the body, and a knowledge of the rules and procedures of the body that can be used to advance or stymie congressional action—in other words, party, position, and procedure. The process of lawmaking is complex; lawmakers who occupy key positions of authority and understand the intricacies of the legislative process can make a dramatic difference in advancing legislation or stopping it in its tracks.

Party

Political parties control the leadership positions in both houses and the flow of legislation. The majority party—the party with the most seats in that chamber—always controls the most important offices of leadership in that body. The majority party always has more seats than the minority party on every legislative entity that passes on bills, and every leader of those bodies is likewise always a member of the majority party. The majority party also controls the rules in that chamber that allow it more easily to control the flow of their legislative agenda. The minority party plays a role, but its impact is small by comparison, especially if the majority party also controls the White House. When partisan control changes hands, positions of power and authority can be expected to be upended in favor of the new majority.

In 2018, Democrats took back control of the House of Representatives, gaining more than 33 seats, the largest Democratic midterm gains since 1974, just after President Nixon resigned from office. Republicans maintained control of the Senate, reinstating divided partisan control of Congress.

The 2018 midterm elections were unusual in several regards. First, voter turnout was unusually high for an off-year election. Spurred by divisive rhetoric and a polarized political environment, voters turned out in numbers more like those seen in presidential years. Turnout for early voting was especially high in many states and young voters between the ages of 18 and 29 made their strongest showing in a midterm election in over a quarter century, with a majority favoring Democratic candidates. Secondly, the amount of money spent skyrocketed. It is estimated that over $5 billion was spent by the parties and by outside groups, with Democrats holding the financial edge. Much of this money was raised through small contributions. Finally, more women and minorities ran in this midterm than ever before, resulting in a more representative looking body in the 116th Congress. Over 100 women took their seats in the House, the most ever.

The new Congress reflects the polarized state of the electorate. Democrats gained seats in suburban areas surrounding already largely Democratic cities—especially in the Northeast and West. Republicans added to the gains they made in recent years in rural areas. Women increased their participation rates, showing strong preference for the Democrats; a majority of men voted Republican, continuing to add to a long running gender gap. On the whole, those with higher levels of education voted Democratic, while those with only a high school education or less voted Republican. Our nation's racial divide continues to be evident with minorities overwhelmingly favoring Democrats and whites voting Republican. These partisan divisions are reflected in a split partisan control of Congress that has occurred six times since 2000, often resulting in gridlock.

Just as a closely divided electorate has produced divisive partisan campaigns, a closely divided Congress has produced a highly charged partisan environment in both chambers. As discussed earlier in this chapter, the ideological gulf between Democrats and Republicans has grown in recent years. Democrats and Republicans in both chambers now vote with members of their own party about 90 percent of the time, with few members crossing party lines to forge bipartisan consensus. This has often resulted in stalemate and gridlock. Those bills that do make it into law, such as several appropriations bills needed to keep the government operating, require the leaders in each House to break with some of their own members, angering the most extreme voices within their own parties. But some of the most pressing matters, like addressing looming future deficits and dealing with burgeoning entitlements, have been placed on the back burner with no bipartisan consensus in sight.

Divided government, when one party controls one or both houses of Congress and the other party controls the White House, has become more frequent in recent decades. We experienced divided government seventeen of the last twenty-four sessions of Congress (1973–2021). Some political scientists believe that about the same amount of legislation passes under divided government as under unified government.[33] There have been some notable legislative successes in periods of divided rule. For example, President Clinton worked with Republicans after they took control of Congress in 1994 to pass landmark welfare reform. President George W. Bush worked across party lines with Senator Ted Kennedy (D-MA) to produce the No Child Left Behind Act at a time of divided party control. Voters often tell pollsters that they prefer divided government because it acts as an additional check on legislative excess. However, divided government may slow down the legislative process and dilute legislation.[34] It may also result in the failure to enact really significant legislation—especially when the legislation is initiated by Congress and opposed by the sitting president of the opposition party.[35]

> **divided government** Control of the White House by one party while the opposition party controls one or both houses of Congress.

Even when the same party controls both chambers as well as the White House, passing legislation in recent years has not been easy because of cracks within the majority party as well as efforts by the minority to scuttle majority initiatives. With the exception of a short period of time after 9/11 when Democrats and Republicans seemed to work together, partisan rancor stymied many initiatives during periods of unified rule. With Democratic control in both chambers, Barack Obama faced great difficulty getting his signature health-care law passed and was forced to rely on executive orders that don't require congressional action in order to push immigration reforms. Under Donald Trump, a Republican Congress was unable to dismantle the Affordable Care Act. In the era of partisan polarization, it seems that even being in the majority does not ensure legislative success.

Speaker of the House The most powerful leader of the House of Representatives.

Committee on Rules In the House of Representatives, the committee charged with determining rules for debate, amendment, and vote on bills brought to the floor.

Position

Control of the chamber confers advantages on majority-party members by tipping the balance of power in their favor. Majority status gives members of that party access to the key leadership positions in that body and to control of the workings of the many committees that take center stage in the lawmaking process.

Leadership in the House The most powerful leader in the lower chamber is the **Speaker of the House**. The majority party selects one of its members to be Speaker, subject to approval by the entire House membership. The Speaker refers bills to committees for consideration and appoints members of the majority party to sit on some of the most powerful House committees. Perhaps the most significant appointments are to the **Committee on Rules**, which sets conditions for debate. Rules can be an important source of power. Rules that extend debate can be an invitation to compromise; rules that limit debate may silence dissent. The Speaker schedules legislation for floor consideration and may choose to preside over sessions of the body, although this is frequently delegated to another member of the majority party. The Speaker helps control the flow of debate and exercises wide discretion in interpreting and applying parliamentary rules. As the one individual with a commanding view of the entire legislative process, the Speaker is in a position to know the status of all legislation at all times and has the ability to influence its course. Although the

House and Senate Leadership Structure

House Leadership

Speaker of the House
Elected by the whole of the House of Representatives, the Speaker acts as leader of the House, presiding officer and administrative head of the House, and chief spokesperson for the majority party in the House.

Majority Party

Majority Leader
Represents majority party on the House floor, assists Speaker in advancing majority-party agenda, and generates support for party positions.

Majority Whip
Assists leadership in managing party's legislative program.

Minority Party

Minority Leader
Represents minority party on the House floor and plans strategy to advance party positions.

Minority Whip
Assists leadership in managing party's legislative program.

Senate Leadership

Vice President of the United States
President of the Senate. Votes only in case of tie; rarely presides.

President Pro Tempore
Senior-most member of the majority, who theoretically presides in the absence of the vice president

Majority Party

Majority Leader
Represents majority party on the Senate floor, responsible for advancing party's legislative agenda, and spokesperson for Senate majority members.

Majority Whip
Assists leadership in managing party's legislative program.

Minority Party

Minority Leader
Represents minority party on the Senate floor and plans strategy to advance party positions.

Minority Whip
Assists leadership in managing party's legislative program.

Speaker is entitled to debate and vote on all legislation, she or he typically votes only on matters of great importance or when his or her vote would be decisive.

Throughout congressional history, the power of the Speaker has risen and fallen. The House has a long history of Speakers who have wielded considerable authority, such as "Uncle Joe" Cannon, who dictated House policy at the turn of the twentieth century. Sam Rayburn (D-TX) served as Speaker three times from 1940 to 1961, with two interruptions of service when Republicans controlled the chamber. Rayburn won notoriety and respect for using his command of House rules to win passage of civil rights reform despite the opposition of southern Democrats. Newt Gingrich (R-GA), who served from 1995 to 1999, engineered the modern resurgence of the Republican Party in Congress and set the tone for a more partisan Congress in which power migrated from committee chairs to party leadership. Party control was also strong when Nancy Pelosi (D-CA), the first woman ever to assume the position, served as Speaker from 2007 to 2011. The ultimate success of any Speaker depends on weighing the demands of vocal ideological or regional factions within one's party with the needs of securing enough votes in the chamber to pass needed legislation.

The second in command for the majority party in the House is the **House majority leader**, who assists the Speaker in setting the legislative agenda and in securing the votes to achieve the party's goals. The majority leader works to generate support for the positions of party leaders, acts as a spokesperson for the party's legislative program, helps shepherd the party's legislation through the lawmaking process, and assists in scheduling floor action and the flow of debate. Majority leaders can enforce voting discipline among party members by influencing appointments to important committees, responding to staffing requests, and lending support to a member's legislation. Of course, the majority leader can also withhold favors from a member who fails to support the party's legislative agenda. Tom DeLay (R-TX), who assumed the position of majority leader in 2002, earned the nickname "The Hammer" because of his power in enforcing discipline among party members.

The minority party—the party with fewer seats in the chamber—also selects a leader to advance its own agenda in the legislative process. This is not an easy job when the opposition holds the levers of power. Nevertheless, the **House minority leader** can speak out on issues important to members, put pressure on majority-party leaders to hold hearings on controversial issues, and organize floor debate among minority-party members. The majority party may consult the minority leader on scheduling and developing procedures for floor debate, but the minority rarely has an equal voice in negotiations. Both majority and minority leaders work with elected **whips** to keep their respective parties united on roll call votes.

Leadership in the Senate The leadership structure in the Senate is similar to that of the House, with only a few differences at the very top. The Constitution specifies that the vice president of the United States serves as the president of the Senate, with the authority to preside over the body and to vote in case of a tie. Beyond this, the vice president exercises little real authority in the Senate. Instead, the Senate selects a **president pro tempore**, a Latin term meaning "for a time" or temporary, to preside over meetings. Most often, the position goes to the member of the majority party who has served the longest. In practice, even this individual rarely carries out the duties of **presiding officer**. Most often, the position rotates among junior members.

The Senate's most influential member is the **Senate majority leader**, who exercises responsibilities much like the Speaker of the House and the House majority leader rolled into one. Like the Speaker of the House, the Senate majority leader controls the body's agenda and the flow of legislation. Chosen by party members, the majority leader maps the party's legislative strategy in the Senate and acts as party spokesperson. The minority party has its own leader as well, chosen by the party caucus. The **Senate minority leader** has far less influence over the Senate agenda. However, he or she can place substantial hurdles in the way of the majority party. We will discuss some of these, like the filibuster and the hold, later in the chapter. As in the House, both parties employ whips to monitor and secure support for votes.

Senators pride themselves on their independence, making the Senate majority leader's job more difficult than that of the Speaker of the House. The Senate majority leader is considered only "first among equals." The Senate has seen its share of notable leaders. Among the most powerful was Lyndon Johnson, famous for his command of chamber rules and his ability to cajole, barter, and lecture his way into obtaining members' support for his party's agenda—even if he had to shadow them into the men's room to do so.

House majority leader The leader of the majority party in the House of Representatives, responsible for organizing the body and marshaling support for the party's agenda.

House minority leader The leader of the minority party in the House, responsible for marshaling support from party members for the party's agenda.

whips Assistant party leaders in each house whose jobs include ensuring that party members are present for floor votes and prepared to vote as the party prefers.

president pro tempore The second-highest-ranking official in the U.S. Senate.

presiding officer The individual who presides over Senate debate, enforcing order and decorum. The presiding officer will at times be the vice president of the United States or the president pro tempore.

Senate Majority Leader The leader of the majority party in the Senate, responsible for organizing the body and marshaling support for the party's agenda. The Senate majority leader exercises powers similar to those of both the Speaker and the majority leader in the House combined.

Senate minority leader The leader of the minority party in the Senate, responsible for marshaling support from party members for the party's agenda.

©Paul Schutzer/The LIFE Picture Collection/Getty Images

Senate majority leader Lyndon Johnson had a reputation for "getting in your face" when he needed support for his party's legislative agenda. Johnson (right) is shown here with House Speaker Sam Rayburn (D-TX).

Subcommittees of the Senate Committee on Foreign Relations

- Subcommittee on Western Hemisphere, and Global Narcotics Affairs

- Subcommittee on Near Eastern and South and Central Asian Affairs

- Subcommittee on African Affairs

- Subcommittee on East Asian and Pacific Affairs

- Subcommittee on International Organizations, Human Rights, Democracy, and Global Women's Issues

- Subcommittee on European Affairs

- Subcommittee on International Development and Foreign Assistance, Economic Affairs, International Environmental Protection, and Peace Corps

Each committee in Congress is broken down into smaller units called subcommittees, enabling members to tackle specialized matters within the purview of the whole committee.

Source: U.S. Senate.

The Committee System The principal function of the legislative branch is to make laws. To perform this function more efficiently, Congress divides its workload among smaller bodies called **committees**, which review legislation, investigate the operation of government agencies, and recommend courses of action for each chamber. Committees may be further divided into **subcommittees**. These are subunits of a congressional committee charged with considering specialized matters within the committee's jurisdiction and reporting findings back to the full committee. For example, the Senate Foreign Relations Committee is charged with overseeing America's foreign policy with other nations. But even this charge is very broad. So, the committee is broken down into smaller bodies called subcommittees, which specialize in dealing with certain regions of the globe, as the figure "Subcommittees of the Senate Committee on Foreign Relations" illustrates. The committee system allows members of Congress to scrutinize policies and legislation in depth, enabling committee members to develop expertise in certain topic areas.

The real work of lawmaking occurs in these committees, which is why they are sometimes called "little legislatures." At one time, the committees and their chairs were almost autonomous centers of power in the lawmaking process. Today, party leaders like the Speaker of the House and the Senate majority leader have a much greater say in what bills committees consider and whether or not committee bills make it into law. Still, committee chairs are not without the authority to determine the agenda and pace of committee action, the list of witnesses who might be called before them to testify, and the likelihood that a bill under consideration will even get a hearing.

Four basic types of committees do the bulk of the work in Congress: standing, select, joint, and conference. We discuss each of them here.

Standing Committees Standing committees are permanent bodies within each House specializing in the consideration of particular subject areas. For example, there are committees that deal with budgets and taxes, committees that deal with foreign affairs, and so on. In the 115th Congress (2017–2019), there were sixteen standing committees in the Senate and twenty in the House (see "Standing Committees in the House and the Senate"). Committee size varies depending on jurisdiction, with the House average near forty committee members and the Senate about half that number.

A member of the House may sit on as many as two full standing committees and four subcommittees, although members sitting on the most influential and time-consuming committees, like Appropriations, have fewer assignments. Senators may serve on even more committees, depending on the importance of the committee's role in the legislative process. Because each committee must meet at least once a month, members stay busy familiarizing themselves with bills under consideration and working with committee staff in order to stay on top of their workload.

The majority party controls the majority of the seats on each committee, including the leadership positions. The distribution of committee seats usually reflects party balance in the body as a whole, as do subcommittees. Committees that deal with the ethical behavior of members are exceptions to these rules, containing equal numbers of Republicans and Democrats.

Both the House and the Senate employ party committees to nominate members for open seats on standing committees. For Republicans, the Steering Committee performs this function

committees Bodies within each house that review legislation, investigate the operation of government agencies, and recommend courses of action for the chamber.

subcommittee A subunit of a congressional committee charged with considering specialized matters within the committee's jurisdiction and reporting its findings back to the full committee.

standing committees Permanent bodies within each House specializing in the consideration of particular subject areas

Standing Committees in the House and the Senate

House Standing Committees	Senate Standing Committes
Agriculture	Agriculture, Nutrition, and Forestry
Appropriations	Appropriations
Armed Services	Armed Services
Budget	Banking, Housing, and Urban Affairs
Education and the Workforce	Budget
Energy and Commerce	Commerce, Science, and Transportation
Ethics	Energy and Natural Resources
Financial Services	Environment and Public Works
Foreign Affairs	Finance
Homeland Security	Foreign Relations
House Administration	Health, Education, Labor, and Pensions
Judiciary	Homeland Security and Governmental Affairs
Natural Resources	Judiciary
Oversight and Government Reform	Rules and Administration
Rules	Small Business and Entrepreneurship
Science, Space, and Technology	Veterans' Affairs
Small Business	
Transportation and Infrastructure	
Veterans' Affairs	
Ways and Means	

Each House has its own standing committees where members debate the merits of bills within the committee's jurisdiction.

Source: U.S. House of Representatives; U.S. Senate.

in the House, and the Committee on Committees does so in the Senate. Democrats employ a Steering Committee in each chamber for purposes of assigning members to standing committees. Experienced members receive requested committee appointments more often than do freshman representatives, although this is not guaranteed. A freshman's chance of attaining a desired assignment depends on a number of factors, including party control of the body, interest and expertise, the size and importance of his or her legislative district, and the member's ties to leadership. Leaders sometimes intervene to ensure that newly elected members from districts considered important for party control get slots that maximize their public exposure and showcase their talents to constituents back home. Once assigned to a committee, members are expected to develop expertise on the subject of the committee's concern, usually with the aid of policy specialists on the committee staff, and to advance the party's agenda.

Not all standing committees have equal status or power. Committees dealing with spending and taxes, such as the Appropriations and Ways and Means committees in the House and the Budget Committee in the Senate, are considered the most powerful. These committees determine how much we are taxed and how much money is spent on government programs. These committees can be crucial for serving the reelection needs of members because they approve federal funding for specific projects located in various congressional districts across the country. Sending federal dollars back to one's home district allows members to show that they are making a tangible impact on the lives of constituents, and voters often reward these members with reelection. Many of these projects, like bridges and road construction, are vital to local communities; others, like money for the improvement of sports complexes or research into esoteric subjects, have been criticized as wasteful spending and are sometimes described as **pork barrel projects**. For many years, congressional leaders would set aside funds for such projects, called **earmarks**, often without debate on merit, as a means of rewarding members for supporting a party's key legislative initiatives. Faced with mounting criticism of such spending in the media, members of both parties promised to ban them from future budgets. Nevertheless, critics argue that Congress has created new loopholes as a means for hiding earmarks within massive spending bills that are hundreds of pages long. Recently, President Trump called for their return as a way to induce members to compromise on needed legislation.

In the House, the Committee on Rules is of special importance because of the role it plays in fashioning the terms for debate and amendment of bills coming to the floor. Often these rules mean the difference between passage and defeat, and the majority party guards its control of procedures by having the Speaker assign two-thirds of the members to this body. The Rules Committee also may initiate legislation on its own; Congress gives immediate consideration to measures the Rules Committee brings to the floor.

Special or Select Committees

Special or Select Committees The leadership of each house can create **special or select committees** to handle matters that do not routinely fit into areas usually covered by existing standing committees. These are typically established on a temporary basis. For example, the House in 2014 created the Select Committee on Events Surrounding the 2012 Terrorist Attack on Benghazi. This highly visible committee conducted hearings focused on the role then–secretary of state Hillary Clinton played in responding to attacks on U.S. government facilities in Benghazi, Libya.

Select committees can also include members from both the House and the Senate, as occurred with the creation of the Joint Select Committee on Deficit Reduction after the 2011 debt-ceiling crisis to find ways to slash the budget. The activity of temporary select committees usually culminates with official reports that the members may or may not use to generate legislation to be considered by other committees.

Some few select committees have permanent standing. For example, the House Permanent Select Committee on Intelligence, first created in 1977, continues to hold hearings on various aspects of intelligence gathering and threats to national security. This committee was charged with investigating allegations of Russian interference in the 2016 presidential election.

Joint Committees

Joint Committees **Joint committees** include members from both houses and can be either temporary or permanent. Most do not handle legislation, but monitor and report on activities of government agencies. For example, the Joint Committee on Taxation reviews tax policy and the operation of the Internal Revenue Service. Party leaders in each house appoint the members to joint committees.

pork barrel projects The term applied to spending for pet projects of individual members of Congress.

earmarks Funding for specific projects added by members of Congress to appropriations bills, usually without oversight or public debate.

special or select committees Committees in either house set up to handle matters that do not routinely fit into areas covered by existing standing committees.

joint committees Committees including members from both houses with jurisdiction over narrow areas and generally limited to powers of oversight.

Conference Committees Before sending legislation to the president for approval, the House and the Senate must pass identical versions of the same bill. When conflicting versions emerge, the leadership in each house selects members for a **conference committee** that attempts to resolve differences. Only after both the House and the Senate approve the conference reports of these committees can legislation move to the president's desk. When a single party controls both houses of Congress, conference committees concentrate mainly on accommodating the wishes of majority-party members in both chambers. In such cases, the opposition can be relied on to complain about being excluded. When congressional control is divided, stalemate and gridlock are not uncommon.

Committee Leadership **Committee chairs** enjoy substantial powers to facilitate action on the thousands of bills and resolutions introduced each session (between 8,000 and 10,000 in the House; between 3,100 and 4,500 in the Senate). Chairs can direct bills to subcommittees, appoint subcommittee chairs, set subcommittee staff and budget levels, and decide which bills get a hearing and, consequently, which are eligible for a vote of the entire chamber.

With few exceptions like the Rules Committee whose chair is appointed by the Speaker, the chairs of most other standing committees in the House have traditionally been selected on the basis of **seniority**. Accordingly, the chair goes to the most senior member of the majority party on a committee. Although the seniority system continues to predominate, the practice was curtailed when Republicans imposed a limit of three two-year terms for committee chairs in the 1990s. The practice is not always followed when the Democrats control the House. Chairs also must be ratified by the majority party caucus but the Speaker can intervene in the selection process in the interest of advancing the party's legislative goals.

In the Senate, committee members of the majority party select a chair via a secret ballot, which must be affirmed by another secret ballot of majority-party members in the entire chamber. Powers and limits of Senate chairs are comparable to those of their House counterparts and—despite the greater independence of members in this chamber—chairs have come under increasing pressure by party leaders to toe the party line. Studies show that committee chairs are among the most ideological members of their party.[36] As in the House, Republicans have imposed a six-year term limit for committee chairmen and ranking minority members when their party controls the chamber.

The highest-ranking member of the minority party on a committee is called the **ranking minority member**. Usually the senior minority member on the committee, he or she shares few of the powers of the chair but can sometimes draw attention to issues and viewpoints that differ from those of the majority party. Since they have no power to convene meetings or issue subpoenas for witnesses on their own, ranking minority members have sometimes staged "mock" hearings to air their party's positions.

Procedures

A twenty-year veteran of Congress, Rep. Robert S. Walker (R-PA), offered this piece of advice about Congress: "Those who understand the rules can control the process."[37] The Constitution authorizes each house to determine its own rules and procedures. Rules are especially important in the House of Representatives because of the sheer number of members and the number of bills introduced during each two-year session. For example, House committee chairs or party leaders can bottle up legislation without releasing it to the floor for a vote. The only vehicle for freeing the legislation is a **discharge petition**, requiring the signatures of 218 members. This strategy is difficult to effect. Success requires maneuvers by a member who is particularly adroit in amassing support and invoking chamber rules.

Once a bill is voted out of the authorizing committees, the House usually considers the legislation under rules adopted by the Committee on Rules. This committee acts something like a traffic cop who determines when cars can go and how quickly. The committee sets the procedures under which floor debate on each bill will occur. These include rules concerning the length of time allotted for debate and whether or not members may propose amendments. Drafted in accord with the wishes of the majority leadership, the rules frequently affect the outcome of the vote. In recent years, both parties have begun new sessions with a pledge for adherence to "open" rules. Open rules allow the opposition an

conference committees Committees including a small number of members from both houses assembled for the explicit purpose of ironing out differences between versions of the same bill before final approval by both chambers.

committee chairs The leaders of congressional committees, usually members of the majority party with the most seniority on that committee.

seniority The length of service in the body (House or Senate) and on a committee.

ranking minority member A leader of the minority party on a committee.

discharge petition A method for freeing legislation from a committee in the House that requires the signatures of 218 members.

opportunity to amend legislation on the floor. The pledge is often cut short, however, when the opposition floods the floor with amendments and the majority retreats to more-limited debate time or fills all the available amendment slots with their own. In the House, all floor debate must be germane, that is, pertinent to the topic at hand, so that members cannot stall by diverting attention to other matters.

Senate rules are more flexible—but potentially more potent—reflecting the body's historic preference for deliberation rather than speed. As in the House, they can affect the outcome of legislative action. Since there is no Rules Committee in the Senate, the Senate majority leader will schedule and bring matters to the floor for debate, sometimes in consultation with the minority leader. The majority leader can request—and usually receives—unanimous consent to waive rules that permit extensive debate. If senators object, however, debate may be unlimited. Such debate may take the form of a **filibuster**, in which opponents of the legislation threaten to carry on unlimited floor debate in hopes of keeping the bill from passage. In addition, the Senate has no rule requiring **germaneness**. As a result, a senator may discuss matters unrelated to the bill. Strom Thurmond (R-SC) holds the record for the longest single filibuster speech. He spoke continuously for twenty-four hours and eighteen minutes in his successful effort to defeat a civil rights bill in 1957.[38] Ted Cruz spoke on the Senate floor for more than twenty-one hours in his 2013 effort to kill the Affordable Care Act, filling the time with various stories including a recitation of Dr. Seuss's *Green Eggs and Ham*. (Although unlimited debate is not normally permitted in the House, it is the prerogative of the Speaker, majority leader, and minority leader to hold the floor as long as they like, a provision Nancy Pelosi, House minority leader, took advantage of in 2018 when she spoke for over eight hours straight in an attempt to get House approval of a path to citizenship for undocumented immigrants known as Dreamers.)

Members can end a filibuster through a procedure known as **cloture**. To invoke cloture, at least sixteen members must sign a petition to close debate. Within two days of filing the petition, sixty senators (a three-fifths majority) must vote to end debate. If cloture succeeds, debate is limited to an additional thirty hours. In recent years, partisan divisions have caused the number of filibuster threats and cloture votes to skyrocket. Whereas fifty-eight cloture votes were taken during the last years of the Clinton presidency, that number swelled to over two hundred in the 113th Congress (2013–2015).[39] Today, even the threat of a filibuster is an effective way to kill proposed legislation that the minority opposes.

The threat of filibusters has also been used to delay or stop presidential appointees from being confirmed. In 2013, majority leader Harry Reid pushed through a change in the filibuster rule, reducing the threshold from sixty votes to fifty-one votes for Senate approval of executive and judicial nominees with the exception of Supreme Court nominees. The change allowed more nominees to move through the pipeline to confirmation but created hard feelings on the part of Republicans and did nothing to limit filibusters as far as legislation is concerned.

Even a lone senator can use procedures to stymie action. For example, an individual senator can place a **hold** on an issue before the membership votes on it. The hold prevents any action from being taken on the issue until the leadership consults with the senator and addresses his or her concerns. It is only recently that the Senate ended the practice of secret holds by which a single anonymous senator could hold up confirmation of presidential appointments.

filibuster The Senate practice of continuous debate, often employed to stop pending legislative action.

germaneness Refers to the requirement that debate be strictly limited to the subject matter at hand. The House requires all debate and amendments be germane; the Senate does not.

cloture The procedure that ends a filibuster with sixty votes of the Senate.

hold A parliamentary procedure of the Senate that allows one or more senators to prevent a motion from reaching a vote on the Senate floor.

EXERCISING CONGRESSIONAL POWER

Lawmaking is the preeminent power of Congress, but the body also exercises the powers to declare war, to monitor the actions of the executive agencies it creates, to impeach and try federal officials, and to fund the federal government through the budget process. In addition, the Senate ratifies treaties and confirms presidential appointments.

Lawmaking

Former congressman Lee Hamilton (D-IN) blanches when he sees diagrams illustrating how laws are made. "How boring! How sterile!" he complains. Indeed, what diagrams miss are the intricacies of interpersonal relations necessary to win support for one's cause.

> You don't just have an idea, draft it in bill form, and drop it in the House hopper or file it at the Senate desk. Developing the idea is very much a political process—listening to the needs and desires of people and then trying to translate it into a specific legislative proposal. Even the earliest stages of drafting a bill involve much maneuvering. The member needs to consult with colleagues, experts, and interest groups to refine and sharpen the idea; gauge the political impact and viability of the proposal (especially with constituents); determine how to formulate the idea so it appeals to a majority of colleagues; study how it differs from and improves upon related proposals introduced in the past; decide how broadly or narrowly to draft it (to avoid it being sent to too many committees); and decide how to draft it so it gets sent to a sympathetic rather than an unsympathetic committee.[40]

Although Congress has veered away from regular procedures for passing bills in recent years, the formal process remains in place. Before we discuss the reasons for recent deviations from this model, we should have some familiarity with the formal steps in the process (see "Formal Procedure: How a Bill Becomes a Law").

Formal Procedure: How a Bill Becomes Law

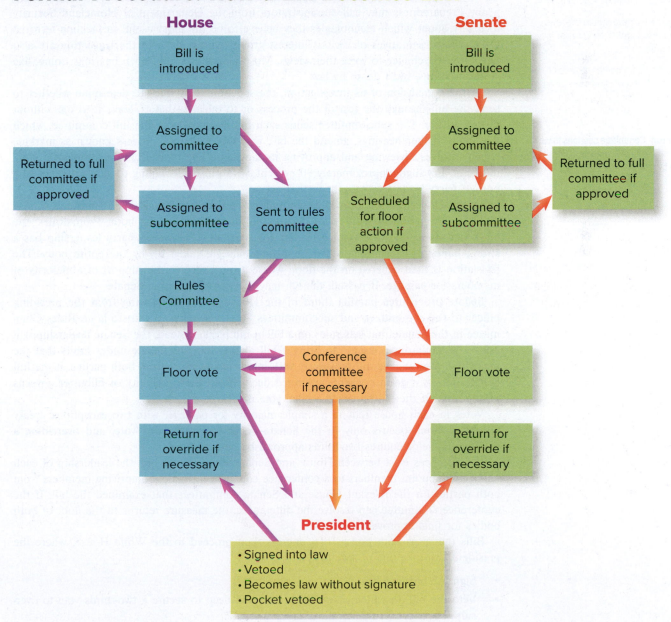

The formal path to legislative success is long and winding, but party leaders can find shortcuts that bypass the usual channels outlined here.

Bills must pass both houses to be eligible for presidential action. Much legislation today actually originates in the White House. In such cases, the president engages faithful party colleagues in the House or the Senate to introduce the bill. With the exception of revenue bills that must originate in the House of Representatives, all bills can be initially introduced into either chamber. The procedures in each body parallel one another with a few significant differences.

Once introduced, the leadership (Speaker in the House or presiding officer in the Senate) assigns the bill to one or more standing committees, depending on jurisdiction. If the bill involves more than one committee's jurisdiction, the leader may partition it so that different committees address portions of the bill related to their own jurisdictions. Once in committee, the chair of the committee can assign the bill to a subcommittee for more detailed analysis and consideration. For example, a bill dealing with new technology for use by first responders in cases of terrorist attacks may be sent to the Committee on Homeland Security in the House or to the Committee on Homeland Security and Governmental Affairs in the Senate. Chairs of these committees may subsequently direct the bill to appropriate subcommittees (Emergency Preparedness, Response, and Communications in the House or Disaster Recovery and Intergovernmental Affairs in the Senate) for further review.

Generally, subcommittees will request investigations and research reports from various executive branch offices affected by the legislation. The subcommittee can call witnesses to testify about the impact of the bill. In the previous example, the Subcommittee on Emergency Preparedness may call administrators from the Department of Homeland Security to testify about which technologies they believe to be the most useful in tackling terrorist threats. Representatives of various interest groups with a stake in the legislation are also likely to get a chance to voice their views. Most committees hold open hearings; some, like Appropriations, must do so by law.

At the conclusion of its investigation, the subcommittee votes to determine whether to send the bill through the rest of the process or to table it—that is, leave it to die without further action. The subcommittee sends each bill it approves to the full committee, which may hold further hearings, amend the bill, and subject it to a process known as **markup**, which involves reviewing and approving its language. The mortality rate for bills in committee is very high, approximately 90 percent, with most bills failing to gain sufficient support of party leaders to warrant further action.

In the House, bills approved by committees proceed to the Rules Committee, whose members prescribe procedures for debate and amendment on the floor. From Rules, the bill proceeds to one of several calendars for scheduling. However, party leadership has a strong hand in determining when important bills are taken up by the entire body. The legislation is then debated on the floor, where it must receive the support of a majority of members for passage. If passed, the bill may then proceed to the Senate.

Senate procedures parallel those in the House with bills moving from the presiding officer to the committees and subcommittees for review. However, there is no Rules Committee in the Senate that sets rules on a bill-by-bill basis. Instead, the Senate leadership will ask for "unanimous consent" to bring a bill to the floor for debate under limits that the majority leader worked out previously with interested senators from both parties. If the full Senate does not grant consent, unlimited debate with the possibility of filibuster governs floor action. If the bill proceeds, a final vote is taken.

Votes in each house require a simple majority for passage, with two exceptions: treaty approval—which occurs only in the Senate—requires a two-thirds vote, and overriding a presidential veto requires two-thirds approval by both houses.

If differences exist between House and Senate versions of a bill, the leadership of each house will appoint members to a conference committee, usually comprising members from both parties on the relevant House and Senate committees that examined the bill. If the conference committee can resolve the differences, the measure returns to the floor of both bodies for final approval.

Bills that pass both houses of Congress then proceed to the White House, where the president can take one of several actions:

- Sign the bill into law.
- Veto the bill, in which case both houses will need to secure a two-thirds vote to override the veto.

markup Committee sessions in which members review contents of legislation line by line.

- Allow the bill to become law without the president's signature simply by failing to take action within ten days. This tends to occur when the president does not support the legislation but recognizes that it has enough support for a veto override.

- Exercise a **pocket veto** by letting the bill sit unsigned for ten days when there are fewer than ten days left in the legislative session. At this point, the legislation dies. Because many bills do not pass until the end of a session, the potential for pocket veto is substantial.

> **pocket veto** An automatic veto achieved when a bill sits unsigned on a president's desk for ten days when Congress is out of session.

The actual process of lawmaking is much more fluid than this road map can portray. Although most bills still go through committees, committee action is often scripted by party leaders.[41] Members use a great deal of ingenuity in devising ways around whatever roadblocks arise. For example, in recent years, members who were stymied by committees have employed task forces to write their own bills and then substituted their versions on the floor for bills approved by committees. The lawmaking process has become more "unorthodox,"[42] reflecting increased partisan polarization and attempts by party leaders to limit opposition in chambers where majorities are slim.[43] Nevertheless, as we have stressed throughout, legislative success continues to depend on three factors: party support, access to those in top positions, and command over the procedures of the body.

Declaring War

Although the United States has formally declared war only five times in its history, it has entered into hostilities with foreign nations hundreds of times since its founding (see "Declared Wars and Congressionally Authorized Military Actions").[44] The Framers explicitly used the term *declare war* rather than *make war* in designating Congress's powers, because they wanted to leave the president free to repel a sudden attack.[45] In fact, the Framers divided the war power by granting the president the power to deploy troops as commander in chief of the armed forces (see Chapter 12), but reserving to Congress the power to declare war. Because both Congress and the president play a role in going to war, the proper role of the executive and legislative branches remains a topic of intense debate to this day.

The debate was particularly acute at the time of the Vietnam War in the late 1960s and early 1970s. Congress authorized the war by a granting of extensive power to the president, but without a formal declaration. As the war dragged on and public support dwindled, members of Congress sought to reclaim congressional authority with the War Powers Resolution. The act, passed over a presidential veto in 1973, requires the president to inform Congress within forty-eight hours of the deployment of military forces. Unless Congress approves of the president's action or formally declares war, troops must be removed after sixty days.

Since its passage, every president—liberal and conservative, Democrat and Republican—has held the act to be an unconstitutional restraint on presidential power; in 2008, several former secretaries of state called upon Congress to rewrite the law. In situations requiring the use of force that have arisen since its passage, both Congress and the president have either ignored the act or passed additional legislation authorizing the president to use force. The wars in Iraq and Afghanistan were sanctioned by congressional authorization after the 9/11 terrorist attacks but dragged on for years. Although the War Powers Resolution

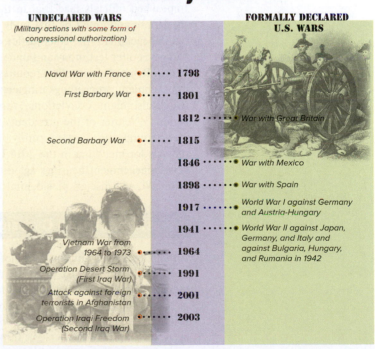

Declared Wars and Congressionally Authorized Military Actions

UNDECLARED WARS (Military actions with some form of congressional authorization)		FORMALLY DECLARED U.S. WARS
Naval War with France	1798	
First Barbary War	1801	
	1812	War with Great Britain
Second Barbary War	1815	
	1846	War with Mexico
	1898	War with Spain
	1917	World War I against Germany and Austria-Hungary
	1941	World War II against Japan, Germany, and Italy and against Bulgaria, Hungary, and Rumania in 1942
Vietnam War from 1964 to 1973	1964	
Operation Desert Storm (First Iraq War)	1991	
Attack against foreign terrorists in Afghanistan	2001	
Operation Iraqi Freedom (Second Iraq War)	2003	

America has been engaged in numerous military actions, but war has been formally declared only five times in U.S. history.

Source: National Archives and Records Administration.

has never been tested in the courts, the Supreme Court has insisted that congressional support for military action does not give the president a blank check. For example, the president cannot simply create new procedures for dealing with enemy combatants that violate established law without congressional authorization.[46]

Ending a conflict once it has started is difficult, because members of Congress do not want to be seen as failing to support our troops. Nevertheless, Congress can effectively end combat operations by cutting the funds for a war. In 1973, Congress passed a joint resolution (H.J.Res. 636) prohibiting further appropriation or expenditure of any funds for combat in, over, or from the shores of Vietnam and its neighbors. Repeated efforts by a Democratic majority brought to power in 2006, in large part because of public discontent over the war in Iraq, failed to bring about a similar cut in funding in the war against the Taliban.

President Obama ordered additional troops into Afghanistan in 2009 with little congressional opposition. When the president decided to assist NATO as it came to the aid of Libyan rebels, however, the House passed a measure rebuking the president for failing to secure congressional approval. In 2014, the president obtained congressional approval for funding to arm and train Syrian rebels and for U.S. air strikes in the battle against Islamic terrorists known as ISIL (Islamic State of Iraq and the Levant); but he did not specifically request authorization for military operations, arguing that previous authorizations in the war against terror were sufficient. President Trump has similarly relied on previous legislative authority in increasing U.S. troop buildup in Afghanistan.

Impeachment

Article I of the U.S. Constitution gives the House of Representatives the sole power to **impeach**—that is, bring formal charges against—federal officials. However, it grants the Senate the power to try, and possibly remove, impeached officials from office. The House may impeach an official for three offenses: treason, bribery, or "high crimes and misdemeanors." The first two of these offenses are straightforward; the latter, however, allows Congress substantial leeway for interpretation. Congress has cited "high crimes and misdemeanors" as its reason for impeachment against two presidents: Andrew Johnson in 1868 and Bill Clinton in 1998.

Procedurally, the House Judiciary Committee drafts and votes on charges warranting impeachment. A simple majority of votes in the House is sufficient to pass the measure. Impeached officials face trial in the Senate, with senators acting as jury and members of the House appointed by that body's leadership acting as prosecutors. In cases of presidential impeachment, the chief justice of the United States presides over the trial, during which witnesses offer testimony and undergo examination and cross-examination, just as in a court of law. Removal from office requires a two-thirds majority. The Senate has conducted formal impeachment proceedings nineteen times, most involving federal judges, resulting in seven acquittals, eight convictions, three dismissals, and one resignation with no further action.[47] Neither of the presidents who faced impeachment was removed from office. President Trump came under scrutiny by a special prosecutor for possible collusion with Russian officials for meddling in the 2016 U.S. presidential election. This raised the specter of possible impeachment hearings against Trump as the nation headed into midterm elections in 2018. We will discuss presidential impeachments in more detail in Chapter 12.

Investigation and Oversight

Although the Constitution does not explicitly grant Congress the power to investigate, it has long been accepted that Congress has the authority to make sure that government agencies it creates by law operate and spend taxpayer money in ways the Congress intended. The power to review, monitor, and supervise executive agency operation is known as **oversight**. Oversight is not an enumerated power, but it is implied by the system of checks and balances. Congress exercises its power of oversight through a wide variety of activities and mechanisms.

Congress may exercise this power by conducting investigations to examine policy implementation or to scrutinize the activities of government personnel and officeholders. Congress has the power to subpoena witnesses to testify under oath, although witnesses can, of course, refuse to testify under rights granted by the Fifth Amendment. After an attack on the U.S. diplomatic mission in Benghazi, Libya, in which the U.S. ambassador and three other Americans were killed in 2012, Congress opened a series of hearings into what the State Department knew in advance and whether it had engaged in a cover-up to prevent criticism of the Obama administration in an election year. The hearings dragged on for years and demonstrate the potential for partisan use of the oversight power when one party uses the proceedings to embarrass the other.

Following an attack on the U.S. diplomatic mission in Benghazi, Libya, Congress held a prolonged series of hearings in order to determine if the Obama administration had attempted to disguise their lack of preparedness in an election year. Hillary Clinton was then secretary of state.

Congressional committees also exercise oversight by monitoring budgets and holding hearings on how executive agencies are spending the money Congress has authorized. The authorization of budgets is potentially Congress's most powerful tool for influencing an agency's operations. Often, however, this power is quite fragmented. For example, because many committees and subcommittees share oversight of the many individual programs run by the Department of Homeland Security, it is difficult to know exactly how well the department as a whole is doing in keeping us safe and spending our money wisely. In addition, the executive branch often resists congressional oversight, arguing for autonomy in matters under its principal jurisdiction.

Very often, when Congress passes a bill, it leaves implementation of that bill up to executive branch agencies. For example, when Congress approves a clean air bill, it does not specify how many particles of soot from a coal plant are permissible before it poses a health hazard. It leaves that decision up to the Environmental Protection Agency (EPA), which it charges with that task. Until 1983, if the EPA made a rule Congress disapproved, it could exercise a select veto of that provision known as the **legislative veto**. This type of veto nullifies the agency's action but without having Congress pass a law to that effect and without presidential approval. Although the Supreme Court ruled in 1983 that this power was an unconstitutional infringement on the powers of the executive branch,[48] Congress has instituted *informal* accommodations with agencies that allow it to continue to reject certain agency decisions.[49]

Similar to the legislative veto, the power of **congressional review** permits Congress to nullify agency regulations after sixty days by passage of a joint resolution by both houses and approval by the president. In 2017, Congress used its power of congressional review to nullify fourteen rules involving teacher training, coal mining runoff, and bear hunting in Alaska, each proposed in the waning days of the Obama administration.[50]

Budgeting

Although the president makes recommendations regarding the administration's budget priorities, the Constitution gives Congress alone the authority to decide how the money is spent. In addition, it specifies that all bills to raise revenues must originate in the House of Representatives.

The budgeting process begins when the president sends Congress a proposed budget (usually after the annual State of the Union message each January or February). The proposed budget is for the period known as a fiscal year, which begins October 1 of that year. A special independent agency, the Congressional Budget Office, then reviews all spending proposals and makes detailed estimates of expenditures needed to accomplish the president's policy objectives. Budget committees in both houses consult with executive branch representatives and develop a **budget resolution** that acts like a blueprint projecting revenue and spending to meet each of the president's policy goals. As we will see, these figures may be adjusted later. Both houses must pass this budget resolution by April 15 of each year, but it does not require a presidential signature.

The next step involves the Appropriations Committees in each house. These committees must now decide how to distribute total funds available to the government to each of the fifteen

legislative veto A congressional action nullifying an executive branch agency's action but without having Congress pass a law to that effect and without presidential signature. This device was declared unconstitutional in 1983.

congressional review Congressional action, requiring approval by both houses and the president, that can stop implementation of executive branch regulations.

budget resolution Early step in the budgeting process, in which both houses of Congress set spending targets to meet the president's priorities.

©Tom Williams/CQ Roll Call/Getty Images

agencies that make up the executive branch of government while meeting the president's priorities. For example, the president may decide he wants to spend about $600 billion on defense. At this point, the Appropriations Committee, operating through various subcommittees, must decide how to allocate this money among the branches of the armed forces and make decisions about what types of military hardware they can afford to fund. If the need arises, Congress can adjust funding targets for various programs within the budget without going beyond the overall spending limits set by the original budget resolution. For example, Congress may decide to cut some money from defense in order to increase spending on social services. This amending process is known as **reconciliation**. Reconciliation operates under special rules and, in the Senate, requires only a majority vote without the opportunity for filibuster.

Final passage of spending bills is supposed to occur just prior to the beginning of the government's fiscal year on October 1. Often, however, Congress does not meet the deadline. One option at this point is to pass a **continuing resolution** that allows agencies to operate at the previous year's funding levels until the new budget is passed. Another option is to fold spending for all programs into a single bill, known as an **omnibus bill**, instead of passing separate appropriations for each of the fifteen executive branch agencies. Omnibus bills are massive, as you might imagine, and often contain hidden last-minute provisions added to win support from particular members.

It should be noted that a large part of the U.S. budget is already committed to programs like Medicare and Social Security. These programs are known as **entitlements** because citizens who meet certain qualifications are entitled to receive them. These programs amount to about two-thirds of the money spent by the government. As a result, most of the budget battles in Congress occur over the roughly 30 percent of the budget allotted for discretionary or new spending.

When the government spends more than it takes in, it runs a deficit. When this occurs, Congress must also authorize the borrowing of money to meet federal obligations. This is known as raising the debt ceiling. Disputes over the debt ceiling have been repeated and heated in recent years, with some Republicans resisting such measures unless accompanied by cuts in federal programs. Disputes over the debt ceiling have resulted in temporary government shutdowns and placed the credit rating of the United States in jeopardy.

Senatorial Powers

The Constitution accords additional powers to the U.S. Senate alone. These include confirmation of presidential appointments and approval of treaties. The first of these requires a simple majority vote; the second, two-thirds approval.

Confirmation of Presidential Appointments The Constitution (Article II, Section 2) states that the president shall seek the "advice" and obtain the "consent" of the Senate before nominees to the federal bench and other "officers of the United States," including Cabinet officers, are confirmed. In other words, the Senate must review and approve of the president's nominees. The Framers saw the Senate's power of **advice and consent** as a way for Congress to check presidential power. The use of the Senate for this purpose—rather than the House—ensured that the interests of both large and small states would be respected, because each state has equal representation in the Senate. Today, the Senate is asked to confirm thousands of civilian and military nominations during each two-year session of Congress. Although it has confirmed the vast majority of these in blocks, controversial nominees do engender significant debate. This is particularly true with respect to Supreme Court nominees, who enjoy lifetime appointments. We will discuss these at length in Chapter 14.

Much of the controversy over Senate approval of presidential appointments centers around the proper application of "advice and consent." Some scholars and senators believe Congress should reject presidential appointees only if the nominee is deficient in competence or character. Others believe the Senate should have the discretion to deny appointment for any reason whatsoever, including disagreements over policy or political perspective. Differences in interpretation and application have led to many battles over presidential nominees. In 1987, the Democratic majority in the Senate refused to confirm Ronald Reagan's Supreme Court nominee Robert Bork largely because they considered his views too extreme. During

---

reconciliation The process of amending spending bills to meet budget targets.

continuing resolution A vehicle for funding government operations at the previous year's levels of support when a new budget is delayed.

omnibus bill A bill that folds spending for all executive agencies into one legislative package.

entitlements Programs promising aid without time limit to anyone who qualifies.

advice and consent The constitutional requirement that the president seek Senate approval for certain appointees and treaties.

the last year of the Obama presidency, Republicans in the Senate refused to take up the president's nominee to replace Justice Antonin Scalia, who had died in February 2016, arguing that the nomination should be delayed in a presidential election year until the next president took office, a position with no exact precedent. Following this rebuke of Obama, Senate Republicans pushed through two of President Trump's Supreme Court appointees.

Recently, the Senate has increased the use of holds in the confirmation process, allowing individual members to delay confirmation of presidential appointments indefinitely. This has led to backlogs in the appointment of federal judges and top administration personnel. Changes limiting the use of the filibuster and anonymous holds for appointments other than Supreme Court nominees has made confirmation somewhat easier but not entirely put an end to delays.

When Congress fails to approve a presidential nominee for an administrative post, the president can make what is called a **recess appointment**. This allows the president to fill the vacancy when Congress is not in session, say, over an end-of-the-year break. Congress can counter this move by simply opening and quickly closing each daily session with the strike of a gavel and without conducting any substantive business. In June 2014, the Supreme Court ruled this practice permissible over the objections of President Obama, who sought to install a nominee whose confirmation had been held up by his congressional rivals.[51]

recess appointment A political appointment made by the president when Congress is out of session.

Approval of Treaties The Constitution provides that the president "shall have Power, by and with the Advice and Consent of the Senate, to make Treaties, provided two-thirds of the Senators present concur." Ever since George Washington visited the Senate in 1789 to confer with members about a series of agreements negotiated with Native American tribes, presidents have employed a number of tactics to win Senate support for treaties. Some presidents have involved senators in the negotiation process itself, as William McKinley did in negotiating a peace treaty with Spain in 1898. Woodrow Wilson, by contrast, paid a price for his failure to include senators in negotiations for the Treaty of Versailles, which ended World War I. The Senate twice refused to ratify the treaty. More recently, presidents have conferred with Senate leaders during the negotiating process. This approach worked particularly well for Ronald Reagan in winning approval for an arms control treaty in 1987.

Woodrow Wilson paid a price for his failure to include senators in negotiations for the Treaty of Versailles ending World War I. The Senate twice refused to ratify it.

The Senate generally has been reluctant to reject treaties, approving more than fifteen thousand while turning down just twenty-one.[52] Still, presidents frequently are reluctant to subject their international negotiations to Senate scrutiny. Some have circumvented the process by adopting executive agreements with other nations that carry the same force of law as treaties but do not require Senate approval. In 2015, President Obama joined with other international partners in removing sanctions on Iran in order to obtain a reduction in that country's nuclear capabilities. Some in the Senate believed they should have been consulted first; but the president indicated the removal of sanctions was an international act not equivalent to a treaty negotiation between the United States and Iran. We will discuss the increasing use of alternative agreements in Chapter 12. More recently, President Trump used his executive authority to unilaterally withdraw from some international agreements, such as the 2016 Paris Agreement on climate change and the Iran nuclear arms reduction agreement.

CONGRESS AND CIVIC ENGAGEMENT TODAY

Congress today appears poorly equipped to find broad-based solutions to problems Americans deem important, such as controlling discretionary spending, balancing the budget, dealing with economic inequality, and providing affordable health care for all. The skillful use of casework may ensure the loyalty of some voters, but the public expresses general dissatisfaction with the institution of Congress as a whole for its inability to solve social problems. Many citizens believe Congress is dysfunctional, inefficient, laggard, and unresponsive, and that it has lost touch with the public.[53] Over the past decade, the number of Americans expressing trust in Congress has rarely exceeded a third of the population.[54] Fewer than half of eligible voters turn out for midterm congressional elections. Two veteran Congress-watchers have characterized the current state of partisan gridlock in Congress in the title of their book: *It's Even Worse Than It Looks*.[55]

These attitudes are, in part, understandable reactions to the political dynamics of the institution today. In a closely divided Congress, bipartisan consensus takes a backseat to partisan politics as members of each party seek to please groups most important to their electoral success. Debate becomes shriller. Compromise and reconciliation of differences become more difficult to achieve. Each party pursues the politics of winning at any cost.[56] Gerrymandering, the high cost of campaigning, and incumbent privileges keep turnover low. Voters are turned off. A number of reforms could help change this picture.

First, since competitive elections tend to increase citizen interest and turnout, we could change practices that protect incumbents in order to level the playing field for challengers. Campaign spending reform would help to increase competition because most money flows to incumbents. Spending reform might range from allowing all candidates free media time, to public financing for congressional contests. Today, more than two dozen states and localities provide some type of public funding for elections.[57] These programs limit the influence of large donors and allow candidates to spend more time with constituents and less time chasing money. To be sure, this is not a cure-all and there is some evidence that public financing may have the unintended consequence of increasing polarization.[58] Nevertheless, campaign finance reform would go a long way toward increasing public confidence in elected officials and decreasing the public perception of corruption.

We should consider expanding the use of a "top-two" primary system like the one used in California. As we discussed in Chapter 9, this system lists all candidates for office on the same ballot regardless of party. The top two candidates then face off against each other in the general election even if both are from the same party. There is evidence that this system has resulted in more moderate legislators being elected to office by limiting the polarizing impact of party primaries where candidates try to outdo each other for attracting the most extreme and loyal wing of the party.[59]

A growing number of states are replacing partisan redistricting with nonpartisan redistricting commissions to draw congressional boundaries. Districts drawn by nonpartisan bodies experience more competition on average than those drawn by partisan legislatures, according to some studies.[60] Independent commissions drawn from the general population have the additional effect of engaging citizens more fully in the legislative process. When California passed a measure creating a citizen redistricting committee, more than thirty thousand residents applied for fourteen positions on the board, which sorted through population figures and election boundaries to ensure that residents of the most-populous state are fairly represented. Although the process was not without controversy, it was "a sharp departure from the incumbent-oriented approach that defined the previous rounds of line-drawing,"[61] and it opened up the 2012 congressional races to new faces. Shaun Bowler, a professor of political science at the University of California, Riverside, told reporters, "This is just a sign of just how engaged or enraged people are by the political process."[62] To be sure, partisan redistricting is not the sole cause for noncompetitive elections. The fact that citizens have increasingly sorted themselves geographically into safe partisan enclaves is another factor. Nevertheless, political gerrymandering by those in office who may benefit from the way district lines are drawn contributes to a lack of confidence in the legislative process, leading some commentators to conclude that citizens no longer pick their lawmakers—instead, lawmakers pick their constituents.[63]

Reforms within Congress are overdue. Although the recent change in the use of the filibuster for delaying some judicial confirmations has quickened the appointment process, further changes are needed to make sure that government business gets conducted while preserving adequate time for debate. A variety of ideas have been advanced to further reform the filibuster without eliminating it. For instance, instead of allowing a single senator to filibuster and then requiring sixty votes to shut it down, rules could be instituted that would require forty members to initiate a filibuster and then requiring at least forty-one votes to continue talking at various stages as debate proceeds. The reform would put the onus of the filibuster on those who wish to use it instead of on those who wish to stop it, as the current practice does.[64]

Ultimately, making lawmakers more attentive to long-standing problems that citizens want resolved will require greater initiative and engagement by citizens themselves. Although over 90 percent of Americans believe it is their duty to communicate with their representatives in Congress, only one-fifth have actually contacted their House member or one of their senators.[65] We already know from Chapter 7 that those who do communicate are not representative of the public at large. Instead, they represent the higher social and economic tiers of the population. As a result, lawmakers hear quite a lot about the concerns of the well-to-do but very little from the poor, children, or the uninsured. It is no wonder that studies show that legislators are vastly more responsive to the views of affluent constituents than to constituents of modest means.[66]

Nevertheless, a recent report by the Congressional Management Foundation found that legislators and staff believe constituent communication is a vital factor in decision making. Most important is personal contact either in person or by well-crafted letter.[67]

We also need to place more attention on civic education beyond the ballot box. Students should learn not just the value of voting but also the value of following up with elected officials to check on their political investment. Don't assume that your vote communicates any information about each of your issue preferences. The only sure way for lawmakers to know what you think is for you to let them hear directly from you. Members of Congress do pay attention to constituents; after all, they are doing our business.

Thinking It Through >>>

Learning Objective: Describe the sources of congressional power.

Review: Keys to Political Power

Describe how each of the keys to political power in Congress—party, position, and procedure—can be used either to facilitate or to stymie the lawmaking process. Which of these factors do you believe most contributes to the partisan gridlock we see in Congress today?

Summary

1. **What powers does Congress have?**
   - Our bicameral Congress has enumerated powers granted by the Constitution. These include lawmaking, budgeting, declaring war, impeachment, oversight, and advice and consent.
   - Congress has implied powers granted by the elastic clause of the Constitution.
   - Revenue bills must be initiated in the House. The Senate alone has the additional powers of ratifying treaties and approving presidential appointments.
   - Congressional power has developed in response to periods of national change. At first, Congress sought to build its own institutional status; it underwent reform in the Progressive Era; its power waned in the twentieth century as executive power grew; and it helped expand rights for minorities during the rights revolution of the 1950s and 1960s.
   - Members of Congress represent the people. There is some debate as to whether they should serve as delegates, trustees, or politicos. There is also the question of whether Congress is really a representative body reflecting the diversity of the American public.

2. **What are some factors affecting election to Congress?**
   - Candidates must have access to resources. They need to have the time to spend countless hours campaigning, and they need access to great amounts of money.
   - Incumbents have an advantage in raising funds and in name recognition because of the franking privilege, the credit they can claim for projects they bring their districts, the casework they perform for grateful constituents, and their access to the media.
   - House members are faced with additional hurdles, including frequent elections, lower turnout in midterm elections, and periodic redistricting. Most incumbents are returned to office partly because they run in safe districts that have been drawn by partisans in the state legislature and partly because Americans have assorted themselves into districts that repeatedly favor one party or the other.

3. **What are the keys to political power in Congress?**
   - The keys to political power in Congress are party, position, and procedure.
   - Power is largely in the hands of the majority party, which controls positions of leadership and the flow of the legislative process.
   - Party leaders have become more important in recent years in engineering legislative success in each chamber. However, committee chairpersons retain substantial power on committees that review legislation.
   - Command of parliamentary rules and procedures like the Senate filibuster is an important element in legislative success.
   - The lawmaking process is characterized by specialized committees that review and approve legislation before debate on the floor of each chamber.

Chapter 12

The Presidency
Power and Paradox

Donald Trump has set an unprecedented tone in his approach to the presidency. Is this the new normal?

THE UNPRECEDENTED PRESIDENT

He came to office promising to change the way Washington works, and it didn't take long for him to make his mark. Within his first eighteen months in office, President Trump cancelled the United States's participation in the Paris Agreement on climate change; withdrew from the Iran nuclear deal that placed limits on Iran's nuclear program in exchange for sanctions relief; approved construction of the Keystone XL and Dakota Access pipelines, which the Obama administration had halted for environmental reasons; signed an executive order blocking travelers from seven Muslim-majority countries; signed executive orders rolling back portions of the Dodd-Frank financial package passed in the wake of the Great Recession to protect consumers; withdrew from the Trans-Pacific Partnership, which would have created trade ties between the United States and several East Asian countries; and took the unprecedented step of meeting with North Korean leader Kim Jong-un in an attempt to get the country to denuclearize. In addition, he stretched or broke any number of norms related to presidential leadership by striking out at the media as "fake news," attacking his own intelligence community and FBI for attempting to undermine his presidency, and posting incendiary tweets taking aim at his enemies.

President Trump has historians and political scientists wondering if his behavior in office has changed the presidency forever or whether the Trump style is a blip that will be forgotten when the next president assumes office.

Presidential historian Michael Beschloss notes: "You've got someone who is defining the presidency very differently. Trump is essentially saying, 'I'm not going to operate just within the boundaries that the founders might have expected or people might have expected for 200 years. I'm going to operate within the boundaries of what is strictly legal, and I'm going to push those boundaries if I can.'"[1]

As You READ

- **What is the path to the presidency?**
- **What are the major constitutional duties and roles of the president?**
- **What agencies and personal factors help to produce a successful presidency?**

According to Jeffrey Engel, director of the Center for Presidential History at Southern Methodist University, "[Trump] has already laid the seeds of fundamentally changing the presidency. . . . Nobody is going to trust norms in the same way that we did before."[2]

Every president leaves his mark on the presidency, and Donald Trump is destined to do the same. Like Trump, future presidents may take to Twitter to convey their innermost thoughts or to stoke controversy as a negotiating tactic.

Institutional forces have traditionally restrained presidential powers in peacetime. The courts can restrain presidential ambitions, as they did in limiting the impact of Trump's travel ban. The party out of power can use parliamentary procedures to block presidential initiatives, as the Democrats did in opposing the president's dismantling of the Affordable Care Act. The press can expose inaccuracies of presidential pronouncements, despite claims about "fake news." And the justice system can pursue claims of wrongdoing, despite attempts to shut it down.

But Donald Trump has waged a war on these forces—calling for the justice department to prosecute political enemies, parceling pardons to political allies, failing to implement Congressionally-mandated sanctions against Russia, and threatening to revoke the license of some media outlets that criticized him. His actions have been erratic, causing panic among some members of his staff who claim surreptitiously to have taken measures to thwart him, and raising questions about whether he is fit for office and whether he can survive his own presidency.[3]

The U.S. presidency is the most powerful position in the world. Yet, the Framers sought to place limits on those who occupy the office. Today, the institutions they created to curtail its power are straining under the forces of partisanship and polarization. In this chapter, we will review the history of the office and examine the ways in which presidential power has traditionally functioned within the confines of the checks and balances the Framers envisioned. The presidency of the future is being written today, however, and its evolution depends as much on the way institutions and voters react to the exercise of presidential authority as it does on the occupant of the office. ■

ORIGIN AND POWERS OF THE PRESIDENCY

The Framers were clear about what the presidency shouldn't be but less certain about what exactly the office *should* be. They did not want the president to dominate the government; they had just fought a revolution to free themselves from monarchical rule. Neither, however, did they want a weak and ineffective executive; lack of central leadership had led to dissatisfaction with the Articles of Confederation. Delegates to the Constitutional Convention argued for months before agreeing on the form and powers of the office. They created a single executive with a broad scope of potential powers that were limited by checks and balances. The delegates deliberately sketched only the rough outlines of executive power, preferring to let the person they all knew would first occupy the office work out the details. George Washington did not disappoint.

Constitutional Provisions

Article II of the Constitution outlines the requirements for election to office, as well as the powers, duties, and limits on the authority of the president. It also provides for a vice president to succeed the president in case of death, resignation, or the inability to discharge the powers and duties of the office. To be eligible for the presidency, an individual must be thirty-five years of age, a resident of the United States for fourteen years, and a natural-born citizen. This last requirement is not applicable to other federal officeholders; it reflected the Framers' desire to prevent command of the U.S. military by a foreign-born national.

The term of office is four years, and originally the Constitution placed no restriction on the number of terms a president could serve. The Twenty-second Amendment, ratified in 1951, imposed a limit of two terms. Dispute over the role the voters and the states should play in the election process led to the creation of an Electoral College (discussed later), in which state electors cast the actual ballots for a president and vice president following the popular vote by the people. The Twelfth Amendment, ratified in 1804, altered the process by requiring electors to submit separate ballots for president and vice president. This change came about as a result of one presidential election that produced a president and a vice president from opposing parties (1796) and another that resulted in a tie (1800).

The Constitution grants the president executive authority to take care that laws are faithfully executed; to operate executive departments; and to require written opinions from the officers of these departments. The president also enjoys the power to make appointments, including appointing judges to the Supreme Court and all other federal courts, with the advice and consent of the Senate; to fill inferior offices and vacancies during Senate recess without Senate approval; and to grant reprieves and pardons. The office has legislative powers, including the powers to recommend legislation to Congress for its consideration, to convene both houses of Congress, and to veto legislation. In military matters, the president is the commander in chief of the armed forces. In the diplomatic arena, the chief executive can negotiate treaties and submit them to the Senate for approval upon a two-thirds vote and can appoint ambassadors and ministers with Senate approval. As chief of state, the president receives foreign officials and dignitaries, presents information on the state of the nation, and swears an oath of allegiance to uphold the Constitution. Article II also provides for removing a president by impeachment and trial upon conviction for treason, bribery, or other high crimes and misdemeanors. The twenty-fifth amendment, ratified in 1967, provides a means whereby the vice-president can replace a president who is deemed unable to discharge the powers of the office. We will discuss these powers and limits more fully later in this chapter. However, these formal powers tell only part of the story of presidential power. In reality, the office's occupants have molded the institution in significant ways.

Crafting the Office: From Washington to Roosevelt

Well aware that his actions would guide the future course of presidents, Washington took pains not to overstep the bounds of constitutional authority and to set worthy precedents. He avoided the partisan feud between Federalists and Antifederalists; he was respectful of Congress, but still willing to assert his independence; he respected the rule of law; and he even led U.S. troops in quashing the Whiskey Rebellion of 1794. Washington also established a precedent by refusing to serve more than two terms, a practice that held informally for almost 150 years and is now enshrined in the Twenty-second Amendment. Washington fit the Framers' vision of the ideal president—a respectable gentleman with suitable wealth, experience, and connections. The notion that "any child can grow up to be president" was foreign to them.

Theodore Roosevelt gave voice to popular sentiment by using the presidency as a "bully pulpit" for change.

As national parties came to dominate government and presidential politics in the early 1800s, party leaders in Congress played the leading role in choosing presidential candidates. That began to change in 1831, when the Anti-Masonic and Republican National Parties used nominating conventions composed of state party delegates to select their nominees. The following year the Democrats met in convention to nominate Andrew Jackson to a second term. Jackson built ties with the public, portraying himself as a tribune of the people and using his popularity to build support for his policies.

For a period, presidents such as Jackson, James Polk, and Abraham Lincoln exercised substantial authority, and the president's power as a popular national leader grew. Lincoln, in particular, demonstrated the wide latitude a president has in responding to a crisis. Among the wartime actions he undertook were the suspension of *habeas corpus,* the confiscation of private property without due process or compensation, the blockage of Southern ports, and the trial of civilians in military courts. Lincoln even defied the orders of the federal courts. His actions demonstrate that, as one historian noted, "So long as public opinion sustains the president . . ., he has nothing to fear from the displeasure of the courts."[4]

After the Civil War, the average American looked to local politicians to address his or her problems and had few expectations of national government. Presidents acceded to this view by advancing few initiatives.

The strength of political parties began to diminish around the turn of the twentieth century as people voiced concern about the corruption of local "machine" politics. Americans turned back to the nation's capital for help in addressing labor and health concerns arising from a growing national economy and burgeoning urban life. Theodore Roosevelt gave voice to popular sentiment by using the presidency as a "bully pulpit" for effecting change and giving vent to the "view then emerging among the Progressives that chief executives were also representatives of the people."[5] Woodrow Wilson offered the most straightforward endorsement of the notion that a president is the people's representative, above parochial or partisan interest:

> No one else represents the people as a whole, exercising a national choice. . . . The nation as a whole has chosen him, and he is conscious that it has no other political spokesman. His is the only national voice in affairs . . . (T)here is but one national voice in the country, and that is the voice of the President.[6]

The Modern Presidency

Franklin D. Roosevelt's presidency ushered in a new era of a powerful chief executive. Many of the policies FDR championed, including social welfare and business regulatory programs, involved the national government directly in the lives of individuals and gave the people a stake in presidential performance. The government programs he helped create further undercut the role of local parties by providing many people with direct federal aid. Business groups found it far more effective to lobby executive branch agencies than local politicians or even members of Congress. These changes increased the reach of presidential power and strengthened the bonds between individual citizens and the president.

After World War II, America became a prominent world power and presidents were expected to protect national interests abroad, prevent nuclear catastrophe, and promote world trade. Today, most citizens consider the president personally accountable for the performance of government. The president is the one politician who speaks for and to the entire nation and the one individual in government who has a commanding view of the problems faced by the nation as a whole.

Clearly, the presidency has become a more democratic institution than the Framers intended. Presidents have become custodians of the public trust and are seen by many as tribunes for common causes. The modern presidency has also given rise to an ever-increasing and complex national government that fosters an atmosphere of enlarged expectations about what presidents can accomplish.

THE PATH TO THE PRESIDENCY

Most presidential contenders reflect the dominant characteristics of the traditional electorate: white, male, Anglo-Saxon, and Protestant. The 2008 campaign marked the first time an African American candidate was chosen as the presidential nominee from a major party and only the second time a female was chosen as a vice presidential running mate. The first female vice presidential candidate from a major party was Geraldine Ferraro in 1984. The 2016 campaign cycle witnessed the most sustained race for the presidential nomination by a woman, Hillary Clinton.

Prior government service is another characteristic that presidential candidates typically share. All but five presidents held political office before becoming chief executive; four of these exceptions (George Washington, Andrew Jackson, Ulysses Grant, and Dwight Eisenhower) were military officers. The fifth, businessman Donald Trump, is the first candidate in U.S. history to ascend to the presidency without any prior military or public service experience. Vice presidents have ascended to the presidency fourteen times, nine as a result of the death or resignation of the person they served. Twelve presidents were former governors, including four of the last seven. Sixteen senators have become president; three (Harding, Kennedy, and Obama) moved directly from the Senate to the White House.

GETTING ELECTED

Hurdling legal and societal barriers is only the first of many tests facing a presidential candidate. Eighteen to twenty-four months prior to the presidential election (and often earlier), potential candidates begin to test the waters and amass the resources necessary to mount a credible campaign. The 2016 presidential contest was one of the longest and most expensive in American history. Candidates began meeting with campaign advisors and consultants years before any votes were cast, and they began fundraising in earnest. It was also one of the most unusual campaigns in recent times as deep fissures within each party opened opportunities for insurgent candidates against party establishment figures.

Fundraising

The most important story of the 2016 presidential campaign was the strength of anti-establishment sentiment fueling the candidacies of outsiders Bernie Sanders and Donald Trump. It was clear that large numbers of Americans were disenchanted with politics as usual and were frustrated with candidates financed by large dollar donors and political insiders whom they felt no longer represented their interests. Whereas candidates Hillary

Clinton and Jeb Bush each started their campaigns with a huge financial advantage over their respective rivals, largely due to support from big dollar donors and outside groups, small donors were the source of Bernie Sanders's fundraising success. Donald Trump pumped large sums of his own money into his campaign. Total spending by candidates, parties, and outside groups for the 2016 presidential campaign was impressive, exceeding $2.4 billion, slightly less than the record of $2.6 billion spent in the presidential campaign of 2012.[7]

None of the 2016 presidential candidates tapped the public funds first made available for presidential elections in 1976. Under the public financing law, major-party presidential candidates who demonstrate their viability by raising a certain dollar amount qualify for federal matching funds to run their campaigns. Independent or third-party candidates may collect these funds retroactively if they receive at least 5 percent of the popular vote in the general election. The public funds are raised through $3 contributions taxpayers may designate on their federal income tax returns. Because candidates who accept these public funds must abide by federal spending limits, presidential candidates have tended to refuse these funds in recent election cycles for fear they would be outspent by opponents who raise and spend all of their funds on their own and without limit.

Campaigning in 2016 was also remarkable because of the flood of cash from independent groups made possible by court rulings in *Citizens United v. Federal Election Commission* (2010) and *SpeechNow.org v. Federal Election Commission* (2010). The former decision from the Supreme Court permitted contributions by corporations, labor unions, and trade associations advocating for or against political candidates; the latter case issued by a federal appeals court gave birth to so-called super PACs by permitting *unlimited* contributions by individuals, corporations, and unions so long as these are not coordinated with candidate committees. In 2014, the court once again weakened the rules on contribution limits. In *McCutcheon v. FEC,* the Supreme Court struck down the cap on the total amount an individual can donate to federal candidates in a two-year cycle. These decisions, together with the low spending caps permitted under the public finance law, have rendered the public financing of presidential elections all but obsolete.

Much of the money raised during a campaign is used to get out the vote. In recent elections, political campaigns have developed new techniques for identifying potential voters and mobilizing their support. In 2008 and 2012, Democrats employed data-mining and microtargeting to reach supporters. These techniques identify and segment voters on the basis of hundreds of demographic and consumer variables that are then used to devise themes and advertisements appealing to each voter group.[8] They also pioneered the use of randomized controlled experiments to determine how best to get their supporters to the polls. In 2016, Senator Ted Cruz invested heavily in some of the same techniques during his Republican primary battle. His analytics team used psychological test data and issue surveys to categorize supporters, who then received specially tailored messages, phone calls, and visits.[9] The Trump campaign took advantage of similar techniques, employing the firm *Cambridge Analytica* to collect Facebook data to target American voters with ads designed to mobilize support for the Republican candidate. The same firm came under scrutiny after the election for engaging in potentially unethical behavior.

Although 2016 continued to see most campaigns pour money into TV advertising, it was apparent that returns from this medium were diminishing (see Chapter 10). Some of the candidates who, together with their super PAC supporters, spent heavily on TV, exited the campaign early. Most notable among those departing early were Jeb Bush and Marco Rubio, who combined spent over $150 million on TV before departing from the campaign with little to show for the investment.[10] Donald Trump made news daily with his Twitter feed and received over $2 billion of free publicity during the primary season by making himself a staple of daily news shows. Super PACs and other outside organizations continued to pour money into campaigns, much of it spent on negative ads against their adversaries.

Following the election, it was discovered that during the campaign Russia surreptitiously purchased social media posts designed to mobilize Trump supporters and drive down support

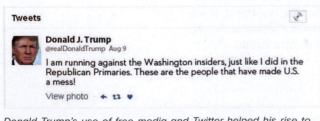

Donald Trump's use of free media and Twitter helped his rise to prominence in the 2016 campaign. As a result, he achieved maximum exposure with a minimum expenditure of campaign cash.

Source: Twitter

for Hillary Clinton. Twitter revealed that the Russian state media agency *Russia Today* spent as much as $247,100 in ads and fake posts targeting U.S. markets during the 2016 campaign.[11] Facebook disclosed that about three thousand ads were purchased for approximately $100,000 by the Internet Research Agency, a Russian company known for trolling, aimed at sowing discord prior to the election.[12] Researchers found that a large number of these ads were placed in swing states.[13] By March 2018, the special counsel entrusted with investigating Russian interference in the 2016 election brought indictments against thirteen Russian nationals and three Russian companies for conducting "information warfare" against the United States in order to influence the election outcome. Although foreign spending on U.S. elections is illegal and these revelations have led to guilty pleas by several defendants, there is no evidence that these social media activities had any effect on the outcome of the election.

JUL 23 **Down With Hillary!**
Sat 1 PM EDT · 1 Pierrepont Plz, New York City, ...
180 people interested · 45 people going   ★ Interested

763 Reactions 76 Comments

👍 Like   💬 Comment

Facebook revealed that thousands of dollars were spent by Russian operatives on ads like this one to influence voter choices in the 2016 election.

Source: Being Patriotic/Facebook post

Primary Sweepstakes

Political scientists have long held that an "invisible primary" takes place in the years and months before a presidential election year.[14] It is a process dominated by activists, resource providers, campaign specialists, and media personnel, who together influence election outcomes by screening candidates for electability and providing some—but not others—with the resources they need to move forward in the campaign. This process, it is thought, allows party insiders to dictate the eventual nominee.[15] The 2016 campaign, dominated as it was by political outsiders, illustrates that this process is not impenetrable. Bernie Sanders and Donald Trump both confounded political pundits as they challenged party favorites and extended the primary season.

During the pre-convention season, candidates run in contests state-by-state. They criss-cross the country, running in primary elections and electoral **caucuses**, local gatherings where townspeople meet to voice their preferences for the candidate they believe can best lead their party. Although voters in these venues express their support for specific presidential candidates, their votes actually determine the composition of pledged delegates that the states send to the party's national convention. The number of delegates each state is allotted is determined by the political parties on the basis of population, as well as each state's performance in delivering the vote in the previous general election.

> **caucus** A voter gathering used to select party candidates to run in the general election.

For Republicans in 2016, early voting states in the primaries divided their allotted delegates proportionately to each candidate based on the popular votes each candidate received. For states voting later in the primary season, Republicans awarded all of a state's delegates to the winner of the popular vote. Democrats awarded delegates on a proportional basis throughout. Some states also use state conventions to allocate a portion of delegates. Once these delegates arrive at the national convention, they are expected to vote for the nominee to whom they are pledged, an expectation that applies to both parties equally.

To win nomination, a candidate must have the support of a majority of delegates attending the national convention. In 2016, the Democratic candidate needed at least 2,382 out of 4,763 delegates to become the party's nominee while the Republican required at least 1,237 out of 2,472 delegates. Because voters select most of the delegates through the primary election process, the public usually knows the identity of each party's nominee long before the conventions. However, each party also sends a number of unelected delegates who are free to vote for the candidate of their choice. It is believed that their votes might steer the convention to the candidate with the best chance of victory in the general election—especially if no one candidate arrives at the convention with enough votes to win on the first ballot. In 2016, the Republicans sent three members of the Republican National Committee from each state to their national convention as **unallocated delegates**. The Democrats sent a much larger number, 712, called **superdelegates** coming from the ranks of elected party officials and state party leaders. Superdelegates, most of whom supported Hillary Clinton, came under criticism from Sanders supporters who believed they posed a threat to the wishes of average voters. At a meeting of the Democratic National Committee in 2018, the party agreed to reduce the influence of superdelegates by eliminating them from first ballot voting.

> **unallocated delegates** Elected officials and party leaders chosen as delegates to the national party conventions with the ability to cast their votes for any candidate regardless of primary election results.
>
> **superdelegates** The term used to refer to Democratic Party leaders and elected officials attending the party convention. The independent influence they played in the nominating process in the past has been recently curbed by changes in party rules.

Not all primaries and caucuses are created equal. Iowa and New Hampshire, for example, are both small states that send few delegates to the party conventions (about 1 percent of the total for each party) and are not representative of the national electorate as a whole.[16] Because they traditionally host the first primaries of a campaign, however, they attract a great deal of media attention and play a disproportionately large role in shaping public opinion about the candidates. Campaigning in these first states allows candidates to hone their messages before small groups of voters gathered in homes and diners throughout the states. The impact of early victories in building momentum can be substantial. In fact, one study found that voters in early primary states had up to five times the influence of voters in late primary states in winnowing the field and helping to choose their party's eventual nominee.[17]

In the 2016 primaries, the Republican candidate pool seeking the nomination was especially large. Seventeen individuals entered the race, forcing television networks hosting debates to split the field into two separate debating stages in the early months of the campaign. Those candidates polling highest at the time of each debate were given prime-time debate slots while those with low poll numbers were relegated to less favorable debating times. Donald Trump racked up a significant number of early wins with a populist appeal stressing the deportation of undocumented immigrants and the closing of U.S. borders to Muslims. His inflammatory and often crude remarks were ratings grabbers that drew media attention. Republican insiders, who believed he was unelectable in a general election, took the unprecedented step of opposing his candidacy and urged voters to support any Republican other than Trump. Mitt Romney delivered a scathing attack on Trump in a televised speech and Republican super PACs poured millions into ads intended to defeat him. Yet Trump's appeal as an outsider in a year when voters expressed distrust for party establishment figures proved irresistible to voters. By May, with a victory in the Indiana primary, Trump had dispatched his opponents and secured the Republican nomination. Although support among party insiders remained tepid at best, he received strong support throughout the campaign from white working-class males without a college education who felt left behind in the wake of a changing economy.[18]

Democratic primary election rules played to Hillary Clinton's early strengths. Every state awarded convention delegates on a proportional basis, making it difficult for a late-surging Bernie Sanders to overcome Clinton's substantial lead, particularly in southern states that held early primaries. Still, Sanders mounted a formidable campaign that defied odds for an outsider claiming to be a "democratic socialist." With a message calling for free health care and free college tuition, Sanders found strong support among youth. He also attracted lower-income white voters with a populist message decrying free trade agreements, which he claimed were responsible for exporting good-paying jobs to low-wage countries. Clinton advanced a more centrist message attracting the support of the party's base electorate including blacks, women, and Hispanics.

Party Conventions

nominating convention A meeting of party delegates to select their presidential nominee.

At one time, the **nominating conventions** were the sites of dramatic battles to determine the parties' platforms and nominees. Some, such as the 1860 Democratic convention, witnessed dozens of votes and extensive backroom deal-making, eventually resulting in a split in the party. Today, conventions are highly orchestrated made-for-TV spectacles where delegates gather to hear candidate and celebrity speeches and to rally around their party as they prepare for the general election contest. Sometimes contentious debates over planks in the party platform are no longer conducted in public on the convention floor. Instead, they occur in a private setting away from the convention where the nominee's representatives exercise control. With most of the decisions about the candidates and the platform completed before the conventions, national television networks have steadily reduced their coverage of these events in recent years. Still, each convention holds the potential for drama, and many voters report they are likely to tune in for long periods of time.

Many delegates are average citizens participating in electoral politics for the first time. Changes in party rules since the 1970s ensure that they represent a diverse mix of individuals. However, elected officials and party workers are also well represented. Many convention delegates are activists who hope to mold the party platform in ways that favor the interests they represent. But the conventions also provide an opportunity for partisans to coalesce and rededicate themselves to the causes the party espouses and to celebrate its historical accomplishments.

Until 2016, each major party could receive public funding for their national nominating conventions. In 2012, this amounted to approximately $18 million. Starting in 2016, the parties were forced to pay for their own conventions but received substantial supplemental funding from political action committees (PACs) and lobbyists.

The party out of power usually holds its convention first, as the Republicans did in 2016, meeting in mid-July in Cleveland, Ohio. Donald Trump attempted to shore up his conservative base by selecting Mike Pence, governor of Indiana, as his running mate. Pence, known for his solid conservative credentials and religious beliefs, provided a stark contrast to Trump's bombastic style and unorthodox ideas. The tone of the convention was dark and foreboding, with speakers warning of terrorist threats and failures of Democrats to protect American citizens at home and abroad. The fissures within the party that had been on display during the primary season were also evident during the convention, with some Republicans notables, such as Texas senator Ted Cruz and John Kasich, governor of Ohio, refusing to endorse the nominee during the convention.

©Mary Altaffer/AP Images

Donald Trump chose Indiana governor Mike Pence as his running mate, a man known as a quiet and reliable conservative, providing a contrast to Trump's own unorthodox style.

The Democratic convention in Philadelphia held its own drama. Sanders's supporters, representing about 45 percent of the elected delegates in attendance, had hoped to dislodge enough superdelegates committed to Hillary Clinton in order to force a floor fight. Although this did not occur, Sanders was able to secure concessions on the party platform, including a pledge to pursue a publicly financed option for health care and a plan to provide free tuition to public colleges for students from families making less than $125,000 a year. Stung by a carefully timed revelation from WikiLeaks that Democratic Party officials had discussed ways to derail the Sanders campaign during the primaries instead of remaining neutral, Sanders's supporters booed some of the prime-time speakers and walked out following the roll call vote that handed Clinton the nomination. The leak also abruptly forced the resignation of Debbie Wasserman Schultz, the chair of the Democratic National Committee, on the opening day of the convention. Despite these controversies, Sanders himself moved that Clinton be nominated by acclamation in an attempt to unify the party. With her nomination, Clinton became the first woman to be nominated by a major political party in the 227-year history of the Republic. Her vice presidential pick, Virginia senator Tim Kaine, had working-class roots and spoke fluent Spanish, making him appealing to the traditional Democratic constituencies Clinton hoped to carry.

The General Election

Immediately following their respective conventions, the nominees mount an intense effort to connect with the public and sell themselves and their ideas to the electorate prior to Election Day. This includes making personal appearances around the country and obtaining maximum exposure in newspapers, radio, and television. Since the Kennedy-Nixon contest in 1960, televised debates have been an important feature of the general election season. All of the campaigns' efforts at this stage are guided by the quest to secure enough Electoral College votes to win the presidency.

The Electoral College Although a candidate's ultimate goal is to collect as many votes as possible, the candidate who receives the most popular votes does not always win the election. That is because presidential elections are won or lost in the Electoral College, a body whose members (called **electors**) cast the deciding votes in presidential elections.

elector Member of the Electoral College.

Representatives of large and small states at the Constitutional Convention of 1787 supported different methods for determining the outcome of presidential elections. Delegates compromised by creating an unorthodox institution that assigns to each state a number of presidential electors equal to its combined total of representatives and senators. This procedure gives delegates from large states a substantial say in the presidential elections while awarding small states two more electoral votes than their population alone would provide. The District of Columbia also has three electors in the college, bringing the total membership to 538; a majority (270) is required for election. Electors generally consist of appointees of state party leaders, party faithful chosen at party conventions, and, in the case of independent candidates, individuals chosen for their loyalty. Electors representing the party whose candidate won the popular vote in each state assemble in their state capitals on the first Monday after the second Wednesday of December to cast official ballots.

unit rule The practice of awarding all of a state's electoral votes to the candidate who wins a plurality of the popular vote in presidential contests.

All but two states in the Electoral College apply the **unit rule** when assigning votes to a candidate. Under this rule, the candidate who receives a plurality of popular votes (more than any competitor) in the state is entitled to all the electoral votes from that state. For instance, if Florida voters award more votes to the Republican candidate than to any other, he or she will receive all twenty-nine of the state's electoral votes. Maine and Nebraska do not use the unit rule; instead, those states award two electors to the candidate who wins the most votes statewide and apportion the remainder according to the popular vote in each congressional district. No elector is under a constitutional obligation, however, to cast a ballot as advertised. This produces the potential for "faithless electors"—electors who cast their votes for someone other than the choice expressed by the electorate. This has occurred more than 150 times in our nation's history, but it has never altered an election result.

If no candidate receives a majority of electoral votes, members of the House of Representatives choose the president from among top vote-getters, with each state receiving one vote. The Senate chooses the vice president. The Framers believed that few candidates would command a majority of the popular vote and felt that the House of Representatives would choose most presidents. They devised the Electoral College to quell political infighting but considered it unlikely to be important in most presidential contests. As it turned out, the House formally selected only two presidents—Thomas Jefferson (1800) and John Quincy Adams (1824).

Originally, each elector submitted a single ballot with two names. The candidate receiving the highest number of votes (but at least a majority of all votes) became president, and the runner-up became vice president. In 1796, this produced a president from one party and a vice president from another. Four years later, it resulted in a tie for the presidency between two candidates from the same party, Thomas Jefferson and Aaron Burr. In response to the political furor caused by these events, Congress enacted the Twelfth Amendment in 1804, requiring electors to cast separate ballots for president and vice president.

The 2016 election demonstrated a potentially more troubling shortcoming with the Electoral College: One candidate can win enough electoral votes to become president while losing the popular vote. Although Clinton won three million more votes than her opponent, Trump won the Electoral College vote. A similar situation occurred in 2000, when Democratic candidate Al Gore won the popular vote by over a half-million votes, but Republican George W. Bush won the presidency by a single electoral vote after a contentious showdown over ballots cast in Florida. A Supreme Court ruling, *Bush v. Gore,* ended the recount process in Florida and gave the victory to Bush. Similar disparities between the popular vote winner and the Electoral College victor arose in the elections in 1824, 1876, and 1888. In those years, votes in the House or last-minute political negotiations between the parties settled the outcome.

The 2000 and 2016 elections were just the most recent, and perhaps the most dramatic, examples of the problems that can arise within our presidential election system. Anomalies such as these have caused some critics to wonder whether the Electoral College has outlived its usefulness and whether it has a dampening impact on political engagement today. Recent Gallup polls show the American public nearly evenly split on whether the Constitution should be amended to replace the institution with the direct election of the president, with partisans supporting the winning candidate more likely to favor keeping things as they are.[19]

Electoral College Strategy Because the Electoral College, not the popular vote, determines the victor, candidates must devise a strategy to ensure that they gather the 270 electoral votes they need to win. This means candidates must determine which states are crucial for their success and plan their campaigns accordingly. First, each party must secure its "base" states, those that reliably vote for that party in general elections. Candidates rarely spend significant time or other resources in their opponents' strongholds. In recent elections, political observers have referred to Republican base states as "red" states and Democratic base states as "blue" states. Red states are generally less populated but more numerous and are spread across the South and Midwest. The more heavily populated blue states are concentrated along the West Coast and in the Upper Midwest and Northeast.

Second, candidates must pick and choose **battleground states**—competitive states where neither side has a major advantage—where they feel they have the best hope of success. As campaigns carefully piece together strategies that focus on the precise combination of states necessary to reach the 270-vote mark, both candidates will be eyeing the battleground states.

battleground state A competitive state where neither party holds an overwhelming edge.

In 2016, the battleground—or most competitive—states included Pennsylvania and Ohio, where the loss of good-paying industrial jobs to foreign competition provided an opportunity for Trump and a challenge for Clinton. States with growing minority populations like Florida were also considered a prize that held a large number of electoral votes. The Clinton campaign, following a traditional campaign script, placed most of its resources in these states, spending lavishly on TV ads and field offices from which it could dispatch workers to knock on doors to get out the vote. Trump, true to his unorthodox approach, failed to match Clinton in traditional outreach, preferring large rallies and TV appearances where his sometimes outlandish statements secured massive amounts of free media. Still, the Republican National Committee and pro-Trump super PACs invested heavily in battleground states and made last-minute appeals to states that had trended Democratic in recent presidential elections but in which a critical mass of disaffected white working-class voters could be identified. This strategy paid huge rewards by squeezing enough votes out of Wisconsin, Michigan, and Pennsylvania to put Trump over the top.

Hillary Clinton spent much of the fall presidential campaign fending off attacks about her use of a private email server while secretary of state, a practice many believed jeopardized U.S. security. The attacks were fueled by both court-ordered releases of documents from the State Department as well as leaked documents secured by WikiLeaks founder Julian Assange. Clinton and the Obama administration suggested the WikiLeaks material was purloined by Russian hackers in an attempt to influence American elections. Clinton also spent time on the campaign trail attempting to reengage President Obama's two-time winning coalition of women, blacks, Hispanics, and youth—constituencies that showed little of the same enthusiasm for Clinton as they did for her former boss. Bernie Sanders and Michelle Obama stumped for Clinton as surrogates on the campaign trail in an effort to build enthusiasm for her candidacy.

The first presidential debate, which drew the largest audience in the history of televised debates, featured Trump taking credit for not paying federal income tax for years as then recently published documents had shown. The second debate featured Trump conjuring up memories of President Bill Clinton's infidelities in response to questions about Trump's own treatment of women after a leaked video showing Trump making lewd remarks. These performances escalated the defection of Republican officeholders and donors away from Trump and, according to polls taken in the aftermath of the debates, seemed to doom his chances for victory. Yet Trump continued to draw huge crowds to his rallies and insisted his support was underreported by pollsters who failed to capture the strength of his support, especially among highly motivated working-class whites without a college degree. His message seemed to resonate particularly well with those outside of the major metropolitan areas.

The End Game As the presidential campaign season began, there was every reason to believe that a Republican would win the White House. Americans rarely award the presidency to the same party after eight years in office. With the exception of Harry Truman's election succeeding Franklin Roosevelt, the last time a Democrat was elected to succeed a two-term president from the same party was in 1836 when Martin Van Buren succeeded Andrew Jackson. The last time the Republicans held the White House for three terms was 1980 to 1992. In addition to this historic trend of party replacement, Republicans seemed prepared to capitalize on discontent with the slow pace of economic recovery under President Obama and the lackluster popular support for the Democratic nominee.

On Election Day, Republican candidate Donald Trump ended up with 306 electoral votes to Clinton's 232. (Two of Trump's electors eventually defected to vote for someone else, while five electors defected from Clinton, yielding an official total of 304 for Trump and 227 for Clinton.) See "Electoral College Maps" to compare the results from 2012 and 2016.

Electoral College Maps

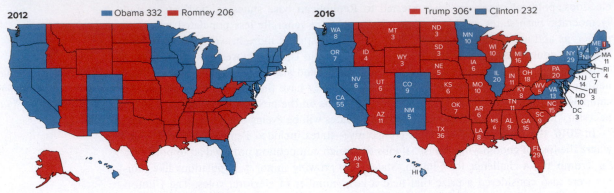

Donald Trump redrew the 2016 electoral map, taking several of the battleground states over Clinton, states that Obama had won in 2008 and 2012.

Source: 2012 and 2016: Edison Research Exit Polls; 2016: Edison/Mitofsky.

Appealing to pockets of resentment against undocumented immigrants, concerns over terrorist threats, suspicion of Washington elites, and a longing to return to the bygone days of prosperity brought on by a manufacturing-based economy, Trump triumphed against his rivals—both within his party and outside—with a combination of persistent and unorthodox live television interviews and the rigorous use of his Twitter feed. In the final days of his campaign, Trump presented a somewhat more reserved demeanor that may have calmed the fears of some undecided voters while still maintaining the enthusiasm of his core supporters. Some observers also attribute Trump's victory to Russian support in the form of social media activity targeted to attract white working-class voters in swing states, as discussed earlier.

In the end, Trump managed to cobble together a coalition of working-class whites without a college education, men, evangelicals, and rural voters who were unhappy with the status quo (see "Portrait of the Electorate, 2016"). Among Trump voters, 83 percent said they chose him because he could bring needed change to Washington. His striking performance was also responsible for helping down-ballot Republicans hold on to the House and the Senate. Finally, his victory may have been helped by the presence of third-party candidates with just enough votes in some states to put him over the top. At the same time, Clinton underperformed among almost all of the constituencies that made up the Obama coalition in 2012, especially minorities and young people, whose turnout was below expectations or who voted for Trump. For example, a plurality (48 percent) of white millennials voted for Trump.

The 2016 election brought with it a populist wave that surprised many seasoned political observers and confounded pollsters. It also brought with it great uncertainty about the future direction of public policy and party alignment.

PRESIDENTIAL POWER

The American presidency has evolved into the most powerful post in the world. Effectively exercising this awesome power requires the ability to diagnose problems, assert priorities, work cooperatively with others, recruit support from other decision makers, shepherd policies through a giant bureaucracy, and communicate effectively with the public. The potential for failure is high, particularly when opponents place roadblocks in the president's path. It is no wonder that Franklin D. Roosevelt, considered to be the architect of the modern presidency, once called the presidency a lonely job. "If you are president," he once commented to an advisor, "you'll be looking at the door over there and knowing that practically everybody that walks through it wants something out of you."[20]

As we discussed earlier, the Framers were wary of executive power. As a result, the Constitution gives presidents few **express powers**, or explicit grants of authority, and places limits on presidential authority through a system of checks and balances. Congress can also

express powers Powers granted to the president by the Constitution.

Portrait of the Electorate, 2016 (percentages)

2016 Vote Choice Among Validated Voters*

Gender	Share of Electorate	Hillary Clinton	Donald Trump
Men	45%	41%	52%
Women	55%	54%	39%

Age	Share of Electorate	Hillary Clinton	Donald Trump
18–29	13%	58%	28%
30–49	30%	51%	40%
50–64	29%	45%	51%
65+	27%	44%	53%

Race/Ethnicity	Share of Electorate	Hillary Clinton	Donald Trump
White	74%	39%	54%
Black	10%	91%	6%
Hispanic	10%	66%	28%
Other/mixed	5%	59%	32%

Race/Ethnicity/Gender	Share of Electorate	Hillary Clinton	Donald Trump
White men	33%	32%	62%
White women	41%	45%	47%
Black men	4%	81%	14%
Black women	6%	98%	1%
Hispanic men	5%	65%	28%
Hispanic women	5%	67%	28%

Education	Share of Electorate	Hillary Clinton	Donald Trump
Postgrad	14%	66%	29%
College grad	23%	52%	41%
Some college	34%	42%	49%
HS or less	30%	44%	51%

Race/Education/Gender	Share of Electorate	Hillary Clinton	Donald Trump
White college grad+	30%	55%	38%
Non-white college grad+	7%	68%	26%
White non-college grad	44%	28%	64%
Non-white non-college grad	19%	77%	18%
White college grad+ men	17%	47%	44%
White college grad+ women	23%	61%	35%
White non-college grad men	28%	23%	73%
White non-college grad women	32%	33%	56%

Marital Status	Share of Electorate	Hillary Clinton	Donald Trump
Married	52%	39%	55%
Unmarried	48%	58%	34%
Married men	27%	32%	62%
Unmarried men	19%	54%	39%
Married women	26%	47%	48%
Unmarried women	29%	60%	31%

Income	Share of Electorate	Hillary Clinton	Donald Trump
$150,000 or more	7%	51%	44%
$100,000–$149,999	11%	48%	45%
$75,000–$99,999	15%	39%	55%
$50,000–$74,999	18%	48%	46%
$30,000–$49,999	20%	42%	54%
Less than $30,000	28%	58%	32%

Residence	Share of Electorate	Hillary Clinton	Donald Trump
Urban	22%	70%	24%
Suburban	50%	45%	47%
Rural	27%	34%	59%

Religion	Share of Electorate	Hillary Clinton	Donald Trump
Protestant	47%	39%	56%
Catholic	20%	44%	52%
Unaffiliated	26%	65%	24%
White evangelical protestant	20%	16%	77%
White mainline protestant	15%	37%	57%
Black protestant	7%	96%	3%
Other race protestant	5%	51%	46%
White non-Hispanic Catholic	14%	31%	64%
Hispanic Catholic	5%	78%	19%
Atheist/Agnostic	12%	69%	20%
Nothing in particular	14%	61%	27%

Party Affiliation	Share of Electorate	Hillary Clinton	Donald Trump
Republican	31%	4%	92%
Democrat	35%	94%	5%
Independent/other	34%	42%	43%
Republican/lean republican	48%	4%	89%
Democrat/lean democrat	51%	89%	5%

Ideology	Share of Electorate	Hillary Clinton	Donald Trump
Very conservative	9%	16%	83%
Conservative	26%	10%	84%
Moderate	38%	55%	36%
Liberal	18%	86%	8%
Very liberal	9%	88%	4%

*Percentages may not add to 100% due to rounding and response rate. Based on 3,014 validated 2016 general election voters. Validated voters are those found to have voted in any of five commercial voter files, corrected for questionable matches. Vote choice is from a post-election survey and excludes those who refused to answer or reported voting for a candidate other than Trump, Clinton, Johnson or Stein. *Source:* Pew Research Center, *A Detailed Look at the 2016 Electorate Based on Voter Records*, August 9, 2018.

Hillary Clinton underperformed among groups that made up the Obama coalition in 2012. By contrast, Donald Trump garnered more support from whites, those without college degrees, and evangelicals than Republican Mitt Romney did four years earlier.

cede powers to the executive that enable the president to enforce laws. Modern presidents use these **delegated powers** to achieve a number of their priorities. When Congress authorizes a clean air law, for example, it does not specify the quantity of pollutants that smokestacks may release into the atmosphere. Instead, it delegates to the executive branch the authority to make rules specifying how rigorous such regulations must be.

The president may also exercise **discretionary powers** associated with carrying out official duties. These are powers granted either expressly or by delegation that give him flexibility in performing the duties of office. Presidents have used their discretionary power to claim extensive authority, especially during times of war or national emergency. In the wake of the September 11, 2001, terrorist attacks, President George W. Bush issued a number of directives in the name of national security to protect the homeland. For example, he authorized the CIA to engage in political assassination of named terrorists, effectively lifting a twenty-five-year ban on such activities. And he authorized the Treasury Department to freeze assets of alleged terrorists.[21] President Barack Obama continued these antiterrorism policies and oversaw an unprecedented expansion of data collection about American citizens' telephone usage. President Donald Trump, too, has wielded discretionary authority by limiting immigration from certain majority-Muslim countries. Presidents must learn how best to use this mix of express, delegated, and discretionary powers in fulfilling the various roles of the office.

Chief Executive

As the nation's chief executive officer, the president oversees a vast bureaucracy that administers countless programs upon which millions of Americans depend. The president exercises his executive power of appointment to hire people to run the day-to-day operations of government and to assist in broader duties, such as budgeting and law enforcement. As chief executive, the president may also issue executive orders to achieve policy goals in the absence of legislation, a long-standing yet controversial practice.

©Doug Mills/AP Images

Presidential powers are both real and ceremonial. The nation looks to the president for leadership in times of crisis. President Bush is seen here shortly after the terrorist attacks in New York City on September 11, 2001, standing on a pile of rubble that was once one of the World Trade Center buildings.

Appointment Even our earliest presidents appointed a substantial number of persons to government jobs. George Washington filled more than one thousand positions from customs collector to surveyor, usually on the basis of statements attesting to the candidate's good character and moral virtue.[22]

The president is free to choose the leaders for top administrative posts, known as the **cabinet**, but must seek the advice and consent of the Senate for their approval (see Chapter 11). Senate committees subject nominees to extensive screening and hearing procedures before the entire body votes on confirmation. The president sometimes personally introduces nominees to senators or solicits suggestions from powerful Senate leaders. Until recently, the Senate rejected few presidential nominees, preferring to defer to the president unless they believed the nominee was genuinely unfit for service. Increased partisan polarization has created a more contentious nomination process. A number of Trump nominees either withdrew or failed to be confirmed because of potential financial conflicts of interest or alleged past indiscretions.

When the Senate does block a nominee, the president may respond by waiting until Congress goes into recess and then appointing the nominee without Senate approval. Such **recess appointments** are effective only until the end of the next Senate session. Recess appointments are not uncommon. Bill Clinton made 139 recess appointments; George W. Bush, 171. President Obama made 32 recess appointments but some were thwarted by Congress's ability to remain formally in session during recess periods without actually performing any work, a practice upheld by the Supreme Court (*N.L.R.B. v Noel Canning*, 2014).

Among the president's most important appointees requiring Senate approval are members of the U.S. Supreme Court. When Supreme Court Justice Antonin Scalia died suddenly in February 2016, the Republican-controlled Senate refused to hold confirmation hearings for Merrick Garland, President Obama's nominee to replace Scalia, taking the unprecedented position that a vacancy occurring in a presidential election year should be filled by a newly elected incoming president. President Trump took advantage of two openings during his first two years in office to appoint conservative justices Neil Gorsuch and Brett Kavanaugh. Supreme Court appointments will be discussed in more detail in Chapter 14.

Budgeting Although the Constitution gives Congress the power to control the purse strings, presidents have taken the initiative in proposing and implementing budgetary priorities. Before 1921, each federal agency submitted a separate budget request directly to the House of Representatives. To impose order on this chaotic process, Congress passed the Budget and Accounting Act of 1921, which requires the president to propose a budget for all agencies and submit to Congress annual estimates of program costs. The Office of Management and Budget (OMB, originally the Bureau of the Budget) was created to coordinate funding requests from various executive branch agencies to ensure they are responsive to the president's priorities. It also conducts cost-benefit analyses of policy recommendations and guides the president's agenda through Washington's bureaucratic maze.[23]

The increased budgetary authority of the executive branch has given presidents immense power to control the political agenda but has also generated heated battles with Congress, which must authorize spending. Until 1974, for example, the president could rein in congressional spending by **impoundment**, or withholding of funds. Responding to what it considered the Nixon administration's overtly partisan use of this tool, Congress placed severe limits on the president's authority to withhold funds already appropriated. The president can request a **rescission**, or cutback, of funds in particular areas, but it must be approved by Congress within a specified period of time. Several presidents have sought the power to simply reject individual items in the budget with which they disagree, a power called a **line item veto**. Governors in most states already have such authority. However, the Supreme Court held that the Constitution does not currently give presidents that option.[24]

The inability of Congress and the president to agree on a budget has led to a series of budget showdowns and government shutdowns since 2010. Even when budgets have been approved, there have been disputes over raising the **debt ceiling**, a procedure that allows the government to borrow additional funds to pay bills for spending Congress has already authorized. In recent years, budgets have often been cobbled together at the last minute by makeshift compromises instead of through an orderly process of debate.

impoundment Presidential refusal to expend funds appropriated by Congress.

rescission Cutback of funds for particular programs that requires congressional approval.

line item veto The executive power to reject a portion of a bill, usually a budget appropriation.

debt ceiling The government's credit limit. If the government seeks to spend more than it has authorized, it must raise its borrowing power.

Law Enforcement Traditionally, law enforcement has been the province of state and local government, but as the federal government has grown and assumed greater responsibilities, the federal executive has played an ever-larger role in law enforcement. Today, executive agencies enforce not only criminal laws but also laws affecting public health, business regulation, civil rights, and immigration, among a host of other areas.

The executive branch attempted to strengthen and centralize its control over federal law enforcement in the wake of the 2001 terrorist attacks. A congressional commission investigating the attacks found that existing criminal law made it difficult, and sometimes impossible, for federal law enforcement agencies to share pertinent information regarding ongoing terrorist investigations. The commission proposed a number of steps to break down interagency barriers. These included creating a National Counterterrorism Center to coordinate intelligence about potential terrorist attacks and establishing a new Office of the Director of National Intelligence to oversee intelligence from a variety of agencies. More controversial were changes permitting the surveillance of domestic citizens. In 2008, Congress placed a check on domestic surveillance by requiring that such activities be approved by a secret court. Revelations by former National Security Agency contractor Edward Snowden of massive government wiretapping forced additional scaling back of surveillance operations.

Through the Department of Justice and the Federal Bureau of Investigation, the executive branch also has the power to investigate alleged violations of civil rights in jurisdictions around the country. Police shootings of black youth in cities like Ferguson, Missouri, Baltimore, Maryland, and Chicago, Illinois have resulted in federal probes into police misconduct and the enforcement of changes in policing practices. The Trump administration has scaled back FBI oversight in these investigations since coming to office. However, Trump has ceded additional powers to the U.S. Immigration and Customs Enforcement (ICE) agency in connection with immigrant surveillance and deportation. His administration also approved a policy that allowed ICE to separate children from immigrants arriving unlawfully at U.S. borders until public reaction and court rulings forced a reversal.

In addition to the power to enforce the law, the president also holds the power to pardon convicted criminals. This power can be far-reaching, as demonstrated by President Gerald Ford's decision to pardon Richard Nixon after the Watergate scandal. President Trump used the power liberally to pardon high profile individuals whom he believed were unfairly treated by authorities and claimed the power to pardon himself if necessary. The Constitution does not limit the use of this power nor require that the president share it with any other branch.

Executive Orders A president may issue **executive orders**, decrees with the force of law but not requiring legislative approval, for a variety of reasons. Although the Constitution does not define these orders, presidents have construed them as lawful instruments for carrying out constitutionally defined executive duties. Presidents also use them during times of crisis to carry out actions deemed essential to national security. Woodrow Wilson, for example, issued nearly two thousand such decrees during World War I.

Many of these orders are mundane, dealing with bureaucratic organization. Others are used to overturn actions of past presidents or to mollify interest groups.[25] Barack Obama issued more than 270 executive orders over the course of his administration, many reversing the policies of his predecessor. For example, Obama ordered the closing of the Guantanamo Bay detention center, a prison facility on the island of Cuba that the Bush administration opened to house prisoners suspected of terrorist activities. He was prevented from doing so, however, by an act of Congress. Obama's order was itself countermanded by an executive order signed in 2018 by President Trump, who pledged to keep the facility operating. President Trump has actively employed executive orders in advancing his own agenda, signing 55 executive orders in his first year in office, the highest figure by a president in a single year since Bill Clinton's 57 in 1993.

Some executive orders break new legal ground and are highly controversial. One of the more than 250 executive orders issued by President George W. Bush (Executive Order 13440, issued in July 2007) exempted captured Taliban, Al Qaeda, and foreign fighters in Iraq from protections of the Third Geneva Convention and authorized the CIA to use interrogation techniques like waterboarding, or simulated drowning, that are more severe

©DOD Photo/Alamy Stock Photo

President Obama's pledge to close the Guantanamo Bay detention center proved popular during the presidential election but difficult to implement after his inauguration, as Congress blocked his efforts.

than those used by military personnel. President Obama revoked this policy with his own executive order just two days into his administration. Interrogations are now limited to those authorized by the Army Field Manuals. But Obama issued controversial executive orders of his own, such as those protecting up to five million undocumented immigrants from deportation, including those who have children who are U.S. citizens or legal residents. President Trump's executive orders included several dealing with border security and limitations on immigration from several majority-Muslim countries. Some of these orders have been challenged in court.

James Madison believed that executive orders threaten the separation of powers by allowing presidents to make their own laws. The Supreme Court has upheld some executive orders, like the one issued by Franklin D. Roosevelt interring Asian Americans (*Korematsu v. United States*, 1944), but it has overturned others, like Harry Truman's seizure of the steel mills to prevent strikes during the Korean War (*Youngstown Sheet & Tube Co. v. Sawyer,* 1952).

Commander in Chief

The Framers understood that the president must have the power to defend the nation and command the troops in times of conflict, but they disagreed about giving the president the power to make war. They compromised by permitting the chief executive to act to repel invasions but not to initiate war.[26] Article II, Section 2, of the Constitution reflects this compromise but has sowed confusion because of its ambiguity.

Although Congress has the constitutional power to declare war (see Chapter 11), it has done so formally only five times (some of these have involved separate declarations against individual countries involved in the same war as in the case of WW II).[27] In most of the conflicts in which the nation has been involved, the president has asserted the authority to act in response to a perceived crisis. Abraham Lincoln, for example, reacted to the Confederate attack on Fort Sumter by raising troops, imposing naval blockades on southern ports, suspending habeas corpus, and trying civilians in military courts—acts that extend presidential power beyond constitutional limits. He failed to convene Congress for months and received support for his actions only retroactively. He agonized over the dilemma but concluded that "measures otherwise unconstitutional might become lawful by becoming indispensable to the preservation of the nation."[28]

Presidents usually can count on wide public support during times of war or when U.S. interests are attacked, a phenomenon known as **rallying around the flag**. The public is willing to give the president a free hand for only a limited time, however. For example, Americans expressed strong support for President George W. Bush's retaliatory attack on Afghanistan after the September 11, 2001, terrorist attacks. He met with more resistance, however, in the lead-up to the war in Iraq. The revelation that Iraq had no weapons of mass destruction—compounded by mounting U.S. casualties—led to a precipitous drop in public support for the operation.

President Obama enjoyed widespread support for his decision to withdraw troops from Iraq and gradually reduce our role in Afghanistan. He also won accolades for the attack on bin Laden's compound in Abbottabad. However, the president's decision to assist NATO forces in aiding resistance fighters in Libya drew criticism. The House of Representatives approved a nonbinding resolution rebuking President Obama for continuing the operation without the express consent of Congress; and up until the final overthrow of Libyan leader Muammar Gaddafi, directed the administration to provide detailed information about the mission's costs and objectives.

During times of crisis, the president may assume **emergency powers** to protect the nation, but their use is also controversial and has led to conflicts over the preservation of civil liberties. Following the U.S. invasion of Afghanistan in 2001, President Bush declared that military tribunals, not civilian courts, would try all **enemy combatants**—enemy fighters captured in battle—whether or not they were members of a national army. Prisoners were not allowed to hear the charges against them and had no access to attorneys. The Supreme Court in 2004 (*Hamdi v. Rumsfeld*) responded to a petition filed on behalf of a prisoner of American descent by holding that the prisoner was entitled to consult with an attorney and to contest his imprisonment before a neutral decision maker. In a companion case,

rallying around the flag The sense of patriotism engendered by dramatic national events such as the September 11, 2001, terrorist attacks.

emergency powers Wide-ranging powers a president may exercise during a time of crisis, or those powers permitted the president by Congress for a limited time.

enemy combatant An enemy fighter captured on the field of battle, whether or not a member of an army.

extraordinary rendition The practice of secretly abducting terror suspects and transporting them to detention camps in undisclosed locations.

diplomatic recognition The presidential power to offer official privileges to foreign governments.

©Getty Images News/Getty Images

President Trump and North Korean leader Kim Jong-un replaced personal insults with dialogue as they met for an unprecedented summit in Singapore in June 2018 to discuss denuclearization of the Korean peninsula. In the aftermath of the meeting, it was not immediately clear how long or whether the talks would bear fruit.

Rasul v. Bush (2004), the Court held that foreign-born detainees can also challenge their detention in U.S. courts. Despite repeated subsequent efforts by the president and Congress to limit detainees' legal rights, the Supreme Court has rejected these efforts, ruling that Guantanamo detainees have a constitutional right under habeas corpus to go to court to challenge their detention.

Another executive action that has been employed since 9/11 is the practice of **extraordinary rendition**, or secretly abducting terrorist suspects and transporting them to detention camps in undisclosed locations. Critics assert that the United States deprives these suspects of due process and that interrogators at the camps torture them. President Obama signed an executive order closing the CIA's foreign prisons, but he left open the door to continued foreign rendition of prisoners. Even more sweeping was Obama's use of targeted assassination of terror suspects. In 2010, he authorized the killing of an American citizen, the radical Muslim cleric Anwar al-Awlaki, a suspected operative of Al Qaeda in the Arabian Peninsula, a move that most scholars believe was extremely rare, if not unprecedented.[29]

Chief Diplomat

The Constitution directs the president to share with the Senate responsibility for making treaties and with Congress the conduct of diplomacy. Historically, however, the president has taken the lead and Congress has then reacted to the decision. Among the tools of foreign policy at the president's disposal are diplomatic recognition, presidential doctrines, executive agreements, and summit meetings.

Diplomatic recognition of foreign officials by a president, an extension of the Constitution's authorization to receive ambassadors and other public officials (Article II, Section 3), can elevate the world status of a nation and entitle it to certain benefits, such as expanded trade. Often, recognition is contentious, especially when it involves former enemies. In 2015, President Obama opened diplomatic relations with Cuba, fifty-four years after Fidel Castro's successful communist takeover, a step that sometimes leads to full diplomatic recognition. President Trump reversed course, however, limiting visitor and business relations with the island.

Presidential doctrines are formal statements that outline the goals or purposes of American foreign policy and the actions the United States is prepared to take in advancing these goals. Presidential doctrines have a venerable history. Perhaps the most famous is the Monroe Doctrine, issued by President James Monroe in 1823 in response to colonial expansion by European powers. It asserted the intention of the United States to resist any attempt by a European power to interfere in the affairs of any country in the Western hemisphere. The Monroe Doctrine has become a foundation on which other presidents have built to define America's interests and role in the world.

In the wake of the September 11, 2001, terrorist attacks, George W. Bush declared a doctrine of preemptive self-defense. According to the highly controversial **Bush Doctrine**, the nation's right of self-defense entitles the United States to attack an enemy it feels presents an imminent threat to national security, even if the enemy has not attacked first. In 2003, the Bush administration utilized this doctrine to justify invading Iraq, arguing that its weapons of mass destruction constituted an imminent and grave threat to our national security. The failure to find those weapons in the war's aftermath only intensified the controversy over this doctrine.

President Obama avoided a doctrinal approach to foreign policy, preferring a more pragmatic and less ideological orientation than his predecessor. Instead, he showed an increased reliance on diplomatic and economic tools, attempting to forge consensus among our allies and avoiding unilateral action whenever possible.[30] For example, joint action with NATO partners was achieved in Afghanistan and Libya. However, Obama was not shy about using American military might, including increased troop deployment in the Afghanistan war and drone strikes in the war against terrorism abroad.

President Trump has adopted a distinctive "America First" policy on the world stage. His administration has withdrawn from global agreements on trade, such as the Trans-Pacific Partnership, and backed out of the Paris Agreement on climate change. He has let it be known that America is more interested in bilateral agreements with other nations rather than international pacts that advance global interests. Trump has downplayed diplomatic initiatives and dramatically reduced staffing of foreign affairs specialists at the State Department. At the same time, he has called for a more muscular military, promising to rebuild the military by increasing the number of ships, aircraft, and ground combat vehicles as well as for modernization of the U.S. nuclear arsenal. (See "Challenges Ahead".) Trump has also ordered a military troop buildup in Afghanistan, reversing course on President Obama's pledge to reduce our troop commitments there.

To a great extent, President Trump has followed through on his pledge to be a disrupter in the arena of international relations. Perhaps his boldest moves involved North Korea and Iran. In the case of North Korea, President Trump signaled his support for on-again-off-again direct talks with North Korean leader Kim Jong-un to discuss dismantling the country's nuclear program. In the case of Iran, President Trump ignored the advice of most of our allies by unilaterally withdrawing from the agreement that ended sanctions in return for a cessation in nuclear arms development. The president also took the controversial step of moving the U.S. embassy in Israel from Tel Aviv to Jerusalem, an action which, while envisioned by U.S. lawmakers as a goal to be implemented once a Mideast peace agreement might be achieved, angered many in the region who believed it setback the peace process.

An **executive agreement** is a pact made between the president and a foreign leader or government that does not undergo the same Senate approval process as a treaty. Many of these agreements involve the fine-tuning or interpretation of details of larger treaties. Although executive agreements, unlike treaties, do not bind future presidents, most represent long-standing commitments to friendly nations that succeeding presidents honor, regardless of party affiliation. Modern presidents often use these agreements to conduct business once reserved for treaties, and the number of executive agreements has escalated in recent years.[31] One type of executive agreement is the status of forces agreement. The United States has negotiated over one hundred of these with foreign nations where the U.S. maintains a military presence. These agreements, created solely by executive action, define the legal status of U.S. defense personnel within the borders of nations where they are stationed and the rights and responsibilities of each party.

Presidents often use the power and prestige of the office to convene **summit meetings**, at which they meet with world leaders to influence the course of world events. Notable summits occurred in 1978, when Egyptian president Anwar el-Sadat and Israeli prime minister Menachem Begin met with President Jimmy Carter to pave the way for a peace treaty between the two nations, and in 1986, when President Ronald Reagan and Soviet general secretary Mikhail Gorbachev met in Reykjavik, Iceland, to discuss the elimination of intermediate-range nuclear missiles. This meeting produced a treaty ratified in 1988. President Obama signed a treaty with Russia aimed at making substantial cuts to their nuclear arsenals at a meeting of world leaders in Prague in the Czech Republic on April 8, 2010. The treaty was ratified by the Senate in the waning days of the 111th Congress. President Trump attended an historic summit in Singapore in 2018 with North Korean leader Kim Jong-un which resulted in promises of denuclearization of the North Korean peninsula over an unspecified period of time. The president also had a controversial summit meeting with Russian leader Vladimir Putin where the two leaders pledged to work on a number of unspecified matters. Trump was criticized for not pushing back more vigorously on Russian interference into U.S. elections.

Chief of State

In addition to being the head of government, the president also serves as the nation's symbolic leader, or chief of state. In some nations, this duty is performed by a monarch.

presidential doctrine A formal statement that outlines the goals and purposes of American foreign policy and the actions to take to advance these goals.

Bush Doctrine The foreign policy position advanced by George W. Bush asserting the U.S. government's right to authorize preemptive attacks against potential aggressors.

executive agreement A pact that is made between the president and a foreign leader of a government and that does not require Senate approval.

summit meeting A high-level meeting of heads of state or government leaders, usually to plan or consummate major pacts or treaties.

IT'S TWO MINUTES 'TIL MIDNIGHT.

That's the assessment of the *Bulletin of Atomic Scientists* regarding doomsday prospects, given the current state of the world's vulnerability to nuclear warfare. Each year, the scientists use the clock metaphor to assess global risks, sometimes moving the hands of the clock backward when risks are ameliorated, or forward when risks intensify. In 2018, the scientists advanced the clock one full minute closer to midnight.

Scientists expressed concern about the buildup of arms by North Korea but also about the "hyperbolic rhetoric and provocative actions"* on the part of both North Korea and the United States that increase the likelihood of nuclear war by accident or miscalculation.

The scientists are also concerned about a planned nuclear arms buildup described in President Trump's *Nuclear Posture Review,*** a legislatively mandated appraisal of the nation's nuclear policy, strategy, and capabilities for the next five to ten years. The latest review calls for increased spending on the nuclear arsenal, including a program that would "create new kinds of small nuclear weapons." The *Review* suggests that nuclear weapons might be used in response to attacks of a nonnuclear nature, including, specifically, cyberattacks against critical U.S. infrastructure.

Today, nearly 9,500 nuclear warheads dot the globe. Although this figure is alarming, it is nowhere near the high of over 64,000 reached at the height of the Cold War. As recently as 1991, the clock was moved back to seventeen minutes before midnight as a result of the Strategic Arms Reduction Treaty that greatly reduced the number of strategic nuclear weapons deployed by Russia and the United States. This was followed by a series of unilateral initiatives to remove most of the intercontinental ballistic missiles and bombers in both countries from hair-trigger alert. Since then, the clock has inched closer to midnight, sometimes as a result

©Ernesto Mastrascusa/LatinContent/Getty Images

of threats from climate change, but more often, as in 2018, principally as the result of fears about the safety and renewed growth of the world's nuclear arsenal.

Scientists call for world leaders to refrain from over-heated rhetoric and to open new channels of communication leading to new rounds of arms reduction. "Leaders react when citizens insist they do so," the scientists write.*** Citizens can insist that leaders rely on facts, and discount nonsense. They can seize the opportunity to make a safer and saner world. They can insist that our national leaders in charge of defense "rewind the clock."

*Science and Security Board of the Bulletin of Atomic Scientists, "It Is 2 Minutes to Midnight: 2018 Doomsday Clock Statement." Retrieved February 8, 2018, from https://thebulletin.org/sites/default/files/2018%20Doomsday%20Clock%20Statement.pdf.

**Office of the Secretary of Defense, *Nuclear Posture Review,* February 2018, https://media.defense.gov/2018/Feb/02/2001872877/-1/-1/1/EXECUTIVE-SUMMARY.PDF.

***Science and Security Board, "It Is 2 Minutes to Midnight."

The Constitution attaches few official duties to this function: taking a formal oath of office, providing Congress with periodic State of the Union messages, and receiving public ministers. Nevertheless, the job of chief of state creates an emotional bond with the electorate that contributes to a president's authority; it also consumes an enormous amount of the president's time. From attending ceremonial events and state funerals, to awarding medals to war heroes, to greeting foreign dignitaries and members of championship sports teams, the president presides over countless events as symbolic leader of the nation. President Trump maintained an active foreign travel schedule in his first years in office, visiting several Middle Eastern countries, including Saudi Arabia and Israel, as well as attending several international conferences such as the twenty-eighth NATO Summit in Brussels, Belgium, and the World Economic Forum in Davos, Switzerland, and a groundbreaking meeting in Singapore with North Korean leader Kim Jong-un that resulted in promises of denuclearization. His meeting with allies at the G7 meeting in Quebec in 2018 did not end well when, refusing to sign the group's final communique, he insulted the Canadian Prime Minister, angered allies by imposing tariffs on some of their exports, and called for readmission of Russia to the group after it had been ousted for annexing Crimea.

As the president's public visibility has risen, the role of chief of state has assumed greater importance. Prior to the 1920s, for example, presidents fulfilled their constitutional duty to

President Trump has alarmed and angered some allies as a result of his "America First" policies like imposing tariffs on goods entering the country.

provide a message on the State of the Union by submitting their report to Congress in writing. Since that time, however, the State of the Union address has become an opportunity for the president to speak to a national audience via radio and television. This increased visibility helps the president highlight the administration's accomplishments and pressure Congress to enact presidential initiatives.

Lawmaker

The president plays a crucial role in the lawmaking process. In addition to the constitutional authority to recommend legislation to Congress and the power of the veto, the president exercises substantial authority through the ability to lobby members of Congress and through his use of the controversial practice of selectively interpreting congressional legislation.

Whereas early presidents enlisted cabinet members or aides to lobby their friends in Congress, twentieth-century presidents took more direct approaches. Teddy Roosevelt employed the bully pulpit, arguing publicly for favored legislation. Franklin D. Roosevelt's radio "fireside chats" to the nation similarly put public pressure on lawmakers to support his initiatives. FDR was also willing to enlist the help of executive agencies to advance his agenda, using the Bureau of the Budget to monitor, screen, and propose legislative action in accord with his New Deal. President Obama invited members of Congress to the White House, held open forums with lawmakers from both parties, and urged supporters to email and tweet members of Congress to pass favored legislation.

The interests of the president and Congress in legislating are not necessarily congruent. The president is the one individual with a truly national constituency and vision and is responsible for the operation of the national bureaucracy that Congress funds. The president is also responsible for national security. It is through his legislative agenda that the president sets the course for the nation. Members of Congress, by contrast, are more attuned to the problems and concerns of their own districts or states. Finding common ground between national and local interests can be somewhat of a challenge, and presidents exert considerable time and effort cultivating legislators to win their support.

The White House maintains an Office of Legislative Affairs, a group of policy and institutional experts that the president can call upon to write legislation, negotiate with members of Congress, and garner legislative support. In winning votes for their agenda, presidents can employ a number of tools. They can offer to direct funds to member districts for discretionary projects; they can help members from their own party raise campaign funds and make personal appearances with them; they can recommend members or their campaign contributors for political appointments. When a popular president has difficulty obtaining cooperation, he can appeal to the public and ask them to pressure Congress, a tactic that worked successfully for Ronald Reagan when he faced congressional opposition. Although the president does wield powerful weapons of personal persuasion in lobbying Congress, members face many pressures that the president is powerless to influence. Studies of presidential influence with Congress show that "presidents operate typically at the margins of coalition building and . . . their legislative skills are essentially limited to exploiting rather than creating opportunities for leadership."[32]

In his "two presidencies" thesis, political scientist Aaron Wildavsky asserted that presidents have more control over legislation in the area of foreign and defense policy than over domestic matters. This may have been the case for the period from World War I until the turn of the century, but foreign policy today has become more partisan and policy success is no longer simply dictated by the president. Success in both foreign and domestic policy depends on factors like partisan control of each branch and presidential skill.[33]

Some presidents are more successful than others in getting their agendas passed. Success depends on a number of factors, including whether Congress is in the hands of the president's own party or the opposition's, as well as on the president's popularity. Presidents generally have an easier time in their first terms when Congress is disposed to give them an opportunity to present their case, and in times of national emergency when the president commands deference. Presidential success also depends on the number of measures on which a president takes an active stand. "The Rise and Fall of Presidential Legislative Success" shows that presidents are more likely to have legislative success during their first year in office and when Congress is controlled by their own party. President George W. Bush had a very high success rate until Congress passed into Democratic control in 2007, when he suffered one of the lowest legislative success rates in recent history. Armed with substantial majorities in both houses of Congress, President Obama enjoyed the second highest level of legislative success during his first year in office of any modern president. Once again, however, when the president lost his legislative majorities in Congress, his success rate plummeted.

President Trump now holds the modern record for the highest level of legislative success for measures on which he took a clear position. With his party in control of both houses of Congress, he was able to prevail on over 98 percent of such votes. However, this achievement

The Rise and Fall of Presidential Legislative Success

This graph illustrates the percentage of the times in the recent past that the president won on roll call votes on which he took a clear position. The data combine House and Senate figures.

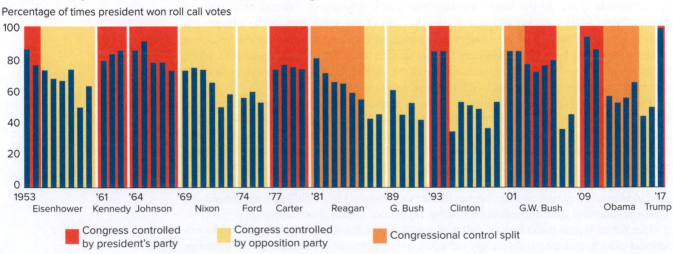

Percentage of times president won roll call votes

Legend:
- Congress controlled by president's party
- Congress controlled by opposition party
- Congressional control split

Source: Adapted from *CQ Magazine*, February 12, 2018.

is tempered by the fact that Trump took fewer clear positions on legislation than his predecessors and many of the successful votes in the Senate were on judicial confirmations made in the wake of rule changes making it easier for the majority to prevail. Like his immediate predecessors in this age of party polarization, Trump's success was borne from overwhelming support from his own majority party in the face of strong opposition from the minority. His most impressive win in year one was on a major tax reduction package.[34]

Even when presidents lose a legislative battle, they can still influence the course of legislation by exercising the veto. Early presidents used the veto sparingly. They generally adhered to the view that Congress should be the principal lawmaking body and tended to veto only those bills they believed violated the Constitution. Andrew Jackson was more inclined to use the veto for political reasons, but the number of presidential vetoes remained relatively small until the Reconstruction battles following the Civil War. Franklin D. Roosevelt pioneered the modern use of the veto as an instrument of legislative policy to thwart attacks on his priorities while advancing his own political agenda.[35] The veto is a powerful tool, because two-thirds of both houses of Congress must vote to override a presidential veto. Of the 2,574 presidential vetoes (including **pocket vetoes**) issued between 1789 and 2017, only 111 (about 4 percent) were overridden.[36] George W. Bush vetoed twelve bills in his two terms and prevailed on eight; President Obama also issued twelve vetoes with only one overridden. No vetoes were issued by President Trump during his first year in office.

Partisan polarization in Congress and congressional rules pose special problems for a president. In cases in which the opposition party controls one or more houses, the president can use the threat of a veto as a bargaining chip to force compromise. Studies show that the use of veto threats has increased markedly under conditions of divided government since the late 1980s.[37] But veto threats can be useful as well when members of the president's own party attempt to move legislation too far from his preferred position.

Even when the president's party controls both chambers, however, a determined minority—especially in the Senate—can hold up or kill legislation the president deems important. Negotiation across the aisle is difficult, as President Trump found when trying to repeal the Affordable Care Act. The president can always try appealing to the public over Congress's objections, but this is only possible when the president's popularity is exceptionally high.

Presidents can have an impact on how laws are interpreted by appending **signing statements** to legislation they approve, but to which they may have some objection or reservation. Sometimes these statements offer the president's interpretation of the act; sometimes they highlight portions that the president reserves the right not to enforce because they may be unconstitutional or infringe on legitimate presidential authority. James Monroe issued the first signing statement in 1822 in connection with a law dealing with presidential appointments. Afterward, they were used infrequently until recent times. Their use increased with the presidency of Ronald Reagan, who issued 250 signing statements, 86 of which contained objections to one or more provisions of law. Bill Clinton issued 381 statements, 70 of which raised constitutional or legal objections. The practice came under public scrutiny after George W. Bush issued 161 signing statements objecting to over one thousand provisions of bills that were signed into law.[38] One of these was attached to a bill passed in 2006 outlawing the torture of detained enemy combatants. According to the statement, the White House reserved the right to waive portions of the bill in the interest of national security.

Legal scholars are divided about the use of signing statements. Some argue that the statements allow presidents flexibility in administering laws;[39] others hold them unconstitutional, arguing that the president must either sign and enforce the entire law or veto it. A 2006 report by the American Bar Association challenged the use of such statements, but presidents are unlikely to abandon the practice unless the Supreme Court acts to halt it. President Obama promised to curtail the use of signing statements but issued over thirty during his two terms in office, including one that reserves the right of the executive branch to transfer Guantanamo detainees to foreign countries despite congressional prohibitions contained in a defense authorization act. President Trump issued seven signing statements during his first year in office. Some were ceremonial, like one supporting the creation of the Frederick Douglass Bicentennial Commission, but some were more substantial, like one objecting to congressionally approved sanctions on Russia for meddling in U.S. elections.[40]

pocket veto An automatic veto achieved when a bill sits unsigned on a president's desk for ten days when Congress is out of session.

signing statement A comment issued by the president upon signing legislation. Some of these are merely ceremonial; others signal an intent not to enforce some provisions because the president believes them to be improper or unconstitutional.

PRESIDENTIAL ROLES

In addition to the constitutionally mandated formal duties already discussed, presidents play a variety of informal roles as leaders of their political parties, economic leaders, and leaders of public opinion. These roles give the president many more opportunities for leading the nation, but they also increase citizen expectations about what the president can accomplish.

Party Leader

The president enjoys unique opportunities to advance the fortunes of fellow party members and the party's ideas through his ability to distribute patronage and to back legislative initiatives. Presidents can reward their party's financial contributors as well by awarding them prestigious honors or coveted positions like ambassadorships to foreign nations.

Because presidential success hinges partly on maintaining party control in Congress, presidents frequently raise funds and campaign for party members running for Congress. When the president is popular, party members seek out opportunities to share the presidential limelight at official ceremonies or campaign rallies. Members of a president's party seek to ride his **coattails** to electoral victory when presidential popularity is high. By contrast, lawmakers tend to avoid associating themselves with an unpopular president. President Trump entered the White House as an outsider to his party. Some Republican members of Congress even opposed him during his campaign for office. Yet, Republicans were able to coalesce around him as he adopted policies more to their liking than those he presented during his presidential campaign. For example, although he indicated he favored higher taxes for the wealthy during the campaign, he supported a massive reduction in taxes for upper-income Americans and corporations once in office, a position more in keeping with his Republican colleagues in both legislative chambers.

coattails The effect a winning candidate at the top of the ticket has in bringing success to those lower on the ballot.

Economic Leader

Since the New Deal, presidents have amassed a vast bureaucracy to monitor economic activity and to control fiscal policy in ways that ameliorate public concerns about the economy. Although the president exerts relatively little direct power over the economy, voters typically punish presidents during times of economic hardship. An economic crisis clearly contributed to the election of Barack Obama in 2008 and set expectations high that he would turn the economy around. His inability to effect a quick recovery, however, cost him popular support and cost his party seats in Congress.

In reality, presidential power over the economy is limited more or less to making proposals about taxing and spending that change the calculations of economic actors. The results of these policies are notoriously difficult to predict with precision and take many years to work themselves through the economy. Often, their full effect is not even felt during the president's own tenure in office. Sometimes presidents are forced to improvise solutions to complex problems as when President George W. Bush proposed a comprehensive bailout for the financial system in response to a crisis precipitated by failures in the mortgage market, a crisis that took several years beyond his term to correct. President Trump's signature economic initiatives have included a tax overhaul bill, the imposition of tariffs on foreign products to encourage the growth of domestic industries including steel, and a revamped trade bill with Mexico and Canada to replace the North American Free Trade Agreement (NAFTA).

Opinion Leader

To be effective, a president must campaign and build public support for the administration's agenda. Following inauguration, the president usually enjoys a **honeymoon period**, during which the public generally abstains from criticism of the administration and gives the president the benefit of the doubt in proposing and passing legislation. Eventually, however, attacks by opponents, the stream of world events, and legislative battles take their toll on presidential approval. President George W. Bush gained public support in the wake of 9/11 and lost it as the war in Iraq dragged on. His approval hit an all-time high just after the attacks, but he left

honeymoon period The period following an election when the public and Congress give the newly elected president the greatest latitude in decision making.

office tied for the lowest approval rating on record. Unlike previous presidents, Donald Trump enjoyed no such honeymoon. Throughout his first years in office, his support was fairly flat, rarely rising above 40 percent (see "Atypical Pattern"). This may be explained by the fact that he rarely tried to reach out to voters beyond his own base.

Presidential approval is filtered through partisan lenses, however. Democrats and Republicans are far more likely to approve of the performance of a president from their own party than from the opposition. President Obama experienced one of the biggest partisan gaps in presidential approval of any president on record. The same can be said of President Trump.

Since the 1930s, presidents have used their own internal polls to track and court public opinion. Franklin D. Roosevelt's administration conducted its own trend polling that offered same-day quick responses to new issues.[41] Richard Nixon's administration used daily polling to track his support among specific demographic groups, to test his popularity against potential electoral opponents, and to explore opposition weaknesses.[42]

Presidents adopt several tactics to rally public support, such as giving speeches promoting their policies and enlisting supporters or administration officials to pitch administration proposals. It is expected that presidents face the scrutiny of the White House press corps, but modern presidents have increasingly looked for ways to communicate more directly with the public so that they may control their own message. Skeptical of the national media, Ronald Reagan gave comparatively few press conferences. Instead, his advisors gave the president and his spokespersons specific daily themes to communicate to the press. Administration spokespersons were directed to "stay on message" no matter how much reporters wished to discuss other issues. The success of this approach helped earn Reagan the moniker "the Great Communicator."

Similarly, President Obama held just 164 news conferences (both individual and joint) during his first seven years in office,[43] averaging fewer per year than any president since Ronald Reagan. In contrast, he gave hundreds of individual interviews, a format he preferred since it allowed him to speak at length on a particular topic and exercise greater control over the dialogue. Obama often used new media like YouTube and Twitter to communicate with followers and appeared regularly on late-night talk shows and even on an Internet episode of *Comedians in Cars Getting Coffee* with comedian Jerry Seinfeld. No president, however, has utilized social media more extensively than Donald Trump, who took to Twitter nearly every day to cajole, criticize, and comment on all manner of political and social issues, to the delight of his loyal supporters. President Trump has also extensively criticized the mainstream media, referring to them as "Fake News" and even pointed to journalists as enemies of the people at public events they were covering. While such rhetoric may have energized the president's base supporters, it may have contributed to negative coverage of the White House.

Atypical Pattern

Trump Job Approval and Disapproval: Weekly Averages

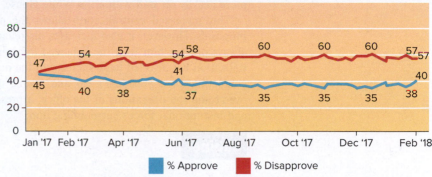

Although most presidents enjoy a honeymoon period with high approval ratings early in the administration, followed by lower ratings as months in office progress, Donald Trump enjoyed no such honeymoon. His approval rating in his first year hovered around 40 percent.

Source: Gallup Organization Daily Tracking.

Donald J. Trump Verified account @realDonaldTrump
FollowFollow @realDonaldTrump
More

The issue of kneeling has nothing to do with race. It is about respect for our Country, Flag and National Anthem. NFL must respect this!

4:39 AM - 25 Sep 2017

President Trump uses daily Twitter posts to comment on a variety of political and social issues, including his opposition to NFL players kneeling in protest during the playing of the National Anthem prior to taking the field before games.

Source: Twitter

THE EXECUTIVE BRANCH

The president oversees a number of agencies and departments that help formulate and implement administration policies. Some, such as the departments that make up the cabinet, are legislatively created; the president has little freedom on his own to change how they are structured. Others are part of White House operations and the president has substantially more discretion in organizing and staffing them. Over time, presidents have come to rely more heavily on staff within the White House, where the president exercises greater control.

This increased centralization allows the president greater supervision over his policy proposals. However, it also increases his reliance on longtime political allies who may not always present him with the balanced information he needs to make wise decisions. Centralization has also led to an increase in the number of advisors within the executive branch competing for a president's ear and raising the potential for bureaucratic infighting.[44] In overseeing the operations of his office, a president needs to carefully balance the political and institutional forces surrounding him.

Cabinet

The cabinet consists of political appointees chosen by the president to lead the most important government departments (see "Composition of the Trump Cabinet"). Cabinet officials preside over an army of **civil service** personnel appointed for their merits or expertise regardless of political affiliation, who carry out the everyday operations of fifteen government departments and several other agencies that manage national and international programs. Ostensibly, cabinet members both advise the president and are responsible for implementing administration policies within their departments or agencies. Since George Washington's day, however, almost all presidents have relied primarily on the secretaries of defense, treasury, and state. The attorney general, who heads the Justice Department and serves as the chief counsel for the government, joins these three secretaries as part of the president's **inner cabinet**, or closest circle of top cabinet officers.

Presidents typically look to fill cabinet positions with individuals from their own party who reflect the president's own priorities and those of valued constituent groups. Many presidents also try to balance the cabinet to reflect significant demographic groups. President Obama's first cabinet appointments were among the most diverse in history, with six women, four African Americans, three Hispanic Americans, and two Asian Americans. President Trump's cabinet is less diverse with fewer than 20 percent women and minorities as opposed to more than 60 percent in Obama's first cabinet.[45] It also contained more former military personnel than earlier cabinets and a number of individuals with no prior government experience, such as Ben Carson, a retired neurosurgeon, who was chosen to lead the Department of Housing and Urban Development. A number of nominees with potential conflicts of interest arising from previous business dealings either withdrew or were forced to divest their holdings before being confirmed. Some Trump appointees are also noted for their ideological opposition to the agencies they head. When he was running for president, Rick Perry called for the abolition of the Department of Energy, the agency that Trump then appointed him to lead. Environmental Protection Agency head Scott Pruitt sued the EPA on multiple occasions in an effort to overturn rules limiting air and water pollution when he served as Oklahoma's attorney general. He was later replaced for alleged ethics and spending violations.

Modern presidents rarely meet with the entire cabinet except for ceremonial occasions. Dwight Eisenhower was the last president to meet regularly with his entire cabinet, and even many insiders considered those meetings

civil service A merit-based system of employment and personnel management that replaced patronage.

inner cabinet The term applied to leaders from the Departments of State, Defense, Treasury, and Justice, with whom the president meets more frequently than other cabinet officials.

Composition of the Trump Cabinet

Environmental Protection Agency
Small Business Administration
Attorney General
Director of National Intelligence
Director of the Central Intelligence Agency
Office of Management and Budget
United Nations Ambassador
Secretary of Agriculture
Secretary of Commerce
Secretary of Defense
Secretary of Education
Secretary of Energy
Secretary of Health and Human Services

Secretary of Homeland Security
Secretary of Housing and Urban Development
Secretary of the Interior
Secretary of Labor
Secretary of State
Secretary of Transportation
Secretary of Treasury
Secretary of Veterans Affairs
U.S. Trade Representative
Vice President
White House Chief of Staff

©ricardoinfante/Getty Images

Source: The White House.

unproductive.[46] Richard Nixon rarely included cabinet officials in high-level meetings; cabinet members sometimes found out about their department's new initiatives from the press. Bill Clinton did not even attend cabinet briefings, leaving that chore to the White House chief of staff. Formal cabinet meetings are rare. Donald Trump met with his cabinet just nine times during his first year in office.[47] Presidents today are more likely to consult with individual cabinet members during meetings of policy groups created and staffed inside the White House, such as the Domestic Policy Council (discussed later in this chapter). The cabinet's role in policymaking has clearly declined. As one insider has noted, "'Cabinet government'—in which each agency manages its own affairs with the president as a general supervisor—is shibboleth, not reality."[48] Power has migrated away from cabinet agencies and become more centralized within the president's inner circle in the White House. This gives the president much more control and flexibility in meeting the demands of the office.

Executive Office of the President

In 1939, Congress created the **Executive Office of the President (EOP)** to help the president manage the growing federal bureaucracy. Over the years, the EOP has expanded through the addition of agencies created by legislative statutes as well as executive orders. The EOP is home to over three dozen entities and subunits, one of which—the White House Office—contains over twenty entities of its own. Together, these entities employ over two thousand appointees. The growth of the EOP represents the increased specialization and centralization of policy expertise within the White House that characterizes the modern presidency (see "Executive Office of the President").[49]

White House Office The White House Office includes political advisors, who attend to matters of daily concern for the administration: policy development, legal affairs, political affairs, press and public communications, legislative affairs, presidential travel, and the increasingly important arena of interest-group relations. These appointees and their staffs, all of whom require no Senate confirmation, review and analyze masses of information to help the president formulate policy proposals. Donald Trump's White House Office employs approximately four hundred people with a payroll of more than $35 million. That figure is about $4 million less than the Obama administration, which employed nearly five hundred staffers and reflects Trump's preference for a leaner operation.[50]

The president's senior advisors, the **White House staff**, are headed by the **chief of staff**, who acts as something of a

Executive Office of the President

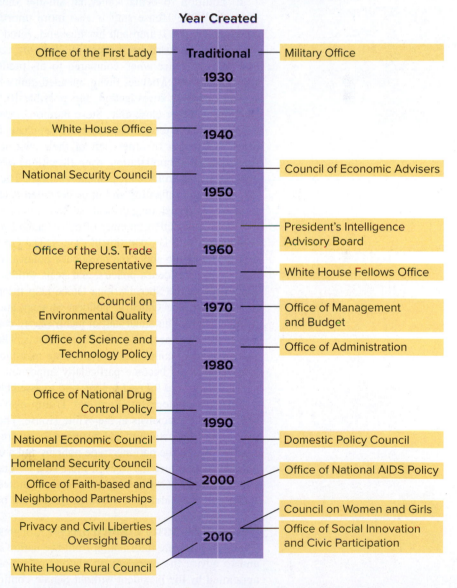

Year Created

Office of the First Lady	**Traditional** — Military Office
	1930
White House Office	**1940**
National Security Council	— Council of Economic Advisers
	1950
	— President's Intelligence Advisory Board
Office of the U.S. Trade Representative	**1960**
	— White House Fellows Office
Council on Environmental Quality	**1970** — Office of Management and Budget
Office of Science and Technology Policy	— Office of Administration
	1980
Office of National Drug Control Policy	
	1990
National Economic Council	— Domestic Policy Council
Homeland Security Council	— Office of National AIDS Policy
Office of Faith-based and Neighborhood Partnerships	**2000**
	— Council on Women and Girls
Privacy and Civil Liberties Oversight Board	— Office of Social Innovation and Civic Participation
	2010
White House Rural Council	

The growth in the operations of the Executive Office of the President represents the increased specialization and centralization of policy expertise within the White House that characterizes the modern presidency.

Source: The White House.

traffic cop to coordinate communication between the president and other staffers. This includes serving as a gatekeeper, deciding what information goes in and out of the Oval Office. The chief of staff is also a confidant whom the president trusts to ensure that the White House staff is carrying out its functions properly, meeting deadlines, determining priorities, maintaining cordial relations with the cabinet and Congress, and smoothly coordinating the actions of the various units of the White House. President Trump's first chief of staff, Reince Priebus, lasted only 189 days, resigning following disagreements with the White House director of communications. Unlike most presidential choices for this post, Priebus was not a long-term friend and ally of the president. He had been chair of the Republican National Committee, and it was hoped he could help the president mend his somewhat frayed ties with members of the president's party in Congress. Priebus was criticized for not properly managing the flow of personnel and information commanding the president's time. He was replaced by retired general John Kelly, who was serving as secretary of homeland security at the time. Kelly brought more order to the president's day and was more successful in focusing the president's attention on pressing policy matters. However, even Kelly had difficulty controlling Trump's schedule and outside contacts, some of which included unscheduled appearances on FOX News.

In addition to being somewhat smaller than more recent administrations, President Trump's White House staff is also more unorthodox. It includes two close relatives: his daughter Ivanka Trump and her husband, Jared Kushner, who both serve as political advisors. There has also been substantially more turnover of Trump's closest staff during his first years in office when compared to his predecessors. Trump's first choice for national security advisor, Michael Flynn, pleaded guilty to lying to the FBI in connection with the special counsel's investigation into possible Russian interference in the 2016 presidential election. Another close aide, Steve Bannon, agreed to leave in the wake of internal discord among Trump's top advisors and his penchant for making controversial statements to the press. A number of others left of their own accord or were forced out during the early stages of the administration, over allegations of improper behavior or possible conflicts of interest arising from their financial dealings. The White House Staff has also been an arena for substantial infighting and unprecedented discord during the Trump administration with frequent leaks including critical public comments regarding the president's fitness for office.

Within the EOP, a number of offices attend to the president's public image and personal relationship with key constituent groups. The Office of the Press Secretary transmits information to the public about the president's political positions and daily activities, addresses criticism of the president's policies, and deals with questions from the White House press corps. Employees in the Speechwriting Office help the president convey ideas with clarity and rhetorical force. The Office of Political Strategy and Outreach is the president's bridge to the political world. This small staff of highly placed confidants walks a thin line between their roles as public employees and political consultants. They work with pollsters, consultants, and the party's national committee to coordinate measures for political success. The Office of Public Engagement has become particularly important as presidents work to reward interest and constituent groups for past support and to assemble ongoing coalitions to meet new challenges.

Like his predecessor, President Trump also created a number of policy "czars," who work as issue specialists in the White House. These specialists often coordinated new initiatives across departments and agencies to ensure policy coherence. For example, there is a czar to oversee the nation's trade policies and a czar to coordinate the nation's drug control policies. Sometimes the roles of these czars overlap with cabinet officials, causing confusion and infighting.[51] Critics of these special appointees often express concern about their special status and their ability to evade congressional oversight, since few require confirmation.

National Security Council In 1947, Congress established the National Security Council (NSC) to integrate information from the nation's domestic and foreign intelligence agencies and to advise the president on matters of national security. The national security advisor, appointed by the president without Senate confirmation, heads the body and provides regular briefings to the president. Traditionally, this body has included the vice president, the secretaries of state and defense, the chairperson of the Joint Chiefs of Staff, and (since the Bush administration) the director of national intelligence. Like presidents before him, President Trump reorganized this body to reflect his own priorities. He created a top-level "principals committee" as the senior interagency forum for national security. Its members include the director of national intelligence and the chairperson of the Joint Chiefs of Staff along with the U.S. secretary of energy, the U.S. representative to the United Nations, and the director of the CIA. The heads of other departments and agencies may also be invited as needed to address issues under consideration.[52] In practice, NSC membership is fluid and the group seldom meets as a whole. Instead, the national security advisor passes information to the president and formulates policy alternatives, acting much as a chief of staff for national security matters.[53]

The national security advisor oversees an operation that has become the largest policy group in the White House, numbering around two hundred. This staff maintains a Situation Room, which collects and analyzes intelligence from around the world, handles liaison with Congress, maintains press relations, and carries on communication with security officers in other nations.

The National Security Council assembles the president's top advisors in matters dealing with foreign policy, intelligence gathering, terrorism, and homeland security.

Source: White House Photo by Shealah Craighead

A major role in national security matters is also played by the director of national intelligence, a position added after the 9/11 attacks. The director oversees the nation's intelligence operations and acts as the principal advisor to the president, the National Security Council, and the Homeland Security Council for intelligence matters.

The composition of President Trump's national security team has been fluid, but it is noteworthy for the record number of military personnel he has tapped for top positions[54] and for the inclusion of political allies and advisors who lacked a top security clearance due to questions arising from their background checks.[55] Whereas President Obama played a "hands-on" role in national security, often chairing weekly meetings and involving himself in the details of operations from troop buildup in Afghanistan to the bin Laden raid,[56] President Trump preferred to concentrate on top-level policy issues while relegating details to his national security team.

Office of Management and Budget Presidents are responsible for managing massive national budgets. They must allocate dollars for the programs administered by executive agencies and ensure that the monies are expended according to the wishes of the Congress that authorizes spending. Congress created the Office of Management and Budget to help with this task. Franklin D. Roosevelt moved the agency, established as a division of the Treasury Department, to the White House in 1939 to assist him in creating an executive budget for Congress. OMB assists the president in preparing the federal budget and supervises the spending of each of the executive agencies of the federal government. Under President Reagan, OMB was also empowered to review every government program to ensure that its benefits outweighed its costs. Because OMB is sometimes seen as helping to advance a president's partisan agenda, Congress relies on its own budget analysts in the Congressional Budget Office (CBO) to provide an independent assessment of policy costs and benefits. Given the rise in partisan polarization, it is not unusual for budget figures generated by OMB and the CBO to be at odds with one another.

Policy Councils Policy councils allow the president to gather experts from both inside and outside the White House into consultative groups organized around policy areas. Among the more notable are the Domestic Policy Council and the National Economic Council. Some presidents rely on these arrangements more than others; Bill Clinton, for example, made extensive use of them. Barack Obama changed the membership of some of these, including the Domestic Policy Council, to reflect priorities such as climate change. Donald Trump created several new councils, including some dealing with infrastructure, innovation, and trade. He also made personnel changes to existing councils to accommodate his policy preferences. One new council dealing with manufacturing and composed of

CEOs from top U.S. businesses was short lived, however. It disbanded following the resignation of some members in response to Trump's confrontational response to a violent white supremacist rally in Charlottesville, Virginia.

PRESIDENTIAL STYLE

Each president has adopted his own management style while in office. John F. Kennedy preferred an informal arrangement, surrounding himself with experts and meeting with advisors to debate policy alternatives. Like the hub of a wheel, Kennedy was at the center of a communication and decision-making network with spokes relatively open to his most trusted advisors.[57] Richard Nixon instituted a hierarchical structure in which his chief of staff, H. R. Haldeman, tightly controlled paper flow, staffing, and access to the president. Only Nixon's national security advisor, Henry Kissinger, had unfettered access to the Oval Office.[58] Obama's style was described as rational, rigorous, and unemotional. Decision making was a lengthy process in which he identified and assembled policy experts, listened as they debated the issues, asked tough questions, and requested the opinions and recommendations of everyone in the room. While pursuing clearly progressive policy ideals, his aim was conciliatory, seeking compromise on the details in order to achieve pragmatic outcomes.[59]

President Trump's style can only be described as unconventional, based on the information available. According to multiple sources, Trump has little patience for extensive meetings or reading long memorandums—even the daily intelligence briefing—preferring instead to rely on oral briefings.[60] Other sources have either denied this or indicated that, despite the mode of delivery, the president has a full grasp of information presented to him.[61] At first, his administration lacked discipline, with many staff entry points and few limits on the individuals or information that received the president's attention. When John Kelly assumed the position of chief of staff, he "immediately set in place a hierarchical system where all staff were expected to go through him before seeing the President."[62] It has also been reported that President Trump often reaches out to acquaintances outside of government for consultation.[63] He demands loyalty from his staff and is impatient with those who fail to support him, leading to widespread turnover of staff. He fired FBI director James Comey for pursuing his investigation into Russian meddling in the 2016 election and openly criticized his attorney general for recusing himself from the investigation. Trump's tendency to give contradictory signals about the bills he supports makes it difficult for members of Congress to reach consensus.[64] And he has rebuffed repeated attempts by close associates to get him to stop posting inflammatory tweets.[65] Nevertheless, the president has had several accomplishments, including a significant tax bill, and he maintains the loyal support of his base voters.

Personality is a crucial component in presidential success, although scholars disagree about which personal traits can make or break a presidency. Studies have identified intelligence, communication skills, decisiveness, respect for democratic principles, optimism, and hope as attributes of achievers.[66] By contrast, character traits linked to failure include compulsiveness, rigidity, defensiveness, and introversion.[67] The public clearly values a president's capacity to rise above adversity. George W. Bush, who demonstrated a lack of sure-footedness in foreign policy during his first presidential

John F. Kennedy practiced a style of leadership that encouraged open debate and discussion with key advisors.

HOW DO YOU RANK THE PRESIDENTS?

Historians, political scientists, and other scholars have long debated what makes a president great. Some believe greatness lies in the individual's fidelity to values; others, in his adaptability. Still others believe a president can only be measured against the demands of his time: Trying times bring out the best. In any case, here are two snapshot views: one from scholars, the other from average citizens.

Poll of Scholars

In 2018, the *New York Times* polled 170 members of the American Political Science Association's Presidents and Executive Politics section, asking them to rank U.S. presidents. Here's their top ten:*

1. Abraham Lincoln
2. George Washington
3. Franklin D. Roosevelt
4. Theodore Roosevelt
5. Thomas Jefferson
6. Harry S. Truman
7. Dwight D. Eisenhower
8. Barack Obama
9. Ronald Reagan
10. Lyndon Baines Johnson

President Donald Trump came in last.

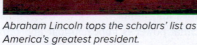

©John Parrot/Stocktrek Images/Getty Images RF

Abraham Lincoln tops the scholars' list as America's greatest president.

Poll of Public

In 2011, Gallup surveyed 1,015 adults nationwide asking, "Who do you regard as the greatest United States president?" Here are the top ten results:**

1. Ronald Reagan
2. Abraham Lincoln
3. Bill Clinton
4. John Kennedy
5. George Washington
6. Franklin Roosevelt
7. Barack Obama
8. Theodore Roosevelt
9. Harry Truman
10. George W. Bush

©Popperfoto/Getty Images

What do you think accounts for the differences in rankings between the scholars and citizens? Does currency matter? Who do you think were the worst presidents?

Ronald Reagan is the public's first choice for greatest president.

*Brandon Rottinhaus and Justin S. Vaughn, "How Does Trump Stack Up Against the Best—and Worst—Presidents?" *The New York Times,* February 19, 2018, https://www.nytimes.com/interactive/2018/02/19/opinion/how-does-trump-stack-up-against-the-best-and-worst-presidents.html.

**Gallup poll, "Americans Say Reagan Is the Greatest U.S. President," February 18, 2011, http://www.gallup.com/poll/146183/Americans-Say-Reagan-Greatest-President.aspx

campaign, received high marks for the strength and resolution with which he responded to the September 11, 2001, terrorist attacks. Ultimately, for long-term success, a president must demonstrate good judgment in balancing strength with wisdom.

ASSESSING PRESIDENTIAL POWER AND ITS LIMITS

In a fast moving world with multiple threats to national security, presidents have amassed a number of powers designed to help them respond swiftly and secretly, often with little input from officials from other branches. Once a president assumes such powers, future presidents are hesitant to abandon them. Nevertheless, presidents are required to work within the framework of constitutional and political limits.

imperial presidency The perspective advanced by some scholars in the 1970s warning about excessive concentration of power in the hands of the chief executive.

unitary executive The theory stressing the importance of giving the president greater authority in foreign policy and in enforcing discipline over members of the executive bureaucracy.

executive privilege The presidential power to shield from scrutiny White House documents and conversations among presidential advisors.

state secrets privilege The assertion of the presidential right to withhold information from the public and from other branches of government for reasons of national security.

Following Vietnam and Watergate, scholars began to raise concerns about the rising powers of the presidency and the wisdom of allowing so much power to accrue to a single office. They argued that this presented the potential for an **imperial presidency**[68]—that is, an institution shielded from criticism and divorced from the world of average citizens. Other scholars have spoken approvingly of a **unitary executive**, claiming that the concentration of presidential power is both inevitable and necessary. They assert that presidents must have the flexibility to act decisively without clear legislative mandate and to enforce discipline and secrecy in dealing with subordinates.[69]

Recent presidents have continued to expand the limits of presidential powers. President George W. Bush followed what his advisors openly acknowledged to be a unitary perspective by regularly appending signing statements to legislation and stretching the bounds of **executive privilege**—the practice of shielding from scrutiny documents and conversations of the president and his advisors—further than previous presidents by claiming it applied to past employees and to conversations with private citizens with whom his staff might have conferred.

Despite promises of greater transparency and consultation, President Obama failed to obtain congressional approval for intervention in Libya, used drone strikes to target and kill suspected terrorists in Afghanistan and Pakistan, and continued to use the same types of surreptitious surveillance employed by his predecessor. He affirmed his right to withhold some information according to the **state secrets privilege**, which asserts the right of the chief executive to keep secret information from the public and from other branches of government for reasons of national security, a privilege usually respected by courts.[70]

President Trump continues to rely on some of these same accrued powers in performing his duties in office. He has continued the use of drone strikes against suspected terrorists abroad; he maintains operations at Guantanamo Bay, where prisoners are denied many due process rights; and he has denied public access to White House visitor logs, scrubbed data from federal websites, refused to divest himself of financial interests that might create conflicts, and zealously pursued government leakers.[71] He also actively sought to undermine the work of Special Counsel Robert Mueller's investigation into Russian meddling into the 2016 presidential election by dubbing it a witch hunt.

Yet our system of checks and balances provides ample means for reigning in presidential power. The president is checked by Congress's ability to stymie legislative initiatives and by the Court's ability to reject the constitutionality of presidential actions. President Trump became well aware of these limits. Repeated attempts to enforce a ban on immigrants from Muslim-majority countries were blocked by the courts, and forced him to adopt a more limited measure, and his efforts to repeal the Affordable Care Act during his first months in office were thwarted by a gridlocked Congress. Ultimately, a president's power derives from the ability to skillfully persuade others, to master the tools of policymaking, and to remain faithful to constitutional duties and limits.[72]

The most severe limit on presidential power is impeachment and removal from office, as discussed in Chapter 11. Congress has impeached two presidents—Andrew Johnson and Bill Clinton—but both survived trial in the Senate and remained in office. Richard Nixon chose to resign rather than face impeachment following revelations that he participated in covering up a break-in at the Democratic Party headquarters during the 1972 presidential campaign. Both the Johnson and Clinton impeachments reflected long-standing political animosities between the president and his opponents and paint a mixed picture of impeachment as a check on presidential power. On the one hand, they illustrate the difficulties in keeping legal charges against the president free of political motivation. However, because neither president was removed from office, these examples also demonstrate that the Senate is reluctant to overturn the will of the electorate unless the charge is serious and the evidence overwhelming. Nevertheless, talk of both impeachment and use of the twenty-fifth amendment to remove Donald Trump from office has persisted throughout his presidency.

THE VICE PRESIDENCY

The vice president has few constitutional duties other than acting as president of the Senate, a position that is more ceremonial than real except when the vice president votes to break ties. The vice president is also the president's designated successor should the president be unable to fulfill the duties of the office due to death, resignation, or removal. Beyond these roles, the vice president serves in a manner dictated by the president, a situation that prompted Benjamin Franklin to recommend that the occupant of the office be called "Your Superfluous Highness."[73]

Presidential candidates choose their vice presidents for a variety of reasons. A vice presidential candidate may help balance the ticket—that is, appeal to different regions of the country or factions within a party. Liberal northeasterner John Kennedy, for example, selected Lyndon Johnson, the Texas Democratic leader of the U.S. Senate, as his running mate—although it was clear that the personalities of the two men were likely to clash. More recently, personal compatibility has become more important in the selection process. George W. Bush chose Dick Cheney, former Defense Department secretary and longtime friend of the Bush family, based largely on personal factors. Cheney was low-key in comparison to Bush's folksy outgoing style; he provided expertise in foreign policy where the former Texas governor was considered weak; and he was extremely loyal, harboring no presidential

©Paul J. Richards/AFP/Getty Images

Dick Cheney exercised unprecedented influence and power as vice president in the George W. Bush White House, particularly in the area of foreign policy.

ambitions of his own. It is widely believed that Barack Obama picked Joe Biden as a running mate both because of his experience in foreign affairs as chairman of the Senate Committee on Foreign Relations and because of his ability to attract white working-class voters during the election. Donald Trump's choice of Mike Pence reflected his need to shore up support from evangelical voters who were concerned about Trump's history of alleged sexual assault as well as his desire to bring policy expertise into the White House due to his own lack of experience in public service. Pence was a favorite of the religious right and served as both a member of Congress and governor of Indiana.

Recent presidents have yielded significant authority to their vice presidents. George W. Bush's vice president, Dick Cheney, may well be considered the most powerful vice president in American history. After the September 11, 2001, terrorist attacks, Cheney played a hands-on role in the planning and implementation of the war on terrorism. He was often personally involved in reviewing intelligence, dealing with foreign governments, planning military operations in Afghanistan, and building support for the invasion of Iraq. He was granted unprecedented authority by George W. Bush, including that of executive privilege. President Obama assigned his vice president, Joe Biden, more traditional duties, including acting as spokesperson for administration policies. The same has held true for Mike Pence in the Trump administration. He has been deployed to defend Trump policies both at home and abroad and has used his legislative background to help sell Trump policies in Congress.

The enhancement of the powers of the office makes it much more likely that a vice president will be prepared to take over quickly should the president become unable to serve a complete term. The Twenty-fifth Amendment, ratified in 1967, formalizes the transition process. Relying on an extensive list of successors to the office first enacted in the 1947 Presidential Succession Act, it also provides for a temporary transfer of presidential power in case of disability. George W. Bush used this provision to transfer authority to Dick Cheney when the president underwent medical procedures in 2002 and 2007. A more controversial, though never yet invoked, provision of the same amendment allows the vice president, along with a majority of the cabinet, to declare a president incapacitated, a provision some Trump opponents have suggested might be used to remove him from office. In such a circumstance, the vice president would serve until the president recovered. The amendment also provides that the president can appoint a successor to the vice president with the consent of a majority of both houses of Congress should that position become vacant. President Nixon used this power to replace Spiro Agnew, who resigned amid tax-evasion charges, with Gerald Ford. Upon ascending to the presidency after Nixon's resignation, Ford used the procedure to name Nelson Rockefeller as his vice president.

THE PRESIDENCY AND CIVIC ENGAGEMENT TODAY

As the institution of the presidency has grown, our expectations of the occupants have grown as well. We look to the president for leadership in times of crisis, for solace in times of grief, for new programs to meet our needs, and for reduced taxes to suit our pocketbooks. Many of our expectations are contradictory: We want defense but not sacrifice; we want better government services but not higher taxes. A famous cartoon by artist Saul Steinberg captures the expectations many Americans have about U.S. presidents today. In the cartoon, George Washington and Abraham Lincoln are seated at a table along with the Easter Bunny, Santa Claus, and the Statue of Liberty. Political scientist Thomas Langston argues that the cartoon captures the modern idea that presidents are imbued with almost magical powers to make our wishes come true. "Like Santa Claus, the Easter Bunny, and witches, presidents are expected to give things to people which they do not have to pay for."[74]

In confronting our expectations, we face a dual challenge. First, we must be realistic in what we think government can accomplish. Because no president can deliver all we expect, it is not uncommon for us to be disappointed in presidential performance. Even when a president succeeds in fulfilling a campaign pledge, the policy may have unintended adverse consequences or fall short of expectations. Disappointment can easily become a rationale for abandoning our responsibilities as citizens rather than a reason for readjusting our expectations. Second, we must resist the temptation to see ourselves as mere consumers of government programs rather than as active participants in self-government. As owners of the many federal agencies and programs the president oversees, citizens must demand responsible stewardship by those we place in charge. The key to achieving both these goals is becoming an alert and informed citizen. There is simply no substitute for an electorate that examines promises and performance, attempts to separate fact from fiction, and realistically appraises what can be accomplished.

As the 2016 presidential campaign revealed, we must also be vigilant about attempts to misguide, incite, and divide us. Russian interference in the election showed how easily Americans can be swayed by false reports and innuendo. The only sure protection against such attempts is arming ourselves with the facts by checking the veracity of news reports, by turning to reliable sources, and by urging others to do the same. As has often been said, the price of liberty is eternal vigilance.[75]

Presidents can increase their own chances of success by presenting frank appraisals of both the costs and the benefits of policies they propose and by enlisting citizens to invest themselves in policy outcomes. In doing so, presidents will be following in the footsteps of Lincoln and Kennedy, who inspired sacrifice. The president must also engage in conversation with the public, recognizing that their support is crucial. With it, he can move his agenda; without it, he will be stymied.

The challenges we face as a nation are daunting—climate change, energy shortages, terrorism, health-care issues, Social Security reform, and economic insecurity, to name a few. Most of these problems cannot be solved with quick fixes or without sacrifice. We must not only remain realistic in our expectations but also demand that the president explain more clearly to the American people where he wants us to go, why we must act now, and the consequences of inaction.

Learning Objective: Describe the presidential election process.

Review: The Path to the Presidency

What are the advantages and disadvantages associated with the way we nominate and elect a president? How would you change the electoral process, if at all? Be sure to discuss all phases of the election process, including: (a) primaries and caucuses; (b) nominating conventions; (c) the general election campaign; and (d) the Electoral College.

Summary

1. **What is the path to the presidency?**

   - The Constitution specifies the requirements for candidates, the term of office (four years), the method of election (Electoral College), and provisions for resolving ties (House selects the president and the Senate selects the vice president). The Twenty-second Amendment limits the president to two terms in office.

   - In the preconvention season, candidates criss-cross the country, running in primary elections and caucuses to amass enough delegates to secure their party's nomination. Unpledged delegates and superdelegates are the only delegates whose support is not tied to primary and caucus results, but their numbers and influence have been reduced recently.

   - Today the party conventions formalize the choice of the nominee and the platform and provide the nominee an opportunity to speak to the nation.

   - The general election is decided by the tallying of electoral votes. Nominees devise strategies to ensure they gather the 270 electoral votes they need to win.

   - The road to the White House requires the amassing of large sums of money, securing the support of the party's base, making strategic decisions about which battleground states to pursue, and crafting a message that can win the support of a majority of voters in targeted states.

2. **What are the major constitutional duties and roles of the president?**

   - The Constitution makes the president the commander in chief, the chief executive, the chief of state, and the chief law enforcement officer. It also gives the president authority to recommend legislation and to carry on diplomacy and requires the taking of an oath of office and the submission of periodic reports on the state of the nation.

   - Congress has delegated substantial powers to the president to implement the laws it makes.

   - Presidents have also exercised an array of discretionary powers that can be quite far-ranging in times of emergency or crisis.

   - Presidential power has grown over time, especially since Franklin D. Roosevelt held the office. Today the president plays a number of roles not specified in the Constitution, including party leader, economic leader, and leader of public opinion.

3. **What agencies and personal factors help to produce a successful presidency?**

   - The president is assisted by the cabinet and the Executive Office of the President, which includes the White House Office, the National Security Council, the Office of Management and Budget, and various policy councils. The quality of advice given to a president can help determine the success of presidential programs.

   - Modern presidents have centralized more power within the White House and have limited their consultation with the cabinet. This centralization allows the president more control but also raises the risk of isolation from needed criticism.

   - Presidential style, which includes a president's management style and personality, can determine the success of a presidency.

Chapter 13

Bureaucracy
Citizens as Owners and Consumers

Today the joy of graduating from college is too often accompanied with the burden of considerable debt.

STUDENT LOANS, DEBT, AND BUREAUCRACY

In 2009, Robert Applebaum became an overnight spokesman for a generation of graduates burdened with student loan debt when the then 35-year-old New York lawyer started a Facebook group called Forgive Student Loan Debt to Stimulate the Economy. "I wanted to rant, so instead of sending an e-mail to a couple of my friends, I decided to start a Facebook group," Applebaum recounted.[1] By the end of the second week, 2,500 people had joined, and within two months the group had grown to 138,500 members.

Applebaum's frustration was born out of his personal experience. After graduating from Fordham law school in 1998, he took a job with the Brooklyn District Attorney's Office. His starting salary was $36,000 a year, an amount so low that he placed his student loans into forbearance for five years. When the time came to start repayment, the accumulated interest caused his student debt total to balloon to more than $100,000. In his words, "Despite having a law degree, I'm middle class and I don't have any money at all. I don't own a house or a car. My only assets are my couch and my television."[2]

Applebaum's plight is still all too common. By 2017, more than 44 million borrowers held student debt surpassing a total of $1.3 trillion. Student debt is now the second highest consumer debt category, trailing only mortgage debt. It is greater than the debt from credit cards, auto loans, and home equity lines of credit (see the figure "Nonmortgage Balances"). Over 12 million borrowers have student loan debt between $10,000 and $25,000, and two million others have student loan debt surpassing $100,000.[3] Groups like StudentLoanJustice.org have emerged as part of a new movement advocating for an overhaul of the country's troubled student-loan system.

Any student who has ever filled out a Free Application for Federal Student Aid (FAFSA) knows that the federal government is involved in the student loan process through the Department of Education. Initially, three basic types of loans were available for undergraduate students. Students could acquire federal loans made by the government directly, federal loans made by banks or other lending institutions that were guaranteed by the federal government, and private loans from private lending institutions.

The most popular federal loans are the Stafford loans, which are dispersed regardless of financial need, and the Perkins loans, which are given to students with the greatest financial need. Under the direct government plan, the federal Department of Education lends a student money—whether through a Stafford, Perkins, or some other type of loan—which is sent directly to the college or university for tuition and fees, with any remaining sums distributed to the student for living expenses. The money is eventually repaid to the Department of Education.

Under the lending system that was known as the Federal Family Education Loan (FFEL) Program, the government paid subsidies to banks and lenders to dole out money to borrowers and reimbursed these companies up to 97 percent of the cost of any loan that was not paid back. (See the figure "Types of Student Loan Programs.") In 2007, scandals were unearthed involving the FFEL Program. Certain lenders were found to be giving kickbacks in money and expensive trips to college officials who steered their students to particular financial lenders. Due largely to the scandals, the FFEL Program was ended in 2010, and colleges and universities were required to start using only the direct loan option for federal student loans.

Nonmortgage Balances
Billions of dollars

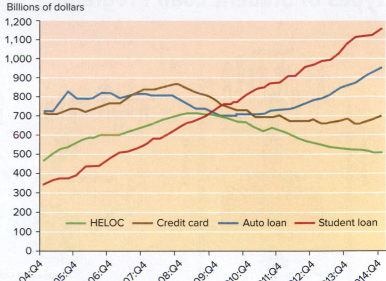

Note: HELOC is home equity line of credit.

Since 2010, student debt surpassed the debt from auto loans, credit cards, and home equity lines of credit.

Source: Federal Reserve Bank of New York Consumer Credit Panel/Equifax.

As You READ

- What is the federal bureaucracy?
- Who are federal bureaucrats, and what do they do?
- What are the sources and limits of bureaucratic power?

Types of Student Loan Programs

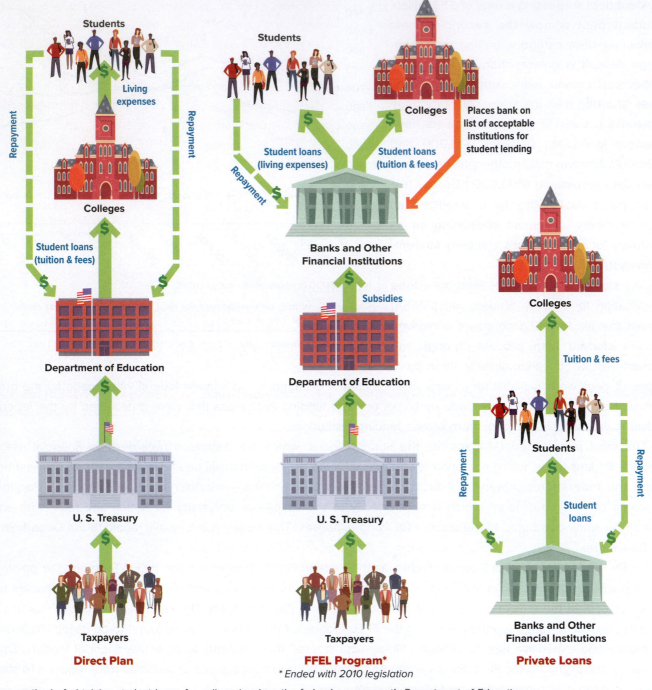

One method of obtaining student loans for college involves the federal government's Department of Education.

In 2012, the Obama administration put a student debt consolidation plan into effect. This plan reduced the payback period from twenty-five years to twenty years (ten years for those working in public service), and reduced the percentage of discretionary income on which income-driven repayments are based (from 15 percent to 10 percent). After twenty years, the remainder of the student debt will be forgiven. It is estimated that the plan could help more than six million borrowers.

The Trump administration in its first year has dealt with only one aspect of the student loan crisis. His Department of Education under the leadership of Betsy DeVos has made it more difficult for students defrauded by for-profit colleges to prove they qualify for federal student loan debt relief. Students now must prove the school intentionally deceived them using the "clear and convincing" standard of guilt rather than the less rigorous "preponderance of the evidence" standard set by the Obama administration.

The national government's role in the student loan process and its response to the student debt problem highlight several realities about the national government's bureaucracy. First, our expectations about the national government have grown immensely. Early citizens expected the government to collect taxes, deliver the mail, and little else—certainly not support their goal of going to college.

Second, a large and complex bureaucracy provides the government services that affect the lives of many citizens. The Department of Education is just one example. Two million federal bureaucrats interact with Americans more often than elected government officials do, and these interactions often lead to complaints about discourtesy, inefficiency, and even dishonesty among these workers. Finally, the president is ultimately responsible for the conduct of the bureaucracy, and he will receive the credit when the bureaucracy functions well and the blame when it does not.

Federal **bureaucrats** today exercise a great deal of power through their ability to make rules that determine how the government implements laws, as well as their authority to mediate disputes. For interest groups, bureaucracy has become a target of lobbying in an effort to shape agency policies for private benefit. For public officials, bureaucracy is often a convenient scapegoat when policies go awry.

> **bureaucrats** The civilian employees of the national government who are responsible for implementing federal laws.

For citizens, bureaucracy is increasingly treated like a business that is expected to provide reliable service while keeping costs, and the taxes that fund them, low. Some scholars worry that we are becoming a nation that treats government like just another provider of services, rather than a nation of citizens who own the government and use it for public purposes. ■

BUREAUCRATIC CHANGES AND EVOLVING CIVIC LIFE

The federal bureaucracy has changed dramatically, both in size and in the manner in which government agencies are staffed. During the 1790s, fewer people worked for the national government than worked at President Washington's Mount Vernon home.[4] The Framers presumed that the tasks of the national government would be rather limited, so they did not envision the need for a large bureaucracy. By 1800, there were still fewer than three thousand civilian employees working for the federal government.

Growth of Bureaucracy

The federal bureaucracy began to expand rapidly following the Civil War, and the pace of growth accelerated during the latter part of the nineteenth century as various groups began to lobby Congress for the promotion and protection of their economic interests. By 1925, the number of federal agencies had expanded from 90 to 170, and the number of federal employees had swollen to six thousand. The federal bureaucracy experienced its greatest expansion in the 1930s under President Franklin D. Roosevelt. In response to the Great Depression, Roosevelt implemented New Deal legislation that greatly increased the role of the federal government in providing services to alleviate the nation's economic hardships. The last significant era of bureaucratic growth came in the 1960s, in response to public demands that the national government do more to promote equal rights, improve working conditions, and protect the environment. Dramatic reductions in bureaucratic size were made in the 1990s during the Clinton years (see "Number of Federal Employees in the Executive Branch"). In recent years, the number of federal employees has been gradually rising again (see "Employment in Government, January 2007-December 2017").

Number of Federal Employees in the Executive Branch

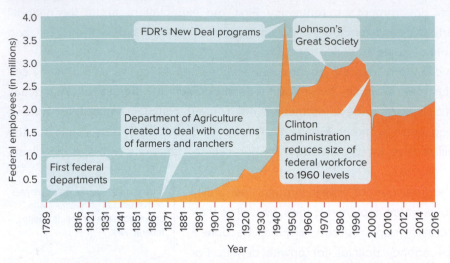

The federal bureaucracy grew most dramatically in size in response to President Franklin D. Roosevelt's New Deal programs and peaked during WWII.

Source: Department of Commerce, U.S. Census Bureau, Historical Statistics of the United States: Colonial Times to 1970 (Washington, DC: U.S. Government Printing Office, 1975); Bureau of Labor Statistics, Monthly Labor Review, November 1988; and Office of Personnel Management, The Fact Book, http://www.opm.gov/feddata/factbook/html/fb-p08.html.

Employment in Government, January 2007–December 2017

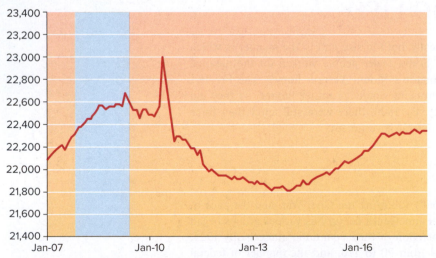

Shaded area represents recession as denoted by the National Bureau of Economic Research. Most recent 2 months of data are preliminary.

In recent years, the number of federal employees has increased gradually.

Source: US Bureau of Labor Statistics, "Current Employment Statistics Highlights: December 2017"

spoils system The expansion of the patronage system to a level of corruption that placed political cronies into all levels of government.

The dramatic growth of the U.S. population and the public's increasing demand for more and better government services have driven the expansion of the federal bureaucracy.[5] At the time of the Constitutional Convention, the United States was a small, rural nation with about 5 million inhabitants; it is now a postindustrial powerhouse of 300 million. As the country has become more complex and diverse, Americans have demanded improved education, better roads, cleaner air, more job training, and more protection of their rights. These demands came most often during sudden changes or crises in the political, economic, cultural, or social environment: the Civil War, the Great Depression, World War II, and the civil rights movement in the 1960s. Politicians are often eager to respond to citizen demands by expanding programs that fuel the growth of the bureaucracy in exchange for greater public approval. Presidents can leave their mark on history by promoting new programs and the larger bureaucracy needed to administer them. Members of Congress can please their constituents by voting for new and larger programs that will have an impact in their districts and states. This desire to please constituents may prove to be a stronger political force than general views concerning the size of government.[6] Bureaucrats desire larger budgets and agencies because an increase in their size is one of the few tangible rewards bureaucrats with limited resources and pay can achieve.

The Early Bureaucracy

Prior to the nineteenth century, government officeholders came from a relatively small pool of prominent gentlemen. Politics was the realm of the elite, and the average citizen lacked the time and the ability to participate directly in national government. George Washington took great pains to ensure that his bureaucratic appointees possessed a high level of competence.[7] This attitude changed with the growth of political parties. By the 1820s, Andrew Jackson was arguing that presidents should make appointments on the basis of patronage, or partisan political loyalty, with little regard for competency. According to Jackson, the simplicity of public work rendered merit and experience unimportant.[8] Under this **spoils system**—which took its name from the slogan "To the victor belong the spoils"—Jackson placed political cronies into all levels of the executive branch.

What Jackson started, his successors in the late 1800s perfected. When James A. Garfield became president in 1880, thousands of job seekers besieged him, hoping to secure government positions. The crush led Garfield to write in his diary: "My day is frittered away with the personal seeking of people when it ought to be given to the great problems which concern the whole country."[9] In a cruel irony, a frustrated job seeker later assassinated Garfield.

The Reform Era

Even before Garfield's assassination, reformers had called for an end to the spoils system. They called for an honest and efficient government whose employees were competent to deliver basic services. In 1883, Congress passed the Pendleton Act, also known as the Civil Service Reform Act, which reduced the number of political appointments the president could make to the executive branch and created the Civil Service Commission. New civil service regulations produced a **merit system** that emphasized an applicant's experience, education, and job performance, as well as scores on competitive exams and performance evaluations. Initially, the merit system applied to only 10 percent of the positions in the civil service, but later legislation and executive orders increased coverage to 90 percent of all federal executive branch employees.

President James Garfield, who wanted to change the spoils system, was assassinated by a frustrated job seeker.

Bureaucracy Today

The composition of today's federal bureaucracy reflects a modern institutional emphasis on professionalism and the treatment of the public as consumers. The federal civil service adopted its current emphasis on professionalism in 1955, recognizing that modern governments face complex problems that require more skilled civil servants. Government work has become more complex, and the civil service now requires employees with advanced degrees in their occupational field. Today's professional bureaucracy is far removed from Jackson's idea of government by the common man. Many highly skilled individuals look on national government service as a rewarding career.

merit system The system that classifies federal civil service jobs into grades to which appointments are made on the basis of performance on competitive exams.

In 1993, President Bill Clinton placed Vice President Al Gore in charge of an effort to improve the performance of the national bureaucracy, called the National Performance Review (NPR). Concerned that bureaucrats often treated the public in a rude and uncaring manner, Clinton believed that the government should act more like a business. It should aim to curb expenses and to treat the public like consumers it values and wishes to retain. Under the rubric of "Reinventing Government," based on the writings of David Osborne and Ted Gaebler,[10] NPR undertook policies designed to cut unnecessary spending, improve public service, treat citizens like customers, and give government employees the power to solve problems.

Despite civil service reform, some political scientists argue that party patronage is not dead but has evolved to meet the conditions of modern bureaucratic life. Rather than trying to influence the outcome of elections, today's parties use patronage to influence the making and implementation of public policy. Rather than mobilizing the public with the promise of patronage jobs, the parties

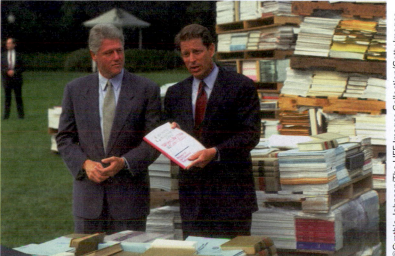

The Clinton-Gore "Reinventing Government" initiative, announced to a special joint session of Congress by President Clinton in March 1993, viewed the public as consumers of government services.

cooperate with allies both inside and outside of the government to bring about changes they desire in government policy.[11] Allies inside government include federal workers with their own views about which policies should be advanced, and outside forces include interest groups with clear policy perspectives. By mobilizing these forces, partisans can either advance their own causes or attempt to undermine the goals of their opposition. Allies of the Democratic Party include the social welfare and regulatory bureaucracies of the federal government, as well as interest groups favoring government support for social welfare spending. The Republican Party is allied with the military, defense contractors, and fundamentalist Protestant churches. These institutional alignments explain why Democrats argued against President George W. Bush's faith-based initiatives and Republicans opposed President Barack Obama's health-care initiatives.

The elites of the two parties can use investigations, revelations of wrongdoing, and criminal prosecutions to disable the institutional allies of the opposition. The acronym for revelation, investigation, and prosecution (RIP) seems fitting for this new age of patronage. These are the type of disputes that are picked up by the media, and this is the type of bitter fighting that alienates citizens from engagement with the political system.

THE NATURE OF BUREAUCRACY

bureaucracy A complex system of organization and control that incorporates the principles of hierarchical authority, division of labor, and formalized rules.

A **bureaucracy** is a complex system of organization and control that incorporates the principles of hierarchical authority, division of labor, and formalized rules. The nature of bureaucracy is based on the principles of Max Weber, summarized in the figure "Weber's Model of a Bureaucracy."

A hierarchy is the chain of command through which those at the top of an organization exercise authority over those below them; those with the least authority are on the bottom. A well-defined chain of command makes clear who is in charge, thus reducing conflict. The division of labor within this hierarchy is a system of job specialization that defines distinct tasks and responsibilities for each position. Division of labor leads to more efficient output of goods and services. In order to run as smoothly as possible, the organization conducts its operations according to formal rules and procedures that allow employees to make quick decisions that are free from personal bias.

Any large organization that is structured hierarchically to carry out specific tasks fits the bureaucratic model. However, there are important differences between private and public bureaucracies. First, private bureaucracies, including corporations such as Microsoft and General Motors, have a single set of bosses called a board of directors. By contrast, government bureaucracies have many bosses—the president, Congress, and the courts. Second, private corporations serve their stockholders, whereas governments are supposed to serve all their citizens. Third, private corporations exist to make a profit; government bureaucracies do not have to worry about profits, although they are supposed to deliver services efficiently and not waste taxpayers' money. Finally, the value of public goods produced by government—a quality education, safe food and water, national defense—is less tangible than the value of a new automobile or a new computer, electronic, or digital product. As a result, citizens are likely to criticize governments for wasting money, even though private bureaucracies actually may waste much more.[12] Remember, however, that

Weber's Model of a Bureaucracy

The concept of hierarchy The organization follows the principle of hierarchy, with each lower office under the control and supervision of a higher one.

Specialized tasks Employees are chosen based on merit to perform specialized tasks within the total operation.

Division of labor Individuals are assigned specialized tasks in order to increase efficiency.

Standard operating procedures Policies are clearly enunciated so that procedures are predictable.

Record keeping Administrative acts and rules are recorded to ensure further predictable performance.

The political economist Max Weber's bureaucratic model includes these five defining characteristics.

Source: Pfiffner, J. M. and Sherwood, F. P. *Administrative Organization* (Englewood Cliffs, NJ: Prentice Hall, 1960), 65–67.

all bureaucracies, public and private, share Weber's basic model. They embrace the concept of hierarchy, with each lower office under the control of a higher one, and they have employees performing specialized tasks according to standard operating procedures designed to ensure predictability.

When carried to an extreme, the very characteristics of bureaucracy intended to enhance efficiency and ensure equal treatment can create the impression that bureaucrats are unresponsive and incompetent. Slavishly following "standard operating procedures" that don't take into account present conditions can lead to decisions that violate common sense and interfere with an organization's ability to respond.[13] Such failures by an organization to serve its intended purposes are called bureaucratic pathologies.[14]

A common form of bureaucratic pathology among government agencies is the drive to expand and to increase responsibilities. When expansion becomes an end in itself, the pathology is known as bureaucratic imperialism. At other times, governmental bureaucracies fail to adapt swiftly when conditions warrant such changes. They may also focus on the task at hand to such an extent that they neglect other legitimate citizen concerns. Some observers, for example, believe that the national security bureaucracy's concentration on terrorism after the September 11, 2001, terrorist attacks led it to neglect basic civil liberties such as privacy and access to the courts. Finally, a bureaucratic agency may begin to display favoritism toward the interests of the groups it is supposed to oversee, rather than serving the interests of the public at large. When any of these pathologies come into public view, they reinforce the generally negative views that many American citizens have concerning bureaucracy.

FEDERAL BUREAUCRATS AND THEIR WORK

Scholars often call the bureaucracy the fourth branch of the government because of the power it wields, but the Framers of the Constitution used very few words to describe it. Article II, Section 2, proclaims, "The President shall be commander in chief of the army and navy of the United States, . . . he may require the opinion, in writing, of the principal officer in each of the executive departments, upon any subject relating to the duties of their respective offices." Beyond these words, the Founders left it to Congress to establish the organization of government and the president to lead it. Nevertheless, they considered the role of the bureaucracy to be vitally important. In *The Federalist* No. 70, Alexander Hamilton wrote that "a government ill executed, whatever it may be in theory, must be, in practice, a bad government."[15]

Who Are They?

Federal bureaucrats may be either political appointees or career civil servants who are allowed to exercise a great deal of power in the tasks they perform. Those with authority to shape policy are generally political appointees, whereas those who maintain the everyday operation and services of the agencies are part of the career civil service. Political appointees, however, come and go, while career civil service employees constitute the permanent bureaucracy.

Political Appointees The most visible federal bureaucrats, who hold the most policy-sensitive positions, are political appointees chosen by the president. They include nearly 400 cabinet secretaries, undersecretaries, assistant secretaries, bureau chiefs, and approximately 2,500 lesser positions, most of whom must be confirmed by the Senate. To fill these posts, presidents seek people with managerial talents, political skills, and ideologies similar to their own. These prestigious jobs are patronage positions, awarded based on political loyalty. These powerful bureaucrats operate what some scholars call a "government of strangers," because on average they leave government work after about twenty-two months on the job.[16]

Civilian Employee Distribution

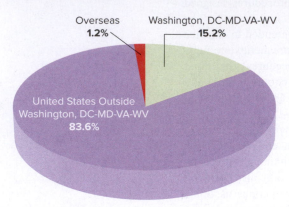

Overseas 1.2%

Washington, DC-MD-VA-WV 15.2%

United States Outside Washington, DC-MD-VA-WV 83.6%

Less than 20 percent of all U.S. federal bureaucrats work in the nation's capital or overseas.

Source: Office of Personnel Management, September 2016.

Once the preserve of white males, the ranks of political appointees have become substantially more diverse. In 1933, Franklin D. Roosevelt appointed the first woman cabinet member, Frances Perkins, to head the Department of Labor. Thirty years later, Lyndon Johnson made Robert Weaver the first African American cabinet member by appointing him secretary of housing and urban development. Today, many women and minorities hold key advisory roles as political appointees. Prior to the Trump administration, three of the last four secretaries of state were women, and the sole male was an African American, Colin Powell. The most notable aspect of Trump's political appointees has been his unwillingness to fill many of the positions. In the spring of 2018, for instance, none of the important undersecretary positions in the state department had been filled.

Career Civil Service Modern federal bureaucrats are primarily white-collar workers performing a variety of professional, managerial, technical, service, and clerical tasks. In the group as a whole, there is a trend toward older employees. Just under two million civil servants work for the federal government, not including the 750,000 postal employees or the millions of workers who compose the proxy administration of the national government. Only 15 percent of the recognized federal employees work in Washington, DC; the rest are stationed in regional offices throughout the nation and abroad (see "Civilian Employee Distribution"). The U.S. government is divided into several bureaucratic regions, and most federal agencies have offices in each region. The term *proxy administration* applies to all the people doing work for the federal government, such as private contractors and state and local government employees who are not counted officially as part of the federal bureaucracy.

civil service system The merit-based employment system that covers most white-collar and specialist positions in the federal government.

As we saw earlier, most federal bureaucrats are hired under a **civil service system** that is designed to promote a nonpartisan and specialist government service. Civil service jobs are assigned a General Schedule (GS) civil service rating ranging from GS 1 (the lowest) to GS 15 (the highest). Their salaries are tied to their assigned level (see "Salary Table 2017-GS"). The nine thousand members of the Senior Executive Service occupy a higher-paying rank, using a separate rating system. These GS positions in the federal bureaucracy constitute nearly 75 percent of all the federal bureaucrats. Approximately 15 percent of all nonpostal federal employees work for agencies that have their own merit systems, such as those in the Coast Guard and career officials in the Foreign Service of the State Department.

To ensure a nonpartisan civil service, the Merit Systems Protection Board makes it difficult to discharge federal bureaucrats for any reason, partisan or otherwise. As a result, fewer than one-tenth of 1 percent of all federal employees have actually been fired for incompetence or misconduct in recent years. Also, most federal bureaucrats may bargain collectively through a labor organizations of their choice.[17] In fact, union membership today is much more prevalent among federal government employees than among private-sector workers. However, when federal agencies were reorganized in the creation of the Department of Homeland Security, many federal employees of the new agency were excluded from collective bargaining protection. The Bush administration argued that it needed greater flexibility in dealing with employees involved in national security. Opponents believed this was merely a ploy to reduce the number of workers protected by employee unions.

At one time, federal bureaucrats gave up some of their political rights in exchange for job security. Today, however, the Hatch Act allows federal employees to run for office in nonpartisan elections, such as for school board or town council, and to contribute money to campaigns in partisan elections.

Salary Table 2017-GS

INCORPORATING THE 1% GENERAL SCHEDULE INCREASE EFFECTIVE JANUARY 2017

GS Level	Entrance Level	Maximum Level
1	$18,526	$23,171
2	20,829	26,213
3	22,727	29,549
4	25,514	33,164
5	28,545	37,113
6	31,819	41,368
7	35,359	45,970
8	39,159	50,904
9	43,251	56,229
10	47,630	61,922
11	52,329	68,025
12	62,722	81,541
13	74,584	96,958
14	88,136	114,578
15	103,672	134,776

Most federal bureaucrats are compensated according to a fixed pay schedule.

Source: U.S. Office of Personnel Management, effective January 2017.

What Do They Do?

The bureaucracy has the extremely important role of policy implementation, which is translating political goals embedded in laws into specific programs.[18] Congress grants it this role through enabling legislation that gives federal agencies the legal authority to carry out congressional laws. Congress relies heavily on the specialists within the bureaucracy to formulate the specific guidelines and rules necessary to implement government policies. Some observers, however, believe that Congress has delegated too much of its legislative authority to the bureaucracy merely to avoid the political pressures of being held accountable by citizens for unpopular policies.[19]

The Environmental Protection Agency writes rules to implement congressional laws regulating air pollution.

Rule Making Bureaucrats play a significant policy role through the administrative process known as **rule making**. Rules are by-products of congressional legislation that specify how to interpret or carry out a policy, and they carry the weight of law. When legislation is fairly clear-cut, it requires little bureaucratic interpretation. For instance, when Congress increases the minimum wage by ten cents an hour over two years, the Labor Department does not need to be very creative in designing rules for employers implementing this change. However, the wording of some laws allows administrative agencies substantial discretion.[20] For example, when Congress orders lower levels of particular pollutants in the smoke emitted by industry smokestacks, it allows the EPA to determine what levels are acceptable. This is not merely a technical matter but a political one as well because compliance with EPA rules can cost industries millions of dollars. In such cases, agency rule makers act as policymakers as well as policy interpreters and enforcers.

The figure "The Paper Trail in Rule Making" illustrates two important characteristics of the rule-making process. First, the Office of Management and Budget (OMB), an agency of the Executive Office of the President, controls the content of the rules issued by federal departments and agencies. Second, the process allows public participation. The agency proposing a new rule must publish the time, place, and nature of the proceedings for rule making in the *Federal Register.* At that time, it must state the purpose of the rule and give interested parties the opportunity to submit written comments. Opening up the rule-making process to citizens increases public participation, which provides bureaucrats with both the information they need to formulate the rules and a sense of popular response to the rule in the affected communities.[21] It also gives greater legitimacy to a process in which unelected bureaucrats, who are not accountable to the public at the ballot box, make the rules. A study of 180 Washington, DC–based interest groups revealed that a large majority of them rate work on rule making as being equal to or more important than lobbying Congress.[22] Government, trade associations, business groups, and labor unions are especially active participants in rule making.[23]

Increased public participation in the rule-making process during the 1960s and 1970s ushered in what one political scientist calls the "participation revolution."[24] During this period, social regulation expanded dramatically, extending the reach of government in such a way that "previously unorganized interests now had more than ample incentive to come together for collective action."[25] Many scholars and activists believe that direct citizen input improves the quality of the decisions.[26] The greater public input has also produced a change in the process itself. A growing number of agencies are encouraging interest groups to become involved directly in the writing of the rules. This process, known as negotiated rule making, was formalized in the Negotiated Rulemaking Act of 1990. Groups affected by a potential new rule can now apply to have their representatives become members of a negotiating committee.

> **rule making** The administrative process that creates rules that have the characteristics of a law.
>
> **Federal Register** A publication of the federal government used to announce public notice of the time, place, and nature of the proceedings to be followed when new agency rules are proposed.

The Paper Trail in Rule Making

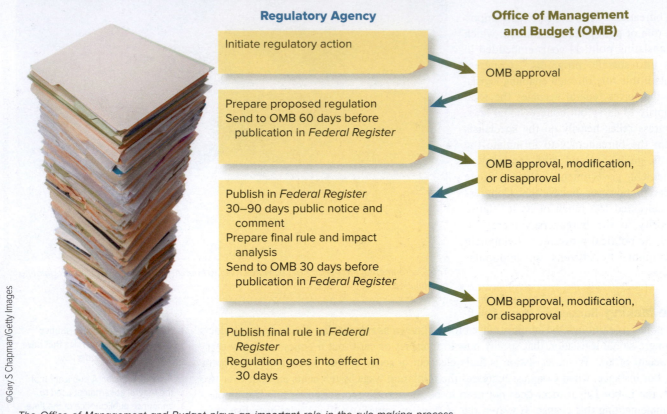

Regulatory Agency

Initiate regulatory action

Prepare proposed regulation
Send to OMB 60 days before
   publication in *Federal Register*

Publish in *Federal Register*
30–90 days public notice and
   comment
Prepare final rule and impact
   analysis
Send to OMB 30 days before
   publication in *Federal Register*

Publish final rule in *Federal
   Register*
Regulation goes into effect in
   30 days

**Office of Management
and Budget (OMB)**

OMB approval

OMB approval, modification,
or disapproval

OMB approval, modification,
or disapproval

The Office of Management and Budget plays an important role in the rule-making process.

Source: From Dumas, K. "Congress or the White House: Who Controls the Agencies?" *Congressional Quarterly Weekly Report,* April 14, 1990, p. 1133.

Adjudicating Disputes Bureaucrats can also make policy through the process of administrative adjudication, a quasi-judicial process for resolving disputes. Agencies use this process to bring parties into compliance with agency rules. The hearings are less formal than a trial, although many agencies use administrative law judges to conduct the hearings. The results of such procedures often set precedents for interpreting the rules in question. In the Social Security Administration alone, administrative law judges decide more than 300,000 cases annually.

Organization of the Federal Bureaucracy

In Chapter 12, we discussed federal agencies that make up the Executive Office of the President, such as the Office of Management and Budget. The remainder of the federal bureaucracy is organized into six major bureaucratic structures: (1) cabinet departments, (2) independent executive agencies, (3) independent regulatory agencies, (4) government corporations, (5) proxy administration, and (6) government-sponsored enterprises. Although the federal bureaucracy may seem like a complex maze of departments, agencies, and faceless individuals, it should be remembered that it was given the primary responsibility for the saving and creation of 1.6 million American jobs under the 2009 stimulus package. It is also within the bureaucracy that decisions are made that can affect citizens in their emotional lives. After the Department of Defense lifted its media blackout on covering the return of fallen soldiers in 2009, citizens could view the somber ceremony of flag-draped coffins being carried from transport planes by soldiers in full dress uniform.

cabinet departments The fifteen major administrative organizations within the federal bureaucracy that are responsible for major governmental functions such as defense, commerce, and homeland security.

Cabinet Departments The fifteen **cabinet departments** are the most visible agencies in the federal government (see "The Cabinet Departments"). Some agencies, such as the State Department and the Defense Department, serve broad national interests. Other agencies, including the Agriculture and Labor Departments, are known as clientele departments

The Cabinet Departments

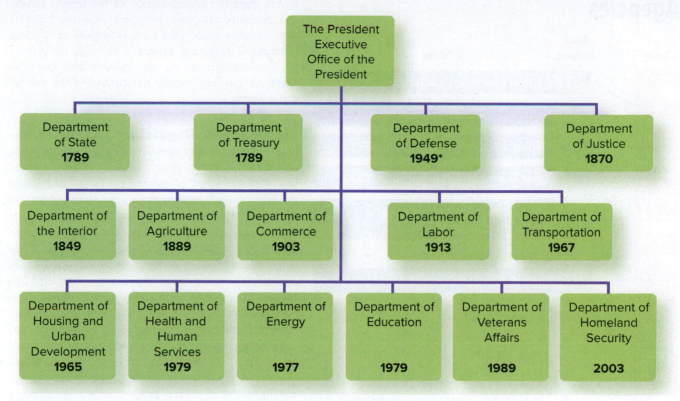

The President
Executive Office of the President

| Department of State **1789** | Department of Treasury **1789** | Department of Defense **1949*** | Department of Justice **1870** |

| Department of the Interior **1849** | Department of Agriculture **1889** | Department of Commerce **1903** | Department of Labor **1913** | Department of Transportation **1967** |

| Department of Housing and Urban Development **1965** | Department of Health and Human Services **1979** | Department of Energy **1977** | Department of Education **1979** | Department of Veterans Affairs **1989** | Department of Homeland Security **2003** |

*Founding date for Department of Defense. It was known as the Department of War when originally founded in 1749.

There are currently 15 cabinet departments in the federal government.

Source: Office of the Federal Register, United States Government Manual 2002–2003 (Washington, DC: U.S. Government Printing Office, 2003), 21.

because many of their services are directed at particular groups. All cabinet departments are **line organizations**, meaning they are directly responsible to the president, who appoints their heads with Senate approval. Each cabinet department is composed of smaller units often known as bureaus, divisions, or offices. These subdivisions are themselves often complex organizations whose members possess a great deal of power and discretion.

Independent Executive Agencies More than two hundred **independent executive agencies** exist outside the fifteen cabinet departments and the Executive Office of the President. The figure "Selected Independent Executive Agencies" presents a partial list of independent executive agencies. These agencies enjoy political independence by virtue of the importance

> **line organization** An administrative organization that is directly accountable to the president.
>
> **independent executive agency** A governmental unit with special responsibilities that is not part of any cabinet department.

citizenship Quiz

Can you pass the U.S. Citizenship Test? See how well you know the content in this chapter covered on the citizenship test required of foreign-born candidates for naturalization.

1. Who is in charge of the executive branch?
2. What does the president's cabinet do?
3. What are two cabinet-level positions?

(1) The president (2) Advises the president (3) See complete list here: http://www.whitehouse.gov /administration/cabinet

Source: United States Citizenship and Immigration Services.

Selected Independent Executive Agencies

Year	Date Formed	Name
1945	1947	Central Intelligence Agency (CIA)
1950	1949	General Services Administration (GSA)
	1950	National Science Foundation (NSF)
1955	1953	Small Business Administration (SBA)
1960	1958	National Aeronautics and Space Administration (NASA)
1965		
1970		
1975	1974	Federal Election Commission (FEC)
1980		
1985		
1990		
1995	1994	Social Security Administration
2000		

Independent executive agencies do not fall under the jurisdiction of any of the cabinet departments.

Source: Supplied by the authors.

independent regulatory agency
An agency existing outside the major departments that regulates a specific economic activity or interest.

of their missions. The Social Security Administration, for example, earned independent status in 1994 to ensure impartial administration of the federal old-age and disability insurance programs. Another independent executive agency, the CIA, is focused on overseas intelligence gathering primarily through the use of human intelligence. As an independent executive agency, it too falls outside the control of the cabinet departments.

Independent Regulatory Agencies The **independent regulatory agencies** make and enforce public policy on specific economic issues. Congress created this "alphabet soup" of government (so-called because we know these agencies mainly by their initials) to provide continuity and expertise in economic policy. For instance, the FCC regulates the broadcast media and the SEC regulates stock market policies. The "Challenges Ahead" feature discusses the role of the FCC in changing the net neutrality policy for regulating the Internet. The organization and administration of these agencies give them independence from the president, Congress, and partisan pressures. Older agencies typically feature a board of five to seven members, selected by the president and confirmed by the Senate. Board members serve longer terms than does the president—usually twelve or fifteen years—that are staggered to increase the chances of a bipartisan composition. The Supreme Court further ensured these agencies' independence in 1935 when it ruled that the president could not remove appointed board members from office.[27] As a result, citizens can interact with these agencies as they do with courts, knowing that those who decide cases are independent of the other branches of government. Newer regulatory agencies such as the Equal Employment Opportunity Commission (EEOC) enjoy less independence because presidents wanted greater control over their operations (see "Selected Independent Regulatory Agencies").

Government Corporations The most recently devised form of bureaucratic organization is the government corporation. Dating from 1933, these are businesses established and sometimes subsidized by Congress to make certain services affordable for average citizens. These corporations typically charge for their services and retain all their profits rather than distributing them as dividends to stockholders. The largest and best-known government corporation is the U.S. Postal Service (see "Selected Government Corporations").

Proxy Administration The federal government does not always carry out its administrative tasks directly; it often delegates the tasks to other parties through contracts, vouchers, grants-in-aid, and mandates. This practice, called proxy administration,[28] makes it difficult to estimate the true size of the national government because countless "shadow employees" do the government's work without officially being members of the federal bureaucracy.[29] In 1996, to great public acclaim, President Clinton announced his plan to shrink the federal bureaucracy, declaring, "the era of big government is over." He neglected to mention, however, the large amount of money the government was spending to pay private firms to perform government services. One political scientist argues that presidents often use "smoke and mirrors" to disguise the real size of the national bureaucracy.[30] Some estimates place the size of the proxy administration as high as eight million employees.

Selected Independent Regulatory Agencies

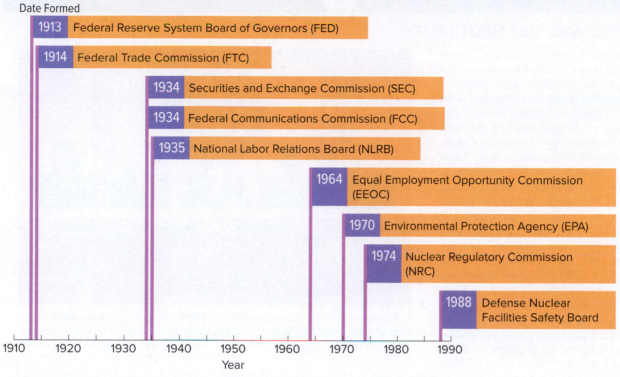

Date Formed

- **1913** Federal Reserve System Board of Governors (FED)
- **1914** Federal Trade Commission (FTC)
- **1934** Securities and Exchange Commission (SEC)
- **1934** Federal Communications Commission (FCC)
- **1935** National Labor Relations Board (NLRB)
- **1964** Equal Employment Opportunity Commission (EEOC)
- **1970** Environmental Protection Agency (EPA)
- **1974** Nuclear Regulatory Commission (NRC)
- **1988** Defense Nuclear Facilities Safety Board

Year: 1910 1920 1930 1940 1950 1960 1970 1980 1990

Independent regulatory commissions have quasi-judicial powers.

Source: Supplied by authors.

Selected Government Corporations

Name	Date formed	Principal functions
Tennessee Valley Authority (TVA) (15,000 employees)	1933	Operates a Tennessee River control system and generates power for a seven-state region and for the U.S. aeronautics and space programs; promotes the economic development of the Tennessee Valley region; controls floods and promotes the navigability of the Tennessee River.
Federal Deposit Insurance Corporation (FDIC) (5,381 employees)	1933	Insures individuals' bank deposits up to $250,000; oversees the business activities of banks.
Export-Import Bank of the United States (EX-IM Bank) (385 employees)	1934	Promotes the sale of American-made goods abroad; grants loans to foreign purchasers of American products.
National Railroad Passenger Corporation (Amtrak) (23,000 employees)	1970	Provides a balanced national and intercity rail passenger service network; controls 23,000 miles of track with 505 stations.
U.S. Postal Service (574,000 employees)	1970	Delivers mail throughout the United States and its territories; is the largest government corporation.

Government corporations like the U.S. Postal Service charge for their services.

THE FCC AND NET NEUTRALITY

The Federal Communications Commission (FCC) is one of the independent regulatory agencies discussed in this chapter. It was created in 1934 to replace the radio regulation functions of the Federal Radio Commission. The FCC has less than two thousand employees and an annual budget funded entirely by regulatory fees. Today the FCC regulates interstate communications by radio, television, wire, satellite, and cable. The agency is directed by five members appointed by the president and confirmed by the Senate. The members serve five-year terms but may continue to serve until the appointment of their replacements. The president designates one of the commissioners to be the chair. By law, only three of the members may be of the same political party.

Traditionally, the agency did not regulate the Internet to any great extent. In 2014, however, President Obama recommended that the FCC reclassify Internet service in order to gain the legal basis necessary to preserve the policy of net neutrality. As defined by its proponents, net neutrality is the basic principle that prohibits Internet service providers from speeding up, slowing down, or blocking any content, websites, or applications. Net neutrality safeguards a user's right to control his or her own Internet experience.* Prior to the FCC's decision on net neutrality in 2015, net neutrality advocates flooded the agency with comments and staged demonstrations in front of its headquarters in Washington. As expected, the Democrat-controlled agency adopted a net neutrality policy.

In 2017, President Trump named Ajit Pai to be the new chairman of the FCC. Pai, a Republican, had been an associate general counsel for Verizon Communications Inc. and was known to be an opponent of net neutrality, saying: "We need to fire up the weed whacker and remove those rules that are holding back investment, innovation, and job creation." Now leading the agency with a new Republican majority, Pai announced that the FCC would reconsider its Internet policy in December 2017. Prior to the meeting, the agency received more than 22 million comments pertaining to the decision, although there were doubts as to how many of these were unique. On his show, *Last Week Tonight,* HBO's John Oliver had implored viewers to submit comments in favor of net neutrality to the agency.[†] A University of Maryland poll showed that 83 percent of the respondents opposed the

Source: Federal Communications Commission

Commissioner Brendan Carr, Commissioner Mignon Clyburn, Chairman Ajit Pai, Commissioner Michael O'Rielly, and Commissioner Jessica Rosenworcel. Voting along straight party lines, they rescinded the net neutrality policy by a vote of three to two.

repeal of net neutrality, including three out of four Republicans.[‡] Despite the outpouring of support, the FCC, voting along party lines, dropped the net neutrality policy by a vote of three to two. Pai argued that competition among Internet providers would prevent any blocking of information to consumers.

The FCC's decision is just one example of the way that bureaucratic agencies can have a profound effect on everyday activities. As of the time this text went to print, computer users were still waiting to see if their Internet experiences would be negatively affected by this change in policy. In 2018, Senate Democrats surpassed the thirty-member threshold required to allow them to use the Congressional Review Act to seek to overrule the new FCC policy. Overruling the FCC would require a majority vote in both the House and the Senate and the president's signature.[§] Our Internet experiences may very well depend on the outcomes of the 2018 and 2020 national elections.

*Free Press, "Net Neutrality: What You Need to Know Now," https://www.freepress.net/issues/free-open-internet/net-neutrality/net-neutrality-what-you-need-know-now.

[†]Ted Johnson, "FCC Chairman Proposes Repeal of Net Neutrality Rules," *Variety,* November 21, 2017.

[‡]Brian Fung, "This Poll Gave Americans a Detailed Case For and Against the FCC's Net Neutrality Plan," *The Washington Post,* December 12, 2017.

[§]See Brian Fung, "Net Neutrality Activists Are Celebrating as Democratic Senators Clear Key Hurdle to Voting Against the FCC," *The Washington Post,* January, 9, 2017.

Government-Sponsored Enterprises The federal government also sets up government-sponsored enterprises (GSEs), which operate as though they were privately owned and operated. For instance, they are primarily responsible to shareholders. Over time, some of these enterprises have become fully privatized. One example is the Student Loan Marketing Association (Sallie Mae), created in 1972 to promote low-cost loans to students and privatized in 2005.

SOURCES OF BUREAUCRATIC POWER

Although federal bureaucrats are not elected, they make important decisions about the direction of public policy. Whereas elected policymakers derive power ultimately from the electorate, the sources of an administrative agency's power include external support, expertise and discretion, longevity and vitality, and strong leadership.

External Support

Americans' historical suspicion of intrusive government has rendered the bureaucracy vulnerable to public attack, and politicians often manipulate this mistrust during elections to gain votes. As a result, bureaucratic agencies seek external support in the form of positive attitudes toward the agency and political agreements to fund their budgets. The more external support an agency possesses, the more power it is able to wield. But agencies can lose public support as quickly as they gain it. Prior to World War II, for example, Americans widely admired the FBI and its director, J. Edgar Hoover. However, revelations of Hoover's illegal surveillance of protest groups in the 1950s and 1960s greatly reduced the FBI's popularity. After constant criticism of its professionalism and objectivity by President Trump, the agency has once again had to become concerned about its external support. The media, with their propensity toward negative news reporting, can also create an environment that does not foster consistent public support for any agency. As a result, agencies must conduct public-relations efforts directed at both the media and the public to put their work in the best possible light.

Because both Congress and the president can curb the power of bureaucratic agencies, bureau chiefs spend considerable time cultivating good relations with members of Congress and the White House. They work primarily with congressional committees and subcommittees, congressional staff members, the Congressional Budget Office, executive department heads, presidential staff members, and the Office of Management and Budget, among others.

It is particularly important for agencies to have the support of the interests that make up their constituency. These interest groups constitute the external support necessary to blunt political opposition.[31] Hence, the Department of Agriculture needs to please farmers, and the Department of Labor needs to satisfy the demands of organized labor.

Expertise and Discretion

Bureaucrats' superior knowledge places them in a position of authority relative to other political actors, who typically lack the same depth of knowledge or understanding of specific policy issues. Researchers employed at the Centers for Disease Control and Prevention, for instance, possess far more knowledge about exotic diseases than Congress members or the president. Thus, they are in a better position to write rules regarding the prevention and treatment of disease. Likewise, during the financial crisis of 2008 and 2009, it was the executive branch leaders with Wall Street experience who developed the plans to rescue the banks and maintain a stable credit market. For bureaucratic agencies, expertise is power.

Agencies like the FBI rely on public support for their continuing power.

The National Aeronautics and Space Administration (NASA), an independent agency, is responsible for the nation's space program.

Because of their expertise, bureaucrats often enjoy great discretion in implementing public policies in the way they feel is most appropriate. In 2004, for example, the Labor Department issued new rules interpreting federal legislation concerning overtime pay. The extent of the changes in the workplace was determined at the Labor Department's discretion rather than at the discretion of Congress. In the Trump administration, the Education Department changed the rules for handling sexual assault cases on college campuses without input by Congress. Remember, the combination of the specialized nature of bureaucratic work with the long tenure afforded bureaucrats allows them to gain expertise over a particular subject matter to a greater extent than members of Congress, the president, or judges.

Longevity and Vitality

The rules of the civil service system make it difficult for political appointees to fire career civil servants for any reason. As a result, civil servants tend to stay in office for a long time, much longer than politicians and their political appointees. This tenure is a source of power because presidents and their appointees must rely on these career civil servants to accomplish their policy objectives. Bureaucrats also have an institutional memory and can view issues in a historical context. Politicians come and go, but the bureaucrats remain and provide stability for the system.[32]

The commitment of its personnel to an agency's mission is another source of bureaucratic strength as employees work together to accomplish agency goals. One way of ensuring vitality is to hire only employees with strong prior commitment to the agency. Another is to create a work environment that fosters loyalty.[33]

Leadership

Good leaders possess the will and talent to translate an agency's resources into power. Good leaders can enhance an agency's expertise and vitality and interact effectively with external groups.[34] Because of the fixed nature of salary schedules and the repetitive nature of some bureau work, bureau chiefs often look for innovative ways to motivate their workers. Bureaucratic leaders must combine the social skills needed to motivate their staff with the skill and determination to gain respect for their agency with external groups. Leaders must also have the innovative skills and knowledge needed to help an agency reach its goals.

CONTROLLING BUREAUCRATIC POWER

In spite of the enormous influence and often independent nature of public bureaucracies, many actors in the political system have some tools to check bureaucratic power. The general unpopularity of bureaucracies among the American public makes it easier for politicians to wield these tools. As James Q. Wilson wrote, "No politician ever lost votes by denouncing the bureaucracy."[35] Denouncing the bureaucracy, however, is easier than controlling it—although Congress, the White House, the courts, and even some bureaucrats have occasionally tried.

Congressional Controls

The implied powers granted under the necessary and proper clause allow Congress to create, abolish, or alter bureaucratic departments, agencies, bureaus, and commissions. Congress can exercise power over the bureaucracy by ordinary legislation. By writing a statute that is very clear and precise, Congress reduces the discretion of the bureaucratic agency to fill in the details. Congress can exercise its authority by passing **sunset laws**, whose provisions automatically expire at a time specified by the statute. Congress also uses legislative veto provisions in some statutes that allow it to veto future bureaucratic interpretation and implementation of a law.

> **sunset laws** Laws that include an expiration date.

Congress can employ the power of the purse to control bureaucratic authority. Authorization legislation sets a maximum amount that a particular agency can spend on a program. After Congress authorizes funds, they must still be appropriated, so agency heads must appear before the House Appropriations Committee to justify their monetary requests. The Appropriations Committee often serves as a budget cutter by decreasing the amount previously authorized by legislative committees.

Congress can also monitor the activities of the federal bureaucracy by exercising its oversight function. The Supreme Court has ruled that the power of Congress to legislate implies the power to conduct investigations and, if necessary, to compel the disclosure of information before legislative hearings.[36] Through such actions, Congress indicates its support for or displeasure with an agency's activities. In April 2008, for instance, the House Transportation and Infrastructure Committee directed its political wrath at the Federal Aviation Administration for creating "a culture of coziness" between the senior agency officials and the airlines they were charged with regulating. The result was a pattern of regulatory abuses and lapses that placed the flying public in danger.[37] In 2017, many Congressional Republicans used committee hearings to voice their displeasure with the special counsel's probe of links between Russia and the Trump campaign. (See the "Current Controversy" feature on the Office of Special Counsel.) There is no way, however, for congressional committees to monitor all the activities of the vast federal bureaucracy. Congress tends to conduct investigations of only those agencies that clearly contradict its will or that have generated a scandal. Congress typically waits for clientele groups, lobbyists, or interest groups to report concerns about an agency and then reacts to those complaints. This pattern suggests that citizen action can exert considerable influence on government policy.

In 1996, Congress provided itself with an additional tool to reduce the power of the bureaucracy. Congressional review gives Congress the power to strike down any newly announced agency rule if both houses pass such a resolution and the president signs it. They almost never use this check, however. As with other laws, Congress can override a presidential veto with a two-thirds vote in each chamber.

Presidential Controls

Without some form of control over the bureaucracy, presidents are at a major disadvantage in advancing their policies. As the national government has grown and become more complex, presidents have delegated increasing power to bureaucrats. Presidents often have a more difficult time selling their programs to the bureaucracy than to Congress.[38]

At the urging of President Jimmy Carter, Congress passed the Service Reform Act of 1978. Among other things, this created the Senior Executive Service. The Senior Executive Service

Current Controversy

The Special Counsel: Outside Regular Bureaucratic Boundaries

When a scandal potentially involves the top officials in the executive branch of government—including the president—the normal agencies and departments of the government bureaucracy may not be the appropriate ones to investigate. Observers may question the ability of the government to lead an inquiry of itself and follow the evidence wherever it leads. As one author expresses it, the justice apparatus could be perceived as a biased arbiter.* To meet this concern, a special counsel outside the regular bureaucratic apparatus may be appointed. This special counsel has two important roles: to figure out what happened and resolve it as appropriate and to reassure the public that the investigation was impartial.†

A special counsel, also referred to at different historical periods as "special prosecutor" or "independent counsel," has been named twenty-nine times in American history. The first one, in 1875, investigated the "Whiskey Ring" scandal in the Grant administration, in which politicians, whiskey producers, and federal employees were accused of stealing tax revenues from alcohol sales. The result of the special counsel's investigation was 110 convictions and $3 million in recovered taxes. A special counsel was appointed one other time in the nineteenth century to examine a bribery scandal in the postal department.‡ Scandals in the presidencies of Theodore Roosevelt, Calvin Coolidge, and Harry Truman also led to the appointment of outside counsels.

The special counsel is currently appointed by the attorney general under regulations adopted by the Department of Justice.

©Orhan Cam/Shutterstock

The most significant employment of a special counsel to date ended the presidency of Richard Nixon. In what became known as the Watergate scandal, members of Nixon's reelection campaign team were caught in a burglary attempt in the national headquarters of the Democratic Party in the Watergate office complex. President Nixon ordered the attorney general to fire the special counsel investigating the case. Both the attorney general and his deputy resigned rather than follow this order and the solicitor general finally complied with the president's order. This so-called Saturday Night Massacre created such a political backlash that the president could not prevent the selection of a second special counsel to continue the Watergate investigation. Evidence was eventually

(SES) is a select group of career federal public administrators who specialize in managing public agencies. They agree to make themselves available for presidential transfers to other agencies that may require their talents in exchange for higher salaries. There are more than six thousand members of this service, and they fill most of the top managerial positions in the federal bureaucracy. The SES provides the president with greater control over the bureaucracy by making it possible to place career civil servants where he wants them.

Another key presidential control on the bureaucracy is the power to submit bureaucratic reorganization plans to Congress, authorized when Congress established the Executive uncovered linking the burglary and subsequent attempts to cover it up to the White House. In 1974, the investigation by the special counsel and probes conducted by congressional committees led the House Judiciary Committee to bring articles of impeachment against President Nixon, who shortly thereafter became the first president to resign.

President Nixon's firing of the first special counsel in the Watergate probe led Congress to pass the Ethics in Government Act in 1978. The act aimed to insulate the office of special counsel by formalizing the appointment process. The provisions of the bill were reauthorized by Congress in 1983 and 1987. Six different special counsel investigated charges against the Reagan administration under the law's provisions. When the law expired in 1992, it was not reinstated for another two years until 1994. Under the 1994 reauthorization of the act, twelve separate inquiries were conducted concerning the Bill Clinton administration. One of them involved the president's lying under oath about having sexual relations with an intern. This led to Clinton's impeachment and eventual acquittal by the Senate. By 1999, when the provisions of the bill expired, both Republicans and Democrats were tired of the numerous investigations and did not extend the Ethics in Government Act.§

Since 1999, the legal authority for a special counsel has rested with the attorney general's office. In 2017, Deputy Attorney General Rod Rosenstein appointed Robert Mueller as special counsel to investigate coordination between the Russian government and Donald Trump's presidential campaign. Attorney General Jeff Sessions had recused himself based

In 2017, Robert Mueller was named special counsel to investigate any cooperation between the Russian government and the Trump campaign during the 2016 presidential election.

©Saul Loeb/AFP/Getty Images

on his earlier activities on behalf of Trump's campaign. A looming question is whether Trump can fire Mueller, following Nixon's example in the Saturday Night Massacre. According to the attorney general's regulations, a special counsel can be removed only by the attorney general—or, in the case of Mueller, by the deputy attorney general—for misconduct, incapacity, conflict of interest, or other good cause. President Trump himself could thus not remove Mueller, but if the Department of Justice rescinded the special counsel regulations, the president could then exercise the removal power. Alternatively, if the attorney general fired Rosenstein, then Trump could appoint a new deputy attorney general and ask this person to fire Mueller. In

either case, the most likely result would be a political firestorm.¶ A lingering question involving the special counsel's powers is whether the office can indict and try a sitting president and whether, in such an instance, Congress would impeach and try that sitting president.

*See Katy Harriger, *The Special Prosecutor in American Politics,* 2nd ed., revised (Lawrence: University Press of Kansas, 2000).

†Ibid.

‡Jeff Nilsson, "Allegation Nation: A Brief History of Presidents and Special Prosecutors," *The Saturday Evening Press,* May 11, 2017.

§See Jonathan S. Tobin, "Against a Special Prosecutor," *National Review,* May 11, 2017.

¶See Simon Bloom and Troy Covington, "Fire the Special Counsel? History Shows It Would Be a Bad Idea," *The Hill,* July 2, 2017.

Office of the President in 1939. President George W. Bush's administration exercised this authority to reorganize several intelligence and law enforcement agencies with the creation of the Department of Homeland Security in 2003. On the whole, however, presidential attempts to reorganize the bureaucracy have not resulted in greater presidential control.[39]

The president does exercise considerable control through his power of appointment.[40] Article II, Section 2, of the Constitution empowers the president to appoint major officials, with confirmation by a majority of the members of the Senate. It also provides that Congress shall decide the means of appointments for minor officials. Under this latter provision,

©MCT via Getty Images

President Obama created the Council on Women and Girls by executive order in 2009 to help government agencies respond to the challenges facing females in the twenty-first century. The Trump administration has demonstrated little enthusiasm for the council.

Congress has empowered the president to choose some minor officials in the executive branch, such as administrative staffers, without the need for Senate approval. This has allowed presidents to build a loyal administrative base by choosing political appointees who will follow their policy wishes. There is a danger in making loyalty the main qualification for appointment, however. "Loyal individuals," one insider writes, "who lack political experience can do the president more harm than good. Motivated by the best of intentions (e.g., serving the president), such officials can produce disastrous political consequences that can ultimately reduce presidential influence."[41] The president also wields the sole power to fire political appointees. This power is limited, however, because it does not extend to the vast majority of bureaucrats whose job security is protected by civil service rules, or to members of independent regulatory commissions.

Like Congress, the president can also use the budget as a tool of administrative control. Gerald Ford stated in his memoirs that "a president controls his administration through the budget. The document reflects his basic priorities."[42] Presidents can set the agenda for their administrations by calling for increases or reductions for specific social programs and by submitting larger or smaller budgets for national defense. They can also influence the fate of a particular agency by proposing increases or reductions in funding, initiating new programs, and vetoing appropriations.[43] Today, the president depends heavily on the Office of Management and Budget to exercise control over the bureaucracy. At the beginning of the budget cycle, OMB assigns each agency a budget limit consistent with the president's directives. After each agency sends OMB its budgetary requests for the fiscal year, OMB reviews the requests and makes changes before sending the budget to Congress. No agency can issue a major rule without an OMB assessment that the rule's benefits outweigh its costs. In addition, no agency can propose legislation to Congress without the approval of OMB.

In 2009, President Obama signed an executive order that created the White House Council on Women and Girls. The mission of the council is to provide a coordinated governmental response to the challenges confronting females. To further that mission, all federal departments and bureaucratic agencies must consider how their programs and policies impact women and families in such areas as economic security, protection from violence, and health. In 2011, the Department of State launched the Women in Public Service Project, and USAID dedicated over $30 million in funding to support women's leadership in a range of sectors. The Women in Public Service Project continues today and is housed at the Woodrow Wilson International Center for Scholars with the goal of training the next generation of women leaders. The future of this policy thrust is uncertain, however, given the lack of attention to women's issues in the Trump administration.

Judicial Controls

The courts' influence on the federal bureaucracy is much less direct than that of Congress or the president. They can intervene only if an aggrieved party files a lawsuit against an administrative agency. When that happens, the courts attempt to ascertain the legislative and presidential intent of the law to evaluate whether the administrative rules are consistent with congressional and presidential wishes. This is a difficult undertaking because, as we have noted, legislation is often purposely vague to allow the specialists in the bureaucracy to fill in the gaps in the policy and to adapt the rules to fit changing and unanticipated conditions. For that reason, the courts tend to support the actions of the bureaucrats if they are at all consistent with the politicians' wishes, and if the bureaucratic rules are consistent with the tenets of due process, ensuring that all parties are treated fairly. In the case of the executive orders that President Trump issued in 2017, banning travelers from Muslim-majority countries, the lower federal courts went against the wishes of the president and bureaucratic agencies when they held the travel bans violated the Constitution. By issuing stays of the president's executive orders, the federal district courts were able to limit what the Immigration and Customs Enforcement division of the Department of Homeland Security could allow its employees to do at airports across the United States with respect to travelers from these countries. (See the "Current Controversy" feature in Chapter 14.)

Whistle-Blowing

A more controversial method of controlling bureaucratic power originates within the bureaucracy itself. Known as **whistle-blowing**, it is the act of calling public attention to inappropriate agency behavior. To encourage whistle-blowing, Congress passed the Whistleblower Protection Act in 1989 to protect employees from retaliation and, in some instances, provide them with a financial reward. Despite the law, many government employees are still afraid to expose corruption for fear of reprisal. Whistle-blowing has uncovered many outrageous cost overruns in government contracts, such as the Defense Department paying $600 apiece for toilet seats.

The 2008 oversight hearings of the Federal Aviation Administration referred to earlier were triggered by two whistle-blowers. One FAA plane inspector, Charalambe Boutris, contacted the congressional committee after his unsuccessful efforts to persuade his superiors to ground Southwest Airlines planes that had cracks in their fuselage. He testified that the cracks "could have resulted in sudden fracture and failure of the skin panels of the fuselage, and consequently cause a rapid decompression which would have a catastrophic impact during flight."[44] A second whistle-blower, Douglas E. Peters, testified after a superior indirectly threatened his family if he did not maintain his silence.

A different type of whistle-blowing occurred in early 2018 when nine of the twelve members of the National Park Service advisory board resigned, citing the secretary of the interior's unwillingness to meet with them. The advisory board was created in 1935 to allow citizen advisers to help the National Park Service. The present-day members represented a breadth of research disciplines from social science to natural research conservation. Their concerns included the Trump administration's rescinding of an Obama 2016 executive order that had called for a focus on climate change in the managing of natural resources in U.S. national parks. The resignations of the nine members was also an opportunity for them to voice their displeasure with downsizing the acreage in some national parks and the Trump administration's plans to open up protected areas of the Arctic and the Atlantic for oil drilling.

The risks and uncertainty involved with whistle-blowing make it an inconsistent means of curbing bureaucratic abuses of power. However, it is just one piece in a larger set of controls—including the congressional, presidential, and judicial means already discussed—on the enormous power and independence exercised by bureaucrats.

> **whistle-blowing** The practice whereby individuals in the bureaucracy bring public attention to gross inefficiency or corruption in the government.

THE BUREAUCRACY AND CIVIC ENGAGEMENT TODAY

Today, citizens have increased the nature and scope of their interactions with government. They now lobby the bureaucracy just as they do their congressional representatives, attempting to influence rules, receive favorable rulings by administrative judges, and demand greater accountability for the way their tax monies are spent. This approach to securing citizen rights has expanded civic engagement in important ways, but at a measurable cost. As citizens attend more to advancing narrow personal interests in government, they risk losing sight of their role as owners of government rather than merely consumers of its policies. Citizens belong to a political community that has a collective existence, whereas customers are people who make individual purchases. Customers are not interested in making changes that benefit citizens collectively.

Many of the changes in today's bureaucracy reflect an increasing government emphasis on privatization. The federal government contracts out a great deal of work to the private sector. Creating voucher systems for some public policy areas such as education creates competitive markets for public services. Some politicians are even advocating privatization of the Social Security system on the basis of dire forecasts that the system will have insufficient funds to pay future benefits when today's workers retire. Under the current system, workers receive a fixed amount of money each month upon retirement, which is based on the number of years worked and the amount of money earned. In a private system, the government would no longer deduct Social Security taxes, leaving workers free to invest this money as they see fit. Such proposals of bureaucratic privatization are likely to increase in frequency in the current political environment.

Thinking It Through »»»

Learning Objective: Outline the ways the federal bureaucracy is held accountable.

Review: Sources of Bureaucratic Power and Controlling Bureaucratic Power

President Trump's first secretary of state, Rex Tillerson, came to office believing that his department needed fewer diplomats and some reorganization to reduce the bureaucracy's undue influence on foreign policy. Discuss how the non-elected bureaucracy wields power and what mechanisms are available to curb that power.

Summary

1. **What is the federal bureaucracy?**
   - The federal bureaucracy is a complex organization of departments, agencies, and corporations that have the characteristics of hierarchy, specialization, and formalized rules.
   - The number of civilians working in the federal bureaucracy has been influenced by the demands citizens have made for government services.
   - The way federal bureaucrats have been chosen has been a reflection of the political system evolving from an elite system, to patronage, and finally to a merit system.
   - Government bureaucracies produce public goods and are not concerned about profits, but they are subject to a variety of pathologies that interfere with their ability to respond.

2. **Who are federal bureaucrats, and what do they do?**
   - Federal bureaucrats are the civilian employees, most of them professionals, who work for the federal government.
   - Most federal bureaucrats are civil servants with job security, but the most visible ones are political appointees who hold the most policy-sensitive positions.

   - Federal bureaucrats exercise much discretion when they formulate the rules for implementing laws and settling disagreements between parties through administrative adjudication.

3. **What are the sources and limits of bureaucratic power?**
   - Bureaucrats draw on external support, their expertise and discretion, longevity on the job, and the vitality and leadership in the agency as sources of power.
   - Congress can limit bureaucratic power by passing laws to reorganize the bureaucracy, enacting sunset laws and legislative vetoes, controlling appropriations, conducting oversight, and practicing congressional review.
   - Presidents can limit bureaucratic power by submitting bureaucratic reorganization plans to Congress, proposing civil service reform, exercising the constitutional appointment and removal powers, and controlling the bureaucracy's budget.
   - The courts and whistle-blowers can limit bureaucratic power on occasion.

Chapter 14

The Courts
Judicial Power in a Democratic Setting

WHAT'S TO COME

Judge Neil Gorsuch became the 113th justice to the United states Supreme Court.

THE TORTUOUS SELECTION OF A SUPREME COURT JUSTICE

On April 7, 2017, Judge Neil Gorsuch was confirmed by the Senate to be a member of the U.S. Supreme Court. Gorsuch filled a vacancy that had lasted for 420 days, the seventh longest period in the Court's history. All of the longer time periods to appoint a new justice had occurred in the nineteenth century.

The 419-day odyssey began on February 13, 2016, when Associate Justice Antonin Scalia died during a hunting trip to Texas. That day, the Court lost its most influential conservative and most provocative justice. Within nine minutes of the announcement of Scalia's passing, the conservative publication *The Federalist* tweeted that the Senate must not confirm his successor in 2016. Four minutes later, a spokesman for a Republican member of the Senate Judiciary Committee tweeted that there was less than a zero percent chance that the Republican-controlled Senate would confirm any nominee named by President Barack Obama. Later in the day, Senate majority leader Mitch McConnell proclaimed the Senate would not hold hearings or take any confirmation vote on any Obama nominee to the Court. At a short news conference, however, the president indicated that he would fulfill his constitutional duty by naming a replacement for Scalia and suggested that the

Senate should also perform its constitutional obligation of holding hearings on his choice and voting on his nominee.

Soon thereafter, the Court vacancy became an issue in the 2016 presidential election campaign. The six remaining Republican candidates all agreed that the Senate should delay confirming any Court nominee so that the winner of the 2016 presidential election would get to choose the next Supreme Court nominee. The two major Democratic candidates, former secretary of state Hillary Clinton and Vermont senator Bernie Sanders, predictably agreed with the president's position. President Obama moved forward the following month with his nomination of Merrick Garland, the chief judge of the D.C. Court of Appeals. Garland had the reputation of being a moderate in his ideology and had been easily confirmed by the Senate for his appellate role. Early public opinion approved of the president's choice, but the Republican leadership in the Senate held fast to their position of holding no hearing and calling for no vote on Judge Garland's confirmation.

As You READ

- **What is the nature of the judicial process?**
- **How are Supreme Court justices selected?**
- **What is the nature of Supreme Court decision making?**

While Judge Garland's name remained before the Senate, Republican candidate Donald Trump released a list of eleven potential nominees he would select if he won the presidency. After issuing the first list in May, he announced a second list of ten potential nominees in September. Both lists were constructed with help from two conservative groups, the Federalist Society and the Heritage Foundation.[1] Leonard Leo of the Federalist Society played a major role in drafting the second list, which included Gorsuch.[2] After winning the election, the Trump White House interviewed four federal appellate judges for the opening. The new president announced his selection of Neil Gorsuch on January 31, 2017.

When Gorsuch's name reached the Senate for confirmation, the partisan divide was palpable. The Democrats were furious about how the majority party had treated the Garland nomination. Although they realized that President Obama's nomination would have had little chance of success—the success rate of presidential nominations to the Supreme Court during the last year of a president's term, particularly when his party does not control the Senate, is very low—Democrats argued that Republican leaders' refusal to vote on the issue was unprecedented. Republicans knew that the minority party had more than enough votes to block the Gorsuch nomination from attaining the required sixty votes for confirmation and invoked the so-called nuclear option, allowing the nomination to be confirmed by a simple majority vote. The Democrats were livid. The Republicans countered that Democratic Senate majority leader Harry Reid had used the nuclear option in 2013 for lower court nominations. Democrats argued that Reid's actions had been necessary because Republicans had blocked President Obama's nominations of highly qualified individuals to the lower federal courts for months.

During three days of hearings before the Senate Judiciary Committee, Gorsuch was hammered by Democratic members concerning one of his appeals court decisions that found against an employee of a truck company. Gorsuch had ruled that the employee's firing was justified when he abandoned cargo to seek safety after losing feeling in his extremities while awaiting help in subzero temperatures. After a party-line vote of 11 to 9 in committee, the nomination moved to the full Senate. On April 7, 2017, the torturous journey to fill the Scalia vacancy ended with a vote of 54 to 45. Three Democrats from conservative states that had voted for Trump in the 2016 election supported the nomination, and one Republican recovering from surgery was absent.

Against this background of bitter partisan divisions over Supreme Court nominations, swing Justice Anthony Kennedy announced his retirement in late June of 2018. His replacement would now cement a new conservative majority on the Court. President Trump nominated Judge Brett Kavannaugh and Senate Republicans pledged to push the nomination through the body before the 2018 midterm elections. Democrats expressed outrage over the rushed process, their inability to receive documents relating to the earlier partisan work of the nominee in the Bush White House, and later the allegations of sexual assault concerning the nominee while he was in high school and college. Those allegations led to an additional hearing before the Senate Judiciary Committee featuring the first accuser and the judge. One Republican on the committee joined with the Democrats in asking for an FBI investigation of the allegations prior to a Senate confirmation vote. A week later after a limited investigation, the Senate confirmed the nomination by only two votes as the nation watched.[3]

When an appointment to the Supreme Court becomes a major issue in a presidential campaign, the Court cannot avoid the charge that it is a political institution making partisan decisions. Yet the Supreme Court has become the institution most likely to determine the extent of personal rights that have become the focus of American democracy. (See Chapters 4 and 5.) It sits atop the nation's dual court system and takes cases from across the nation. The Supreme Court's ability to affect the lives of citizens has heightened public interest in the selection of its members and in the way they make decisions. Their prominence has also created new opportunities for citizens to interact with the Court. ■

NATIONAL COURT STRUCTURE

The national court structure began to take on its present look with the passage of the Judiciary Act of 1789. The Constitution provided for just the Supreme Court and "such inferior courts as the Congress may from time to time ordain and establish." Once the Constitution was ratified, Congress moved quickly to establish a complete national judiciary, including trial courts and other appellate courts. At this time, each state government already had its own system of courts. The existence of one national court system and separate court systems in each of the states is known as a **dual court system**. Citizens of any state are subject to the jurisdiction of both state courts and national courts.

The first bill introduced in the Senate dealt with the unresolved issue of national inferior courts. After considerable debate, Congress passed the law that led to the foundation of the current judicial system. It created a three-tier system of national courts. At the base were thirteen district courts, each presided over by a single district judge. In the middle were circuit courts located in every district. Each circuit court comprised two Supreme Court justices and one district judge. The country was divided into an Eastern, a Middle, and a Southern Circuit. Two justices were assigned to each circuit and traveled to the various courts located within that circuit. At the top of the national structure was the Supreme Court, consisting of a chief justice and five associate justices.

Currently there is a division of responsibilities between the national court system and the state court systems. Most cases that begin in a state court system are resolved in that system. The only way a case can move from a state court system to the national system is by an appeal from the state's highest court to the U.S. Supreme Court. Appeals may not move in the opposite direction. A case that begins in the national court system will be resolved in that system. For the most part, state and national courts have separate jurisdiction. A few cases, such as diversity suits (civil cases that involve parties from different states) brought for amounts greater than $75,000 may be initiated in either system. Once the case is initiated, however, it must stay in that system, except for a possible appeal from the state system to the Supreme Court. The figure "The U.S. Court System" illustrates the American dual court structure.

dual court system The system under which U.S. citizens are subject to the jurisdiction of both national and state courts.

District Courts

Today, the national court system includes ninety-four U.S. district courts. Each state contains at least one district court, and no district court crosses state lines. U.S. district courts are trial courts; they represent the entryway to the national court system. District courts typically deal with cases involving the violation of federal labor, civil rights, Social Security, truth-in-lending, federal crimes, and anti-trust laws. A single judge presides over

The U.S. Court System

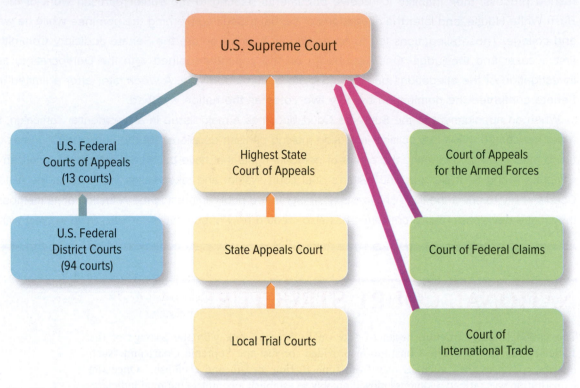

The U.S. Supreme Court sits atop the country's judicial system, which includes both federal and state courts.

the trial, which may or may not have a jury. District courts resolve disputes following the precedents of the U.S. Supreme Court and the appropriate court of appeals in their geographic area; they make few policy innovations themselves.

Federal Judicial Circuits

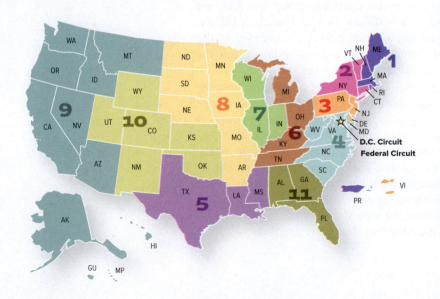

The U.S. judicial system is divided into eleven circuits located around the country, as well as the D.C. Circuit Court and the Federal Circuit, both of which are located in Washington D.C.

Source: Lawrence Baum, *American Courts: Process and Policy* (Boston: Houghton Mifflin Company, 1998), 38.

United States Courts of Appeals

The United States Courts of Appeals are strictly appellate courts. They only examine legal questions, specifically how did lower courts in the federal system apply the law in a particular case. In 1891, Congress passed the Court of Appeals Act creating separate appeals judges serving on nine appellate courts. Today, there are thirteen U.S. courts of appeals; eleven are located in numbered circuits throughout the United States and two—the D.C. Court of Appeals and the Court of Appeals for the Federal Circuit—are in Washington, D.C. (see "Federal Judicial Circuits"). Losing parties in federal trial courts have an automatic right to appeal to these intermediate appellate courts. In resolving cases, appeals courts typically use rotating three-judge panels. The winning litigant in the original case must secure at least two votes in order to prevail; otherwise, the appeals court overturns the original decision. For particularly difficult or important cases, all the judges in a circuit may sit together to hear a case or rehear a case already decided by a three-judge panel. These *en banc* hearings are relatively rare and occur less than a hundred times in an average year. The U.S. Courts of Appeals are unlike the courts featured in the movies and television shows. They have no juries, no witnesses giving testimony, and no more than a single judge. Their concern is to resolve legal questions only.

United States Supreme Court

In many ways, the Supreme Court is the most visible and powerful court in the world. Because of its importance, we will later describe in detail the Court's decision-making process and its role in the American political system.

Specialized Courts

Whereas the district courts, the U.S. Courts of Appeals, and the Supreme Court are considered constitutional courts with broad jurisdiction and permanent judges with life terms, there are additional national courts known as specialized courts. They are created by Congress to help administer specific federal statutes. Specialized national courts such as the Court of Appeals for the Armed Forces, the Court of Federal Claims, and the Court of International Trade hear a limited range of cases, their judges serve varying terms, and some have no permanent judges, borrowing justices from other courts.

Two courts with borrowed judges that have gained attention recently are the Foreign Intelligence Surveillance Court and the Foreign Intelligence Surveillance Court of Review. The former is a secret court formed in 1978 to hear government requests for warrants to conduct surveillance on suspected spies. The borrowed judge hears the request in a secret proceeding conducted in an office in the Justice Department building. In the proceeding, counsel represents the government, but not the person for whom the wiretap is intended. If the district judge denies the application for the warrant, the government may appeal to the Foreign Intelligence Surveillance Court of Review, which consists of three judges borrowed from the courts of appeals. However, this court seldom meets because the government has almost never failed to obtain a warrant. After the terrorist attacks on September 11, 2001, Congress expanded the powers of these courts to grant warrants to obtain evidence that can be used in criminal trials.

In summary, specialized courts have more narrow jurisdiction than the federal district courts, the courts of appeal, and the Supreme Court, and their judges do not have life terms.

NATURE OF THE JUDICIAL PROCESS

The American judicial process is based on a number of principles, many of which were inherited from English law. These principles establish the ground rules for our current system of justice and outline the role of judges, the various types of law, and the types of cases different courts may hear.

Common Law

American colonists brought with them a system of law that had developed in England over several centuries. It consisted of a national judge-made law that was common to the entire country. In time, courts published annual *Yearbooks* that summarized portions of the most important decisions. Under the common law system, judicial decisions in cases served the dual function of settling controversies and establishing **precedents**—previous decisions that have a bearing on current legal cases.[4] In most cases, precedent is followed, although judges do have some discretion over whether to follow a precedent.

precedent A former case that was supported by a majority on an appellate court and provides guidance for the determination of a present case.

The common law tradition not only enhanced the role of judges but also allowed them to use the law to prevent abuse from other political leaders. When a conflict between an act of Parliament and the common law developed in 1610, an English court held that a judge could overturn the act if he determined it violated the basic principles of common law.[5] The common law tradition provided the basis for judicial review in the United States.

Judicial Review

The principle of **judicial review** is not written anywhere in the Constitution. It was first discussed and justified by the Supreme Court's fourth chief justice, John Marshall, in the 1803 case of *Marbury v. Madison.* In explaining the Court's reasoning in the case, Marshall formally enshrined the principle that the Supreme Court has the power to declare acts of Congress unconstitutional. The case arose out of events that transpired in 1801. Near the end of his term as president in 1801, John Adams made a number of last-minute appointments. Among them was William Marbury, whom Adams named justice of the peace for the District of Columbia. Adams's secretary of state did not have time, however, to deliver the written commissions to Marbury and many of the other appointees before Adams's term expired. When Thomas Jefferson assumed the presidency in 1801, he ordered the new secretary of state, James Madison, to void Marbury's commission and that of many of the other late-term appointees whose commissions were undelivered. Marbury sued Madison, arguing that the Judiciary Act of 1789 gave the Supreme Court power to force the president to honor the appointment.

In the unanimous opinion, Chief Justice John Marshall concluded that although the Jefferson administration should have given Marbury his judicial position, the Supreme Court could not help Marbury. He concluded that the portion of the Judiciary Act under which Marbury sued for his commission was at odds with the Constitution. Since the Court could not honor a law that was contrary to the Constitution, it had no power to force Jefferson to honor the appointment. Marshall ruled that the Court had a duty to declare laws null and void if they conflicted with the Constitution, establishing the precedent of Court oversight on congressional statutes. As a result, Marshall turned a partisan dispute into an opportunity to dramatically increase the power of the Supreme Court by allowing it to declare laws passed by Congress and signed by the president to be null and void.

The Supreme Court has used its vast power of judicial review to void a very small fraction of all federal laws (see "Significant Supreme Court Cases"). Since 1803, it has struck down less than two hundred federal statutes. In recent years, this has included the Defense of Marriage Act and sections of the Campaign Reform Act. At the same time, the Court has struck down seven times more state and local laws.

Civil and Criminal Law

The two basic types of law under the American judicial system are civil law and criminal law. Civil law involves disputes between private parties over such matters as contracts, personal injuries, family law, and the buying and selling of property. The parties may be individuals, business corporations, or governments acting in a private capacity. Criminal law involves the prosecution of individuals who commit acts that are prohibited by the government.

The party who initiates a civil case is the *plaintiff.* The person against whom the lawsuit is brought is the *defendant.* Some types of civil

©Joshua Gates Weisburg-Pool/Getty Images

The American judicial process is based on the adversary process, in which lawyers for all parties present evidence in a trial setting.

Significant Supreme Court Cases

Case	Significance
Marbury v. Madison (1803)	Established the principle of judicial review.
McCulloch v. Maryland (1819)	Enlarged the powers of the national government by recognizing its implied constitutional powers.
Gibbons v. Ogden (1824)	Provided a broad interpretation of the federal commerce power.
Schenck v. United States (1919)	Created the clear and present danger test for the free speech cases.
Palko v. Connecticut (1937)	Opened the door for the nationalization of the Bill of Rights.
Brown v. Board of Education (1954)	Ended the separate but equal doctrine for race relations by declaring legally segregated schools unconstitutional.
Baker v. Carr (1962)	Allowed courts to hear cases on legislative apportionment, leading ultimately to the one-person, one-vote rule.
Gideon v. Wainwright (1963)	Recognized the right of poor criminal defendants to have counsel.
Miranda v. Arizona (1966)	Provided criminal suspects with a series of police warnings regarding their constitutional rights.
Roe v. Wade (1973)	Ruled that women's constitutional right to privacy allows abortions.
Bush v. Gore (2000)	Determined the outcome of 2000 presidential election.
NFIB v. Sebelius (2012)	Established the constitutionality of the Affordable Care Act.

Each of the Supreme Court cases shown here had a major impact on the political and legal systems of the United States.

law use the terms *petitioner* and *respondent* instead. Some civil cases may have multiple plaintiffs, multiple defendants, or both. In some situations, plaintiffs may bring a case known as a **class action suit**, in which one or more persons sue on behalf of a larger set of people who share the same situation. The Supreme Court writes the rules that determine how easy or how difficult it is to qualify for a class action suit. The party that initiates criminal cases is the government. The government is the plaintiff in criminal cases, because the government considers crime to be a violation of the interests of society as a whole, not just those of an individual or a group.

Judicial Requirements

The judicial requirements of **jurisdiction** and **justiciability** limit the types of cases that a particular court can hear. Jurisdiction is the power of the court to hear and decide cases. The Constitution grants the U.S. Supreme Court **original jurisdiction** in cases involving ambassadors or states suing other states. The Court has **appellate jurisdiction** in cases involving federal law, cases involving citizens from one state suing citizens from another state (diversity suits), or cases in which the federal government is a litigant.

Justiciability is a less precise term than *jurisdiction*. Chief Justice Earl Warren once referred to "justiciability" as one of "the most amorphous [concepts] in the entire domain of public law."[6] Basically, it means that a court can exclude certain cases from judicial consideration because of the identity of the party bringing the lawsuit or the subject of the lawsuit. For a lawsuit to meet the standard of justiciability, the party bringing the case must have **standing**. That is, the defendant's actions must either harm the plaintiff or threaten the plaintiff with harm. In other words, a litigant must demonstrate a personal stake in the outcome of the case. The Court can make litigation more available to citizens by relaxing the standards of standing. The Supreme Court

class action suit A lawsuit in which one or more persons sue on behalf of a larger set of people claiming the same injury.

jurisdiction The power of a court to hear and decide cases.

justiciability The doctrine that excludes certain cases from judicial consideration because of the party bringing the lawsuit or the nature of the subject matter.

original jurisdiction The power of a court to hear and decide a case first.

appellate jurisdiction The power of a court to receive cases from trial courts for the purpose of reviewing whether the legal procedures were followed properly.

standing Proof that a party has suffered harm or been threatened with harm by the circumstances surrounding a lawsuit.

Access to the U.S Supreme Court

Jurisdiction	The power of the U.S. Supreme Court to hear the particular types of cases.
Federal questions	A lawsuit that involves a federal statute, treaty, or the U.S. Constitution.
Federal party	A lawsuit in which the federal government is either the plaintiff or the defendant.
Diversity of citizenship	A civil lawsuit that involves parties from different states in which the dollar amount exceeds $75,000.

Justiciability	The exclusion of certain lawsuits from consideration because of the party bringing the case or the subject of the lawsuit.
Standing	The party bringing the lawsuit must have suffered real harm.
Mootness	The controversy is no longer alive by the time it reaches the Court.
Ripeness	The case is ready to be litigated because all other avenues of resolution have been exhausted.
Political question	The Court will not resolve cases more properly resolved by Congress or the president.

Class action suits	The ability of a litigant to bring a lawsuit on behalf of a larger set of people who share the same situation.

Amicus curiae briefs	Interest groups can submit their views to the Court even though they are not parties to the lawsuit.

A case may reach the Supreme Court only if it meets certain specifications, but that does not guarantee the case will be heard.

Julia Roberts's movie role as Erin Brockovich, a legal clerk and environmental activist, demonstrated how courts encourage civic engagement through litigation by allowing class action suits.

has ruled, for instance, that federal taxpayers have standing to challenge the constitutionality of federal programs if they can show that a specific expenditure of tax monies violates the Constitution.[7]

The federal courts also will not hear cases that involve **political questions**. The Supreme Court has acknowledged that other branches of the federal government are better equipped to address this class of constitutional issues. The concept, however, is flexible; at one time, the Court said the issue of political reapportionment was a political question,[8] but it later reversed itself in *Baker v. Carr* (1962). The principles that permit access to the Supreme Court are described in the table "Access to the U.S. Supreme Court."

Real Cases and Controversies

When trial judges confront legal questions in the context of a case, they or a jury must first determine the facts of the case, which are not always self-evident. The judicial process in the United States uses the adversary system, in which two opposing parties both present their own interpretation of the facts to ascertain the truth. An impartial third party, a judge or jury, has the responsibility of choosing between the two alternative versions of the facts. When Supreme Court justices receive a case, lower courts have already determined the facts. The job of the Supreme Court justices is to match the facts with the relevant law. When determining the law, the Court may interpret the meaning of a constitutional provision or a statutory provision. Either process allows the justices more discretion than might be imagined, because the meaning of these provisions is often subject to a variety of interpretations.

America is a **litigious** society that increasingly looks to the courts to resolve its disputes.[9] Americans file more lawsuits per capita than the citizens of Japan, Italy, Spain, Germany, and Sweden but about the same number as counterparts in England and Denmark.[10] As more cases are filed in the courts, the Supreme Court has more opportunity to choose which cases to hear on appeal. Congress also has made the courts more accessible to Americans with the passage of legislation that makes it easier to pay for litigation. The 1964 Civil Rights Act allows private citizens who file discrimination claims to collect their attorney's fees from the defendant if they win. Other legislation makes it easier for victims of gender bias and consumer fraud to press their claims in court. Ultimately, however, lower court decisions may be subject to Supreme Court review, and they must clear this hurdle to remain in force.

CHANGING NATURE OF THE SUPREME COURT

political questions Issues determined by the Supreme Court to be better resolved by Congress or the president.

litigious Marked by a tendency to file lawsuits.

The United States had no national judiciary under the Articles of Confederation.[11] It was not until the nation adopted the Constitution in 1787 that the Supreme Court came into existence as an independent and permanent court.[12] At the time, it was the object of much popular suspicion from citizens who feared the power of a national court. Alexander Hamilton was quick to assure readers, in *The Federalist* No. 78, that the new Supreme Court would be the "least dangerous branch" of the new national government. Without the power of the purse to appropriate money, or the power of the sword to enforce the law, the Court would prove no threat to the other branches of government, Hamilton reasoned.[13]

The Early Court

The Supreme Court first met on Tuesday, February 2, 1790, in the Royal Exchange Building located in what is today New York City's Wall Street district. Things began slowly for the justices, elegantly clad in the black and scarlet robes of English tradition: They had no cases to hear that first year.[14] Due to its perceived weakness in the new national government and its small workload, the early Court lacked status. Many men turned down presidential nominations to the Court, and others, including inaugural Chief Justice John Jay, soon left for positions they thought carried more respect.

Marbury v. Madison marked a watershed in the history of the Supreme Court. By establishing the principle of judicial review, the Marshall Court placed the Court squarely in the mainstream of American government and made it a force to reckon with. The Marshall Court used its new power to uphold policies of Congress that enhanced the role of the national government. Such nationalist constitutional rulings created a congenial relationship between the Court, Congress, and the presidency because all were supportive of a greater role for the national government.

John Marshall's successor, Roger Taney, led the Court in a new policy direction of limiting the power of the national government. Under Taney, the Court tilted much more dramatically toward protecting state power from incursion by the federal government. The Taney Court often found itself at odds with the other branches of the federal government. When the Taney Court decided to hear the *Dred Scott* case (discussed in Chapter 5), it caused nearly irreparable damage to the institution. By declaring the Missouri Compromise unconstitutional, the Court provided slave owners with a major political victory and incurred the wrath of abolitionists and the Republican Party. When Republican president Abraham Lincoln took office in 1861, his first inaugural address criticized the Supreme Court in some of the most scathing language ever uttered by a president about another branch of government. Congressional Republicans followed these remarks by attempting to weaken the Court through manipulating the number of justices for political advantage.[15] They also removed some of the Court's appellate

---

citizenship Quiz

Can you pass the U.S. Citizenship Test? See how well you know the content in this chapter covered on the citizenship test required of foreign-born candidates for naturalization.

1. What does the judicial branch do?
2. What is the highest court in the United States?
3. How many justices are on the Supreme Court?
4. Who is the chief justice of the United States?

(1) Reviews laws; explains laws; resolves disputes; decides if a law goes against the Constitution (2) The Supreme Court (3) Nine (4) John Roberts

Source: United States Citizenship and Immigration Services.

jurisdiction.[16] Whereas Marshall strengthened the Court by establishing the power of judicial review and using it to bolster the national government, Taney decided in favor of state governments and ultimately weakened the Court in the *Dred Scott* case.

The Court, Business, and Social Welfare

The Court would face peril again some eighty years later when the laissez-faire economic philosophy of most of its members conflicted with Franklin D. Roosevelt's activist program to combat the Great Depression. When the Court declared eight of the ten legislative proposals of the New Deal unconstitutional in 1935 and 1936, the president introduced his "court-packing" plan. He proposed that for every Supreme Court justice who had reached the age of seventy and chose not to retire, the president could nominate an additional judge to help with the workload. The real purpose of the proposal had nothing to do with helping elderly justices. The Court was typically voting 6 to 3 to invalidate New Deal programs. Five of the six justices voting against the president were at least seventy years of age. If Roosevelt were able to appoint new justices for all those who did not retire, he could turn a 6 to 3 deficit into a 9 to 6 victory. Believing the bill violated the judicial independence of the Supreme Court, however, Congress narrowly defeated its passage. Two members of the Supreme Court understood the politics of the moment and the long-term implications for the Court as an institution. Chief Justice Charles Evans Hughes and Justice Owen Roberts changed their positions and began consistently to uphold New Deal attempts to regulate the economy. Statutes were now surviving on 5 to 4 votes. The two justices understood how close their beloved institution had come to losing its independence.

©TopFoto/The Image Works

President Dwight D. Eisenhower called the nomination of liberal Chief Justice Earl Warren, pictured here, one of his two biggest mistakes as president. The other one, he said, was Justice William Brennan.

The Court and Personal Rights

Since its retreat during the New Deal, the Court has fundamentally changed its emphasis regarding the nature of the cases it hears. Today, the Court's emphasis in the area of constitutional law is civil liberties and civil rights. This modern era of support for rights is most identified with the leadership of Earl Warren, who became chief justice in 1953. The Court's direction, however, did not change dramatically with respect to civil liberties under the leadership of Warren Burger, who became chief justice in 1969, or William Rehnquist, who was chief justice from 1986 to 2005. The Roberts Court, under the leadership of Chief Justice John Roberts, who began his tenure in 2005, has continued the trend of supporting civil liberties, especially free speech, and civil rights generally, but not necessarily affirmative action or voting rights protections.

SUPREME COURT DECISION MAKING

The modern Supreme Court bears little resemblance to the institution that first convened in 1790. Today, the Court meets on a regular basis and turns away work. Its annual term begins on the first Monday in October and continues until late June or early July of the following year. Throughout the term, the schedule alternates between two weeks of sittings and two weeks of recess. During the *sittings,* the justices hear case arguments and announce decisions. During the *recess,* they have time to think, research, and write opinions.

The Supreme Court now functions as nine small and independent law firms, each with a justice as the senior partner aided by four law clerks.[17] The justices spend little time interacting with each other, and such interactions are almost impersonal. As one law clerk observed, "Justices don't think that much about what other justices are doing. They spend little time with them and rarely see each other. They often come in and sit by themselves day after day without really talking to any of the other justices."[18] Most of the communication among them takes the form of a written Memorandum to the Conference (MTTC), and much of it is done by the law clerks. Clerks also provide valuable service to the justices they serve by reviewing petitions from potential appellants and writing the legal opinions explaining the outcomes of cases. All Supreme Court clerks come from top law schools, and many of them clerk in a lower federal court for a year or two before coming to the Supreme Court. Four of the current members of the Court—Chief Justice John Roberts and Associate Justices Stephen Breyer, Elena Kagan, and Neil Gorsuch—were once Supreme Court clerks.

In this section, we will examine how the Supreme Court chooses which cases it will hear, how it decides these cases, and how it justifies its decisions. Once the Court makes and justifies its decisions, others must implement them. We will explore how the Court can help in this process. Finally, we will analyze what factors best explain why Supreme Court justices behave as they do.

Agenda Decisions

The Supreme Court is able to determine its own agenda because it has almost complete discretion in deciding what cases to review. Since 1988, nearly all cases that have made it to the nation's highest court arrived there on a petition for a **writ of certiorari**. *Certiorari* is a legal term that means literally "to be informed." If the Court grants such a writ, the lower court will send a record of the case to the Court for purposes of review. All members of the Court except Justice Samuel Alito participate in the "cert pool." Their eight offices take a portion of the petitions at random, summarize them, and share them with the other participating chambers. Clerks perform the initial substantive review of these petitions, "marking up" the memo based on the interests and values of the individual justices and concluding with a recommendation to grant or deny. Membership in the cert pool is voluntary, and currently Justice Alito prefers to have his own clerks review all the petitions. In recent decades, the Court has granted certiorari and given full consideration to approximately 1 percent of the cases filed with the judicial body for consideration.

writ of certiorari An order issued by a superior court to one of inferior jurisdiction demanding the record of a particular case.

Rule of Four The requirement that a minimum of four justices must vote to review a lower court case by issuing a writ of certiorari.

The chief justice plays a special role in the agenda-setting process. Several times during the term, the chief justice prepares a "discuss list" consisting of the forty to fifty cases he or she believes the Court should consider at the next meeting of the justices. On Friday afternoons during the sittings, the justices gather in conference to review the discuss list. At these private meetings, the justices decide whether to grant or deny certiorari. According to the **Rule of Four**, if at least four of the justices vote to grant certiorari, the Court will hear the case and notify the parties. Since the late 1980s, the Court has been accepting less than half the number of cases for a full hearing than it used to accept, less than one hundred per term.[19]

Most petitions sent to the Court are denied certiorari for a variety of reasons. One scholar asserts that the Court will deny certiorari when (1) the case is frivolous; (2) the case is too fact-bound; (3) insufficient evidence is presented in the briefs; (4) the case involves an issue the justices want to avoid; (5) the legal issue has not percolated enough in the lower courts; (6) the briefs contain disputed facts; (7) a better case is in the pipeline; or (8) the case will fragment the Court.[20]

The question still remains as to which cases the justices will vote to hear. The best insight into which cases the Court is more likely to hear is provided by an examination of Rule 10. The Court itself wrote Rule 10 to govern the process. It specifies that the Court will accept cases that have been decided differently by the various federal circuits, cases that conflict with Supreme Court precedents, and state cases that conflict with federal decisions. Based on interviews with justices and law clerks, one author concluded that the justices follow Rule 10, stating that conflict in the federal circuits is "without a doubt, one of the

This court artist rendering depicts one of the first Supreme Court cases including Justice Sonia Sotomayor, the first Hispanic American woman to serve on the Supreme Court, on the bench. The artist rendering is necessary because the Court does not allow video or photographs during sessions.

most important things to all the justices. All of them are disposed to resolve conflicts when they exist and want to know if a particular case poses a conflict."[21]

The Court, however, does not accept all such cases with conflicts, because there are too many of them.[22] The determination of what cases with conflicts the Court ends up hearing turns on such factors as the subject matter of the case, the number of groups interested in the case's outcome as measured by the number of *amicus curiae,* or "friend of the court," briefs submitted to the Court, and whether the U.S. government as represented by the Office of Solicitor General wants the Court to hear a particular case. First, the subject of the case often determines whether it gets a hearing. During the Vinson and Warren Court eras (1946–1969), the Court was more likely to accept cases dealing with labor relations, civil rights and civil liberties, and federalism.[23] Second, as we saw in Chapter 4, the Court is also more likely to hear a case for which supporters have submitted *amicus curiae* briefs. Finally, the solicitor general, who is responsible for handling most Supreme Court appeals on behalf of the federal government, appears as a party or a friend of the court in more than 50 percent of the cases the Court hears each term.[24] The influence of the solicitor general's office is so great that it has a suite of offices within the Supreme Court building, and its occupant is referred to as the "tenth justice."[25] Because of this special relationship, the Court accepts some 70 to 80 percent of cases the solicitor general's office brings before it, compared to less than 5 percent for all other petitioners.[26]

In summary, Supreme Court decisions to hear cases are based on the characteristics of the case itself, such as whether the issue has been heard enough by the lower courts, whether the issue has created disagreement among the courts of appeals, and whether lower court and state court opinions conflict with previous Supreme Court opinions. Further, outside factors such as attention shown by interest groups and the solicitor general can affect the Court's agenda decision.

Voting Decisions

Only after the Court's law clerks have reviewed hundreds of petitions and four justices have voted to grant certiorari does the Supreme Court move on to the public oral argument stage. Attorneys arguing cases before the Court usually have thirty minutes to present their legal arguments, a rule that is strictly enforced. When the Court voted in 2011 to rule on the constitutionality of President Obama's health-care law, however, they set aside three days and a total of six hours for the oral arguments. A flashing white light signals when the attorney has but five minutes remaining; when the light turns red, time has elapsed. Although attorneys often prepare for weeks, or even months, for their appearance before the Supreme Court, there is no guarantee that they will be able to present all of their arguments. The members of the Court may interrupt at any time with probing questions that can befuddle a lawyer who is not on top of his or her game. An attorney cannot possibly anticipate all the questions the justices may ask, but the experienced ones are able to use these questions to emphasize the points they want to make. Chief Justice Roberts has become quite vocal and hard-edged during oral arguments and in a 2009 session ridiculed a lawyer's argument saying, "That's like the old elephant whistle. You know, I have this whistle to keep away the elephants. Well there are no elephants, so it must work."[27] Justices Breyer and Sotomayor are usually the most active interrogators, whereas Justice Clarence Thomas almost never asks a question.

Late on Wednesday afternoons after hearing oral arguments, and all day on Fridays when the Court is sitting, the justices meet in conference to decide the cases just argued. Since 1836, the justices have begun the conference session with a round of handshaking. It serves as a subtle reminder that they remain colleagues even though they may soon be engaged in a heated exchange of views. The associate justice with the least seniority acts as both official stenographer and doorkeeper.

By tradition, the chief justice presides over the conference and has the task of allowing adequate discussion, while at the same time moving the Court efficiently through its docket of cases. The chief justice speaks first, followed by the eight associate justices in order of seniority. At one time, justices tried to change the minds of others with their comments, but the purpose of the conference session is now just to discover consensus.[28] The late Justice Scalia viewed it as "an exercise in stating your views while the rest of us take notes."[29] The individual justices vote at the same time they discuss the case. At this point, however, the individual votes are still tentative and subject to change. The Court will not deliver a final vote until the completion of the next stage of the process.

The Supreme Court decided the outcome of the Bush-Gore 2000 presidential election when it did not allow a recount of the contested Florida ballots.

©Rob Crandall/The Image Works

Variety of Court Opinions

Majority Opinion	Written by one member of the Court on behalf of at least five members. The only opinion that can serve as a precedent.
Plurality Opinion	Written on behalf of the largest block of the members but fewer than five members.
Concurring Opinion(s)	Written by one or more members who agree with the decision but offers a different rationale.
Dissenting Opinion(s)	Written by one or more members who disagree with decisions and offer their rationale.
Per Curiam Opinion	Written usually by all members of the Court in cases where there is a great deal of consensus. These are unsigned opinions.

In any case it hears, the Supreme Court can hand down a variety of different opinions to explain its decision.

decision The indication of which litigant the court supports and by how large a margin.

opinions Written arguments explaining the reasons behind a decision.

majority opinion An opinion written by a justice who represents a majority of the Court.

concurring opinion An opinion written by one or more of the justices who agree with the decision but for different reasons than those stated in the majority opinion.

plurality opinion An opinion written on behalf of the largest bloc of the justices, representing less than a majority, who agree on the reasons supporting the Court's decision.

dissenting opinion An opinion written by one or more justices who disagree with a decision.

per curiam opinion An unsigned opinion of the Supreme Court that usually signals a high degree of consensus.

Explaining Decisions

After the members of the Court cast their initial votes concerning a case **decision**, their next task is to explain their votes by writing **opinions**. Whereas the decision indicates which litigant the Court supports and by how large a margin, the opinion explains the reasons behind the decision. Only one justice writes the opinion for the Court, but other justices have the option of writing additional opinions. The chief justice decides who will write the opinion if he or she is in the majority on the initial vote in a case. If not, the most senior associate justice in the majority assigns the task.

When John Marshall was chief justice of the Supreme Court, the Court's decision was most often explained in just one opinion. Today, the members of the Court are more likely to be fragmented in their reasoning as well as in their votes. As a result, four different types of opinions may accompany any particular decision. A **majority opinion** is written by one member of the Court on behalf of at least five members of the Court; the reasoning in the opinion can serve as a precedent for future cases. A **concurring opinion** is one written by a justice who agrees with the decision, but offers a different rationale for the Court's finding. A **plurality opinion** is one that is written on behalf of the largest bloc of the justices, but less than a majority, who agree on the reasons supporting the Court's decision. A plurality opinion does not serve as a precedent for future cases. Finally, a **dissenting opinion** is one that is written by one or more justices who disagree with the case decision and the opinion of the majority or plurality of the Court. Occasionally, the Court will submit a **per curiam opinion** to explain its reasoning in a case. These are unsigned opinions that represent the view of the Court in a case where there is a great deal of consensus or in a case where time is a critical factor. The Court issued a per curiam opinion in the case of *Bush v. Gore* (2000). Justices may dissent from such opinions but rarely do so. Per curiam opinons usually represent a high degree of consensus among the judges and, as a result, are short in length.

The combination of opinions that finally accompanies the decision in a particular case is the result of negotiations that begin after one of the jurists in the majority receives the assignment to write the Court's opinion. According to political scientist David O'Brien, "Writing opinions is the justice's most difficult and time-consuming task."[30] Since the original conference vote is not final, a dissenting opinion occasionally becomes the majority opinion, and vice versa. In 1971, for instance, the Court voted 5 to 3 in conference to deny famous boxer Muhammad Ali's conscientious objector claim for refusing induction into the Army. After two months of negotiation, however, the Court ruled for Ali.[31] Ultimately, the bargaining ends, the final votes are recorded in a conference meeting, and the opinions are printed and made public.

Implementing Decisions

Once the Supreme Court has reached its final decision in a case, the decision has to be implemented. The first level of implementation of a Supreme Court decision consists of how judicial decisions are enforced on the parties to the lawsuit. With respect to the litigants, if the Supreme Court affirms a lower court decision, the lower court then enforces its original decision. If the Supreme Court reverses the lower court ruling, the original decision is void. Often, the Supreme Court remands a case—sends it back to the court that originally heard it—with instructions to retry it under proceedings consistent with the Court's opinion. After the Supreme Court ruling in *Miranda v. Arizona* (see Chapter 4), the trial court retried Miranda, but the prosecution was not allowed to use his confession because the Supreme Court had ruled that Miranda's confession was unconstitutional since he had not been informed of his right to remain silent. Even so, the lower court once again found the defendant guilty.

The second level of implementing Supreme Court decisions involves turning them into general public policy. It is a more difficult process than implementing a decision just on the parties to the lawsuit. The Court alone cannot enforce its decisions; it must depend on other public officials who may not always desire to cooperate to do so. When upset with a Supreme Court ruling, President Andrew Jackson is reported to have said, "John Marshall has made his decision; now let him enforce it." In other words, implementation is not an automatic process.

Two political scientists have written that the implementation of a Supreme Court decision depends on several elements.[32] First, there is the *interpreting population,* made up largely of judges and lawyers, who must correctly understand and reflect the intent of the decision in subsequent decisions. Lower judges usually follow the rulings of the Supreme Court, but sometimes they circumvent rulings to pursue their own policy preferences.[33] The federal district court judges in the South, for example, circumvented the *Brown v. Board of Education* decision (see Chapter 5) for years.[34] The second element in the process is the *implementing population,* such as school administrators who implement prayer in school decisions or police departments

President Lyndon B. Johnson nominated the first African American justice, Thurgood Marshall, to the U.S. Supreme Court.

©AP Photo

that implement search and seizure decisions. Finally, a *consumer population* must be aware of these new rights if they are to exercise them. Suspects who are about to be interrogated are the consumers of the *Miranda* decision, and women who want abortions are the consumers of the *Roe v. Wade* decision. The Supreme Court must hope that other actors will respect its moral authority and legal expertise enough to implement its policies. The Court can help itself, however, by writing clear opinions.

In summary, implementing the Court's decisions is more complicated when a decision extends beyond the parties in the lawsuit to the general public. In that instance, the Court must depend on others, such as lower court judges and lawyers, to interpret their opinions; others, such as police departments and school administrators, to implement their decisions; and still others, like criminal suspects and students and their parents, to be aware of and understand the rights granted them in particular decisions.

Understanding Decisions

Scholars today look to a variety of nonlegal factors to understand Supreme Court decisions. Some of these factors are external to the individual justices and comprise the political environment, such as Congress, the president, and public opinion. Other factors, including ideology, perception of their role, and the ability to negotiate with colleagues on the bench, originate with the individual justices.

External Factors When making decisions, the Supreme Court is aware of the many checks the Constitution provides Congress over the behavior of the Court. If Congress is unhappy with a Supreme Court decision, it can propose a constitutional amendment to overturn the decision. The Eleventh, Fourteenth, Sixteenth, and Twenty-sixth Amendments were all passed in response to congressional unhappiness with a Court decision. Congress can also threaten to modify the Court's appellate jurisdiction. If Congress believes the Court has interpreted one of its laws or its legislative intent erroneously, Congress can rewrite the law. In 1993, for example, Congress enacted the Religious Freedom Restoration Act because members believed a Court decision was too restrictive of religious liberty.[35] The Rehnquist Court responded, however, by declaring the law unconstitutional.[36] At other times, the Court clearly responds to congressional wishes, such as when it began to declare New Deal legislation constitutional. Congress can also express its displeasure with Court decisions by withholding funds necessary for implementation of a decision and by careful Senate scrutiny of future Court nominees. In conclusion, Congress is able to exercise some checks over the Court by proposing constitutional amendments, modifying the Court's appellate jurisdiction, rewriting laws it believes the Court has misinterpreted, and withholding funding for the Court.

Presidents exercise control over the Supreme Court by filling vacancies on the Court with nominees who share their beliefs. This is why the question as to whether President Obama could or should select the replacement for Associate Justice Antonin Scalia was such a hot-button issue, as was the question of whether or not the Senate could legally refuse to entertain the president's nomination. In contrast, President Trump easily received compliance from a Republican-led Senate to get his nominee confirmed. The president also often plays a key role in implementing Supreme Court decisions that have broad policy ramifications. If President Eisenhower had not called out the troops to enforce school integration in Little Rock, Arkansas, the implementation of *Brown v. Board of Education* (1954) might have been hopelessly stalled. Presidents also appoint the solicitor general, who has an important relationship with the Court. The solicitor general and staff argue cases before the Court when the national government is a party as well as submit *amicus curiae* briefs to influence decisions. Occasionally, they are asked their procedural position on a case.

Since the American public does not directly elect Supreme Court justices, the justices do not have to worry about constantly analyzing public opinion polls or running for reelection. This does not mean, however, that public opinion has no effect on the Court's behavior. After all, the justices work and live among the rest of us, and social trends influence their attitudes as well. Since popularly elected officials must nominate and approve Supreme Court justices, the justices' views usually reflect those of the majority of Americans. Justices who have been on the Court for a long time may reflect political views that are no longer in vogue, but even they know that a decision at odds with public opinion will produce a backlash and even resistance to obeying the law. In all likelihood, the justices were well aware of Americans' changing public opinions on the issue of same-sex marriage when a majority of them held in *Obergefell v. Hodges* (2015) that such unions were constitutionally protected. There are even times when the Court clearly follows public opinion in making decisions. In its 2002 ruling that executing intellectually disabled criminals constitutes cruel and unusual punishment, the Court noted "powerful evidence that today our society views mentally retarded offenders as categorically less culpable than the average criminal."[37]

Internal Factors Supreme Court justices do not magically rid themselves of all their attitudes and political biases so that they can function as neutral judges. In fact, the president chooses nominees—and the Senate confirms them—largely on doctrinal qualifications. Therefore, it is reasonable to assume that justices often follow their own policy preferences when making legal decisions. Justices with a liberal ideology typically support civil liberties and civil rights claims, back the government in economic regulation cases, and vote for national regulation in federalism cases. Conservatives, of course, cast votes in the opposite direction. Knowledge of the justices' ideology can lead to accurate predictions of their voting patterns. For instance, conservative justices Samuel Alito and Antonin Scalia voted together much of the time, in opposition to liberal justices Ruth Bader Ginsburg and Stephen Breyer. Not all cases, however, can be analyzed neatly on a liberal versus conservative basis. For example, in spite of his reputation as a conservative, Chief Justice Roberts sided with the liberal justices in casting his vote to uphold the constitutionality of most of the Affordable Care Act, including the hotly contested individual mandate provision.

Other studies emphasize that a single justice can accomplish little because a majority of justices must reach the same conclusion to render a decision, and a majority must agree on a single opinion in order to set a precedent. Therefore, a single justice must work strategically in order to advance his or her goals.[38] Such strategic behavior manifests itself in the number of times justices change their votes and revise their opinions. Studies have shown that between the initial vote in conference and the official announcement of the decision, at least one vote switch occurs more than 50 percent of the time.[39] Also, in almost every case, some justice will revise an opinion to please his or her colleagues.[40] It is not unusual for a justice to revise an opinion ten times in order to hold the original majority. Not all justices work strategically, however. One observer believes that, among the current Court, Justice Kagan bases her opinions on attempts to influence her colleagues whereas Justice Sotomayor is more of a sole operator.[41]

Individual justices also hold their own views as to the proper role of a good judge and of the Court. Some justices subscribe to a philosophy of **judicial activism**, arguing that the Court should make public policy and vigorously review the policies of the other branches. Others, convinced that the Court should not become involved in questioning the operations and policies of the elected branches unless absolutely necessary, believe in **judicial restraint**.

> **judicial activism** The belief that the Supreme Court should make policy and vigorously review the policies of other branches.
>
> **judicial restraint** The belief that the Supreme Court should not become involved in questioning the operations and policies of the elected branches unless absolutely necessary.

SUPREME COURT SELECTION

One hundred and thirteen individuals have served on the Supreme Court. Most have been wealthy, white males between the ages of 41 and 60 when they were named to the Court, with Protestant backgrounds. Although the Constitution is silent with regard to qualifications, all have been lawyers and many were federal or state judges or had their own legal practice just prior to nomination. Seven had served as attorney general, and several others had held other high executive offices such as secretary of state. Eight had served in Congress; three had been state governors. Their number has even included a former president, William Howard Taft. Let's now examine the process by which these men and (a few) women have risen to the most powerful court in the land.

Nomination

Until the late 1960s, presidents had personally known about 60 percent of the nominees to the Supreme Court. More recently, however, few nominees had any prior contract with the nominating president. Perhaps modern presidents have not wanted to be tagged with charges of "cronyism." The retirement or death of a sitting justice does give the president a remarkable opportunity to make a lasting impact on the direction of U.S. legal and political practices. The president fills openings for associate justices from a wide pool of candidates, as we will discuss shortly. When the chief justice position becomes vacant, the president may select the new chief justice from among the sitting associate justices. In most cases, however, presidents have chosen someone from outside the Court to fill the position. Only three of the seventeen chief justices came from among sitting associate justices (see "U.S. Supreme Court Chief Justices").

U.S. Supreme Court Chief Justices

Name	Party	Term
John Jay	Federalist	1789–1795
John Rutledge	Federalist	1795–1795
Oliver Ellsworth	Federalist	1796–1800
John Marshall	Federalist	1801–1835
Roger Taney	Democrat	1836–1864
Salmon Chase	Republican	1864–1873
Morrison Waite	Republican	1874–1888
Melville Fuller	Democrat	1888–1910
Edward White*	Democrat	1910–1921
William H. Taft	Republican	1921–1930
Charles Hughes	Republican	1930–1941
Harlan Stone*	Republican	1941–1946
Fred Vinson	Democrat	1946–1953
Earl Warren	Republican	1953–1969
Warren Burger	Republican	1969–1986
William Rehnquist*	Republican	1986–2005
John Roberts	Republican	2005–

*Appointed chief justice while serving as an associate justice.

Seventeen men have served as chief justice of the Supreme Court. With more women being appointed to the Court, perhaps there will be a woman on this list one day soon.

When a president chooses a sitting associate justice to be the new chief justice, an opening is created for a new associate justice.

Presidents play the major role in selecting Supreme Court nominees, although other individuals and groups also influence the selection process. Interest groups close to the administration may participate privately in the selection process, or at least receive consideration of their views. Conservative interest groups and columnists, for example, sank the nomination of Harriet Miers, whom President George W. Bush originally selected to replace Sandra Day O'Connor, claiming that Miers was not conservative enough. Their efforts were rewarded because she was also not considered to have a sufficient judicial background. The American Bar Association (ABA) plays a unique role in the nomination process by assigning nominees a rating of "well qualified," "qualified," or "not qualified." These ratings signal to the public the ABA's assessment of a nominee's legal qualifications. The Ronald Reagan administration did not work with the ABA in choosing its nominees, and George W. Bush announced early in his presidency that he would use the more conservative Federalist Society to investigate his nominees to the federal bench. Obama did not continue the practice of using the Federalist Society, but Trump has returned to it.

To further ensure that damaging information regarding a candidate does not surface and affect the credibility of the president who makes the nomination, the FBI has played an increasingly important role in the selection process. Candidates who pass an initial screening process fill out questionnaires that include information about their personal lives. FBI agents thoroughly examine the potential nominee's life to make sure there are no skeletons in the closet. The examinations, however, do not always turn up every potentially damaging fact about a nominee. The Reagan administration, for instance, withdrew the nomination of Douglas Ginsburg when the media verified that he had smoked marijuana as a youth and as a member of the Harvard University law faculty.

Nomination Criteria

Political scientists disagree about which criteria presidents use when choosing a Supreme Court nominee. Some argue that the relatively high caliber of appointments over time demonstrates that presidents rely primarily on merit and do not want to be embarrassed by choosing unqualified nominees.[42] Others stress that the politics inherent in the selection process outweighs any concern for merit.[43] Herbert Hoover's nomination of Benjamin Cardozo in 1932 shows that the truth lies somewhere between these extremes. Cardozo, a Democrat, was the chief judge of the New York Court of Appeals and author of the universally praised book *The Nature of the Judicial Process.* He was "a man widely regarded as one of America's most brilliant jurists," who enjoyed great support from the legal community and the U.S. Senate.[44] The Republican Hoover drew considerable praise when he crossed party lines to nominate Cardozo. Although it was a merit selection, it was also a political maneuver by the president. At the time, Hoover's administration was struggling to respond to the Great Depression, and he may have seen Cardozo's nomination as a way to restore some luster to his presidency.

There is a high degree of consensus among political scientists, however, on some basic selection criteria. First, the president wants a justice who is capable of doing the work on the Court and working with his or her colleagues. President Woodrow Wilson was chagrined by the fact that one of his nominees, James C. McReynolds, turned out to be one of the most obnoxious individuals ever to serve on the Court. Chief Justice Taft described McReynolds

©AP Photo

Republican President Herbert Hoover, shown here, was praised for his nomination of Democrat Benjamin Cardozo to the Supreme Court.

as "selfish to the last degree, . . . fuller of prejudice than any man I have ever known, . . . one who delights in making others uncomfortable. He has no sense of duty. He is a continual grouch."[45] Presidents also desire predictability, the assurance that nominees will share the president's views on public policy. In this way, presidents can leave their mark on national policy long after leaving the White House.

Because the Supreme Court consists of members who are not elected, it is important that the institution be representative of the people it serves. Scholars believe that citizens will accord a diverse Court greater legitimacy than if "it were dominated by a few rich, old, white Protestant males from the Northeast educated at the Ivy League schools and still effectively wearing the old school tie."[46] By increasing the representativeness of the Court, the president also seeks to win political support and dispense political rewards through the nomination process. Ironically, today there are no Protestants on the Court. It is important to remember that as presidents consider a variety of candidates' professional, doctrinal, and representational qualifications, they very much want a nominee who works well with others, casts a predictable ideological vote, and helps to balance the Court's composition to represent the various demographic groups in the country.

Professional Qualifications Presidents look to professional qualifications to determine whether candidates possess the characteristics necessary to perform the tasks of a Supreme Court justice. These qualifications include not only evidence of an eminent public or private career but also a reputation of high moral character that provides the basis for any valid professional qualifications. Recent Supreme Court appointments would indicate that presidents choose their nominees from some of the nation's most prominent law schools and that they view appellate judicial experience as a vital qualification for service. All but one (Justice Kagan) of the current justices are former federal appeals court judges. Nominees who fall short on professional qualifications may fail Senate confirmation. If they are approved and then serve poorly on the Court, they can be an embarrassment to the appointing president.

Doctrinal Qualifications Presidents seek nominees who share their views about policy. Since the common law tradition leaves the judge with a great deal of discretion to interpret policy, having sympathetic justices on the Court gives the president an advantage in making and implementing policy. As a result, recent presidents have attempted to increase the doctrinal predictability of candidates by nominating appellate judges. Appellate judges, particularly federal ones, hear cases similar to those that will reach the Supreme Court; therefore, they have established a record on those cases that the president can evaluate, and they have opinions that can be analyzed.

Presidents generally have an accurate sense of how a nominee will perform on the Court, but not all their predictions are correct. President Dwight D. Eisenhower was disappointed with liberal decisions by two of his appointees, Democrat William Brennan and Republican Earl Warren. When asked if he had made any mistakes as president, Eisenhower replied, "Yes, two, and they are both sitting on the Supreme Court."[47] More recently, Justices O'Connor, Kennedy, and Souter have not been as conservative as Presidents Ronald Reagan and George H. W. Bush may have hoped. Today the Court has a liberal bloc consisting of Justices Ginsburg, Breyer, Sotomayor, and Kagan and a conservative bloc of Justices Roberts, Gorsuch, Thomas, and Alito. Kennedy represents a "swing vote" who sometimes supports the conservative bloc and sometimes the liberal bloc.

Representational Qualifications Representational qualifications are attributes that link a nominee to significant portions of the American public—political party, age, religion, race, and gender. Presidents almost always choose justices from within their own political party. It provides them opportunities not only to alter the partisan balance on the Court but also to reward leading lawyers and politicians of their own party. Presidents have crossed partisan lines only thirteen times in selecting the 113 successful nominees to the Court.

Presidents typically choose nominees who are old enough to have gained some prominence but also young enough to serve an extended time on the bench. The last five nominees, Roberts, Alito, Sotomayor, Kagan, and Gorsuch were 50, 55, 55, 50, and 49, respectively. Most members of the Supreme Court have been Protestants, but a tradition

In 1981, Sandra Day O'Connor became the first woman to serve on the Supreme Court.

began in the late nineteenth century to have at least one "Catholic seat" on the Court. The tradition has held since that time, except for the period between 1949 and 1956.[48] Today, Justices Kennedy, Thomas, Roberts, Alito, and Sotomayor are Catholics.[49] In 1916, Justice Louis Brandeis became the first Jewish member of the Supreme Court. He was followed on the Court by other Jewish justices, including Cardozo, Felix Frankfurter, Arthur Goldberg, and Abe Fortas. Current Jewish members of the Court include Ruth Bader Ginsburg, Stephen Breyer, and Elena Kagan.

Until the presidency of Lyndon Johnson, all Supreme Court Justices had been white. In 1967, Johnson appointed the famous NAACP lawyer Thurgood Marshall to the bench. Johnson's nomination of Marshall was not only an acknowledgment that Marshall had been successful as an advocate in getting the Supreme Court to change civil rights policy (see Chapter 5) but also a political reward to the African American community that was becoming a solid supporter of the Democratic Party in national elections. When Marshall retired from the bench in 1991, President Bush filled the vacancy with another African American, albeit one with a far more conservative philosophy, Clarence Thomas. In 2009, Justice Sotomayor became the first Hispanic American ever to serve on the nation's highest court.

By the 1970s, interest groups were calling for female representation on the Supreme Court. The number of women graduating from law school and serving on federal and state courts was growing, producing a sufficient pool of qualified women from which to choose a Supreme Court nominee. Facing serious opposition among female voters, presidential candidate Ronald Reagan promised that if he was elected, his first appointment to the Supreme Court would be a woman. He fulfilled his campaign promise by selecting Sandra Day O'Connor. Bill Clinton appointee Ruth Bader Ginsburg became the second woman to serve on the bench of the nation's highest court, and now Sonia Sotomayor and Elena Kagan are the third and fourth.

Senate Confirmation

As we have discussed, the Senate exercises an advise and consent role with respect to presidential nominees. Although presidents do not have to ask the Senate for advice on Supreme Court nominees, these nominees must receive Senate confirmation by a majority vote. A sitting justice nominated to be the new chief justice must also undergo Senate confirmation to assume his or her new position.

Confirmation is not an automatic process. During the nineteenth century, more than 25 percent of Supreme Court nominees failed to receive Senate confirmation. Since that time, the number of unsuccessful nominations has declined. One political scientist attributes this decline to two factors.[50] First, presidents are now aware that the Senate exercises close scrutiny over the process, so they are more inclined to choose nominees who are likely to win confirmation. Second, senators today generally begin the confirmation process with a presumption that the nominee is qualified.

Several factors may weaken the presumption of confirmation, such as strong and widespread opposition to the nominee's views on legal issues. Confirmation is also less likely when the president's party is not in control of the Senate. Confirmation chances are slimmer for nominees chosen near the end of a president's term. In such a situation, senators from the opposition party may desire to keep the vacancy open until after the next election in case their candidate captures the White House. The confirmation process also tends to be more contentious if the Court is split along conservative and liberal lines and the newest member could tilt the ideological balance. As a result, presidents have a greater likelihood of success in the Senate if they are not near the end of their term, if their party controls the Senate, and if the nominee would not change the ideological balance on the Court. President Obama's selection of Judge Garland carried none of those advantages whereas Trump's nomination of Judge Gorsuch had all of them.

Except for the final vote on the president's nominee by the entire Senate, the process of Senate confirmation is done exclusively by the Senate Judiciary Committee, whose jurisdiction includes the consideration of federal judicial nominations. After the president announces a nomination to the Supreme Court, the Senate Judiciary Committee asks the nominee to complete a questionnaire that probes the candidate's work history, judicial philosophy, speeches, media interviews, articles and books, and judicial opinions if the candidate has served as an appellate judge. The committee also contacts potential witnesses to testify concerning the nominee's fitness to serve on the Supreme Court. At this point in the process, interest groups become mobilized for or against a candidacy. When President Reagan announced the nomination of Robert Bork, "more than twenty groups and dozens of individual experts . . . abandoned their families and summer vacations to prepare in-depth analyses and reports that addressed their specific individual and institutional concerns."[51] These groups ran television commercials against the Bork nomination. Spokespersons for eighty-six different interest groups testified before the Senate Judiciary Committee during the Bork confirmation hearings, helping to sink his confirmation.[52]

In 1939, Felix Frankfurter set a precedent by appearing in person before the committee and answering questions pertaining to his qualifications. All subsequent nominees have followed the tradition except one: Sherman Minton, a U.S. senator from Indiana. The 1981 nomination of the first woman to the Supreme Court, Sandra Day O'Connor, drew the interest of the television networks; since that time, all the hearings have been televised. Following the hearings, the Judiciary Committee makes a recommendation to the full Senate on the question of whether the nominee should be confirmed. Most recent nominees have won overwhelming approval from the Senate, including unanimous votes for O'Connor, Stevens, Scalia, and Kennedy. By contrast, Clarence Thomas was confirmed by a 52 to 48 vote, the closest in over a century. Justice Gorsuch was also confirmed by a close vote, 54 to 45. (See the chapter introduction.)

LOWER COURT SELECTION

Congress established the same process for the selection of lower federal court judges as the Constitution set for Supreme Court justices. Traditionally, presidents have been less involved in these selections because of the geographic decentralization of these courts and their lesser importance. Beginning with Ronald Reagan, however, presidents have been more directly involved in the process. The White House has become particularly interested in selections to the various federal courts of appeal. They realize that these courts handle very important issues, that they often make the final determination, and that these judgeships have become stepping stones to seats on the U.S. Supreme Court.

Presidents have the constraint of **senatorial courtesy** when naming lower court judges, particularly district court judges. Under this tradition, the Senate defers to the wishes of the senators from the home state of the judicial nominee, particularly if they are members of the president's party. The senator or senators have almost a veto power because the full Senate can deny confirmation as a courtesy to the one or two senators of the president's party from the state of the nominee.

senatorial courtesy In the selection of lower federal court judges, the deference shown to home-state senators who are of the same party as the president.

Although home-state senators still have near veto power, their support of a candidate no longer guarantees an easy confirmation. "This change seems to derive partly from a general decline in senators' deference to each other and partly from the growing recognition that lower-court judgeships are important."[53] This trend is particularly clear at the court of appeals level. In 1997, Republican senators held up Bill Clinton's appointment of Sonia Sotomayor to a federal appeals court for over a year, believing correctly that as a Hispanic American appellate judge, she would be a formidable candidate for the Supreme Court. In

Current Controversy

Lower Federal Courts and the Travel Bans

Immigration policy emerged as a major issue in the 2016 presidential election and remained so in President Trump's first term. When the president used an executive order to issue his first travel ban during the second week of his presidency, it dramatically affected the lives of many immigrants and travelers. The controversy that developed revealed the important role played by lower federal courts in immediately addressing a crisis in people's lives. The controversy also illuminated the fact that a range of federal courts, not just the Supreme Court, can serve as a check on presidential power.

In January 2017, the president issued his first travel ban. His executive order, which went into effect immediately, barred all travelers from Iran, Iraq, Syria, Yemen, Libya, Somalia, and Sudan from entering the country. It included all persons even if they had green cards, valid visas, or refugee status. The immediate result was confusion and protests at U.S. airports. At least 746 people were temporarily detained at U.S. airports. Some were deported back to their home countries, and many others were prevented from boarding their flights at airports overseas.* Within days, federal district court judge Ann Donnelly addressed a case brought by two Iraqi men detained in New York. She issued a stay that temporarily prevented federal agents from deporting anyone who entered the United States with a valid visa.

After the announcement of the first Trump travel ban, protests occurred at airports across the United States.

©Carlos Fernandez/Alamy Stock Photo

Soon thereafter, a district judge in Boston entered a similar temporary stay. In Seattle, a district judge heard a case brought by the states of Washington and Minnesota. District judge James Robart issued a nationwide temporary restraint on the travel ban. The Trump administration filed an appeal with the U.S. Court of Appeals for the Ninth Circuit. In February 2017, that court ruled unanimously, 3 to 0, to maintain the freeze on President Trump's immigration order. In a twenty-nine-page opinion, the judges rejected the government's argument that the freeze order should be lifted immediately for national security reasons, forcefully asserting their ability to serve as a check on the president's

power. The court said it was too early to determine the legal question of whether the ban was meant to discriminate against Muslims.[†]

A month later, President Trump released a revised travel ban order. Travel ban 2.0 narrowed the list of countries to Iran, Libya, Somalia, Sudan, Syria, and Yemen. It called for a 90-day ban on travelers from these six countries and 120 days for refugees. It excluded, however, visa and green card holders, deleted a section from the earlier ban that had given preference to Christian minorities, and included a waiver process for those claiming undue hardship. The order was blocked by a federal judge in Hawaii hours before it was to

2005, the minority Democrats in the Senate held up seventeen of President Bush's nominees by threatening filibusters. Their actions were supposedly in response to Republican actions against a similar number of the judicial nominees of President Clinton. After the Senate majority leader threatened to change the rules on cloture votes for filibusters on judicial nominees, seven moderates from each party got together and reached a compromise. They agreed not to change the filibuster rules in exchange for allowing most of the Bush nominees to face a vote.

In 2013, however, after excessive delays in confirming Obama judicial nominees, the Democratic majority in the Senate did change the rules on cloture votes for judicial confirmations by requiring only fifty-one votes rather than sixty votes to end a filibuster. This go into effect, as well as by another federal judge in Maryland. Trump's Justice Department appealed both cases. The appeals court for the Maryland case struck down the ban on constitutional grounds, holding that it discriminated against Muslims by targeting only countries with large Muslim majorities. The appeals court hearing the Hawaii case ruled against the ban on statutory grounds, declaring it violated federal immigration law by targeting people from certain countries without proving that it enhanced national security.

At this point, the Supreme Court got involved. In June 2107, it agreed to let the travel ban go into effect for some travelers, reversing the actions of lower federal courts that had put the plan completely on hold.[‡] The Court also announced it would rule on the legality of the second travel ban in October 2017.

That ruling never occurred because President Trump introduced his third travel ban on September 25, 2017. It would be that ban that eventually came before the nation's highest court. Travel ban 3.0 targeted travelers from eight nations, six of them predominantly Muslim. Under the order, most citizens of Iran, Libya, Syria, Yemen, Somalia, Chad, and North Korea were barred indefinitely from entering the United States, along with some groups from Venezuela. The executive order contained a few exceptions, however, like granting some student visas to Iranian nationals, and Chad was later removed from the list. The cycle was repeated for a third time, with lower federal courts in Hawaii and Maryland stopping the presidential travel ban from taking effect.

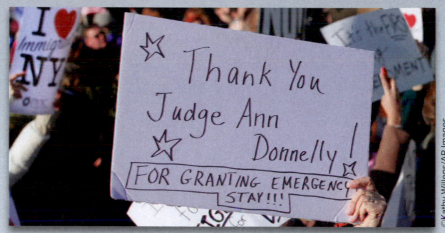

Federal judge Ann Donnelly issued a stay to temporarily prevent the enforcement of President Trump's first travel ban.

In December 2017, the Supreme Court urged the lower courts of appeal to reach a decision on the merits of travel ban 3.0 so that it could hear an appeal in April 2018. Later that month, the Ninth Circuit Court of Appeals affirmed the Hawaii district court's decision striking down the third travel ban. It based its decision on the rule of separation of powers, arguing that the president cannot change existing immigration law, only Congress can. In February 2018, the Fourth Circuit ruled against the travel ban as well, arguing that its anti-Muslim foundation violates the establishment clause.

The saga of the three Trump travel bans shows how important the lower federal courts are in adjudicating legal issues that affect the lives of many people. The decisions made by these courts provided reassurance and hope for people stranded in airports, unsure of their fate as well as that of their loved ones. Usually decisions of lower federal courts are final. Very few decisions are appealed. The travel ban issue was atypical, however, in that the Justice Department was intent on fulfilling one of the president's key campaign pledges, so it asked the Supreme Court to intervene. The Supreme Court did ultimately intervene in the case of Trump v. Hawaii upholding the president's last travel ban.

---

[*]See Colin Dwyer, "Of Courts and Confusion: Here's the Reaction to Trump's Immigration Freeze," NPR, January 29, 2017.
[†]See Matt Zapotosky, "Federal Appeals Court Rules 3 to 0 Against Trump on Travel Ban," *The Washington Post,* February 9, 2017.
[‡]Richard Wolf and Alan Gomez, "Supreme Court Reinstates Trump's Travel Ban, But Only for Some Immigrants," *USA Today,* June 26, 2017.

---

policy ended when the Republicans regained control of the Senate. The result was an unprecedented delay in the filling of judicial vacancies during the Obama administration. In the first year of the Trump administration, the new president was successful in getting four times more federal judges confirmed than Obama in his first year. In terms of demographics, only one of Trump's first eighty-seven successful nominees was African American and only one was Hispanic. In contrast, more than one-third of Obama's confirmed judicial nominees were representatives of minority groups.[54]

Who is selected to serve on the lower federal courts is also very important because these judges can have a impact on individuals immediate problems. See the "Current Controversy" section.

Since the 1981 nomination of Sandra Day O'Connor to the Supreme Court, all Supreme Court nomination hearings have been televised, stimulating greater public interest in the process.

THE JUDICIARY AND CIVIC ENGAGEMENT TODAY

Today, individuals and interest groups actively use the courts to shape public policy. In today's political environment, lawsuits provide interest groups with an easier means of achieving their goals than elections. In the 1950s and 1960s, liberal groups used the courts to achieve expanded civil liberties, civil rights, and environmental protections. By the 1980s, conservative groups were using litigation to further the interests of crime victims, private property owners resisting government regulation, and plaintiffs claiming "reverse discrimination" in affirmative action cases.[55]

The expanding role of the courts in making public policy has been the product of decisions made by both Congress and the Supreme Court. In 1988, Congress passed Public Law 100-352, which gives the Supreme Court almost complete discretion in choosing its agenda. The act allows the Court to choose cases with the greatest public policy implications, as measured by the number of *amicus curiae* briefs submitted to the justices. Title II of the 1964 Civil Rights Act also contributed to the expansion of judicial policy making by designating plaintiffs who filed suits under the statute as "private attorneys general." The act defined their actions as contributions to the enforcement of federal law and made plaintiffs eligible to collect attorneys' fees if they prevailed at trial.[56] This practice, known as fee-shifting, expanded under the 1976 Civil Rights Attorney's Fee Award Act that allowed for the recovery of attorneys' fees for actions brought under all civil rights laws enacted since 1876.

Other legislation that has expanded access to the courts to address political and social issues includes the 1990 Americans with Disabilities Act, which opened the path for extensive litigation by interest groups supporting the rights of people with disabilities, and the 1991 Civil Rights Act, which gave the victims of gender bias access to the federal courts. A number of regulatory statutes passed by Congress in the 1970s also allowed public interest groups to challenge the decisions of executive agencies in consumer fraud and environment cases.

Today, the Supreme Court decides cases that affect the personal lives of citizens, including those with specific challenges that make access to public facilities difficult.

The Equal Access to Justice Act in 1980 gave business groups the same access to challenge government regulations.

Ultimately, the Court's role in addressing political issues and social issues will be dependent on how it is perceived by the members of the society. See the ensuing "Challenges Ahead" section for a reading of the public's confidence in the Court.

Supreme Court decisions also have expanded the role of the courts in making public policy. We have seen that the Court relaxed the rules governing justiciability by allowing taxpayers to have standing. It has modified the Rules of Civil Procedure to facilitate class action suits.[57] Court rulings, however, have limited class action suits brought by advocates for immigrants and by Legal Services lawyers on behalf of poor persons. For others, the class action suit remains an important political weapon.[58]

The Court has all but abandoned three of the four parts of the political question test, ruling it always has a duty to rule on the constitutionality of political decisions of the president or Congress if there are manageable judicial standards.[59] The Court also effectively has dropped the doctrine under which federal courts decline to hear cases not yet resolved by state courts. As a result, "Stretching the legal concept of justiciability has broadened the range of issues subject to judicial settlement and allowed a wider range of litigants access to the courts."[60]

Therefore, the Supreme Court has been able to expand its public policy role by relaxing some of the rules of justiciability such as allowing standing for class action suits and weakening the political question doctrine for bypassing certain lawsuits. In other words, the Court has relaxed some of its own self-imposed restraints in order to allow itself to resolve public policy issues that involve millions of people.

The expanded role of courts in this era, which emphasizes personal rights, presents questions of propriety. Do the courts permit groups with narrow interests to affect national policy without having to create broader coalitions of support? Does litigation allow for a full consideration of the range of alternative views? Does policymaking by judges, who are

CONFIDENCE IN THE SUPREME COURT

The U.S. Supreme Court heads the least-known branch of the national government. Its members are not elected and much of its work is completed outside of public view. It decides cases that define our rights and affect the quality of our lives. Because every case produces winners and losers, the Court faces the potential for eroding public confidence at any time.

When asked in 2017 whether they approve of the way Supreme Court is handling its job, 49 percent of respondents approved of its work and 40 percent disapproved. The approval rating represented a small decline since 2016 but an improvement from two years earlier (see "Supreme Court Approval Ratings"). Remember that the Court's approval rating was measured at a time of declining public confidence in all national institutions.

In June 2017, Gallup poll respondents were asked whether they had confidence in each of several institutions. Only three institutions (the military, small business, and the police) had confidence ratings higher than 50 percent. More respondents expressed confidence in the Supreme Court (40 percent) than in the presidency (32 percent) or Congress (12 percent) (see "Confidence in Institutions: 2016 and 2017").

This might appear to be relatively good news for the Supreme Court, but another 2017 Gallup poll revealed that the federal government had the least positive image of any business or industry measured.* The Gallup authors believe that low confidence in Congress drags down the people's confidence in the Supreme Court. Supporting this observation is a scholarly article that suggests public opinion concerning the high court depends more on trends in opinions about Congress and the presidency than on controversial Supreme Court decisions or appointments to the Court itself.†

*Jeffrey M. Jones, Frank Newport, and Lydia Saad, "How Americans Perceive Government in 2017," Gallup, November 1, 2017.

†Sofi Sinozich, "Public Opinion on the U.S. Supreme Court, 1973–2015," *Public Opinion Quarterly* 81:1 (2017): 173–195.

Supreme Court Approval Ratings

Do you approve or disapprove of the way the Supreme Court is handling its job?

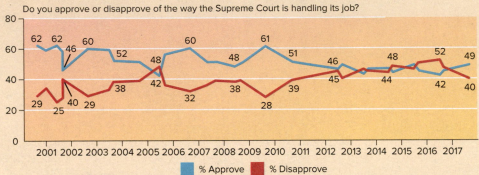

% Approve   % Disapprove

The Supreme Court has an approval rating of nearly 50 percent.

Source: Gallup Poll, http://news.gallup.com/poll/4732/supreme-court.aspx.

Confidence in Institutions: 2016 and 2017

	June 2016	June 2017	Change: 2016 to 2017
	%	%	pct. pts.
Newspapers	20	27	7
Public schools	30	36	6
Banks	27	32	5
Organized labor	23	28	5
U.S. Supreme Court	36	40	4
Criminal justice system	23	27	4
Congress	9	12	3
Television news	21	24	3
Big business	18	21	3
Small business	68	70	2
Police	56	57	1
Church or organized religion	41	41	0
Military	73	72	−1
Medical system	39	37	−2
Presidency	36	32	−4
News on the internet	n/a	16	n/a

The Supreme Court has a higher confidence rating than the presidency and Congress.

Source: Jones, J. M. "Confidence in U.S. Institutions Still Below Historical Norms," Gallup, June 15, 2015, http://news.gallup.com/poll/183593/confidence-institutions-below-historical-norms.aspx.

not elected, circumvent democracy? The answers to these questions are complex and require a consideration of just how democratic the other branches of government are today. We know that accommodating the participation of interest groups in submitting *amicus curiae* briefs has allowed the Court to view issues in ways similar to the other branches. These provide the Court with a great deal of factual material, focus its attention on the broader interests involved, allow the Court to better assess the probable consequences of its actions, and illuminate the unwillingness of the other branches to deal with certain political issues.[61] *Amicus curiae* briefs serve as a link between engaged citizens and members of the Supreme Court.

Thinking It Through >>>

Learning Objective: Demonstrate knowledge of the Supreme Court's judicial process.

Review: Nature of the Judicial Process

During the first weeks of the Trump administration, lawsuits presented before federal judges asserted that the president's executive order banning Muslims from traveling to the United States violated the freedom of religion clause of the First Amendment. Opponents of the president's policies were hopeful that the federal courts would serve as a check on what they viewed to be unwise use of presidential power. Which aspects of the judicial process allow the courts to curb presidential power? Which aspects make this task difficult?

Summary

1. **What is the nature of the judicial process?**
   - Judges have considerable discretion in deciding issues contained in real cases, but they are limited by the rules of jurisprudence and justiciability as to which cases they can hear.
   - Federal judges exercise their power in the judicial process in district courts, courts of appeal, specialized courts, and the U.S. Supreme Court.
   - With its use of judicial review, the Supreme Court has evolved from its early days into a court with great power that has at times angered presidents and Congress.
   - Today, the Court's role in the judicial process emphasizes personal rights in its constitutional law cases.

2. **How are Supreme Court justices selected?**
   - Supreme Court justices are appointed by the president and confirmed by the Senate for terms of good behavior, which is the equivalent of a life term because no justice has been both impeached by the House and removed from office by the Senate.
   - In making nominations, presidents consider a variety of professional, doctrinal, and representational qualifications.
   - Confirmation by the Senate is not assured, but the likelihood is greater if the president's party has a majority in the Senate and the nomination is not made in the last year of a president's term.
   - Today, nominees appear before the Senate Judiciary Committee in person to answer questions, and the hearings are televised.

3. **What is the nature of Supreme Court decision making?**
   - The Supreme Court follows the Rule of Four in making agenda decisions.
   - After hearing cases during oral argument, the justices take an initial vote during the conference. Votes can be changed after the justices read each other's opinions, and it takes a majority vote to decide a case.
   - Opinions are written to explain the votes of the justices, and they are often the result of negotiation because of the fluidity of the votes until the final pronouncements are made.
   - The Court must depend on others to implement its decisions, but it can aid implementers by writing clear opinions.
   - In making decisions, justices are motivated not only by the law but also by external factors, such as Congress, the president, and public opinion, and by internal factors, such as personal attitudes, strategic behavior, and conceptions of their judicial role.

Chapter 15

Public Policy
Responding to Citizens

©Carlos Chavez/Los Angeles Times via Getty Images

Many plants like this aerospace facility in Downey, California have closed down in recent years due to global competition, widening the gap between rich and poor.

THE WIDENING GAP

In 2007, Bob Thompson retired from his job at the North American Rockwell plant after forty-two years of service. He began his career at the high-tech aerospace company's plant in his hometown of Downey, California, in 1965, making nearly double the minimum wage at $2.95 an hour, and worked his way up to fabricator, a position paying $24.95 an hour plus benefits. Thompson knew he had punched his ticket to the middle class: good work at decent wages. From his first day at the plant, Thompson said, "I thought I was a king."[1]

Toward the end of his career, defense cuts hit the factory, the plant closed, and Thompson was forced to relocate to another Rockwell plant in southern California. Still, he considered himself to be lucky. At least he had a job. His hometown was not as lucky. Downey turned the factory site into a shopping mall, but the jobs it created were not high paying. The once thriving middle-class community finds itself wondering about its future.[2]

Thompson's story is not unique. A once-thriving middle class has been buffeted by multiple economic shocks, ranging from the globalization of industries that were once solely U.S. based to a financial crisis in 2007 that continues to take its toll on American families. Whereas 61 percent of U.S. households earned incomes placing them in the middle class in 1971, that number had contracted to just 50 percent in 2015 and the share of households in the lower income tier rose from 25 percent to 29 percent.[3] An uptick in the U.S. economy in the past few years

has meant somewhat higher employment rates and an amelioration of conditions for the poor and middle classes, but their condition relative to the more affluent has not improved.

The number of lower income households has grown, but so also has the number of higher income households. In fact, while the ranks of the lower income tier have grown by 4 percent, the share living in the upper income tier has risen by 7 percent, from 14 percent in 1971 to 21 percent in 2015. Whereas incomes for the poorest fifth of Americans rose just four-tenths of a percent from 2015 to 2016, incomes for the wealthiest fifth rose 2.5 percent during the same period, marking a continuation of the trend toward greater income inequality.[4]

Scholars are greatly concerned about the anxiety the middle class is feeling. Since the time of Aristotle, political thinkers have considered a vital middle class essential for political stability. A fragile, downtrodden middle class may be prone to appeals from demagogues and mass movements. The 2016 presidential campaign illustrated the power of the income inequality issue for forces on both the left and the right of the political spectrum.

As You READ

- **What is public policy, how is it made, and how can we explain policy outcomes?**
- **What is domestic policy, and what are some of the problems it addresses?**
- **How is economic policy made and implemented?**

Policymakers have begun to wrestle with the mix of factors that have led to the decline of our middle class. Some propose a guaranteed minimum income for all Americans that would provide every citizen enough money for basic living expenses.[5] Others have promoted trade barriers to restrict the outsourcing of jobs and to preserve good-paying jobs at home. Still others call for a dramatic rise in the minimum wage as a cushion for low-wage workers. Each of these solutions has its merits, but each has consequences that affect economic growth and efficiency.

In this chapter, we will examine how public policies are made and the trade-offs policymakers weigh in forging solutions to our nation's problems. When the government decides it must take action, it has to balance the interests of a wide variety of players, some with a much larger stake in the outcome than others and some with more political clout than others. The people of Downey, California, and the middle-class citizens across the country they exemplify, are hoping their interests will prevail. ■

THE NATURE AND SCOPE OF PUBLIC POLICY

Public policy pervades our lives; it is impossible to go through the day without being affected by programs issuing from federal, state, and local governments. If you go to a university, even a private one, you may participate in student loan programs, Pell grants, and work-study opportunities that pay at least the federally mandated minimum wage. If you attend a public university, the state bears a large share of the cost of your education, and a host of state laws and programs affect everything on campus from curriculum to traffic safety. Even the air you breathe is subject to quality standards set by the Environmental Protection Agency and monitored by state government agencies. In return for these services, you pay taxes to all of these governmental units.

Simply put, **public policy** is anything the government chooses to do or not to do.[6] This can include tangible actions, such as providing student grants or imposing taxes, as well as symbolic gestures, such as creating a legal holiday to commemorate the birthday of Martin Luther King, Jr. Governments assert policy even when they fail to act. For example, congressional failure to pass meaningful climate change legislation means that reducing greenhouse gas emissions is a lower priority than is keeping energy costs low.

public policy Anything the government chooses to do or not to do.

POLICYMAKING AND EVALUATION

A host of actors, including both government officials and private citizens, shape the policy making process. Their options are limited by a number of factors, including the availability of resources and political control of the instruments of power (such as which party controls Congress and the presidency). Tradition and public opinion serve as additional constraints. For example, even if it were possible to eliminate poverty by placing limits on how much property an individual could own, few Americans would agree to such a policy. It simply is not part of the American tradition, nor does it reflect the guiding ideology of either major political party. The process sometimes moves very slowly, at other times with great speed. With these caveats in mind, let us review the basic stages in the policymaking process.

Problem Recognition

The first step in policymaking is identifying and defining a problem as something the government can and should do something about. Some problems are easy to identify, such as the 2010 BP oil spill in the Gulf of Mexico that began with the explosion of the Deepwater Horizon rig. The threat to our coastal waters and shoreline was clear and immediate; the impact on fishing and tourism jobs was devastating. In other situations, we may only dimly or gradually perceive a problem and government's role in addressing it. For example, even though some scientists have long warned that greenhouse gas emissions caused by human activity are producing climate change, many lawmakers remain reluctant to involve government in devising solutions.

Agenda Setting

After identifying a problem, we need to determine how important it is and how urgent it is for us to act. Problems such as a massive oil spill require immediate action as well as long-range planning to prevent further occurrences. Following the BP disaster, the government took immediate steps to clean coastal waters, but various government agencies also began exploring long-range plans to reduce the probability of future spills.

Crises such as the BP oil spill in the Gulf of Mexico require immediate action as well as long-range planning.

Competing political actors often have different agendas as they jockey for national attention. The president commands the national spotlight when he speaks, but so do members of Congress and interest groups—all of whom can sound alarms about problems they want confronted; and states have their own priorities and solutions that may be at odds with the federal agenda.

Policy Formation

Once an item has been determined to be of significant importance for government action, the next step is to review possible solutions and select those most likely to be successful. Potential solutions come from a variety of sources, including lawmakers, scholars and think tanks, politicians, interest groups, and even average citizens who suggest ideas to lawmakers. In most cases, experts within government agencies present their own ideas to Congress and members of the executive branch.

As policymakers sorted through proposals about paying for the Deepwater cleanup and avoiding future recurrences, various government agencies such as the U.S. Coast Guard, the Environmental Protection Agency, the Interior Department, and others dispatched workers and volunteers to contain the spill and prevent its spread. Whereas there may have been debate and disagreement over how to handle the spill, there was no debate about the government's role or ability to do something about it. Necessity and public opinion demanded quick action on the part of government officials. However, on many policy fronts, debate over policy options continues for years, often until a crisis demands action or until consensus is reached about how best to address the problem.

Following the BP spill, President Barack Obama proposed a moratorium on new offshore wells until their safety could be guaranteed. He also conducted talks with the oil giant about compensation for the spill. Members of Congress, particularly those from the Gulf region, offered their own solutions, many of them seeking to reverse the president's moratorium on new drilling. Eventually, President Obama removed some of these exploration restrictions. President Trump later re-opened nearly all offshore waters to drilling.

Policy Adoption

Elected leaders are responsible for choosing which of the available policy options to adopt and how to put them into effect. At the federal level, this generally includes presidential actions and congressional lawmaking. After the immediate cleanup response by federal agencies, President Obama set up a commission to investigate the cause of the spill and worked with BP officials to set up a $20 billion fund to compensate victims and cover cleanup costs. Congress offered a variety of legislative responses as well, including bills to eliminate caps on oil company liability for spills and to improve oversight of federal agencies that are supposed to protect wildlife and the environment.

Policy Implementation

As we discussed in Chapter 13, government bureaucracies usually carry out the task of executing policy. In carrying out policy directives in the BP disaster, the Department of Homeland Security played a lead role in coordinating the government's response by overseeing the activities of a host of other government agencies, including the U.S. Coast Guard and the Environmental Protection Agency. Meanwhile, the president used an executive order to establish the National Commission on the BP Deepwater Horizon Oil Spill and Offshore Drilling, which issued a final report on the causes of the spill in January 2011; appointed an independent body, the Gulf Coast Claims Facility (GCCF), to receive and pay claims for compensation from the newly established BP fund; and ordered federal agencies to monitor and respond to potential public-health and environmental concerns in the Gulf region. Congress also held hearings about the lax oversight of agencies such as the now-defunct Minerals Management Service, which regulated offshore drilling.

In implementing policies, officials must be sensitive to the effects policies may have on multiple constituencies. The Obama administration ran into opposition from energy company executives who believed the moratorium on new deepwater wells was an overreaction; environmentalists who believed the president should call for an outright ban on deep-sea wells; and state government officials who believed the federal response was too slow and cumbersome. Eventually, the president lifted the moratorium earlier than planned. On assuming office, President Trump went further by allowing extensive offshore oil and gas exploration despite resistance from some coastal states.

The courts play a role in the policy process as well. Once the GCCF began accepting requests for compensation from the BP fund, a lawsuit was filed in Louisiana claiming the agency was making misleading statements to claimants about their right to sue BP on their own for restitution. The GCCF was forced to revise its practices to conform to a court order.

Policy Evaluation

Ideally, the government will try to determine whether a policy solves the problem for which it was designed. Once policies are in place, their impact should be assessed to determine their continued utility. Once again, bureaucracies play a vital role by collecting statistics and conducting studies to measure the progress of these policies. The president and Congress use this information to reauthorize programs and to make changes to fine-tune their impact.

Political factors may be as important as objective measures of success in the decision to continue, change, or abandon a policy. Each policy has a constituency that supports it and individuals who benefit from its operation—whether permanent or not it works as intended. After the BP oil spill, environmentalists called for a permanent ban on offshore drilling. The oil industry wanted drilling to restart as soon as possible. Each of these constituencies pressured the White House and Congress to promote its own point of view. Ultimately, the president relented by permitting new offshore drilling permits but put new safety restrictions in place to minimize the recurrence of a major spill. Because it is difficult to accommodate many competing interests, it is not surprising that most policymaking involves **incremental change** rather than wholesale change. Large changes are more likely to meet resistance, whereas small changes are more likely to be acceptable to a wider array of interests.

incremental change Small, gradual steps that characterize most policy changes due to the need to reconcile many competing interests.

Policies often have unintended consequences that are not always apparent at the time they are adopted. For example, the Deepwater commission found that splitting jurisdictional authority for matters such as granting drilling permits and selecting ecological sites for protection diminishes the kind of interagency cooperation that may have limited drilling in the affected area. Policymakers can minimize unintended consequences by carrying on conversations about proposed policies with constituencies and administrative agencies *before* the policy is enacted. As policies are evaluated and changes adopted, they continue to cycle through the policymaking process. Rarely does policymaking produce a finished product that escapes revisiting.

Types of Policy Outcomes

Benefits

	Widely Distributed	Concentrated
Widely Distributed	Social Security Defense Policy	Aid to Public Education Agriculture Subsidies
Concentrated	Air Pollution Controls Auto Fuel Economy	Tax Policy Telecommunications

Costs

Policy outcomes depend on the extent to which policy costs and benefits are shared.

Source: Adapted from James Q. Wilson, *Political Organizations* (Princeton NJ: Princeton University Press, 1995), 332–337.

Explaining Policy Outcomes

Whether or not government adopts a policy, as well as the types of policy that might be adopted, depends largely on the costs the policy imposes and the benefits it confers (see "Types of Policy Outcomes"). How the policy allocates costs and benefits plays a significant role in determining whether the policy is adopted, how well it is accepted, and how easily it can be altered. The figure illustrates different ways to classify the allocation of costs and benefits, and it gives some examples of policies that fit each classification.[7]

Policies that allocate costs and distribute benefits widely are often easiest to sustain. The popularity of Social Security, despite questions about its long-term sustainability, provides an example. The costs of the program are widely distributed across millions of American workers, and most citizens will eventually receive its benefits. Conversely, when the costs of widespread benefits are borne by a relatively concentrated population, those who pay most of the bill will lobby intensely against it. For example, energy companies are generally unhappy when they are forced to meet strict pollution standards, even though disgruntled stockholders will be among the beneficiaries of cleaner air.

Policies with widely distributed costs but concentrated benefits receive strong support from individuals and groups that benefit from them but tend to raise little organized opposition because no one group or class pays the entire cost. For example, all taxpayers support public schools and colleges, even though the benefits go primarily to parents and children. When both costs and benefits are concentrated, narrow interests may clash and the government must mediate the resulting disputes. Conflicts of this sort often occur when Congress writes tax legislation. There is perhaps no other policy that draws the attention of so many interests, each petitioning for advantages benefiting its own members. Ski lodge owners who have lost income because of warm winter weather, military contractors who desire long-term tax deferrals for military contracts, and home builders and owners who want to protect federal tax write-offs for mortgage payments are all examples of the interests jockeying for favorable treatment when tax bills are written.

Sometimes the actions that advance policy goals in one area create policy problems in another. For example, Americans have long embraced the goal of energy independence. A drilling technique known as hydraulic fracturing, or *fracking,* is being employed in many states with the aim of freeing vast deposits of oil and natural gas, thus lessening the nation's reliance on foreign oil. However, the technique, which involves pumping large amounts of water and chemical additives underground to free up energy trapped between layers of rock, has raised environmental concerns, including the potentially adverse impact of the process on groundwater quality and wildlife survival. Environmentalists call for stricter controls; energy companies balk at the prospect of the increased costs that regulation would entail.

DOMESTIC POLICY

Domestic policy consists of government action (and inaction) that most directly affects citizens within the United States. Each branch of the American government and many bureaucratic agencies at all levels are involved in formulating domestic policy, which includes a wide variety of initiatives such as police and environmental protection, public education, fair housing laws, income security programs, and antidiscrimination policies, to name but a few. However, in an era of globalization, the actions of other nations and those of international agencies may also have a strong impact on domestic policies, even though the levers that control their actions are further removed and often more difficult to access. We will examine more closely two areas of domestic policy that are sources of continuing controversy: environmental protection and antipoverty programs.

Protecting the Environment

Americans have long appreciated the beauty of the natural environment and sought to preserve its wilderness areas. President Theodore Roosevelt (1901–1909) was an early champion of government involvement in conservation, creating the country's first national parks and establishing the National Park Service to protect them. The rapid advance of industrialization in the twentieth century, however, produced enormous amounts of pollution and chemical toxins that threatened human health and wildlife. By the middle of the twentieth century, naturalists sounded the alarm about the damage pollution was doing to the environment. In her controversial 1962 book, *Silent Spring,* author and naturalist Rachel Carson alerted the nation to the dangers of pesticides and urged Americans to seek protection for our fragile ecosystem.

regulatory negotiation The process of shared decision making in which representatives of industries meet with policymakers to develop policies and regulations.

cap and trade A market-based system of pollution control whereby individual businesses can buy and sell emission credits even while the total level of industry pollution is capped at some level.

Government Responds By 1970, environmental activists had managed to elevate environmental protection to prominence in the political arena and claimed two major victories: the creation of the Environmental Protection Agency (EPA) and the passage of the Clean Air Act. The EPA's mission is to develop and enforce regulations to protect the nation's air, water, and soil. Today, it employs more than eighteen thousand individuals, including many scientists working at monitoring stations and labs across the nation. The Clean Air Act of 1970 gave the EPA the authority to identify major sources of pollution, to determine permissible levels of toxins that businesses can emit into the atmosphere, and to enforce regulations against polluters. The EPA also has been influential in requiring auto manufacturers to produce cleaner-burning engines and to increase automobile fuel efficiency. Congress enacted additional statutes to regulate pollution in waters and streams (Clean Water Act of 1972) and to protect various endangered species of wildlife (Endangered Species Act of 1973). It also amended the Clean Air Act in 1977 and again in 1990 to deal with additional environmental threats, including acid rain and ozone depletion.

Since the federal government enacted these measures, the nation has witnessed a substantial reduction in pollution. According to its ongoing study of ambient air quality, the EPA reports that emissions of each of the six major air pollutants have declined significantly since 1990. Emissions of sulfur dioxide (SO_2), which has been linked to acid rain, have declined by 89 percent since 1990.[8] Many rivers and streams that were once overwhelmed with pollution—such as Cleveland's Cuyahoga River, which caught fire in 1969—have responded to cleanup efforts and again support wildlife. A number of once-endangered species, including the peregrine falcon, have returned to viability with help from recovery programs operated by the U.S. Fish and Wildlife Service.

Environmental regulations concentrate the costs of cleanup on polluting industries, while distributing the benefits of cleaner air and water to everyone. As we discussed earlier, such policies tend to elicit resistance from those who bear the costs. The government has employed several different techniques to enforce compliance. In some cases, it has negotiated with polluters to build consensus about how quickly and how significantly they must reduce emissions, a policy known as **regulatory negotiation**. In other cases, the government has allowed polluters to bargain among themselves about how they will meet pollution standards, with those industries that are slower to achieve designated limits purchasing pollution credits from those that meet the standards more quickly, a policy known as **cap and trade**. Both policies have industry and environmental critics, but both policies have also contributed to a reduction in overall pollution.

Acting more aggressively to combat climate change than his predecessors had, President Obama initiated unilateral action on several fronts, including ordering a reduction of carbon pollution from the nation's coal-fired plants by 30 percent by the year 2030 and mandating greater fuel efficiency for all autos sold in the United States. Some of these actions were successfully overturned by the courts during Obama's tenure. The Trump administration has mounted a more serious challenge by repealing the coal plant directive and slowing compliance with the fuel standards rule. Most significantly, Trump forced cuts in the EPA's budget for enforcement and named an ardent opponent of the agency, Scott Pruitt, as the agency's head. Pruitt revamped agency priorities and ordered the removal of climate change references and information from the agency's website prior to his removal from the job for suspected ethics violations.[9]

The Trump administration has similarly reversed Obama-era policies on gas and oil exploration as well as development of solar power initiatives. Trump approved plans for building the Keystone XL pipeline, connecting vast oil sands deposits in Canada with refineries along the Texas Gulf, a plan Obama had rejected on grounds that it would inflict environmental damage. Trump also imposed tariffs on solar equipment made outside the United States, a move many believe would slow the implementation of solar power in the United States as a viable replacement for other forms of electrical generation.

Greenhouse Gas Polluters

Source: NASA/JPL

Per-Capita Fossil Fuel Emission Rates*

Metric tons of carbon per capita

Rank	Country	Metric tons of carbon per capita
1	Qatar	13.54
2	Curacao	10.30
3	Trinidad and Tobago	9.32
4	Kuwait	6.93
5	United Arab Emirates	6.34
6	Bahrain	6.28
7	Brunei (Darussalam)	5.95
8	Saint Martin (Dutch Portion)	5.31
9	Saudi Arabia	5.31
10	Falkland Islands (Malvinas)	5.16
11	Luxembourg	4.73
12	New Caledonia	4.50
13	Gibraltar	4.50
14	United States of America	4.43
15	Australia	4.17

Energy-Related Carbon Dioxide Emissions by Country or Region (2012–2040)

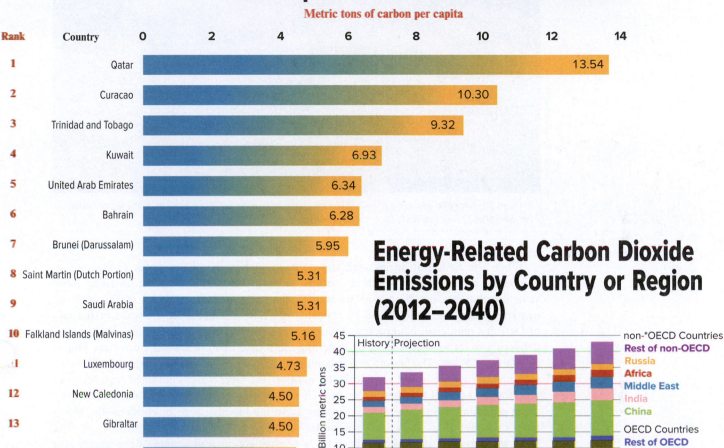

*Per–capita estimates are expressed in metric tons of carbon (not CO_2).

*OECD stands for Organization for Economic Co-operation and Development. The thirty-five member countries include many of the world's most advanced nations but also emerging countries such as Mexico, Chile, and Turkey.

Although many smaller countries have a higher rate of per-capita greenhouse gas emissions (top chart), larger countries like the United States and China have a larger impact on total worldwide emissions (bottom chart).

Sources: Top figure: Carbon Dioxide Information Analysis Center, 2017, "Ranking of the World's Countries by 2014 Per Capita Fossil-Fuel CO_2 Emission Rates," http://cdiac.ess-dive. lbl.gov/trends/emis/top2014.cap. Bottom figure: U.S. Energy Information Administration, "Projected Growth in CO_2 Emissions Driven by Countries Outside the OECD," May 16, 2016, https://www.eia.gov/todayinenergy/detail.php?id=26252.

According to the latest information available from the EPA, the United States emitted 4,998 million metric *tons* of carbon dioxide in 2015, second only to China's emissions of 9,040 million metric tons. Most of these emissions were from burning fossil fuels to generate electricity and to power our cars. The remaining emissions included industrial chemicals and methane from wastes in our landfills, raising livestock, natural gas pipelines, and coal.

Questions:

1. What factors might account for the extent of carbon dioxide emissions from each of the top fifteen greenhouse gas polluters?
2. Explain why the United States is second in overall carbon dioxide emissions but fourteenth in per-capita emissions.
3. Which geographic areas pose the greatest long-term threat in carbon dioxide emissions? What might be the reasons for this?

Although the scientific evidence of global warming due to human activities mounts, debate continues over who should pay the costs for a greener planet.

While the nation struggles with the question of how many resources to commit to combating air and water pollution, we also face serious challenges from an aging infrastructure that has not been well maintained. The most recent reminder of this was the drinking water emergency faced by residents of Flint, Michigan. In the wake of the city of Detroit's municipal bankruptcy, state-appointed managers sought to reduce the costs of delivering water to nearby Flint by switching the source of Flint's water from Lake Huron to the Flint River. The water, which contained high levels of contaminants, was treated incompletely by the use of chemicals. In addition, the river water contained high levels of chloride, a chemical that has a corrosive effect on pipes and leached lead out of the city's aging plumbing. When lead began showing up in the bloodstreams of children—the group most critically affected by lead poisoning—state and federal authorities stepped in. The Flint water system was switched back to its original source and a state of emergency was declared. Thousands of residents were given bottled water, water filters, and water test kits as a stop-gap measure. It will take years, however, to flush the water pipes of contaminants and even longer to build a planned new system for water delivery.

The residents of Flint, Michigan, faced a drinking water emergency when a switch in their water source resulted in toxic levels of lead leaching from aging pipes.

Environmental Protection in a Global Context

After years of failed attempts to achieve worldwide agreement on ways to reduce the emission of greenhouse gases that contribute to climate change, 196 nations struck a deal in Paris in December 2015. Signatory nations pledged to cut or limit emissions from fossil-fuel burning within a framework of rules that provides for monitoring and verification as well as financial and technical assistance for developing countries. The stated goal is to reduce pollution levels so that the rise in global temperatures is limited to no more than 2 degrees Celsius (3.6 degrees Fahrenheit) above pre-industrial averages. World leaders, including President Obama, hailed the Paris agreement as a turning point in the effort to stem global warming. Earlier efforts to reach worldwide consensus in

Rio de Janeiro in 1992, in Kyoto in 1997, and in Copenhagen in 2009 met with only limited success in securing binding pledges on carbon reduction.

Once again, however, the Trump administration has reversed course, announcing the withdrawal of the United States from the Paris agreement after the president met with world leaders in Italy in May 2017.[10] Trump argued that the agreement placed undo economic burdens on the United States without demanding enough from developing nations. He left open the possibility, however, of entering into a renegotiated agreement at a later date. The remaining signatories of the agreement made clear their continuing commitment to the goals of the accord, and some U.S. cities and states pledged continued support for the agreement's environmental goals.

Helping the Poor and the Elderly

The "social safety net," designed to protect the health and welfare of American citizens, offers an example of a dramatic change in government policy over time. Prior to the turn of the twentieth century, few laws protected American workers and private charitable organizations provided virtually all relief to the poor. The dangerous conditions in early twentieth-century factories gave rise to the first laws against child labor, laws improving sanitation, and laws favorable to the formation of labor unions as a means to increase wages. All of these initiatives, first enacted for the most part by the states, played a part in relieving poverty among urban populations.

The widespread unemployment and financial panic triggered by the Great Depression of the 1930s forced the federal government to take a more active role in alleviating suffering. Many programs now basic to American society, such as unemployment compensation and Social Security, emerged as part of the massive Social Security Act of 1935. The major provision of the act, the federal Old-Age and Survivors Insurance Trust Fund (currently known as Social Security), provides retirement income to the elderly, financed by employer and employee contributions. Another provision of the act, known as the Supplemental Security Income program (SSI), provides supplemental income to those who are blind, aged, or disabled. Unemployment compensation, also financed through a combination of employer contributions and federal and state funding, provides temporary and partial wage replacement for those who have been involuntarily laid off from their jobs.

In 1965, the government added health-care coverage for the elderly through a program known as Medicare, financed again through a combination of employer and employee contributions. This was followed shortly thereafter by a companion program of medical care for the poor called Medicaid, financed with funds from both the federal and state governments. The government designed these programs to attack the major causes of wide-spread poverty: unemployment, disability, and old age.

These programs have had considerable success in reducing poverty, especially among the elderly. Whereas the poverty level in the 1950s stood at about 30 percent, by the 1970s it had fallen to about 11 percent.[11] Since then, there have been marginal increases and declines based on a number of factors, including the amount of funds available for antipoverty programs and the state of the U.S. economy. In 2016, the official poverty rate stood at 12.7 percent, meaning that 40.6 million Americans were living on income at or below the poverty threshold of $24,563 for a family of four.[12] The highest percentage of poverty occurs among children, minorities, and urban populations. Even so, in absolute numbers, there are more white adults between the ages of 18 and 64 living in poverty than any other single group.

Our social safety net for the poor also includes short-term assistance for those temporarily out of work through no fault of their own. Unemployment insurance is a cooperative program using federal and state dollars to provide temporary income to those

In 2016, over 40 million Americans lived below the poverty threshold of $24,563 a year for a family of four.

©Mario Tama/Getty Images

Who Are the Poor?

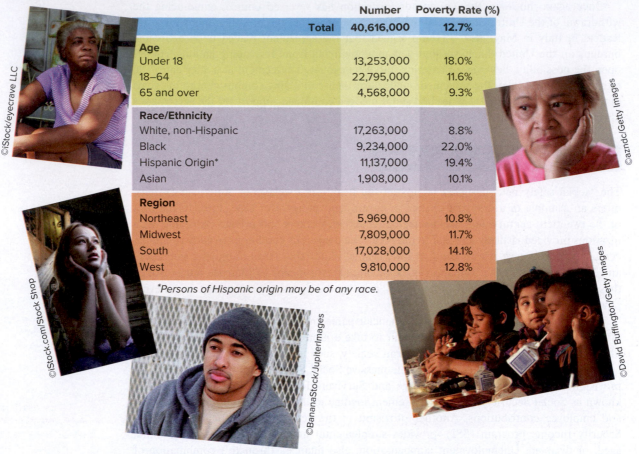

		Number	Poverty Rate (%)
	Total	**40,616,000**	**12.7%**
Age			
Under 18		13,253,000	18.0%
18–64		22,795,000	11.6%
65 and over		4,568,000	9.3%
Race/Ethnicity			
White, non-Hispanic		17,263,000	8.8%
Black		9,234,000	22.0%
Hispanic Origin*		11,137,000	19.4%
Asian		1,908,000	10.1%
Region			
Northeast		5,969,000	10.8%
Midwest		7,809,000	11.7%
South		17,028,000	14.1%
West		9,810,000	12.8%

Persons of Hispanic origin may be of any race.

Minorities have disproportionately high rates of poverty, as do some regions of the country, like the South.

Source: U.S. Census Bureau, Current Population Survey, 2016 and 2017 Annual Social and Economic Supplements.

looking for work. Most states provide up to twenty-six weeks of aid, and short-term extensions are also possible. The poor can also receive help through the Supplemental Nutrition Assistance Program (SNAP), sometimes known as food stamps. Benefits are based on family size and monthly income (see "Who Are the Poor?").

The Trump administration has signaled its intent to revisit and alter many of these safety net programs. For example, instead of providing cash for food assistance through SNAP, Trump has advocated sending each qualifying family a "harvest box" of shelf-stable foods.

The problem with social safety net programs is their burgeoning cost. These programs, known as **entitlements** because anyone who qualifies is entitled to receive benefits, account for approximately two-thirds of the federal budget. Such **mandatory expenditures** represent a promise made to those who are eligible to receive benefits.

Programs for the elderly, Social Security and Medicare, constitute the largest portion of mandatory federal spending. As our population ages, mandatory expenditures will continue to increase dramatically. On our current budget trajectory, this will leave little money for discretionary programs in other areas the government seeks to pursue, like education, transportation, and the environment (see "The Escalating Share of Mandatory Spending").

Welfare Reform Unlike Social Security, for which both costs and benefits are widely dispersed, programs for the poor provide concentrated benefits that are secured only through well-organized pressure. But the poor lack the political clout to advance their programs. They are not as active politically as are the elderly. Although a variety of interest groups such as

entitlements Programs promising aid without time limit to anyone who qualifies.

mandatory expenditures Budget expenditures guaranteed by Congress to all beneficiaries meeting eligibility requirements.

the Children's Defense Fund exist to speak for the poor, interests that are more vocal and active than America's poor dominate lobbying for government funds. As a result, programs to aid the poor undergo particular scrutiny as policymakers seek to cut costs and ensure those deemed as the undeserving poor are excluded from benefits.

The biggest changes in antipoverty policy have come in the form of public assistance programs—generally known as **welfare**. From the New Deal until the mid-1990s, the principal program for poor families was Aid to Families with Dependent Children (AFDC). This entitlement program provided payments to families with children who either had no income or earned below the annually adjusted standard poverty level established by the Bureau of Labor. Responding to complaints that

The Escalating Share of Mandatory Spending

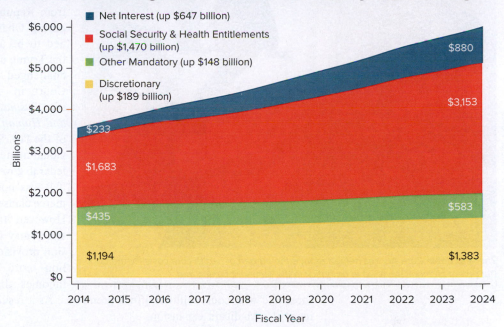

Spending on programs like Social Security and Medicare are projected to consume a growing share of government expenditures, leaving less and less money for programs like education and transportation.

Source: Congressional Budget Office, January 2015.

AFDC generated welfare dependency and thwarted self-sufficiency, Congress passed a reform measure in 1996 that ended welfare's status as an entitlement. Under the new program, **Temporary Assistance for Needy Families** (TANF), the federal government provides a fixed amount of money in the form of block grants (see Chapter 3) to the states, which decide work requirements, payment levels, and time limits within guidelines set by Congress. These guidelines specify that the state must cap continuous cash benefits at two years and lifetime benefits at five years. In 1997, Congress passed amendments to the program to ensure that cash payments under TANF did not go below previous AFDC benefit levels.

Scholars debate the overall success of welfare reform. One study showed that those who fared best after welfare reform found additional government programs—food stamps, job counseling, child care, and various state-sponsored medical programs for children—to supplement their TANF income.[13] As states struggle to control poverty, they are having difficulty in sustaining funding for programs, especially medical programs, that have proven critical to the success of welfare reform. State officials are also concerned about the growing number of working families who are poor but do not qualify for many government programs. The Bureau of Labor Statistics reports that more than five million American families living in poverty had at least one member working in the labor force for more than half a year.[14] Many of the workers in these families are the most vulnerable to changes in the workforce generated by recession and the outsourcing of jobs associated with globalization.

Health Care and Poverty In 2013, 44 million Americans lacked health-care coverage. With the adoption and implementation of the Affordable Care Act (ACA), the number of uninsured nonelderly Americans declined to less than 28 million as of the end of 2016.[15] The reduction was spurred by an increase in the number of young persons up to age 26 now covered by their parents' policies and by the number of low-income individuals who made use of government subsidies to buy insurance. Gains have been particularly sharp for minorities, especially Hispanics, who accounted for nearly a third of the increase in adults with insurance.[16] The law included a mandate that individuals obtain coverage through an employer, private carriers, or state Medicaid programs for those in poverty. Those who don't comply were required to pay a tax penalty. Even with the adoption of the ACA, the United States still lags behind most industrialized nations that provide universal coverage.

welfare The term characterizing the wide variety of social programs developed during the New Deal to help the poor, unemployed, disabled, and elderly.

Temporary Assistance for Needy Families A program funded by federal and state governments to provide financial assistance to pregnant women and families with one or more dependent children to help pay for necessities such food and shelter.

The Affordable Care Act has helped reduce the burden of health care costs for the poor, but recent changes have led to an uptick in the number of uninsured.

©Monika Graff/The Image Works

The expansion of health care coverage under the ACA met with strong resistance from Republicans when it was first passed during Obama's presidency, and it continued to be attacked and scaled back under the Trump administration. The act itself was challenged in the courts. The Supreme Court, in *National Federation of Independent Business v. Sebelius, Secretary of Health and Human Services,* upheld most portions of the law. Specifically, it held that the individual mandate was constitutional under the federal government's taxing authority even if it was not constitutional under the commerce clause, as the administration intended. However, the Court also ruled that the states may opt out of the Medicaid expansion provision intended to cover several million more lower-income Americans with incomes slightly higher than the poverty threshold who could still not afford premiums. As a result, many states refused to implement the Medicaid expansion.

The Trump administration came to office having promised to repeal and replace the ACA. When Congress failed to do so, the administration adopted a series of proposals designed to weaken the program. For example, it eliminated the government mandate, removing one of the supports that made the program financially stable. Trump also permitted states to weaken the plan benefits required under the original program and allowed states to impose work requirements on Medicaid recipients who received ACA benefits. By the end of Trump's first year in office, the number of uninsured persons rose by over three million but remained well below the number of uninsured prior to implementation of the ACA.[17]

ECONOMIC POLICY

The federal government has played a role in economic activity since its inception, collecting taxes, funding the construction of roads and canals, and granting licenses to companies, all in the name of economic development. The Great Depression, however, triggered the most extensive expansion of government activity into the economic realm through the creation of programs that provided income security to millions of Americans.

Many factors contributed to the Great Depression. Increases in productivity outpaced wages, leading to a surplus of goods many Americans could not afford. Restrictive international trade practices worsened this situation, as overseas sales by U.S. firms plummeted. Investors overspeculated in the booming stock market of the 1920s, and investors who lost money stopped supplying capital for business expansion. Laid-off workers defaulted on mortgages and cut back on purchases, further depressing business activity and investor confidence. More than a quarter of the labor force was out of work. Banks began to fail as depositors demanded their savings and banks were unable to collect on outstanding loans fast enough to provide liquidity. Food riots were not uncommon, and lines of men, women, and children waiting for help at soup kitchens stretched for blocks.

Franklin Roosevelt's New Deal attempted to prop up the failing economy, reassure financial markets, and provide hope for the legions of unemployed. Social Security insurance helped millions of elderly retire without facing destitution. Unemployment insurance provided short-term relief for those thrown out of work by adverse economic conditions. Short-term job creation programs like the Works Progress Administration (WPA) put thousands of unemployed Americans to work building roads, buildings, and bridges. The Tennessee Valley Authority brought electricity and jobs to millions living in the rural South. And savings were guaranteed under the Federal Deposit Insurance Corporation. Although scholars debate the overall economic effectiveness of these policies, they agree that the New Deal marked a significant change in the nature of federal intervention in the economy. Under Roosevelt, the national government took the direct hand in promoting, directing, and regulating economic activity that it maintains today.

Some of the same factors that led to the Great Depression contributed to the economic recession that began in 2007, although the recession was not nearly as deep, and some of the tools developed in the New Deal kept the recession from becoming even worse. The recession was triggered by multiple factors. For one, many Americans had become hooked on easy credit. Abetted by low interest rates and creative financial instruments, Americans bought more than they could afford. Financial institutions extended credit—especially in the form of home mortgages—to many who simply could not afford it, believing that losses could be prevented by repackaging mortgages and selling them to other financial institutions in chunks certified as secure by Wall Street ratings agencies. Many of these new banking practices escaped government regulators. When home sales began to lag, home buyers began to default and financial institutions were unable to recoup their losses, producing a crisis in confidence among banks that bought and sold the repackaged debt. In this environment, banks became wary of lending—even to other banks—and credit began to evaporate. With less credit, Americans cut back their spending and businesses were forced to lay off workers. Particularly hard hit were auto companies that carried the additional burden of paying for health care and pensions for retired workers as well as for their current workforce, something foreign competitors did not face. These factors cascaded, and the financial system began to unravel amid rumors of the potential failure of Wall Street behemoths like Bear Stearns and Lehman Brothers. When these and other financial giants, deemed "too big to fail," saw their stock values plummet and faced bankruptcy, a number of federal agencies moved in to prevent a global banking failure.

> **fiscal policy** Taxing and spending policies prescribed by Congress and the president.

In attacking recessions, the government relies on a number of tools that were developed in the wake of the Great Depression and are now well developed. For example, since 1933, depositors have been protected against bank failures by the Federal Deposit Insurance Corporation (FDIC). Since its creation, the insurance limit has been raised and expanded to $250,000 for a variety of accounts. However, policymakers also find it necessary to improvise when the usual weapons for improving economic performance fail to work as designed.

Fiscal Policy

Fiscal policy consists of the use of the government's taxing and spending authority to influence the national economy. By virtue of its sheer size, the government's fiscal policies can dramatically affect the direction of the economy. Government regulations, such as those that ensure the quality of food and drugs and protect workers, also affect economic activity.

Tools for Fiscal Policy Fiscal policy is made by the president, who proposes a yearly budget for the U.S. government, and by Congress, which authorizes taxing and spending through a process discussed in Chapter 11. The pie charts in "Federal Revenue and Spending, 2018" show expenditures and revenue projections for fiscal year 2018. A fiscal year is the 12-month period covered by the budget, usually from October 1 to the following September 30.

Much of the thinking about the goals and effects of fiscal policy was outlined early in the twentieth century by British economist John Maynard Keynes (1883–1946). Keynes argued that fiscal policy can be used as a discretionary tool to moderate

Federal Revenue and Spending, 2018

Fiscal Year 2018 Federal Revenues

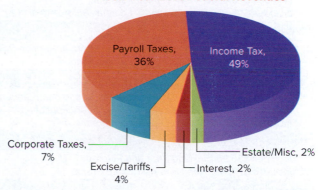

Fiscal Year 2018 Federal Spending

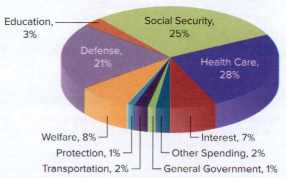

The charts above illustrate sources of revenue (top chart) and expenditure (lower chart) for the federal budget.

Source: National Priorities Project, Institute for Policy Studies, https://www.nationalpriorities.org.

Would You Like a Receipt for Your Taxes?

2016 Federal Income Tax Receipt
Average Federal Income Taxes Paid in the United States
April 15, 2017
Inflation adjusted to 2015 dollars

Health	**$2,910.82**
* Includes $1,235.24 for Medicaid	
* Includes $1,140.55 for Medicare	
* Includes $48.52 for Children's Health Insurance Program	
Military	**$2,341.48**
* Includes $497.07 for Military Personnel	
* Includes $121.14 for Lockheed Martin	
* Includes $64.62 for Nuclear Weapons	
Interest on Debt	**$1,322.77**
Unemployment and Labor	**$748.85**
* Includes $55.14 for Temporary Assistance for Needy Families	
* Includes $22.02 for Job Training and Employment Programs	
Veterans Benefits	**$595.39**
* Includes $269.91 for Payments for disability, death, etc.	
* Includes $233.37 for Veterans Health Administration	
Food and Agriculture	**$448.86**
* Includes $261.97 for SNAP (food stamps)	
* Includes $31.24 for Federal Crop Insurance	
Government	**$421.66**
* Includes $44.65 for Border Protection	
* Includes $23.43 for Federal Prison System	
* Includes $18.44 for Immigration & Customs Enforcement (ICE)	
Transportation	**$321.02**
* Includes $16.62 for Transportation Security Administration (TSA)	
* Includes $7.10 for Federal Aviation Administration	
Education	**$283.04**
* Includes $98.98 for Pell Grants, Work Study, and other Student Aid	
* Includes $77.54 for Elementary and Secondary Education	
* Includes $0.51 for National Endowment for the Arts	
Housing and Community	**$207.89**
* Includes $36.95 for Head Start and Related	
* Includes $7.61 for Homeless Assistance Grants	
Energy and Environment	**$159.63**
* Includes $26.67 for Environmental Protection Agency	
* Includes $7.14 for Energy efficiency and renewable energy	
International Affairs	**$134.96**
* Includes $101.15 for Department of State	
* Includes $20.17 for USAID (foreign aid)	
Science	**$103.61**
* Includes $62.51 for NASA	
* Includes $23.05 for National Science Foundation	
TOTAL	**$10,000**

Some tax experts suggest that providing taxpayers with a receipt showing exactly how their taxes are spent will give Americans a better idea of the size and cost of government programs.

Source: National Priorities Project, Institute for Policy Studies, "2016 Tax Receipt," https://www.nationalpriorities.org/interactive-data/taxday/2016/taxespaid/10000/.

cycles of inflation and unemployment, known as the business cycle. By varying the amount of taxes they levy or spending they authorize, Keynes asserted, governments can control overall economic demand. For example, government can respond to **recessions**—periods of high unemployment and reduced demand—in one of two ways. It can either buy more goods and services itself, thereby putting income into the hands of workers who will, in turn, increase their own spending, or decrease taxes so that consumers can keep and spend more of their own money. Either way, demand will rise, absorbing excess production and raising economic activity. To combat **inflation**, a rise in prices that occurs when the demand for goods and services outstrips the supply, government must slow aggregate demand. It can do so either by cutting back on its own spending and reducing the income it pumps into the economy or by raising taxes to suppress consumer spending. Of course, no one likes their taxes raised but taxes support programs most Americans like. (See Would you Like a Receipt for Your Taxes?)

A different take on fiscal policy emerged in response to the unusual scenario of *stagflation,* simultaneously high unemployment and high inflation, produced by an oil crisis in the late 1970s. President Ronald Reagan's team of economists called for government to concentrate on factors that increase aggregate supply, an approach known as **supply-side economics**. Reagan's economists argued that if the goods and services people want are available at the right price, consumers will buy them without the need for direct government intervention. Under this theory, the government's main economic role should consist of keeping prices low by reducing regulations that increase the costs of production and by keeping taxes low so as to increase consumer spending on goods and services. Some supply-side supporters estimate, for example, that federal regulations regarding safety and fuel efficiency add about $3,000 to the price of a new car.[18] A reduction in regulation, they claim, will reduce prices and create incentives for consumers to buy more products. When this happens, businesses will produce more and employ more people. Supply-siders also believe that high taxes act as a disincentive for workers who would rather forgo increases in income than pay higher taxes when their income increases. Thus, reducing taxes should encourage people to work more, boosting productivity.

Supply-side economics has a checkered track record. After a severe recession in the early 1980s, the country experienced a period in which both inflation and unemployment declined. Despite reduced tax revenues, government spending continued to climb under Reagan, resulting in historically high federal deficits. When Bill Clinton took office in January 1993, he raised taxes. By the end of his second term, the nation had undergone a dramatic economic expansion, and the federal government was running a surplus. The election of President Bush in 2000 marked a return to supply-side thinking with passage of one of the largest tax cuts in history. Once again, however, the government failed to match tax cuts with reductions in federal spending, largely because of expenditures related to the war on terror, the war in Iraq, and a failure to substantially reduce spending on domestic programs. A return to deficits ensued followed by the worst credit crisis since the Great Depression.

Entering office during the twin crises of a deepening recession and a near credit collapse, President Obama worked with then- Federal Reserve chair Ben Bernanke to stabilize financial institutions, to pump capital into banks to spur lending, and to encourage mortgage providers to renegotiate terms with borrowers who could not pay. They infused money into Chrysler and General Motors on the condition that they reorganize and become more efficient. And they helped design a $787 billion stimulus plan to stem the loss of jobs. Since then, many of the loans to banks have been repaid, and the auto companies are returning to profitability. Technically, the recession brought on by the financial crisis ended in 2009 and unemployment dropped to around 5 percent by 2016. Nevertheless, wages remained stagnant, and many Americans continued to feel financially insecure.

President Trump and the Republican Congress attacked the sluggish economy by slashing corporate and individual taxes, arguing that the infusion of money into the pockets of industry and consumers would increase wages and consumption. However, this approach was implemented at a time when the economy was recovering, albeit slowly, and unemployment was low. It fell below 4% by 2018. Many economists believed the policies adopted by the Trump administration could overstimulate the economy and spur inflationary pressures. In crafting the budget deal for fiscal year 2019, Congress also agreed to higher spending on both defense and domestic programs. Combined with the massive tax cuts, these policies appeared to be paving the way to higher and higher deficits.

Deficits The **deficit** is the one-year difference between the government's income and spending. When the government spends more than it takes in, it finances the deficit by selling U.S. Treasury bonds to financial institutions, individuals, and even foreign governments. Purchasers see these bonds as a good investment because they pay competitive interest rates and are backed by the full faith and credit of the U.S. government. Deficits may be acceptable and appropriate in times of economic recession as a way of stimulating economic activity, but deficits have become an almost omnipresent feature of the American economy. Are deficits good, are they bad, or don't they make a difference?

Whether a deficit is a weight on the nation's economy depends on several factors: the deficit's size, its sustainability, its impact on economic investment, and the faith of its creditors. The Congressional Budget Office estimated the budget deficit for fiscal year 2018 at about $833 billion. This may appear to be a very large number, but it is almost $600 billion less than the deficit in 2009, during the depths of the recession.

The budget deficit today stands at around 4 percent of the **gross domestic product (GDP)**, the value of all goods and services produced in the United States. This is well below the level reached during the worst of the recession in 2009, the largest since World War II (see "The Federal Budget in CBO's Extended Baseline"). Nevertheless, the deficit is expected to rise significantly in the coming years as a result of the Trump administration tax cuts.

Spending must also be measured against the long-term **national debt**, which includes mandatory obligations for programs such as Medicare, Medicaid, and Social Security. These long-term obligations are now expected to grow from roughly 77 percent of GDP in 2018 to 150 percent by 2047.[19] In light of future demographic trends, the government will have to cut programs, raise taxes, and borrow more. When the government borrows, it must pay interest to its creditors. Some economists argue that government's borrowing diverts investment from private businesses and slows economic growth. Others worry that more than half of the creditors buying U.S. securities are foreign investors, an increase of about 20 percent since the 1970s. Should world events or global financial markets take a turn for the worse, we might not be able to attract these investors and might not be able to pay for the things their money finances.

The one thing economists of all stripes can agree on is that the United States must come to grips with its long-term debt in the coming years. As the number of elderly rises, Social Security and Medicare costs will burgeon, placing a heavy burden on younger workers. Each year, Congress must raise the debt ceiling to allow more borrowing to pay our bills. In

recession A period of the business cycle characterized by high levels of unemployment.

inflation An economic condition in which the supply of money overwhelms our capacity to produce, creating rising prices.

supply-side economics An approach to economic policymaking focusing on lowering the barriers to production on the assumption that supplies at the right price will create their own demand.

deficit The difference between expenditures and income in any given year.

gross domestic product (GDP) A measure of the value of all goods and services produced in the United States.

national debt The total financial obligations of the U.S. government measured over many years.

The Federal Budget in CBO's Extended Baseline

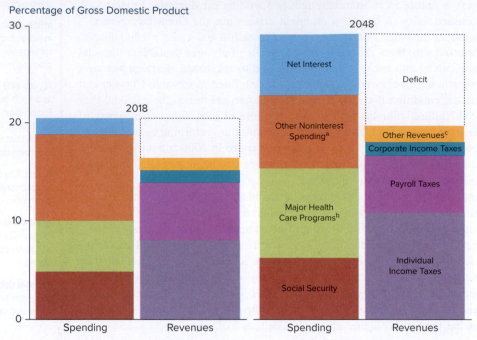

Percentage of Gross Domestic Product

The federal budget deficit (the difference between the government's income and expenditures) is expected to grow from around 4% of GDP in 2018 to about 9.5% in 2048 in the wake of Trump administration's 2018 tax reform bill.

Source: Congressional Budget Office, The 2018 Long Ter Budget Outlook

recent years, the debt ceiling has been the occasion for partisan gridlock. Republicans have insisted that the debt be reduced by spending cuts alone while Democrats wanted a combination of tax increases and spending hikes. Conflicts such as these are likely to recur until the long-term debt is brought under control.

Monetary Policy

Government can also regulate economic activity by controlling the availability of money. Like any other commodity, money has a price that increases when the supply is scarce and decreases when supplies are plentiful. That price is the interest rate that lenders charge to those who want to borrow money. When the supply of money is plentiful, interest rates fall, encouraging consumers to borrow more. Conversely, when the money supply is tight, interest rates rise, discouraging borrowers from taking on more debt.

By varying the money supply, government can alleviate the impact of recession or inflation. When more money is available in the form of inexpensive loans, the economy will expand. An expanding economy should put unemployed workers back into the active labor force. Similarly, when businesses are incapable of producing enough goods and services to meet demand, making loans more expensive is one way to force consumers to reduce spending and relieve inflationary pressures.

Making Monetary Policy A quasi-independent agency called the Federal Reserve, or simply the Fed, controls the supply of money. President Woodrow Wilson and Congress created the Fed in 1913 to regulate the money supply and establish confidence in the nation's banking system. A seven-member board of governors, appointed by the president and confirmed by the Senate, oversees the Fed. Governors serve fourteen-year terms, and appointments are staggered so that no one president will be able to control all appointments. This procedure removes the board somewhat from politically motivated policymaking. The chair of the Federal Reserve is selected to serve a four-year term by the president of the United States, with Senate confirmation, from among sitting Fed governors. President

Trump appointed Jerome Powell as Fed chair for a term commencing in 2018, replacing Janet Yellen, the first woman ever to head the agency.

The Fed consists of twelve regional banks, each run by a board of nine directors (see "Twelve Regions Served by Fed Banks"). All nationally chartered banks must belong to the Federal Reserve system; state-chartered banks may join if they wish. Member banks in each region elect six of the directors; the Fed's board of governors appoints the other three. Member banks buy stock in the Fed and pay for its operation. In return, they receive various benefits for joining, including the privilege of borrowing from the Fed member banks at attractive rates. The

Twelve Regions Served by Fed Banks

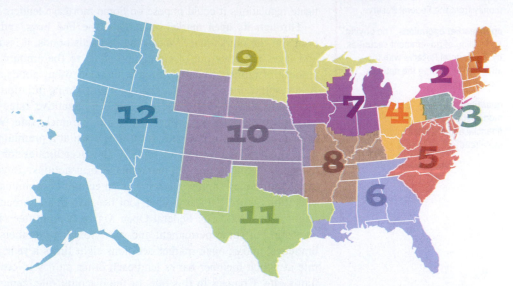

The Fed consists of twelve regional banks, each run by a board of nine directors.

Source: Federal Reserve Bank.

Fed also provides check-clearing services, processing the millions of checks consumers and businesses use in their daily financial transactions. The Fed acts essentially as a kind of credit union in which member banks hold shares. The Fed is also the U.S. government's bank, maintaining accounts and providing services for the Treasury Department. The regional Reserve banks work with the board of governors to establish and implement **monetary policy** and are responsible for supervising the operation of member banks.

The chair of the Fed frequently appears before budget-writing committees in Congress. Members of that body look to the chair for informal advice about fiscal policy.

Tools for Making Monetary Policy The Fed uses several tools to effect changes in monetary policy: the reserve requirement ratio, the discount rate, the federal funds rate, and open market operations. The **reserve requirement ratio** is the amount of money the Fed requires banks to keep on hand to meet their liabilities. Even a small change in this requirement can dramatically affect the amount of money a bank can lend to its borrowing customers. An increase in the requirement limits the money available to borrowers; a decrease expands the supply of money. The Fed has been working recently to increase the reserve requirements in order to ensure enough liquidity to cover bad loans. The **federal funds rate** is the interest rate banks charge one another for lending money. When banks fall short of cash, they turn to other banks just like the rest of us. The **discount rate** is the interest rate the Fed charges to its members on a short-term basis to cover shortfalls in their reserves. This rate is usually somewhat higher than the federal funds rate and is seen as a last resort for borrowing. A change in either of these rates can alter the amount of money banks make available to borrowers. Faced with concerns about the potential economic fallout from

monetary policy The control of economic growth through management of the money supply by the Federal Reserve.

reserve requirement ratio The amount of money the Fed requires banks to keep on hand to meet their liabilities. Its size helps determine how much banks can lend.

federal funds rate The interest rate banks charge other banks for borrowing money.

Jerome Powell was named by President Trump as chair of the Federal Reserve in 2018 to serve a four-year term. Powell was first appointed to the board of governors by President Obama in 2012 to fill an unexpired term and reappointed to a full term in 2014.

defaults in risky mortgages made by some lenders, the Fed repeatedly cut rates in late 2007 and early 2008 in an attempt to stem a drop in investor confidence. The Fed also agreed to investigate regulations it could impose on home mortgage lenders to improve home loan practices.

Through its **open market operations**, the Fed buys and sells government securities or bonds in the marketplace. When the Fed sells bonds, it issues a certificate to the purchaser and takes currency out of circulation equal to the amount of the bonds. This reduces the amount of money available to make loans or to buy goods and services in the marketplace. As a result, selling bonds is a good tool for fighting inflation. Individuals and member banks buy these securities because they yield competitive rates of interest and because, being backed by the U.S. government, they are extremely safe. When the economy is slumping, the Fed will offer to buy back securities, often at a premium—that is, above their face value. This encourages investors to trade in their certificates for cash, which they can then use for making loans and for marketplace transactions. Buying bonds should result in an expanded money supply and serve as an economic stimulus. The Fed employs open market operations more than any other tool because this approach has a more subtle impact on financial markets. The Federal Open Market Committee (FOMC), a twelve-member body consisting of some permanent and some rotating members from the Fed's twelve regional branches, makes open market decisions eight times a year. The FOMC can also adjust the rate at which member banks lend each other money to cover short-term needs, the federal funds rate. Changes in this rate, or the discount rate, generally trickle down to consumers, affecting loans for things like automobiles and credit card purchases.

For several reasons, the Fed generally is more successful fighting inflation than recession. First, it is easier to curtail spending by drying up the money supply—the policy recommended in times of inflation—than it is to encourage spending simply by placing more money in circulation—a policy usually taken in times of recession. When loan rates increase, consumers who cannot afford the higher rates will be unable to qualify for loans and not able to make purchases like cars and homes. But there is no guarantee that consumers will spend more when interest rates fall, especially if they are still recovering from an economic setback. Lower interest rates alone will not guarantee that we will buy more, and banks may be reluctant to lend even when they are flush with cash for fear that borrowers will be unable to cover their debts.

Second, since the Fed is primarily responsive to member banks, it worries more often about inflation than recession because of the impact inflation has on the banking community. Although people borrow less during recessions, banks are still able to make money by collecting on existing loans. However, when inflation reduces the value of money over time, borrowers are repaying banks with money borrowed at a lower rate than it was when the bank lent it. As a result, banks will be making less money and put pressure on federal policymakers to take those measures likely to rein in inflation.

Financial Innovation During the recent financial crisis, then–Fed chair Bernanke, who was appointed by President George W. Bush and reappointed by President Obama, demonstrated an important feature of policymaking: Policymakers sometimes find it necessary to act boldly when a crisis hits, even if there is little precedent. A student of the Great Depression in his graduate studies and scholarly writings, Bernanke wanted to ensure that credit problems stemming from financial failures did not dry up needed capital and cripple economic growth. As a result, he worked diligently behind the scenes to orchestrate the sale of some large financial players facing bankruptcy, to distribute TARP (Troubled Asset Relief Program) money to bail out troubled banks, and to inject credit into markets to stave off collapse. Finally, he engaged in what is known as **quantitative easing**, a procedure by which the Fed floods the markets with additional reserves by buying government securities and other financial assets in an effort to spur financial activity when low interest rates alone are not enough. By creating even more liquidity than provided by other tools at its disposal, the Fed hopes to spur more economic activity when the economy is depressed. These actions helped stabilize markets, but some economists warn they risk inflation.

Financial reform was another consequence of the recent recession. Reacting to the sometimes reckless manner in which financial institutions lent money, Congress imposed new regulations, including the requirement that banks hold on to greater reserves for use in a downturn, and prohibitions against the use of federally insured depositor cash for speculative investments. Another step was the creation of the Consumer Financial Protection Bureau, which serves as a watchdog for consumers of financial products. Hostile reaction to these reforms by financial institutions resulted in an effort by the Trump administration to scale back and, in some cases, dismantle these consumer protections.

Global Economic Policy

President Trump's decisions to withdraw from world trade agreements and to impose tariffs on foreign-made steel and aluminum caused global alarm. That is because the nations of the world have worked over the past few decades to promote free trade across national boundaries. Trade policies such as the 1994 **North American Free Trade Agreement** (NAFTA), supported by Democrats and Republicans alike, created the world's largest free trade zone by removing most trade barriers among the United States, Canada, and Mexico. The proposed Trans-Pacific Partnership, originally agreed to by President Obama but then rescinded by President Trump, proposed reduced tariffs and increased trade among twelve countries that border the Pacific Ocean. Together, these nations represent roughly 40 percent of the world's economic output. Trump's insistence that NAFTA was one of the worst trade deals the U.S. ever made led to an effort to rework the deal with our partners in Mexico and Canada on terms more favorable to the Untied States. A revised pact dubbed the United States-Mexico-Canada Agreement, or USMCA, was submitted to Congress for review and approval late in 2018.

Trump's actions may have rattled financial markets and raised concerns among world political and economic leaders, but not everyone was upset. Although globalization of markets has resulted in more goods at lower prices for U.S. consumers, it has also had a negative impact on some segments of the U.S. economy. Especially hard hit have been jobs in the manufacturing sector. Recent years have seen a loss of auto manufacturing jobs to Mexico, a loss of jobs in making furniture to China, and job losses in textile manufacturing to Indonesia and other developing countries. These countries provide labor at much lower costs than the United States.

But globalization also has the potential for increasing markets for U.S. goods and services. We sell millions of dollars worth of aircraft, pharmaceuticals, and food to the rest of the world, not to mention entertainment in the form of movies and television shows. This results in gains for certain industries but not others. Globalization produces winners among some sectors of the labor market, such as the financial industry, and losers among others, such as manufacturing.

One potential response to world competition is **protectionism**, the use of taxes and tariffs to protect domestic production by limiting the products we buy from other nations. This is the route President Trump took with regard to steel and aluminum imports. Protectionist policies, however, can lead to retaliation as foreign countries build walls to limit the importation of American goods. Some economists believe tariff policies lead inevitably to recessions and even depressions.

Several international bodies have emerged to bring stability to world markets and to coordinate world economic policy. One of these is the **G20**, a group of world leaders from the twenty largest developed and developing economies. The group meets periodically to consider steps aimed at producing global economic stability and sustainability as well as financial regulation. Another important world body is the **World Trade Organization** (WTO). An offspring of the **General Agreement on Tariffs and Trade**, or GATT, an international trade agreement created in the wake of World War II, the WTO has become the principal world body responsible for negotiating trading agreements, monitoring compliance, and adjudicating trade disputes among 164 member nations. The WTO's top-level decision-making body is the Ministerial Conference, which

North American Free Trade Agreement A 1994 trade agreement eliminating trade barriers among the United States, Canada, and Mexico.

protectionism The policy of using taxes and tariffs to limit the kinds and amounts of foreign goods entering the nation.

G20 Annual meeting of nineteen countries plus the European Union, at which members discuss strengthening the global economy.

World Trade Organization The international body concerned with negotiating the rules of trade among nations.

General Agreement on Tariffs and Trade An international agreement following World War II designed to eliminate tariffs and trading barriers.

Meetings of the World Trade Organization have been the focus of much protest by workers and environmentalists unhappy with the trade policies the WTO has adopted.

International Monetary Fund An international organization based in Washington, D.C., designed to foster monetary cooperation and trade among nations.

meets at least once every two years. Decisions are made by the entire membership, typically by consensus. The United States fields a team of negotiators that works with the WTO and with individual trading partners through the Office of the United States Trade Representative, whose chief administrator is appointed by the president with Senate confirmation. Another important global financial agency is the **International Monetary Fund** (IMF), whose 189 member nations make loans and help promote economic growth in developing nations.

These world organizations have been the targets of hostility among those who have lost jobs and opportunities during the era of globalization. The WTO, for example, has been the focus of much protest by workers and environmentalists from around the world. Recent WTO meetings have been greeted by thousands of demonstrators and even by violence. Protesters believe that global organizations like the WTO remove important decisions from the hands of the citizens in democratic nations and turn them over to bureaucrats more interested in advancing the interests of multinational corporations than those of workers or environmentalists. Free trade advocates respond by pointing out that democratic institutions are not being subverted by WTO decisions. Trade representatives are responsible to the president and Congress, who are ultimately accountable to the American electorate. Nevertheless, debate about the role of global institutions is likely to continue as the uneven effects of trade rules are felt by various interests throughout the world.

PUBLIC POLICY AND CIVIC ENGAGEMENT TODAY

Opportunities to address social problems in our communities abound. Every year, millions of Americans volunteer to feed the poor, build shelters for the homeless, assist the sick and the elderly, and clean up the environment. In 2016, over 62 million volunteers contributed over 7.8 billion hours to these efforts.[20] This number includes 16.9 million millennials and 19.9 million Gen Xers.[21] These efforts improve the lives of countless more millions of Americans, and they supplement the efforts of government in alleviating human suffering and improving the quality of life.

Opportunities for political involvement are plentiful as well. We can lobby our elected officials for causes we espouse, protest government actions we oppose, and send clear signals to the business community about how we view their impact on the health and welfare of our communities. In each of these areas, youth are making a real difference.

Following the mass shooting at a high school in Parkland, Florida, in 2018, students rallied at the state capitol, sent representatives to talk with federal officials in Washington, and took to the airwaves and to social media to demand action on gun reform. Although the students did not get everything they wanted, they convinced the Florida legislature to strengthen some gun control measures and they raised the consciousness of the American people about gun violence in the United States. Equally important, they sent a message to policymakers that these young people intended to stay involved until all the changes they sought are enacted into law. Youth are also taking to the streets in greater numbers to protest policies they oppose, a phenomenon that cuts across national borders. A study of protest in the United States, Britain, Canada, and Australia found that, by significant margins, young people in each country were more likely to attend demonstrations than their elders. In the United States, young people were more than twice as likely as older people to attend a demonstration.[22] Youth are making a difference in economic policy as well through efforts such as boycotting and buycotting. These activities are particularly popular among youth and alert manufacturers and commercial interests to the political preferences of their future customers.

If we are to solve the many policy problems we reviewed in this chapter, we will need to bring even more citizens into the political process. Community organizations, churches, labor groups, and other mobilizing agents are already hard at work implementing innovative ideas to make this happen in hundreds of communities nationwide. A number of online forums where citizens can share experiences, gain policy expertise, and explore ideas for expanding citizen participation also exist.[23] Until our discussion is enriched by participants from all sectors of the political community, the true promise of citizenship for all will be unfulfilled. The good news is that there is no shortage of ideas and energy among Americans already hard at work to make this happen.

Thinking It Through >>>

Learning Objective: Describe the major income security programs.

Review: Helping the Poor and the Elderly

Social Security and Medicare provide needed benefits to millions of elderly Americans. However, costs for these programs will continue to rise as the elderly population grows. To control costs, economists warn, we must cut benefits, raise the retirement age, increase tax contributions, or implement some combination of these reforms. Analyze the costs and benefits of each of these options and present an argument to support the choice you believe is best for both the welfare of the elderly and the economic health of the nation.

Summary

1. **What is public policy, how is it made, and how can we explain policy outcomes?**
   - Public policy is anything the government chooses to do or not to do.
   - The policy process includes problem recognition, agenda setting, policy formation, policy adoption, policy implementation, and policy evaluation.
   - Policy outcomes can be explained by considering the distribution of costs and benefits to various groups affected by the policies.
   - Both costs and benefits can be either widely distributed or concentrated.

2. **What is domestic policy, and what are some of the problems it addresses?**
   - Domestic policy consists of government action (and inaction) that affects citizens within the United States.
   - Each branch of the American government and many bureaucratic agencies at all levels are involved in formulating domestic policy.
   - Climate change, energy production, and pollution of our air, land, and water are all growing and controversial areas that domestic policymakers must address. Some agencies such as the Department of Energy and the Environmental Protection Agency specialize in dealing with these problems.

   - Poverty and the rising costs of Social Security and health care are domestic policy areas that have resisted easy solutions because they are expensive and affect many diverse interests. The Affordable Care Act produced a dramatic reduction in the number of uninsured, but recent attempts to weaken its protections may reverse this trend.

3. **How is economic policy made and implemented?**
   - The major tools of economic policy are fiscal and monetary policy.
   - Fiscal policy consists of the use of the government's taxing and spending power to influence the nation's economy.
   - Fiscal policy is made by the president and Congress through their taxing and spending decisions.
   - Monetary policy uses changes in the supply of money to influence the nation's economy.
   - The Federal Reserve uses the tools of the reserve requirement ratio, the discount rate, the federal funds rate, and open market operations to direct monetary policy.
   - American economic policy is also affected by global economic policies that often divide political leaders into positions of protectionism versus free trade.

Chapter 16

Foreign and Defense Policy
Protecting American Interests in the World

Refugees fleeing poverty and war face death and uncertain futures as they seek asylum in countries that are increasingly hostile about their arrival.

©Tony Comiti/Corbis via Getty Images

FLIGHT AND FIGHT

In October 2013, an estimated 368 migrants died in the sinking of two boats near the Italian island of Lampedusa. Desperate to escape poverty, famine, and war in their native countries in the Middle East and Africa, many of these migrants paid smugglers thousands of dollars to ferry them to the perceived safety of Western Europe, where they hoped to forge a brighter future. Instead, one vessel caught fire and capsized, expelling the migrants into the waters of the Mediterranean.[1] The other shipwrecked seventy-five miles from Lampedusa, and at least thirty-four more migrants were drowned.

This event focused the attention of Western nations on the plight of migrants seeking to escape deadly conditions in their native lands. Since then, the number of migrants seeking asylum in the West has skyrocketed. More recently, the exodus has been greatest from war-torn Syria (see "Refugees by Major Country of Origin, as of 2016"), where the nation's president, Bashar al-Assad, backed by Russian allies, has brutally assailed rebel forces with no consideration for the innocent and vulnerable people caught in between.[2]

At first, some European countries, like Sweden and Germany, accepted responsibility for sheltering the refugees. Others, like the Netherlands and Slovakia, balked; some, like Hungary, built walls to keep out the migrants.[3] As the flow of refugees has continued almost unabated over the past few years, even those countries that had

originally provided safe haven for these desperate foreigners experienced a political backlash as the costs of sheltering the migrants grew. Workers in these countries feared the migrants would take their jobs. Such fears led to the growth of nativist politics and the rise of right-wing fringe groups demanding an end to immigration, as well as, in the case of Great Britain, the severing of ties with the European Union, whose governing body made acceptance of the immigrants a condition of membership.[4]

The United States has experienced similar tensions arising from the simultaneous growth in migration over our southern borders and the lackluster performance of our economy in securing jobs for those with little formal education. A country that was once proud to call itself a nation of immigrants has called for building walls to keep our neighbors out. The current flow of migrants around the world points to the difficulty every nation has in balancing its ideals with the very real economic and social limits that give rise to internal political discord.

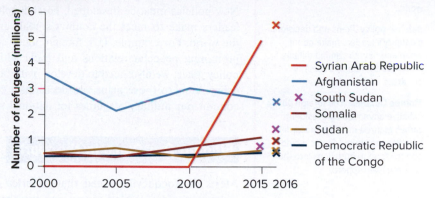

Refugees by Major Country of Origin, as of 2016

Although the number of refugees from various countries has risen in recent years, those escaping from the revolution in Syria far outnumber those from other countries.

Source: International Organization for Migration, *World Migration Report* 2018 (Geneva, Switzerland: IOM, 2017), http://www.iom.int/wmr/world-migration-report-2018.

As You READ

• **What are the major goals of American foreign policy?**

• **Who are the principal actors in the foreign-policy-making process?**

• **What are the tools that foreign policy makers have at their disposal?**

In this chapter, we will discuss the foreign policy dilemmas that the United States faces in an increasingly uncertain world. We will examine the institutions charged with assessing and formulating policies to protect the American homeland and the tools at their disposal to carry them out. Along the way, we will identify the role citizens can and must play to protect the ideals we value. ■

DEFENSE AND FOREIGN POLICY IN HISTORICAL PERSPECTIVE

The world has changed dramatically during your lifetime. Most of you were born after the collapse of the Soviet Union in 1991, which marked the end of the Cold War. Many observers believed that a period of world peace would follow. A bloody war in the Balkans, the bombing of the World Trade Center in 1993, attacks on U.S. embassies in Kenya and Tanzania in 1998, and most especially the events of September 11, 2001, shattered that dream and ushered in a period of increased global terrorism.

foreign policy Plans a nation's leaders make to meet their goals and objectives in dealing with other nations in the world.

defense policy Plans and decisions a country's leaders make about when and how to commit military resources for national security purposes.

Monroe Doctrine The foreign policy initiative advanced by President James Monroe in 1823, according to which the United States would oppose foreign intrusions into the Western Hemisphere.

The requirements for defending the nation change dramatically depending on the source and the nature of the enemies it faces. Defense and foreign policies that promoted peace and security during the Cold War may not meet the challenges of the "age of terrorism." New policies must be developed. **Foreign policy** refers to the plans and decisions a nation's leaders make to meet the country's goals and objectives in dealing with other nations in the world. For example, U.S. foreign policy seeks to keep Americans safe from attack while promoting peaceful relations and trade with the rest of the world. To meet our foreign policy goals, we also need to develop plans about the strategic use of military force. **Defense policy** refers to those plans and decisions a country's leaders make about when and how to commit our military resources for national security purposes.

Finding Our Place in the World

Alexis de Tocqueville noted that America's prosperity rested in part on its geographic isolation, its defensible borders, and the absence of passion for war:

> The Americans have no neighbors and consequently no great wars, financial crises, invasions, or conquests to fear; they need neither heavy taxes nor a numerous army, nor great generals; they have also hardly anything to fear from something else which is a greater scourge for democratic republics than all these others put together, namely, military glory.[5]

He went on to observe that the foreign policy of early American presidents took advantage of the country's relative isolation and was guided by a defensive posture that steered clear of entangling alliances.[6]

Despite George Washington's admonition in his farewell address to avoid embroilment in the affairs of other nations, it soon became clear that America could not isolate itself from the world, especially since much of the North American continent was still in the hands of European nations. Early on, presidents were called upon to deal with naval skirmishes that interfered with free trade and hostilities with Native Americans that were instigated or exacerbated by foreign powers. Americans soon began to develop an active foreign policy aimed at expanding American territorial frontiers at home and defending American commercial interests abroad against ambitious Europeans.[7] Presidents became the prime movers in foreign policy-making as the nation continued to grow in power and prestige. In order to make their intentions clear to the rest of the world, presidents sometimes issued proclamations or doctrines outlining their foreign policy objectives. Since the Revolution, Americans have paid dearly in both lives and dollars in defense of our borders and our values. (See "Military Costs of Major U.S. Wars.")

By the time James Monroe became president in 1817, America's western frontier had already been pushed almost halfway across the continent. Faced with the dual threat of Russian incursions in the Pacific Northwest and European designs on reacquiring recently liberated countries in Central and South America, Monroe presented a new foreign policy to Congress on December 2, 1823. The **Monroe Doctrine**, as it came to be known, warned that the United States would consider any attempt by European powers to expand their territorial control to the Western Hemisphere as a threat to the nation's peace and safety. In return for European restraint, the United States would refrain from interference in the internal affairs of Europe. In subsequent years, this doctrine was used to ward off European powers and to justify U.S. expansion to the Pacific.

In the second quarter of the nineteenth century, America supplemented its westward territorial expansion with international economic expansion. Diplomatic relations with the rest of the world continued to grow, along with American prestige; but the domestic fight over slavery consumed most of the nation's energy, and in 1861 the growing schism between slave states and free states led to the Civil War.

Becoming an International Power

When the Civil War ended, the United States once again turned its gaze outward. Unlike many European nations, America sought to achieve economic expansion without acquiring political outposts. By the turn of the twentieth century, it was becoming a world power, exercising military might to protect its interests in the Western Hemisphere and expanding its influence in the South Pacific. America also began carving out a larger role for itself on the international stage. The **Open Door policy**, initiated by John Hay, secretary of state in the administration of President William McKinley, declared that all nations trading with China should have equal privileges and also opposed China's partition by foreign powers.

In 1904, President Theodore Roosevelt issued his **Roosevelt Corollary**, an expansion of the Monroe Doctrine, reasserting U.S. opposition to European intervention in this hemisphere. It also asserted America's right to intervene in the domestic affairs of its neighbors if they proved unable to protect their borders from foreign encroachments on their own. The corollary was used by the United States to justify intervention in a number of Caribbean countries, including Cuba, Haiti, and the Dominican Republic. The United States consolidated its dominance in the hemisphere with the opening of the Panama Canal in 1914.

Eventually, the United States was dragged into playing an even larger role. Despite President Woodrow Wilson's determination to keep the country out of World War I, the sinking of American merchant vessels by German submarines compelled America to join the fight. After the war, Wilson's efforts to prevent future wars by establishing the League of Nations, one of his Fourteen Points for international cooperation, failed to gain traction either at home or abroad, and the Treaty of Versailles he helped negotiate to end the war was not even ratified by the U.S. Senate.

During this period, the involvement of American citizens in executing foreign policy decisions expanded. The military draft was initiated in 1917 as a democratic response to the need for military personnel. Wealthy citizens could no longer buy their

Despite President Woodrow Wilson's determination to keep the country out of World War I, the sinking of American merchant vessels by German submarines compelled the United States to join the fight.

way out of military service as they could in earlier eras. A peacetime draft was instituted just before the United States entered World War II—a conflict that the country had tried to avoid but could not. The Selective Training and Service Act of 1940 required all men between the ages of 21 and 35 to register with the Selective Service System and to remain available for service regardless of wealth or education. Deferments were available in the case of hardship, and those who opposed war on religious grounds were given the opportunity for alternative service. After that long and bloody war, in which thousands of American soldiers died, the Allies met in Yalta and subsequent conferences to partition the world in ways they believed would bring stability. That goal was not realized, however, as the Soviets expanded their reach and nations under first world control sought independence.

The Nuclear Age

After World War II, the United States and the Soviet Union were the world's preeminent powers; both possessed large nuclear arsenals and could dispatch conventional military forces quickly anywhere in the world. In 1947, President Harry Truman issued the **Truman Doctrine**, declaring the intention of the United States to support countries attempting to resist communist expansion. This doctrine informed the U.S. policy of **containment**, referring to U.S. efforts to limit or contain the communist sphere of influence. In our efforts to stop communism, the United States involved itself in a number of conflicts the government believed were inspired by the Soviet Union's desire to spread its ideology. One of these conflicts was Vietnam.

Vietnam marked another change in citizen involvement in war. Deferments for those who could afford to go to college led to disenchantment with the way the Selective Service operated. In response, a draft lottery that limited deferment opportunities was initiated in 1969. In 1973, as the Vietnam War was winding down, the draft was replaced by a system of voluntary military enlistment. Today, the all-volunteer army includes a growing number

Open Door policy The foreign policy initiative advanced by Secretary of State John Hay in 1899 proposing to keep China open to free trade with all nations on an equal basis and denying any one nation from total control of trade.

Roosevelt Corollary The foreign policy pronounced by President Theodore Roosevelt asserting the United States' right to intervene in the domestic affairs of its neighbors if they proved unable to protect their borders from foreign encroachments on their own.

Truman Doctrine The foreign policy position advanced by President Harry Truman asserting the United States' intention to prevent Soviet expansion after World War II.

containment American policies designed to limit the expansion of Soviet power around the world during the Cold War.

Military Costs of Major U.S. Wars

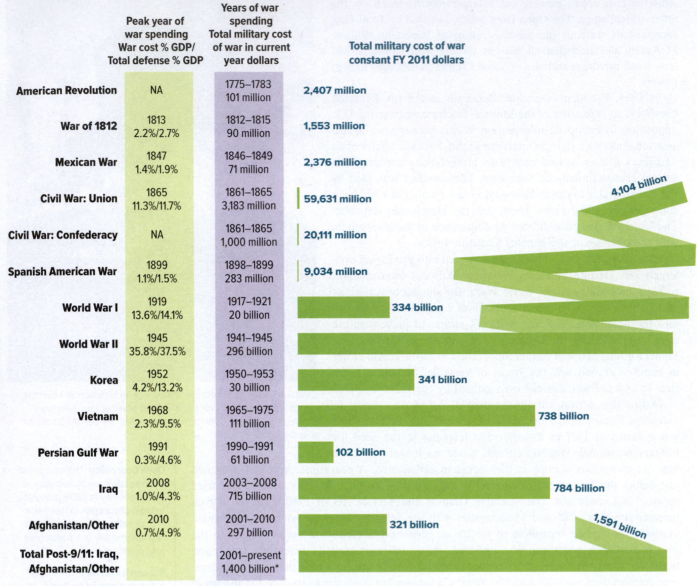

	Peak year of war spending War cost % GDP/ Total defense % GDP	Years of war spending Total military cost of war in current year dollars	Total military cost of war constant FY 2011 dollars
American Revolution	NA	1775–1783 101 million	2,407 million
War of 1812	1813 2.2%/2.7%	1812–1815 90 million	1,553 million
Mexican War	1847 1.4%/1.9%	1846–1849 71 million	2,376 million
Civil War: Union	1865 11.3%/11.7%	1861–1865 3,183 million	59,631 million
Civil War: Confederacy	NA	1861–1865 1,000 million	20,111 million
Spanish American War	1899 1.1%/1.5%	1898–1899 283 million	9,034 million
World War I	1919 13.6%/14.1%	1917–1921 20 billion	334 billion
World War II	1945 35.8%/37.5%	1941–1945 296 billion	4,104 billion
Korea	1952 4.2%/13.2%	1950–1953 30 billion	341 billion
Vietnam	1968 2.3%/9.5%	1965–1975 111 billion	738 billion
Persian Gulf War	1991 0.3%/4.6%	1990–1991 61 billion	102 billion
Iraq	2008 1.0%/4.3%	2003–2008 715 billion	784 billion
Afghanistan/Other	2010 0.7%/4.9%	2001–2010 297 billion	321 billion
Total Post-9/11: Iraq, Afghanistan/Other		2001–present 1,400 billion*	1,591 billion

Wars are costly not just in lives but in dollars, too.

Note: The current year dollar estimates are converted to constant prices using estimates of changes in the consumer price index (CPI) for years prior to 1940 and using Office of Management and Budget and Department of Defense estimates of defense inflation for years thereafter. The CPI estimates used here are from a database maintained at Oregon State University. The database periodically updates figures for new official CPI estimates of the U.S. Department of Commerce.

Sources: Stephen Daggett, "Cost of U.S. Major Wars," *CRS Report for Congress,* June 29, 2010; Neta C. Crawford, "U.S. Costs of Wars Through 2014: $4.4 Trillion and Counting Summary of Costs for the U.S. Wars in Iraq, Afghanistan and Pakistan," June 25, 2014, http://watson.brown.edu/costsofwar/files/cow/imce/figures/2014/Costs%20 of%20War%20Summary%20Crawford%20June%202014.pdf.

of women. In 2013, the government lifted its long-held ban on women in combat, recognizing the important role women play on and off the battlefield and opening new opportunities for them in special forces.

U.S. nuclear policy during the Cold War was informed by a principle of **mutually assured destruction** (MAD). Architects of the MAD theory held that the buildup of nuclear arsenals by the United States and the Soviet Union assured that neither side would launch a first strike because it would face massive retaliation. In other words, massive nuclear arsenals on each side would force a stalemate in which both sides might lose but neither could win. The certainty of destruction would act as a deterrent. The discomfort many Americans felt living under the threat of nuclear annihilation was reflected in the popular culture of the 1960s. Movies such as *Dr. Strangelove or: How I Learned to Stop Worrying and Love the Bomb* poked fun at living in a world of permanent nuclear stalemate.

mutually assured destruction The arms policy followed by the superpowers during the Cold War, in which each side maintained sufficient fire power to destroy its adversary if that adversary struck first.

Stanley Kubrick's 1964 film, *Dr. Strangelove or: How I Learned to Stop Worrying and Love the Bomb*, spoofed Cold War relations between the United States and Russia at a time when nuclear warfare posed a very real threat.

A period of **détente** opened in the 1970s when the United States and the Soviet Union attempted to ease tensions by undertaking a number of cooperative actions like signing treaties to limit the arms race. The United States also began discussions with other formerly hostile nations such as China. By the time of the Ronald Reagan administration, however, the fervor for détente had waned, and America commenced an arms buildup that the Soviets could not match. The Soviets' failure to keep pace with America, coupled with internal economic problems, contributed to the collapse of the Soviet empire in the early 1990s.

détente An easing of tensions among nations.

The Growing Threat of Terrorism

The breakup of the Soviet Union and the Soviet bloc ended the Cold War, but the role that the sole surviving superpower would play in this new era was uncertain. President George H. W. Bush helped bring former Soviet satellites into Western alliances like the North Atlantic Treaty Organization (NATO) at this time. He also asserted U.S. commitment to global stability by assembling a multinational coalition with the authorization of the United Nations to aid Kuwait after it was invaded by Iraq in 1990. Coalition forces liberated Kuwait in just forty-two days. President Bill Clinton continued President Bush's policy of building alliances with former Soviet states and intensified diplomatic efforts in the Middle East, attempting unsuccessfully to end the long and bitter conflict between Israel and the Palestinians.

While the United States sought to redefine its role in the post–Cold War era, it was confronted by an increase in terrorism around the world led by such groups as Al Qaeda, which found refuge in various Asian and Middle Eastern nations. In 1993, U.S. interests were hit by terrorists when a bomb in the World Trade Center killed six and wounded nearly a thousand; in 1998, simultaneous bombings took American as well as African lives at U.S. embassies in Tanzania and Kenya. The most serious assaults came in New York and Washington, D.C., on September 11, 2001, when attacks using hijacked airplanes killed nearly three thousand Americans. The United States retaliated by invading Afghanistan and removing the Taliban government, which had supported Osama bin Laden, the mastermind behind the operation.

The "war on terrorism" was the centerpiece of President George W. Bush's national security policy. It was envisioned as a global war against unseen enemy terrorists, some of whom travel within U.S. borders. It produced a reorganization of the federal bureaucracy and a shakeup in the nation's intelligence-gathering operations, as well as a change in official military policy from the use of force only to counter imminent threats to a doctrine of **preemption**. President Bush outlined this new approach shortly after the September 11 attacks. According to this doctrine, the United States has a right to attack terrorist groups or nations in order to disrupt plans they may have to attack us.[8] The new policy was implemented when the United States invaded Iraq over fears of an alleged buildup of weapons of mass destruction.

Even though President Barack Obama articulated a national security strategy that was more collaborative and less narrowly focused on fighting terrorism than his predecessors, he maintained a U.S. presence in Afghanistan and ordered the execution of Al Qaeda leaders including Osama bin Laden. He escalated the use of drone strikes to take out suspected terrorists—even American citizens such as Anwar al-Awlaki, a U.S. citizen living in Yemen. By the end of his second administration, chaos remained in the Middle East, however, as a new threat, known as ISIS, the Islamic State in Iraq and Syria (sometimes known as ISIL, the Islamic State in Syria and the Levant), destabilized several nations, including Syria, which was undergoing its own revolution spurred by the actions of its brutal dictator. ISIS's strongholds became a training ground for radicalized Muslims from around the world. Obama also sought to restructure our foreign and military policy by "pivoting" or "rebalancing" toward the Asia-Pacific region through increased trade and enhanced military readiness in the area.

President Donald Trump entered office announcing a new policy of "America First," in which the United States would curtail its role as the world's police and concentrate on securing its own borders. It would also withdraw from global commercial treaties it deemed unfair and forge bilateral agreements with individual nations more favorable to U.S. interests. Nevertheless, Trump increased troop commitments in Afghanistan and commenced a buildup of America's nuclear arsenal to confront the evolving capabilities of other nuclear powers.

DEFENDING U.S. INTERESTS IN A CONSTANTLY CHANGING WORLD

Foreign and defense policy experts often explain the positions they advocate in terms of protecting national interests. What are national interests? How do we determine what will best serve these interests? And how do we achieve our interests when other nations' interests may clash with ours? To answer these question, we must first address the sometimes conflicting nature of the interests that we seek to protect as well as the dynamics of nation-state interactions.

Defining National Interests

The most important foreign policy goal facing any nation is maintaining its own security in the face of potential threats. Security comes in many forms. First is physical security from attacks like those of September 11, 2001. Nations must ensure the protection of their citizens and the integrity of their borders. Second is secure access to the resources needed for economic well-being. For example, until new sources of energy are abundantly available, the economic integrity of the United States depends on access to oil around the globe. Third is promotion of values that maintain domestic institutions and that contribute to a world environment supportive of those values. For example, one of the stated goals of U.S. foreign policy is to support fledgling democracies. Democracies, we believe, tend to favor negotiated solutions over the violent resolution of conflict. Taken together, this constellation of military, economic, and ideological concerns about security constitute a country's **national interests**.

It is easy to see how security interests may clash. For example, even though our stated goal is to support democracies, the United States often has tolerated and even supported dictatorial regimes such as that of the shah in Iran (1941–1979), who served as a reliable ally and militant anticommunist in the oil-rich Middle East. The Nixon administration helped overthrow the democratically elected president of Chile, Salvador Allende, whom it viewed as hostile to U.S. business interests even though Chile's people had installed him through democratic elections.[9] In fashioning foreign policy, we must weigh the relative importance of these different interests and understand how each contributes to our national security. It also requires that we understand how nations perceive the actions of others in a constantly changing world.

Understanding Nation-State Dynamics: Foreign Policy Theories

Foreign policy is generally guided by the assumption that nations act in a world that is anarchic, that is, one that lacks a recognized arbiter with the authority to settle disputes. As a result, each nation is limited in the pursuit of its own interests only by the strength of its own resources and the countervailing power of other nations.[10] Each nation weighs the military power, resources, and goodwill at its disposal and assesses how best to advance its interests. These assessments are guided by theories about how nations behave and how best to achieve our national interests in light of that understanding. Three of the most prominent theories of foreign policy are realism, liberalism, and idealism.

Foreign policy **realism** is the theory that emphasizes the need for a strong military as a deterrent to other nations. According to foreign policy realists, nations always act in their own self-interest and must have sufficient military resources to defend those interests from foreign threats. Foreign policy realism is one of the most venerable and persistent theories held by foreign policy professionals, although it exists in a variety of shades. Although realists place a premium on nations' ability to take coercive action when necessary, they realize that alliances and peace treaties may also serve our interests. Nevertheless, peace, they believe, can be achieved only through the maintenance of a strong defense as a credible deterrent.[11]

Foreign policy **liberalism** is a theory that focuses on the potential for cooperation among nations in meeting common goals such as prosperity and peace. Franklin D. Roosevelt's efforts to build the United Nations as a vehicle for averting war and the Truman administration's Marshall Plan to rebuild war-torn Europe are examples of liberal commitment to internationalism and the proposition that a stable world order is necessary for nations to grow and prosper. Foreign policy liberals believe that our national interests are best secured by building alliances that strengthen the bonds among nations, making conflict more costly than cooperation.

Closely aligned to liberalism is foreign policy **idealism**, which emphasizes the promotion of American values such as democracy, freedom, and cultural diversity. Such promotion, idealists believe, will attract nations wishing to emulate our success and to gain our support. Often foreign aid is contingent on the recipient's accepting these principles and making tangible efforts to institutionalize them. Idealists believe spreading our values allows us to influence the actions other nations take as long as they believe that we are truly guided by them ourselves.[12] U.S. foreign policy idealists of the twentieth century include former presidents Woodrow Wilson and Jimmy Carter.

Of course, any given president must choose his preferred course based not on theoretical considerations alone but also on world events as they unfold. Although some political leaders rely more heavily on one of these perspectives than others, most foreign policy decisions are guided by a combination of approaches.

> **realism** The theory that holds that nations always act in their own self-interest and must have sufficient military resources to defend those interests.
>
> **foreign policy liberalism** The theory that holds that national interests are best secured by building alliances and making conflict more costly than cooperation.
>
> **idealism** The theory that advocates American values such as democracy, freedom, and cultural diversity as the best way to promote our national interests.

MAKING FOREIGN POLICY

Foreign policy links diplomatic, intelligence, economic, and military operations into a coherent framework for achieving American goals in the world. As we saw in earlier chapters, the constitutional authority for making and conducting such policies is shared by Congress and the president. However, the executive branch is in charge of day-to-day operations, and its role in the formation and execution of foreign policy decisions has grown steadily.

The Primacy of the Executive Branch

Overseeing the operations of agencies dealing with foreign and defense policies has been a feature of executive branch power since George Washington was president. For the most part, Americans are highly deferential to the president in his capacity as foreign policy chief (see Chapter 12). However, Congress, interest groups, and public opinion can significantly limit the president's options. The president relies on a wide range of departments and agencies to provide guidance on national security, as described in the sections that follow.

National Security Council Established in 1947 by Congress and made part of White House operations in 1949, the National Security Council (NSC) serves both to advise the president on defense and foreign policy matters and to coordinate the implementation of policy among various government agencies. Membership includes the president; the vice president; the secretaries of state, defense, and the treasury; the chairman of the Joint Chiefs of Staff, who represents the military leaders of each branch of the armed forces; the director of national intelligence; and the national security advisor to the president. The president can also invite heads of other agencies to join these meetings if he believes they possess valuable information about national security matters.

Allegations that the Trump campaign colluded with the Russians in the 2016 election caused a rift between President Trump and his foreign policy and intelligence teams from the very start of his presidency, impacting relations with foes and allies alike. Often it appeared as if he and his advisors would deliver quite different messages to the world community. Ordinarily, the president and his national security team work seamlessly to ensure that messages to other nations are uniform and consistent.

Department of State The State Department is the chief diplomatic arm of the U.S. government. It is responsible for leading and coordinating U.S. representation abroad and for conveying U.S. foreign policy to foreign governments and international organizations. It operates abroad through diplomatic offices or embassies in approximately 180 countries and through mission offices that act as liaisons with international organizations such as the United Nations. Its staff negotiates agreements and treaties on issues ranging from trade to nuclear weapons (see "U.S. Department of State"). Domestically, it is in charge of issuing passports and visas to U.S. citizens traveling abroad and, with the Justice Department, for monitoring the issuance of visas granted to foreign visitors.

Foreign Service Corps of U.S. diplomats stationed around the world.

The secretary of state, appointed by the president with Senate confirmation, oversees the conduct of agency business by civil servants and the staffing of the **Foreign Service**, the diplomatic corps that represents U.S. interests abroad. Although top diplomats to foreign countries are political appointees, the experts who staff the embassies are drawn from Foreign Service professionals who undergo intensive training within the agency. Secretaries of state are often eager to reflect their agency's positions when they offer advice to the president. Whether or not their views make their way into policy depends on a number of factors, including their personal relationship with the president, consistency between their views and presidential priorities, and the strength of personalities with whom they must compete. In the days leading to the American invasion of Iraq, then-secretary of state Colin Powell's views were often overlooked in favor of stronger voices within the White House, such as Vice President Dick Cheney, and in the Department of Defense, such as Secretary Donald Rumsfeld. President Trump downplayed the role of the State Department in foreign affairs, leaving many positions in the agency unfilled. He preferred to rely on those closest to him in the White House, including son-in-law Jared Kushner, with whom he entrusted such diplomatic missions as securing peace in the Middle East.

U.S. Department of State

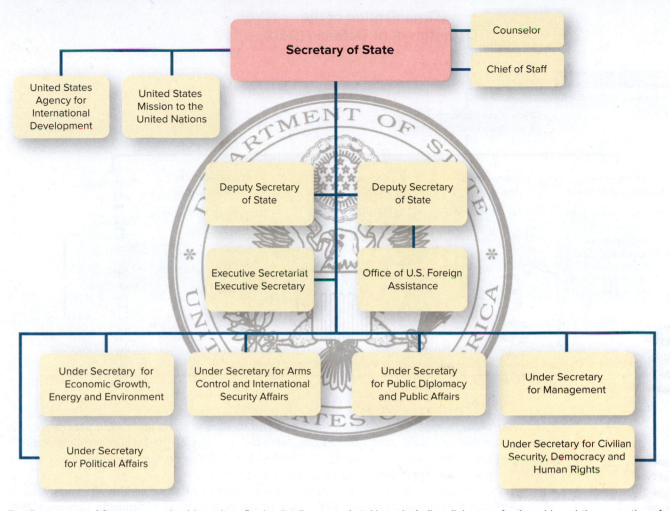

The Department of State is organized by units reflecting its diverse undertakings, including diplomacy, foreign aid, and the promotion of democratic ideals.

Source: U.S. Department of State

Department of Defense Like the Departments of State and Treasury, the Department of Defense is as old as the Republic. However, it is constantly adapting to new technologies and strategies in carrying out its primary mission of maintaining combat readiness to defend the nation. It employs more than 650,000 civilians and 1.3 million active-duty service personnel. The secretary of defense reports to the president and sits atop a defense structure in which each branch of the armed services is represented (see "U.S. Department of Defense"). The Joint Chiefs of Staff, appointed by the president and confirmed by the Senate for nonrenewable four-year terms, are the military leaders of the army, navy, air force, and marines. The chairman of the Joint Chiefs is eligible for two renewable two-year terms. Reporting to the Joint Chiefs of Staff are leaders of command operations in various military theaters as well as officers in charge of special units.

Intelligence Community In response to intelligence failures regarding the existence of weapons of mass destruction in Iraq, Congress passed the Intelligence Reform and Terrorism Prevention Act of 2004. A key provision of the act was the creation of the Office of the Director of National Intelligence, which is responsible for coordinating intelligence from a variety of domestic and foreign sources and reporting findings to the president. As

U.S. Department of Defense

Organization of the Department of Defense (DoD)

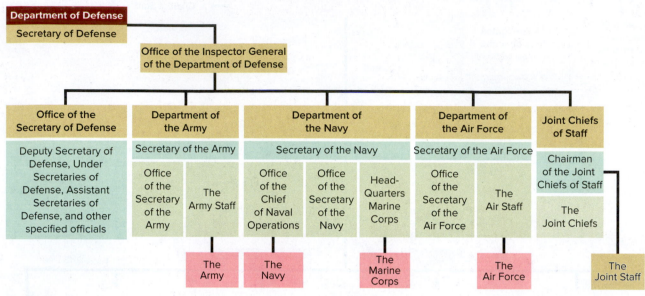

The Department of Defense oversees the operations of all of the nation's fighting forces.

Source: Department of Defense.

titular head of the intelligence community, the director oversees and coordinates intelligence gathering from sixteen agencies (see "Member Agencies of the Intelligence Community"). This office is also responsible to the legislative branch that created it, and the director often reports to select intelligence committees in each house.

Perhaps the best-known member of the nation's intelligence community is the Central Intelligence Agency (CIA). The CIA grew out of the Office of Strategic Services (OSS), which was created by Franklin D. Roosevelt in 1942 to collect and manage strategic information during World War II. The National Security Act of 1947 gave rise to its current moniker and function in providing national security intelligence to senior U.S. policymakers. Headed by a director who is appointed by the president and confirmed by the Senate, the agency collects intelligence through human and electronic sources, evaluates it, and provides assessments of threats to the nation's security. Although some agents in the field perform hazardous duty by infiltrating terrorist organizations and spying on foreign governments, the bulk of CIA employees spend their time translating and analyzing foreign newspapers, checking websites, and evaluating aerial maps and photographs.

Intelligence that has a bearing on national security is also gathered by other agencies in the Department of Defense, including various branches of

Member Agencies of the Intelligence Community

Central Intelligence Agency

Office of Intelligence and Counterintelligence (Department of Energy)

Intelligence and Analysis (Department of Homeland Security)

Intelligence and Research (Department of State)

Office of Intelligence and Analysis (Department of Treasury)

Defense Intelligence Agency (DOD)

Drug Enforcement Administration (DEA)

Federal Bureau of Investigation

National Geospatial Intelligence Agency (DOD)

National Reconnaissance Office (DOD)

National Security Agency (DOD)

Intelligence, Surveillance, and Reconnaissance (U.S. Air Force)

Military Intelligence (U.S. Army)

Coast Guard Intelligence

Marine Intelligence

Naval Intelligence

A multitude of government agencies attached to various cabinet offices aid in gathering intelligence that contributes to national security.

Source: U.S. Intelligence Community, http://www.intelligence.gov/mission/member-agencies.html.

the military; by the Federal Bureau of Investigation (FBI) and the Drug Enforcement Administration (DEA), which are both part of the Justice Department; and by other bodies. According to the 9/11 Commission, which investigated the attacks on the World Trade Center and the Pentagon, the failure of the intelligence community to identify and track the perpetrators was due in part to the lack of intelligence sharing among these agencies.[13] Reorganization under the supervision of the Office of the Director of National Intelligence was meant to integrate foreign, military, and domestic intelligence in defense of the homeland and of U.S. interests abroad.

Extensive surveillance operations were begun in the administration of George W. Bush following the 9/11 attacks and continued virtually unabated in the Obama and Trump administrations. Congress and presidents have jousted over the years in an attempt to bring government surveillance under control. Legislation in 2008 limited the use of wiretaps to terrorism and espionage cases and called for greater oversight, including advance approval by a secret court created under the Foreign Intelligence Surveillance Act of 1978. The **FISA court** is staffed by eleven judges appointed by the chief justice of the U.S. Supreme Court to serve seven-year terms. Legislation extending the life of the court and its jurisdiction has been passed several times since.

Civil libertarians have long been concerned that enhanced surveillance techniques used by intelligence agencies could be used for domestic spying. Their worst fears were realized when a former contract employee for the National Security Agency leaked information about the intelligence community's massive data-gathering operations. Edward Snowden released documents showing the government's collection of phone records from millions of U.S. citizens indiscriminately and in bulk—regardless of whether they were suspected of any wrongdoing. The Snowden revelations spurred investigation by an Obama-appointed commission that issued a three-hundred-page report listing forty-six recommendations, including one requiring the government to meet tougher standards before it can order a telecommunications company to turn over customer records. However, Congress voted to kill this rule, along with a series of other Internet privacy rules, in 2018.

Foreign Intelligence Surveillance Act court (FISA court) The secret court housed in the Justice Department and used to oversee requests by federal agencies for surveillance warrants based on suspected espionage or terrorism.

Other Executive Agencies

In an era dominated by concerns about global terror and the global economy, virtually no executive agency is without some role in advancing U.S. foreign policy goals. The Departments of Commerce and the Treasury help expand peaceful trade; the Drug Enforcement Administration attempts to interdict drug shipments; the Departments of Energy, Defense, and Commerce all monitor the types of technology we transfer to potentially hostile nations; and the Department of Health and Human Services provides technical support to nations combating HIV/AIDS. All of these activities advance the national security goal of creating "a more secure and prosperous world that benefits the American people and the world community."[14]

Congress's Role

Congress can play a key role in foreign and defense policy even if it is sometimes overshadowed by executive branch power. In Chapter 11, we learned that the Framers split authority for national security by authorizing the president to take immediate action to defend against attacks on U.S. interests but reserved to Congress the prerogative to declare war. We also learned that presidents have usually managed to secure authorization from Congress for waging war short of formal declarations. Nevertheless, Congress is not powerless to oppose presidential powers related to defense and security. Congress can cut off funding for war; it can reject presidential requests for authority to commence hostile activities; it can expand or reject presidential requests for foreign aid; and, by holding hearings on presidential policies and procedures, Congress can convey its own preferences. The House Permanent Select Committee on Intelligence and the Senate Select Committee on Intelligence receive briefings from the intelligence community, conduct oversight hearings, and authorize budgets for intelligence operations. In addition, the Senate can reject treaties with other nations. These checks on presidential authority are not merely hypothetical. In 2010, Congress barred the transfer of prisoners

Congressional Actions Influencing War Operations

Year	Congressional Action
1801	Amended treaty ending quasi-war with France, forced further negotiations
1919	Rejected Versailles Treaty that ended World War I
1919	Tie vote on resolution calling for withdrawal of U.S. troops intervening in Soviet Russia, prompting order for withdrawal within days
1923	Voted on resolution asking for immediate return of U.S. occupation troops from Germany, prompting withdrawal announcement within days
1970	Barred further military operations in Cambodia following U.S. withdrawal
1973	Forced U.S. air combat operations in Southeast Asia to end
1975	Rejected last-minute requests for aid to South Yemen
1993	Wrote into law Clinton administration promise to withdraw troops from Somalia
2011	House rebuked Obama for not obtaining congressional consent for military operations in Libya

Congress has only infrequently chosen to take actions curtailing war operations or to defy military operations undertaken by the president.

Sources: Adapted from Charles A. Stevenson, Congress at War: The Politics of Conflict Since 1789 (Dulles, VA: Potomac Books, 2007), 68; Carol M. Highsmith Archive, Library of Congress (LC-DIG-highsm-16167).

from Guantanamo Bay to the United States for trial, which President Obama sought in his effort to close down the facility.

Congress has successfully reined in presidential authority on a number of occasions (see "Congressional Actions Influencing War Termination"). Nevertheless, in times of international tension, support for presidential authority is sometimes difficult for congressional opponents to overcome. Such was the case in 2007, when a newly elected Democratic Congress repeatedly tried unsuccessfully to end the war in Iraq by rejecting President Bush's call for the infusion of more troops. In 2011, the House rebuked President Obama for not obtaining congressional consent before committing resources to a military operation in Libya designed to protect the civilian population. However, they did not take any direct action to end our involvement in the NATO-led mission.

One of Congress's principal foreign policy functions is to provide funding for military, diplomatic, and foreign aid programs. The cost of being a world superpower is enormous. Approximately 21 percent of the fiscal year 2018 federal budget (about $700 billion) is devoted to direct expenditures on national defense. This reflects a reversal of Obama-era reductions in defense spending when his administration emphasized a leaner but more flexible military and greater reliance on diplomacy. Trump-era budgets include large increases for modernizing battlefield weaponry and missile defense systems as well for upgrading our arsenal of nuclear weapons.

Other Actors

You will recall from Chapter 15 that the costs and benefits of national security are dispersed widely. As a result, policymakers receive advice from many segments of the political community. Both nonpartisan and partisan groups can play a significant advisory role. For example, the Council on Foreign Relations is a well-respected, nonpartisan body composed of scholars, corporate and government leaders, and other interested citizens who study foreign policy and try to influence its course through publications and meetings with policymakers. Think tanks with particular ideological perspectives also weigh in. The conservative Heritage Foundation and the more liberal-leaning Brookings Institution are among the most influential. Political movements sometimes spawn think tanks as incubators for new policies to advance their worldviews.

When it comes to policies dealing with particular countries or specific weapons, national security policy often involves the concentrated costs and benefits that generate intense competition by groups with an immediate interest in their outcomes. For example, political action committees, such as the powerful American Israel Public Affairs Committee, regularly donate millions of dollars to candidates who support the defense of Israel, whereas a number of smaller, vocal Muslim American groups espouse the cause of Islamic nations in the Middle East. Defense contractors are also active participants in foreign policy debates.

The Public's Role

Ultimately, foreign and defense policy is guided by the limits of public opinion. As we saw in Chapter 6, for the most part Americans display far less knowledge and interest in international and foreign affairs than in domestic policy matters. Some public opinion experts have employed the term **cognitive misers** in explaining the selective attention of Americans to foreign affairs and to the likelihood that they will employ mental shortcuts in fashioning opinions about foreign policy.[15] For example, the terms *hawk* or *dove* are shortcuts for those who advocate, respectively, military might or the use of diplomacy.

Even when Americans do express views on foreign policy, differences are sometimes sharp and yield mixed messages for policymakers. For example, there are generational differences in the way we view the role of military and diplomatic efforts to ensure peace. Whereas younger individuals see diplomacy as the best way to secure American interests, older generations are inclined to see military strength as the guarantor of our safety (see "Millennials Increasingly View 'Good Diplomacy' as Best Way to Ensure Peace").[16]

Although Americans give their leaders wide latitude in making foreign and defense policy decisions, they will react when they feel policies are counterproductive. Americans gave President Bush strong support for the war in Afghanistan following the September 11, 2001 attacks, but support was more muted for the war in Iraq, which many Americans could not directly connect with the events of September 11. Despite the quick victory over Saddam Hussein, national support dwindled as the occupation in Iraq dragged on and insurgent resistance increased. By April 2008, Gallup reported that 63 percent of the American public believed that the war was a mistake; and dissatisfaction with the war was partly responsible for Barack Obama's presidential victory over his Republican rival, John McCain.[17] Policymakers do not slavishly follow polls when dealing with national security issues; however, they do understand that the options they pursue must attract popular support in order for the policies to succeed, especially when those policies involve the possibility of American casualties.

Millennials Increasingly View 'Good Diplomacy' As Best Way to Ensure Peace
% who say diplomacy, rather than military strength, is the best way to ensure peace.

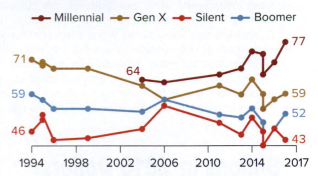

American youth are more likely than their elders to believe we should rely more heavily on good diplomacy than military might to ensure peace.

Source: Pew Research Center, Survey of U.S. adults conducted June 8-18, 2017.

> **cognitive misers** Term referring to mental shortcuts Americans sometimes use to simplify their understanding of government policies, particularly in the arena of foreign affairs. For example, the terms "hawk" or "dove" are shortcuts respectively for those who advocate military might or the use of diplomacy.

TOOLS OF FOREIGN POLICY

Nations, particularly those with significant resources, have a variety of means for influencing the actions of others. Military power is the bluntest weapon in any nation's foreign policy arsenal; and nuclear weaponry, for those who have it, inspires the most fear. However, nations also attempt to influence the actions of others through diplomacy, the promise of financial aid, and support from international organizations.

Military Power

You may have heard the saying that "War is the continuation of politics by other means." The author was the Prussian military historian and theorist Carl von Clausewitz (1780–1831), who was reflecting the realist position that military power is a nation's most potent resource in furthering its interests. Military might is both an offensive weapon and a powerful deterrent. Enemies can be dissuaded from using military force if their opponent has clear military superiority. As a result, one of the most important jobs of a nation's leaders is to ensure that the nation has sufficient military power to dissuade others from attacking and to successfully defend the country if it is attacked.

Defense Spending

Global military and arms expenditures are currently running at several trillion annually—and rising. The figure here lists some of the world's top spenders in 2016. Defenders of U.S. spending point out that our nation provides protection for many other countries and contributes to global stability. Critics argue that our allies should pick up more of the tab for their own defense and that current levels of spending are unsustainable given the current level of debt.

Questions:

1. How many top spenders are traditional U.S. allies?
2. How might our allies respond if the United States cut back on its own military spending?
3. Why do relatively small countries like Saudi Arabia and Japan spend so much on defense?
4. What factors might account for China's rise to second place (behind the United States) in military spending?

Billions in 2016 Dollars

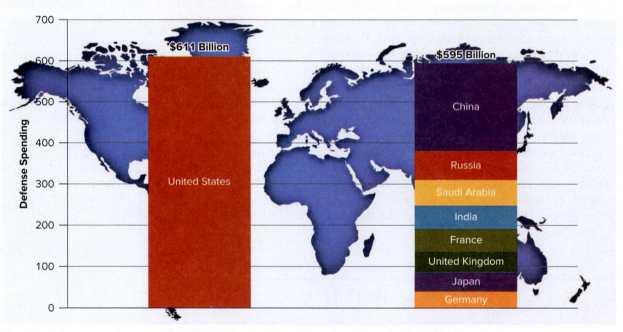

The United States spends more on the military than the next eight top spending nations combined.

Source: Stockholm International Peace Research Institute, SIPRI Military Expenditure Database, April 2017. Data are for 2016. Compiled by Peter G. Peterson Foundation

Nations spend enormous sums on national defense. Even small nations with anemic economies find it necessary to spend significant sums in order to ward off potential aggressors. The defense budget of the United States, however, dwarfs those of all other nations. In 2016, the United States spent more on defense than the next eight highest defense spending nations combined (see "Global Perspectives").[18] Relative to total gross domestic product (GDP), however, the United States spends about 3.3 percent of GDP on military operations; by comparison, the Russian Federation, another superpower, spends about 5 percent of its GDP. Some smaller nations, among them Saudi Arabia and Oman, spend 10 percent or more.[19]

Where does all of this money go? For the United States, the biggest expenditure is for personnel, about 1.3 million active-duty military troops and thousands of civilian employees stationed here and at bases in 150 nations around the world. Operations maintenance and weapons procurement are the next highest costs, with smaller amounts going to research, nuclear programs, and construction.[20] In addition, there are scores of bombs and missiles and new weaponry—including an air defense system and low-yield nuclear weapons—currently under development. This impressive array of human and material resources has purchased a high level of security. But, as September 11, 2001, made clear, no nation's defenses are impenetrable.

Despite these impressive assets, the war in Iraq strained some of our resources, especially military personnel. The war required more personnel and money than its architects in the White House foresaw. Although Saddam Hussein was toppled from power in a relatively short time, the insurgency that resulted from the subsequent U.S. occupation proved long and deadly. Our experiences in fighting terrorism led the Obama administration to call for a more mobile and technologically nimble military with reduced expenditures on Cold War–era weaponry. The Trump administration has reversed course and called for an increase in expenditures for military and nuclear hardware.

Diplomacy

Diplomacy is the practice of using peaceful means to resolve conflict. It involves the use of incentives and deterrents in order to build alliances and support for a nation's policies. Often, diplomacy involves the use of personal persuasion, as when the president or secretary of state meets with world leaders to explain our positions and build support for our policies. Presidents have met regularly in recent years with Israeli and Palestinian leaders in an attempt to broker a lasting peace, although none has proved enduring. Sometimes diplomacy involves working with other nations as intermediaries. Other times, diplomacy involves the use of multinational coalitions to provide joint security. For example, the North Atlantic Treaty Organization (NATO), founded in 1949, seeks to provide mutual deterrence and defense against common enemies as well as to promote consultation, crisis management, and economic partnerships among member nations. Since the breakup of the former Soviet Union, NATO membership has expanded to include Estonia, Latvia, and Lithuania, as well as several formerly communist nations that were part of the Soviet sphere, among them the Czech Republic, Hungary, Poland, Bulgaria, Romania, Slovakia, and Slovenia.

Diplomacy, usually the domain of specialists in the Department of State, is a subtle weapon of foreign policy. Success depends on a number of factors, including the skillful deployment of rewards and punishments, the willingness of parties to negotiate, and domestic pressures faced by national leaders. Diplomats, like skilled chess players, must think several moves ahead, recognizing that any action they take will evoke a response for which they must be prepared.

diplomacy The practice of using peaceful means to resolve conflict.

Foreign Aid

As the richest nation in the world, the United States can make friends and influence the policies of other nations by making loans and grants available to them. Some of this money is designated as military aid; the recipient can use it to enhance its own internal security in ways approved by the United States. Often, military aid is returned to the United States when it is used to buy weaponry and armaments from American firms. Grants and loans may enhance the security of both donor and receiver. For example, the United States gives some Middle Eastern countries money for law enforcement designed to stem terrorism and provides funds to Latin American countries to curb drug trafficking. The United States also makes money available to developing countries to assist them in expanding their economies, particularly when cash infusions provide a measure of social stability for the impoverished. Assistance is given for humanitarian causes such as combating the spread of HIV/AIDS. Finally, the United States provides assistance to multinational organizations such as the United Nations and the World Bank to accomplish many of these same objectives.

In all, the United States provides assistance to over 180 countries and international bodies. Among the largest recipients in recent years have been Israel, Egypt, and Afghanistan. Since September 11, 2001, aid has increased for Pakistan, Jordan, Indonesia, and countries in sub-Saharan Africa, which are seen as key partners in the war on terrorism.

Foreign Aid as a Percentage of the U.S. Budget

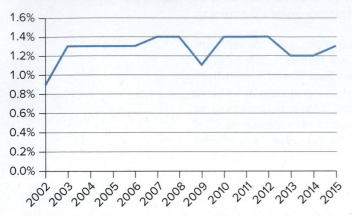

Although the United States has increased nonmilitary foreign assistance in recent years, foreign aid continues to consume approximately 1 percent of the U.S. budget.

Source: USAID.

These programs are administered by a variety of agencies including the U.S. Agency for International Development (USAID), the Treasury Department, the Department of Defense, and the State Department. The House International Relations Committee and the Senate Foreign Relations Committee have primary congressional responsibility for authorizing foreign aid programs, whereas the Appropriations Committee in each house appropriates the funds.[21]

Polls have shown that many Americans are not convinced of the effectiveness of aid programs. In fact, it is often difficult to prove that these funds achieve the desired ends. Nevertheless, ending these programs would limit the tools available to policymakers for achieving U.S. security goals and could push some nations into alliance with our enemies. Although the dollar amount of foreign aid has increased in recent years, after a long period of decline, it still constitutes just about 1 percent of the national budget (see "Foreign Aid as a Percentage of the U.S. Budget"). The United States is the largest international economic aid donor in absolute terms, but when aid is calculated as a percentage of gross domestic product, it is the smallest contributor among the major donor governments.[22]

Working with International Partners

The threats that our nation faces are not solely military in nature. We face economic threats in the form of oil-supply disruptions, public health threats like Zika virus, and threats to the security of our friends and neighbors caused by political upheaval or rampant poverty. To cope with such threats, the United States works with a variety of international organizations to share information and resources, to influence world opinion, and to develop solutions to problems that cross national boundaries.

In coping with potential health crises, for example, the United States works closely with the World Health Organization (WHO), an arm of the United Nations. WHO monitors disease outbreaks, assesses the performance of health systems around the globe, serves as a repository for research on major diseases affecting the international community, and provides technical support to countries coping with medical emergencies. For example, it assists nations facing the Zika virus with medical care and advice. In recent years, WHO played a leading role in combating the swine flu pandemic and the Ebola outbreak in West Africa.

Another international partner is the World Bank, which offers financial and technical assistance to developing countries. Comprising 189 member nations, the World Bank provides low-interest loans, interest-free credit, and grants to developing countries for education, health, infrastructure development, communications, and many other purposes. By tradition, the bank's president is a U.S. national and is nominated by the United States, the bank's largest shareholder.

Diplomats in the State Department build support for American policy through bilateral discussions with individual nations and through multilateral organizations such as NATO. But it is also necessary at times to engage all nations in dialogue in order to avert war, broker solutions to international crises, or work cooperatively to address humanitarian needs. The United Nations (UN) provides a forum for such activities. Chartered in 1945, the UN was intended to promote international peace and security as well as to facilitate cooperation in solving international economic, social, cultural, and humanitarian problems. The Security Council, which is charged with settling disputes and authorizing military action, comprises ten rotating member nations and five permanent members: China, France, Russia, the United Kingdom, and the United States. Any permanent member nation can prevent action by exercising its veto power.

The United States has met with varying degrees of success in securing UN support for its foreign policy agenda. At the urging of the United States, the Security Council voted in August

The UN Security Council is charged with settling international disputes and authorizing military action. It comprises ten rotating member nations and five permanent members: China, France, Russia, the United Kingdom, and the United States.

1990 to condemn Iraq's invasion of Kuwait, and subsequently to use UN armed forces to oppose Iraq's occupation of its neighbor. U.S. commanders led multinational forces in the Persian Gulf War, which lasted six weeks and resulted in the Iraqi withdrawal from Kuwait. Subsequently, the UN agreed to monitor Iraq's compliance with a resolution requiring the country to eliminate its weapons of mass destruction. The United States and the UN also have cooperated in a number of peacekeeping operations, including a 1999 mission in Kosovo. In 2003, however, the United States was unable to persuade the UN to authorize a mission to disarm Iraq of the weapons of mass destruction it suspected Iraq of having. Although UN members supported the use of economic sanctions, Security Council members, including France, Russia, and Germany, questioned the reliability of intelligence estimates on such weapons and declined to support a military invasion. Instead, the United States formed its own "coalition of the willing," including Great Britain, Australia, Italy, and many smaller nations, to topple the Iraqi regime. The UN has been more willing to consider sanctions against North Korea and Iran in order to stop their development of nuclear weapons. The UN has also sponsored negotiating conferences to bring warring parties together, such as the government of Syrian president Bashar al-Assad and rebel leaders engaged in the Syrian civil war.

CONFRONTING THE FUTURE

From the end of World War II until the dismantling of the Berlin Wall in 1989, the world was dominated by two superpowers in a bipolar world. Each held the other in check with the threat of sufficient nuclear force to obliterate it. The superpowers often fought each other by proxy, taking up the cause of surrogates, as in Vietnam and in Afghanistan during the 1979 Soviet invasion, which pitted the various opposition groups known as mujahideen against the Red Army. Since the demise of the Soviet empire, nations have struggled to come to grips with the fact that there remains but one major superpower in a unipolar world.

That is not to say that the United States can automatically get its way. It continues to rely on its allies to advance its trade and security interests, and upon all countries to confront global threats such as terrorism.[23] And the rise of a unipolar world with the United States as its leader has not gone unchallenged. Russia's invasion of neighboring Georgia in

©Majid Saeedi/Getty Images

Hassan Rouhani, president of Iran, entered into an agreement to halt the country's nuclear program with six major world powers, but the future of the agreement was cast into doubt when President Trump withdrew U.S. support for the pact.

2008 as a response to the U.S.-instigated expansion of NATO into former Soviet territories, its seizure of Ukraine's Crimean peninsula in order to shore up its hold of the Ukraine region, and its intervention on the side of dictator Bashar al-Assad in the Syrian civil war all underscore that Russia has not given up its global ambitions. And its interference in elections in Europe and the United States indicate Russian aims to subvert democratic institutions abroad while strengthening its influence over former Soviet states. The United States must also address the growing challenges it faces from new sources such as China, whose rapid rise poses risks to our nation's dominance as an economic and military power.

The Nuclear Threat

Since the end of the Cold War, the United States and Russia have destroyed a significant portion of the nuclear arsenals that they once maintained. Nevertheless, the United States still has more than four thousand operational weapons and nuclear weapon stockpiles. It is estimated that Russia maintains about the same number of active and stockpiled nuclear warheads. Weapons once maintained in former territories were all to have been returned to Russia.[24]

Despite treaties signed as recently as 2010 calling for the continued reduction of nuclear warheads by Russia and the United States, both nations have signaled their intention to bypass these agreements and renew the nuclear arms race. Russia has unveiled plans for "nuclear-powered, nuclear-tipped cruise missiles with nearly infinite range and nuclear-armed underwater drones designed to creep up on enemy ports before destroying them."[25] The United States has responded by calling for an upgrade of its own nuclear arsenal to include small-scale nuclear weapons that might be used in response to attacks of a nonnuclear nature, including cyber attacks against critical U.S. infrastructure.[26] President Trump has also signaled his intention to withdraw as well from the Intermediate Nuclear Force Treaty (INF) negotiated by President Ronald Reagan and Soviet leader Mikhail Gorbachev in 1987 which led to the elimination of an entire category of nuclear missiles and the removal of more than 2,500 missiles from installations across Europe.

The escalation of nuclear weapons development reverses decades of progress made to reduce the nuclear threat across the globe. Under a treaty signed in 1968 and reaffirmed in 1995, the world's largest nuclear powers instituted measures to prevent countries without nuclear weapons from initiating weapons production. The Treaty on the Non-Proliferation of Nuclear Arms secured the pledges of 191 nations including five nuclear-weapon states to resist nuclear development. Today, at least eight nations are part of the "nuclear club": the United States, Russia, the United Kingdom, France, China, India, Pakistan, and most likely Israel. South Africa has dismantled the nuclear arsenal that it once maintained. Some of the nuclear players are located in the most unstable regions of the world. India and Pakistan, for example, harbor long-standing grievances stemming from the partition of the subcontinent by Great Britain in 1947.

Perhaps the greatest threats come from autocratic countries in critical regions of the world that aspire to join the nuclear club. North Korea's leader, Kim Jong-un, has test-fired missiles capable of carrying nuclear warheads to the shores of the United States and is believed to already have a small cache of nuclear weapons along with enough uranium to produce an additional six nuclear bombs each year.[27] President Trump has entered into talks with Kim Jong-un ostensibly designed to dismantle North Korea's nuclear program, but the long-term success of these discussions is in doubt.

Iran's nuclear ambitions are also a major concern for the world. Iran has for some time developed reactor-grade plutonium, which it claimed was to be used for energy production, but some commentators have portrayed this as a step in the creation of weapons-grade nuclear material. In 2015, President Obama and the leaders of five other nations signed a nuclear agreement with Iran to restrict the production of weapons-grade nuclear material, reduce its current stockpile, limit research and development, and severely cut back the number of centrifuges used in the enrichment of uranium. In addition, the agreement allowed inspections of nuclear sites by an international monitoring agency. In return, signatory nations agreed to lift economic sanctions that had crippled the Iranian economy. Under the fifteen-year agreement, sanctions could be reimposed at any time if Iran did not meet its responsibilities. The Trump administration expressed skepticism about Iran's fulfillment of the agreement and announced in May 2018 that the United States was withdrawing from the agreement.

Perhaps even more disconcerting than the prospect of unstable nations obtaining nuclear weaponry is the threat of non-nation-state actors, such as extremist groups, gaining access to nuclear material. Although security experts believe extremist groups would not be able to develop a nuclear bomb—let alone the means of delivering one—they could mix radioactive material with other explosive agents in a "dirty bomb," should they be able to obtain the raw materials. The U.S. Nuclear Regulatory Commission has determined that although the explosive impact of a "dirty bomb" would not be much greater than that of a conventional bomb, such an explosion could create widespread panic, contaminate property, and necessitate costly cleanup.[28]

Since the Reagan administration, the United States has been developing a missile defense system that would potentially shield America and its allies from incoming nuclear missiles by exploding them in midflight. The Bush administration proposed deploying components of the system in the former Soviet satellites of Poland and the Czech Republic. The Obama administration announced it would scrap the deployment of missile defenses in Eastern Europe and instead develop a more mobile and flexible system designed to shoot down short- and medium-range missiles likely to be delivered by rogue states with nuclear ambitions.

The Terrorist Threat

The roots of terrorism are many and complex. They include, but are not limited to, extremist ideology, feelings of powerlessness, and lack of economic opportunity. The nature of the terrorist threat facing the United States today is linked to Islamic fundamentalism, which grew in response to the partition of Palestine and the establishment of Israel under UN General Assembly Resolution 181 in 1947 (see the discussion in "Threats Posted by Regional Conflicts," later in this chapter). Palestinians who were displaced by the resolution were dealt another blow in 1967, when Israel's army preempted Egypt's call for an Arab invasion by capturing Arab territories in the Six-Day War. Unable to match the firepower of Israel and its Western allies, Islamic militants supporting the reclamation of Palestinian territories developed a sophisticated network of terrorist supporters in Muslim countries throughout the Middle East and South Asia. Often aided by state sponsors such as Iran and Syria, these militants spread terrorist techniques worldwide, organizing the attacks on Israeli athletes at the Munich Olympics in 1972; the bombing of Pan Am Flight 103 in 1988; the bombing of U.S. embassies in Kenya and Tanzania in 1998; the attack on the USS Cole in 2000; and, of course, the attacks on the World Trade Center and the Pentagon on September 11, 2001. Although the terrorist network comprises various distinct factions and movements, it is united by an animus for Israel and the Western nations supporting it.

Until 2001, the United States had treated terrorism much like a criminal activity, protecting targets as best it could and prosecuting terrorists as criminals. For example, suspects were prosecuted and convicted in U.S. courts for their role in the 1993 World Trade Center bombing and the 1998 U.S. embassy bombings in Kenya and Tanzania. The trials produced significant evidence implicating Al Qaeda and Osama bin Laden in terrorist crimes. After September 11, 2001, American strategy changed. Given the evidence that the attacks were directed by bin Laden and that he was being harbored by the Taliban regime in Afghanistan, the United States and a coalition of allies—with widespread international support—attacked that country, replacing the Taliban government with a new regime led by Hamid Karzai. However, there was less international support for the second phase of the American response, the invasion of Iraq.

The Iraq War proved hugely unpopular with both world and American public opinion, especially after waves of sectarian violence resulted in thousands of American and Iraqi deaths. The violence was abetted by Syrians, Iranians, and Saudis who streamed over the porous borders of Iraq to exploit the chaos and foment discontent with the American

U.S. drone strikes into Pakistan have been a continuous source of tension between the two countries.

occupiers. The new government, installed with American help, lacked the cohesion necessary to enhance security and rebuild the country. Nevertheless, as the Bush administration came to an end, Iraqi prime minister Nouri al-Maliki was eager to negotiate an end to the American occupation, even while violence in neighboring Afghanistan was once again on the rise.

The United States retained a small contingent of troops in Iraq after the official end of its combat mission in August 2010 in the hopes that the newly installed government would be able to provide for its own security. However, continued violence in the region drove President Trump to increase the American troop level to over 14,000 and to step up U.S. airstrikes against radical Islamists aligned with the Taliban.

The unstable political environment proved fertile ground for the rise of militant groups, the most extreme of which, ISIS, plunged the country into civil war and expanded the conflict into regional warfare involving Iraq's neighbors. By late 2014, the United States commenced air strikes in Syria and the president received authority from Congress to arm and train Syrian rebels in an attempt to contain the ISIS threat. Although ISIS-held territories have since been scaled back, ISIS remains a threat, both in this region riven by sectarian divisions and globally, due to its commitment to using terrorist tactics to strike abroad as bombings in Paris, Brussels, and elsewhere attest.

Pakistan poses an equally daunting threat, as terrorist groups have increased their presence there. The raid on Osama bin Laden in 2011 revealed that his mansion was located near a military school, raising questions about whether that country had been harboring the 9/11 mastermind. The situation in Pakistan is particularly dangerous because Pakistan is a nuclear power, and world leaders worry about the possibility that terrorists might gain access to nuclear materials. U.S. relations with Pakistan have been frayed as a result of repeated U.S. drone strikes into Pakistan, some of which have resulted in the deaths of innocent Pakistanis.

Threats Posed by Regional Conflicts

As we have learned, the world system is anarchic in the sense that there is no designated umpire to settle regional conflicts. At the same time, nations today are connected by a vast array of economic, communication, and transportation networks, so that upheavals in one region are likely to have an impact elsewhere. A serious conflict in the Middle East is likely to disrupt oil supplies and send world markets reeling. An infectious disease outbreak in Africa or Asia can result in a pandemic that all nations must confront. Globalization has tied the fate of nations much more closely together than in the past. Regional problems that once might not have drawn close scrutiny by a major power can no longer be ignored.

Middle East The roots of Middle East tensions are numerous, complex, and not easily resolved. Although Jews have long claimed religious roots in the Middle East, modern Israel emerged from a conflict between Zionists emigrating from Russia in the early twentieth century to escape persecution and Palestinians already settled in the region. Although both groups laid claim to the territory, Britain was awarded control of the region after World War I by the League of Nations. Britain attempted to mediate ongoing conflict between Jews and Arabs but abandoned the territory in 1947 when the United Nations Special Commission on Palestine recommended the partition of Palestine into separate Jewish and Arab states. The Jewish state was officially established on May 14, 1948, when the Jewish fighters secured military control of the region the UN had partitioned for them. Nevertheless, fighting between Arab and Jewish settlers continued unabated and many Arabs called for the destruction of Israel.

In 1967, a Six-Day War broke out, spawned by border disputes between Israel and her neighbors. Israel captured the Golan Heights from Syria, the West Bank from Jordan, and the Gaza Strip and Sinai Peninsula from Egypt, displacing thousands of Palestinians. Despite efforts by the United Nations to arrange a trade of captured lands for a peace agreement, the Palestinian Liberation Organization (PLO), which claimed leadership of those displaced by the war, refused to drop its support for the destruction of Israel. Shortly thereafter, Israelis began building permanent settlements in the occupied regions, intensifying Palestinian resentment.

Over the next few decades, American presidents made numerous attempts to broker agreements among regional leaders. One major breakthrough occurred in 1979 when President Jimmy Carter arranged a peace treaty between Egypt and Israel. A second major breakthrough occurred in 1993 with the signing of the Oslo Accords, in which the PLO recognized Israel's right to exist in exchange for the promise of Israeli withdrawal from unspecified territory in the West Bank and the Gaza Strip. Talks implementing the accords with the goal of creating a two-state solution—a secure Israel with official recognition by previously belligerent nations, and an independent Palestinian state—were intended to continue for a number of years until a final settlement was reached. Since then, Israel has ceded some local control to Palestinians in the occupied territories, but neither side has been willing to bring negotiations to a conclusion. Israel has complained about continuing Palestinian terrorism, and the Palestinians have complained about Israeli foot-dragging and settlement expansion in regions that were supposed to be returned to Palestinian control.

President Obama made repeated overtures to both Israeli and Palestinian leaders to reopen a peace initiative in the region with the express goal of achieving the two-state solution. Peace efforts were complicated in 2011 with the reconciliation of two rival Palestinian factions, one of which (Hamas) is a sworn enemy of Israel. The revolution in Egypt that brought down the regime of Hosni Mubarak raised additional uncertainties as militant forces hostile to Israel gained political muscle and threatened the long-standing peace between the two nations.

In 2017, President Trump recognized Jerusalem as Israel's capital and announced plans to relocate the U.S. embassy there, a controversial move since the Palestinians also claim the city as their capital. Trump's plan upended years of U.S. foreign policy, which held that the status of Jerusalem would be determined only after peace in the region had been secured. By making the move now, Trump reasoned he could jump-start stalled negotiations between the Israelis and the Palestinians.

Africa Africa has been riddled by civil wars pitting ethnic and tribal rivals against each other and resulting in displacement, starvation, and massive loss of life. Conflict in the Darfur region of Sudan between Arabs and non-rebels (some of them supported by the government of Sudan) resulted in more than 400,000 deaths from violence, while disease and displacement led to as many as 2.5 million more deaths. Like the ethnic conflict between Hutus and Tutsis in Rwanda years earlier, the carnage in the Darfur region has been called genocide by the U.S. government. In 2006, a peace agreement was reached between Sudan and some rebel groups, and the United Nations sent a peacekeeping force to the region. However, Sudan objected to the presence of peacekeepers, and violence continued between various factions and tribes. A referendum in early 2011 led to the partitioning of the nation. In July 2011, South Sudan became the world's newest country. However, internal conflicts led to civil war until a power sharing agreement between warring parties was reached in 2018. Nevertheless, peace in the region remains exceptionally fragile.

Other recent conflicts have involved Uganda (1987–present), Angola (1974–2002), Sierra Leone (1991–2002), Liberia (1999–2003), and the Democratic Republic of Congo (1998–2004). The death toll in these conflicts has been enormous. Over four million deaths have been attributed to the Congo wars alone, with most victims dying from starvation and disease. The lack of economic development, slow progress toward modernization, and the persistence of tribal and ethnic rivalries plague the region. Even once-stable nations such as Kenya and Zimbabwe have experienced instability in recent years. Zimbabwe's former

The Nigerian terrorist group Boko Haram has claimed responsibility for kidnapping nearly four hundred school girls from their homes in the northeastern part of the state.

president Robert Mugabe, who helped bring independence to his country, led a regime that became increasingly repressive and corrupt. Mugabe won his seventh term as president in 2013 in an election fraught with charges of fraud and corruption. A military takeover in the country ended his thirty-seven-year rule in 2017. Continued political instability has made many Western nations reluctant to make needed investments in the region.

Nigeria has witnessed high levels of violence in recent years as well. A terrorist group known as Boko Haram seeks to overthrow the current government and replace it with an Islamist state. The group has attacked Christians and bombed schools and public facilities. Its tactics include kidnapping. They have claimed responsibility for taking nearly four hundred girls from schools in the northeastern part of the state, though many were later released.

Events in Africa may not present an immediate threat to American national security, but widespread unrest and poverty breed extremism as well as disease. A widespread outbreak of the Ebola virus in 2014 killed thousands, forcing some countries to close their borders and mobilizing world leaders in an effort to prevent a global pandemic. These conditions present opportunities for terrorists to exploit tensions and build safe harbors for their ideologies of hatred. As a result, American policymakers cannot afford to ignore the challenges posed by events on this continent.

The Rise of China

The People's Republic of China will play an increasingly important role in world affairs in the coming decades. Despite its communist government, China has adapted since the death of its founder, Mao Zedong, to a Western-style commercial economy, one that has been growing rapidly in the recent past. China has quickly become the second-largest economy in the world, behind only the United States. Reasons for this growth include China's ability to keep costs of production low, to attract foreign capital, and to build huge trade surpluses with other nations that buy its relatively inexpensive products. In 2015, Americans spent some $375 billion more on Chinese goods than the Chinese spent on U.S. products, and until a recent slowdown in China, the gap was growing by more than 25 percent per year.[29] President Trump has frequently criticized China for "dumping" cheap goods on the world market while keeping out American products. In response, he placed a series of tariffs on some of China's leading exports.

With the money that it receives, China is able to flex its military and economic muscles. China is now the second-largest military spender, behind only the United States. It has increased its military spending by double digits every year since 1993. Military analysts say that China is purchasing increasingly sophisticated weaponry. They note, for example, a recent successful test of an antisatellite missile, which destroyed a defunct Chinese weather satellite, and the deployment of a state-of-the-art jet fighter, the J-10, which Chinese and foreign experts have described as a breakthrough for the Chinese defense industry.

China is also using its financial clout to finance U.S. debt. China is now second only to Japan as a foreign holder of U.S. securities. These securities include Treasury debt, U.S. agency debt, U.S. corporate debt, and U.S. equities. Given the United States' relatively low savings rate, the U.S. economy depends heavily on foreign capital inflows from countries with high savings rates, such as China, to help promote growth and to fund the nation's federal budget deficit, as we discussed in Chapter 15.[30] China's rapid economic growth is also an increasing concern for those worried about climate change.

In addition to trade, two flash points continue to dominate U.S.-China relations: territorial disputes over islands in the South China Sea and China's record on human rights. China considers several island chains off its coast part of its own territory, sparking disputes with Taiwan, Malaysia, and the Philippines regarding maritime rights in the area. These tensions have placed the United States in a difficult position since it wishes to maintain peace in the region and keep sea lanes open for its own vessels. With regard to human rights, American diplomats seem content to lecture Chinese leaders on the importance of human rights without letting the subject interfere with negotiations on other matters such as trade.

©Peter Dazeley/Getty Images

FOREIGN POLICY AND CIVIC ENGAGEMENT TODAY

As we have seen, Americans appear to pay less attention to matters of foreign policy than to domestic policy, except during major crises or catastrophes such as the terrorist attacks of September 11, 2001. One reason for this relative inattention is that most Americans believe there is little they can do to make a difference in this arena. Of course, voters can voice their preferences at the polls. But, as we learned in earlier chapters, elections are blunt instruments that do not address the complexities of policymaking. Even when the voters register their disagreement with a policy, as they did in 2006 and 2008 when opposition to the Iraq War produced electoral change, altering course in foreign policy is not easily or quickly accomplished. Still, there are ways in which individual Americans can make a positive contribution to the lives of others and enhance the humanitarian reputation of the United States throughout the world.

Each year, voluntary citizens' groups called **nongovernmental organizations (NGOs)** send volunteers and money all over the world to feed the hungry, alleviate poverty, combat disease, educate the young, and provide expertise to help local populations build civil societies and the infrastructure needed to succeed in development. NGOs perform a variety of service and humanitarian functions, bring citizen concerns to governments, advocate and monitor policies, and encourage political participation.

nongovernmental organizations (NGOs) Voluntary citizens' groups organized for a variety of charitable and humanitarian purposes.

NGOs offer many and varied opportunities for Americans interested in working to help others in foreign lands. Some NGOs are well known, such as the American Red Cross and Save the Children. Many are associated with religious organizations, such as the Quakers. For instance, the American Friends Service Committee operates summer internships around the globe.

soft power The ability to persuade others without coercion.

Such opportunities not only provide direct help to those in need but also spread goodwill. This goodwill is part of **soft power**, the ability to shape the preferences of others without coercion.[31] Soft power is spread through the sharing of American values, customs, and culture. Through civic outreach, we foster cooperation and inspire others to share our concerns for fairness and just outcomes. We motivate others to want the same outcomes that we want.

Thinking It Through >>>

Learning Objective: Describe potential challenges to U.S. foreign policy.

Review: Confronting the Future

Describe the challenges facing U.S. foreign policy makers in each of the areas listed below. Identify what you believe to be the greatest of these challenges, and state your reasons for holding that position.

- ISIS
- Terrorism
- Nuclear proliferation
- Tensions in the Middle East

Summary

1. **What are the major goals of American foreign policy?**
   - Foreign policy seeks to secure the nation's defense and to promote its economic and ideological interests.
   - Defining a country's national interest involves making strategic choices about how best to use military, economic, and moral strength to keep the nation safe and secure.
   - Foreign policy is guided by theories such as realism, foreign policy liberalism, and idealism

2. **Who are the principal actors in the foreign-policy-making process?**
   - The president plays the primary role in foreign policy making through executive agencies that include the National Security Council, the Director of National Intelligence, the Department of State, and the Department of Defense.

   - Congress also plays a role through its appropriations and approval of international treaties by the Senate.
   - Foreign policy making can also involve interest groups, defense contractors, think tanks, nongovernmental organizations, and the general public, whose support is needed to sustain policies.

3. **What are the tools that foreign policy makers have at their disposal?**
   - Foreign policy makers employ military powers, diplomacy, and foreign aid in advancing U.S. interests.
   - They also seek to forge ties with other nations and with multinational organizations to achieve shared objectives.
   - Foreign policy makers will use these tools to confront such future challenges as the terrorist threat, the nuclear threat, regional conflicts, and the rise of China as a major economic and military power.

Appendix

★ The Constitution of the United States of America (Annotated)

©Tetra Images/Corbis

The Constitution of the United States of America[1]

>> See Chapter 1 for a comparison of the democratic form of government with other forms and reasons for civic engagement.

We the People of the United States, in Order to form a more perfect Union, establish Justice, insure domestic Tranquility, provide for the common defence, promote the general Welfare, and secure the Blessings of Liberty to ourselves and our Posterity, do ordain and establish this Constitution for the United States of America.

ARTICLE I

SECTION 1

All legislative Powers herein granted shall be vested in a Congress of the United States, which shall consist of a Senate and House of Representatives.

SECTION 2

>> The states set suffrage requirements subject to the Fourteenth, Fifteenth, Nineteenth, Twenty-fourth, and Twenty-sixth Amendments.

The House of Representatives shall be composed of Members chosen every second Year by the People of the several States, and the Electors in each State shall have the Qualifications requisite for Electors of the most numerous Branch of the State Legislature.

No Person shall be a Representative who shall not have attained to the Age of twenty five Years, and been seven Years a Citizen of the United States, and who shall not, when elected, be an Inhabitant of that State in which he shall be chosen.

>> The three-fifths compromise was made obsolete by the Thirteenth and Fourteenth Amendments.

[Representatives and direct Taxes[2] shall be apportioned among the several States which may be included within this Union, according to their respective Numbers, which shall be determined by adding to the whole Number of free Persons, including those bound to Service for a Term of Years, and excluding Indians not taxed, three fifths of all other Persons.][3] The actual Enumeration shall be made within three Years after the first Meeting of the Congress of the United States, and within every subsequent Term of ten Years, in such Manner as they shall by Law direct. The Number of Representatives shall not exceed one for every thirty Thousand, but each State shall have at Least one Representative; and until such enumeration shall be made, the State of New Hampshire shall be entitled to chuse three, Massachusetts eight, Rhode-Island and Providence Plantations one, Connecticut five, New-York six, New Jersey four, Pennsylvania eight, Delaware one, Maryland six, Virginia ten, North Carolina five, South Carolina five, and Georgia three.

When vacancies happen in the Representation from any State, the Executive Authority thereof shall issue Writs of Election to fill such Vacancies.

The House of Representatives shall chuse their Speaker and other Officers; and shall have the sole Power of Impeachment.

SECTION 3

>> See Chapter 11 for differences between the House of Representatives and the Senate.

The Senate of the United States shall be composed of two Senators from each State, chosen by the Legislature thereof for six Years; and each Senator shall have one Vote.

>> This clause was modified by the Seventeenth Amendment that provides for the direct election of senators.

Immediately after they shall be assembled in Consequence of the first Election, they shall be divided as equally as may be into three Classes. The Seats of the Senators of the first Class shall be vacated at the Expiration of the second Year, of the second Class at the Expiration of the fourth Year; and of the third Class at the Expiration of the sixth Year, so that one third may be chosen every second Year; and if Vacancies happen by Resignation, or otherwise, during the Recess of the Legislature of any State, the Executive thereof may make temporary Appointments until the next Meeting of the Legislature, which shall then fill such Vacancies.

No Person shall be a Senator who shall not have attained to the Age of thirty Years, and been nine Years a Citizen of the United States, and who shall not, when elected, be an Inhabitant of that State for which he shall be chosen.

The Vice President of the United States shall be President of the Senate, but shall have no Vote, unless they be equally divided.

The Senate shall chuse their other Officers, and also a President pro tempore, in the Absence of the Vice President, or when he shall exercise the Office of President of the United States.

The Senate shall have the sole Power to try all Impeachments. When sitting for that Purpose, they shall be on Oath or Affirmation. When the President of the United States is tried, the Chief Justice shall preside: And no person shall be convicted without the Concurrence of two thirds of the Members present.

Judgment in Cases of Impeachment shall not extend further than to removal from Office, and disqualification to hold and enjoy any Office of honor, Trust or Profit under the United States: but the Party convicted shall nevertheless be liable and subject to Indictment, Trial, Judgment and Punishment, according to Law.

SECTION 4

The Times, Place and Manner of holding Elections for Senators and Representatives, shall be prescribed in each State by the Legislature thereof; but the Congress may at any time by Law make or alter such Regulations, except as to the Places of chusing Senators.

The Congress shall assemble at least once in every Year and such Meeting shall be on the first Monday in December, unless they shall by Law appoint a different Day.

>> Congress based the Voting Rights Act of 1965 on this section to protect the right to vote. See Chapter 5.

>> The Twentieth Amendment has invalidated this paragraph.

SECTION 5

Each House shall be the Judge of the Elections, Returns and Qualifications of its own Members, and a Majority of each shall constitute a Quorum to do Business; but a smaller number may adjourn from day to day, and may be authorized to compel the Attendance of absent Members, in such Manner, and under such Penalties, as each House may provide.

Each House may determine the Rules of its Proceedings, punish its Members for disorderly Behaviour, and, with the Concurrence of two thirds, expel a Member.

Each House shall keep a Journal of its Proceedings, and from time to time publish the same, excepting such Parts as may in their Judgment require Secrecy; and the Yeas and Nays of the Members of either House on any question shall, at the Desire of one fifth of those Present, be entered on the Journal.

Neither House, during the Session of Congress, shall, without the Consent of the other, adjourn for more than three days, nor to any other Place than that in which the two Houses shall be sitting.

SECTION 6

The Senators and Representatives shall receive a Compensation for their Services, to be ascertained by Law, and paid out of the Treasury of the United States. They shall in all Cases, except Treason, Felony and Breach of the Peace, be privileged from Arrest during their Attendance at the Session of their respective Houses, and in going to and returning from the same; and for any Speech or Debate in either House, they shall not be questioned in any other Place.

No Senator or Representative shall, during the Time for which he was elected, be appointed to any civil Office under the Authority of the United States, which shall have been created, or the Emoluments whereof shall have been encreased, during such time; and no Person holding any Office under the United States shall be a Member of either House during his continuance in Office.

SECTION 7

All Bills for raising Revenue shall originate in the House of Representatives; but the Senate may propose or concur with Amendments as on other bills.

Every Bill which shall have passed the House of Representatives and the Senate, shall, before it becomes a Law, be presented to the President of the United States: If he approve he shall sign it, but if not he shall return it, with his Objections to that House in which it shall have originated, who shall enter the Objections at large on their Journal, and proceed to reconsider it. If after such Reconsideration two thirds of that House shall agree to pass the Bill, it shall be sent, together with the Objections, to the other House, by which it shall likewise be reconsidered, and if approved by two thirds of that House, it shall become a Law. But in all such Cases the Votes of both Houses shall be determined by Yeas and Nays, and the Names of the Persons voting for and against the Bill shall be entered on the Journal of each House respectively. If any Bill shall not be returned by the President within ten Days (Sundays excepted) after it shall have been presented to him, the Same shall be a Law, in like Manner as if he had signed it, unless the Congress by their Adjournment prevent its Return, in which Case it shall not be a Law.

Every Order, Resolution, or Vote to which the Concurrence of the Senate and House of Representatives may be necessary (except on a question of Adjournment) shall be presented to the President of the United States; and before the Same shall take Effect, shall be approved by him, or being disapproved by him, shall be repassed by two thirds of the Senate and House of Representatives, according to the Rules and Limitations prescribed in the Case of a Bill.

SECTION 8

>> This general clause gives the national government the authority to pursue the domestic and foreign policies discussed in Chapters 15 and 16.

The Congress shall have Power To lay and collect Taxes, Duties, Imposts and Excises, to pay the Debts and provide for the common Defence and general Welfare of the United States; but all Duties, Imposts and Excises shall be uniform throughout the United States;

To borrow Money on the credit of the United States;

To regulate Commerce with foreign Nations, and among the several States, and with the Indian Tribes;

To establish a uniform Rule of Naturalization, and uniform Laws on the subject of Bankruptcies throughout the United States;

To coin Money, regulate the Value thereof, and of foreign Coin, and fix the Standard of Weights and Measures;

To provide for the Punishment of counterfeiting the Securities and current Coin of the United States;

To establish Post Offices and post Roads;

To promote the Progress of Science and useful Arts, by securing for limited Times to Authors and Inventors the exclusive Right to their respective Writings and Discoveries;

To constitute Tribunals inferior to the supreme Court;

To define and punish Piracies and Felonies committed on the high Seas, and Offences against the Law of Nations;

To declare War, grant Letters of Marque and Reprisal, and make Rules concerning Captures on Land and Water;

To raise and support Armies, but no Appropriation of Money to that Use shall be for a longer Term than two Years;

To provide and maintain a Navy;

To make Rules for the Government and Regulation of the land and naval Forces;

To provide for calling forth the Militia to execute the Laws of the Union, suppress Insurrections and repel Invasions;

>> The listing of the enumerated powers of the national government serves as the basis for the extent of national power with respect to the states (Chapter 3), with respect to civil liberties (Chapter 4), and with respect to congressional and presidential powers (Chapters 11 and 12).

To provide for organizing, arming, and disciplining the Militia, and for governing such Part of them as may be employed in the Service of the United States, reserving to the States respectively, the Appointment of the Officers, and the Authority of training the Militia according to the discipline prescribed by Congress;

To exercise exclusive Legislation in all Cases whatsoever, over such District (not exceeding ten Miles square) as may, by Cession of particular States, and the Acceptance of Congress, become the Seat of the Government of the United States, and to exercise like Authority over all Places purchased by the Consent of the Legislature of the State in which the Same shall be, for the Erection of Forts, Magazines, Arsenals, dock-Yards, and other needful Buildings;—And

To make all Laws which shall be necessary and proper for carrying into Execution the foregoing Powers, and all other Powers vested by this Constitution in the Government of the United States, or in any Department or Officer thereof.

>> This clause served as the basis for the Supreme Court's implied powers doctrine first espoused in *McCulloch v. Maryland*.

SECTION 9

The Migration or Importation of such Persons as any of the States now existing shall think proper to admit, shall not be prohibited by the Congress prior to the Year one thousand eight hundred and eight, but a tax or duty may be imposed on such Importation, not exceeding ten dollars for each Person.

The privilege of the Writ of Habeas Corpus shall not be suspended, unless when in Cases of Rebellion or Invasion the public Safety may require it.

>> These limitations on congressional power reveal a heritage of rights and liberties that existed before the addition of the Bill of Rights. See Chapter 4.

No Bill of Attainder or ex post facto Law shall be passed.

No Capitation, or other direct, Tax shall be laid, unless in Proportion to the Census or enumeration herein before directed to be taken.

>> The poll tax was invalidated by the Twenty-fourth Amendment.

No Tax or Duty shall be laid on Articles exported from any State.

No Preference shall be given by any Regulation of Commerce or Revenue to the Ports of one State over those of another; nor shall Vessels bound to, or from, one State, be obliged to enter, clear, or pay Duties in another.

No Money shall be drawn from the Treasury, but in Consequence of Appropriations made by Law; and a regular Statement and Account of the Receipts and Expenditures of all public Money shall be published from time to time.

No Title of Nobility shall be granted by the United States: And no Person holding any Office of Profit or Trust under them, shall, without the Consent of the Congress, accept of any present, Emolument, Office, or Title, of any kind whatever, from any King, Prince, or foreign State.

SECTION 10

No State shall enter into any Treaty, Alliance, or Confederation; grant Letters of Marque and Reprisal; coin Money; emit Bills of Credit; make any Thing but gold and silver Coin a Tender in Payment of Debts; pass any Bill of Attainder, ex post facto Law, or Law impairing the Obligation of Contracts, or grant any Title of Nobility.

No State shall, without the Consent of the Congress, lay any Imposts or Duties on Imports or Exports, except what may be absolutely necessary for executing it's inspection Laws: and the net Produce of all Duties and Imposts, laid by any State on Imports or Exports, shall be for the Use of the Treasury of the United States; and all such Laws shall be subject to the Revision and Control of the Congress.

No state shall, without the Consent of Congress, lay any duty of Tonnage, keep Troops, or Ships of War in time of Peace, enter into any Agreement or Compact with another State, or with a foreign Power, or engage in War, unless actually invaded, or in such imminent Danger as will not admit of delay.

ARTICLE II

SECTION 1

The executive Power shall be vested in a President of the United States of America. He shall hold his Office during the Term of four years, and, together with the Vice President, chosen for the same Term, be elected, as follows:

Each State shall appoint, in such Manner as the Legislature thereof may direct, a Number of Electors, equal to the whole Number of Senators and Representatives to which the State may be entitled in the Congress: but no Senator or Representative, or Person holding an Office of Trust or Profit under the United States, shall be appointed an Elector.

>> Limits on a presidential term were added in the Twentieth Amendment.

>> This selection clause was modified by the Twelfth Amendment.

[The Electors shall meet in their respective States, and vote by Ballot for two Persons, of whom one at least shall not be an Inhabitant of the same State with themselves. And they shall make a List of all the Persons voted for, and of the Number of Votes for each; which List they shall sign and certify, and transmit sealed to the Seat of the Government of the United States, directed to the President of the Senate. The President of the Senate shall, in the Presence of the Senate and House of Representatives, open all the Certificates, and the Votes shall then be counted. The Person having the greatest Number of Votes shall be the President, if such Number be a Majority of the whole Number of Electors appointed; and if there be more than one who have such Majority, and have an equal Number of Votes, then the House of Representatives shall immediately chuse by Ballot one of them for President; and if no Person have a Majority, then from the five highest on the List the said House shall in like Manner chuse the President. But in chusing the President, the Votes shall be taken by States, the Representation from each State having one Vote; a quorum for this purpose shall consist of a Member or Members from two thirds of the States, and a Majority of all the States shall be necessary to a Choice. In every Case, after the Choice of the President, the Person having the greatest Number of Votes of the Electors shall be the Vice President. But if there should remain two or more who have equal Votes, the Senate shall chuse from them by Ballot the Vice President.][4]

The Congress may determine the Time of chusing the Electors, and the Day on which they shall give their Votes; which Day shall be the same throughout the United States.

No person except a natural born Citizen, or a Citizen of the United States, at the time of the Adoption of this Constitution, shall be eligible to the Office of President; neither shall any Person be eligible to that Office who shall not have attained to the Age of thirty five years, and been fourteen Years a Resident within the United States.

>> This disability and transfer of power clause was modified by the Twenty-fifth Amendment.

In Case of the Removal of the President from Office, or of his Death, Resignation, or Inability to discharge the Powers and Duties of the said Office, the Same shall devolve on the Vice President, and the Congress may by Law provide for the Case of Removal, Death, Resignation, or Inability, both of the President and Vice President, declaring what Officer shall then act as President, and such Officer shall act accordingly, until the Disability be removed, or a President shall be elected.

The President shall, at stated Times, receive for his Services, a Compensation, which shall neither be increased nor diminished during the Period for which he shall have been elected, and he shall not receive within that Period any other Emolument from the United States, or any of them.

Before he enter on the Execution of his Office, he shall take the following Oath or Affirmation:—"I do solemnly swear (or affirm) that I will faithfully execute the Office of President of the United States, and will to the best of my Ability, preserve, protect and defend the Constitution of the United States."

SECTION 2

The President shall be Commander in Chief of the Army and Navy of the United States, and of the Militia of the several States, when called into the actual Service of the United States; he may require the Opinion, in writing, of the principal Officer in each of the executive Departments, upon any Subject relating to the Duties of their respective Offices, and he shall have Power to grant Reprieves and Pardons for Offences against the United States, except in Cases of Impeachment.

He shall have Power, by and with the Advice and Consent of the Senate, to make Treaties, provided two thirds of the Senators present concur; and he shall nominate, and by and with the Advice and Consent of the Senate, shall appoint Ambassadors, other public Ministers and Consuls, Judges of the supreme Court, and all other Officers of the United States, whose Appointments are not herein otherwise provided for, and which shall be established by Law: but the Congress may by Law vest the Appointment of such inferior Officers, as they think proper, in the President alone, in the Courts of Law, or in the Heads of Departments.

The President shall have Power to fill up all Vacancies that may happen during the Recess of the Senate, by granting Commissions which shall expire at the End of their next Session.

SECTION 3

He shall from time to time give to the Congress Information of the State of the Union, and recommend to their Consideration such Measures as he shall judge necessary and expedient; he may, on extraordinary Occasions, convene both Houses, or either of them, and in Case of Disagreement between them, with Respect to the Time of Adjournment, he may adjourn them to such Time as he shall think proper; he shall receive Ambassadors and other public Ministers; he shall take Care that the Laws be faithfully executed, and shall Commission all the Officers of the United States.

SECTION 4

The President, Vice President and all civil Officers of the United States, shall be removed from Office on Impeachment for, and Conviction of, Treason, Bribery, or other high Crimes and Misdemeanors.

ARTICLE III

SECTION 1

The judicial Power of the United States shall be vested in one supreme Court, and in such inferior Courts as the Congress may from time to time ordain and establish. The Judges, both of the supreme and inferior Courts, shall hold their Offices during good Behaviour, and shall, at stated Times, receive for their Services a Compensation, which shall not be diminished during their Continuance in Office.

SECTION 2

The judicial Power shall extend to all Cases, in Law and Equity, arising under this Constitution, the Laws of the United States, and Treaties made, or which shall be made, under their Authority;—to all Cases affecting ambassadors, other public Ministers and Consuls;—to all cases of admiralty and maritime Jurisdiction;—to Controversies to which the United States shall be a Party;—to Controversies between two or more states;—between a State and Citizens of another State,[5]—between Citizens of different States,—between Citizens of the same State claiming Lands under Grants of different States, and between a State, or the Citizens thereof, and foreign States, Citizens or Subjects.

>> The power of judicial review is not mentioned among the Court's powers.

In all Cases affecting Ambassadors, other public Ministers and Consuls, and those in which a State shall be Party, the supreme Court shall have original Jurisdiction. In all the other Cases before mentioned, the supreme Court shall have appellate Jurisdiction, both as to Law and Fact, with such Exceptions, and under such Regulations as the Congress shall make.

The trial of all Crimes, except in Cases of Impeachment, shall be by Jury; and such Trial shall be held in the State where the said Crimes shall have been committed; but when not committed within any State, the Trial shall be at such Place or Places as the Congress may by Law have directed.

SECTION 3

Treason against the United States, shall consist only in levying War against them, or in adhering to their Enemies, giving them Aid and Comfort. No Person shall be convicted of Treason unless on the Testimony of two Witnesses to the same overt Act, or on Confession in open Court.

The Congress shall have Power to declare the Punishment of Treason, but no Attainder of Treason shall work Corruption of Blood, or Forfeiture except during the Life of the Person attainted.

ARTICLE IV

SECTION 1

Full Faith and Credit shall be given in each State to the public Acts, Records, and judicial Proceedings of every other State. And the Congress may by general Laws prescribe the Manner in which such Acts, Records and Proceedings shall be proved, and the Effect thereof.

SECTION 2

The Citizens of each State shall be entitled to all Privileges and Immunities of Citizens in the several States.

A Person charged in any State with Treason, Felony, or other Crime, who shall flee from Justice, and be found in another State, shall on Demand of the executive Authority of the State from which he fled, be delivered up, to be removed to the State having Jurisdiction of the Crime.

No Person held to Service or Labour in one State, under the Laws thereof, escaping into another, shall, in Consequence of any Law or Regulation therein, be discharged from such Service or Labour, but shall be delivered up on Claim of the Party to whom such Service or Labour may be due.

>> The Thirteenth Amendment eliminated the fugitive slave clause.

SECTION 3

New States may be admitted by the Congress into this Union; but no new State shall be formed or erected within the Jurisdiction of any other State; nor any State be formed by the Junction of two or more States, or Parts of States, without the Consent of the Legislatures of the States concerned as well as of the Congress.

The Congress shall have Power to dispose of and make all needful Rules and Regulations respecting the Territory or other Property belonging to the United States; and nothing in this Constitution shall be so construed as to Prejudice any Claims of the United States, or of any particular State.

SECTION 4

The United States shall guarantee to every State in this Union a Republican Form of Government, and shall protect each of them against Invasion; and on Application of the Legislature, or of the Executive (when the Legislature cannot be convened) against domestic Violence.

ARTICLE V

The Congress, whenever two thirds of both Houses shall deem it necessary, shall propose Amendments to this Constitution, or, on the Application of the Legislatures of two thirds of the several States, shall call a Convention for proposing Amendments, which, in either Case, shall be valid to all Intents and Purposes, as Part of this Constitution, when ratified by the Legislatures of three fourths of the several States, or by Conventions in three fourths thereof, as the one or the other Mode of Ratification may be proposed by the Congress; Provided that no Amendment which may be made prior to the Year One thousand eight hundred and eight shall in any Manner affect the first and fourth Clauses in the Ninth Section of the first Article; and that no State, without its Consent, shall be deprived of its equal Suffrage in the Senate.

>> The Constitution may also be changed by informal means. See Chapter 2.

ARTICLE VI

All Debts contracted and Engagements entered into, before the Adoption of this Constitution, shall be as valid against the United States under this Constitution, as under the Confederation.

This Constitution, and the Laws of the United States which shall be made in Pursuance thereof; and all Treaties made, or which shall be made, under the Authority of the United States, shall be the supreme Law of the Land; and the Judges in every State shall be bound thereby, any Thing in the Constitution or Laws of any State to the Contrary notwithstanding.

The Senators and Representatives before mentioned, and the Members of the several State Legislatures, and all executive and judicial Officers, both of the United States and of the several States, shall be bound by Oath or Affirmation to support this Constitution; but no religious Test shall ever be required as a Qualification to any Office or public Trust under the United States.

ARTICLE VII

The Ratification of the Conventions of nine States, shall be sufficient for the Establishment of this Constitution between the States so ratifying the Same.

The Word, "the," being interlined between the seventh and eighth Lines of the first Page, the Word "Thirty" being partly written on an Erazure in the fifteenth Line of the first Page, The Words "is tried" being interlined between the thirty second and thirty third Lines of the first Page and the Word "the" being interlined between the forty third and forty fourth Lines of the second Page.

Attest William Jackson Secretary

Done in Convention by the Unanimous Consent of the States present the Seventeenth Day of September in the Year of our Lord one thousand seven hundred and Eighty seven and of the Independence of the United States of America the Twelfth In witness whereof We have hereunto subscribed our Names.[6]

George Washington
*President and deputy
  from Virginia*

New Hampshire
John Langdon
Nicholas Gilman

Massachusetts
Nathaniel Gorham
Rufus King

Connecticut
William Samuel Johnson
Roger Sherman

New York
Alexander Hamilton

New Jersey
William Livingston
David Brearley
William Paterson
Jonathan Dayton

Pennsylvania
Benjamin Franklin
Thomas Mifflin
Robert Morris
George Clymer
Thomas FitzSimmons
Jared Ingersoll
James Wilson
Gouverneur Morris

Delaware
George Read
Gunning Bedford, Jr.
John Dickinson
Richard Bassett
Jacob Broom

Maryland
James McHenry
Daniel of St. Thomas
  Jenifer
Daniel Carroll

Virginia
John Blair
James Madison, Jr.

North Carolina
William Blount
Richard Dobbs Spaight
Hugh Williamson

South Carolina
John Rutledge
Charles Cotesworth
  Pinckney
Charles Pinckney
Pierce Butler

Georgia
William Few
Abraham Baldwin

Articles in Addition to, and Amendment of, the Constitution of the United States of America, Proposed by Congress, and Ratified by the Legislatures of the Several States, Pursuant to the Fifth Article of the Original Constitution[7]

AMENDMENT I

Congress shall make no law respecting an establishment of religion, or prohibiting the free exercise thereof; or abridging the freedom of speech, or of the press; or the right of the people peaceably to assemble, and to petition the Government for a redress of grievances.

>> The first nine amendments are the basis of citizens' civil liberties protections. See Chapter 4. The First Amendment, in particular, is the legal basis for political participation (see Chapter 7), and the role of interest groups (see Chapter 8), political parties (see Chapter 9), and the media (see Chapter 10).

AMENDMENT II

A well regulated Militia, being necessary to the security of a free State, the right of the people to keep and bear Arms, shall not be infringed.

AMENDMENT III

No Soldier shall, in time of peace be quartered in any house, without the consent of the Owner, nor in time of war, but in a manner to be prescribed by law.

AMENDMENT IV

The right of the people to be secure in their persons, houses, papers, and effects, against unreasonable searches and seizures, shall not be violated, and no Warrants shall issue, but upon probable cause, supported by Oath or affirmation, and particularly describing the place to be searched, and the persons or things to be seized.

AMENDMENT V

No person shall be held to answer for a capital, or otherwise infamous crime, unless on a presentment or indictment of a Grand Jury, except in cases arising in the land or naval forces, or in the Militia, when in actual service in time of War or public danger; nor shall any person be subject for the same offence to be twice put in jeopardy of life or limb; nor shall be compelled in any criminal case to be a witness against himself, nor be deprived of life, liberty, or property, without due process of law; nor shall private property be taken for public use, without just compensation.

AMENDMENT VI

In all criminal prosecutions, the accused shall enjoy the right to a speedy and public trial, by an impartial jury of the State and district wherein the crime shall have been committed, which district shall have been previously ascertained by law, and to be informed of the nature and cause of the accusation; to be confronted with the witnesses against him; to have compulsory process for obtaining witnesses in his favor, and to have the Assistance of Counsel for his defence.

AMENDMENT VII

In Suits at common law, where the value in controversy shall exceed twenty dollars, the right of trial by jury shall be preserved, and no fact tried by a jury, shall be otherwise re-examined in any Court of the United States, than according to the rules of the common law.

AMENDMENT VIII

Excessive bail shall not be required, nor excessive fines imposed, nor cruel and unusual punishments inflicted.

AMENDMENT IX

The enumeration of the Constitution, of certain rights, shall not be construed to deny or disparage others retained by the people.

AMENDMENT X

The powers not delegated to the United States by the Constitution, nor prohibited by it to the States, are reserved to the States respectively, or to the people.

AMENDMENT XI [1795]

The Judicial power of the United States shall not be construed to extend to any suit in law or equity, commenced or prosecuted against one of the United States by Citizens of another State, or by Citizens or Subjects of any Foreign State.

AMENDMENT XII [1804]

The Electors shall meet in their respective States and vote by ballot for President and Vice-President, one of whom, at least, shall not be an inhabitant of the same State with themselves; they shall name in their ballots the person voted for as President, and in distinct ballots the person voted for as Vice-President, and they shall make distinct lists of all persons voted for as President, and of all persons voted for as Vice-President, and of the number of votes for each, which lists they shall sign and certify, and transmit sealed to the seat of the government of the United States, directed to the President of the Senate;—the President of the Senate shall, in the presence of the Senate and House of Representatives, open all the certificates and the votes shall then be counted;—The person having the greatest number of votes for President, shall be the President, if such number be a majority of the whole number of Electors appointed; and if no person have such majority, then from the persons having the highest numbers not exceeding three on the list of those voted for as President, the House of Representatives shall choose immediately, by ballot, the President. But in choosing the President, the votes shall be taken by states, the representation from each state having one vote; a quorum for this purpose shall consist of a member or members from two-thirds of the states, and a majority of all the states shall be necessary to a choice. And if the House of Representatives shall not choose a President whenever the right of choice shall devolve upon them, before the fourth day of March next following, then the Vice-President shall act as President, as in the case of the death or other constitutional disability of the President.—The person having the greatest number of votes as Vice-President, shall be the Vice-President, if such number be a majority of the whole number of Electors appointed, and if no person have a majority, then from the two highest numbers on the list, the Senate shall choose the Vice-President; a quorum for the purpose shall consist of two-thirds of the whole number of Senators, and majority of the whole number shall be necessary to a choice. But no person constitutionally ineligible to the office of President shall be eligible to that of Vice-President of the United States.

AMENDMENT XIII [1865]

SECTION 1

Neither slavery nor involuntary servitude, except as a punishment for crime whereof the party shall have been duly convicted, shall exist within the United States, or any place subject to their jurisdiction.

SECTION 2

Congress shall have power to enforce this article by appropriate legislation.

AMENDMENT XIV [1868]

SECTION 1

All persons born or naturalized in the United States, and subject to the jurisdiction thereof, are citizens of the United States and of the State wherein they reside. No State shall make or enforce any law which shall abridge the privileges or immunities of citizens of the United States; nor shall any State deprive any person of life, liberty, or

>> The due process clause is the basis of the incorporation doctrine (see Chapter 4), and the equal protection clause is the constitutional basis of equality cases (see Chapter 5).

property, without due process of law; nor deny to any person within its jurisdiction the equal protection of the laws.

SECTION 2

Representatives shall be apportioned among the several States according to their respective numbers, counting the whole number of persons in each State, excluding Indians not taxed. But when the right to vote at any election for the choice of electors for President and Vice-President of the United States, Representatives in Congress, the Executive and Judicial officers of a State, or the members of the Legislature thereof, is denied to any of the male inhabitants of such State, being twenty-one years of age, and citizens of the United States, or in any way abridged, except for participation in rebellion, or other crime, the basis of representation therein shall be reduced in the proportion which the number of such male citizens shall bear to the whole number of male citizens twenty-one years of age in such State.

SECTION 3

No person shall be a Senator or Representative in Congress, or elector of President and Vice-President, or hold any office, civil or military, under the United States, or under any State, who, having previously taken an oath, as a member of Congress, or as an officer of the United States, or as a member of any State legislature, or as an executive or judicial officer of any State, to support the Constitution of the United States, shall have engaged in insurrection or rebellion against the same, or given aid or comfort to the enemies thereof. But Congress may by a vote of two-thirds of each House, remove such disability.

SECTION 4

The validity of the public debt of the United States, authorized by law, including debts incurred for payment of pensions and bounties for services in suppressing insurrection or rebellion, shall not be questioned. But neither the United States nor any State shall assume or pay any debts or obligation incurred in aid of insurrection or rebellion against the United States, or any claim for the loss or emancipation of any slave; but all such debts, obligations and claims shall be held illegal and void.

SECTION 5

The Congress shall have the power to enforce, by appropriate legislation, the provisions of this article.

AMENDMENT XV [1870]

SECTION 1

The right of citizens of the United States to vote shall not be denied or abridged by the United States or by any State on account of race, color, or previous condition of servitude.

SECTION 2

The Congress shall have the power to enforce this article by appropriate legislation.

AMENDMENT XVI [1913]

The Congress shall have power to lay and collect taxes on incomes, from whatever source derived, without apportionment among the several States, and without regard to any census or enumeration.

AMENDMENT XVII [1913]

The Senate of the United States shall be composed of two Senators from each State, elected by the people thereof, for six years; and each Senator shall have one vote. The electors in each State shall have the qualifications requisite for electors of the most numerous branch of the State legislatures.

When vacancies happen in the representation of any State in the Senate, the executive authority of such State shall issue writs of election to fill such vacancies: *Provided*, That the legislature of any State may empower the executive thereof to make temporary appointments until the people fill the vacancies by election as the legislature may direct.

This amendment shall not be so construed as to affect the election or term of any Senator chosen before it becomes valid as part of the Constitution.

AMENDMENT XVIII [1919]

SECTION 1

After one year from the ratification of this article the manufacture, sale, or transportation of intoxicating liquors within, the importation thereof into, or the exportation thereof from the United States and all territory subject to the jurisdiction thereof for beverage purposes is hereby prohibited.

SECTION 2

The Congress and the several States shall have concurrent power to enforce this article by appropriate legislation.

SECTION 3

This article shall be inoperative unless it shall have been ratified as an amendment to the Constitution by the legislatures of the several States, as provided in the Constitution, within seven years from the date of the submission hereof to the States by the Congress.

AMENDMENT XIX [1920]

The right of citizens of the United States to vote shall not be denied or abridged by the United States or by any State on account of sex.

Congress shall have power to enforce this article by appropriate legislation.

>> The amendment was the result of the second national women's rights movement.

AMENDMENT XX [1933]

SECTION 1

The terms of the President and Vice President shall end at noon on the 20th day of January, and the terms of Senators and Representatives at noon on the 3d day of January, of the years in which such terms would have ended if this article had not been ratified; and the terms of their successors shall then begin.

SECTION 2

The Congress shall assemble at least once in every year, and such meeting shall begin at noon on the 3d day of January, unless they shall by law appoint a different day.

SECTION 3

If, at the time fixed for the beginning of the term of the President, the President elect shall have died, the Vice President elect shall become President. If a President shall not have been chosen before the time fixed for the beginning of his term, or if the President elect shall have failed to qualify, then the Vice President elect shall act as President until a President shall have qualified; and the Congress may by law provide for the case wherein neither a President elect nor a Vice President elect shall have qualified, declaring who shall then act as President, or the manner in which one who is to act shall be selected, and such person shall act accordingly until a President or Vice President shall have qualified.

SECTION 4

The Congress may by law provide for the case of the death of any of the persons from whom the House of Representatives may choose a President whenever the right of choice shall have devolved upon them, and for the case of the death of any of the persons from whom the Senate may choose a Vice President whenever the right of choice shall have devolved upon them.

SECTION 5

Sections 1 and 2 shall take effect on the 15th day of October following the ratification of this article.

SECTION 6

This article shall be inoperative unless it shall have been ratified as an amendment to the Constitution by the legislatures of three-fourths of the several States within seven years from the date of its submission.

AMENDMENT XXI [1933]

SECTION 1

The eighteenth article of amendment to the Constitution of the United States is hereby repealed.

SECTION 2

The transportation or importation into any State, Territory, or Possession of the United States for delivery or use therein of intoxicating liquors, in violation of the laws thereof, is hereby prohibited.

SECTION 3

This article shall be inoperative unless it shall have been ratified as an amendment to the Constitution by conventions in the several States, as provided in the Constitution, within seven years from the date of the submission hereof to the States by the Congress.

AMENDMENT XXII [1951]

SECTION 1

No person shall be elected to the office of the President more than twice, and no person who has held the office of President, or acted as President, for more than two years of a term to which some other person was elected President shall be elected to the office of the President more than once. But this Article shall not apply to any person holding the office of President when this Article was proposed by the Congress, and shall not prevent any person who may be holding the office of President, or acting as President, during the term within which this Article becomes operative from holding the office of President or acting as President during the remainder of such term.

SECTION 2

This article shall be inoperative unless it shall have been ratified as an amendment to the Constitution by conventions in the several States, as provided in the Constitution, within seven years from the date of the submission hereof to the States by the Congress.

AMENDMENT XXIII [1961]

SECTION 1

The District constituting the seat of Government of the United States shall appoint in such manner as the Congress may direct:

A number of electors of President and Vice President equal to the whole number of Senators and Representatives in Congress to which the District would be entitled if it were a State, but in no event more than the least populous State; they shall be in addition to those appointed by the States, but they shall be considered, for the purposes of the election of President and Vice President, to be electors appointed by a State; and they shall meet in the District and perform such duties as provided by the twelfth article of amendment.

SECTION 2

The Congress shall have power to enforce this article by appropriate legislation.

AMENDMENT XXIV [1964]

SECTION 1

The right of citizens of the United States to vote in any primary or other election for President or Vice President, for electors for President or Vice President, or for Senator or Representative in Congress, shall not be denied or abridged by the United States or any State by reason of failure to pay any poll tax or other tax.

SECTION 2

The Congress shall have the power to enforce this article by appropriate legislation.

AMENDMENT XXV [1967]

SECTION 1

In case of the removal of the President from office or of his death or resignation, the Vice President shall become President.

SECTION 2

Whenever there is a vacancy in the office of the Vice President, the President shall nominate a Vice President who shall take office upon confirmation by a majority vote of both Houses of Congress.

SECTION 3

Whenever the President transmits to the President pro tempore of the Senate and the Speaker of the House of Representatives his written declaration that he is unable to discharge the powers and duties of his office, and until he transmits to them a written declaration to the contrary, such powers and duties shall be discharged by the Vice President as Acting President.

SECTION 4

Whenever the Vice President and a majority of either the principal officers of the executive departments or of such other body as Congress may by law provide, transmit to the President pro tempore of the Senate and the Speaker of the House of Representatives their written declaration that the President is unable to discharge the powers and duties of his office, the Vice President shall immediately assume the powers and duties of the office as Acting President.

Thereafter, when the President transmits to the President pro tempore of the Senate and the Speaker of the House of Representatives his written declaration that no inability exists, he shall resume the powers and duties of his office unless the Vice President and a majority of either the principal officers of the executive departments or of such other body as Congress may by law provide, transmit within four days to the President pro tempore of the Senate and the Speaker of the House of Representatives their written declaration that the President is unable to discharge the powers and duties of his office. Thereupon Congress shall decide the issue, assembling within forty-eight hours for that purpose if not in session. If the Congress, within twenty-one days after receipt of the latter written declaration, or, if Congress is not in session, within twenty-one days after Congress is required to assemble, determines by two-thirds vote of both Houses that the President is unable to discharge the powers and duties of his office, the Vice President shall continue to discharge the same as Acting President; otherwise, the President shall resume the powers and duties of his office.

AMENDMENT XXVI [1971]

SECTION 1

The right of citizens of the United States, who are eighteen years of age or older, to vote shall not be denied or abridged by the United States or by any State on account of age.

SECTION 2

The Congress shall have the power to enforce this article by appropriate legislation.

AMENDMENT XXVII [1992]

No law, varying the compensation for the service of Senators and Representatives, shall take effect, until an election of representatives shall have intervened.

Glossary

501(c) groups   Tax-exempt organizations considered advocacy groups whose primary purpose is to promote "social welfare."

527 groups   Tax-exempt organizations set up by interest groups to engage in political activities.

adversarial or attack journalism   A form of interpretive journalism that adopts a hostile position toward government, politics, and political figures.

advice and consent   The constitutional requirement that the president seek Senate approval for certain appointees and treaties.

advocacy groups   Groups organized around broad public goals but without local chapters and often without formal membership.

affirmative action   Programs that attempt to provide members of disadvantaged groups enhanced opportunities to secure jobs, promotions, and admission to educational institutions.

amicus curiae brief   Legal briefs filed by organized groups to influence the decision in a Supreme Court case.

Antifederalists   Opponents of the ratification of the Constitution.

appellate jurisdiction   The power of a court to receive cases from trial courts for the purpose of reviewing whether the legal procedures were followed properly.

astroturf lobbying   Using deceptive practices and lack of transparency to manufacture grassroots support for an issue important to a particular set of unidentified interests.

bad tendency test   The free speech test that prohibits speech that could produce a bad outcome, such as violence, no matter how unlikely the possibility the speech could be the cause of such an outcome.

battleground state   A competitive state where neither party holds an overwhelming edge.

benchmark survey   A campaign poll that measures a candidate's strength at the time of entrance into the electoral race.

biased pluralism   The view positing that power and public policies tilt largely in the direction of the well-off.

bicameral   Composed of two houses.

Bill of Rights   The freedoms listed in the first ten amendments to the U.S. Constitution.

blanket primary   An election in which voters can choose from among potential nominees in both parties; currently outlawed by the U.S. Supreme Court.

block grants   Federal programs that provide funds for broad categories of assistance such as public health programs or law enforcement.

bloggers   Citizens who create online diaries and forums for the posting of opinions and personal viewpoints.

budget resolution   Early step in the budgeting process, in which both houses of Congress set spending targets to meet the president's priorities.

bureaucracy   A complex system of organization and control that incorporates the principles of hierarchical authority, division of labor, and formalized rules.

bureaucrats   The civilian employees of the national government who are responsible for implementing federal laws.

Bush Doctrine   The foreign policy position advanced by George W. Bush asserting the U.S. government's right to authorize preemptive attacks against potential aggressors.

buycotting   Using purchasing decisions to support the policies of businesses that make these products.

cabinet   Presidential appointees to the major administrative units of the executive branch.

cabinet departments   The fifteen major administrative organizations within the federal bureaucracy that are responsible for major governmental functions such as defense, commerce, and homeland security.

cap and trade   A market-based system of pollution control whereby individual businesses can buy and sell emission credits even while the total level of industry pollution is capped at some level.

casework   The practice of finding solutions to constituent problems, usually involving government agencies.

categorical grants   Federal assistance that provides funds for specific programs such as flood assistance.

caucus   A voter gathering used to select party candidates to run in the general election.

chief of staff   The official in charge of coordinating communication between the president and other staffers.

civic engagement   Involvement in any activity aimed at influencing the collective well-being of the community.

civic life   Participation in the collective life of the community.

civil rights   The protection of historically disadvantaged groups from infringement of their equality rights by discriminatory action.

Civil Rights Act of 1964   Historic legislation that prohibited racial segregation in public accommodations and racial discrimination in employment, education, and voting.

civil rights movement   The litigation and mobilization activities of African Americans in the second half of the twentieth century that led to a greater realization of equality for all disadvantaged groups.

civil service   A merit-based system of employment and personnel management that replaced patronage.

civil service system The merit-based employment system that covers most white-collar and specialist positions in the federal government.

class action suit A lawsuit in which one or more persons sue on behalf of a larger set of people claiming the same injury.

clear and present danger test The free speech test that prohibits speech that produces a clear and immediate danger.

closed primary An election in which voters can choose from potential nominees only within their own party.

cloture The procedure that ends a filibuster with sixty votes of the Senate.

coattails The effect a winning candidate at the top of the ticket has in bringing success to those lower on the ballot.

cognitive misers Term referring to mental shortcuts Americans sometimes use to simplify their understanding of government policies, particularly in the arena of foreign affairs. For example, the terms "hawk" or "dove" are shortcuts respectively for those who advocate military might or the use of diplomacy.

cohort The members of one's own generation.

collective goods Goods that are not owned privately but benefit all citizens equally, such as clean air.

committee chairs The leaders of congressional committees, usually members of the majority party with the most seniority on that committee.

Committee on Rules In the House of Representatives, the committee charged with determining rules for debate, amendment, and vote on bills brought to the floor.

committees Bodies within each house that review legislation, investigate the operation of government agencies, and recommend courses of action for the chamber.

comparable worth The notion that individuals performing different jobs that require the same amount of knowledge, effort, skill, responsibility, and working conditions should receive equal compensation; the proposal would elevate the pay structure of many jobs traditionally performed by women.

concurrent powers Powers shared by both state and national governments.

concurring opinion An opinion written by one or more of the justices who agree with the decision but for different reasons than those stated in the majority opinion.

conference committees Committees including a small number of members from both houses assembled for the explicit purpose of ironing out differences between versions of the same bill before final approval by both chambers.

Congressional Budget Office The nonpartisan agency created by Congress to review and assess the impact of proposed budget items.

congressional caucuses Unofficial party or special interest groups formed by like-minded members of Congress to confer on issues of mutual concern.

Congressional Research Service A congressional agency providing nonpartisan policy and legal analysis to committees and members of both the House and the Senate.

congressional review Congressional action, requiring approval by both houses and the president, that can stop implementation of executive branch regulations.

conservatism A political philosophy that rests on the belief in traditional institutions and a minimal role for government in economic activity.

constituents The citizens from a state or district that an elected official represents.

containment American policies designed to limit the expansion of Soviet power around the world during the Cold War.

continuing resolution A vehicle for funding government operations at the previous year's levels of support when a new budget is delayed.

contrast ad Advertising that draws attention to differences that clearly distinguish each candidate.

conventional participation Traditional forms of participation like voting that citizens have relied upon to make their voices heard and to impact governmental decisions.

cooperative federalism The federal-state relationship characteristic of the post–New Deal era that stressed state and federal partnership in addressing social problems.

creative federalism The federal-state relationship that sought to involve local populations and cities directly in addressing urban problems during the 1960s and 1970s.

credit claiming The practice of personally taking credit for some action of government, like announcing the award of federal funds to one's constituents, in order to receive acclaim.

critical elections Elections signaling realignments, often sweeping the opposition party into control of the presidency and Congress.

dark money Spending by a group that is meant to influence the decision of voters, where the donor is not disclosed and the source of the money is unknown.

de facto segregation Segregation that occurs because of past economic and social conditions such as residential racial patterns.

de jure segregation Segregation mandated by law or decreed by government officials.

dealignment A falloff in electoral support for both major political parties.

debt ceiling The government's credit limit. If the government seeks to spend more than it has authorized, it must raise its borrowing power.

decision The indication of which litigant the court supports and by how large a margin.

defense policy Plans and decisions a country's leaders make about when and how to commit military resources for national security purposes.

deficit The difference between expenditures and income in any given year.

delegate style A style of representation stressing the lawmaker's role as a tribune of the people who reflects their views on issues of the day.

delegated powers Powers ceded by Congress to the president.

descriptive representation The idea that our representatives should reflect the demographic makeup of the population and not just our political interests.

détente An easing of tensions among nations.

devolution A movement begun in the 1980s to grant states greater authority over the local operation of federal programs and local use of federal funds.

diplomacy The practice of using peaceful means to resolve conflict.

diplomatic recognition The presidential power to offer official privileges to foreign governments.

direct democracy A form of government in which decisions about public policy extend to the entire citizenry.

direct initiatives Procedure that enables citizens to place proposals for laws and amendments directly on the ballot for voter approval.

direct mobilization   The process by which citizens are contacted personally by candidate and party organizations to take part in political activities.

direction   The attribute of an individual's opinion that indicates a preference for or against a particular issue.

discharge petition   A method for freeing legislation from a committee in the House that requires the signatures of 218 members.

discount rate   The interest rate at which member banks can borrow money from the Federal Reserve.

discretionary powers   Powers granted the president either expressly or by delegation that do not require action but permit the action at his discretion, giving him greater authority and flexibility in performing the duties of office.

dissenting opinion   An opinion written by one or more justices who disagree with a decision.

divided government   Control of the White House by one party while the opposition party controls one or both houses of Congress.

dual court system   The system under which U.S. citizens are subject to the jurisdiction of both national and state courts.

dual federalism   An approach to federal–state relationships that envisions each level of government as distinct and authoritative within its own sphere of action.

Duverger's law   The principle that asserts single-member district elections lead to two-party systems.

early voting   A practice used in some states in which voters are allowed to cast votes days before Election Day. The practice was begun to enhance voter access and convenience.

earmarks   Funding for specific projects added by members of Congress to appropriations bills, usually without oversight or public debate.

earned media   Media attention for which candidates do not pay; associated with major events like debates.

elastic clause   The provision of Article I of the Constitution authorizing Congress to make those laws necessary and proper for carrying out the other laws it passes.

elector   Member of the Electoral College.

Electoral College   The assemblage of state electors constitutionally charged with casting the deciding votes in presidential elections. With the exception of Maine and Nebraska, the candidate who wins the popular vote in a state is entitled to all the electoral votes from that state (with some exceptions). It takes the vote of 270 of these electors to declare a president the winner.

elites   Individuals in a position of authority, often those with a higher level education than the population at large.

emergency powers   Wide-ranging powers a president may exercise during a time of crisis, or those powers permitted the president by Congress for a limited time.

enemy combatant   An enemy fighter captured on the field of battle, whether or not a member of an army.

entitlements   Programs promising aid without time limit to anyone who qualifies.

enumerated powers   The list of specific powers granted to Congress by Article I, Section 8, of the Constitution.

Equal Rights Amendment   The proposed constitutional amendment that would have prohibited national and state governments from denying equal rights on the basis of sex.

equal time rule   The rule that requires that all broadcasters provide airtime equally to all candidates if they choose to provide it to any.

equilibration   The tendency toward regular alterations in party control of the White House and Congress.

establishment clause   The First Amendment prohibition against the government's establishment of a national religion.

exclusionary rule   The judicial barring of illegally seized evidence from a trial.

executive agreement   A pact that is made between the president and a foreign leader of a government and that does not require Senate approval.

Executive Office of the President   Close presidential advisors, including the White House staff, the national security advisor, the chief of staff, and members of various policy councils.

executive order   A decree with the force of law but not requiring legislative approval.

executive privilege   The presidential power to shield from scrutiny White House documents and conversations among presidential advisors.

exit poll   Interviews of voters as they leave the polling place.

express powers   Powers granted to the president by the Constitution.

expressive participation   Engaging the political world by expressing to others one's views by words or actions. Common forms include the use of social media to promote one's stance, boycotting, and buycotting.

external political efficacy   An individual's belief that his or her activities will influence what the government will do or who will win an election.

extraordinary rendition   The practice of secretly abducting terror suspects and transporting them to detention camps in undisclosed locations.

factions   Groups—most often driven by economic motives—that place their own good above the good of the nation as a whole.

fairness doctrine   The law that formerly required broadcasters to present contrasting views on important public issues.

federal funds rate   The interest rate banks charge other banks for borrowing money.

federal mandates   Federal requirements imposed on state and local governments, often as a condition for receiving grants.

Federal Register   A publication of the federal government used to announce public notice of the time, place, and nature of the proceedings to be followed when new agency rules are proposed.

federalism   Power-sharing arrangement between the national and state governments in which some powers are granted to the national government alone, some powers are reserved to the states, some powers are held concurrently, and other powers are prohibited to either or both levels of government.

Federalists   Supporters of the Constitution and its strong central government.

Fifteenth Amendment   The Civil War amendment that extended suffrage to former male slaves.

fifth party system   The period, beginning in 1932 and continuing at least until the mid-1960s, characterized by the dominance of the Democratic Party and its New Deal coalition.

filibuster   The Senate practice of continuous debate, often employed to stop pending legislative action.

first party system The period from the founding until about 1824 that gave birth to the Federalist Party and the Democratic-Republican Party (later known simply as the Democrats).

fiscal policy Taxing and spending policies prescribed by Congress and the president.

Foreign Intelligence Surveillance Act court (FISA court) The secret court housed in the Justice Department and used to oversee requests by federal agencies for surveillance warrants based on suspected espionage or terrorism.

foreign policy Plans a nation's leaders make to meet their goals and objectives in dealing with other nations in the world.

foreign policy liberalism The theory that holds that national interests are best secured by building alliances and making conflict more costly than cooperation.

Foreign Service Corps of U.S. diplomats stationed around the world.

Fourteenth Amendment The Civil War amendment that provided all persons with the privileges and immunities of national citizenship; the guarantee of equal protection of the laws by any state; and the safeguard of due process to protect one's life, liberty, and property from state government interference.

fourth party system The period from about 1896 until 1932 in which the Republican Party dominated American politics.

franking privilege Free postage for members of Congress to communicate with constituents.

free exercise clause The First Amendment provision intended to protect the practice of one's religion free from government interference.

free riders Those who enjoy the benefits from activities without paying the costs of participation.

full faith and credit The constitutional provision requiring each state to recognize legal transactions authorized in other states.

G20 Annual meeting of nineteen countries plus the European Union, at which members discuss strengthening the global economy.

gender gap The systematic variation in political opinions that exists between males and females.

General Agreement on Tariffs and Trade An international agreement following World War II designed to eliminate tariffs and trading barriers.

generational effects The impact of events experienced by a generational cohort on the formation of common political orientations.

germaneness Refers to the requirement that debate be strictly limited to the subject matter at hand. The House requires all debate and amendments be germane; the Senate does not.

gerrymandering The practice of drawing congressional boundaries to the advantage of one party.

government The body (or bodies) charged with making official policies for citizens.

Government Accountability Office The congressional agency that investigates how the federal government spends taxpayer dollars and the performance of agencies funded by the government.

grassroots mobilization The practice of organizing citizen support for a group's policy or candidate preferences.

Great Compromise The agreement at the Constitutional Convention to split the legislature into two bodies—one apportioned by population, the other assigning each state two members.

Gregg v. Georgia The Supreme Court decision that upheld the death penalty in the United States.

gross domestic product (GDP) A measure of the value of all goods and services produced in the United States.

hard money Campaign money received by candidates or parties that can be used for any purpose and is subject to federal limits and regulations.

hashtag activism Using social media to draw attention to a cause.

hate speech Prejudicial and hostile statements toward another person's innate characteristics such as race and ethnicity.

hold A parliamentary procedure of the Senate that allows one or more senators to prevent a motion from reaching a vote on the Senate floor.

home style Those actions that link members of Congress to their constituents. These include mail, the use of electronic communication, visits to the district, and town hall meetings.

homophobia Irrational fear and hatred directed toward persons who are homosexuals.

honeymoon period The period following an election when the public and Congress give the newly elected president the greatest latitude in decision making.

House majority leader The leader of the majority party in the House of Representatives, responsible for organizing the body and marshaling support for the party's agenda.

House minority leader The leader of the minority party in the House, responsible for marshaling support from party members for the party's agenda.

House of Burgesses The first legislative assembly in the American colonies.

idealism The theory that advocates American values such as democracy, freedom, and cultural diversity as the best way to promote our national interests.

ideological parties Minor parties organized around distinct ideological principles.

ideologue One who thinks about politics almost exclusively through the prism of his or her ideological perspective.

ideology Ideas, values, and beliefs about how governments should operate.

impeach To bring formal charges against a federal official, including the president.

imperial presidency The perspective advanced by some scholars in the 1970s warning about excessive concentration of power in the hands of the chief executive.

implied powers Powers necessary to carry out constitutionally enumerated functions of government.

impoundment Presidential refusal to expend funds appropriated by Congress.

incremental change Small, gradual steps that characterize most policy changes due to the need to reconcile many competing interests.

incumbent The current occupant of an office.

independent executive agency A governmental unit with special responsibilities that is not part of any cabinet department.

independent regulatory agency An agency existing outside the major departments that regulates a specific economic activity or interest.

indirect initiatives Citizen-initiated procedure for placing proposals on the ballot, requiring legislative action before submission to voters.

indirect mobilization The process by which political leaders use networks of friends and acquaintances to activate political participation.

inflation An economic condition in which the supply of money overwhelms our capacity to produce, creating rising prices.

informational support The attribute of an individual's opinion that measures his or her amount of knowledge concerning the issue.

inherent powers Those powers that are part of the very nature of the institution and necessary for the institution to do the job for which it was created. For example, the president must have the power to use force as part of his duties as commander in chief.

inner cabinet The term applied to leaders from the Departments of State, Defense, Treasury, and Justice, with whom the president meets more frequently than other cabinet officials.

intensity The attribute of an individual's opinion that measures how strongly it is held.

interest group Any formally organized association that seeks to influence public policy.

intergovernmental lobbies Professional advocacy groups representing various state and local governing bodies.

intermediate scrutiny test The equal protection test used by the Supreme Court that requires the government to prove that the use of classifications such as age, gender, or race is substantially related to an important government objective.

internal political efficacy An individual's self-confidence in his or her ability to understand and participate in politics.

International Monetary Fund An international organization based in Washington, D.C., designed to foster monetary cooperation and trade among nations.

interstate compacts Cooperative agreements made between states, subject to congressional approval, to address mutual problems.

iron triangle A decision-making structure dominated by interest groups, congressional committees, and executive agency personnel who create policies that are mutually beneficial.

issue evolution Changes in the issue agendas of each party that often result in a re-balancing of voter support for one or another party.

issue networks Decision-making structures consisting of policy experts, including lobbyists, members of Congress, bureaucrats, and policy specialists from think tanks and universities.

Jim Crow laws Legislation in the South that mandated racial segregation in public facilities such as restaurants and restrooms.

joint committees Committees including members from both houses with jurisdiction over narrow areas and generally limited to powers of oversight.

judicial activism The belief that the Supreme Court should make policy and vigorously review the policies of other branches.

judicial restraint The belief that the Supreme Court should not become involved in questioning the operations and policies of the elected branches unless absolutely necessary.

judicial review The power of the U.S. Supreme Court to review the acts of other political institutions and declare them unconstitutional.

jurisdiction The power of a court to hear and decide cases.

justiciability The doctrine that excludes certain cases from judicial consideration because of the party bringing the lawsuit or the nature of the subject matter.

Korematsu v. United States The 1944 Supreme Court decision that upheld the constitutionality of the U.S. government's internment of more than one hundred thousand Americans of Japanese descent during World War II.

leadership PACs Political action committees set up by political leaders as a means to finance the campaigns of political allies who they believe will reciprocate with support for their own political ambitions.

leading question A question worded to suggest a particular answer desired by the pollster.

legislative referendum Ballot measure aimed at securing voter approval for some legislative acts, such as changes to a state's constitution.

legislative veto A congressional action nullifying an executive branch agency's action but without having Congress pass a law to that effect and without presidential signature. This device was declared unconstitutional in 1983.

***Lemon* test** The three-part test for establishment clause cases that a law must pass before it is declared constitutional: It must have a secular purpose; it must neither advance nor inhibit religion; and it must not cause excessive entanglement with religion.

libel Written statements that are false and injure another's reputation.

liberal democracy An ideology stressing individual rights and expressing faith in popular control of government.

liberalism A political philosophy that combines a belief in personal freedoms with the belief that government should intervene in the economy to promote greater equality.

libertarianism A political philosophy that espouses strong support for individual liberty in both social and economic areas of life.

life cycle effects The impact of age-related factors in the formation of political attitudes, opinions, and beliefs.

line item veto The executive power to reject a portion of a bill, usually a budget appropriation.

line organization An administrative organization that is directly accountable to the president.

litigious Marked by a tendency to file lawsuits.

lobbying A tactic for influencing public decisions for private purposes, often employing personal contact with elected officials.

majority opinion An opinion written by a justice who represents a majority of the Court.

majority rule The requirement that electoral majorities determine who is elected to office and that majorities in power determine our laws and how they are administered.

majority-minority district A district in which minority members are clustered together, producing a majority of minority voters in the district.

mandatory expenditures Spending that is mandated by law such as entitlements which are guaranteed to eligible individuals.

markup Committee sessions in which members review contents of legislation line by line.

mass media The total array of mass communication, including television, radio, newspapers, magazines, and the Internet.

merit system The system that classifies federal civil service jobs into grades to which appointments are made on the basis of performance on competitive exams.

microtargeting The practice of mining databases containing information about consumer interests and behaviors to design personal appeals to voters.

***Miller* test**   The current judicial test for obscenity cases that considers community standards, whether the material is patently offensive, and whether the material taken as a whole lacks serious literary, artistic, political, or scientific value.

minority rights   Protections beyond the reach of majority control guaranteed to all citizens.

***Miranda* rights**   The warning police must administer to suspects so that the latter will be aware of their right not to incriminate themselves. The rights include the right to remain silent, the right to know statements will be used against them, and the right to have an attorney for the interrogation.

mobilizing the grass tops   Mining databases for high-status community leaders for purposes of contacting legislators in key districts regarding sponsoring a group's position.

monetary policy   The control of economic growth through management of the money supply by the Federal Reserve.

Monroe Doctrine   The foreign policy initiative advanced by President James Monroe in 1823, according to which the United States would oppose foreign intrusions into the Western Hemisphere.

mutually assured destruction   The arms policy followed by the superpowers during the Cold War, in which each side maintained sufficient fire power to destroy its adversary if that adversary struck first.

narrowcasting   Programming targeted to one small sector of the population, made possible by the emergence of cable television and the Internet.

national convention   An event held every four years by each political party to formally anoint its presidential candidate and to signal the initiation of the general election campaign.

national debt   The total financial obligations of the U.S. government measured over many years.

national interests   The constellation of military, economic, and ideological concerns surrounding a nation's security.

negative advertising   Advertising that attacks one's opponents, usually on the basis of issue stance or character.

New Deal coalition   The constellation of social groups that became the core base of support for the Democratic Party after the election of Franklin D. Roosevelt.

New Jersey Plan   William Paterson's proposal for a national government consisting of a unicameral legislature in which every state had equal representation and a plural executive body chosen by the legislature.

nominating convention   A meeting of party delegates to select their presidential nominee.

nonattitudes   Uninformed responses triggered by requiring survey respondents to answer whether or not they know about the subject in question.

nongovernmental organizations (NGOs)   Voluntary citizens' groups organized for a variety of charitable and humanitarian purposes.

norms   Informal standards about what constitutes acceptable social behavior.

North American Free Trade Agreement   A 1994 trade agreement eliminating trade barriers among the United States, Canada, and Mexico. NAFTA was renegotiated in 2018 and renamed the United States-Mexico-Canada Agreement, or USMCA.

nullification   The doctrine that asserted the right of states to disregard federal actions with which they disagreed.

omnibus bill   A bill that folds spending for all executive agencies into one legislative package.

Open Door policy   The foreign policy initiative advanced by Secretary of State John Hay in 1899 proposing to keep China open to free trade with all nations on an equal basis and denying any one nation from total control of trade.

open market operations   The buying and selling of government securities by the Federal Reserve with the intention of altering the nation's money supply.

open primary   An election in which voters can choose from among potential nominees from their own party or those from the other major political party.

opinion persistence   Stability of an erroneous opinion even in the face of disconfirming evidence.

opinions   Written arguments explaining the reasons behind a decision.

opposition research   The practice of searching for events in candidates' records or personal lives that can be used to attack them during elections.

original jurisdiction   The power of a court to hear and decide a case first.

outside spending   Political expenditures made by organizations and individuals other than the candidate campaigns themselves.

oversight   Congressional authority to investigate and monitor the actions and spending of executive agencies it creates.

paid media   Media access for which candidates or the party must pay a fee; advertisements.

partisan polarization   The term used to describe the growing ideological divide separating our two major political parties.

party caucus   A meeting of party members in closed sessions for the purposes of setting legislative agendas, selecting committee members, and holding elections to choose various floor leaders.

patronage   The practice of providing jobs or favors in exchange for political loyalty.

per curiam opinion   An unsigned opinion of the Supreme Court that usually signals a high degree of consensus.

platform   The statement of political principles and campaign promises generated by each party at its national convention.

pluralism   The view positing that various groups and coalitions constantly vie for government favor and the ability to exercise political power but none enjoys long-term dominance.

plurality opinion   An opinion written on behalf of the largest bloc of the justices, representing less than a majority, who agree on the reasons supporting the Court's decision.

pocket veto   An automatic veto achieved when a bill sits unsigned on a president's desk for ten days when Congress is out of session.

policy diffusion   The spread of policy innovation across jurisdictions.

political action committees (PACs)   Organized financial arms of interest groups used to collect and distribute money to candidates for elective office.

political culture   The dominant values and beliefs of a political community.

political cynicism   The view that government officials look out mostly for themselves.

political disadvantage theory   The view positing that groups are likely to seek remedies in courts if they do not succeed in the electoral process.

political efficacy   The belief that an individual can understand and influence political affairs.

political engagement   Active interest and participation in political activities.

political entrepreneur An individual who develops support for latent causes or projects that have not yet gained widespread popularity.

political ideology A cohesive set of beliefs that form a general philosophy about the role of government.

political information A measure of the amount of political knowledge an individual possesses concerning political issues, political figures, and the workings of the political system.

political interest An attribute of political participation that measures one's concern for an election outcome and the positions of the candidates on the issues.

political machine A strong party organization that maintained control by giving favors in return for votes.

political mobilization The process whereby citizens are alerted to participatory opportunities and encouraged to become involved.

political movement An organized constellation of groups seeking wide-ranging social change.

political participation Taking part in activities aimed at influencing the policies or leadership of government.

political party An organization created for the purpose of winning elections and governing once in office.

political power The ability to get things done by controlling or influencing the institutions of government.

political questions Issues determined by the Supreme Court to be better resolved by Congress or the president.

political socialization The process by which individuals come to adopt the attitudes, values, beliefs, and opinions of their political culture.

politico A style of representation in which the lawmaker attempts to balance the views of constituents, interest groups, and party leaders with his or her own ideological leanings.

politics The process by which we choose government officials and make decisions about public policy.

popular referendum A device that allows citizens to approve or repeal measures already acted on by legislative bodies.

population The people whose opinions are being estimated through interviews with samples of group members.

populist A political philosophy expressing support for greater equality and for traditional social values.

pork barrel projects The term applied to spending for pet projects of individual members of Congress.

precedent A former case that was supported by a majority on an appellate court and provides guidance for the determination of a present case.

precinct The geographic area served by a polling place and organized by local party units.

preemption The doctrine espoused by President George W. Bush, according to which the United States has a right to attack terrorist groups or nations in order to disrupt plans they may have to attack us.

president pro tempore The second-highest-ranking official in the U.S. Senate.

presidential doctrine A formal statement that outlines the goals and purposes of American foreign policy and the actions to take to advance these goals.

presiding officer The individual who presides over Senate debate, enforcing order and decorum. The presiding officer will at times be the vice president of the United States or the president pro tempore.

primary election An election in which voters choose candidates to represent the political parties in the general election.

prior restraint The practice that would allow the government to censor a publication before anyone could read or view it.

privileges and immunities A constitutional phrase interpreted to refer to fundamental rights, such as freedom to make a living, and access to the political and legal processes of the state.

probability sampling A sample design showing that each individual in the population has a known probability of being included in the sample.

probable cause A practical and nontechnical calculation of probabilities that is the basis for securing search warrants.

Progressive Era The period of social activism from roughly the 1890s to the 1920s, resulting in widespread political reform.

prohibited powers Powers denied one or both levels of government.

proportional representation A system of representation in which seats for office are apportioned according to the proportion of votes received by candidates or parties.

prospective voting Voting choice made on the basis of anticipated results if the candidate of choice is elected.

protectionism The policy of using taxes and tariffs to limit the kinds and amounts of foreign goods entering the nation.

public interest groups Those advocating policies they believe promote the good of all Americans and not merely the economic or ideological interests of a few.

public opinion Opinions held by private individuals that governments find it prudent to heed.

public policy Anything the government chooses to do or not to do.

push poll A campaign tactic that attacks an opponent while pretending to be a poll.

quantitative easing Additions to the money supply by the Fed to increase financial activity when interest rates are already close to zero.

racial gerrymandering The practice of redrawing legislative districts in a manner that minimizes the likelihood that minorities will be able to elect their preferred candidate.

rallying around the flag The sense of patriotism engendered by dramatic national events such as the September 11, 2001, terrorist attacks.

random digit dialing A procedure whereby pollsters select the initial portions of a telephone exchange and append randomly selected digits to complete the number. The procedure ensures that even those holding unlisted numbers have an equal chance of being selected for interview.

ranked choice voting A form of voting where voters can rank order their choice of candidates and those failing to achieve high levels of support are eliminated until one candidate is determined to have secured a majority.

ranking minority member A leader of the minority party on a committee.

rational actor theory The theory that choices are based on our individual assessment of costs and benefits.

rational basis test The equal protection test used by the Supreme Court that requires a complainant to prove that the use of a classification such as age, gender, or race is not a reasonable means of achieving a legitimate government objective.

realignments Periodic changes in party strength, composition, and direction.

realism The theory that holds that nations always act in their own self-interest and must have sufficient military resources to defend those interests.

reapportionment The periodic reallocation of 435 House seats among the states as population shifts from one region to another.

recall Procedure whereby citizens can remove and replace a public official before the end of a term.

recess appointment A political appointment made by the president when Congress is out of session.

recession A period of the business cycle characterized by high levels of unemployment.

reconciliation The process of amending spending bills to meet budget targets.

redistricting The practice of drawing congressional district boundaries to accord with population changes.

Regents of the University of California v. Bakke The 1978 Supreme Court case that declared unconstitutional the use of racial quotas to achieve a diverse student body but allowed the use of race as one of many factors in admissions decisions.

regulatory negotiation The process of shared decision making in which representatives of industries meet with policymakers to develop policies and regulations.

representative democracy A form of government in which popular decision making is restricted to electing or appointing the public officials who make public policy.

rescission Cutback of funds for particular programs that requires congressional approval.

reserve requirement ratio The amount of money the Fed requires banks to keep on hand to meet their liabilities. Its size helps determine how much banks can lend.

reserved powers Powers constitutionally allocated to the states.

retail politics A campaign style emphasizing close personal contact between the candidate and voters.

retrospective voting Voting on the basis of the candidate's or party's record in office.

revenue sharing A grant program begun in 1972 and ended in 1987 that funneled money directly to states and local governments on the basis of formulas that combined population figures with levels of demonstrated need.

reverse discrimination The argument that the use of race as a factor in affirmative action programs constitutes unconstitutional discrimination against the majority population.

revolving door A term referring to the back-and-forth movement of individuals between government and interest group employment.

Roe v. Wade The Supreme Court case that legalized abortions in the United States during the first two trimesters of a pregnancy.

Roosevelt Corollary The foreign policy pronounced by President Theodore Roosevelt asserting the United States' right to intervene in the domestic affairs of its neighbors if they proved unable to protect their borders from foreign encroachments on their own.

rule making The administrative process that creates rules that have the characteristics of a law.

Rule of Four The requirement that a minimum of four justices must vote to review a lower court case by issuing a writ of certiorari.

ruling elite theory The view positing that wealthy and well-educated citizens exercise a disproportionate amount of influence over political decision making.

runoff elections A second election between the top two vote-getters in a race that did not produce a majority winner.

safe district An electoral district in which the candidate from the dominant party usually wins by 55 percent or more.

safe seats Legislative districts that regularly remain in the hands of the same candidate or party.

salience The attribute of an individual's opinion that indicates how central it is to her or his daily concerns.

sample The individuals whose opinions are actually measured.

sampling error The measure of the degree of accuracy of a poll based on the size of the sample.

scientific polls Any poll using proper sampling designs.

second party system The period from the late 1820s until about 1854 in which the Democrats dominated American politics and in which the Whig Party became ascendant.

selective incorporation The process of applying some of the rights in the Bill of Rights to the states through the due process clause of the Fourteenth Amendment.

Senate Majority Leader The leader of the majority party in the Senate, responsible for organizing the body and marshaling support for the party's agenda. The Senate majority leader exercises powers similar to those of both the Speaker and the majority leader in the House combined.

Senate minority leader The leader of the minority party in the Senate, responsible for marshaling support from party members for the party's agenda.

senatorial courtesy In the selection of lower federal court judges, the deference shown to home-state senators who are of the same party as the president.

seniority The length of service in the body (House or Senate) and on a committee.

service learning programs Learning strategy that incorporates service to community with classroom education.

sexual harassment The practice of awarding jobs or job benefits in exchange for sexual favors, or the creation of a hostile work or education environment by unwarranted sexual advances or sexual conversation.

signing statement A comment issued by the president upon signing legislation. Some of these are merely ceremonial; others signal an intent not to enforce some provisions because the president believes them to be improper or unconstitutional.

simple random sampling The technique of drawing a sample for interview in which all members of the targeted population have the same probability of being selected for interview.

single issue or candidate Minor parties arising in electoral response to important issues not addressed by major-party candidates or around a strong personality.

single-member district An electoral system in which the candidate receiving a plurality of votes wins the election to represent the district.

slander Oral statements that are false and injure another's reputation.

social capital Bonds of trust and reciprocity between citizens that form the glue that holds modern societies together.

social class   The perceived combination of wealth, income, education, and occupation that contributes to one's status and power in society.

soft money   Unlimited sums of money raised from corporations, unions, and wealthy individuals used to support party activities. Political parties are no longer able to raise this type of funds.

soft power   The ability to persuade others without coercion.

sound bites   News programs' short video clips of politicians' statements.

sovereign   Independent.

Speaker of the House   The most powerful leader of the House of Representatives.

special or select committees   Committees in either house set up to handle matters that do not routinely fit into areas covered by existing standing committees.

spin   A campaign's favorable interpretation of their campaign and unfavorable view of their opponent's activities.

spin doctors   Political campaign operatives who interpret campaign events in the most favorable light to their candidate.

splinter parties   Political parties that are formed as offshoots of major political parties, usually by dissenters.

spoils system   The expansion of the patronage system to a level of corruption that placed political cronies into all levels of government.

stability   The attribute of an individual's opinion that measures how consistently it is held.

standing   Proof that a party has suffered harm or been threatened with harm by the circumstances surrounding a lawsuit.

standing committees   Permanent bodies within each House specializing in the consideration of particular subject areas.

state secrets privilege   The assertion of the presidential right to withhold information from the public and from other branches of government for reasons of national security.

strategy   A group's overall plan for achieving its goals.

straw poll   An unscientific survey of popular views.

strength of party identification   The degree of loyalty that an individual feels toward a particular political party.

strict scrutiny test   The equal protection test used by the Supreme Court that places the greatest burden of proof on the government to prove that classifications such as age, gender, or race are the least restrictive means to achieve a compelling government goal.

subcommittee   A subunit of a congressional committee charged with considering specialized matters within the committee's jurisdiction and reporting its findings back to the full committee.

Sullivan **rule**   The standard requiring public officials and public figures in defamation suits to prove that allegedly libelous or slanderous statements are both false and made with malice.

summit meeting   A high-level meeting of heads of state or government leaders, usually to plan or consummate major pacts or treaties.

sunset laws   Laws that include an expiration date.

Super PACs   Independent expenditure-only committees that are permitted to accept unlimited contributions and make unlimited expenditures to help elect or defeat federal candidates.

superdelegates   The term used to refer to Democratic Party leaders and elected officials attending the party convention who may pledge support to a candidate prior to the convention.

supply-side economics   An approach to economic policymaking focusing on lowering the barriers to production on the assumption that supplies at the right price will create their own demand.

supremacy clause   Provision of Article VI stipulating that the federal government, in exercising any of the powers enumerated in the Constitution, must prevail over any conflicting or inconsistent state exercise of power.

swing voter   A voter lacking strong attachment to one party or another and who likely votes across party lines.

symbolic speech   Ideas expressed by actions or symbols rather than words.

systematic sampling   A sample design to ensure that each individual in the population has an equal chance of being chosen after the first name or number is chosen at random.

tactics   Specific actions that groups take to implement strategies.

Temporary Assistance for Needy Families   A program funded by federal and state governments to provide financial assistance to pregnant women and families with one or more dependent children to help pay for necessities such as food and shelter.

test case   The practice by which a group deliberately brings a case to court in order to secure a judicial ruling on a constitutional issue.

third party   A minor party that runs a slate of its own candidates in opposition to major-party organizations in an election.

third party system   The period from about 1854 to the late 1890s in which the newly formed Republican Party gained prominence while the Democrats split into factions. This period was marked by very high levels of voter turnout and corruption.

Thirteenth Amendment   The Civil War amendment that specifically prohibited slavery in the United States.

top-two primary   A primary election in which voters choose from a list of all candidates regardless of party, with the top two facing off in the general election.

tracking polls   Campaign polls that measure candidates' relative strength on a daily basis.

trial heat survey   A campaign poll that measures the popularity of competing candidates in a particular electoral race.

Truman Doctrine   The foreign policy position advanced by President Harry Truman asserting the United States' intention to prevent Soviet expansion after World War II.

trustee style   A style of representation stressing the lawmaker's own judgment in legislative decision making.

unallocated delegates   Elected officials and party leaders chosen as delegates to the national party conventions with the ability to cast their votes for any candidate regardless of primary election results.

unconventional participation   Less common forms of participation that often challenge or defy authority.

unfunded mandates   Requirements imposed on state and local governments for which the federal government provides no funds for compliance.

unicameral   Single-body legislature.

unit rule   The practice of awarding all of a state's electoral votes to the candidate who wins a plurality of the popular vote in presidential contests.

unitary executive   The theory stressing the importance of giving the president greater authority in foreign policy and in enforcing discipline over members of the executive bureaucracy.

Virginia Plan   Edmund Randolph's proposal at the Constitutional Convention for a strong central government comprising a two-house legislative body apportioned by population with the power to make and enforce laws and collect taxes.

voter fatigue   A tendency to tire of the process of voting as a result of frequent elections.

Voting Rights Act of 1965   Federal legislation that outlawed literacy tests and empowered federal officials to enter southern states to register African American voters; the act dismantled the most significant barriers to African Americans' suffrage rights.

welfare   The term characterizing the wide variety of social programs developed during the New Deal to help the poor, unemployed, disabled, and elderly.

whips   Assistant party leaders in each house whose jobs include ensuring that party members are present for floor votes and prepared to vote as the party prefers.

whistle-blowing   The practice whereby individuals in the bureaucracy bring public attention to gross inefficiency or corruption in the government.

White House staff   Senior leadership advising the president.

World Trade Organization   The international body concerned with negotiating the rules of trade among nations.

writ of certiorari   An order issued by a superior court to one of inferior jurisdiction demanding the record of a particular case.

Endnotes

Chapter 1: Citizenship: In Our Changing Democracy

1. U.S. Census Bureau, "Millennials Outnumber Baby Boomers and Are Far More Diverse, Census Bureau Report," June 25, 2015, https://www.census.gov/newsroom/press-releases/2015/cb15-113.html.

2. Ibid.

3. Niki Graf, "Today's Young Workers Are More Likely Than Ever to Have A Bachelor's Degree," Pew Research Center, May 16, 2017, http://www.pewresearch.org/fact-tank/2017/05/16/todays-young-workers-are-more-likely-than-ever-to-have-a-bachelors-degree/.

4. National Association of Realtors, *Home Buyer and Seller Generational Trends Report,* March 7, 2017, https://www.nar.realtor/sites/default/files/reports/2017/2017-home-buyer-and-seller-generational-trends-03-07-2017.pdf.

5. U.S. Census Bureau, *1980–2016 Voting and Registration Supplements,* 2017, https://census.gov/content/dam/Census/library/visualizations/2017/comm/voting-rates-age.pdf.

6. Paul Taylor and Scott Keeter, eds., *Millennials: A Portrait of Generation Next,* Pew Research Center, February 2010, 78, http://www.pewsocialtrends.org/files/2010/10/millennials-confident-connected-open-to-change.pdf.

7. Cathy Cohen, Joseph Kahne, Benjamin Bowyer, Ellen Middaugh, and John Rogowski, *Participatory Politics: New Media and Youth Political Action* (Oakland, CA: MacArthur Research Network on Youth and Participatory Politics, June 2012), http://ypp.dmlcentral.net/sites/all/files/publications/YPP_Survey_Report_FULL.pdf.

8. Aaron J. Martin, *Young People and Politics: Political Engagement in the Anglo-American Democracies* (New York: Routledge, 2012), 93–94.

9. Rebecca Jacobsen and Tamara Wilder Linkow, *The Engaged Citizen Index: Examining the Racial and Ethnic Civic Political Engagement Gaps of Young Adults* (Tufts University Center for Research on Civic Learning and Engagement, February 2012), http://civicyouth.org/featured-the-engaged-citizen-index-examining-the-racial-and-ethnic-civic-and-political-engagement-gaps-of-young-adults/.

10. Jennifer L. Lawless and Richard L. Fox, *Running from Office: Why Young Americans Are Turned Off to Politics* (New York: Oxford, 2015), 109.

11. Lawless and Fox, 27.

12. Jeffrey M. Jones, "Americans' Trust in Political Leaders, Public at New Lows," Gallup News, September 21, 2016, http://news.gallup.com/poll/195716/americans-trust-political-leaders-public-new-lows.aspx.

13. Robert D. Putnam, *Bowling Alone: The Collapse and Revival of American Community* (New York: Simon & Schuster, 2000).

14. See, for example, C. Everett Ladd, *The Ladd Report* (New York: Free Press, 1999).

15. Aaron J. Martin, *Young People and Politics: Political Engagement in the Anglo-American Democracies* (New York: Routledge, 2012), especially 87–101.

16. See, for example, C. Wright Mills, *The Power Elite* (New York: Oxford University Press, 1956); Michael Parenti, *Democracy for the Few,* 7th ed. (Belmont, CA: Wadsworth Publishing, 2001); Gaetano Mosca, *The Ruling Class* (Boston: McGraw-Hill, 1959); see also Peter Bachrach, *The Theory of Democratic Elitism: A Critique* (Boston: Little-Brown, 1967).

17. Robert Dahl, *A Preface to Democratic Theory: How Does Popular Sovereignty Function in America?* (Chicago: University of Chicago Press, 1963).

18. Martin Gilens and Benjamin I. Page, "Testing Theories of American Politics: Elites, Interest Groups, and Average Citizens," *Perspectives on Politics* 12 (2014): 564–581.

19. Joseph Losco and Leonard Williams, *Political Theory: Classic and Contemporary Readings,* vol. 2, 2d ed. (Los Angeles: Roxbury Press, 2003).

20. Russel Thornton, *American Indian Holocaust and Survival: A Population History Since 1492* (Norman: University of Oklahoma Press, 1990), 43.

21. Myron Orfield and Thomas Luce, *America's Racially Diverse Suburbs: Opportunities and Challenges* (Minneapolis: Institute for Metropolitan Opportunity, University of Minnesota Law School, July 20, 2012), 2, http://www.law.umn.edu/uploads/e0/65/e065d82a1c1d-a0bfef7d86172ec5391e/Diverse_Suburbs_FINAL.pdf.

22. Paul Taylor and Richard Fry, "The Rise of Residential Segregation by Income," Pew Research Center, August 1, 2012, http://www.pewsocialtrends.org/2012/08/01/the-rise-of-residential-segregation-by-income/.

23. Amy Widestrom, "Building Civic Environments to Empower Citizens," *PS: Political Science and Politics* 50:4 (October 2017), 997–999.

24. Michael Olander, Emily Hoban Kirby, and Krista Schmitt, *Attitudes of Young People Towards Diversity,* Fact Sheet of the Center for Information and Research on Civic Learning and Engagement, February 2005.

25. Aaron Smith, "Record Number of Americans Now Own Smartphones, Have Home Broadband," Pew Research Center, January 12, 2017, http://www.pewresearch.org/fact-tank/2017/01/12/evolution-of-technology/.

26. See Lee Rainie, "Cell Phone Ownership Hits 91% of Adults," Pew Research Center, June 6, 2013, http://www.pewresearch.org/fact-tank/2013/06/06/cell-phone-ownership-hits-91-of-adults/; and Cecilia Kang, "Number of Cell Phones Exceeds US Population," *Washington Post,* November 11, 2011.

27. Organization for Economic Co-operation and Development, *Income Inequality,* 2015. Accessed on March 23, 2018 at https://data.oecd.org/inequality/income-inequality.htm.

28. Lael Brainard, "Labor Market Disparities and Economic Performance," Board of Governors of the Federal Reserve System, September 27, 2017, https://www.federalreserve.gov/newsevents/speech/brainard20170927a.htm; see also Emmanuel Saez, "Striking It Richer: The Evolution of Top Incomes in the United States (updated with 2015 preliminary estimates)," June 30, 2016, https://eml.berkeley.edu/~saez/saez-UStopincomes-2015.pdf.

29. Alfred Stepan and Juan J. Linz, "Comparative Perspectives on Inequality and the Quality of Democracy in the United States," *Perspectives on Politics* 9:4 (December 2011): 852.

30. Hertz, Tom. "Understanding Mobility in America," *Report for Center for American Progress,* April 2006, 32.

31. Patricia Atkins, Pamela Blumenthal, Adrienne Edisis, Alec Friedhoff, Leah Curran, Lisa Lowry, Travis St. Clair, Howard Wial, and Harold Wolman, *Responding to Manufacturing Job Loss: What Can Economic Development Policy Do?* (Washington, DC: Brookings Institution, June 2011), http://www.brookings.edu/~/media/Files/rc/

papers/2011/06_manufacturing_job_loss/06_manufacturing_job_loss.pdf on March 6, 2012.

32. "Poll: Public Service Valued; Politics—Not So Much," *USA Today,* July 21, 2013. See also, Lawless and Fox.

33. Dave Harker, "Political Consciousness but Not Political Engagement: Results from a Service Learning Study," *Michigan Journal of Community Service Learning* (Spring 2016): 31–47, http://files.eric.ed.gov/fulltext/EJ1137442.pdf.

34. See Alison Rios Millet McCartney, "Introduction." *Teaching Civic Education Across the Disciplines* (Washington, DC: American Political Science Association, 2017), 3–10.

35. Ibid.

Chapter 2: The Constitution: The Foundation of Citizens' Rights

1. Gallup Organization, "Americans' Support for Electoral College Rises Sharply," December 2, 2016, http://news.gallup.com/poll/198917/americans-support-electoral-college-rises-sharply.aspx.

2. Dionne, E.J. Jr., Ornstein, N.J. and Mann, T.E., *One Nation After Trump: A Guide to the Perplexed, the Disillusioned, the Desperate, and the Not-Yet Deported* (New York: St. Martins, 2017), 29.

3. Philip Bump, "The Senate May Be Developing an Electoral College Issue," *The Washington Post,* April 10, 2017, https://www.washingtonpost.com/news/politics/wp/2017/04/10/the-senate-may-be-developing-an-electoral-college-issue/.

4. For examples of the range of proposals being floated for a new constitution, see Alex Seitz-Wald, "The U.S. Needs a New Constitution—Here's How to Write It," *The Atlantic,* November 2, 2013, https://www.the-atlantic.com/politics/archive/2013/11/the-us-needs-a-new-constitution-heres-how-to-write-it/281090/.

5. David S. Law and Mila Versteeg, "The Declining Influence of the United States Constitution," *New York University Law Review,* 87 (2012), http://ssrn.com/abstract=1923556.

6. Charles Beard, *An Economic Interpretation of the Constitution of the United States* (New York: Macmillan, 1913).

7. John P. Roche, "The Founding Fathers: A Reform Caucus in Action," *American Political Science Review* 55 (1961): 816.

8. Congressional Quarterly, *Origins and Development of Congress,* 2d ed. (Washington, DC: Congressional Quarterly, 1982).

9. Roche, 816.

10. Madison, J. "Federalist 51," *The Federalist Papers,* Clinton Rossiter, ed. (New York: Mentor, 1961), 322.

11. Ibid., 323.

12. Keenan, Joseph J. *The Constitution and the United States: An Unfolding Story,* 2d ed. (Chicago: Dorsey Press, 1988), 27.

13. Henry, P. "Against the Federal Constitution: June 5, 1788," *American Rhetorical Movements to 1900.* Retrieved from http://www.wfu.edu.

14. James Madison, "Federalist 10," *The Federalist Papers,* Clinton Rossiter, ed. (New York: Mentor, 1961), 77–84.

15. Quoted in Keenan, 35.

16. Daniel Diller and Stephen H. Wirls, "Commander in Chief," in *Powers of the Presidency,* 2d ed. (Washington, DC: CQ Press, 1997), 165.

17. Hamilton, A. "Federalist 78," *The Federalist Papers,* Clinton Rossiter, ed. (New York: Mentor, 1961), p. 467.

18. *Roe v. Wade,* 410 U.S. 113 (1973)

19. Frederick Jackson Turner, *The Frontier in American History* (New York: Holt, 1920).

20. Pub. L. 108–447, *Consolidated Appropriations Act,* 2005.

Chapter 3: Federalism: Citizenship and the Dispersal of Power

1. John Burnett, "Border Patrol Arrests Parents While Infant Awaits Serious Operation," National Public Radio, September 20, 2017, http://www.npr.org/2017/09/20/552339976/border-patrol-arrests-parents-while-infant-awaits-serious-operation.

2. H. Robert Baker, "A Brief History of Sanctuary Cities," Tropics of Meta, February 2, 2017, https://tropicsofmeta.wordpress.com/2017/02/02/a-brief-history-of-sanctuary-cities/.

3. U.S. Census Bureau, *Governments Integrated Directory, 2007.* Retrieved March 8, 2018, from http://www.census.gov/govs/www/gid2007.html.

4. Madison, James, "Federalist 51", *The Federalist Papers,* Clinton Rossiter, ed. (New York: Mentor, 1961), 232.

5. Steven Macedo, Yvete Alex-Assensoh, Jeffrey M. Berry, Michael Brintnall, David E. Campbell, Luis Ricardo Fraga, Archon Fung, William A. Galston, Christopher F. Karpowitz, Margaret Levi, Meira Levinson, Keena Lipsitz, Richard G. Niemi, Robert D. Putnam, Wendy M. Rahn, Rob Reich, Robert R. Rogers, Todd Swanstrom, and Katherine Cramer Walsh, *Democracy at Risk: How Political Choices Undermine Citizen Participation and What We Can Do About It* (Washington, DC: Brookings Institution, 2005), 68–73.

6. *McCulloch v. Maryland,* 4 Wheaton 316 (1819).

7. *McCulloch v. Maryland,* 4 Wheaton 316 (1819).

8. For an excellent discussion of the legacy of Jefferson's nullification movement and its contribution to factional strife leading to the Civil War, see Garry Wills, *A Necessary Evil: A History of American Distrust of Government* (New York: Simon & Schuster, 1999).

9. *Dred Scott v. Sandford,* 60 U.S. 393 (1857).

10. *Hammer v. Dagenhart,* 247 U.S. 251 (1918).

11. *U.S. v. E.C. Knight Co.,* 156 U.S. 1 (1895).

12. *Lochner v. New York,* 198 U.S. 45 (1905).

13. *Schechter Poultry Co. v. U.S.,* 295 U.S. 495 (1935).

14. *U.S. v. Butler,* 297 U.S. 1 (1936).

15. *Brown v. Board of Education of Topeka,* 347 U.S. 483 (1954).

16. *Roe v. Wade,* 401 U.S. 113 (1973).

17. See, for example, *Gideon v. Wainwright,* 372 U.S. 335 (1963).

18. *South Carolina v. Katzenbach,* 383 U.S. 301 (1966).

19. *United States v. Lopez,* 514 U.S. 549 (1995).

20. *Printz v. United States,* 521 U.S. 898 (1997).

21. *Kimel v. Florida Board of Regents,* 528 U.S. 62 (2000).

22. *Board of Trustees v. Garrett,* 531 U.S. 356 (2001).

23. Donald Boyd, "2006 Rockefeller Institute Reports on State and Local Government Finances," Rockefeller Institute for Government, May 2006.

24. Ben Canada, *Federal Grants to State and Local Government: A Brief History* (Washington, DC: Congressional Research Service, 2003).

25. Robert Jay Dilger, *Federal Grants to State and Local Governments: A Historical Perspective on Contemporary Issues* (Washington, DC: Congressional Research Service, 2015).

26. The first block grant, the Partnership for Public Health, was created by Congress in 1966. See Canada, 2003, 11.

27. Dilger, 2015, 24.

28. Kenneth Finegold, Laura Wherry, and Stephanie Schardin, "Block Grants: Historic Overview and Lessons Learned," *New Federalism: Issues and Options for States,* Series A, No. A-63 (Washington, DC: Urban Institute, 2004).

29. Dilger, 2015, 37.

30. David C. Nice and Patricia Fredericksen, *The Politics of Intergovernmental Relations,* 2d ed. (Chicago: Nelson-Hall, 1995), 35.

31. See, for example, Paul E. Peterson, "Federalism, Economic Development, and Redistribution," in J. David Greenstone, ed., *Public Values and Private Power in American Politics* (Chicago: University of Chicago Press, 1982). Also see Grant McConnell, *Private Power and American Democracy* (New York: Knopf, 1966).

32. *Obergefell et al. v. Hodges, Director, Ohio Department of Health, et al.,* 576 U.S. ____ (2015).

33. *Arizona v. U.S.,* 567 U.S. ____ (2012).

34. *Garcia v. San Antonio Metropolitan Transit Authority,* 469 U.S. 528 (1985).

35. *United States v. Lopez,* 514 U.S. 549 (1995).

36. *United States v. Morrison,* 529 U.S. 598 (2000).

37. *National Federation of Independent Business v. Sebelius,* 567 U.S. ____ (2012).

38. *National League of Cities v. Usery,* 426 U.S. 833 (1976).

39. *New York v. United States,* 505 U.S. 144 (1992).

40. *Printz v. United States,* 521 U.S. 898 (1997).

41. *Gonzales v. Raich,* 545 U.S. 1 (2005).

42. *Alden v. Maine,* 527 U.S. 706 (1999)

43. *Kimel v. Florida Board of Regents,* 528 U.S. 62 (2000).

44. *Tennessee v. Lane,* 541 U.S. 509 (2004).

45. *District of Columbia v. Heller,* 554 U.S. 570 (2008).

46. *Obergefell v. Hodges.*

47. *Virginia v. Maryland,* 540 U.S. 56 (2003).

48. Nice and Fredericksen, 122.

49. *New State Ice Co. v. Liebmann,* 285 U.S. 262 (1932)

50. Jack L. Walker, "The Diffusion of Innovations Among the American States," *American Political Science Review 63,* no. 3 (1969): 880–899. For somewhat differing analyses and a discussion of the methodological problems involved in measuring innovation and diffusion, see Virginia Gray, "Innovation in the States: A Diffusion Study," *American Political Science Review 67* (1973): 1174–1185; Jack L. Walker, "Comment: Problems in Research on the Diffusion of Policy Innovation," *American Political Science Review 67* (1973): 1186–1191; John L. Foster, "Regionalism and Innovation in the American States," *Journal of Politics* 40:1 (1978): 179–187; and David C. Nice, *Policy Innovation in the States* (Ames: Iowa State University Press, 1994).

51. Andrew Karch, *Democratic Laboratories: Policy Diffusion Among the American States* (Ann Arbor, MI: University of Michigan Press, 2010), 51; Daniel J. Elazar, *Federalism: A View from the States,* 3d ed. (New York: HarperCollins, 1984).

52. Susan Welch and Kay Thompson, "The Impact of Federal Incentives on State Policy Innovation," *American Journal of Political Science* 24:4 (1980): 715–729.

53. Macedo, S., et al., *Democracy at Risk: How Political Choices Undermine Citizen Participation, and What We Can Do About It,* (Brookings Institution Press, 2006).

54. Tocqueville, Alexis de. Trans. Lawrence, George edited by Mayer, J.P., *Democracy in America,* (New York: HarperCollins, 1969,) 164.

Chapter 4: Civil Liberties: Citizens' Rights versus Security

1. Barnes, R., "The Spurned Gay Couple, the Colorado Baker and Years Spent Waiting for the Supreme Court, *"The Washington Post,* August 14, 2017. https://www.denverpost.com/2017/08/14/colorado-gay-wedding-cake-case/

2. Daniel J. Elazar, "How Present Conceptions of Human Rights Shape the Protection of Rights in the United States," in Robert A. Licht, ed., *Old Rights and New* (Washington, DC: AEI Press, 1993), 39.

3. Daniel A. Farber and Suzanna Sherry, *A History of the American Constitution* (St. Paul, MN: West Publishing Company, 1990), 221–222.

4. Alexander Hamilton, John Jay, and James Madison, *The Federalist Papers,* Benjamin F. Wright, ed. (New York: Metro Books, 1961), 535.

5. Of the two that were rejected, one provided that states add a representative to the House each time their population grew by 30,000 and the other called for an intervening congressional election before any pay raise for members of Congress could take effect. The latter became the Twenty-Seventh Amendment nearly two hundred years later.

6. *Barron v. Mayor & City Council of Baltimore,* 32 U.S. 243 (1833)

7. Highlighting supplied by the authors.

8. Farber and Sherry, *A History of the American Constitution,* 122–123.

9. Although the establishment clause is mentioned first in the First Amendment, the free exercise clause is dealt with first because its interpretation is easier for students to understand.

10. Letter quoted in *Reynolds v. United States* (1879)

11. *Cantwell v. Connecticut* (1940).

12. *Reynolds v. United States* (1879) and *Employment Division, Department of Human Resources of Oregon v. Smith* (1990).

13. *Sherbert v. Verner* (1963).

14. *Wisconsin v. Yoder* (1972).

15. *Goldman v. Weinberg* (1986)

16. *City of Boerne v. Flores* (1997).

17. Frank Newport, "Religion Remains a Strong Marker of Political Identity in U.S.," Gallup, July 28, 2014, http://www.gallup.com/poll/174134/religion-remains-strong-marker-political-identity.aspx.

18. Malbin, *Religion and Politics.*

19. *Lemon v. Kurtzman* (1971).

20. *Walz v. Tax Commission of the City of New York* (1970).

21. *Epperson v. Arkansas* (1968).

22. *Edwards v. Aguillard* (1987).

23. *Widmar v. Vincent* (1981).

24. *Engel v. Vitale,* 370 U.S. 421 (1962)

25. *School District of Abington Township v. Schempp* (1965).

26. Lee Epstein, Jeffrey A. Segal, Harold J. Spaeth, and Thomas G. Walker, *The Supreme Court Compendium: Data, Decisions, and Developments* (Washington, DC: Congressional Quarterly, 2003), Tables 8–23.

27. *Wallace v. Jaffree* (1985).

28. *Lee v. Weisman* (1992).

29. *Santa Fe Independent School District v. Doe* (2000).

30. *Town of Greece v. Galloway.*

31. *Zobrest v. Catalina Foothills School District* (1993).

32. *Agostini v. Felton* (1997).

33. *Zelman v. Simmons-Harris* (2002).

34. *County of Allegheny v. ACLU* (1989).

35. *Lynch v. Donnelly* (1984).

36. *Van Orden v. Perry* (2005).

37. *McCreary County v. ACLU of Kentucky* (2005).

38. John Stuart Mill, *Essential Works of John Stuart Mill,* Max Lerner, ed. (New York: Bantam Books, 1961).

39. *Schenck v. United States* (1919).

40. *Whitney v. California* (1927).

41. *Gitlow v. New York* (1925)

42. *Brandenburg v. Ohio* (1969).

43. *Buckley v. Valeo* (1976).

44. *Virginia State Board of Pharmacy v. Virginia Citizens Consumer Council, Inc.* (1976).

45. *Bates v. State Bar of Arizona* (1977).

46. *United States v. O'Brien* (1968).

47. *Tinker v. Des Moines School District* (1969).

48. *Texas v. Johnson* (1989).

49. *United States v. Eichman,* 496 U.S. 310 (1990)

50. *Jacobellis v. Ohio* (1964)

51. *Miller v. California* (1973)

52. *Snyder v. Phelps* (2011).

53. *Blackstone's Commentaries on the Laws of England,* vol. 4 (London, 1765–1769), 151–152.

54. *Smith v. Daily Mail Publishing Company* (1979)

55. *Nebraska Press Association v. Stuart* (1976).

56. *Miami Herald Publishing v. Tornillo* (1974).

57. *Branzburg v. Hayes* (1972).

58. *Houchins v. KQED* (1978).

59. *Wilson v. Layne* (1999).

60. *Gannett Company v. DePasquale* (1979).

61. *Edwards v. South Carolina,* 372 U.S. 229 (1963)

62. *Cox v. Louisiana* (1965).

63. *Adderley v. Florida* (1966).

64. *Madsen v. Women's Health Center, Incorporated* (1994).

65. *Hill v. Colorado* (2000).

66. *NAACP v. Button* (1963).

67. *Board of Directors of Rotary International v. Rotary Club of Duarte* (1987).

68. *New York State Club Association v. City of New York* (1988).

69. *Hurley v. Irish-American Gay, Lesbian and Bisexual Group of Boston* (1995).

70. *Boy Scouts of America v. Dale,* 530 U.S. 640 (2000)

71. Highlighting supplied by the authors.

72. *United States v. Miller* (1939).

73. *District of Columbia v. Heller* (2007).

74. *McDonald v. City of Chicago* (2010)

75. The taking clause of the Fifth Amendment that guarantees a citizen the right to just compensation for property taken by the government is the only provision not related to the rights of the accused in the Fourth, Fifth, Sixth, and Eighth Amendments.

76. *Messerschmidt v. Millender* (2012).

77. *Chimel v. California* (1969).

78. *United States v. Knights* (2001).

79. *Warden v. Hayden* (1967).

80. *Illinois v. Wardlow* (2000).

81. *Cupp v. Murphy* (1973).

82. Ibid.

83. *Ferguson v. City of Charleston* (2001) and *Vernonia School District 47J v. Acton* (1995).

84. *Hester v. United States* (1924).

85. *Florida v. Riley* (1988).

86. *Kyllo v. United States* (2001).

87. *City of Indianapolis v. Edmond* (2000).

88. *Weeks v. United States* (1914) and *Mapp v. Ohio* (1961).

89. *United States v. Leon* (1984).

90. *Dickerson v. United States* (2000).

91. *Powell v. Alabama* (1932).

92. *Gideon v. Wainwright* (1963).

93. *Argesinger v. Wainwright* (1972).

94. *Scott v. Illinois* (1979).

95. *Alabama v. Shelton* (2002).

96. *Strauder v. West Virginia* (1880) for African Americans and *Taylor v. Louisiana* (1975) for women.

97. *Batson v. Kentucky* (1986), *Georgia v. McCullum* (1992), and *J.E.B. v. Alabama ex rel. T.B.* (1994).

98. *Williams v. Florida* (1970).

99. *Johnson v. Louisiana* (1972) and *Apodaca v. Oregon* (1972).

100. *Furman v. Georgia* (1972).

101. *Gregg v. Georgia* (1976).

102. *Atkins v. Georgia* (2002).

103. *Roper v. Simmons* (2005).

104. *Baze v. Rees* (2008).

105. *Kennedy v. Louisiana* (2008).

106. *Griswold v. Connecticut* (1965).

107. By the time her case reached the Supreme Court, McCorvey had already given birth to the baby and put it up for adoption.

108. Charles S. Franklin and Liane Kosaki, "The Republican Schoolmaster: The Supreme Court, Public Opinion, and Abortion," *American Political Science Review* 83 (1989): 751–772.

109. *Akron, Ohio v. Akron Center for Reproductive Health* (1983).

110. *Webster v. Reproductive Health Services* (1989).

111. *Beal v. Doe (1977)* and *Harris v. McRae* (1980).

112. *Gonzales v. Carhart* (2007).

113. *Cruzan v. Director, Missouri Department of Health* (1990).

114. *Watchtower Bible and Tract Society v. Stratton* (2002).

115. Gregory A. Calderia and John R. Wright, "Organized Interests and Agenda Setting in the U.S. Supreme Court" *Political Science Review* 82 (1988): 1109.

Chapter 5: Civil Rights: Toward A More Equal Citizenry

1. See Larkin, M. *"The Obama Administration Remade Sexual Assault Enforcement on Campus. Could Trump Unmake It?"* November 26, 2016, http://www.wbur.org/edify/2016/11/25/title-ix-obama-trump.

2. Miriam Gleckman-Krut and Nicole Bedera, "Who Gets to Define Campus Rape?" *The New York Times,* September 18, 2017, https://www.nytimes.com/2017/09/18/opinion/campus-sexual-assault-devos.html.

3. See Max Larkin, "The Obama Administration Remade Sexual Assault Enforcement on Campus."

4. Ben Sisario, Hawes Spencer, and Sydney Ember, "Rolling Stone Loses Defamation Case over Rape Story," *The New York Times,* November 5, 2016, https://www.nytimes.com/2016/11//05/business/medi/rolling-stone-rape-story-case-guilty.html.

5. Christopher Krebs and Christine Lindquist, "Setting the Record Straight on '1 in 5'," *Time,* December 15, 2014, http://time.com/3633903/campus-rape-1-in-5-sexual-assault-setting-record-straight/.

6. Lydia Wheeler, "DeVos Ignites Backlash with Rewrite of Sexual Assault Policy," *The Hill,* September 7, 2017, http://thehill.com/homenews/administration/349647-devos-to-change-obama-era-campus-sexual-assault-policy.

7. For an excellent discussion of the difference between civil liberties and civil rights, see John C. Domino, *Civil Rights and Liberties in the 21st Century,* 2d ed. (New York: Longman Publishers, 2003), 1–5.

8. *Dred Scott v. Sanford* (1857).

9. "Jim Crow" was the stereotypical name given to African Americans in a nineteenth-century minstrel song.

10. See Woodward, Vann C. "The Case of the Louisiana Traveler", in Garraty, J. A. ed., *Quarrels That Shaped the Constitution* (New York: Harper & Row: 1987), 157–174.

11. The grandfather clause denied the right to vote to anyone whose grandfather did not vote before the Reconstruction period.

12. For an excellent discussion of the NAACP's strategy, see Richard Kluger, *Simple Justice* (New York: Vintage Books, 1975).

13. The decision in *Missouri ex. Rel. Gaines v. Canada* (1938) led to the group's success in *Sweatt v. Painter* (1950).

14. *McLaurin v. Oklahoma* (1950).

15. *Brown v. Board of Education II* (1955)

16. *Swann v. Charlotte-Mecklenberg County Schools* (1971).

17. *Missouri v. Jenkins* (1995).

18. Southern Democratic senator Strom Thurmond conducted an eight-week filibuster to hold up the voting on the bill. It is the longest filibuster in the history of the United States.

19. *Heart of Atlanta Motel v. United States* (1964).

20. Margery Turner, "How Wide Are the Racial Opportunity Gaps in Your Metro," Urban Institute, February 2, 2012.

21. *San Antonio Independent School District v. Rodriguez* (1973).

22. *United Steelworkers of America v. Weber* (1979).

23. *United States v. Paradise* (1987).

24. *Local 28 of the Sheet Metal Workers v. EEOC* (1986) and *Johnson v. Transportation Agency of Santa Clara County, California* (1987).

25. *Aderand Constructors v. Pena* (1995).

26. John F. Kain, Daniel M. O'Brien, and Paul A. Jargowsky, *Hopwood and the Top 10 Percent Law: How They Affected The College Enrollment Decisions of Texas High School Graduates,* The Texas Schho Project, May 25, 2005.

27. *Meredith v. Jefferson Country Board of Education* (2007) and *Parents Involved in Community Schools v. Seattle School District No. 2* (2004).

28. For a criticism of affirmative action programs, see John David Skrentny, *The Ironies of Affirmative Action: Politics, Culture, and American Justice in America* (Chicago: The University of Chicago Press, 1996).

29. Harry Holzer and David Newmark, "Assessing Affirmative Action," *Journal of Economic Literature* 38 (2000): 245–269.

30. Rennard Strickland, "Native Americans," in Kermit Hall, ed., *The Oxford Companion to the Supreme Court of the United States* (New York: Oxford University Press, 1992), 557.

31. Dee Brown, *Bury My Heart at Wounded Knee* (New York: Holt, Rinehart, and Winston, 1971).

32. Joanne Nagel, *American Indian Ethnic Renewal: Red Power and the Resurgence of Identity and Culture* (New York: Oxford University Press, 1996).

33. David Pfeiffer, "Understanding Disability Policy," *Policy Studies Journal* (1996): 157–174.

34. *Cedar Rapids v. Garret F.* (1999).

35. *Bregdon v. Abbot* (1998).

36. *Sutton v. United Air Lines* (1999), *Albertsons v. Kirkinburg* (1999), and *Murphy v. United Parcel Service* (1999).

37. *O'Connor v. Consolidated Coil Casterers Corp.* (1996).

38. *Massachusetts Board of Retirement v. Murgia* (1976).

39. *Reeves v. Sanderson* (2000).

40. *Kimel v. Florida Board of Regents* (2000).

41. *CBOCS v. Humphries* (2007).

42. See Diane Helene Miller, *Freedom to Differ: The Shaping of the Gay and Lesbian Struggle for Civil Rights* (New York: New York University Press, 1998).

43. *Romer v. Evans* (1996).

44. *Bowers v. Hardwick* (1986).

45. *Boy Scouts of America v. Dale* (2000).

46. *Baehr v. Lewin* (1993).

47. Since women are the majority gender and yet have had to struggle to gain equal rights, the term "minority group" is inappropriate when applied to them.

48. See Judith A. Baer, *Equality Under the Constitution: Reclaiming the Fourteenth Amendment* (Ithaca, NY: Cornell University Press, 1983), 44–47.

49. See Nancy E. Glen and Karen O'Connor, *Women, Politics, and American Society,* 2d ed. (Upper Saddle River, NJ: Prentice Hall, 1998).

50. *Minor v. Happersett* (1875).

51. Robert Putnam sees this as one of the positive aspects of the Progressive Era in his *Bowling Alone* (New York: Simon & Schuster, 2000), chap. 23.

52. See Glen and O'Connor, *Women, Politics, and American Society,* 6–10.

53. *Hoyt v. Florida* (1961).

54. Orr v. Orr (1979)

55. *Mississippi University for Women v. Hogan* (1982).

56. *JEB v. Alabama ex rel.* (1996).

57. *Michael M. v. Superior Court of Sonoma County* (1981).

58. *Rotsker v. Goldberg* (1981).

59. Sara M. Evans and Barbara J. Nelson, *Wage Justice: Comparable Worth and the Paradox of Technocratic Reform* (Chicago: The University of Chicago Press, 1989).

60. *Meritor Savings v. Vinson* (1986).

61. *Burlington Industries v. Ellerth* (1998).

Chapter 6: Public Opinion

1. Bodenner, C. "How Could Obama Voters Vote for Trump?" *The Atlantic,* November 21, 2016, https://www.theatlantic.com/notes/2016/11/obama-voters-for-trump/508292/.

2. Ibid.

3. Federal Election Commission, "Official 2016 Presidential Election Results," November 8, 2016, https://transition.fec.gov/pubrec/fe2016/2016presgeresults.pdf.

4. Arthur Delaney, "Donald Trump Won Voters Who Said Trade Costs Jobs," *HuffPost,* November 9, 2016, https://www.huffingtonpost.com/entry/donald-trump-trade_us_582350ade4b0aac62488a5f2.

5. John Sides, "Race, Religion, and Immigration in 2016: How the Debate over American Identity Shaped the Election and What It Means for a Trump Presidency," Democracy Fund Voter Study Group, June 2017, https://www.voterstudygroup.org/publications/2016-elections/race-religion-immigration-2016.

6. Ibid.

7. Key, V. O. Jr. *Public Opinion and American Democracy* (New York: Alfred Knopf, 1961) 14.

8. Gabriel Almond and Sidney Verba, *The Civic Culture: Political Attitudes and Democracy in Five Nations* (Princeton, NJ: Princeton University Press, 1963). See also a series of critiques of the political culture thesis in Gabriel Almond and Sidney Verba, eds., *The Civic Culture Revisited* (Newbury Park, CA: Sage, 1989).

9. Herbert McClosky and John Zaller, *The American Ethos: Public Attitudes Toward Capitalism and Democracy* (Cambridge, MA: Harvard University Press, 1984).

10. Hamilton, A. *The Federalist Papers,* No. 71, Clinton Rossitor, ed. (New York: Mentor, 1961), 432.

11. Forrest McDonald, *The American Presidency: An Intellectual History* (Lawrence: University of Kansas Press, 1994), 216.

12. Michael Schudson, *The Good Citizen: A History of American Civic Life* (New York: Free Press, 1998), 121.

13. Tom W. Smith, "The First Straw? A Study of the Origin of Election Polls," *The Public Opinion Quarterly* 54 no. 1 (1990): 27.

14. Bernard Hennessey, *Public Opinion,* 4th ed. (Monterrey, CA: Brooks/Cole, 1981), 43.

15. See Fred I. Greenstein, *Children and Politics* (New Haven: Yale University Press, 1965); Robert D. Hess and Judith V. Torney, *The Development of Political Attitudes in Children* (Chicago: Aldine, 1967); and David Easton, *Children in the Political System: Origins of Political Legitimacy* (New York: McGraw-Hill, 1969).

16. David O. Sears, "Political Socialization," in Fred I. Greenstein and Nelson Polsby, eds., *Micropolitical Theory* (Reading, MA: Addison-Wesley, 1975), 93–153.

17. Ibid., 119.

18. M. Kent Jennings and Richard G. Niemi, "The Persistence of Political Orientations: An Over Time Analysis of Two Generations," *British Journal of Political Science* 8, no. 3 (1978): 333–363.

19. Richard G. Niemi and Jane Junn, *Civic Education: What Makes Students Learn?* (New Haven, CT: Yale, 1998).

20. Sidney Verba, Kay Lehman Schlozman, and Henry E. Brady, *Voice and Equality: Civic Voluntarism in American Politics* (Cambridge, MA: Harvard University Press, 1995), 422–426.

21. Michael T. Rogers, "The History of Civic Education in Political Science: The Story of a Discipline's Failure to Lead," in Elizabeth C. Matto, Alison Rios Millet McCartney, Elizabeth A. Bennion, and Dick Simpson, eds., *Teaching Civic Engagement Across the Disciplines* (Washington, DC: American Political Science Association, 2017), 85.

22. M. Kent Jennings, "Political Knowledge Across Time and Generations," *Public Opinion Quarterly* 60 (2006): 228–252.

23. Howe, Neil., and Nadler, R. *Yes We Can: The Emergence of Millennials as a Political Generation* (Washington, DC: New America Foundation, 2009), 18, https://www.lifecourse.com/assets/files/yes_we_can.pdf.

24. Paul Allen Beck, "The Role of Agents in Political Socialization," in Stanley Allen Renshon, ed., *Handbook of Political Socialization* (New York: Free Press, 1977), 117.

25. Lake, Snell, Perry, and Associates and the Tarrance Group, Inc., "Short-Term Impacts, Long-Term Opportunities: The Political and Civic Engagement of Young Adults in America," *Analysis and Report for the Center for Information and Research in Civic Learning & Engagement, The Center for Democracy and Citizenship, the Partnership for Trust in Government, and the Council for Excellence in Government,* March 2002, http://www.civicyouth.org/research/products/National_Youth_Survey/summary.pdf.

26. Jennifer L. Lawless and Richard L. Fox, *Running from Office: Why Young People Are Turned Off to Politics* (New York: Oxford, 2015), 62.

27. Lake, Snell, Perry and Associates, 2002.

28. Pew Research Center, "U.S. Public Becoming Less Religious," Nov. 3, 2015. Accessed on August 4, 2018 at http://assets.pewresearch.org/wp-content/uploads/sites/11/2015/11/201.11.03_RLS_II_full_report.pdf.

29. Verba, Schlozman, and Brady, *Voice and Equality,* 228–268.

30. Lake, Snell, Perry, and Associates and the Terrance Group, Inc. See also Bipartisan Policy Center/*USA Today* National Survey on Public Service, July 22, 2013, http://bipartisanpolicy.org/library/research/bpcusa-today-national-survey-public-service.

31. David E. Campbell, *Why We Vote: How Schools and Communities Shape Our Civic Life* (Princeton, NJ: Princeton University Press, 2006). See also, Rogers, "The History of Civic Education in Political Science," 87.

32. See Paul Lazarsfeld, Bernard Berelson, and Hazel Gaudet, *The People's Choice* (New York: Columbia University Press, 1948); and Bernard Berelson, Paul Lazarsfeld, and William McPhee, *Voting* (Chicago: University of Chicago Press, 1954).

33. Pew Research Center, *In Changing News Landscape, Even Television Is Vulnerable,* September 27, 2012, http://www.people-press.org/files/legacy-pdf/2012%20News%20Consumption%20Report.pdf. See also Doris Graber, *Processing the News* (New York: Longman, 1988).

34. Ibid.

35. Pew Research Center, *Millennials and Political News,* June 1, 2015, http://www.journalism.org/files/2015/06/Millennials-and-News-FINAL-7-27-15.pdf.

36. Franklin D. Gilliam, Jr., and Shanto Iyengar, "Prime Suspects: The Influence of Local Television News on the Viewing Public," *American Journal of Political Science* 44:3 (2000): 560–573.

37. American National Election Studies SETUPS: Voting Behavior: The 2012 Election. Analysis run on December 19, 2013 (08:14 AM EST) using SDA 3.5: Tables.

38. Pew Research Center, "The Rise of Asian Americans," June 19, 2012, http://www.pewsocialtrends.org/2012/06/19/the-rise-of-asian-americans/.

39. CNN. *Exit Polls.* November 23, 2016. Accessed on November 14, 2017 at http://www.cnn.com/election/results/exit-polls/national/president.

40. Myriam Miedaian, *Boys Will Be Boys: The Link Between Masculinity and Violence* (New York: Doubleday, 1991).

41. Michael X. Delli-Carpini and Scott Keeter, *What Americans Know About Politics and Why It Matters* (New Haven, CT: Yale University Press, 1996), 203–209.

42. Sidney Verba, Nancy Burns, and Kay Lehman Schlozman, "Knowing and Caring about Politics: Gender and Political Engagement," *The Journal of Politics* 59 (1997): 1055.

43. Kay Lehman Schlozman, Sidney Verba, and Henry E. Brady, *The Unheavenly Chorus: Unequal Political Voice and the Broken Promise of American Democracy* (Princeton, NJ: Princeton University Press, 2012), see esp. 137–146, 188–192.

44. Lawless and Fox, *Running from Office,* 29.

45. Frank Newport, "Majority Still Extremely Proud to Be American," Gallup Organization, July 3, 2006, http://news.gallup.com/poll/23557/majority-still-extremely-proud-american.aspx.

46. Daniel Elazar, *American Federalism: A View from the States,* 3d ed. (New York: Harper Collins, 1984).

47. Bill Bishop, *The Big Sort: Why the Clustering of Like-Minded Americans Is Tearing Us Apart* (Boston: Mariner Books, 2009); Alan I. Abramowitz and Kyle L. Saunders, "Ideological Realignment in the U.S. Electorate," *Journal of Politics* 60:3 (1998): 634–652; and Corey Lang and Shanna Pearson-Merkowitz, *Partisan Sorting in the United States, 1972–2012: New Evidence from a Dynamic Analysis, Political Geography* 48 (2015), 119–129.

48. Jesse Sussell, "New Support for the Big Sort Hypothesis: An Assessment of Partisan Geographic Sorting in California, 1992–2010," *PS: Political Science and Politics* 46:4 (2013): 768–773.

49. Gamio, L. "Urban and Rural America Are Becoming Increasingly Polarized," *The Washington Post,* November 17, 2016 https://www.washingtonpost.com/graphics/politics/2016-election/urban-rural-vote-swing/?noredirect=on.

50. See, for example, Brendan Nyhan and Jason Reifler, "When Corrections Fail: The Persistence of Political Misperceptions," *Political Behavior* 32:2 (June 2010): 303–330.

51. Jonas T. Kaplan, Sarah I. Gimbel, and Sam Harris, "Neural Correlates of Maintaining One's Political Beliefs in the Face of Counterevidence," *Scientific Reports* 6 (2016), https://www.nature.com/articles/srep39589.pdf.

52. American Association of Public Opinion Research, *An Evaluation of 2016 Election Polls in the U.S.* 2017, https://www.aapor.org/

Education-Resources/Reports/An-Evaluation-of-2016-Election-Polls-in-the-U-S.aspx.

53. John Sides, "Which Was the Most Accurate National Poll in the 2016 Presidential Election?" *The Washington Post,* December 5, 2016, https://www.washingtonpost.com/news/monkey-cage/wp/2016/12/05/which-was-the-most-accurate-national-poll-in-the-2016-presidential-election/?noredirect=on.

54. Herbert Asher, *Polling and the Public: What Every Citizen Should Know,* 6th ed. (Washington, DC: Congressional Quarterly Press, 2004), 28.

55. Annenberg Public Policy Center, *2017 Annenberg Constitution Day Civics Survey,* https://www.annenbergpublicpolicycenter.org/americans-are-poorly-informed-about-basic-constitutional-provisions/.

56. Delli-Carpini and Keeter, *What Americans Know About Politics and Why It Matters,* 238.

57. Council on Foreign Relations and NatGeo, *What College-Aged Students Know About the World: A Global Literacy Survey,* September 2016, https://www.cfr.org/content/newsletter/files/CFR_NatGeo_ASurveyonGlobalLiteracy.pdf.

58. Markus Prior, "Political Knowledge After September 11," *PS: Politics and Society* (September 2002): 523–529.

59. Seymour Martin Lipset and William Schneider, *The Confidence Gap: Business, Labor, and Government in the Public Mind* (New York: The Free Press, 1983), 43.

60. Prysby, Charles, Carmine Scavo, American Political Science Association, and Inter-university Consortium for Political and Social Research. *SETUPS: Voting Behavior: The 2016 Election.* ICPSR36853-v1. Ann Arbor, MI: Inter-university Consortium for Political and Social Research [distributor], 2017-08-25. https://doi.org/10.3886/ICPSR36853.v1.

61. Pew Research Center, "Millennials in Adulthood," March 2014. Accessed on August 5, 2018 at http://assets.pewresearch.org/wp-content/uploads/sites/3/2014/03/2014-03-07_generations-report-version-for-web.pdf.

62. Recent empirical evidence has confirmed this assessment. See Luke Keele, "Social Capital and the Dynamics of Trust in Government," *American Journal of Political Science* 51:2 (2007): 241–254.

63. See Aaron J. Martin, *Young People and Politics: Political Engagement in the Anglo-American Democracies* (New York: Routledge, 2014). See also Pippa Norris, ed., *Critical Citizens: Global Support for Democratic Governments* (New York: Oxford Press, 1999); Ronald Inglehart, *Modernization and Postmodernization* (Princeton, NJ: Princeton University Press, 1997); and Stein Ringen, "Wealth and Decay: Norway Funds a Massive Political Self-Examination and Finds Trouble for All," *Times Literary Supplement* (February 13, 2004), 3–5.

64. Angus Campbell, Gerald Gurin, and Warren E. Miller, *The Voter Decides* (New York: Harper & Row, 1954), 187.

65. See Samuel Stouffer, *Communism, Conformity and Civil Liberties* (New York: Doubleday, 1955); and Herbert McClosky, "Consensus and Ideology in American Politics," *American Political Science Review* 58 (1964): 361–382.

66. John E. Meuller, "Trends in Political Tolerance," *Public Opinion Quarterly* 52 (1988): 1–25; and John L. Sullivan, James E. Pierson, and George E. Marcus, *Political Tolerance and American Democracy* (Chicago: University of Chicago Press, 1982).

67. See Carol Pateman, *Participation and Democratic Theory* (New York: Cambridge University Press, 1970); Benjamin R. Barber, *Strong Democracy: Participatory Politics for a New Age* (Berkeley: University of California Press, 1984); and Jack L. Walker, "A Critique of the Elitist Theory of Democracy," *American Political Science Review* 60 (1966): 285–295.

68. Pew Center for the People and Press, *Evenly Divided, Increasingly Polarized: 2004 Political Landscape* (Washington, DC: Pew Research Center, 2003), Table T-6.

69. Gallup Organization, *Civil Liberties.* Retrieved February 10, 2006, from http://www.galluppoll.com.

70. Alan D. Monroe, "Public Opinion and Ideology," in Samuel L. Long, ed., *The Handbook of Political Behavior,* vol. 4 (New York: Plenum, 1981), 155–196.

71. See, for example, Joseph Carroll, "Many Americans Use Multiple Labels to Describe Their Ideology," Gallup Organization, December 6, 2006, http://news.gallup.com/poll/25771/many-americans-use-multiple-labels-describe-their-ideology.aspx. See also Nate Silver, "There Are Few Libertarians. But Many Americans Have Libertarian Views," FiveThirty Eight, April 9, 2015, https://fivethirtyeight.com/features/there-are-few-libertarians-but-many-americans-have-libertarian-views/.

72. Lydia Said, "Social Liberals Nearly Tie Social Conservatives in the U.S.," Gallup Organization, July 28, 2017, http://news.gallup.com/poll/214598/social-liberals-nearly-tie-social-conservatives.aspx.

73. Center for Information and Research on Civic Learning and Engagement, *Millennials After 2016: Post Election Poll Analysis* (Medford, MA: Tufts University, 2017), https://civicyouth.org/wp-content/uploads/2017/03/Millennials-after-2016-Post-Election-Poll-Analysis.pdf.

74. American National Election Studies, *SETUPS: Voting Behavior: The 2016 Election.*

75. Pew Research Center, "Political Polarization in the American Public," June 2014, http://www.people-press.org/2014/06/12/section-1-growing-ideological-consistency/. See also Pew Research Center, "The Partisan Divide on Political Values Grows Even Wider," October 2017, http://www.people-press.org/2017/10/05/the-partisan-divide-on-political-values-grows-even-wider/.

76. Alan Abramowitz, *The Disappearing Center: Engaged Citizens, Polarization, and American Democracy* (New Haven, CT: Yale University Press), 2011; and Morris P.

Fiorina and Samuel J. Abrams, "Political Polarization in the American Public," *Annual Review of Political Science* 11 (2008): 563–588. See also Samuel J. Abrams and Morris P. Fiorina, "'The Big Sort' That Wasn't: A Skeptical Reexamination," *PS: Political Science and Politics* 45: 2 (2012): 203–210.

77. See, for example, J. W. Kingdon, *Agendas, Alternatives, and Public Policies* (New York: Harper Collins, 1995); and Christopher Wlezien and Stuart N. Soroka, "The Relationship Between Public Opinion and Policy," in Russell J. Dalton and Hans-Dieter Klingmann, eds., *Oxford Handbook of Political Behavior* (New York: Oxford University Press, 2009): 799–817.

78. Eileen Lorenzi McDonagh, "Constituency Influence on House Roll Call Votes in the Progressive Era, 1913–1915," *Legislative Studies Quarterly* 18: 2 (May 1993), 185–210.

79. Page, B. I. and Shapiro, R. Y. "Effects of Public Opinion on Policy," *The American Political Science Review* 77:1 (1983): 175–190.

80. See Alan D. Monroe, "Public Opinion and Public Policy, 1980–1993," *The Public Opinion Quarterly* 62:1 (1998): 6–28; and Lawrence Jacobs and Robert Y. Shapiro, "Public Opinion, Institutions, and Policy Making," *PS: Political Science and Politics* 27:1 (1994): 9–17.

81. Martin Gilens and Benjamin I. Page, "Testing Theories of American Politics: Elites, Interest Groups, and Average Citizens," *Perspectives on Politics* (Fall 2014).

82. See, for example, John R. Hibbing and Elizabeth Theiss-Morse, *Stealth Democracy: Americans' Beliefs About How Government Should Work* (New York: Cambridge University Press, 2002).

83. Based on interview by Gerrow, R. University of Texas at Austin Online Newsletter, 2003, http://www.utexas.edu/features/archive/2003/polling.html.

84. James Fishkin, Thad Kousser, Robert C. Luskin, and Alice Siu, "Deliberative Agenda Setting: Piloting Reform of Direct Democracy in California," *Perspectives on Politics* 13:4 (December 2015): 1030–1042.

85. Molly Worthen, "Where in the World Can We Find Hope," *The New York Times,* February 18, 2017, SR 9.

86. Ibid.

Chapter 7: Political Participation: Equal Opportunities And Unequal Voices

1. Zach Friedman, "This 27-Year-Old California Mayor Wants to Pay Residents $500 Cash Per Month," *Forbes,* November 10, 2017, https://www.forbes.com/sites/zackfriedman/2017/11/10/stockton-universal-basic-income/#2ab130a67a23.

2. Roger Phillips, "Foundation Provides Additional $250,000 to Stockton Basic Income Program," Recordnet.com, November 16, 2017, http://www.recordnet.

com/news/20171116/foundation-provides-additional-250000-to-stockton-basic-income-program/1.

3. City of Stockton, Mayor Michael D. Tubbs, Biography. Retrieved November 29, 2017, from http://www.stocktongov.com/government/council/mayor.html.

4. Blavity Team, "This California Mayor Is Spearheading an Initiative That Gives Basic Income to Help Residents Live," November 12, 2017, https://blavity.com/this-california-mayor-is-spearheading-an-initiative-that-gives-basic-income-to-help-residents-live.

5. Dylan Scott, "Millennials in the Mayor's Seat," *Governing,* January 2013, http://www.governing.com/topics/politics/gov-millennial-mayors.html.

6. Sidney Verba, Kay Lehman Schlozman, and Henry E. Brady, *Voice and Equality: Civic Voluntarism in American Politics* (Cambridge, MA: Harvard University Press, 1995), 115.

7. Alexis de Tocqueville, *Democracy in America,* trans. George Lawrence, ed. J. P. Mayer (New York: Perennial Classics, 1969), 520–521.

8. Verba et al., *Voice and Equality,* 38.

9. This section roughly follows the "Civic Volunteerism Model" developed by Verba et al., *Voice and Equality,* 1995.

10. Kay Lehman Schlozman, Sidney Verba, and Henry E. Brady, *The Unheavenly Chorus: Unequal Political Voice and the Broken Promise of American Democracy* (Princeton, NJ: Princeton University Press, 2012), 247.

11. See Sidney Verba and Norman H. Nie, *Political Participation in America: Political Democracy and Social Equality* (New York: Harper & Row, 1972).

12. Steven J. Rosenstone and John Mark Hansen, *Mobilization, Participation and Democracy in America* (New York: Macmillan, 1993), 77.

13. Scott Keeter, Cliff Zukin, Molly Andolina, and Krista Jenkins, *The Civic and Political Health of the Nation: A Generational Portrait,* report prepared for the Center for Information and Research on Civic Learning and Engagement (September 19, 2002), 32. See also Elizabeth C. Matto, Alison Rios, Millett McCartney, Elizabeth A. Bennion, and Dick Simpson, eds., *Teaching Civic Engagement Across the Disciplines* (Washington, DC: American Political Science Association, 2017).

14. Verba et al., *Voice and Equality,* 320–333.

15. Thom File, "The Diversifying Electorate— Voting Rates by Race and Hispanic Origin in 2012 (and Other Recent Elections)," *Current Population Survey Reports,* P20-569 (Washington, DC: U.S. Census Bureau, 2013).

16. Mark Hugo Lopez and Paul Taylor, *Dissecting the 2008 Electorate: Most Diverse in U.S. History* (Washington, DC: Pew Research Center, April 30, 2009), 255.

17. Frederick Solt, "Economic Inequality and Democratic Political Engagement," *American Journal of Political Science* 52 (January 2008): 48–60.

18. Verba et al., *Voice and Equality,* 345–348.

19. See Robert E. Lane, *Political Life: Why and How People Get Involved in Politics* (New York: Free Press, 1959).

20. Michael McDonald, "Preliminary VEP Turnout Estimates," United States Election Project. Retrieved November 9, 2016, from www.electproject.org on.

21. File, "The Diversifying Electorate."

22. Jennifer L. Lawless and Richard L. Fox, *Running from Office: Why Young Americans Are Turned off to Politics* (New York: Oxford, 2015), 36.

23. Center for Information and Research on Civic Learning and Engagement, Tufts University, *The Youth Vote in 2012,* http://www.civicyouth.org/wp-content/uploads/2013/05/CIRCLE_2013FS_outhVoting2012FINAL.pdf.

24. U.S. Census Bureau, *Current Population Survey,* May 2017, https://www.census.gov/newsroom/blogs/random-samplings/2017/05/voting_in_america.html.

25. Ibid.

26. Wendy Weiser and Lawrence Norden, *Voting Law Changes in 2012* (New York: Brennan Center, 2012), 25, http://www.brennancenter.org/sites/default/files/legacy/Democracy/VRE/Brennan_Voting_Law_V10.pdf.

27. Project Vote, *Factsheet: Same Day Registration,* February 2015. Accessed on August 14, 2018 at http://www.projectvote.org/wp-content/uploads/2015/06/SameDayFactSheet-PV-Feb2015.pdf.

28. Center for Information and Research on Civic Learning and Engagement, Tufts University, "Youth Voting," http://www.civicyouth.org/quick-facts/youth-voting/.

29. Michael McDonald, *A Brief History of Early Voting,* December 6, 2017. Accessed on August 14, 2018 at https://www.huffingtonpost.com/michael-p-mcdonald/a-brief-history-of-early_b_12240120.html

30. For a discussion of the effects of early voting, see Joseph D. Giammo and Brian J. Brox, "Reducing the Costs of Participation: Are States Getting a Return on Early Voting?" *Political Research Quarterly* 63:2 (June 2010): 295–303. For a more extensive treatment, see Paul Gronke, Eva Galanes-Rosenbaum, and Peter A. Miller, "Early Voting and Turnout," *PS: Political Science and Politics* 40:4 (October 2007): 639–645.

31. Francis Fox Piven and Richard A. Cloward, *Why Americans Don't Vote* (New York: Pantheon, 1989).

32. See discussion by Rosenstone and Hansen, *Mobilization, Participation and Democracy in America,* 179–183.

33. Richard R. Beeman, "Deference, Republicanism, and the Emergence of Popular Politics in Eighteenth-Century America," *William and Mary Quarterly* 49:3 (July 1992), 417.

34. Michael E. McGerr, *The Decline of Popular Politics: The American North, 1865-1928* (New York: Oxford University Press, 1986).

35. Michael Lewis-Beck, William G. Jacoby, Helmut Norpoth, and Herbert F. Weisberg, *The American Voter Revisited* (Ann Arbor: University of Michigan Press, 2008).

36. Steven A. Jesse, "Spatial Voting in the 2004 Presidential Election," *American Political Science Review* 103:1 (February, 2009): 59–81.

37. Michael Tomz and Robert Van Houweling, "The Electoral Implications of Candidate Ambiguity," *American Political Science Review* 103:1 (February 2009): 83–98.

38. G. Patrick Lynch traces the impact of retrospective economic voting on presidential election outcomes back to 1872 in "Presidential Elections and the Economy 1872 to 1996: The Times They Are A'Changin or the Song Remains the Same?" *Political Research Quarterly* 52:4 (December 1999): 825–844.

39. See, for example, James E. Campbell's review of forecasting models in the 2016 presidential election in "A Recap of the 2016 Election Forecasts." *PS: Political Science and Politics* 50:2 (April 2017): 331–338.

40. Some studies contend that voters are more likely to vote for candidates who reflect their own demographic characteristics. See, for example, Eric Plutzer and John F. Zipp, "Identity Politics, Partisanship, and Voting for Women Candidates," *Public Opinion Quarterly* 60:1 (Spring 1996): 30–57. See also Jan E. Leighley and Arnold Vedlitz, "Race, Ethnicity and Political Participation: Competing Models and Contrasting Explanations," *Journal of Politics* 61:4 (November 1999): 1092–1114. For contrasting findings and explanations, see Richard Seltzer, Jody Newman, and Melissa Voorhees Leighton, *Sex as a Political Variable: Women as Candidates and Voters in U.S. Elections* (Boulder, CO: Lynne Reinner, 1997), esp. ch. 5; and Monika L. McDermott, "Race and Gender Cues in Low-Information Elections," *Political Research Quarterly* 51:4 (December 1998): 895–918.

41. Michael S. Lewis-Beck, Charles Tien, and Richard Nadeau, "Obama's Missed Landslide: A Racial Cost?" *PS: Political Science and Politics* 43:1 (January 2010): 69–76.

42. See Samuel H. Barnes, Max Kaase et al., *Political Action: Mass Participation in Five Western Democracies* (Beverly Hills: Sage, 1979), 541–542.

43. Verba et al., *Voice and Equality,* 115.

44. Aaron J. Martin, *Young People and Politics: Political Engagement in the Anglo-American Democracies* (New York: Routledge, 2012).

45. Verba et al., *Voice and Equality,* 186–227.

46. Keeter et al., 20–22.

47. Stephen Shaffer, "Policy Differences Between Voters and Nonvoters in American Elections," *Western Political Quarterly* 35: 4 (1982): 496–510. See also Verba, Schlozman, and Brady, *Voice and Equality;* and Raymond E. Wolfinger and Steven J. Rosenstone, *Who Votes?* (New Have: Yale University Press,1980).

48. See also Stephen Earl Bennett and David Resnic, "The Implications of Nonvoting for Democracy in the United States," *American Journal of Political Science* 34:3 (August 1990): 771–802.

49. Jan E. Leighy and Jonathan Nagler, *Who Votes Now? Demographics, Issues, Inequality, and Turnout in the United States* (Princeton, NJ: Princeton University Press, 2013).

50. Sidney Verba, "Would the Dream of Political Equality Turn Out to Be a Nightmare?" *Perspectives on Politics* 1:4 (2003): 671.

51. Solt,"Economic Inequality and Democratic Political Engagement," 58.

52. Bartels, L. "Economic Inequality and Political Representation," revised paper presented at the Woodrow Wilson School of Public and International Affairs, Princeton, NJ, August 2005, http://www.princeton.edu/~bartels/economic.pdf.

53. Verba, "Would the Dream of Political Equality Turn Out to Be a Nightmare?" 675.

54. This conforms to the views of many writers. See Thomas R. Dye and Harmon Zeigler, *The Irony of Democracy* (Pacific Grove, CA: Brooks/Cole, 1990); Seymour Martin Lipset, *Political Man* (Garden City, NY: Doubleday, 1963); and William Kornhauser, *The Politics of Mass Society* (Glencoe, IL: Free Press, 1959).

55. See Emily Hoban Kirby and Mark Hugo Lopez, *State Voter Registration and Election Day Laws,* paper prepared for the Center for Information and Research on Civic Learning and Engagement. Retrieved June 24, 2006 from http://www.civicyouth.org. See also Raymond E. Wolfinger, Benjamin Highton, and Megan Mullin, "Mailed Ballots Might Increase Youth Vote," *Institute of Governmental Studies Public Affairs Report* 43:4 (2002).

56. Martin Wattenberg, *Is Voting for Young People?* (New York: Pearson Education, 2007).

57. American Political Science Association's Standing Committee on Civic Education and Engagement, *Democracy at Risk: Reviewing the Political Science of Citizenship* (Chicago: American Political Science Association Meeting, 2004), 33.

58. Rosenstone and Hansen, *Mobilization, Participation and Democracy in America,* 227.

Chapter 8: Interest Groups in America

1. Elliott, P., Edwards, H.S., and Alter, C. "After the Massacre," *Time,* October 16, 2017.

2. Joe Gandleman, "How the NRA Won," The Week, April 9, 2013, http://theweek.com/article/index/242411/how-the-nra-won/

3. Glen H. Utter, *Encyclopedia of Gun Control and Gun Rights* (Westport, CT: Greenwood, 2000), 99–100, 162.

4. Stein, S. and Blumenthal, P. "Why the NRA is the Baddest Force in Politics," *Huffington Post,* December 17, 2002, www.huffingtonpost.com/2012/12/17/gun-lobby-nra_n_2317885.html.

5. Center for Responsive Politics, "Gun Rights vs. Gun Control," 2017, https://www.opensecrets.org/news/issues/guns.

6. Center for Responsive Politics, "Gun Rights," 2017, https://www.opensecrets.org/industries/indus.php?ind=q13.

7. Tyler Fisher, Sarah Frostenson, and Lily Mihalik, "The Gun Lobby: See How Much Your Representative Gets," Politico, October 2, 2017, https//www.politico.com/interactives/2017/gun-lobbying-spending-in america-congress/.

8. Center for Responsive Politics, "Gun Rights vs. Gun Control."

9. Elliott et al., "After the Massacre."

10. PollingReport.com, "Guns," November 2017, http://www.pollingreport.com/guns.htm.

11. CBS News, "CBS News Poll: Will Gun Violence Increase in the Next Decade?" March 13, 2016.

12. The classic definition of an interest group offered by political scientist David Truman is "any group that, on the basis of one or more shared attitudes, makes certain claims upon other groups in the society for the establishment, maintenance, or enhancement of forms of behavior that are implied by the shared attitudes." David Truman, *The Governmental Process* (New York: Alfred Knopf, 1951), 33.

13. Madison, J. "Federalist No. 10," in *Federalist Papers,* ed. Clinton Rossiter (New York: New American Library, 1961), 78.

14. Sidney Verba, Kay Lehman Scholzman, and Henry E. Brady, *Voice and Equality: Civic Voluntarism in American Politics* (Cambridge, MA: Harvard University Press, 1995), 72–73. But see somewhat contradictory data from Steven J. Rosenstone and John Mark Hansen, *Mobilization, Participation, and Democracy in America* (New York: Macmillan, 1993), chap. 3. Theda Skocpol, *Diminished Democracy: From Membership to Management in American Civic Life* (Norman: University of Oklahoma Press, 2003) argues that much of this activity is managed by Washington professionals.

15. Arthur M. Schlesinger, "Biography of a Nation of Joiners," *American Historical Review* 50:1 (1944): 25.

16. Shirley J. Yee, *Black Women Abolitionists: A Study in Activism 1828–60* (Knoxville: University of Tennessee Press, 1992).

17. Matthew A. Crenson and Benjamin Ginsberg, *Downsizing Democracy* (Baltimore, MD: Johns Hopkins University Press, 2002), 107.

18. Robert D. Putnam, *Bowling Alone: The Collapse and Revival of American Community* (New York: Simon & Schuster, 2000), 80–92.

19. Michael Schudson, *The Good Citizen: A History of American Civic Life* (New York: Free Press, 1988), 245.

20. Michael Pertschuk, *Giant Killers* (New York: W. W. Norton, 1996).

21. Kay Lehman Schlozman, Sidney Verba, and Henry E. Brady, *The Unheavenly Chorus: Unequal Political Voice and the Broken Promise of American Democracy* (Princeton and Oxford: Princeton University Press, 2012), 267, 319.

22. Skocpol, *Diminished Democracy.*

23. Schlozman, Verba, and Brady, *The Unheavenly Chorus: Unequal Political Voice and the Broken Promise of American Democracy,* 321.

24. Ibid., 330.

25. See, for example, Jack L. Walker, "The Origins and Maintenance of Interest Groups in America," *American Political Science Review* 77 (1983): 390–406.

26. Kay Lehman Schlozman, "What Accent the Heavenly Chorus? Political Equality and the American Pressure System," *Journal of Politics* 46 (1984): 1009.

27. Ibid., 1022–1024.

28. Alex Altman, "The Suite of Power: Why Donald Trump's Washington Hotel Is the Capital's Swamp," *Time,* June 19, 2017.

29. Ibid.

30. Political scientist David Truman coined the term *latent interests* to refer to the ever-present possibility that new groups will arise at any time to meet yet unforeseen challenges. See Truman, *The Governmental Process,* 1951.

31. James Q. Wilson, *Political Organizations* (New York: Basic Books, 1973).

32. Rosenstone and Hansen, *Mobilization, Participation, and Democracy in America.*

33. Mancur Olson, *The Logic of Collective Action* (Cambridge, MA: Harvard University Press, 1965).

34. Jack L. Walker, *Mobilizing Interest Groups in America* (Ann Arbor: University of Michigan Press, 1991), 87–89. This result is confirmed by the research of Verba, Schlozman, and Brady.

35. Verba, Schlozman, and Brady, *Voice and Equality,* 121–127.

36. Jonathan D. Salant, "The Lobbying Game Today," *Extensions: A Journal of the Carl Albert Congressional Research and Studies Center* (2006): 19.

37. Center for Responsive Politics, "Revolving Door: Members of the 114th Congress," 2017.

38. See Timothy M. LaPira, Herschel F. Thomas III, and Frank R. Baumgartner, "The Two Worlds of Lobbying: The Core-Periphery Structure of the Interest Group Structure," January 12, 2012, https://papers.ssrn.com/sol3/papers.cfm?abstract_id=2245065.

39. Ibid.

40. Frank R. Baumgartner, Jeffrey M. Berry, Marie Hojnacki, David C. Kimball, and Beth L. Leech, *Lobbying and Policy Change: Who Wins, Who Loses, and Why* (Chicago: University of Chicago Press, 2009).

41. See Clyde Wilcox, "The Dynamics of Lobbying the Hill," in Paul Herrnson, Ronald G. Shaiko, and Clyde Wilcox, eds., *The Interest Group Connection* (Chatham, NJ: Chatham House, 1998), 89–90.

42. Ornstein, N. J., Elder, S. *Interest Groups, Lobbying and Policymaking* (Washington, DC: Congressional Quarterly Press, 1978), 77–78.

43. Ibid.

44. See John E. Chubb, *Interest Groups and the Bureaucracy* (Stanford, CA: Stanford University Press, 1983), for a good discussion of the relationship between interest groups and the bureaucracy in the energy policy field.

45. Kay Lehman Schlozman and John T. Tierney, *Organized Interests and the Bureaucracy* (New York: Harper & Row, 1986), 333.

46. For an excellent discussion of research into "capture theory," see James Q. Wilson, *The Politics of Regulation* (New York: Basic Books, 1980).

47. Robert H. Salisbury, John Heinz, Robert L. Nelson, and Edward O. Laumann, "Triangles, Networks, and Hollow Cores: The Complex Geometry of Washington Interest Representation," in Mark Petracca, ed., *Interest Group Politics* (Washington DC: Congressional Quarterly Press, 1995), 131.

48. See Walker, *Mobilizing Interest Groups in America,* 125.

49. William T. Gromley, Jr., "Interest Group Interventions in the Administrative Process: Conspirators and Co-conspirators," in Paul S. Herrnson, Ronald G. Shaiko, and Clyde Wilcox, eds., *The Interest Group Connection* (Chatham, NJ: Chatham House, 1998), 213–223.

50. Frank R. Baumgartner, Jeffrey M. Berry, Marie Hojnacki, David C. Kimball, and Beth L. Leech, *Lobbying and Policy Change: Who Wins, Who Loses, and Why* (Chicago: University of Chicago Press, 2009).

51. Quoted in Makinson, L. *Speaking Freely: Washington Insiders Talk About Money in Politics* (Washington, DC: Center for Responsive Politics, 2003), 85.

52. Schlozman and Tierney, *Organized Interests and the Bureaucracy,* 221.

53. *McConnell v. Federal Election Commission* (2003) and *FEC v. Wisconsin Right to Life* (2007).

54. Schlozman and Tierney, *Organized Interests and the Bureaucracy,* 333.

55. David Levinthal, "How Super PACs Got Their Name," *Politico,* January 10, 2012, http://www.politico.com/news/stories,01/12/71285.html.

56. Matea Gold, "It's Bold, but Legal: How Campaigns and Their Super PAC Backers Work Together," *The Washington Post,* July 6, 2015, https://www.washingtonpost.com/politics/here-are-the-secret-ways-super-pacs-and-campaigns.

57. Ibid.

58. Editorial, "When Other Voices Are Drowned Out," *The New York Times,* March 25, 2012.

59. Center for Responsive Politics, "Ideological/Single Issue Section," 2013, http://www.opensecrets.org/lobby/indus.php?id=Q&year=2013.

60. For an analysis of the general reliability of this finding, see Thomas Brunell, "The Relationship Between Political Parties and Interest Groups: Explaining Patterns of PAC Contributions to Candidates for Congress," *Political Research Quarterly* 58 (2005): 681–688.

61. Center for Responsive Politics, "Who Gives to Republicans, Who Gives to Democrats," http://www.opensecrets.org/pacs/sectors, 2013.

62. Jane Mayer, *Dark Money: The Hidden History of the Billionaires Behind the Rise of the Radical Right* (New York: Random House, 2016).

63. Robert Maguire, "How 2014 Is Shaping Up to Be the Darkest Money Election to Date," Center for Responsive Politics, April, 30, 2014, https://www.opensecrets.org/news/2014/04/2014-is-shaping-up-to-be-the-darkest-money-elections-to-date.

64. Leah McGrath Goodman, "As Dark Money Floods U.S. Elections, Regulators Turn a Blind Eye," *Newsweek,* September 30, 2014.

65. Editorial, "Dark Money Helped Win the Senate," *The New York Times,* November 8, 2014.

66. Karen O'Connor, *Women's Organizations' Use of the Courts* (Lexington, MA: Lexington Books, 1980).

67. Stuart Scheingold, *The Politics of Rights* (New Haven: Yale University Press, 1974).

68. Karen O'Connor and Lee Epstein, "The Role of Interest Groups in Supreme Court Policymaking," in Robert Eyestone, ed., *Public Policy Formation* (Greenwich, CT: JAI Press, 1984) 63–81.

69. See Lucius J. Barker, "Third Parties in Litigation: A Systemic View of the Judicial Function," *Journal of Politics* 29 (1967): 41–69.

70. See Gregory A. Calderia and John R. Wright, "Organized Interests and Agenda Setting in the U.S. Supreme Court," *American Political Science Review* 82 (1988): 1109–1127.

71. James G. Gimpel, "Grassroots Organizations and Equilibrium Cycles in Group Mobilization and Access," in Paul Herrnson, Ronald G. Shaiko, and Clyde Wilcox, eds., *The Interest Group Connection* (Chatham, NJ: Chatham House, 1998), 100–115.

72. Emily Cadei, "Advocacy Groups Employ Web's Extended Reach," *CQ Weekly,* May 4, 2009, 1015.

73. Kenneth M. Goldstein, *Interest Groups, Lobbying, and Participation in America* (New York: Cambridge University Press: 1999), 62.

74. Gimple, "Grassroots Organizations and Equilibrium Cycles," 104.

75. See Kevin Hula, "Rounding Up the Usual Suspects: Forging Interest Group Coalitions in Washington," in Allan J. Cigler and Burdett A. Loomis, eds., *Interest Group Politics* (Washington, DC: Congressional Quarterly Press, 1995), 239–258.

76. Verba et al., *Voice and Equality,* 189–191.

77. Crenson and Ginsberg, *Downsizing Democracy,* 151.

78. Ibid.

79. Ibid., 194.

80. E. E. Schattschneider, *The Semisovereign People* (New York: Holt, Rinehart, & Winston, 1960), 35.

Chapter 9: Parties and Political Campaigns: Putting Democracy into Action

1. Tovia Smith, "When Dating in the Era of Divisive Politics, Both Sides Stick to Themselves," NPR, February 14, 2017, https://www.npr.org/2017/02/14/515179534/when-dating-in-the-era-of-divisive-politics-both-sides-stick-to-themselves.

2. William Cummings, "Trump's in the White House, Turkey's on the Table: What to Do If You Don't Want to Talk Politics," *USA Today,* November 22, 2017, https://www.usatoday.com/story/news/nation/2017/11/17/trump-era-holiday-survival-guide/864764001/.

3. Huber, G. A. and Malhotra, N. "Political Homophily in Social Relationships: Evidence from Online Dating Behavior," *Journal of Politics* 79:1 (2017): 269–283.

4. Dan Kahan, Ellen Peters, Erica Cantrell Dawson, and Paul Slovic, "Motivated Numeracy and Enlightened Self-Government," *Behavioral Public Policy* 1:1 (May 2017): 54–86.

5. E. E. Schattschneider, *Party Government* (New York: Holt, Rinehart, & Winston, 1942), 1.

6. V. O. Key, Jr., *Politics, Parties, and Pressure Groups,* 5th ed. (New York: Crowell, 1964).

7. Anthony Downs, *An Economic Theory of Democracy* (New York: Harper & Row, 1957), 25.

8. E. E. Schattschneider, "Intensity, Visibility, Direction, and Scope," *American Political Science Review* 51:4 (December 1957): 933–942.

9. Kathleen Bawn, Martin Cohen, David Karol, Seth Masket, Hans Noel, and John Zaller, "A Theory of Political Parties: Groups, Policy Demands and Nominations in American Politics," *Perspectives on Politics* 10:3 (September 2012): 571–597.

10. See, for example, Morris Fiorina, "The Decline of Collective Responsibility in American Politics," *Daedalus* 109 (Summer 1980): 25–45. See also American Political Science Association, *Toward a More Responsible Two-Party System* (New York: Rinehart, 1950).

11. Alexis de Tocqueville, *Democracy in America,* trans. George Lawrence, ed. J. P. Mayer (New York: Perennial Classics, 1969), 174.

12. Maurice Duverger, *Political Parties: Their Organization and Activity in the Modern State* (New York: Wiley, 1954).

13. For a more thorough examination of other voting systems and their potential effects, see Joseph F. Zimmerman, "Alternative Voting Systems for Representative Democracy," *PS: Political Science and Politics* 27:4 (December 1994): 674–677.

14. At the time of publication, fourteen states and the District of Columbia provided some form of public financing option for campaigns. Details differ from state to state. For a comprehensive examination of state policies, see National Conference of State Legislatures, "Overview of State Laws on Public Financing," http://www.ncsl.org/research/elections-and-campaigns/public-financing-of-campaigns-overview.aspx.

15. John H. Aldrich, *Why Parties? The Origins and Transformation of Political Parties in America* (Chicago: University of Chicago Press, 1995), 70–82.

16. Ibid., 99.

17. See discussion in Frances Fox Piven and Richard A. Cloward, *Why Americans Don't Vote* (New York: Pantheon, 1989).

18. John C. Green, *The American Religious Landscape and Political Attitudes: A Baseline for 2004,* Pew Forum, June 28, 2012, http://users.clas.ufl.edu/billrad/Behave_Fall_2006/green-full.pdf.

19. See, for example, Susan J. Carroll, "Women's Autonomy and the Gender Gap: 1980 and 1982," in Carol M. Mueller, ed., *The Politics of the Gender Gap: The Social Construction of Political Influence* (Beverly Hills, CA: Sage, 1988).

20. V. O. Key, Jr., "A Theory of Critical Elections," *Journal of Politics* 17 (1955): 3–18; Walter Dean Burnham, *Critical Elections and the Mainsprings of American Politics* (New York: Norton, 1970); Paul Allen Beck, "A Socialization Theory of Partisan Realignment," in Richard Niemi, ed., *The Politics of Future Citizens* (San Francisco: Jossey-Bass, 1974).

21. A. James Reichley, "The Future of the American Two-Party System After 1996," in John C. Green and Daniel M. Shea, eds., *The State of the Parties: The Changing Role of Contemporary American Parties,* 3rd ed. (Lanham, MD: Rowman & Littlefield, 1999), 10–27.

22. See, for example, Larry M. Bartels, "Electoral Continuity and Change, 1868–1996," *Electoral Studies* 17:3 (1998): 301–326; and David R. Mayhew, *Electoral Realignments: A Critique of an American Genre* (New Haven, CT: Yale University Press, 2002).

23. Edward G. Carmines and Michael W. Wagner, "Political Issues and Party Alignments: Assessing the Issue Evolution Perspective" *Annual Review of Political Science* 9 (2006): 67–81.

24. See, for example, Martin P. Wattenberg, *The Decline of American Political Parties, 1952-1996* (Cambridge, MA: Harvard University Press, 1998); Paul Allen Beck, "The Changing American Party Coalitions," in Green and Shea, eds., *The State of the Parties,* 28–49.

25. Larry M. Bartels, "Partisanship and Voting Behavior, 1952-1996," *American Journal of Political Science* 44:1 (January 2000): 35–50. See also Michael Lewis-Beck, William G. Jacoby, Helmut Norpoth, and Herbert F. Weisberg, *The American Voter Revisited* (Ann Arbor: University of Michigan Press, 2008).

26. Ed Kilgore, "Polarization and History," *The Democratic Strategist,* April 10, 2009, https://thedemocraticstrategist.org/2009/04/polarization_and_history/.

27. For a full discussion of these factors and controversy surrounding them, see Morris P. Fiorina and Samuel J. Abrams, *Disconnect: The Breakdown of Representation in American Politics* (Norman: University of Oklahoma Press, 2009), especially 102 ff.

28. For the view that voters are as polarized as elites on a host of issues, see Alan Abramowitz and Kyle L. Saunders, "Why Can't We All Get Along? The Reality of a Polarized America," *The Forum* (Berkeley, CA: Bee Press, 2005), https://www.degruyter.com/view/j/for.2005.3.2_20120105083450/for.2005.3.2/for.2005.3.2.1076/for.2005.3.2.1076.xml. For the contrasting view that voters are more moderate but have been driven to make choices among available polarized options, see Fiorina, *Disconnect.*

29. Shanto Iyengar, Gaurav Sood, and Yphtach Lelkes, "Affect, Not Ideology: A Social Identity Perspective on Polarization," *Public Opinion Quarterly* 76:3 (Fall 2012): 405–431.

30. Paul S. Herrnson, "The Roles of Party Organizations, Party-Connected Committees, and Party Allies in Elections," *Journal of Politics* 71:4 (2009): 1207–1224.

31. John F. Bibby, "Party Networks: National-State Integration, Allied Groups, and Issue Activists," in Green and Shea, eds., *The State of the Parties,* 69–85.

32. Malcolm Jewell and David Olson, *American State Political Parties and Elections,* rev. ed. (Homewood, IL: Dorsey Press, 1982).

33. Marjorie Randon Hershey, *Party Politics in America,* 15th ed. (Boston: Pearson, 2013), 53.

34. Third parties have been categorized in a number of ways. Key speaks of short-lived and doctrinal parties (Key, *Politics, Parties, and Pressure Groups,* 1964). Orren lists principled, personalistic, and protest as third-party types. See Gary R. Orren, "The Changing Styles of American Party Politics," in Joel L. Fleishman, ed., *The Future of American Political Parties* (Englewood Cliffs, NJ: Prentice Hall, 1982). Here we employ the categories splinter, ideological, and issue candidate.

35. Christopher J. Devine and Kyle C. Kopko, "5 Things You Need to Know About How Third-Party Candidates Did in 2016," *The Washington Post,* November 15, 2016, https://www.washingtonpost.com/news/monkey-cage/wp/2016/11/15/5-things-you-need-to-know-about-how-third-party-candidates-did-in-2016/? See also Marc J. Hetherington, "The Election: The Allure of the Outsider," in *The Elections of 2016,* Michael Nelson, ed.(Thousand Oaks, CA: Sage), 2017, 72. Hetherington notes that the election was so close that a case could be made that a number of factors cost Clinton the election, including the impact of third parties in some states.

36. *SpeechNow.org v. Federal Election Commission,* 599 F.3d 686 (D.C. Cir. 2010); *Citizens United v. Federal Election Commission,* 130 S. Ct. 876 (2010).

37. Marian Currinder, "Campaign Finance: Where Big Money Mattered and Where It Didn't," in Michael Nelson, ed., *The Elections of 2016* (Thousand Oaks, CA: Sage, 2017), 139.

38. Ibid.

39. Clyde Wilcox, "Internet Fundraising in 2008: A New Model?" *The Forum* 6:1, http://www.bepress.com/forum/vol6/iss1/art1. Also see Richard L. Hasen, "Political Equality, the Internet, and Campaign Finance Regulation," *The Forum* 6:1, Article 7, https://www.degruyter.com/view/j/for.2008.6.1_20120105083453/for.2008.6.1/for.2008.6.1.1228/for.2008.6.1.1228.xml.

40. Erika Franklin Fowler, Travis N. Ridout, and Michael M. Franz, "Political Advertising in 2016: The Presidential Election as Outlier?" *The Forum* 2016; 14(4): 445–469. See also, Ken Goldstein, John McCormick and Andre Tartar, "Candidates Make Last Ditch Ad Spending Push Across 14 State Electoral Map," *Bloomberg Politics,* November 2, 2016, https://www.bloomberg.com/politics/graphics/2016-presidential-campaign-tv-ads/.

41. Kurt Wagner, "Donald Trump and Hillary Clinton Spent $81 Million on Facebook Ads Before Last Year's Election," Recode.net, November 1, 2017, https://www.recode.net/2017/11/1/16593066/trump-clinton-facebook-advertising-money-election-president-russia.

42. *California Democratic Party v. Jones, 530 U.S. 567* (2000).

43. Wattenberg, *The Decline of American Political Parties,* 35.

44. Thomas E. Patterson, *The Vanishing Voter: Public Involvement in an Age of Uncertainty* (New York: Knopf, 2002), 99–127.

45. Erika Franklin Fowler and Travis N. Ridout, "Negative, Angry, and Ubiquitous: Political Advertising in 2012," *The Forum* 10:4 (February 2013): 51–61.

46. Gina M. Garramone, Charles K. Atkin, Bruce E. Pinkleton, and Richard T. Cole, "Effects of Negative Political Advertising on the Political Process," *Journal of Broadcasting and the Electronic Media* 34 (1990): 299–311.

47. John Sides and Lynn Vavreck, *The Gamble: Choice and Chance in the 2012 Presidential Election* (Princeton, NJ: Princeton University Press, 2013).

48. Stephen Ansolabehere and Shanto Iyengar, *Going Negative: How Political Advertisements Shrink and Polarize the Electorate* (New York: Free Press, 1995). But see Robert Jackson, Jeffrey J. Mondak, and Robert Huckfeldt, "Examining the Possible Corrosive Impact of Negative Advertising on Citizens' Attitudes Toward Politics," *Political Research Quarterly* 62 (March 2009): 55–69. Jackson et al. find no evidence to support the claim that negative ads erode voter attitudes other than efficacy.

49. Steven E. Finkel and John G. Geer, "A Spot Check: Casting Doubt on the Demobilizing Effect of Attack Advertising," *American Journal of Political Science* 42:2 (April 1998): 573–595.

50. Patterson, *The Vanishing Voter,* 51.

51. Yale University Institution for Social and Policy Studies, *Lessons from GOTV Experiments.* Retrieved December 12, 2017, from https://isps.yale.edu/node/16698.

52. Tom Curry, "Early Voting Transforms Strategy," October 4, 2010, http://www.nbcnews.com/id/39444285/ns/politics-decision_2010/t/early-voting-transforms-strategy/#.W3WmZehKhPY.

53. Ibid.

54. David Mayhew, *Partisan Balance: Why Political Parties Don't Kill the U.S. Constitutional System* (Princeton, NJ: Princeton University Press, 2013).

55. National Conference of State Legislatures, "Overview of State Laws on Public Financing."

56. Neil Malhotra, "The Impact of Public Financing on Electoral Competition: Evidence from Arizona and Maine," *State Politics and Policy Quarterly* 8:3 (2008): 263–281.

57. Mimi Marziani, Laura Moy, Adam Scaggs, and Marcus Williams, *More Than Combating Corruption: The Other Benefits of Public Financing* (New York: Brennan Center for Justice), https://www.brennancenter.org/analysis/more-combating-corruption-other-benefits-public-financing.

58. Mann and Ornstein, *It's Even Worse Than It Looks,* 162.

59. Seattle.gov, Democracy Voucher Program. Retrieved December 12, 2017, from https://www.seattle.gov/democracyvoucher/about-the-program. See also Editorial Board, "Voters Morph into Donors in Seattle," *The New York Times,* November 8, 2015, SR 10.

60. Eric McGhee and Boris Shor, "Has the Top Two Primary Elected More Moderates," *Perspectives on Politics* 15:4 (2017): 1053–1066.

Chapter 10: Media: Tuning in or Tuning Out

1. Frank Newport, "Americans Confidence in Institutions Edges Up," Gallup News, June 26, 2017.

2. See AP, NORC, and American Press Institute, *A New Understanding: What Makes People Trust and Rely on News,* The Media Insight Project, April 2016, http://www.mediainsight.org/PDFs/Trust/TrustFinal.pdf.

3. Robert Zemsky, *Merchants, Farmers, and River Gods: An Essay on Eighteenth-Century American Politics* (Boston: Gambit, 1971), 59.

4. Frank Luther Mott, *American Journalism: A History 1690–1960* (New York: Macmillan, 1962), 52.

5. Michael Schudson, *The Good Citizen* (New York: Free Press, 1998), 40.

6. Culver H. Smith, *The Press, Politics, and Patronage* (Athens: University of Georgia Press, 1977), 52.

7. Walter Lippman, "Two Revolutions in the American Press," *Yale Law Review* 20 (1931): 433–441.

8. Mott, *American Journalism,* 539.

9. Paul H. Weaver, *News and the Culture of Lying* (New York: The Free Press, 1994), 35.

10. Schudson, *The Good Citizen,* 179.

11. George Jurgens, *Joseph Pulitzer and the New York World* (Princeton, NJ: Princeton University Press, 1966), 239.

12. Doris Graber, *Mass Media and American Politics,* 3d ed. (Washington, DC: CQ Press, 2002), 12.

13. https://www.statista.com/statistics/183408/number-of-us-daily-newspapers-since-1975/

14. Amy Mitchell, Jeffrey Gottfried, and Katerina Eva Matsa, "Political Interest and Awareness Lower Among Millennials," Pew Research Center, June 1, 2015, http://www.journalism.org/2015/06/01/political-interest-and-awareness-lower-among-millennials/.

15. Reuters Institute, University of Oxford, "Social Networks and Their Role in News," Digital News report, 2015, http://www.digitalnewsreport.org/survey/2015/social-networks-and-their-role-in-news-2015/.

16. Ibid., 1.

17. Amy Mitchell, "Political Interest and Awareness Lower Among Millennials," Pew Research Center, June 1, 2015.

18. See AP, NORC, and American Press Institute, *How Millennials Get News: Inside the Habits of America's First Digital Generation,* The Media Insight Project, March 2015, http://www.mediainsight.org/PDFs/Millennials/Millennials%20Report%20FINAL.pdf.

19. Richard Davis, *The Press and American Politics* (Upper Saddle River, NJ: Prentice Hall, 1996), 13.

20. Stephen Ansolabehere, Roy Behr, and Shanto Iyengar, *The Media Game: American Politics in the Television Age* (New York: Macmillan, 1993), 28–29.

21. Christina Holtz-Bacha and Lynda Lee Kaid, "A Comparative Perspective on Political Advertising," in *Political Advertising in Western Democracies,* ed. Linda Lee Kaid and Christina Holz-Bacha (Thousand Oaks, CA: Sage, 1995), 13.

22. Ibid.

23. Ibid.

24. Isaac, M. "Amazon's Jeff Bezos Explains Why He Bought *The Washington Post,*" The New York Times, December 2, 2014, http://bits.blogs.nytimes.com/2014/12/02/amazons-bezos-explains-why-he-bought-the-washington-post/?_r=0.

25. Lukas I. Alpert and Jack Marshal, "Bezos Takes Hands-On Role at Washington Post," *The Wall Street Journal,* December 20, 2015, http://www.wsj.com/articles/bezos-takes-hands-on-role-at-washington-post-1450658089.

26. See Robert McChesney, *Rich Media, Poor Democracy* (New York: New York Press, 1999).

27. *Near v. Minnesota* (1931).

28. *New York Times v. Sullivan* (1964).

29. Speech given by Robert McNeil at the University of South Dakota, Vermillion, SD, Wednesday, October 16, 1996. Cited in Jeremy Iggers, *Good News, Bad News* (Boulder, CO: Westview Press, 1998), 2.

30. James Fallows, *Breaking the News* (New York: Pantheon Books, 1996), chap. 3.

31. Ibid., 105.

32. Lichter, S. R., and Noyes, R. E. *Good Intentions Make Bad News* (Lanham, MD: Rowman & Littlefield, 1955), 3.

33. Michael Schudson, *Discovering the News* (New York: Basic Books, 1973), 178–181.

34. "The Times and Iraq," *The New York Times,* May 26, 2004.

35. S. Robert Lichter, Stanley Rothman, and Linda S. Lichter, *The Media Elite* (Bethesda MD: Adler & Adler, 1986), 21–25.

36. Dave D'Alessio and Mike Allen, "Media Bias in Presidential Elections: A Meta-Analysis," *Journal of Communication* 50:4 (2000): 133–156.

37. See Graham Browning, "Too Close for Comfort?" *National Journal* (1992): 2243.

38. "Amid Criticism, Support for Media's 'Watchdog' Role Stands Out, Overview," Pew Research Center, August 8, 2013, poll taken July 20–24, 2013.

39. Ibid.

40. Amy Mitchell, Jeffrey Gottfried, Galen Stocking, Katerina Eva Matsa, and Elizabeth Greico, "Covering President Trump in a Polarized Media Environment," Pew Research Center, October 2, 2017, http://www.journalism.org/2017/10/02/covering-president-trump-in-a-polarized-media-environment/.

41. Sides, "Why Trump Is Surging? Blame the Media." Also see John Sides and Lynn Vareck, *The Gamble: Choice and Chance in the 2012 Presidential Election* (Princeton, NJ: Princeton University Press, 2013).

42. Thomas E. Patterson, *The Vanishing Voters: Public Involvement in an Age of Uncertainty* (New York: Knopf, 2002), 57.

43. Graber, *Mass Media and American Politics,* 248–249.

44. Kate Kaye, "Interpreting the 2016 Presidential Ads Online," *Ad Age,* April 1, 2016, http://adage.com/article/campaign-trail/inter-preting-2016-presidential-ads-online/303358/.

45. Paula Minardi, "How Will Political Campaigns Reach Voters Who Are Avoiding Ads?" Ad Exchanger, January 26, 2016, https://adexchanger.com/politics/how-will-political-campaigns-reach-voters-who-are-avoiding-ads/.

46. Gina M. Garramone, Charles K. Atkin, Bruce E. Pinkleton, and Richard T. Cole, "Effects of Negative Political Advertising on the Political Process," *Journal of Broadcasting and the Electronic Media* 34 (1990): 299–311.

47. Stephen Ansolabehere and Shanto Iyengar, *Going Negative: How Political Advertisements Shrink and Polarize the Electorate* (New York: Free Press, 1995).

48. Steven E. Finkle and John G. Geer, "A Spot Check: Casting Doubt on the Demobilizing Effect of Attack Advertising," *American Journal of Political Science* 42:2 (1998): 573–595.

49. eBiz MBA Rank, July 2017.

50. Kurtz, H. "Blogging Without Warning," *The Washington Post,* June 9, 2008, 1.

51. Staci D. Kramer, "CBS Scandal Highlights Tension Between Bloggers and News Media," USC *Annenberg Online Journalism Review,* October 10, 2004.

52. Andrew Guess, Brendan Nyhan, and Jason Reifler, "Selective Exposure to Misinformation: Evidence from the Consumption of Fake News During the 2016 Presidential Campaign," January 9, 2018. Paper sponsored by Poynter Institute, Knight Foundation, American Press Institute, and the European Research Council.

53. Thomas E. Patterson, *Out of Order* (New York: Vintage Press, 1993), 57.

54. Ibid., 116.

55. Fallows, *Breaking the News,* 181.

56. See Roderick Hart, *Seducing America: How Television Charms the Modern Voter* (New York: Oxford University Press, 1995).

57. Larry Sabato, *Feeding Frenzy* (New York: Free Press, 1991), 68.

58. See Kenneth T. Walsh, *Feeding the Beast* (New York: Random House, 1996) for an excellent treatment of the relationship between the president and the media.

59. Ibid., 23.

60. Ibid., 28.

61. Ibid., 77–78.

62. See Everette E. Dennis and Robert Snyder, eds., *Covering Congress* (New Brunswick, NJ: Transaction, 1998).

63. See John Hibbing and Elizabeth Theiss-Morse, *Congress as Public Enemy: Political Attitudes Toward American Political Institutions* (New York: Cambridge University Press, 1995).

64. Solomon Messing, Patrick van Kessel, and Adam Hughes, "Sharing the News in a Polarized Congress," Pew Research Center, December 18, 2017, http://www.people-press.org/2017/12/18/sharing-the-news-in-a-polarized-congress/.

65. Quoted in Stephen Macedo et al., *Democracy at Risk: How Political Choices Undermine Citizen Participation and What We Can Do About It* (Washington, DC: Brookings Institution, 2005), 42.

66. Mitchell, Gottfried, and Matsa, "Political Interest and Awareness Lower Among Millennials."

67. See Joseph N. Capella and Kathleen Hall Jamieson, *Spiral of Cynicism: The Press and the Public Good* (New York: Oxford University Press, 1997).

68. Pew Center for People and the Press, *Public Wants Neutrality and Strong Point of View: Strong Opposition to Media Cross Ownership Emerges* (Washington, DC: Pew Center for People and the Press, July 13, 2003), 5.

69. Macedo et al., *Democracy at Risk,* 42.

70. AP, NORC, and American Press Institute, *How Millennials Get News,* 31.

Chapter 11: Congress: Doing The People's Business

1. Philips, A. "Al Franken's Defiant, Unapologetic Resignation Speech, Annotated," *The Washington Post,* December 7, 2017, https://www.washingtonpost.com/news/the-fix/wp/2017/12/07/al-frankens-defiant-unapologetic-resignation-speech-annotated/?utm_term=.9b02f66f4c56.

2. The U.S. Census Bureau put the figure at 50.8 percent for 2016.

3. For the 115th Congress (2017–2019).

4. See, for example, Craig Volden, Alan E. Wiseman, and Dana E. Wittmer, "When Are Women More Effective Lawmakers Than Men," *American Journal of Political Science* 57:2 (April 2013), 326–341. See also Stefano Gagliarducci and M. Daniele Paserman, *Gender Differences in Cooperative Environments? Evidence from the U.S. Congress,* National Bureau of Economic Research Working Paper No. 22488 (August 2016), http://www.nber.org/papers/w22488.

5. Quoted in Congressional Quarterly, Inc., *Origins and Development of Congress,* 2d ed. (Washington, DC: Congressional Quarterly, 1982), 43.

6. Ibid., 219.

7. For an excellent review of the history of these changes, see Barbara Sinclair, *Party Wars: Polarization and the Politics of National Policy Making* (Norman: University of Oklahoma Press, 2006), esp. chapters 2–4.

8. Thomas E. Mann and Norman J. Ornstein, *It's Even Worse Than It Looks: How the American Constitutional System Collided with the New Politics of Extremism* (New York: Basic Books, 2012), 51.

9. Keith Poole and Howard Rosenthal have tracked ideological votes in Congress for years. See, for example, "Measuring Polarization Through Chamber and Party Medians over Time (1879–2012)," *Voteview Blog,* March 2, 2012, http://voteview.com/blog.

10. Center for Responsive Politics, "Most Expensive Races." Retrieved January 3, 2018 from https://www.opensecrets.org/overview/topraces.php?cycle=2016&display=allcandsout.

11. Rep. McCollum, B. in Makinson, L. *Speaking Freely: Washington Insiders Talk About Money in Politics,* 2d ed. (Washington, DC: Center for Responsive Politics, 2003), 36–37.

12. Center for Responsive Politics, "Personal Finances." Retrieved January 3, 2018, from https://www.opensecrets.org/personal-finances/.

13. Center for Responsive Politics, "PAC Dollars to Incumbents, Challengers, and Open Seat Candidates." Retrieved January 3, 2018, from https://www.opensecrets.org/overview/pac2cands.php?cycle=2016. See also Paul Herrnson, "Money and Motives: Spending in

House Elections," in Lawrence C. Dodd and Bruce L. Oppenheimer, eds., *Congress Reconsidered*, 6th ed. (Washington, DC: Congressional Quarterly, 1997), 100–131.

14. *Baker v. Carr,* 369 U.S. 186 (1962); *Reynolds v. Sims,* 377 U.S. 533 (1964); *Westberry v. Sanders,* 376 U.S. 1 (1964). States use total population as a base for drawing districts. A conservative group challenged this approach in *Evenwell v. Abbott* in 2016, arguing that the basis for drawing districts should be eligible voters instead, since children, felons, and undocumented immigrants cannot vote. The Supreme Court rejected the challenge.

15. *League of United Latin American Citizens et al. v. Perry,* 548 U.S. (2006).

16. *Davis v. Bandemer,* 478 U.S. 109 (1986).

17. Andrew Gelman and Gary King, "Enhancing Democracy Through Legislative Redistricting," *American Political Science Review* 88 (1994): 541–559.

18. Alan Abramowitz, Brad Alexander, and Matthew Gunning, "Don't Blame Redistricting for Uncompetitive Elections," *PS: Politics and Society* 39 (2006): 87ff.

19. *Shelby County v. Holder,* 133 S. Ct. 2612 (2013).

20. See, for example, *Shaw v. Reno,* 509 U.S. 630 (1993); *Alabama Legislative Black Caucus v. Alabama,* 575 US _ (2015).

21. Public Policy Institute of California, "Voter Turnout in Majority Minority Districts," *Research Brief* 46 (June 2001).

22. See a full discussion of this matter in David Epstein and Sharyn O'Halloran, "Measuring the Electoral and Policy Impact of Majority-Minority Voting Districts," *American Journal of Political Science* 43:2 (1999): 367–395.

23. See, for example, Neil Riemer, *The Representative: Trustee, Delegate, Partisan, Politico?* (Boston: DC Heath, 1967).

24. Richard Fenno, *Home Style: Members in Their Districts* (Boston: Little Brown, 1978), 50ff.

25. Matthew E. Glassman, "Tweet Your Congressman: The Rise of Electronic Communications in Congress," in *The Evolving Congress* (Washington, DC: Congressional Research Service, 2014), 101. See also Michael Losco, "Homestyle 2.0: House Members Online in the 21st Century," unpublished thesis, Georgetown University, May 2010.

26. Matt Glassman, "On Writing Your Congressman," *My Blog,* April 2, 2012, http://www.mattglassman.com/?p=3139.

27. Robert S. Erikson and Gerald C. Wright, "Voters, Candidates, and Issues in Congressional Elections," in Lawrence C. Dodd and Bruce L. Oppenheimer, eds., *Congress Reconsidered,* 6th ed. (Washington, DC: Congressional Quarterly, 1997), 143.

28. David Mayhew, *Congress: The Electoral Connection,* 2d ed. (New Haven, CT: Yale University Press, 2004).

29. Whitehurst, W. G. "Lobbies and Political Action Committees: A Congressman's Perspective," in Frey, L. Jr., and Hayes, M. T. eds., *Inside the House: Former Members Reveal*

How Congress Really Works (Lanham, MD: University Press of America, 2001), 210.

30. Ibid.

31. Lee Drutman and Steven Teles, "Why Congress Relies on Lobbyists Instead of Thinking for Itself," *The Atlantic,* March 10, 2015, https://www.theatlantic.com/politics/archive/2015/03/when-congress-cant-think-for-itself-it-turns-to-lobbyists/387295/.

32. Barbara Sinclair, *The Transformation of the U.S. Senate* (Baltimore, MD: Johns Hopkins University Press, 1989), 101.

33. See, for example, David Mayhew, *Divided We Govern* (New Haven, CT: Yale University Press, 1991); Charles O. Jones, *The Presidency in a Separated System* (Washington, DC: Brookings Institution Press, 1994).

34. See, for example, James L. Sundquist, *Constitutional Reform and Effective Government,* rev. ed. (Washington, DC: Brookings Institution Press, 1992); Samuel Kernell, "Facing an Opposition Congress: The President's Strategic Circumstance," in Gary W. Cox and Samuel Kernall, eds., *The Politics of Divided Government* (Boulder, CO: Westview Press, 1991).

35. George C. Edwards III, Andrew Barrett, and Jeffrey Peake, "The Legislative Impact of Divided Government," *American Journal of Political Science* 41:2 (1997): 545–563.

36. Lawrence A. Becker and Vincent G. Moscardelli, "Congressional Leadership on the Front Lines: Committee Chairs, Electoral Security, and Ideology," *PS: Political Science and Politics* 41 (January 2008): 77–82.

37. Robert S. Walker, "A Look at the Rules of the House," in Frey and Hayes, 250.

38. *Origins and Development of Congress,* 261.

39. U.S. Senate, "Senate Actions on Cloture Motions." Retrieved February 20, 2016, from http://www.senate.gov/pagelayout/reference/cloture_motions/clotureCounts.htm.

40. Hamilton, L. *How Congress Works and Why You Should Care* (Bloomington, IN: Indiana University Press, 2004), 55–56.

41. Sinclair, *Party Wars,* 148.

42. Barbara Sinclair, *Unorthodox Lawmaking: New Legislative Processes in the U.S. Congress* (Washington, DC: Congressional Quarterly Press, 1997).

43. See, for example, Hong Min Park, Steven S. Smith, and Ryan J. Vander Wielen, *Politics over Process: Partisan Conflict and Post-Passage Processes in the U.S. Congress* (Ann Arbor: University of Michigan Press, 2018).See also Bruce Bartlett, "How Congress Used to Work: The Deep Roots of Republicans' Failure on Capitol Hill," *Politico,* April 4, 2017, https://www.politico.com/magazine/story/2017/04/how-congress-used-to-work-214981.

44. Congressional Research Service, *Instances of Use of United States Armed Forces Abroad, 1798–2001* (Report RL30172).

45. This sentiment is traced to Roger Sherman. See *Origins and Development of Congress,* 62.

46. *Hamdan v. Rumsfeld,* 548 U.S. (2006).

47. Senate Historical Office, "United States Senate: Powers and Procedures," http://www.senate.gov/artandhistory/history/common/briefing/ Senate_Impeachment_Role.htm.

48. *Immigration and Naturalization Service v. Chadha,* 454 U.S. 812 (1983).

49. Louis Fisher, *Legislative Vetoes After Chadha* (CRS Report RS22132), May 2, 2005, http://www.loufisher.org/docs/lv/4116.pdf.

50. Stephen Dinan, "GOP Rolled Back 14 of 15 Obama Rules Using Congressional Review Act," *The Washington Times,* May 15, 2017, https://www.washingtontimes.com/news/2017/may/ 15/gop-rolled-back-14-of-15-obama-rules-using-congres/.

51. *N.L.R.B. v. Noel Canning*

52. Senate Historical Office, "Treaties." Retrieved July 30, 2006, from http://www.senate.gov.

53. Frank Newport, "Dysfunctional Gov't Surpasses Economy as Top U.S. Problem," Gallup Organization, October 9, 2013, http://news.gallup.com/poll/165302/dysfunctional-gov-surpasses-economy-top-problem.aspx. See also John R. Hibbing and Elizabeth Theiss-Morse, *Congress as Public Enemy* (Cambridge, UK: Cambridge University Press, 1995).

54. Art Swift, "Congress Approval Rating Remains at 16 percent in September," Gallup Organization, September 13, 2017, http://news.gallup.com/poll/218984/congress-approval-remains-september.aspx.

55. Mann and Ornstein, *It's Even Worse Than It Looks.*

56. Thomas Mann and Norman Ornstein, *The Broken Branch: How Congress Is Failing America and How to Get It Back on Track* (New York: Oxford University Press, 2006).

57. National Conference of State Legislatures, *Overview of State Laws on Public Financing,* http://www.ncsl.org/research/elections-and-campaigns/public-financing-of-campaigns-overview.aspx.

58. Andrew Hall, *How The Public Funding of Elections Increases Candidate Polarization.* Paper presented at the 2014 annual meeting of the Southern Political Science Association, August 13, 2014, http://www.andrewbenjamin-hall.com/Hall_publicfunding.pdf.

59. Eric McGhee and Boris Shor, "Has the Top Two Primary Elected More Moderates?" *Perspectives on Politics* 14:4 (December 2017): 1053–1066.

60. Jamie L. Carson, Michael H. Crespin, and Ryan D. Williamson, "Reevaluating the Effects of Redistricting on Electoral Competition, 1972–2012," *State Politics & Policy Quarterly* 14:2 (2014): 165–177.

61. Alex Isenstadt, "California Redistricting Plan Finalized," *Politico,* July 31, 2011, http://www.politico.com/news/stories/0711/60250.html.

62. Jennifer Steinhauer, "Californians Compete for a Shot at Redistricting," *The New York Times,* March 4, 2010, A18.

63. Franklin D. Gilliam, Jr., "Influences on Voter Turnout for U.S. House Elections in Non-presidential Election Years," *Legislative Studies Quarterly* 10:3 (1985): 339–351.

64. Mann and Ornstein, *It's Even Worse Than It Looks,* 168.

65. Steven E. Gottlieb, "Incumbents Rules," *The National Law Journal,* February 25, 2002, A21.

66. Larry Bartels, *Unequal Democracy: The Political Economy of the New Gilded Age* (Princeton, NJ: Princeton University Press, 2008).

67. Congressional Management Foundation, "Citizen-Centric Advocacy: The Untapped Power of Constituent Engagement," 2017, http://www.congressfoundation.org/projects/communicating-with-congress/citizen-centric-advocacy-2017.

Chapter 12: The Presidency: Power and Paradox

1. Baker, P. "A Year of Reinventing the Presidency," *The New York Times,* December 31, 2017, https://www.nytimes.com/2017/12/31/us/politics/trump-reinventing-presidency.html.

2. Gillman, T. J. "Shattered Norms: In Just One Year Has Donald Trump Changed the Presidency Forever?" *The Dallas Morning News,* January 14, 2018, https://www.dallasnews.com/news/politics/2018/01/14/shattered-norms-trump-changed-presidency-forever.

3. For discussion of the presidential actions mentioned here, see, for example: Celeste Katz, "Can Donald Trump Really Have the FBI Investigate His Political Enemies?" Newsweek, November 3, 2017. Accessed on September 6, 2018 at https://www.newsweek.com/donald-trump-fbi-justice-department-investigations-twitter-701117. Adam Liptak, "How Far Can Trump Go in Issuing Pardons," The New York Times, May 31, 2018. Accessed on September 6, 2018 at https://www.nytimes.com/2018/05/31/us/politics/pardons-trump.html. Max Bergmann and James Lamond, "Trump's Attitude Toward Russia Sanctions Makes a Mockery of the United States," Foreign Policy, March 1, 2018. Accessed on September 6, 2018 at https://foreignpolicy.com/2018/03/01/trumps-attitude-toward-russia-sanctions-makes-a-mockery-of-the-united-states/. Louis Nelson and Margaret Harding McGill, "Trump Suggests Challenging NBC's Broadcast License," Politico, October 11, 2017. Accessed on September 6, 2018 at https://www.politico.com/story/2017/10/11/trump-nbc-broadcast-license-243667. For a discussion of concern about the president's actions inside the White House, see Bob Woodward, Fear: Trump in the White House (New York: Simon and Schuster, 2018); Anonymous, "I Am Part of the Resistance Inside the Trump Administration," The New York Times, September 5, 2018. Accessed on September 6, 2018 at https://www.nytimes.com/2018/09/05/opinion/trump-white-house-anonymous-resistance.html?action=click&module=Top%20Stories&pgtype=Homepage.

4. Bass, H. F. Jr., "The President and Political Parties," in *The President, the Public, and the Parties* (Washington, DC: Congressional Quarterly Press, 1997), 33.

5. D. Robert Dahl, "Myth of the Presidential Mandate," *Political Science Quarterly* 105 (1990): 359.

6. Ibid.

7. Christopher Ingraham, "Somebody Just Put a Price-Tag on the 2016 Election. It's a Doozy," *The Washington Post,* April 14, 2017, https://www.washingtonpost.com/news/wonk/wp/2017/04/14/somebody-just-put-a-price-tag-on-the-2016-election-its-a-doozy/?noredirect=on. See also Center for Responsive Politics, "2012 Presidential Race," retrieved February 3, 2018, from https://www.opensecrets.org/pres12/.

8. Sasha Issenberg, "The Death of the Hunch," *Slate,* May 22, 2012, http://www.slate.com/articles/news_and_politics/victory_lab/2012/05/obama_campaign_ads_how_the_analyst_institute_is_helping_him_hone_his_message_.html.

9. Tom Hamburger, "Cruz Campaign Credits Psychological Data and Analytics for Its Rising Success," *The Washington Post,* December 13, 2015, https://www.washingtonpost.com/politics/cruz-campaign-credits-psychological-data-and-analytics-for-its-rising-success/2015/12/13/4cb0baf8-9dc5-11e5-bce4-708fe33e3288_story.html?noredirect=on.

10. Alex Leary, "Jeb Bush and Marco TV Spending," *Tampa Bay Times,* February 9, 2016, http://www.tampabay.com/jeb-bush-and-marco-tv-spending-in-south-carolina-124-million/2264705.

11. Twitter Public Policy, "Update: Russian Interference in 2016 US Election, Bots, & Misinformation," September 28, 2017, https://blog.twitter.com/official/en_us/topics/company/2017/Update-Russian-Interference-in-2016-Election-Bots-and-Misinformation.html.

12. Scott Shane and Vindu Goel, "Fake Russian Facebook Accounts Bought $100,000 in Political Ads," *The New York Times,* September 6, 2017, https://www.nytimes.com/2017/09/06/technology/facebook-russian-political-ads.html.

13. Philip Howard, Bruce Kollanyi, Samantha Bradshaw, and Lisa-Maria Neudert, "Social Media, News and Political Information during the US Election: Was Polarizing Content Concentrated in Swing States?" DATA MEMO 2017.8. Oxford, UK: Project on Computational Propaganda, September 28, 2017, http://comprop.oii.ox.ac.uk/research/working-papers/social-media-news-and-political-information-during-the-us-election-was-polarizing-content-concentrated-in-swing-states/.

14. John Aldrich, "The Invisible Primary and Its Effect on Democratic Choice," *PS: Political Science and Politics* 42 (January 2009): 33–38. See also Marty Cohen, David Karol, Hans Noel, and John Zaller, *The Party Decides: Presidential Nominations Before and After Reform* (Chicago: University of Chicago Press, 2008).

15. Cohen, Karol, Noel, and Zaller, *The Party Decides.*

16. But see Michael Lewis Beck and Peverill Squire, "Iowa: The Most Representative State?" *PS: Political Science and Politics* 42 (January 2009): 39–44. The authors claim that although the demographics of the state are not a microcosm of the nation as a whole, on many important social, political, and economic indicators it ranks about the midpoint of many states.

17. Brian Knight and Nathan Schiff, "Momentum and Social Learning in Presidential Primaries," *Journal of Political Economy,* NBER Working Paper No. 13637, November 2007, http://www.nber.org/papers/w13637.

18. George Packer, "How Donald Trump Is Winning Over the White Working Class," *The New Yorker,* May 16, 2016, http://www.nytimes.com/2016/05/06/upshot/bernie-sanderss-legacy-the-left-may-no-longer-need-the-rich.html?_r=0.

19. Art Swift, "Americans' Support for Electoral College Rises Sharply," *Gallup News,* December 2, 2016, https://news.gallup.com/poll/198917/americans-support-electoral-college-rises-sharply.aspx.

20. Quoted in Pfiffner, J. *The Modern Presidency* (New York: St. Martin's Press, 1994)

21. William G. Howell, *Power Without Persuasion: The Politics of Direct Presidential Action* (Princeton, NJ: Princeton University Press, 2003), chap. 1.

22. Sidney M. Milkis and Michael Nelson, *The American Presidents: Origins and Development, 1776–1993* (Washington, DC: CQ Press, 1994), 77.

23. Paul C. Light, *The President's Agenda: Domestic Policy Choice from Kennedy to Clinton* (Baltimore, MD: Johns Hopkins Press, 1999), 230.

24. *Clinton v. City of New York,* 524 U.S. 417 (1998).

25. W. Craig Bledsoe, Christopher J. Bosso, and Mark J. Rozell, "Chief Executive," in *Powers of the Presidency,* 2d ed. (Washington, DC: CQ Press, 1997), 41.

26. Milkis and Nelson, *The American Presidents,* 45.

27. Daniel Diller and Stephen H. Wirls, "Commander in Chief," in *Powers of the Presidency,* 2d ed. (Washington, DC: CQ Press, 1997), 165.

28. Abraham Lincoln, "Letter to Albert Hodges," in *The Complete Works of Abraham Lincoln.,* ed. John Nicolay and John Hay (New York: Francis Tandy, 1891), 10–66.

29. Scott Shane, "U.S. Approves Targeted Killing of American Cleric," *The New York Times,* April 7, 2010, A12.

30. Jonathan Wilkenfeld, "Structural Challenges for American Foreign Policy in the Obama Administration," in James A. Thurber, ed., *Obama in Office* (Boulder, CO: Paradigm, 2011), 227–242.

31. Daniel Diller and Stephen H. Wirls, "Chief Diplomat," in *Powers of the Presidency,* 2d ed. (Washington, DC: CQ Press, 1997), 140.

32. Edwards, G. III, *At the Margins: Presidential Leadership in Congress* (New Haven: Yale University Press, 1989), 212.

33. See Aaron Wildavsky, "The Two Presidencies," *Society* 35:2 (January/February 1998): 23–31. For a contrasting view, see John R. Bond and Richard Fleisher, *The President in the Legislative Arena* (Chicago: University of Chicago Press, 1992), esp. ch. 6.

34. "CQ Vote Studies: Presidential Support—Trump Divided, Conquered," *CQ Magazine* (February 12, 2018), http://library.cqpress.com/cqweekly/weeklyreport115-000005263239.

35. Christopher J. Bosso, "Legislative Leader," in *Powers of the Presidency*, 2d ed. (Washington, DC: CQ Press, 1997), 86.

36. U.S. Senate, "Summary of Bills Vetoed 1789–Present," February 11, 2018, https://https://www.senate.gov/reference/Legislation/Vetoes/vetoCounts.htm.

37. Barbara Sinclair, *Party Wars: Polarization and the Politics of National Policy Making* (Norman: University of Oklahoma Press, 2006), 246.

38. Todd Garvey, *Presidential Signing Statements: Constitutional and Institutional Implications* (Washington, DC: Congressional Research Service, January 4, 2012).

39. Samuel A. Alito, Jr., Office of Legal Counsel, U.S. Department of Justice, "Using Presidential Signing Statements to Make Fuller Use of the President's Constitutionally Assigned Role in the Process of Enacting Law," February 5, 1986, 1.

40. Donald J. Trump, "Statement by President Donald J. Trump on Signing the 'Countering America's Adversaries Through Sanctions Act'," The White House, August 2, 2017, https://www.whitehouse.gov/briefings-statements/statement-president-donald-j-trump-signing-countering-americas-adversaries-sanctions-act/.

41. Jeremy D. Mayer and Lynn Kirby, "The Promise and Peril of Presidential Polling: Between Gallup's Dream and the Morris Nightmare," in Stephen J. Wayne, ed., *Is This Any Way to Run a Democratic Government?* (Washington, DC: Georgetown University Press, 2004), 103.

42. Lawrence R. Jacobs and Melinda S. Jackson, "Presidential Leadership and the Threat to Popular Sovereignty," in *Polls and Politics: The Dilemmas of Democracy,* ed. Michael A. Genovese and Matthew J. Streb (Albany, NY: State University of New York Press, 2004).

43. Gerhard Peters, "Presidential News Conferences," in John T. Woolley and Gerhard Peters, eds., *The American Presidency Project.* Retrieved February 11, 2018, from www.presidency.ucsb.edu/data/news-conferences.php.

44. John P. Burke, "The Institutional Presidency," in Michael Nelson, ed., *The Presidency and the Political System,* 10th ed. (Los Angeles: Sage, 2014), 349–373.

45. Jasmine C. Lee, "Trump's Cabinet So Far Is More White and Male Than Any First Cabinet Since Reagan's," *The New York Times,* March 10, 2017, https://www.nytimes.com/interactive/2017/01/13/us/politics/trump-cabinet-women-minorities.html.

46. These were the sentiments of Richard Nixon, who was included in cabinet deliberations. Quoted in Pfiffner, *The Modern Presidency,* 12.

47. Allan Smith, "Why Trump's Sycophantic Cabinet Meetings Seem So Oddly Familiar," *Business Insider,* December 22, 2017, http://www.businessinsider.com/trump-praise-filled-cabinet-meetings-sound-like-the-apprentice-2017-12.

48. Bradley Patterson, Jr., *The White House Staff: Inside the West Wing and Beyond* (Washington, DC: The Brookings Institution, 2000), 11.

49. John P. Burke, "The Institutional Presidency," pp. 349–373.

50. Tamara Keith, "Trump White House Staff Payroll Nearly $36 Million and Top-Heavy," *National Public Radio,* June 30, 2017, https://www.npr.org/2017/06/30/535069910/trump-white-house-staff-payroll-nearly-36-million-and-top-heavy.

51. James P. Pfiffner, "Organizing the Obama White House," in James A. Thurber, ed., *Obama in Office* (Boulder, CO: Paradigm, 2011), 78.

52. The White House, *National Security Presidential Memorandum,* April 4, 2017, https://s3.amazonaws.com/public-inspection.federalregister.gov/2017-07064.pdf.

53. B. Patterson, *The White House Staff,* 62.

54. Jennifer Rubin, "Why It's Dangerous to Have So Many Generals in the Trump Cabinet," *The Washington Post,* April 19, 2017, https://www.washingtonpost.com/blogs/right-turn/wp/2017/04/19/why-its-dangerous-to-have-so-many-generals-in-the-trump-cabinet/.

55. Jim Geraghty, "Why the Trump Administration Still Has Personnel Troubles," *National Review,* February 13, 2018, http://www.nationalreview.com/corner/456359/jared-kushner-still-doesnt-have-full-security-clearance-and-trump-administration-still.

56. Pfiffner, "Organizing the Obama White House," 79.

57. This model was advocated by advisors Clark Clifford and Richard Neustadt. See James Pfiffner, *The Strategic Presidency* (Chicago: Dorsey Press, 1988), 23–25.

58. Pfiffner, *Strategic Presidency,* 67.

59. Stephen J. Wayne, "Obama's Personality and Performance," in James A. Thurber, ed., *Obama in Office* (Boulder, CO: Paradigm, 2011), 69–70.

60. Carol D. Leonnig, Shane Harris and Greg Jaffe, "Breaking with Tradition, Trump Skips President's Written Intelligence Report and Relies on Oral Briefings," *The Washington Post,* February 9, 2018, https://www.washingtonpost.com/politics/breaking-with-tradition-trump-skips-presidents-written-intelligence-report-for-oral-briefings/2018/02/09/b7ba569e-0c52-11e8-95a5-c396801049ef_story.html.

61. Jacqueline Thomsen, "Trump Prefers Oral Report to Reading Daily Intel Briefing: Report," *The Hill,* February 9, 2018, http://thehill.com/homenews/administration/373124-trump-prefers-oral-report-to-reading-daily-intel-briefing-report.

62. Baker Institute for Public Policy, *The White House Transition Project,* 2001–2017, Report 2017–10. Rice University, Houston, TX, p. 2.

63. Jeremy Diamond, "How Trump Works: A Network of Friends and Advisers on the Outside," *CNN Politics,* April 25, 2017, https://www.cnn.com/2017/04/25/politics/donald-trump-phone-outsiders/index.html. See also Maggie Haberman and Glenn Thrush, "Trump Reaches Beyond West Wing for Counsel," *The New York Times,* April 23, 2017, A1.

64. George Edwards III, "No Deal: Donald Trump's Leadership of Congress," paper prepared for delivery at the annual meeting of the American Political Science Association, San Francisco, September 2, 2017.

65. Josh Siegel, "John Kelly Wants Trump to Stop Making Policy on Twitter: Report," *Washington Examiner,* August 4, 2017. Accessed on May 14, 2018 at https://www.washingtonexaminer.com/john-kelly-wants-trump-to-stop-making-policy-on-twitter-report/article/2630696.

66. See, for example, Edward Hargrove, "What Manner of Man?" in James David Barber, ed., *Choosing the President* (New York: Prentice-Hall, 1974). Also see Thomas E. Cronin and Michael A. Genovese, *The Paradoxes of the American Presidency* (New York: Oxford, 1998), 33–38.

67. James David Barber, *The Presidential Character,* rev. ed. (New York: Prentice-Hall, 1992).

68. Arthur M. Schlesinger, Jr., *The Imperial Presidency* (Boston: Houghton Mifflin, 1973).

69. See, for example, Steven G. Calabresi and Christopher S. Yoo, "The Unitary Executive During the Second Half-Century," *Harvard Journal of Public Policy* 668 (2003).

70. The state secret privilege was upheld by the Supreme Court in *United States v. Reynolds,* 345 U.S. 1 (1953).

71. James Eli Shiffer, "Trump White House Confounds, Confuses Transparency Advocates," *Star Tribune,* October 28, 2017, http://www.startribune.com/search/q=Trump+White+House+Confounds2C+Confuses+Transparency+Advocates.

72. Richard Neustadt, *Presidential Power and the Modern Presidents: The Politics of Leadership from Roosevelt to Reagan* (New York: Free Press, 1991).

73. Quoted in Cronin and Genovese, *The Paradoxes of the American Presidency,* 317.

74. Langston, T. S. *With Reverence and Contempt: How Americans Thinks About Their President* (Baltimore, MD: Johns Hopkins University Press 1995), xi.

75. Although this quote has frequently been attributed to Thomas Jefferson, this assertion has been challenged by historians. The librarian at Monticello traced a similar phrase to Thomas Charlton in a biography of Major General James Jackson. See Anna Berkes, "Eternal Vigilance," *Jefferson Library Blog,* August 23, 2010, https://jefferson library.wordpress.com/2010/08/23/eternal-vigilance/.

Chapter 13: Bureaucracy: Citizens as Owners and Consumers

1. Damast, A. "Asking for Student Loan Forgiveness," *BusinessWeek,* February 24, 2010.

2. Ibid.

3. Zack Friedman, "Student Loan Debt in 2017: A $ 1.3 Trillion Crisis," *Forbes,* February 21, 2017, https://www.forbes.com/sites/zackfriedman/2017/02/21/student-loan-debt-statistics-2017/#36518ae95dab.

4. Joyce Appleby, "That's General Washington to You," *The New York Times Book Review,* February 14, 1993, 11.

5. Herbert Kaufman, *Red Tape: Its Origins, Uses, and Abuses* (Washington, DC: The Brookings Institution, 1977), 11.

6. See David A. Stockman, *The Triumph of Politics: How the Reagan Revolution Failed* (New York: Harper & Row, 1986).

7. Frederick C. Mosher, *Democracy and the Public Service* (New York: Oxford University Press, 1968), 57.

8. James D. Richardson, *Messages and Papers of the Presidents, Volume II* (Washington, DC: Bureau of National Literature and Art, 1903), 438.

9. Caldwell, R. C., *James A. Garfield* (Hamden, CT: Archon Books, 1965).

10. David Osborne and Ted Gaebler, *Reinventing Government: How the Entrepreneurial Spirit Is Transforming the Public Sector* (Reading, MA: Addison-Wesley, 1992).

11. Matthew A. Crenson and Benjamin Ginsberg, *Downsizing Democracy* (Baltimore, MD: Johns Hopkins University Press, 2002), 86.

12. Mark Green and John Berry, *The Challenge of Hidden Profits: Reducing Corporate Bureaucracy and Waste* (New York: William Morrow, 1985).

13. See an interview in Ralph P. Hummel, *The Bureaucratized Experience* (New York: St. Martin's Press, 1977), 23.

14. Gerald E. Caiden, "What Is Maladministration?" *Public Administration Review,* 51:6 (1991): 486–493.

15. Alexander Hamilton, James Madison, and John Jay, *The Federalist,* ed. Benjamin F. Wright (New York: Metro Books, 2002), 451.

16. Hugh Helco, *A Government of Strangers: Executive Politics in Washington* (Washington, DC: Brookings Institution, 1997).

17. Postal workers have their own organization but are not allowed to strike. There are other federal workers, such as federal air traffic controllers, who are not allowed to strike. Political appointees, unlike career civil servants, serve at the pleasure of the president.

18. Robert Lineberry, *American Public Policy: What Government Does and What Difference It Makes* (New York: Harper & Row, 1977).

19. Theodore Lowi, *The End of Liberalism* (New York: W. W. Norton, 1969).

20. See Cornelius M. Kerwin, *Rulemaking: How Government Agencies Write Law And Make Public Policy* (Washington, DC: CQ Press, 1994).

21. Ibid., 162.

22. Ibid., 194.

23. Ibid., 196.

24. Ibid., 170–171.

25. Ibid., 170.

26. Ibid., 170.

27. *Humphrey's Executor v. United States* (1935).

28. Donald D. Kettl, *Government by Proxy: (Mis)Managing Federal Programs* (Washington, DC: CQ Press, 1998).

29. Paul C. Light, *The True Size of Government* (Washington, DC: Brookings Institution, 1999).

30. Ibid., 9.

31. B. Dan Wood and Richard W. Waterman, *Bureaucratic Dynamics: The Role of Bureaucracy in a Democracy* (Boulder, CO: Westview Press, 1994), 105.

32. See Patricia W. Ingraham and David H. Rosenbloom, *The Promise and Paradox of Civil Service Reform* (Pittsburgh: University of Pittsburgh Press, 1992), 4.

33. Wood and Waterman, *Bureaucratic Dynamics,* 104.

34. John Brehm and Scott Gates, *Working, Shirking, and Sabotage: Bureaucratic Response to a Democratic Public* (Ann Arbor: University of Michigan Press, 1997).

35. James Q. Wilson, *Bureaucracy: What Government Agencies Do and Why They Do It* (New York: Basic Books, 1989), 236.

36. *McGrain v. Daugherty* (1972).

37. Johanna Neuman, "FAA's 'Culture of Coziness' Targeted in Airline Safety Hearing," *Los Angeles Times,* April 4, 2008, 1.

38. See Clinton Rossiter, *The American Presidency* (New York: Harcourt, Brace, and World, 1960).

39. James G. March and Johan P. Olson, "Organizing Political Life: What Administrative Reorganization Tells Us About Government," *American Political Science Review* 77 (1983): 281–296.

40. Richard W. Waterman, *Presidential Influence and the Administrative State* (Knoxville: The University of Tennessee Press, 1989), 27.

41. Waterman, R. W. *Presidential Influence and the Administrative State* (Knoxville: The University of Tennessee Press, 1989), 27.

42. Gerald Ford, *A Time to Heal: The Autobiography of Gerald R. Ford* (New York: Harper & Row, 1979), 352.

43. Waterman, *Presidential Influence and the Administrative State,* 37.

44. Ibid., 1–2.

Chapter 14: The Courts: Judicial Power in A Democratic Setting

1. Shane Goldmacher, Elina Johnson, and Josh Gerstein, "How Trump Got to Yes on Gorsuch," *Politico,* January 31, 2017.

2. Eric Lipton and Jeremy W. Peters, "In Gorsuch, Conservative Activist Sees Test Case for Reshaping the Judiciary," *The New York Times,* March, 19, 2017.

3. Henry Gass, "Neil Gorsuch Heads to a Supreme Court Changed by his Appointment," *The Christian Science Monitor,* April 4, 2017.

4. Edward D. Re, *Stare Decisis* (Washington, DC: Federal Judicial Center, 1975), 2.

5. See Charles Rembar, *The Judicial Process* (New York: Oxford University Press, 1968), 12.

6. *Flast v. Cohen* (1968).

7. Ibid.

8. *Colegrove v. Green* (1946).

9. Jethro K. Lieberman, *The Litigious Society* (New York: Basic Books, 1983), viii.

10. See Christopher E. Smith, *Courts, Politics, and the Judicial Process,* 2d ed. (Chicago: Nelson Hall, 1997), 330.

11. Howard Abadinsky, *Law and Justice: An Introduction to the American Legal System* (Chicago: Nelson Hall, 1995), 55.

12. Article III, Section 1, of the Constitution.

13. Alexander Hamilton, John Jay, and James Madison, *The Federalist Papers,* ed. Benjamin F. Wright (New York: Metro Books, 1961), 490–491.

14. Bernard Schwartz, *A History of the Supreme Court* (New York: Oxford University Press, 1993), 15.

15. The number of justices on the Supreme Court is set by Congress because no set number was specified in the Constitution.

16. *Ex parte McCardle* (1869).

17. All the justices today have four clerks.

18. Quoted in Perry, H. W. *Deciding to Decide: Agenda Setting in the U.S. Supreme Court* (Cambridge, MA: Harvard University Press, 1992), 144.

19. For a discussion of the reasons for a dwindling Supreme Court caseload, see Lawrence Baum, *The Supreme Court,* 12th ed. (Washington, DC: CQ Press, 2016), chap. 3.

20. Ibid., 222.

21. Quoted in Perry, H. W. *Deciding to Decide: Agenda Setting in the U.S. Supreme Court* (Cambridge, MA: Harvard University Press, 1992), 144.

22. See Lawrence Baum, *The Supreme Court,* 6th ed. (Washington, DC: CQ Press, 1998), 114.

23. Doris M. Provine, "Deciding What to Decide: How the Supreme Court Sets Its Agenda" *Judicature* 64: 7 (1981): 320.

24. See Adam Chandler, "The Solicitor General of the United States: Tenth Justice or Zealous Advocate?" *Yale Law Journal* 121 (December 2011): 733.

25. See Lincoln Caplan, *The Tenth Justice: The Solicitor General and the Rule of Law* (New York: Vintage Books, 1987).

26. See Rebecca Mae Salokar, *The Solicitor General: The Politics of Law* (Philadelphia: Temple University Press, 1992), 3.

27. Toobin, J. "No More Mr. Nice Guy", *The New Yorker,* May 25, 2009, 2.

28. David O'Brien, *Storm Center* (New York: Norton, 1986), 294.

29. Brian Lamb, Susan Swain, and Mark Farkas, eds., *The Supreme Court: A C-SPAN Book Featuring the Justices in Their Own Words* (New York: Public Affairs, 2010), 63.

30. Ibid., 313.

31. Bob Woodward and Scott Armstrong, *The Brethren* (New York: Simon & Schuster, 1979), 136–139.

32. Charles A. Johnson and Bradley C. Canon, *Judicial Policies: Implementation and Impact,* 2d ed. (Washington, DC: Congressional Quarterly Press, 1999), chap. 1.

33. See Richard L. Pacelle, Jr., and Lawrence Baum, "Supreme Court Authority in the Judiciary," *American Politics Quarterly* 20 (1992): 169–191.

34. J. W. Peltason, *Fifty-Eight Lonely Men: Southern Federal Judges and School Desegregation,* 2d ed. (Urbana: University of Illinois Press, 1971), 246.

35. *Employment Division, Department of Human Resources v. Smith* (1990).

36. *City of Boerne v. Flores* (1997).

37. *Atkins v. Virginia* (2002).

38. See Lee Epstein and Jack Knight, *The Choices Justices Make* (Washington, DC: CQ Press, 1998); Forest Maltzman, Paul J. Wahlbeck, and Jack Spriggs, *Crafting Law on the Supreme Court: The Collegial Game* (New York: Cambridge University Press, 2000); and Walter F. Murphy, *Elements of Judicial Strategy* (Chicago: University of Chicago Press, 1964).

39. Saul Brenner, "Fluidity on the Supreme Court, 1956–1967," *American Journal of Political Science* 90 (1996): 581.

40. Epstein and Knight, *The Choices Justices Make,* chap. 3.

41. Joan Biskupic, *Breaking In: The Rise of Sonia Sotomayor and the Politics of Justice* (New York: Farrar, Straus, & Giroux, 2014), 11.

42. See Henry J. Abraham, *Justices and Presidents,* 2d ed. (New York: Oxford University Press, 1985).

43. See O'Brien, *Storm Center.*

44. Abraham, *Justices and Presidents,* 191.

45. Mason, A. T. *William Howard Taft: Chief Justice* (New York: Simon & Schuster, 1965), 215–216.

46. Cooper, P. and Ball, H. *The United States Supreme Court: From the Inside Out* (Upper Saddle River, NJ: Prentice-Hall, 1996), 50.

47. Robert G. Scigliano, *The Supreme Court and the Presidency* (New York: Free Press, 1971), 147–148.

48. Roger Taney was a Catholic who served on the Court from 1835 until 1864, but the tradition of a Catholic seat did not begin with him, because his replacement was not a Catholic.

49. It is unclear whether Justice Gorsuch considers himself a Catholic or an Episcopalian.

50. Lawrence Baum, *American Courts,* 4th ed. (Boston: Houghton Mifflin, 1998), 106.

51. Pertschuk, M. and Schaetzel, W. *People Rising* (New York: Thunder's Mouth Press, 1989), 68.

52. See Karen O'Connor, "Lobbying the Justices for Justice," in Paul S. Herrnson, Ronald G. Shaido, and Clyde Wilcox, eds., *The Interest Group Connection* (Chatham, NJ: Chatham House, 1998), 273.

53. Baum, L. *American Courts,* 4th ed. (Boston: Houghton Mifflin, 1998).

54. Richard Wolf, "Trump's Judge Selection Skews White," *USA Today,* February 15, 2018.

55. Lee Epstein, *Conservatives in Court* (Knoxville: University of Tennessee Press, 1985).

56. In *Newman v. Piggie Park Enterprises Inc.* (1968), the Supreme Court upheld the fee-shifting provision.

57. See Stephen C. Yeazell, *From Medieval Group Litigation to the Modern Class Action* (New Haven, CT: Yale University Press, 1987).

58. Samuel Issacharoff, "Goverance and Legitimacy in the Law of Class Actions," *Supreme Court Review* (1999): 337.

59. *Powell v. McCormack* (1969).

60. Crenson, M. A. and Ginsberg, B. *Downsizing Democracy: How America Sidelined Its Citizens and Privatized Its Public* (Baltimore: Johns Hopkins University Press, 2002), 154.

61. See Lucius J. Barker, "Third Parties in Litigation: A Systematic View of the Judicial Function," *The Journal of Politics* 29: 1 (1967): 54–60.

Chapter 15: Public Policy: Responding to Citizens

1. Jim Tankersley, "Why America's Middle Class Is Lost," *The Washington Post,* https://www.washingtonpost.com/sf/business/2014/12/12/why-americas-middle-class-is-lost/?noredirect=on.

2. Ibid.

3. Pew Research Center, "The American Middle Class Is Losing Ground: No Longer the Majority and Falling Behind Financially," Washington, DC, December 2015, http://www.pewsocialtrends.org/2015/12/09/the-american-middle-class-is-losing-ground/.

4. U.S. Census Bureau, *Income and Poverty in the United States: 2016* (September 12, 2017). The figures are for equivalence-adjusted income.

5. This idea has undergone experimentation in some European countries like Finland which recently ended the program and is considering changes to the manner in which it was run. (See CBS News, "Finland's Flirtation with 'Free' Money for the Jobless to End," accessed on June 11, 2018 at https://www.cbsnews.com/news/finland-universal-basic-income-experiment-to-end-after-two-years/.) In the United States, the idea is currently undergoing experimentation in Oakland, California. See the story in Chapter 7's opening vignette of the young Oakland mayor who is experimenting with this approach.

6. Thomas R. Dye, *Understanding Public Policy,* 10th ed. (Upper Saddle River, NJ: Prentice-Hall, 2002), 1.

7. This section draws heavily on the work of James Q. Wilson, whose typology is described. See James Q. Wilson, *Political Organizations* (Princeton, NJ: Princeton University Press, 1995), 332–337.

8. Environmental Protection Agency, "Air Quality Trends," https://www.epa.gov/air-trends.

9. Julia Manchester, "Pruitt Personally Monitored Removal of Climate Change Info from EPA Sites: Report," *The Hill,* February 2, 2018, http://thehill.com/homenews/administration/371955-pruitt-personally-monitored-removal-of-climate-change-info-from-epa.

10. White House, "Statement by President Trump on the Paris Climate Accord," June 1, 2017, https://www.whitehouse.gov/briefings-statements/statement-president-trump-paris-climate-accord/.

11. Dye, *Understanding Public Policy,* 106.

12. U.S. Census Bureau, "Income, and Poverty in the United States, 2016," September 12, 2017, https://www.census.gov/content/dam/Census/library/publications/2017/demo/P60-259.pdf.

13. Urban Institute, *Assessing the New Federalism: Eight Years Later* (Washington, DC: Urban Institute, 2005).

14. Bureau of Labor Statistics, *A Profile of the Working Poor,* July 2015, https://www.bls.gov/opub/reports/working-poor/2015/home.htm.

15. Henry K. Kaiser Family Foundation, *Key Facts about the Uninsured Population,* November 29, 2017, https://www.kff.org/uninsured/fact-sheet/key-facts-about-the-uninsured-population/.

16. Sabrina Tavernise and Robert Gebeloff, "Immigrants, the Poor and Minorities Gain Sharply under Health Act," *The New York Times,* April 18, 2016, A1.

17. Zac Auter, "U.S. Uninsured Rate Steady at 12.2% in Fourth Quarter of 2017," Gallup Sharecare Well-Being Index, January 16, 2018, http://news.gallup.com/poll/225383/uninsured-rate-steady-fourth-quarter-2017.aspx.

18. Stephen Moore, ed., *Restoring the Dream: The Bold New Plan by House Republicans* (Washington, DC: Times Books, 1995), 156.

19. Congressional Budget Office, *The 2017 Long-Term Budget Outlook,* March 2017.

20. Corporation for National and Community Service, *Volunteering and Civil Life in America.* Retrieved March 5, 2018, from https://www.nationalservice.gov/vcla.

21. Ibid.

22. Aaron J. Martin, *Young People and Politics: Political Engagement in the Anglo-American Democracies* (New York: Routledge, 2012).

23. See, for example, the Center for Deliberative Democracy at Stanford University (cdd.stanford.edu) and the Deliberative Democracy Consortium (www.deliberative-democracy.net).

Chapter 16: Foreign and Defense Policy: Protecting American Interests in the World

1. Jim Yardley and Elisabetta Povoledo, "Migrants Die as Burning Boat Capsizes Off Italy," *The New York Times,* October 3, 2013, https://www.nytimes.com/2013/10/04/world/europe/scores-die-in-shipwreck-off-sicily.html.

2. International Organization for Migration, *World Migration Report 2018* (Geneva, Switzerland: IOM, 2017), http://www.iom.int/wmr/world-migration-report-2018.

3. Megan Gibson, "What Happens After Europe Allows the Migrants In?" *Time,* September 15, 2015, http://www.iom.int/wmr/world-migration-report-2018.

4. Harold D. Clarke, Matthew Goodwin and Paul Whiteley, *Brexit: Why Britain Voted to Leave the European Union* (Cambridge, UK: Cambridge University Press, 2017).

5. Tocqueville, A. D. *Democracy in America,* trans. George Lawrence, ed. J.P. Mayer (New York: Harper and Row, 1969), 278.

6. Ibid., 227.

7. H. William Brands, *The United States in the World: A History of American Foreign Policy,* vol. 1 (Boston: Houghton Mifflin, 1994), 110.

8. George W. Bush, "President Bush Delivers Graduation Speech at West Point," White House website. Accessed at https://georgewbush-whitehouse.archives.gov/news/releases/2002/06/20020601-3.html.

9. The Kissinger Telcons: Kissinger Telcons on Chile, *National Security Archive Electronic Briefing Book No. 123,* edited by Peter Kornbluh, posted May 26, 2004. This particular dialogue can be found at TELCON: September 16, 1973, 11:50 a.m. Kissinger Talking to Nixon. Accessed online November 26, 2006 at https://nsarchive2.gwu.edu/NSAEBB/NSAEBB123/.

10. See, for example, Robert J. Lieber, *No Common Power: Understanding International Relations* (Boston: Scott Foresman, 1988).

11. See, for example, the excellent discussion of the school of realism in Bruce W. Jentleson, *American Foreign Policy: The Dynamics of Choice in the 21st Century,* 2d ed. (New York: W. W. Norton, 2004).

12. See, for example, Joseph Nye, *The Power to Lead: Soft, Hard, and Smart* (New York: Oxford University Press, 2008).

13. National Commission on Terrorist Attacks, *The 9/11 Commission Report: Final Report of the Commission on Terrorist Attacks upon the United States* (New York: W. W. Norton, 2004).

14. U.S. Department of State, "Mission Statement." Retrieved May 1, 2005, from https://www.state.gov/s/d/rm/rls/dosstrat/2004/23503.htm.

15. Ole R. Holsti, *Public Opinion and American Foreign Policy,* rev. ed. (Ann Arbor: University of Michigan Press, 2007), 55.

16. Pew Research Center, "Millennials Increasingly View 'Good Diplomacy' as Best Way to Ensure Peace," March 1, 2018. Accessed on March 9, 2018 at http://www.people-press.org/2018/03/01/3-u-s-foreign-policy-and-americas-global-standing-islam-and-violence-nafta/030118_3_1/.

17. Gallup Organization, "Gallup's Pulse of Democracy: The War in Iraq," April 18–20, 2008 survey, https://news.gallup.com/poll/1633/iraq.aspx.

18. Peter G. Peterson Foundation, "U.S. Defense Spending Compared to Other Countries," June 1, 2017, https://www.pgpf.org/chart-archive/0053_defense-comparison.

19. World Bank, "Military Expenditures as % of GDP," March 9, 2018, https://data.world-bank.org/indicator/ms.mil.xpnd.gd.zs.

20. Brad Plumer, "America's Staggering Defense Budget in Charts," *The Washington Post,* January 7, 2013, https://www.washingtonpost.com/news/wonk/wp/2013/01/07/everything-chuck-hagel-needs-to-know-about-the-defense-budget-in-charts/?noredirect=on.

21. Foreign Aid Dashboard, May 4, 2016, https://explorer.usaid.gov/aid-dashboard.html.

22. Center for Global Development, "Foreign Assistance and the U.S. Budget," May 4, 2016, http://www.cgdev.org/page/foreign-assistance-and-us-budget.

23. Joseph S. Nye, *Soft Power: The Means to Success in World Politics* (New York: Public Affairs, 2004), 4.

24. Arms Control Association, "Who Has What at a Glance," May 5, 2016, https://www.armscontrol.org/factsheets/Nuclearweapons whohaswhat.

25. "Russia's Nuclear Weapons Are Technically Plausible... But practically Dubious, "*The Economist,* March 8, 2018, https://www.econo-mist.com/science-and-technology/2018/03/08/russias-new-nuclear-weapons-are-technically-plausible.

26. U.S. Department of Defense, *2018 Nuclear Posture Review* (February 2018), https://media.defense.gov/2018/Feb/02/2001872886/-1/-1/1/2018-NUCLEAR-POSTURE-REVIEWFINAL-REPORT.PDF.

27. Al Jazeera, "North Korea's Nuclear Weapons: What We Know," February 20, 2018, https://www.aljazeera.com/news/2017/05/north-korea-testing-nuclear-weapons-170504072226461.html.

28. United States Nuclear Regulatory Commission, "Fact Sheet on Dirty Bombs," February 9, 2008, https://www.nrc.gov/reading-rm/doc-collections/fact-sheets/fs-dirty-bombs.html.

29. U.S. Census Bureau, "Foreign Trade Statistics," March 13, 2018, https://www.census.gov/foreign-trade/index.html.

30. Wayne M. Morrison and Marc Labonte, "China's Holdings of U.S. Securities: Implications for the U.S. Economy," *Congressional Research Service Report for Congress,* August 19, 2013, https://fas.org/sgp/crs/row/RL34314.pdf.

31. Nye, *Soft Power,* 5–11.

Index

Bold page numbers indicate key terms. Page numbers followed by *f* indicate figures.

voters
demographics of, 170–174, 170*f*
home-style politics with, 284
mobilization of, 236–237
voting, 170–177
candidate as basis for, 176–177
compulsory, 184*f*
and demographics of voters, 170–174, 170*f*
early, **236**
Electoral College, 33, 176, 216, 309, 315–319
by House in presidential election, 316
issues as basis for, 175–176, 176*f*
political party as basis for, 174–175
prospective, 175
retrospective, 175
by Supreme Court, 376–377
voter registration, 171–173
and voter turnout, 170–171, 172*f*, 183–184, 184*f*
voting rights, 36–37, 109, 124–125
Voting Rights Act of 1965, **112,** 124–125, 280

W

Wallace, George, 228
warrantless searches, 89–90
Warren, Earl, 51, 110, 371, 374, 374*f*, 376, 383
war(s). *See also names of specific wars*
declarations of, 34–35, 299–300, 299*f*, 323
military costs of, 418*f*
termination of, 426*f*
Washington, George, 46
Constitution, 23–24
Continental Congress, 20
public opinion, 138
Watergate scandal, 153, 181, 230, 251, 263, 322
wealth, and political participation, 165–166, 166*f*, 179–182

Weber's model of bureaucracy, 348*f*
welfare, 402–**403**
Whig Party, 228
whips, **291**
whistle-blowing, **363**
White House Office, 333–334
White House Staff, **333**–334
Williams, Roger, 19
Wilson, Woodrow, 322, 417, 417*f*
women
civil rights for, 36–37, 126–133
in Congress, 128–129, 275, 275*f*, 283
earnings of men *vs.,* 129*f*, 130*f*, 131*f*
in military, 132*f*, 133, 133*f*
in politics, 275, 283
programs for, 362
and sexual harassment, 131–132
as Supreme Court justices, 384
voting rights, 36–37
workplace equity for, 129–131
women's movements, 127–129
workplace
equity for women in, 129–131
and political participation, 166–167
World Bank, 430
World Health Organization (WHO), 430
World Trade Organization, **411**–412, 411*f*
World War I, 191, 303, 417
World War II, 120–121, 417
writ of certiorari, **375**

Y

Yellen, Janet, 409
yellow journalism, 244–245

![McGraw Hill Education] **connect**® | Students—study more efficiently, retain more and achieve better outcomes. Instructors—focus on what you love—teaching.

SUCCESSFUL SEMESTERS INCLUDE CONNECT

FOR INSTRUCTORS

You're in the driver's seat.

Want to build your own course? No problem. Prefer to use our turnkey, prebuilt course? Easy. Want to make changes throughout the semester? Sure. And you'll save time with Connect's auto-grading too.

65%

Less Time Grading

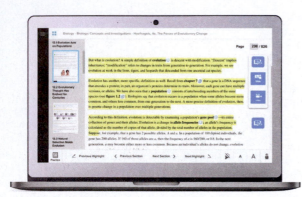

They'll thank you for it.

Adaptive study resources like SmartBook® help your students be better prepared in less time. You can transform your class time from dull definitions to dynamic debates. Hear from your peers about the benefits of Connect at **www.mheducation.com/highered/connect**

Make it simple, make it affordable.

Connect makes it easy with seamless integration using any of the major Learning Management Systems—Blackboard®, Canvas, and D2L, among others—to let you organize your course in one convenient location. Give your students access to digital materials at a discount with our inclusive access program. Ask your McGraw-Hill representative for more information.

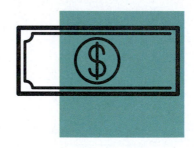

©Hill Street Studios/Tobin Rogers/Blend Images LLC

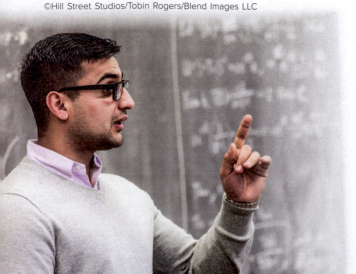

Solutions for your challenges.

A product isn't a solution. Real solutions are affordable, reliable, and come with training and ongoing support when you need it and how you want it. Our Customer Experience Group can also help you troubleshoot tech problems—although Connect's 99% uptime means you might not need to call them. See for yourself at **status.mheducation.com**